Motus mixti et compositi

Intersections

INTERDISCIPLINARY STUDIES IN EARLY MODERN CULTURE

General Editor

Karl A.E. Enenkel (*Chair of Medieval and Neo-Latin Literature*
Universität Münster
e-mail: kenen_01@uni_muenster.de)

Editorial Board

W. de Boer (*Miami University*)
S. Bussels (*University of Leiden*)
A. Dlabačová (*University of Leiden*)
Chr. Göttler (*University of Bern*)
J.L. de Jong (*University of Groningen*)
W.S. Melion (*Emory University*)
A.C. Montoya (*Radboud University Nijmegen*)
R. Seidel (*Goethe University Frankfurt am Main*)
P.J. Smith (*University of Leiden*)
J. Thompson (*Queen's University Belfast*)
A. Traninger (*Freie Universität Berlin*)
C. Zittel (*Ca' Foscari University of Venice / University of Stuttgart*)
C. Zwierlein (*Bonn*)

VOLUME 90 – 2025

The titles published in this series are listed at *brill.com/inte*

Motus mixti et compositi

The Portrayal of Mixed and Compound Emotions in the Visual and Literary Arts of Europe, 1500–1700

Edited by

Karl A.E. Enenkel
Walter S. Melion

BRILL

LEIDEN | BOSTON

Cover illustration: Housebook Master, Crowd beneath the Cross, detail from Calvary scene, central panel of a Passion Altarpiece, 1480–1485. Tempera and oil on pine panels, 131 × 173 cm (central panel). Freiburg im Breisgau, Augustinermuseum. Photo © Augustinermuseum, Michael Jensch, CC BY 4.0.

Library of Congress Cataloging-in-Publication Data

Names: Enenkel, K. A. E., editor. | Melion, Walter S., editor.
Title: Motus mixti et compositi : the portrayal of mixed and compound emotions in the visual and literary arts of Europe, 1500–1700 / edited by Walter S. Melion, Karl A.E. Enenkel.
Description: Leiden ; Boston : Brill, 2025. | Series: Intersections, 1568–1181; volume 90 – 2025 | Includes bibliographical references and index.
Identifiers: LCCN 2024036256 (print) | LCCN 2024036257 (ebook) | ISBN 9789004694606 (hardback ; acid-free paper) | ISBN 9789004694613 (ebook)
Subjects: LCSH: Emotions in literature. | Affect (Psychology) in literature. | European literature—Renaissance, 1450–1600—History and criticism. | European literature—17th century—History and criticism. | Emotions in art. | Affect (Psychology) in art. | Painting, European—16th century. | Painting, European—17th century
Classification: LCC PN56.E6 M68 2025 (print) | LCC PN56.E6 (ebook) | DDC 700/.453—dc23/eng/20240828
LC record available at https://lccn.loc.gov/2024036256
LC ebook record available at https://lccn.loc.gov/2024036257

Typeface for the Latin, Greek, and Cyrillic scripts: "Brill". See and download: brill.com/brill-typeface.

ISSN 1568-1181
ISBN 978-90-04-69460-6 (hardback)
ISBN 978-90-04-69461-3 (e-book)
DOI 10.1163/9789004694613

Copyright 2025 by Karl A.E. Enenkel and Walter S. Melion. Published by Koninklijke Brill BV, Leiden, The Netherlands.
Koninklijke Brill BV incorporates the imprints Brill, Brill Nijhoff, Brill Schöningh, Brill Fink, Brill mentis, Brill Wageningen Academic, Vandenhoeck & Ruprecht, Böhlau and V&R unipress.
Koninklijke Brill BV reserves the right to protect this publication against unauthorized use. Requests for re-use and/or translations must be addressed to Koninklijke Brill BV via brill.com or copyright.com.

This book is printed on acid-free paper and produced in a sustainable manner.

Contents

Acknowledgements IX
List of Illustrations X
Notes on the Editors XXI
Notes on the Contributors XXIII

1 Introduction: *Motus mixti et compositi* – the Portrayal of Mixed and Compound Emotions in the Visual and Literary Arts of Europe, 1500–1700 1
Walter S. Melion

PART 1
Portraying Mixed Emotions in the Literary Arts

SECTION A
Mixed Emotions in Dutch and Latin Drama

2 All Motion Discovers Us: Moral Discernment and the Role of the Passions in Willem van Nieulandt's *Nero* (1618) 47
Bart Ramakers

3 Staging the In-Between: Compound, Conflicting and Shifting Emotions in Seventeenth-Century Neo-Latin Drama from the Dutch Republic 105
Lukas Reddemann

SECTION B
Mixed Emotions in Neo-Latin and French Poetry

4 Between Fleeting and Compound Emotions in Neo-Latin Lyric Poetry on 'Turks': Georgius Sisgoreus' *Elegia de Sibenicensis agri vastatione* 151
Ludovica Sasso

5 Shifting Emotions in Neo-Latin Psalm Poetry and Erotic Elegy: George Buchanan and Janus Lernutius 184
Carolin A. Giere

CONTENTS

6   On Red and White Cheeks: Jakob Balde's Poetic Ekphrases on a
Triptych by Christoph Schwarz in the Light of the Scholastic Theory
of the Passions   220
    Aline Smeesters

7   Mixed Motives: the Art of Joachim Du Bellay, 1549–1558   250
    Tom Conley

SECTION C
Mixed Emotions in Prose Literature

8   Tears of Love and Sorrow: the Affective Regime of the European
Pastoral Tradition   283
    Anita Traninger

9   'How We Weep and Laugh at the Same Thing': Conflicting Emotions
in Rabelais and Montaigne   310
    Paul J. Smith

10   The Troubles of Christian Perfection: Berinzaga, Gagliardi,
Borromeo   327
    Wietse de Boer

PART 2
Portraying Mixed Emotions in the Visual Arts

SECTION A
Mixed Emotions in Image-based Spiritual Exercises

11   *O vos omnes*: Recognition, Tragic Emotion,
and the Passerby Topos in Northern European Art around 1500   369
    Mitchell Merback

12   Mixed Emotion and Spiritual Perfection in Abraham Bloemaert's
Sylva anachoretica of 1619   410
    Walter S. Melion

CONTENTS VII

13 Spiritual Joy in the Face of Death: Compound Emotions in Texts and Images of the Martyrs of the Japan Mission 502
Raphaèle Preisinger

14 Materialities of Mixed Emotions and Spiritual Martyrdom between the Grand Duchy of Lithuania and Grand Duchy of Tuscany 537
Ruth Sargent Noyes

SECTION B
Heuristic and Sanative Images of Mixed Emotions

15 *Francisci chorda traxit ad se plurima corda*: 'Drawing' the Heart's Emotions in Jan Provoost's Diptych of *Christ Carrying the Cross* 573
Elliott D. Wise

16 'Symbolic Anatomies': Hendrick Goltzius and the Ambiguities of Early Modern Disability 615
Barbara A. Kaminska

17 Exploring Complex Emotions through the Portrayal of Dialogic Exchange: Pieter Lastman's *Paul and Barnabas in Lystra* of 1617 647
Graham R. Lea

18 Between Despair and Hope: Raising Emotions with Dutch Seventeenth-Century Marine Paintings and Prints 675
Stijn Bussels and Bram Van Oostveldt

Index Nominum 695

Acknowledgements

This volume consists of essays redacted from papers originally delivered at the colloquium, "*Motus mixti et compositi*: The Portrayal of Mixed and Compound Emotions in the Visual and Literary Arts of Europe, 1500–1640", held at Emory University on April 7th–9th, 2022. Organised under the aegis of the Art History Department's Lovis Corinth Endowment, the colloquium was the twelfth in the ongoing series of such events convened at Emory. Kay Corinth and her sister Mary Sargent established the endowment to honor the memory of Kay's father-in-law, the celebrated painter Lovis Corinth. The Corinth Colloquia provide an interdisciplinary forum for the comparative study of early modern northern art. Sarah McPhee, Samuel Candler Dobbs Professor of Art History and Chair of the Art History Department, encouraged and facilitated "*Motus mixti et compositi*: The Portrayal of Mixed and Compound Emotions in the Visual and Literary Arts of Europe" amidst the many complications attendant upon a post-pandemic conference. For her administrative support, I am beholden to Blanche Barnett, Academic Department Administrator. Corinth Graduate Associates Annie McEwen Maloney and Alexandra Zigomalas assisted in preparing and implementing the colloquium, and Dr. Maloney served afterward as an ideal editorial assistant. This is the third time I have worked closely with Dr. Maloney, now affiliated with Brown University, whose intelligence and unfailing good will ensured the colloquium's success. I also want to thank Chris Sawula, the department's former Visual Resources and Spatial Art History Librarian, and Hannah Plank, Digital Image Specialist, for consulting with the IT team tasked with managing the colloquium. Chris Higa, in his capacity as Corinth Administrative Associate, not only liaised with the IT experts but also ably monitored the day-to-day operations of the colloquium. Finally, an immeasurable debt of thanks is owed once again to Linnea Harwell, Graduate Program Coordinator in Art History, the person without whom the colloquium could never have been realised. The co-organisers of "*Motus mixti et compositi*", Karl Enenkel and I, relied at every turn on Ms. Harwell, whose intelligence, *sangfroid*, and attention to detail are nonpareil.

Illustrations

1.1   Pieter Bruegel the Elder, *Massacre of the Innocents*, ca. 1565–1567. Oil on panel, 109.2 × 105.1 cm. Royal Collection Trust, Windsor RCIN 405787   8

1.2   *Groenendael Passion*, fol. 23v: Articles 41 and 42 of the *Hondert articulen der passion Iesu Christi* and fol. 24r: Israhel van Meckenem, *Flagellation of Christ*. Album: late fifteenth century; each folio ca. 260 × 204 mm. Metropolitan Museum of Art, 2003.476   15

1.3   Israhel van Meckenem, *Flagellation of Christ in the Presence of Pilate, with Christ Brought before Herod*, from *Große Passion*, ca. 1480. Engraving, highlighted in gold, with touches of pen and red ink (on Christ's feet), ca. 205 × 151 mm. Metropolitan Museum of Art   16

1.4   Jan David, s.j., *Pancarpium Marianum, Septemplici Titulorum serie distinctum; ut in B. Virginis odorem curramus, et Christus formetur in nobis.* (Antwerp, Balthasar and Jan Moretus: 1607; repr. ed., 1618). Engraving by Theodoor Galle, 150 × 90 mm. Courtesy of The Newberry Library, Chicago: Case W. 1025.22   18

1.5   Jan David, s.j., "Tituli quinquaginta partitio, prout in praesenti Tractatu sunt digesti", in *Pancarpium Marianum* (Antwerp, Balthasar and Jan Moretus: 1607; repr. ed., 1618), fol. + 8v. Courtesy of The Newberry Library, Chicago: Case W. 1025.22   20

1.6   Theodoor Galle, Emblem 5: "Mater pulchrae dilectionis", in Jan David, s.j., *Pancarpium Marianum* (Antwerp, Balthasar and Jan Moretus: 1607; repr. ed., 1618). Engraving, 156 × 90 mm. Courtesy of The Newberry Library, Chicago: Case W. 1025.22   21

1.7   Theodoor Galle, Emblem 42: "Lapis adiutorii", in Jan David, s.j., *Pancarpium Marianum* (Antwerp, Balthasar and Jan Moretus: 1607, repr. ed., 1618). Engraving, 158 × 91 mm. Courtesy of The Newberry Library, Chicago: Case W. 1025.22   22

1.8   Peter Paul Rubens and Workshop, *Return of Briseis*, ca. 1630–1635. Oil on panel, 107.5 × 163 cm. Museo del Prado, Madrid P002566   23

1.9   Peter Paul Rubens, *The Negotiations at Angouleme*, 1622–1625. Oil on canvas, 394 × 295 cm. Musée du Louvre, Paris. (Photo: Art Resource)   24

1.10   *Veturia, Mother of Coriolanus* (also known as *Thusnelda*). Marble, over life size. Loggia dei Lanzi, Florence. (Photo: Art Resource)   25

1.11   Diego Velázquez, *Joseph's Blooded Coat Presented to Jacob*, 1630. Oil on canvas, 213.5 × 284 cm. Nuevos Museos, El Escorial. (Photo: Art Resource)   26

2.1   Willem van Nieulandt II, *The Death of Nero* (1618). Title page of *Claudius Domitius Nero* (Antwerp, Guilliam van Tongheren: 1618). The Hague, Koninklijke Bibliotheek, KW 851 D 31   51

ILLUSTRATIONS

2.2   Jean Meyssens, *Willem Nieulandt II* (1662). Engraving, 162 × 113 mm. Cornelis de Bie, *Het gulden cabinet vande edele vry schilder-const*, 3 vols. (Antwerp, Joannes Meyssens and Juliaen van Montfort, 1662), vol. 1, 63. Amsterdam, Rijksmuseum, RP-P-OB-23.603   52

2.3   Johann Theodor de Bry after Dirck Volckertszoon Coornhert after Maarten van Heemskerck, *Democritus and Heraclites* (1596). Engraving, 100 × 100 mm. *Emblemata Saecularia* [...] (Frankfurt am Main, J.T. de Bry & J.I. de Bry: 1596). Amsterdam, Rijksmuseum, RP-P-BI-5187   57

2.4   Peter Paul Rubens, *The Four Philosophers* (1611–1612). Oil on panel, 167 × 143 cm. Florence, Galleria Palatina. Image © SCALA, Florence; Ministero Beni e Att. Culturali   84

2.5   Peter Paul Rubens, *The Death of Seneca* (1612–1613). Oil on panel, 185 × 154,7 cm. Münich, Bayerische Staatsgemäldesammlungen – Alte Pinakothek   87

2.6   Frans Francken the Younger, *The Painter's Cabinet* (*c*.1627). Oil on panel, 54 × 69 cm. Private collection, Las Arenas, Getxo, Spain   88

2.7   Frans Francken the Younger, *The Painter and the Poet* (1618). Pen with brown and blue ink, brown wash on paper, 29.1 × 19.8 cm. Paris, Musée du Louvre, inv. no. 19981. Image © RMN-Grand Palais/Art Resource, New York   89

2.8   Jan Saenredam after Hendrick Goltzius, *Mercury* (1596). Engraving, 257 × 180 mm. Amsterdam, Rijksmusueum, RP-P-OB-10.599   91

3.1   Peter Paul Rubens (workshop of), *Alboin and Rosamund*, painted ca. 1615. Oil on canvas, 202 × 132 cm. Vienna, Kunsthistorisches Museum. Public Domain   118

3.2   Philips Galle after Maarten van Heemskerck, *Amnon rapes Tamar* from the series *Geschiedenis van Tamar en Amnon*, 1559. Engraving, 24,5 × 20,3 cm. Public Domain   126

3.3   Eustache Le Sueur, *The Rape of Tamar*, painted ca. 1640. Oil on canvas, 189.2 × 161.3 cm. New York, Metropolitan Museum of Art. Public Domain   127

3.4a–b   Duym, *Het moordadich stuck*, fols. G iii v. and <D iiii> r   141

6.1   Christoph Schwarz, *Marienaltar*, 1580–1581. Triptych with St. Catherine of Alexandria, the Virgin and Child in a Glory of Clouds, and St. Jerome, painted for the Jesuit College of Munich. Oil on wood, 183.1 × 64.4 cm – 197.6 × 152.8 cm – 181.8 × 64.2 cm. Nuremberg, Germanisches Nationalmuseum. Image © Germanisches Nationalmuseum, Nuremberg. Loan from Bayerischen Staatsgemäldesammlungen München   224

6.2   Christoph Schwarz, *St. Catherine of Alexandria*, 1580–1581. Part of Schwarz's *Marienaltar*, painted for the Jesuit College of Munich. Left panel. Oil on wood, 183,1 × 64,4 cm. Image © Germanisches Nationalmuseum, Nuremberg. Loan from Bayerischen Staatsgemäldesammlungen München   225

6.3   Christoph Schwarz, *The Virgin and Child in the Glory of the Clouds*, 1580–1581. Part of Schwarz's *Marienaltar*, painted for the Jesuit College of Munich. Center

	panel. Oil on wood, 197,6 × 152,8 cm. Image © Germanisches Nationalmuseum, Nuremberg. Loan from Bayerischen Staatsgemäldesammlungen München 226
7.1	Sonnets 22 and 23 of *L'Olive* (Paris: Arnoul l'Angelier, 1549) 257
7.2	Incipit to *L'Olive* (Paris: Arnoul l'Angelier, 1550) 259
7.3	Title page, *Recueil de poesie* (Paris: Cavellat, 1558) 260
7.4	*L'Olive*, 1549, sonnet 23 and catchword (n.p.) 262
7.5	"Dialogue d'un amoureux et d'Echo," *Recueil de poesie* (1549), n.p. 265
7.6	*Divers Ieux rustiques*, 1558, title page 276
10.1	Gagliardi Achille, *Breve compendio intorno alla perfettione Christiana, dove si vede una prattica mirabile per unire l'anima con Dio* (Naples, per Gio. Giacomo Carlino: 1614), frontispiece. © Bayerische Staatsbibliothek, Munich, Asc. 1988, urn:nbn:de:bvb:12-bsb10262716-1 329
10.2	Pellegrini Lelio, *De affectionibus animi noscendis et emendandis commentarius* (Rome, apud Vincentium Pelagallum: 1598), frontispiece. © The British Library Board, 0 Coll DRT Dig Store 716.a.2. By permission of the British Library 335
11.1	Upper Rhine, Christ in Misery, *c.*1480. Limewood with traces of polychromy, 81.6 cm in height. Cologne, Kolumba. Image: © Lothar Schnepf; Kolumba, Cologne 371
11.2	North German, Passion Scenes, inner face of the left wing of a Passion Altarpiece known as the *Goldene Tafel*, *c.*1410–18. Mixed technique on oak panel, 231 × 184 cm (wing dimensions). Hannover, Landesmuseum. Image: Landesmuseum Hannover – ARTOTHEK 372
11.3	Hans Holbein the Elder, Christ in Repose before the Crucifixion, panel from the *Gray Passion*, *c.*1495–1500. Oil on panel, 88.5 × 88 cm. Stuttgart, Staatsgalerie. Image © Staatsgalerie Stuttgart 374
11.4	Hans Holbein the Elder, Mary and Christ at Rest on Golgotha, *c.*1503–04. Oil on limewood panel, 41.5 × 32.8 cm. Hannover, Landesmuseum. Image: Landesmuseum Hannover – ARTOTHEK 375
11.5	Housebook Master, Crowd beneath the Cross, detail from Calvary scene, central panel of a Passion Altarpiece, 1480–85. Tempera and oil on pine panels, 131 × 173 cm (central panel). Freiburg im Breisgau, Augustinermuseum. Photo © Augustinermuseum, Michael Jensch, CC BY 4.0 377
11.6	Workshop of Cornelis Engebrechtsz, Christ in Repose with Nun and Saint Augustine, *c.*1500. Oil on panel, 52 × 41 cm. Antwerp, KMSKA. Photo: Collection KMSKA – Flemish Community, Public Domain Mark 1.0 378
11.7	Late Byzantine (Constantinople), Micromosaic Icon of the King of Glory, early 14th century. Colored stones, 13 × 19 cm. Rome, Basilica di Santa Croce in Gerusalemme. Photo: Soprintendenza Speciale per il Patrimonio Storico, Artistico ed Etnoantropologico, Rome 382

ILLUSTRATIONS   XIII

11.8   Israhel van Meckenem, Man of Sorrows Standing in the Tomb, later
        15th century. Engraving, 10 × 7.6 cm. Vienna, Albertina. Photo: Albertina,
        Public Domain Mark 1.0   383

11.9   Wolf Traut, Man of Sorrows and Mother of Sorrows, indulgenced broadsheet
        published by Hieronymus Höltzel in Nuremberg, 1512, with typographical text.
        Woodcut highlighted with red ink, 42.5 × 26 cm. Washington, DC, National
        Gallery of Art, Rosenwald Collection. Photo © National Gallery of Art   384

11.10   Jacob Binck, Man of Sorrows – Ecce Homo, 1520–30. Hand-colored engraving
        on a manuscript leaf, 133 × 96 mm, from a disassembled Flemish prayerbook.
        London, British Museum. Photo © Trustees of the British Museum   385

11.11   South German, Man of Sorrows between Mary and Saint John, c.1500.
        Elephant ivory with paint and gilding, 8.6 × 6.5 × 1.0 cm. New York,
        Metropolitan Museum of Art. Photo courtesy of the Metropolitan Museum
        of Art, www.metmuseum.org   386

11.12   Claus Sluter, Jeremiah, from the Well of Moses, c.1400–06. Dijon, Chartreuse de
        Champmol. Artwork in the public domain; photograph by the author   388

11.13   Jan van Eyck and workshop assistant, Christ as Judge, detail from Last
        Judgment, ca. 1430. Oil on canvas, transferred from wood, 56.5 × 19.7 cm (one
        panel of a diptych). New York: Metropolitan Museum of Art. Photo courtesy of
        the Metropolitan Museum of Art, www.metmuseum.org   397

11.14   Middle Rhenish, Mass of Saint Gregory, second half of 15th century, with
        16th-century indulgence text. Oil on panel, 141.5 × 71.5 cm. St. Petersburg,
        The State Hermitage Museum. Photo © The State Hermitage Museum   398

11.15   Jan Mostaert, Calvary, c.1530. Oil on panel, 114.6 × 74.6 cm. Philadelphia,
        Philadelphia Museum of Art. Photo: The John G. Johnson Collection,
        Philadelphia Museum of Art (cat. 411), public domain   405

12.1   Abraham Bloemaert, Title-Page: Sacra eremus ascetarum (Antwerp, Hendrik
        Aertssens: 1619), quarto. Rijksmuseum, Amsterdam   413

12.2   Boëtius à Bolswert after Abraham Bloemaert, Frontispiece: Ad sacrum
        speculum, ca. 1612/reissued 1619. Engraving, ca. 125/30 × 85/88 mm.
        Rijksmuseum, Amsterdam   414

12.3   Boëtius à Bolswert, Similis factus sum pellicano solitudinis: Wooded Landscape
        with Hermits, ca. 1612/reissued 1619. Engraving, ca. 145 × 90 mm. Rijksmuseum,
        Amsterdam   415

12.4   Boëtius à Bolswert after Abraham Bloemaert, Jesus is led into the desert:
        Temptation of Christ, ca. 1612/reissued 1619. Engraving, ca. 125/30 × 85/88 mm.
        Rijksmuseum, Amsterdam   416

12.5   Boëtius à Bolswert after Abraham Bloemaert, Saint John the Baptist, ca. 1612/
        reissued 1619. Engraving, ca. 125/30 × 85/88 mm. Rijksmuseum, Amsterdam   417

12.6	Boëtius à Bolswert after Abraham Bloemaert, *Saint Paul Hermit*, ca. 1612/ reissued 1619. Engraving, ca. 125/30 × 85/88 mm. Rijksmuseum, Amsterdam	418
12.7	Boëtius à Bolswert after Abraham Bloemaert, *Saint Anthony Hermit*, ca. 1612/ reissued 1619. Engraving, ca. 125/30 × 85/88 mm. Rijksmuseum, Amsterdam	419
12.8	Boëtius à Bolswert after Abraham Bloemaert, *Saint Hilarion*, ca. 1612/reissued 1619. Engraving, ca. 125/30 × 85/88 mm. Rijksmuseum, Amsterdam	420
12.9	Boëtius à Bolswert after Abraham Bloemaert, *Saint Malchus*, ca. 1612/ reissued 1619. Engraving, ca. 125/30 × 85/88 mm. Rijksmuseum, Amsterdam	421
12.10	Boëtius à Bolswert after Abraham Bloemaert, *Saint Onuphrius*, ca. 1612/reissued 1619. Engraving, ca. 125/30 × 85/88 mm. Rijksmuseum, Amsterdam	422
12.11	Boëtius à Bolswert after Abraham Bloemaert, *Saint Pachomius*, ca. 1612/reissued 1619. Engraving, ca. 125/30 × 85/88 mm. Rijksmuseum, Amsterdam	423
12.12	Boëtius à Bolswert after Abraham Bloemaert, *Saint Macarius Aegyptius*, ca. 1612/reissued 1619. Engraving, ca. 125/30 × 85/88 mm. Rijksmuseum, Amsterdam	424
12.13	Boëtius à Bolswert after Abraham Bloemaert, *Saint Macarius Alexandrinus*, ca. 1612/reissued 1619. Engraving, ca. 125/30 × 85/88 mm. Rijksmuseum, Amsterdam	425
12.14	Boëtius à Bolswert after Abraham Bloemaert, *Saint Abraham Hermit*, ca. 1612/reissued 1619. Engraving, ca. 125/30 × 85/88 mm. Rijksmuseum, Amsterdam	426
12.15	Boëtius à Bolswert after Abraham Bloemaert, *Saint Basil the Great*, ca. 1612/reissued 1619. Engraving, ca. 125/30 × 85/88 mm. Rijksmuseum, Amsterdam	427
12.16	Boëtius à Bolswert after Abraham Bloemaert, *Saint Ephraem*, ca. 1612/reissued 1619. Engraving, ca. 125/30 × 85/88 mm. Rijksmuseum, Amsterdam	428
12.17	Boëtius à Bolswert after Abraham Bloemaert, *Saint Simeon Stylita*, ca. 1612/reissued 1619. Engraving, ca. 125/30 × 85/88 mm. Rijksmuseum, Amsterdam	429
12.18	Boëtius à Bolswert after Abraham Bloemaert, *Saint Frontonius*, ca. 1612/reissued 1619. Engraving, ca. 125/30 × 85/88 mm. Rijksmuseum, Amsterdam	430
12.19	Boëtius à Bolswert after Abraham Bloemaert, *Saint John in Lyco*, ca. 1612/reissued 1619. Engraving, ca. 125/30 × 85/88 mm. Rijksmuseum, Amsterdam	431

ILLUSTRATIONS

XV

12.20 Boëtius à Bolswert after Abraham Bloemaert, *Saint Elias Aegyptius*,
ca. 1612/reissued 1619. Engraving, ca. 125/30 × 85/88 mm. Rijksmuseum,
Amsterdam   432

12.21 Boëtius à Bolswert after Abraham Bloemaert, *Saint Theonas*,
ca. 1612/reissued 1619. Engraving, ca. 125/30 × 85/88 mm. Rijksmuseum,
Amsterdam   433

12.22 Boëtius à Bolswert after Abraham Bloemaert, *Saint Helenus*,
ca. 1612/reissued 1619. Engraving, ca. 125/30 × 85/88 mm. Rijksmuseum,
Amsterdam   434

12.23 Boëtius à Bolswert after Abraham Bloemaert, *Saint Ammon Nitriota*,
ca. 1612/reissued 1619. Engraving, ca. 125/30 × 85/88 mm. Rijksmuseum,
Amsterdam   435

12.24 Boëtius à Bolswert after Abraham Bloemaert, *Saint Paul Simplex*,
ca. 1612/reissued 1619. Engraving, ca. 125/30 × 85/88 mm. Rijksmuseum,
Amsterdam   436

12.25 Boëtius à Bolswert after Abraham Bloemaert, *Saint Arsenius*,
ca. 1612/reissued 1619. Engraving, ca. 125/30 × 85/88 mm. Rijksmuseum,
Amsterdam   437

12.26 Boëtius à Bolswert after Abraham Bloemaert, *Saint Bonosus*,
ca. 1612/reissued 1619. Engraving, ca. 125/30 × 85/88 mm. Rijksmuseum,
Amsterdam   438

12.27 Boëtius à Bolswert after Abraham Bloemaert, *Saint Jerome*,
ca. 1612/reissued 1619. Engraving, ca. 125/30 × 85/88 mm. British Museum,
London   439

12.28 Boëtius à Bolswert after Abraham Bloemaert, *Title-Page: Sacra eremus
ascetriarum*, ca. 1612/reissued 1619. Engraving, ca. 125/30 × 85/88 mm.
Rijksmuseum, Amsterdam   440

12.29 Boëtius à Bolswert after Abraham Bloemaert, *Virgin Mary, Mother of God*,
ca. 1612/reissued 1619. Engraving, ca. 125/30 × 85/88 mm. Rijksmuseum,
Amsterdam   441

12.30 Boëtius à Bolswert after Abraham Bloemaert, *Saint Mary Magdalene*,
ca. 1612/reissued 1619. Engraving, ca. 125/30 × 85/88 mm. Rijksmuseum,
Amsterdam   442

12.31 Willem de Passe after Abraham Bloemaert, *Angel Gabriel*, ca. 1610. Engraving,
273 × 186 mm. Rijksmuseum, Amsterdam   443

12.32 Crispijn van de Passe after Abraham Bloemaert, *Virgin Annunciate*, ca. 1610.
Engraving, 275 × 187 mm. Rijksmuseum, Amsterdam   444

12.33 Willem van Swanenburg after Abraham Bloemaert, *Peter Mourning his
Betrayal of Christ*, from *Biblical Penitents*, 1609–1611. Engraving, 268 × 171.
Rijksmuseum, Amsterdam   445

12.34	Willem van Swanenburg after Abraham Bloemaert, *Paul's Contrition over his Former Persecution of Christ*, from *Biblical Penitents*, 1609–1611. Engraving, 267 × 170 mm. Rijksmuseum, Amsterdam 446
12.35	Willem van Swanenburg after Abraham Bloemaert, *Zachaeus Grieving over his Riches*, from *Biblical Penitents*, 1609–1611. Engraving, 272 × 173 mm. Rijksmuseum, Amsterdam 447
12.36	Willem van Swanenburg after Abraham Bloemaert, *Repentant Mary Magdalene in the Wilderness*, from *Biblical Penitents*, 1609–1611. Engraving, 271 × 174 mm. Rijksmuseum, Amsterdam 448
12.37	Jan Saenredam after Abraham Bloemaert, *Ahijah Divides his Cloak before Jeroboam*, from *Prophecies of Ahijah*, 1604. Engraving, 270 × 199 mm. Rijksmuseum, Amsterdam 449
12.38	Jan Saenredam after Abraham Bloemaert, *Ahijah Predicts the Fall of Jeroboam*, from *Prophecies of Ahijah*, 1604. Engraving, 270 × 194 mm. Rijksmuseum, Amsterdam 450
12.39	Jan Saenredam after Abraham Bloemaert, *Expulsion*, from *History of Adam and Eve*, 1604. Engraving, 278 × 200 mm. Rijksmuseum, Amsterdam 451
12.40	Jan Saenredam after Abraham Bloemaert, *Lamentation of Adam and Eve*, *from History of Adam and Eve*, 1604. Engraving, 279 × 200 mm. Rijksmuseum, Amsterdam 452
13.1	The 26 Japan Martyrs of 1597 on the Way to their Crucifixion, 1599, engraving. From: Guzmán Francisco Tello de, *Relation, Auß befelch Herrn Francisci Teglij Gubernators, vnd general Obristens der Philippinischen Inseln* [...] (Munich, Adam Berg: 1599), fol. A iv r. Munich, Bayerische Staatsbibliothek Res/4 H.eccl. 870,49, 10. CC BY-NC-SA 4.0, https://creativecommons.org/licenses /by-nc-sa/4.0/ 506
13.2	The Crucifixion of 1597 in Nagasaki, 1599, engraving. From: Guzmán Francisco Tello de, *Relation, Auß befelch Herrn Francisci Teglij Gubernators, vnd general Obristens der Philippinischen Inseln* [...] (Munich, Adam Berg: 1599), fol. B ii r. Munich, Bayerische Staatsbibliothek Res/4 H.eccl. 870,49, 14. CC BY-NC-SA 4.0, https://creativecommons.org/licenses/by-nc-sa/4.0/ 507
13.3	Title page of Fróis Luís, *Drey Japponische Schreiben* [...] (Mainz, Johan Albin: 1599). Munich, Bayerische Staatsbibliothek 4 Jes. 268. Photo courtesy of Bayerische Staatsbibliothek München 508
13.4	St. Francis Lovingly Embracing a Crucifix, engraving. From: Guzmán Francisco Tello de, *Relation, Auß befelch Herrn Francisci Teglij Gubernators, vnd general Obristens der Philippinischen Inseln* [...] (Munich, Adam Berg: 1599), fol. A i v. Munich, Bayerische Staatsbibliothek Res/4 H.eccl. 870,49, 5. CC BY-NC-SA 4.0, https://creativecommons.org/licenses/by-nc-sa/4.0/ 510

ILLUSTRATIONS   XVII

13.5 Jacques Callot, The Crucifixion of the 23 Franciscan Martyrs of 1597 in Japan, 1627 or later, etching, 11,4 × 16,8 cm, Amsterdam, Rijksmuseum, object number RP-P-1925-15. CC0 1.0, https://creativecommons.org/publicdomain/zero/1.0/deed.en   513

13.6 The Crucifixion of the 23 Franciscan Martyrs of 1597 in Japan, 1627, oil on canvas, ca. 220 × 350 cm, Francavilla Fontana, Santa Maria della Croce, Fototeca SABAP-BA n. inv. 205091 cat.D. Su autorizzazione della Soprintendenza Archeologia, Belle Arti e Paesaggio per la città metropolitana di Bari – MiC   515

13.7 Raphaël Sadeler II, The Crucifixion of the 23 Franciscan Martyrs of 1597 in Japan, 1627–1632, engraving, 39 × 48,9 cm, Amsterdam, Rijksmuseum, object number RP-P-1926-631. CC0 1.0, https://creativecommons.org/publicdomain/zero/1.0/deed.en   517

13.8 The Martyrs of 1597 Preparing for Crucifixion, 1608, engraving. From: Ricci Bartolomeo, *Triumphus Jesu Christi crucifixi* (Antwerp, Joannes Moretus: 1608), fol. B iv r, Vienna, Österreichische Nationalbibliothek. Public domain: http://rightsstatements.org/vocab/NoC-NC/1.0/   519

13.9 Matthäus Greuter and Paul Maupin, *Effigies et nomina quorundam è societate Jesu qui pro fide vel pietate sunt interfecti* [...], 1608, engraving, 182,5 × 50 cm, middle section of the print, Paris, Bibliothèque nationale de France, BnF ms. Français 15782, Fol. 423r   520

13.10 Wolfgang Kilian, *Drey Seelige Martyrer der Societet Jesu* [...], 1628, engraving, 14,5 × 27 cm, Munich, Bayerische Staatsbibliothek Einbl. VII,24 l. Photo courtesy of Bayerische Staatsbibliothek München   524

13.11 Hieronymus Wierix, The 'True Effigy' of St. Francis Xavier, before 1619, engraving, 7,3 × 11 cm, Paris, Musée du Louvre. Photo © Musée du Louvre, Dist. RMN-Grand Palais / Martine Beck-Coppola   527

13.12 Schelte Adamsz. Bolswert after Peter Paul Rubens, Saint Francis Xavier and Saint Ignatius of Loyola, ca. 1633–1659, engraving, 24,1 × 34,2 cm, New York, The Metropolitan Museum of Art, Accession Number: 51.501.7129. CC0 1.0, https://creativecommons.org/publicdomain/zero/1.0/deed.en   528

13.13 Schelte Adamsz. Bolswert after Abraham van Diepenbeeck, The Crucifixion of the Three Jesuit Martyrs of 1597, 1628–1659, engraving, 27,1 × 43 cm, Amsterdam, Rijksmuseum, object number RP-P-BI-2563. CC0 1.0, https://creativecommons.org/publicdomain/zero/1.0/deed.en   530

13.14 After Abraham van Diepenbeeck, The Crucifixion of Jesuit and Franciscan Martyrs in Japan in 1597, 1667, engraving, Wellcome Collection, Reference: 11014i. Public Domain Mark, https://creativecommons.org/publicdomain/mark/1.0/. Source: Wellcome Collection   531

XVIII   ILLUSTRATIONS

13.15 *Drij ghekruijste Japonoisen*, oil on canvas, 117,5 × 89 cm, Kyushu National
       Museum. Source: ColBase (https://colbase.nich.go.jp/collection_items
       /kyuhaku/A27?locale=ja) 533

13.16 Guido Cagnacci, *Tre martiri del Giappone*, 1635, oil on canvas,
       250 × 140 cm, Rimini, San Francesco Saverio. Reproduced with the
       permission of Commissione Diocesana per l'Arte Sacra e i Beni Culturali,
       Diocesi di Rimini 533

14.1   Danzig (Gdańsk) workshop, Reliquary of St. Kazimierz Jagiellończyk,
       c.1677–1678. Wooden core, amber, silver, ivory, metal. 35 × 56 × 20 cm. Front
       view. Florence, Palazzo Pitti, Tesoro dei Granduchi. Image © Gallerie degli
       Uffizi 542

14.2   Danzig (Gdańsk) workshop, Reliquary of St. Kazimierz Jagiellończyk,
       c.1677–1678. Wooden core, amber, silver, ivory, metal. 35 × 56 × 20 cm.
       Back view. Florence, Palazzo Pitti, Tesoro dei Granduchi. Image © Gallerie
       degli Uffizi 542

14.3   Woodcut frontispiece portrait of Kazimierz Jagiellończyk. In Ferreri Zaccaria,
       Vita Beati Casimiri Confessoris [n.p]. Image in the public domain 546

14.4   Carlo Dolci, Portrait of St. Kazimierz, 1670–1671. Oil on canvas, 95 × 79 cm.
       Image © Gallerie degli Uffizi 547

15.1   Jan Provoost, Interior of *Christ Carrying the Cross and Portrait of a
       Fifty-Four-Year-Old Franciscan*, (1522). Oil on panel, 40 cm × 49.5 cm.
       Sint-Janshospitaal, Bruges (inv. no. 0000.SJ0191.I). Artwork in the
       public domain 575

15.2   Jan Provoost, Exterior of *Christ Carrying the Cross and Portrait of a
       Fifty-Four-Year-Old Franciscan*, (1522). Oil on panel, 40 cm × 49.5 cm.
       Sint-Janshospitaal, Bruges (inv. no. 0000.SJ0191.I). Artwork in the
       public domain 575

15.3   Hieronymus Bosch or Follower of Hieronymus Bosch, *Christ Carrying the Cross*,
       (ca. 1510–ca. 1516). Oil on panel, 76.7 × 83.5 cm, Museum voor Schone Kunsten,
       Ghent (inv. 1902-H). Artwork in the public domain 586

15.4   Titian/Giorgione, *Christ Carrying the Cross*, (1505). Oil on canvas,
       68.2 cm × 88.3 cm, Scuola Grande di San Rocco, Venice. Image
       © Cameraphoto Arte, Venice / Art Resource, NY 588

15.5   Bernardino Luini, *Christ Carrying the Cross and the Virgin*, (1520/1530).
       Oil on wood, 50.6 cm × 49.7 cm, Museo Poldi Pezzoli, Milan, (inv. no. 1624).
       © Museo Poldi Pezzoli, Milan 589

15.6   Jan Provoost, *Sacred Allegory*, (ca. 1500). Oil on wood, 50 cm × 40 cm, Musée
       du Louvre, Paris (inv. no. RF 1973 44). © 2017 RMN-Grand Palais (Louvre) /
       Tony Querrec 592

ILLUSTRATIONS   XIX

15.7   Master of 1499, Interior right panel of *Diptych of Abbot Christiaan de Hondt*,
        (1499). Oil on panel, 31 cm × 29 cm, Koninklijk Museum voor Schone Kunsten,
        Antwerp (inv. no. 255-256-530-531). Artwork in the public domain   597

15.8   Antonio Leonelli da Crevalcore, *St. Francis as the Man of Sorrows*, (ca. 1490).
        Tempera on wood panel, 74.5 cm × 56 cm, Princeton University Art Museum,
        Princeton, Museum purchase, Carl Otto von Kienbusch Jr., Memorial Collection
        (inv. no. y1956–3). Artwork in the public domain   605

15.9   Antonio Leonelli da Crevalcore, Reverse of *St. Francis as the Man of Sorrows*,
        (ca. 1490). Tempera on wood panel, 74.5 cm × 56 cm, Princeton University Art
        Museum, Princeton, Museum purchase, Carl Otto von Kienbusch Jr., Memorial
        Collection (inv. no. y1956–3). Artwork in the public domain   606

16.1   Philips Galle after Pieter Bruegel the Elder, *Caritas*, 1559–1560. Engraving,
        22.3 × 29.1 cm. Amsterdam, Rijksmuseum. Image © Public Domain   622

16.2   Anonymous, *Cripples* (*The Crippled Bishop*), ca. 1570. Engraving, 30.3 × 21.9 cm.
        Amsterdam, Rijksmuseum. Image © Public Domain   623

16.3   Hendrick Goltzius, [*Goltzius'*] *Right Hand*, 1588. Pen and brown ink on paper,
        22.9 × 32.8 cm. Haarlem, Teylers Museum. Image © Public Domain   626

16.4   Hendrick Goltzius, *Self-Portrait*, 1589. Silverpoint with graphite, with grey and
        blue-grey wash, on yellow-prepared vellum, 14.6 × 10.4 cm. London, British
        Museum. Image © The Trustees of the British Museum   627

16.5   Hendrick Goltzius, *Four Studies of* [*Goltzius'*] *Right Hand*, 1588–1589. Black and
        red chalk, on slightly tinted ribbed laid paper, 30.9 × 20.7 cm. Frankfurt am
        Main, Städel Museum. Image © Public Domain   628

16.6   Hendrick Goltzius, *Mucius Scaevola*, 1586. Engraving, 36.7 × 23.5 cm.
        Amsterdam, Rijksmuseum. Image © Public Domain   637

16.7   Hendrick Goltzius, *Sine Cerere et Libero Friget Venus*, 1606. Pencil, pen, and
        brown wash on grounded canvas, 220 × 170 cm. St. Petersburg, The Hermitage.
        Image © Public Domain   639

17.1   Pieter Lastman, *Paul and Barnabas in Lystra* (1617). Oil on panel. 76 × 115 cm.
        Amsterdam Museum, Amsterdam. Public Domain   649

17.2   Pieter Lastman, *Paul and Barnabas in Lystra* (1617). Oil on panel. 76 × 115 cm.
        Detail of apostles. Amsterdam Museum, Amsterdam. Public Domain   652

17.3   Pieter Coecke van Aelst, *The Sacrifice at Lystra* (ca. 1529–1530). Pen and brown
        ink. 29.5 × 45.7 cm. J. Paul Getty Museum, Los Angeles. Public Domain   654

17.4   Pieter Coecke van Aelst, *The Sacrifice at Lystra* (ca. 1529–1530). Pen and brown
        ink. 29.5 × 45.7 cm. Detail of sacrifice. J. Paul Getty Museum, Los Angeles.
        Public Domain   655

17.5   Marten de Vos, *Paul and Barnabas in Lystra* (ca. 1568). Oil on panel.
        140 × 185 cm. Château d'Olivier, Gironde; as illustrated in

ILLUSTRATIONS

Jonckheere K. – Suykerbuyk R. (eds.), *Art after Iconoclasm: Painting in the Netherlands between 1566 and 1585* (Turnhout, 2012) 39   656

17.6   Marten de Vos, *Paul and Barnabas in Lystra* (ca. 1568). Oil on panel. 140 × 185 cm. Details of apostles. Château d'Olivier, Gironde; as illustrated in Jonckheere – Suykerbuyk (eds.), *Art after Iconoclasm* 39   657

17.7   Jan Saenredam after Karel van Mander, *Paul and Barnabas in Lystra* (1589–1607). Engraving. 26.7 × 41 cm. Rijksmuseum, Amsterdam. Public Domain   658

17.8   Jan Saenredam after Karel van Mander, *Paul and Barnabas in Lystra* (1589–1607). Engraving. 26.7 × 41 cm. Detail of apostles. Rijksmuseum, Amsterdam. Public Domain   659

18.1   Hendrick Staets, *Ships Wrecked on a Rocky Shore*, 1655. Oil on panel, 50,8 × 68,6 cm. National Maritime Museum, Greenwich, London   676

18.2   Detail from Hendrick Staets, *Ships Wrecked on a Rocky Shore*   677

18.3   Jacob Bellevois, *A Fishing Boat off a Rocky Coast in a Storm with a Wreck*, c.1665. Oil on canvas, 82,5 × 121,9 cm. National Maritime Museum, Greenwich, London   679

18.4   Detail from Jacob Bellevois, *A Fishing Boat off a Rocky Coast in a Storm with a Wreck*   680

18.5   Claes Jansz. Visscher (printmaker), *Frustra qui iterum, emblem XLVII*, in Visscher Roemer, *Sinnepoppen* (Amsterdam, Willem Jansz. Blaeu, 1614), Rijksmuseum   683

18.6   Pieter Nolpe, *Shipwreck: The Month March and the Element water*, 1640s or early 1650s. Engraving, 405 × 519 mm. Rijksmuseum, Amsterdam   685

18.7   Detail from Pieter Nolpe, *Shipwreck: The Month March and the Element water*   686

18.8   Hans Savery the Elder (attr.), *The Wreck of the* Amsterdam, ca. 1630. Oil on canvas, 125,7 × 177,8 cm. National Maritime Museum, London   689

18.9   Detail from Hans Savery the Elder (attr.), *The Wreck of the* Amsterdam   690

Notes on the Editors

Karl A.E. Enenkel
is Professor of Medieval Latin and Neo-Latin at the University of Münster (Germany). Previously he was Professor of Neo-Latin at Leiden University (Netherlands). He is a member of the *Royal Netherlands Academy of Arts and Sciences*. He has published widely on international Humanism, early modern culture, paratexts, literary genres 1300–1600, Neo-Latin emblems, word and image relationships, and the history of scholarship and science. Among his major book publications are *Francesco Petrarca: De vita solitaria, Buch 1.* (1991); *Die Erfindung des Menschen. Die Autobiographik des frühneuzeitlichen Humanismus von Petrarca bis Lipsius* (2008); *Die Stiftung von Autorschaft in der neulateinischen Literatur (ca. 1350–ca. 1650). Zur autorisierenden und wissensvermittelnden Funktion von Widmungen, Vorworttexten, Autorporträts und Dedikationsbildern* (2015); *The Invention of the Emblem Book and the Transmission of Knowledge, ca. 1510–1610* (2019), and *Ambitious Antiquities, Famous Forebears. Constructions of a Glorious Past in the Early Modern Netherlands and Europe* (with Koen Ottenheym, 2019). He has (co)edited and co-authored some 35 volumes on a variety of topics; key topics are addressed in *Modelling the Individual. Biography and Portrait in the Renaissance* (1998), *Recreating Ancient History* (2001), *Mundus Emblematicus. Studies in Neo-Latin Emblem Books* (2003), *Cognition and the Book* (2004), *Petrarch and his Readers* (2006), *Early Modern Zoology* (2007), *Meditatio – Refashioning the Self. Theory and Practice in Late Medieval and Early Modern Intellectual Culture* (2011), *Portuguese Humanism* (2011), *The Authority of the Word* (2011), *Discourses of Power. Ideology and Politics in Neo-Latin Literature* (2012), *The Reception of Erasmus* (2013), *Transformation of the Classics* (2013), *Neo-Latin Commentaries and the Management of Knowledge* (2013), *Zoology in Early Modern Culture* (2014), *Iohannes de Certaldo. Beiträge zu Boccaccios lateinischen Werken und ihrer Wirkung* (2015), *Discourses of Anger in the Early Modern Period* (2015), *Jesuit Image Theory* (2016), *Emblems and the Natural World* (2017), *The Figure of the Nymph in Early Modern Culture* (2018), *Solitudo. Spaces, Places, and Times of Solitude in Late Medieval and Early Modern Cultures* (2018), *The Quest for an Appropriate Past in Literature, Art and Architecture* (2018), *Artes Apodemicae and Early Modern Travel Culture, 1550–1700*, and *Reinventing Ovid's Metamorphoses. Pictorial and Literary Transformation in Various Media, 1500–1800*. He has founded the international series *Intersections. Studies in Early Modern Culture* (Brill); *Proteus. Studies in Early Modern Identity Formation*; *Speculum Sanitatis: Studies in Medieval and Early Modern Medical Culture (500–1800)* (both Brepols),

and *Scientia universalis. Studien und Texteditionen zur Wissensgeschichte der Vormoderne* (LIT-Münster). He is currently preparing a critical edition of and a commentary on Erasmus's *Apophthegmata*, books V–VIII.

Walter S. Melion

is Asa Griggs Candler Professor of Art History at Emory University in Atlanta, where he directed the Fox Center for Humanistic Inquiry between 2017 and 2023. He is the author of three monographs and a critical edition of Karel van Mander's Foundation of the Noble, Free Art of Painting, co-author of two exhibition catalogues, editor or co-editor of more than twenty-five volumes, and has published more than one hundred articles. Melion is also editor of two book series: Brill's Studies on Art, Art History, and Intellectual History and Lund Humphries' Northern Lights. He was elected Foreign Member of the Royal Netherlands Academy of Arts and Sciences in 2010 and Fellow of the American Academy of Arts and Sciences in 2023. He is president emeritus of the Sixteenth Century Society, current president of the Historians of Netherlandish Art, and a board member of the Print Council of America.

Notes on the Contributors

Stijn Bussels
is Professor Art History before 1800 at the Leiden University Centre for the Arts in Society. His research focusses on the impact of the arts and the theatre in the early modern Low Countries. He is the author of *The Antwerp Entry of Prince Philip in 1549* (Amsterdam: 2012), and *The Animated Image* (Berlin: 2012) and the editor of, among other book volumes, *Theatricality in Early Modern Art and Architecture* (London: 2011), *Translations of the Sublime* (Leiden: 2012), *Magnificence in the Seventeenth Century* (Leiden: 2020), and *The Amsterdam Town Hall* (London: 2021).

Tom Conley
is Lowell Professor in Harvard University's Departments of Art, Film & Visual Studies and Romance Languages & Literatures and author of *The Graphic Unconscious in Early Modern French Writing* (1991, French translation, 2000), *The Self-Made Map: Cartographic Writing in Early Modern France* (1996/2007); *An Errant Eye: Poetry and Topography in Early Modern France* (2011), *À fleur de page: Voir et lire le texte de la Renaissance* (2016). His studies of cinema include *Film Hieroglyphs* (1991/2007); *Cartographic Cinema* (2007), and *Action, Action, Action: The Early Cinema of Raoul Walsh* (2022). He has translated and edited works by Michel de Certeau, Gilles Deleuze, and others.

Wietse de Boer
is the Phillip R. Shriver Professor of History at Miami University (Ohio). His research interests are focused on the religious and cultural history of early modern Italy. His books include *The Conquest of the Soul: Confession, Discipline, and Public Order in Counter-Reformation Milan* (2001), *Art in Dispute: Catholic Debates at the Time of Trent* (2022), and seven edited volumes, including *Religion and the Senses in Early Modern Europe*, co-edited with Christine Göttler (2013), *Jesuit Image Theory*, co-edited with Karl A.E. Enenkel and Walter S. Melion (2016), and *La ghianda e la quercia. Saggi per Adriano Prosperi*, co-edited with Vincenzo Lavenia and Giuseppe Marcocci (2019). Another volume, co-edited with Christine Göttler, entitled *The Eschatological Imagination: Space, Time, and Experience (1300–1800)*, is forthcoming from Brill. The book project, *The Windows of the Soul: Sensory Culture and Religious Conflict in Early Modern Italy*, is in an advanced stage of preparation.

Carolin A. Giere

studied Latin, Arts, and Italian Studies at the University of Osnabrück. She received her M.Ed. in 2018 and was thereafter a Research Associate at the University of Göttingen. Since 2022 she has been academic coordinator of the School of Medieval and Neo-Latin Studies at the University of Freiburg. Her research focuses on intertextuality and interdependencies of ancient and early modern literature, with special regard for 15th- and 16th-century Europe. For her Ph.D. project, she is preparing the first critical edition, with introduction and commentary, of the manuscript of the song-book *Lucina* (1474), written by Aurelius Laurentius Albrisius of Pavia.

Barbara A. Kaminska

Ph.D. in History of Art and Architecture from the University of California Santa Barbara (2014), is an Associate Professor of Art History at Sam Houston State University in Huntsville, Texas. Her research focuses on interconfessional networks in sixteenth-century Antwerp, the history of charity and hospitality in Northern Europe ca. 1600, and the intersections of early modern art theory and disability studies, in particular the historiography of Netherlandish painters with deafness. She is the author of *Pieter Bruegel the Elder: Religious Art for the Urban Community* (2019) and *Images of Miraculous Healing in the Early Modern Netherlands* (2021).

Graham R. Lea

is an art historian trained in late medieval, renaissance, and early modern art of the Low Countries, and he specialises in art and art theory of the Netherlands, 1500–1650. He received a Ph.D. in art history from Emory University and a Ph.D. in art history from the University of Groningen in 2022, a J.D. from the University of Memphis in 2012, and a B.A. in art history and classics from Vanderbilt University in 2006.

His current research interests revolve around the relationship between visual art, theatre, humanism, rhetoric, and theology. He presently works on a project exploring the biblical history paintings by Hendrick Goltzius (1558–1617) and Pieter Lastman (1583–1633), specifically focusing on how these Dutch painters assimilate local rhetorical dramaturgy and performance practices found in the work of local rhetoricians (*rederijkers*).

Mitchell Merback

is the William Arnell and Everett Land Professor in the History of Art at Johns Hopkins University, and has also taught at DePauw University, Indiana

University, and the University of Pennsylvania. His art-historical work centers on northern Europe during the Later Middle Ages, Early Modern and Reformation periods, with a focus on Germany, Austria, and the Low Countries. He is the author of *The Thief, the Cross and the Wheel: Pain and the Spectacle of Punishment in Medieval and Renaissance Europe* (1999); *Pilgrimage and Pogrom: Violence, Memory, and Visual Culture at the Host-Miracle Shrines of Germany and Austria* (2013); and *Perfection's Therapy: An Essay on Albrecht Dürer's* Melencolia I (2017), and edited *Beyond the Yellow Badge: Anti-Judaism and Antisemitism in Medieval and Early Modern Visual Culture* (2008). He is currently completing a book on the expanded role of late medieval devotional images in fostering meditation, inner dialogue, care of the self, and the pursuit of ethical-spiritual wisdom. A longer-term book project, *Radical German Renaissance: Art, Dissent, and Freedom in the Era of Reform*, examines the work of painter-printmakers whose lives intersected in fateful ways with the radical religious movements of the early Reformation.

Ruth Sargent Noyes

is 2020–2023 Marie Skłodowska-Curie EU Senior Research Fellow at the National Museum of Denmark in Copenhagen. From 2024 she will be a lecturer at the Estonian Academy of Arts in Tallinn, Estonia. Author of a number of books and articles and recipient of a number of international research grants and awards, her recent research investigates art and architecture of the Baltic region from the late Middle Ages through the Enlightenment in its global context.

Bram Van Oostveldt

is Professor Theatre History at Ghent University. He has published widely on seventeenth, eighteenth and nineteenth-century theater history, often related to the visual arts and early modern art theory. With Stijn Bussels he was the guest editor of a special issue on the sublime in the Dutch Golden Age in the *Journal of Historians of Netherlandish Art* in 2016, and of *Lias, Journal of Early Modern Intellectual Culture and its Sources* in 2017. He has written two monographs on Brussels theater life in the eighteenth century *Tranen om het alledaagse* (Hilversum: 2013) and *The Theatre de la Monnaie and Theatre Life in the 18th Century Austrian Netherlands* (Ghent: 2001). With Caroline van Eck and Stijn Bussels, he co-edited a book on the historical reactions to the Amsterdam Town Hall (*The Amsterdam Town Hall in Words and Images. Constructing Wonder*, London, 2021).

Raphaèle Preisinger

received her Ph.D. degree in Art History and Media Theory from the Karlsruhe University of Arts and Design in 2012. She is currently Assistant Professor and Principal Investigator of the research project *Global Economies of Salvation: Art and the Negotiation of Sanctity in the Early Modern Period*, funded by the European Research Council (ERC) and the Swiss National Science Foundation (SNSF), at the University of Zurich. While her current research centres on the global circulation of images and objects in the early modern period, she maintains a major focus on image and piety in the Middle Ages. Her first book is titled *"Lignum vitae". Zum Verhältnis materieller Bilder und mentaler Bildpraxis im Mittelalter* (2014).

Bart Ramakers

is Professor of Historical Dutch Literature at the University of Groningen. He specialises in the drama of the Netherlandish rhetoricians, particularly in the relation between theatre, art, and humanism. His publications include *The Knowledge Culture of the Netherlandish Rhetoricians* (special issue *Renaissance Studies* 32.1 [2018]), co-edited with Arjan van Dixhoorn and Samuel Mareel; *Art and Death in The Netherlands, 1400–1800* (Netherlands Yearbook for History of Art 2022), co-edited with Edward H. Wouk; and *Het Land van Belofte: Het tafelspel van Schipper, Pelgrim en Post* (2022), an edition of a sixteenth-century Dutch dinner play.

Lukas Reddemann

is a Research Associate with the Department of Medieval Latin and Neo-Latin Philology at the University of Münster. In 2023, he completed his Ph.D. programme in Neo-Latin Philology with a thesis on a series of early modern descriptions of states in the Dutch Republic, the so-called 'Republics'. His monograph *Staatenkunde als Weltbeschreibung* appeared in 2024. His main areas of scholarly interest are Dutch late humanism, the reception of the classics, the history of emotions, and intersections of book history, university history and intellectual history in early modern times.

Ludovica Sasso

studied Classical Philology and Ancient Cultures (with a specialisation in Medieval History and Neo-Latin Philology) at the University of Naples. She worked from 2018 until August 2021 as *Wissenschaftliche Mitarbeiterin* and Ph.D. Student at the University of Dresden in the Collaborative Research Centre 1285 *Invektivität. Konstellationen und Dynamiken der Herabsetzung*. Her Ph.D. dissertation, *Invettive agonali nell'Umanesimo italiano. Poggio Braccolini e*

NOTES ON THE CONTRIBUTORS

i suoi "nemici" was defended in December 2021 and published in April 2023. With Uwe Israel and Marius Kraus, she is co-editor of the volume *Agonale Invektivität. Konstellationen und Dynamiken der Herabsetzung im italienischen und deutschen Humanismus* (2021). Since 2021 she is a Research Associate at the University of Münster, participating in the project *Türkenlyrik. Der europäische Osmanendiskurs in der lateinischen Okkasionalpoesie des Renaissancehumanismus*. Her research interests include social and political history in Renaissance Italy, polemical discourse in Italian Renaissance humanism, and Neo-Latin literature.

Aline Smeesters

is FNRS Research Associate at the UCLouvain (Louvain-la-Neuve, Belgium), where she co-directs the research centre GEMCA (Group for Early Modern Cultural Analysis). She specializes in Neo-Latin literature, poetry and poetics. In 2017–2023, she co-promoted the project "Schol'Art", investigating the impact of scholasticism on early modern letters and arts theories. She is author of the monograph *Aux rives de la lumière: la poésie de la naissance chez les auteurs néo-latins des anciens Pays-Bas* (2011) and co-editor of the volumes *Poésie latine à haute voix* (2013, with L. Isebaert), *Otto Van Veen, 'Theologicae et Physicae Conclusiones', 1621* (2017, with. A. Catellani, R. Dekoninck, E. Granjon, A. Guiderdoni), *Le Poète face au Tableau, de la Renaissance au Baroque* (2018, with R. Dekoninck) and *Arma victricia. Une pièce de théâtre jésuite des Pays-Bas espagnols* (2022, with G. Ems, R. Dekoninck, C. Drèze, C. Heering and D. Kiss).

Paul J. Smith

is Emeritus Professor of French literature at Leiden University. His has published widely on 16th-, 17th-, and 20th-century French literature, its reception in the Netherlands, French and Dutch fable and emblem books, literary rhetoric, intermediality, and early modern zoology. His main book publications include *Voyage et écriture. Etude sur le* Quart Livre *de Rabelais* (1987); *Het schouwtoneel der dieren. Embleemfabels in de Nederlanden (1567–ca. 1670)* (2006); *Dispositio. Problematic Ordering in French Renaissance Literature* (2007); and *Réécrire la Renaissance, de Marcel Proust à Michel Tournier. Exercices de lecture rapprochée* (2009). He edited *Éditer et traduire Rabelais à travers les âges* (1997), and co-edited, among other works, *Le paradoxe en linguistique et en littérature* (1996); *Montaigne and the Low Countries (1580–1700)* (2007); *Early Modern Zoology. The Construction of Animals in Science, Literature and the Visual Arts* (2007); *Emblems and the Natural World* (2017); *Natural History in Early Modern France* (2019); *Langues hybrides. Expérimentations linguistiques et littéraires* (2019); and *Early Modern Catalogues of Imaginary Books* (2020).

Anita Traninger

is Full Professor of Romance Literatures at Freie Universität Berlin, Germany. Her research focuses on the shape of knowledge, predominantly in the early modern period, and specifically with a view to European literatures in a global context. She has published on the history and theory of rhetoric as well as the history of reading, books, and media. Further areas of research include the history of gender and institutions, and historical shifts of the fact/fiction divide. Her books include: *Disputation, Deklamation, Dialog* (Stuttgart: Steiner 2012); *The Emergence of Impartiality* (ed. with Kathryn Murphy, Leiden: Brill 2014); *Discourses of Anger in the Early Modern Period* (ed. with Karl A.E. Enenkel, Leiden: Brill 2015); *The Figure of the Nymph in Early Modern Culture* (ed. with Karl A.E. Enenkel, Leiden: Brill 2018); Copia / *Kopie: Echoeffekte in der Frühen Neuzeit* (Hannover: Wehrhahn 2020).

Elliott D. Wise

is Associate Professor of Art History at Brigham Young University. He completed his doctoral studies under Walter Melion at Emory University, having spent a semester at the University of Leiden and a year in New York City as a fellow at The Metropolitan Museum of Art. His research and publications focus on the devotional function of late medieval and early modern art. In particular, he is interested in art and liturgy, Eucharistic piety, representations of the suffering Christ and the Virgin Mary, and the visual culture of the great mendicant and monastic orders. He recently completed a co-edited volume, *Mary, Mother of God: Devotion and Doctrine in the Visual Arts (1450–1700)* (Brill), and ongoing projects include a monograph that explores the affinity between vernacular mystical literature in the Low Countries and fifteenth-century panel paintings by Rogier van der Weyden and Robert Campin.

CHAPTER 1

Introduction: *Motus mixti et compositi* – the Portrayal of Mixed and Compound Emotions in the Visual and Literary Arts of Europe, 1500–1700

Walter S. Melion

This book examines the representation of affective complexity in the literary and pictorial arts of Northern Europe between the sixteenth and seventeenth centuries, asking how and why, by what means and to what ends alloyed or multilayered emotions were showcased. Although early modern humoral treatises acknowledged that states of feeling, much like their material sources – the four elements, the four qualities, and the four humours – could and often did mix, and treatises on art commented explicitly on the phenomenon, the portrayal of mixed and compound emotions remains little studied by historians of art or literature. And yet, there were few emotional communities (to use Barbara Rosenwein's handy terminology) that either lacked terms to describe such experiences or failed to give serious thought to them.[1] Take this Puritan testimonial, signed L.P. by a likely follower of the evangelical pastor Henry Walker and published in *Spiritual experiences, of sundry beleevers* (London, n.p.: 1653): 'The peace I finde with my God in my soule, which is sweet, though not without much heaviness of spirit for my failings'.[2] Spiritual delectation here admixes with anxious remorse about the attestant's sinful condition, the emotional mix verifying the signatory's Reformed bona fides. Or, crossing the confessional divide, take this description of the liturgical spectacle staged in Douai to celebrate the canonisation of Ignatius of Loyola,

---

1 On emotional communities, see Rosenwein B.H., *Anger's Past: The Social Uses of an Emotion in the Middle Ages* (Ithaca: 1998); eadem, *Emotional Communities in the Early Middle Ages* (Ithaca: 2006); and eadem, "Problems and Methods in the History of Emotions", *Passions in Context: Journal of the History and Philosophy of the Emotions* 1.1 (2010), at www.passionsin context.de/index.php/?id=557 (accessed 26 September 2023). Also see Karant-Nunn S., *The Reformation of Feeling: Shaping the Religious Emotions in Early Modern Germany* (Oxford: 2010); Mullaney S., *The Reformation of Emotions in the Age of Shakespeare* (Chicago: 2015); and Lynch A., "Emotional Community", in Broomhall S. (ed.), *Early Modern Emotions: An Introduction* (Milton Park – Abingdon: 2017) 3–6.

2 Cited in Rosenwein B.H., "Despair and Happiness", in eadem, *Generations of Feeling: A History of Emotions, 600–1700* (Cambridge: 2015) 248–287, at 268.

© WALTER S. MELION, 2025 | DOI:10.1163/9789004694613_002

s.j. and Francis Xavier, s.j. in 1622: 'Candles shone brightly from every place on the multi-stepped substructure; but above, [there were] three triumphal arches, its artful shadows eliciting sacred horror and reverence for God in the souls of the praying supplicants'.[3] The vast apparatus, made up of twin stages, one on each side of the main altar, served as a base for enthroned effigies of Saints Ignatius and Francis Xavier, whose presence, enhanced by the brilliant chiaroscuro, filled beholders with a mixture of dread/terror and reverent awe. The term *sanctus* (or *sacer*) *horror* denotes an experience of fear so great that it sets a person quivering, but that terror heightens rather than impedes the experience of worshipful, wonder-struck piety. Both citations, the one Protestant, the other Roman Catholic, utilise mixed emotion to approximate the sensation of divine presence, secured in one case through meditative prayer, in the other through the public encounter with a scenographic affirmation of the intercessory power of two newly minted saints. Mixed emotions could also be marshalled under more mundane circumstances to signify strong, sincerely felt affection, such as the altruistic love of concerned friends tried by adversity. Writing to Samuel Pepys, who had survived a shipwreck, John Evelyn asseverates:

> I have ben both very Long, and very-much concern'd for you, since your Northern Voyage [...] and that the dismal Accident was past, which gave me apprehensions for you, and a mixture of Passions, not realy to be Express'd, 'til I was assur'd of your Safty; and I now give God Thankes for it with as much Sincerity, as any Friend you have alive.[4]

So great was the danger or, more precisely, Evelyn's imagining of the danger, that it occasioned 'apprehensions' beyond the scope of any single definable passion. All three examples describe complex emotion to insist on the intensity and authenticity of what has been felt, and also to give the reader pause, so that s/he pays more than passing attention to what the person speaking claims to have seen and/or heard or, in the case of Evelyn, anxiously envisioned.

These two functions of showing mixed emotion – to make readers (or viewers) mindful of affective experience and to intensify their sense of the affects being conveyed – become all the more consequential when the poet or painter

---

3 Cited in Dekoninck R. – Delfosse A., "*Sacer Horror*: The Construction and Experience of the Sublime in the Jesuit Festivities of the Early Seventeenth-Century Southern Netherlands", *Journal of the Historians of Netherlandish Art* 8.2 (2016) 1–6, at https://jhna.org/articles/sacer-horror-construction-experience-sublime-jesuit-festivities-early-seventeenth-century-southern-netherlands/ (accessed 26 September 2023).
4 Cited in Rosenwein, "Despair and Happiness" 285.

INTRODUCTION: *MOTUS MIXTI ET COMPOSITI*

dwells on episodes of affective complexity, making them pivotal to the development of story and character. The essays gathered in this volume concentrate on the representation of such instances of alloyed or multi-sided emotion, or alternatively, on situations wherein emotions are observed to shift so rapidly and multiply that they appear almost to overlap, proving difficult to disentangle. Our joint purpose is not only to suggest the frequency with which these episodes occurred in early modern art and literature but, more importantly, to consider the whys and wherefores of their application to push a story forward or delineate its protagonists. What sort of literary or pictorial device was this? How was it deployed to shore up the poet's or painter's *ethos* (credibility or authority as a conveyor of story and character) and, complementarily, to produce *pathos* by inciting feelings of sympathy or antipathy? And what meaningful effects was the representation of mixed emotions intended to procure?

Before embarking on a summary account of some of the literary and art theoretical places where mixed emotion regularly surfaces as a potent affective appliance between 1500 and 1700, we want to acknowledge our debt to the many recent studies on early modern emotions, in particular the groundbreaking work of Barbara Rosenwein, Susan Broomhill,[5] Brian Cummings and Freya Sierhuis,[6] Stephanie Dickey and Herman Roodenburg,[7] Penelope Gouk and Helen Hills,[8] Richard Meek and Erin Sullivan,[9] Gail Kern Paster,[10] and Johann Steiger.[11] In thinking about mixed emotion, we have greatly benefitted from Kern Paster's attempts to construct an historical phenomenology of early modern emotions apropos the doctrine of psychophysiological causation of

---

5   Broomhall S., *Emotions in the Household* (Basingstoke – New York: 2008); eadem, *Gender and Emotions in Medieval and Early Modern Europe* (Farnham: 2015); and eadem, "Emotions of the Past in Catherine de Medici's Correspondence", in Marculescu A. – Moran Métivier C.-L. (eds.), *Affective and Emotional Economies in Medieval and Early Modern Europe*, Palgrave Studies in the History of Emotions (Cham: 2018) 87–104.

6   Cummings B. – Sierhuis F. (eds.), *Passion and Subjectivity in Early Modern Culture* (Farnham – Burlington, VT: 2013).

7   Dickey S. – Roodenburg H. (eds.), *The Passions in the Arts of the Early Modern Netherlands*, Nederlands Kunsthistorisch Jaarboek 60 (Zwolle: 2010).

8   Gouk P. – Hills H. (eds.), *Representing Emotions: New Connections in the Histories of Art, Music, and Medicine* (Aldershot – Burlington, VT: 2005).

9   Meek R. – Sullivan E. (eds.), *The Renaissance of Emotion: Understanding Affect in Shakespeare and his Contemporaries* (Manchester: 2015).

10 Kern Paster G., *Humoring the Body: Emotions and the Shakespearean Stage* (Chicago: 2004); and Kern Paster G. – Rowe K. – Floyd-Wilson M. (eds.), *Reading the Early Modern Passions: Essays in the Cultural History of Emotion* (Philadelphia: 2004).

11 Steiger J.A. (ed.), *Passion, Affekt, und Leidenschaft in der frühen Neuzeit*, Wolfenbütteler Arbeiten zur Barockforschung 43, 2 vols. (Wiesbaden: 2005).

the passions.[12] Equally important as a complement to Kern Paster have been Meeks and Sullivan's efforts to shift scholarly emphasis away from humoral explanations towards 'other belief systems and literary and dramaturgical styles', such as the philosophical and theological commitments of authors who wrote about the affective dimensions of spiritual life, or the linguistic and rhetorical usages that shaped conceptions of such affective terms as 'spleen, sympathise, and happiness', or again, the performative traditions in respect of which the affects were enacted on courtly or public stages with the aim of moving their respective audiences.[13] Gouk and Hills's volume was one of the first to explore the historicization of the emotions as an interpretative problem common to art history, musicology, and the history of medicine, especially as pertains to the study of spiritual passion, affective modes of bodily address, and the disciplinary functions of constrained emotional expression. And for the study of northern art, Dickey and Roodenburg's *The Passions in the Arts of the Early Modern Netherlands* launched the study of affects as a central topic in scholarship on Dutch and Flemish art: whereas the majority of essays in their volume looked carefully at how painters tended to enforce gendered emotional norms, fixing their attention on moments when emotional ambiguity resolves into mastery over the passions, others instead centered on the portrayal of *beweeglijkheid* (enlivened emotion keyed to liveliness of motion) and *staetveranderinge* (Joost van den Vondel's term for Aristotelian *peripeteia*, broadly defined by him as a 'change of state' akin to Ovidian metamorphosis).[14] However, Zirka Z. Filipczak's essay, to be discussed below, broached several issues central, too, to our volume: namely, the manner and meaning of Peter Paul Rubens's adaptations of classical sculpture for the purpose of ambiguating emotional expression.[15]

All the publications just enumerated make use of the full range of early modern terminology for felt experience: in particular, affect, passion, and, to some extent, emotion. The consensus on the etymology of these terms or, better, categories is that 'passion', which derives from the Greek *pathe* and the Latin *patior*, sometimes retained its ties to the notion of suffering passively. This implication, as Susan James, and Meek and Sullivan have argued, perhaps

---

12 Kern Paster, *Humoring the Body* 1–76.

13 Meek – Sullivan (eds.), "Introduction", in *Renaissance of Emotion* 13, 15, 16; as regards performative traditions, see Part 3, in ibid. 177–263.

14 See, respectively, Roodenburg H., "*Beweeghlijkheid* Embodied: On the Corporeal and Sensory Dimensions of a Famous Emotion Term", in Dickey – Roodenburg (eds.), *Passions in the Arts* 307–319; and Sluijter E.J., "Rembrandt's Portrayal of the Passions and Vondel's '*staetveranderinge*'", in ibid. 285–306.

15 Filipczak Z.Z., "Rubens Adapts the Poses of Classical Sculptures for Deliberately Ambiguous and Other Emotions", in Dickey – Roodenburg (eds.), *Passions in the Arts* 125–149.

INTRODUCTION: *MOTUS MIXTI ET COMPOSITI*

derives from Aristotle's understanding of passion and sensation as reactive states stimulated by external forces.[16] 'Affect', from the Latin *afficio*, can refer to a state of body or mind produced by some active influence and was often associated, as Kern Paster notes, with desire or affection.[17] In their analysis of the terms *affectus* and *affectio*, Raphaele Garrod, Michael Champion, and Juanita Ruys, with reference to Francisco Suárez, s.j.'s commentary on Thomas Aquinas's *Prima secundae*, define them as motions in the senses of the appetitive power, and thus distinguish them from *passio*, which connotes not these motions per se but the effects – often accompanied by physical changes – produced by motions of sense, upon instigation from an external catalyst.[18] Much less common was the word 'emotion', a derivative from *moveo* and *emoveo*, which, as Meek and Sullivan hypothesize on the basis of Jean François Senault's critique of *passio*'s passive implications, adverts to the 'motive power of the passions'.[19] In "Towards a History of Emotion, 1562–1660", David Thorley charts the early French and English uses of 'emotion' to signify the overlapping senses of a physical movement from one place to another, a political tumult or commotion, and a mental sensation indexing concerted agitation of the mind and of the humours or spirits.[20] Michel de Montaigne's *Essais* (Paris, Simon Millanges – Jean Richer: 1580) popularised this tripartite usage of *émotion*, which further circulated in the English-language translation by John Florio.[21] Randle Cotgrave's *Dictionarie of the French and English Tongues* (London, Islip: 1611), perhaps the first lexicon to attempt an experiential definition of the term, elucidates *esmotion* as the emphatic motion of the body, mind, and/or spirit: 'commotion, sudden, or turbulent stirring; an agitation of the spirit, violent motion of the thoughts, vehement inclination of the mind'.[22]

---

16   James S., *Passion and Action: The Emotions in Seventeenth-Century Philosophy* (Oxford: 1997), 1–26, esp. 11, 41; and Meek – Sullivan (eds.), "Introduction", in *Renaissance of Emotion* 10–11.

17   Kern Paster, *Humoring the Body* 10.

18   Champion M. – Garrod R. – Ruys J., "But were they talking about emotions? *Affectus, affectio,* and the History of Emotions", *Rivista storica italiana* 128.2 (2016) 521–543, esp. 536–537.

19   Meek – Sullivan, "Introduction", in *Renaissance of Emotion* 11. Cf. Senault Jean François, *The Use of the Passions*, trans. Henry Earl of Monmouth (London, J.L. Moseley – Humphrey Moseley: 1649) 18, which refers to motions of the soul and body so 'violent [...] that they do hardly deserve the name of passions'.

20   Thorley D., "Towards a History of Emotion, 1562–1660", *The Seventeenth Century* 28.1 (2013) 3–19.

21   Montaigne Michel de, *The Essayes or Morall, Politike and Millitarie discourses of Lo: Michaell de Montaigne*, trans. John Florio (London: E. Blount, 1603) 147, 206, 234, 235, 239, 274, 394, 400, 424, 426, 432, 461, 715, as discussed by Thorley, "Towards a History of Emotion" 8–9.

22   Cotgrave, *Dictionarie* n.p.

In practice, however, differences in meaning, even between 'passion' and 'affect', let alone 'passion' and 'emotion', were not strictly enforced, as is evident from the definitions offered in Cornelis Kiliaen's *Etymologicum Teutonicae linguae* (Antwerp, Ex Officina Plantiniana: 1573), which renders *affectie* as 'animus, studium, voluntas, affectio', *passie* as 'passio, aegritudo, affectio, affectio animi, perturbatio'.[23] This dictionary draws a residual distinction between the two terms: it suggests that *affectie* can involve the faculty of will ('voluntas' and also 'studium' in the sense of zealous effort), whereas *passie* can be tied to affliction ('aegritudo', grief, sorrow, care, but also illness and the suffering it brings); but the two terms also overlap since they both share the cognate 'affectio'. Moreover, 'animus' appears with *affectie*, 'affectio animi' with *passie*. Although no Dutch equivalent for emotion is given, the Latin noun *emotio* and past participle *emotus* are comprised by the definitions of the strong feelings *verbaestheyd/verschricktheyd* (shock, dismay) and *verruckinghe der sinnen* (sensory rapture): the former's cognates are 'ecstasis: consternatio: stupor, emotio mentis';[24] the latter's are 'ecstasis, mentis excessus, abstractio mentis a corpore: mentis emotio, vulgo raptus'.[25] *Emotus* also forms part of the definition of *dulhuys* (madhouse): 'locus in quo mente emoti, vincti aut inclusi tenentur' (place in which the mentally disturbed are held bound or imprisoned).[26] These applications of *emotio* and *emotus* suggest the terms' association with strongly felt passion, not only because *emotus* is used to define a setting linked with illness and disquietude, but also because *emotio* appears in tandem with the term 'consternatio' (dismay, disquiet, disorder, consternation) that resembles 'perturbatio' (disorder, disquiet, perturbation). The essays in this volume therefore utilise affect, passion, and emotion judiciously rather than strictly, applying them to accord with the sources cited on a case by case basis.

Discussions of mixed emotion primarily occur in two types of didactic text: psychophysiological treatises on the humours and temperaments, especially descriptive-therapeutic accounts of melancholy such as Robert Burton's *The Anatomy of Melancholy* (Oxford, J. Lichfield – J. Short: 1621), and art treatises such as Karel van Mander's *Den Grondt der Edel vry Schilder-const* (Foundation of the Noble, Free Art of Painting), Book 1 of his six-part *Schilder-Boeck* (Book on Painting) (Haarlem, Paschier van Wesbusch: 1604).[27] Let us begin with Van Mander, the chief source of whose interest in mixed emotion, the theorist

---

23   Kiliaen C., *Etymologicum teutonicae linguae*, ed. F. Claes, s.J. (Mouton – The Hague: 1972), respectively, 692, 713.

24   Ibid. 581.

25   Ibid. 600.

26   Ibid. 102.

27   On the *Grondt* (Foundation or, alternatively, Groundwork), see Melion W.S., *Karel van Mander and his* Foundation of the Noble, Free Art of Painting (Leiden – Boston: 2022). On

INTRODUCTION: *MOTUS MIXTI ET COMPOSITI*

Gian Paolo Lomazzo's *Trattato dell'arte della pittura, scultura ed architettura* (Milan, Paolo Gottardo Pontio for Pietro Tini: 1585), was the first printed treatise to contain a chapter specifically focusing on the representation of mixed emotions.[28]

Dutch and Flemish art treatises published in the wake of Van Mander's *Schilder-Boeck* (1604) invariably emulate him by devoting much attention to the passions (*affecten, passien*) and how to portray them. These texts, ranging from Franciscus Junius's Latin, English, and Dutch redactions of *De pictura veterum* (1637, 1638, and 1641) to Samuel van Hoogstraeten's *Inleyding tot de hooge schoole der schilderkonst* (1678) and Arnold Houbraken's *De groote schouburgh* (1718), generally give prominence to what Van Mander called the '*motus* des lichaems van buyten', that is, the motions of the body as indices of the motions of the spirit, and consider how these 'affections, passions, inclinations, and afflictions' may effectively be conveyed and propagated.[29] Theoreticians were especially fascinated with the transitional, volatile, ephemeral, and flexible character of certain emotions, which often results in the production of mixed, composite, complex, or ambivalent emotional states. Van Mander, in chapter 6, stanza 54 of the *Grondt* lavishly praises Pieter Bruegel for his ability, in the *Massacre of the Innocents*, to describe the ambivalence of Herod's herald, who appears jointly obdurate and compassionate, inwardly remorseful and outwardly remorseless [Fig. 1.1]:

> Further, in a *Massacre of the Innocents*
> By the subtle, faultless Bruegel is to be seen
> A cadaverously pale Mother, straitened and swooning,
> Yea an entire grief-stricken family,
> Pleading with a Herald for a child's life,
> In whom a modicum of compassion is discernible,
> But who yet promulgates the King's Placard, though with senses mortified
> That one may be merciful to no one.[30]

---

the *Schilder-Boeck*, see Melion W.S., *Shaping the Netherlandish Canon: Karel van Mander's* Schilder-Boeck (Chicago: 1991).

28 On the *Trattato*, see Tramelli B., *Giovanni Paolo Lomazzo's* Trattato dell'Arte della Pittura: *Color, Perspective, and Anatomy*, Nuncius Series 1 (Leiden – Boston: 2017).

29 On the '*motus* des lichaems van buyten', see Van Mander, *Grondt*, chapter 6, stanza 35, in *Schilder-Boeck*, fol. 25v; and Melion, *Karel van Mander's* Foundation 135–136, 437. Chapter 6 is titled "Wtbeeldinghe der Affecten, passien, begeerlijckheden, en lijdens der Menschen" (Portrayal of the Affects/affections, passions, desires/inclinations, and sorrows/afflictions of Persons).

30 Van Mander, *Grondt*, chapter 6, stanza 54, in *Schilder-Boeck*, fol. 27r:
 'Van den aerdighen brueghel sonder faute.

FIGURE 1.1   Pieter Bruegel the Elder, *Massacre of the Innocents*, ca. 1565–1567. Oil on panel, 109.2 × 105.1 cm. Royal Collection Trust, Windsor RCIN 405787

The herald combines two registers of expression codified by Quintilian in *Institutio oratoria* VI.ii.8–9: *pathos*, i.e., *adfectus* (passion), which he defines as the description of 'the more violent emotions', and *ethos*, i.e., *mores* (morals, habits of conduct, standards of behavior based in felt experience), which he characterises as more 'subdued', 'calm and gentle'. Whereas *pathos* aims to 'command and disturb', *ethos* aims to 'persuade and induce a feeling of goodwill'.[31] He adds, in VI.ii.12, that *pathos* and *ethos* are often linked, being different more in degree than kind: 'Indeed I would add that *pathos* and *ethos* are

---

   Noch in een Kinderdoodingh is te siene,
   Dootverwich een Moeder benout in flaute,
   Iae een droevich gheslacht, tot den Heraute,
   Om een kindts leven verbidden, aen wiene
   Wel ghenoech melijden is te bespiene,
   Maer toont s'Conings Placcaet met sinnen smertich,
   Datmen over geen en mach zijn barmhertich'.
   On this stanza, see Melion, *Karel van Mander's* Foundation 136–137, 441–442.
31 Quintilian, *The* Institutio oratoria, trans. H.E. Butler, 4 vols. (London – Cambridge, MA: 1939) 2:420–423.

INTRODUCTION: *MOTUS MIXTI ET COMPOSITI* 9

sometimes of the same nature, differing only in degree; love for instance comes under the head of *pathos*, affection of *ethos*'.[32] Disturbed by his own cruelty, the herald is thus an epitome of mixed emotion: feeling a modicum of compassion, yet constrained to show no mercy, and troubled as a result by fruitless compunction, he holds true to a habit of conduct even while falling prey to the vagaries of *pathos*. The encounter between Bruegel's herald and the peasants accosting him functions something like a commonplace for the depiction of emotions jostling for the upper hand, or, alternatively, of admixed emotions – implacable cruelty tempered by the mortifying sensation of compassion.

Van Mander's interest in emotional complexity of this sort probably derived, at least partly, from his familiarity with Lomazzo's *Trattato*, Book 2, chapter 18 of which, "Of the concord and discord of the motions, and of their uniting", concerns the nature and representation of mixed emotions.[33] Lomazzo is chiefly interested in passions of the mind that are susceptible to bodily expression through 'certaine motions'. As these motions are reactive to the apprehension of some thing, so these apprehensions are threefold – namely, sensitive, rational, or intellectual: sensitive when an object is judged good or evil 'under the shewe of that which is profitable or unprofitable, pleasant or offensive'; rational when an object is considered good or evil 'in maner of virtue or vice, praise of dispraise, honestie or dishonestie'; intellectual when a good object is regarded as true, an evil object as false.[34] Sensitive apprehension is the painter's purview, and from it issue two principal passions, desire and its concupiscible derivatives or anger and its irascible derivatives. Taken together, these derivatives constitute the 'eleven passions or affections in the minde, which are these: Love, Hatred, Desire, Feare, Joy, Sorrowe, Hope, Despayre, Audacities, Timorousnes and Anger'.[35] Lomazzo treats these eleven passions as unalloyed, mainly discoursing on them in Book 2, chapter 3. Chapter 18, on the other hand discusses the hybrid configurations of passion that ensue when sensitive apprehension is applied under conditions of humoral mixing. His account is

---

32   Ibid. 422–423.

33   Lomazzo Giovanni Paolo, "Of the concord and discord of the motions, and of their uniting", in *A Tracte containing the artes of curious Paintinge, Carvinge and Buildinge*, trans. Richard Haydocke (Oxford, Joseph Barnes for Richard Haydocke: 1598) 77–79. Cf. Lomazzo G.P., *Trattato dell'arte della pittura, sculture ed architettura*, in Ciardi R.P. (ed.), *Gian Paolo Lomazzo, Scritti sulle arti*, 2 vols. (Florence: 1974) 2:152–153.

34   Lomazzo, "Of the passions of the minde, their originall and difference", in *Tracte containing the artes*, trans. Haydocke 9. Cf. Lomazzo, *Trattato*, ed. Ciardi 2:102.

35   Lomazzo, "Passions of the minde", in *Tracte*, trans. Haydocke 9–10. Cf. Lomazzo, *Trattato*, ed. Ciardi 2:102.
      Lomazzo never explains in what respect the inferior power of the mind he identifies as Desire differs from the derivative also called Desire.

exceedingly detailed, so, a brief excerpt should suffice to give some sense of its tenor and scope; he keeps history painting always in view as he sets about the task of enumerating possible mixtures:

> On the other side these agree: viz. anxiety, heavines, sadnes, stubbournnes, and roughnesse, with timidity, simplicity, humility, purity, and mercifulnes, and may be united (but never with that facility and sympathy) with violence, rage, arrogancy, audacity, cruelty, and fiercenes; temperatnes, modesty, gratiousnes, royalnes, clemency, and cheerfulness, may accord with timiditye, simplicity, humility, purity, and mercifulness, as also with audacity, fiercenes, magnanimity, liberality, comelinesse, wantonnesse; and so through all the other motions wee shall easily finde out all their agreements, and disagreements: which being perceived and understood, wee shal afterwards easily couple the motions together, and represent them in countenances in such sorte, as shalbee fit for Histories, and for the effects, from whence they springe: as for example, in *Abraham* when hee must sacrifice his sonne to God, both piety and obedience; and in *Isaac* both those, but mixed with feare and sorrow.[36]

Even motions/emotions that Lomazzo considered inimical could under certain circumstances be combined by association with a *tertium comparationis*: 'boldenesse' and 'feare' are 'enemies in the highest degree, and yet notwithstanding may agree with some other, and by this meanes agree together with them in the same subiect'. This is because boldness and fear, howsoever contradictory between themselves, agree with both 'honesty and wantonnesse'.[37] Chapter 18 concludes by declaring that mixed emotions are the true currency of pictorial excellence; surprising as these mixtures may be, they in no way contravene the rule of decorum, as Lomazzo makes clear by differentiating the mixed emotions of a painted Jupiter or Christ:

> And thus whosoever shall ioyne the motions together, according unto this method of concord and discorde, which I have shewed to be found in them, shall not onely attaine unto the easinesse of representing whatsoever hee list, but also to the commendation of a good Painter. As for example, in representing Jupiter most kindly courting and embracing Io,

---

36 Lomazzo, "Passions of the minde", in *Tracte*, trans. Haydocke, 77–78. Cf. Lomazzo, *Trattato*, ed. Ciardi 2:152.

37 Lomazzo, "Passions of the minde", in *Tracte*, trans. Haydocke, 78. Cf. Lomazzo, *Trattato*, ed. Ciardi 2:152.

INTRODUCTION: *MOTUS MIXTI ET COMPOSITI* 11

hee shall expresse, that pleasaunt cheerefulnesse which agreeth with his milde nature, mixed and tempered with maiesty, boldenesse, and wantonnesse: though I say hee were naturally and by occasion pleasaunt and cheerefull. For if hee shoulde bee otherwise described, hee woulde not easily bee taken for Jupiter: so that you may also resemble in a childe kindenesse, but with an action, of basenesse, and rudenesse, which if wee shoulde expresse in Christ, woulde be most absurd.[38]

Noteworthy is the fact that Lomazzo is talking about the representational mixing or layering of emotions, rather than distinguishing, in the manner of philosophers such as Robert Burton, between emotions by nature, i.e., inherently, either simple or mixed. Burton writes about good and bad affections and perturbations, identifying melancholy as a 'simple' offshoot of the bad; by contrast, good affections are simple not mixt:

The *Bad* are *Simple* or *mixt*: *Simple* for some bad object present, as sorrow which contracts the Heart, macerates [that is, torments] the Soule, subverts the good estate of the Body, hindering all the operations of it, causing Melancholy, and many times death it selfe; or future, as fear. Out of these two [i.e., sorrow and fear] arise those mixed affections and passions of anger, which is a desire of revenge; hatred, which is inveterate anger; zeal, which is offended with him who hurts that he loves; and *épichairechachía* [flattery], a compound affection of joy and hate, when we rejoice at other men's mischief, and are grieved at their prosperity, pride, self-love, emulation, envy, shame, etc.[39]

Melancholy, as it turns out, is a complex emotion, not 'mixt' in the sense above but more like what we in this volume have designated as mixed; it consists of a layering of 'simples', in threes, fours, sixes, or paired opposites:

Nothing so prosperous and pleasant, but it hath some bitterness in it, some complaining, some grudging; it is all *glykypikron* [bittersweet], a mixed passion, and like a chequer table black and white: men, families,

---

38 Ibid. 79.

39 Burton R., *The Anatomy of Melancholy* (Philadelphia, E. Claxton: 1883) 103–104. On this passage and its basis in the Thomist distinction between the concupiscible and irascible powers of the sensory appetite, see Rosenwein, *Generations of Feeling* 260.

cities, have their falls and wanes; now trines, sextiles, then quartiles and oppositions.[40]

René Descartes, in *Les passions de l'âme* (Paris, Henry Le Gras: 1649) would later systematise the distinction between 'mixt' and mixed, calling the former derivatives, the latter, consisting of simple primitives, compounds. In the "69th Article" he identifies six simple, primitive passions; every other passion either derives from one of them or is compounded of two or more of them.

> But the number of those which are simple, and primitive is not very great; for doe but review all those I have cast up, and it may easily be noted, that there are but six such, to wit, Admiration, Love, Hatred, Desire, Joy, and Sadnesse: and that all the other are compounded of some of these six, or are sorts of them.[41]

In the "196th Article", for example, he says about indignation that it can attach either to pity or derision, depending on whether one is well- or ill-disposed toward the perpetrator of some offense; consequently, he imagines such a person as a chimaera whose mixed emotions transform him into Democritus and Heraclitus combined:

> TO doe an evill, is also in some respects to receive one, from whence it comes that some with their Indignation joyn Pity, and others derision: according as they bear a good or ill Will towards those whom they see commit faults. Thus the laughter of Democritus, and the weeping of Heraclitus, might proceed from the same cause.[42]

By the same token, although sadness often accompanies indignation, it can also mingle or merge with joy, even hilarity:

> Indignation is also oftimes accompanied with Admiration. For we use to think that all things shall be done in the same manner we conceive they ought to be done, that is, after that manner which we esteem good. Wherefore when it falls out otherwise it surprizeth us, and we Admire it. Nor is it incompatible with Joy, although it most commonly be joyned with Sadnesse. For when the evill we bear an Indignation against cannot

---

40   Ibid. 94.
41   Descartes René, *The passions of the soule in three books*, trans. s.n. (London, J. Martin – J. Ridley: 1650) 54–55.
42   Ibid. 159.

INTRODUCTION: *MOTUS MIXTI ET COMPOSITI* 13

hurt us, and we consider that we would not doe the like, it gives us some delight: and this may be one of the causes of Laughter, which sometimes accompanies this Passion.[43]

Baruch de Spinoza, in *Ethica* (Amsterdam, Jan Rieuwertsz.: 1677), argued that all emotions must ultimately resolve into only three fundamental ones – desire, pleasure, or pain – of which the first, desire, is inextricable from individual nature, whereas the other two, pleasure and pain, are passionate tendencies. In *Ethics*, Part 3, note 59 he proposes that every other emotion and, by implication, the greater part of emotional experience is compounded of these three or of other emotions in almost infinite measure:

> For by the same method as has been employed above, we can easily show that love is sometimes united to repentance, to disdain, to shame, etc. Nay, I think it must be clear to all from what has been said, that the emotions can be compounded one with another in so many ways, and so many variations may thence arise, that it is impossible to specify their number.[44]

Descartes, unlike Spinoza, gives serious consideration to exterior signs of the passions, especially 'gestures of the eyes and face' (Article 113), changes of complexion (114–117), and tears (128), but his interest in affective bodily traces pertains mainly to the simpler passions, and only to those expressed by persons themselves, not to images of them. Our volume, on the other hand, deals with literary and pictorial approaches to complex forms of emotional representation.

The passage from Van Mander's *Grondt*, cited above, is a case in point: he comments on a pivotal figure, the herald, who epitomises Bruegel's command of complex emotional expression, as lodged in that figure's paradoxical attitude, at once responsive *and* unresponsive, compassionate *and* implacable, toward the villagers. There were, of course, other ways of describing mixed and/or shifting emotions; for example, an image's emotional range could be made contingent on its relation to adjacent images or texts that contextualise it. Here is an early example of this phenomenon. Compiled in late fifteenth-century Brabant for the Augustinian monks of Groenendael Priory, Metropolitan Museum Album 2003.476, known as the *Groenendael Passion*, is a customised manuscript prayerbook organised around first-state impressions of

---

43   Ibid. 159–160.

44   Spinoza B. de, *Ethics Proved in Geometrical Order, Divided into Five Parts*, trans. A. Boyle (London: 1910; repr. ed., 1941) 127.

the *Grosse Passion*, a series of twelve prints designed, engraved, and published ca. 1480 by the master engraver-goldsmith Israhel van Meckenem [Fig. 1.2].[45] The book takes the form of a *rapiaria*, a collection of religious texts gathered from various sources in order to facilitate pious devotion and prayerful edification. The book's texts are written in Latin and Dutch. The Dutch extracts, taken from such sources as the *Secret Passion*, the *Christi Leiden*, and *Extendit-Manum-Passion*, minutely focus on the bloody wounds of Christ, dissolving or, better, anatomizing his body into its torn and shredded particulars, and recounting the pain, grief, anxiety, and other torments of Christ.[46] The Latin excerpts, sourced from Ludolphus's *Vita Christi*, are incarnational in a more strictly theological sense: they anchor episodes from the Passion in the whole of the *verum corpus* and, implicitly, in the mind, heart, and spirit of Christ that inhere in this incarnate body and remain fully, calmly cognizant of his redemptive vocation.[47] Directly inscribed on the versos of the engravings, these extracts are modally distinct from the more aggressive Dutch texts amidst which Van Meckenem's prints were interfoliated.[48] The Latin moderates the horrors of the Passion, constantly reminding the votary to consider the relation between the *vita mortalis* and *vita vitalis* (i.e., *spiritualis*) of Christ. By contrast, the Dutch externalises and exacerbates the bodily horrors of the Passion, harping on the hundreds of cuts, bruises, and wounds, administered

---

45   On the *Groenendael Passion*, see Melion W.S., "Meditating the Unbearable in a Fifteenth-Century Manuscript Prayerbook with Printed Images", in Dlabačová A. – Leerdam A. van – Thompson J. (eds.), *Vernacular Books and their Readers in the Early Age of Print (c. 1450–1600)*, Intersections 85 (Leiden – Boston: 2023) 328–393.

46   On the sobriquet *Secret Passion*, used to refer to extra-scriptural Passion narratives such as the *Heimelike Passie*, the *Christi leiden in einer Vision geschaut*, and Heinrich of St. Gallen's *Die Extendi-manum-Passion*, see Marrow J.H., *Passion Iconography in Northern European Art of the Late Middle Ages and Early Renaissance*, Ars Neerlandica 1 (Kortrijk: 1979) 24, 259, n. 100; and Ampe A., "Naar een geschiedenis van de passie-beleving vanuit Marrows' *Passie-boek*", *Ons geestelijk erf* 58 (1984) 130–175, esp. 132–149. On these and other amplified *Lives of Christ*, also see Goudriaan K., "Middle Dutch Meditative *Lives of Jesus* on the Early Printing Press: An Exploration of the Field", in idem, *Piety in Practice and Print: Essays on the Late Medieval Religious Landscape*, ed. A. Dlabačová – A. Tervoort (Hilversum: 2016) 219–239.

47   On the *Vita Christi*, see Baier W., *Untersuchungen zu den Passionsbetrachtungen in der 'Vita Christi' des Ludolfs von Sachsen: Ein Quellenkritischer Beitrag zu Leben und Werk Ludolfs und zur Geschichte der Passionstheologie*, Analecta Cartusiana 44, 3 vols. (Salzburg: 1977). Also see, on Middle-Dutch redactions of the *Vita Christi*, Deschamps J., "De 'Vita Christi' van Ludolf van Saksen in het Middelnederlands", in *Historia et spiritualitas cartusiensis. Colloquii quarti internationalis acta, Gandavi Antverpiae Brugis 16–10 Sept. 1982* (Destelbergen: 1983) 157–176.

48   Only the *Ecce Homo* incorporates an inscription on the recto side.

INTRODUCTION: *MOTUS MIXTI ET COMPOSITI* 15

FIGURE 1.2   *Groenendael Passion*, fol. 23v: Articles 41 and 42 of the *Hondert articulen der passion Iesu Christi* and fol. 24r: Israhel van Meckenem, *Flagellation of Christ*. Album: late fifteenth century; each folio ca. 260 × 204 mm. Metropolitan Museum of Art, 2003.476

violently and repetitively, that ultimately lead to the inhuman death of Christ. Van Meckenem's plates function as the common ground for both manners and modes of Passion meditation: viewed in conjunction with its associated texts, Jesus can be seen as calm and/or tormented, sanguine and/or anguished; and the same holds true of the reader-viewer, whose emotional responses, too, become profoundly mixed as he dwells now on the bodily suffering of Christ, now on his transcendent spirit, and strives to embrace the fullness of the Lord's personhood. Indeed, one might argue that the narrative coherence of these semi-liturgical, bi-modal meditative exercises derives from Van Meckenem's images, which depict the Passion as a series of scripturally-based events susceptible to the kinds of extra-scriptural, affective elaboration on show in the Latin and Dutch texts.

The Dutch texts also revel in modal shifts of affect. Take the meditative exercises on the *Flagellation*: they particularise the punishments visited on Christ by the three kinds of scourges – respectively formed of rods, cords knotted with metal hooks, and dried ox-sinews – wherefrom blood spurted everywhere, flooding the floors, while thick lumps of flesh adhered to the scourges [Fig. 1.3].

FIGURE 1.3 Israhel van Meckenem, *Flagellation of Christ in the Presence of Pilate, with Christ Brought before Herod*, from *Große Passion*, ca. 1480. Engraving, highlighted in gold, with touches of pen and red ink (on Christ's feet), ca. 205 × 151 mm. Metropolitan Museum of Art

INTRODUCTION: *MOTUS MIXTI ET COMPOSITI*

The emphasis falls on the horror of the scene, felt most intensely by Jesus, at the climax of which 'the Lord was pitiable to see, for then from the crown of his head to the soles of his feet there was nothing that had not been thoroughly wounded'.[49] Suddenly, the votary is then urged to think of Jesus as his bridegroom, who holds himself still, both in body and soul, amidst all this suffering, which he feels more grievously from within than from without, and yet gladly, even joyfully accepts for love of his spouse (viz., the penitent votary). The abrupt swing to the bridal imagery of the *Song of Songs*, and the concomitant adjuration, 'attend to your bridegroom Jesus with your inward eyes', brief yet insistent, serve to foster contemplative devotion even as they shock the votary into acknowledging his sinful guilt and shame. He has betrayed his beloved, thrown him to the wolves now devouring him. As Jesus falls prey to pain and terror, and yet epitomises tender love and unselfish desire, so the exercitant finds himself longing for the spouse whom he cruelly and selfishly immiserates. Mixed emotion intensifies his sense of sinful abjection compounded with grateful remorse and loving compunction.

Another example of this type of contextually produced effect of mixed emotion comes from one of the first and most elaborate of all Marian emblem books. Distinctive in form, function, and argument, Jan David, s.j.'s *Pancarpium Marianum* (Marian Garland) (Antwerp, Balthasar and Jan Moretus: 1607) was the first emblem book entirely devoted to the Virgin Mary [Fig. 1.4].[50] It consists of fifty emblems subdivided into seven groups of seven (plus a closing fiftieth emblem) that expound the dual intercessory agency of Mary who is seen jointly to have brought Christ forth into the world and to mediate his coming forth internally within the votary's heart. Each emblematic cluster attaches to a Marian *titulus*, which David construes multiply, not merely as a commemorative inscription or personal title, but also as a claim to glory, fame, or honor, and as a head under which an action and affect, or better, class of affective action is sanctioned. As he puts it, his emblem book operates like an intaglio press that deeply imprints the reader-viewer with images of the Virgin's sevenfold relation to Christ, but more than this, the *Pancarpium*, if properly utilized, brings about the reader-viewer's conversion into a living Marian image, causing her/him actively to reenact and feel Mary's septenary relation to the

---

49 *Groenendael Passion*, fol. 25r–v: 'Och hoe deerlijc was ons here doen aen te siene. Want hi niet geheels en hadde vander cruynen sijns hoefs totten planten sijnre voeten ten was al doe[r]wont'.

50 On the *Pancarpium Marianum*, see Melion W.S., "*De Virgine natalitia ad rapientem*: Marian Maternity, Militancy, and Mimesis in the First Marian Emblem Book – Jan David, s.j.'s *Pancarpium Marianum* of 1607", *Emblematica: Essays in Word and Image* 4 (2021) 139–209.

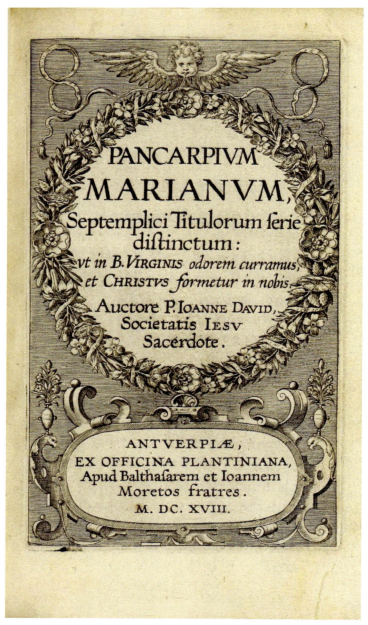

FIGURE 1.4 Jan David, s.j., *Pancarpium Marianum, Septemplici Titulorum serie distinctum; ut in B. Virginis odorem curramus, et Christus formetur in nobis*. (Antwerp, Balthasar and Jan Moretus: 1607; repr. ed., 1618). Engraving by Theodoor Galle, 150 × 90 mm
COURTESY OF THE NEWBERRY LIBRARY, CHICAGO: CASE W. 1025.22

INTRODUCTION: *MOTUS MIXTI ET COMPOSITI* 19

Lord. The book's sequence of Marian *tituli* is also a sequence of Marian affects: Mary, in her commerce with Christ, is portrayed consecutively as 'giving birth' (*natalitia*), 'nourishing' (*nutritia*), 'provisioning / ornamenting' (*ornans*), 'defending' (*tutelaris*), 'enticing / ensnaring' (*alliciens*), 'fortifying' (*corroborans*), and finally, 'seizing / taking captive' (*rapiens*) [Fig. 1.5].[51] In a curious paradox, the emblems become increasingly dynamic, indeed martial, evoking military imagery even as they come more fully to signify how through Mary the votary is subsumed into the love of Christ [Figs. 1.6 & 1.7]. David conceived of the titular sequence not as a series of discrete episodes, each the epitome of an affective inflection, but as a kind of Marian *scala* or edifice comprising mutually constitutive experiential layers from which an increasingly complex felt image of the Virgin (and the Marian votary) is constructed. On this account, Mary becomes a peerless epitome of *motus mixti*, her relation to her Son and to the votary almost preternaturally multilayered, always loving but also infused or inundated with successive (and often concomitant) waves of feeling modulated by the fifty Marian *tituli*.

The ancient sculptural canon, as Filipczak has shown, constituted an affective norm against which inflections in the emotional register could be measured. For examples, she adduces Peter Paul Rubens's oil sketches, *The Return of Briseis* (ca. 1630–1635), in which Achilles is posed like the *Apollo Belvedere*, but off balance, to indicate that he is caught between two emotions, waning grief for the dead Patroclus (who lies dead in the tent behind Achilles) and rising joy in the presence of Briseis, toward whom he reaches ardently [Fig. 1.8];[52] and *The Negotiations at Angouleme* (1622–1625), from the *Marie de' Medici* series, in which the allegorical figure of Vigilance, modeled on the *Veturia* (mother of Marcus Coriolanus), a famous statue in the Medici sculpture collection, encodes maternal grief, layering this passion onto the adjacent figure of Marie [Figs. 1.9 & 1.10].[53] Marie's seeming impassivity, readable in this context as a possible sign of good grace and even biddability, is thus overlain with the traces of anxious care. Rubens occasionally substituted the figural inventions of Titian for the ancient sculptural canon: in the oil sketch *Perseus*

---

51 See David Jan, S.J., "Titulorum quinquaginta partitio, prout in praesenti Tractatu sunt digesti", in idem, *Pancarpium Marianum*, fol. + 8v. The *Pancarpium* constitutes the second part of David's bipartite emblem book, *Paradisus Sponsi et Sponsae*, of which part 1, focusing on the Passion, is titled *Messis myrrhae et aromatum, ex instrumentis ac mysterijs Passionis Christi colligenda, ut ei commoriamur* (Harvest of myrrh and spices, fit to be gathered from the instruments and mysteries of the Passion of Christ, that we may die with him) (Antwerp, Balthasar and Jan Moretus: 1607).

52 See Filiczak, "Rubens Adapts the Poses" 131.

53 See ibid. 138–146.

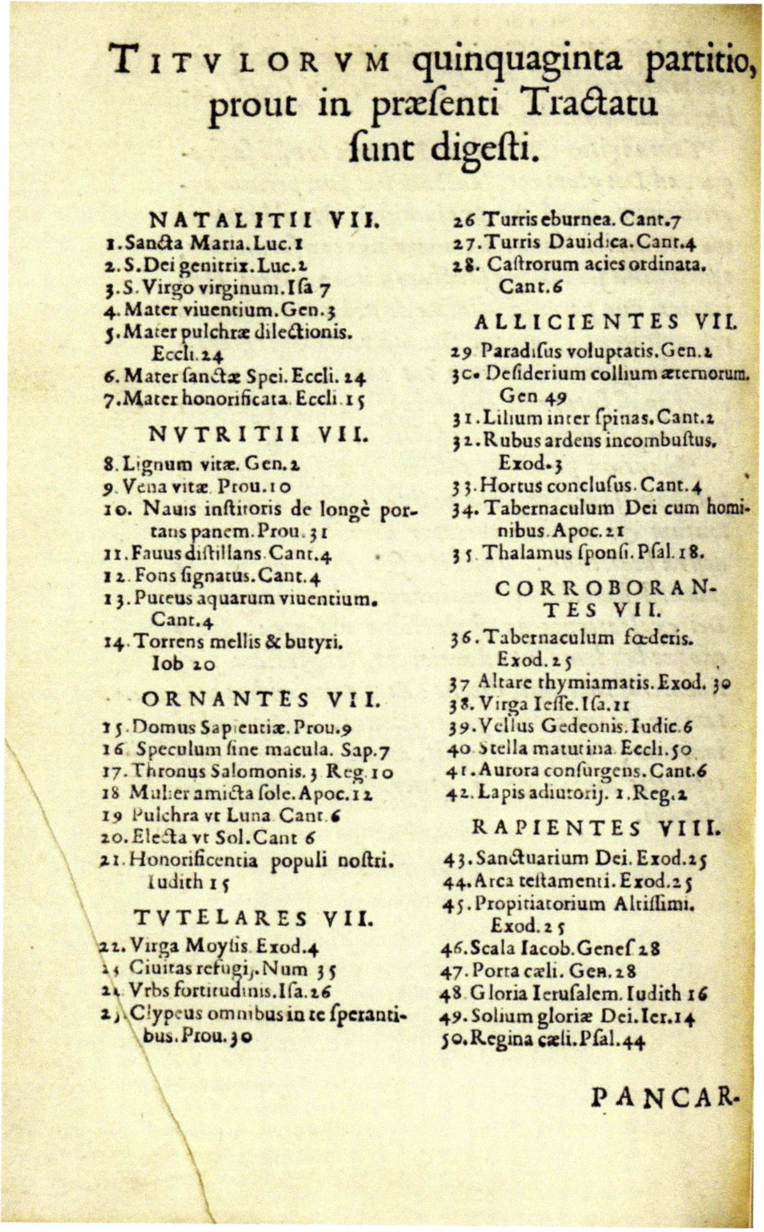

TITVLORVM quinquaginta partitio, prout in præfenti Tractatu funt digesti.

NATALITII VII.

1. Sancta Maria. Luc. 1
2. S. Dei genitrix. Luc. 2
3. S. Virgo virginum. Ifa 7
4. Mater viuentium. Gen. 3
5. Mater pulchræ dilectionis. Eccli. 24
6. Mater fanctæ Spei. Eccli. 24
7. Mater honorificata. Eccli. 15

NVTRITII VII.

8. Lignum vitæ. Gen. 2
9. Vena vitæ. Prou. 10
10. Nauis inftitoris de longè portans panem. Prou. 31
11. Fauus diftillans. Cant. 4
12. Fons fignatus. Cant. 4
13. Puteus aquarum viuentium. Cant. 4
14. Torrens mellis & butyri. Iob 20

ORNANTES VII.

15. Domus Sapientiæ. Prou. 9
16. Speculum fine macula. Sap. 7
17. Thronus Salomonis. 3 Reg. 10
18. Mulier amicta fole. Apoc. 12
19. Pulchra vt Luna. Cant. 6
20. Electa vt Sol. Cant 6
21. Honorificentia populi noftri. Iudith 15

TVTELARES VII.

22. Virga Moyfis. Exod. 4
23. Ciuitas refugij. Num 35
24. Vrbs fortitudinis. Ifa. 26
25. Clypeus omnibus in te fperantibus. Prou. 30

26. Turris eburnea. Cant. 7
27. Turris Dauidica. Cant. 4
28. Caftrorum acies ordinata. Cant. 6

ALLICIENTES VII.

29. Paradifus voluptatis. Gen. 2
30. Defiderium collium æternorum. Gen 49
31. Lilium inter fpinas. Cant. 2
32. Rubus ardens incombuftus. Exod. 3
33. Hortus conclufus. Cant. 4
34. Tabernaculum Dei cum hominibus. Apoc. 21
35. Thalamus fponfi. Pfal. 18.

CORROBORANTES VII.

36. Tabernaculum fœderis. Exod. 25
37. Altare thymiamatis. Exod. 30
38. Virga Ieffe. Ifa. 11
39. Vellus Gedeonis. Iudic. 6
40. Stella matutina. Eccli. 50
41. Aurora confurgens. Cant. 6
42. Lapis adiutorij. 1. Reg. 2

RAPIENTES VIII.

43. Sanctuarium Dei. Exod. 25
44. Arca teftamenti. Exod. 25
45. Propitiatorium Altiffimi. Exod. 25
46. Scala Iacob. Genef 28
47. Porta cæli. Gen. 28
48. Gloria Ierufalem. Iudith 16
49. Solium gloriæ Dei. Ier. 14
50. Regina cæli. Pfal. 44

PANCAR-

FIGURE 1.5   Jan David, S.J., "Tituli quinquaginta partitio, prout in praesenti Tractatu sunt digesti", in *Pancarpium Marianum* (Antwerp, Balthasar and Jan Moretus: 1607; repr. ed., 1618), fol. + 8v
COURTESY OF THE NEWBERRY LIBRARY, CHICAGO: CASE W. 1025.22

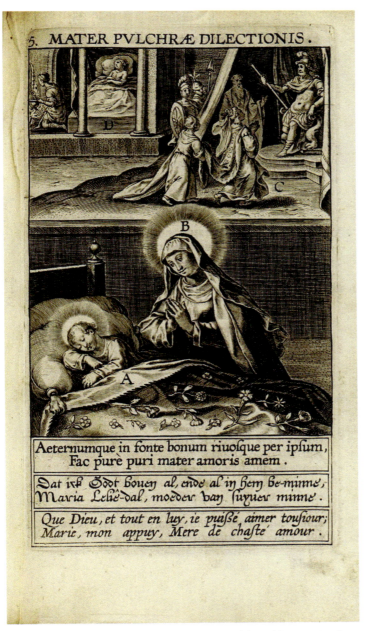

FIGURE 1.6 Theodoor Galle, Emblem 5: "Mater pulchrae dilectionis", in Jan David, s.j., *Pancarpium Marianum* (Antwerp, Balthasar and Jan Moretus: 1607; repr. ed., 1618). Engraving, 156 × 90 mm
COURTESY OF THE NEWBERRY LIBRARY, CHICAGO: CASE W. 1025.22

FIGURE 1.7 Theodoor Galle, Emblem 42: "Lapis adiutorii", in Jan David, s.j., *Pancarpium Marianum* (Antwerp, Balthasar and Jan Moretus: 1607, repr. ed., 1618). Engraving, 158 × 91 mm
COURTESY OF THE NEWBERRY LIBRARY, CHICAGO: CASE W. 1025.22

INTRODUCTION: *MOTUS MIXTI ET COMPOSITI*

FIGURE 1.8 Peter Paul Rubens and Workshop, *Return of Briseis*, ca. 1630–1635. Oil on panel, 107.5 × 163 cm. Museo del Prado, Madrid P002566

and Andromeda (1636), he emulated an early version of Titian's *Perseus and Andromeda* (ca. 1553–1562), raising Andromeda's bound arms to indicate fearful grief while turning her face and body toward Perseus to bespeak incipient hope.[54] Rubens introduced these elaborations upon his pictorial and sculptural models to evoke complex emotional states that situate the empathetic viewer between competing impulses. Liminality allowed him to explore pivotal narrative moments when a situation and the feelings it arouses begin to change, shifting toward a new situation and its attendant feelings.

Diego Velázquez's *Joseph's Bloodied Coat Presented to Jacob*, one of two large figural subjects dating from the painter's first Roman sojourn, executed to demonstrate his peerless command of history painting in the Italian manner, reveals the extent to which mastery of the *istoria* entailed the ability to portray mixed and/or shifting emotions [Fig. 1.11].[55] Following upon his now

---

54 See ibid. 135–137.
55 The other painting, dated 1629–1630, depicts *The Forge of Vulcan*; in choosing this subject, Velázquez surely wished to show that he was as skilled at painting mythology as biblical history. On *Joseph's Bloodied Coat* as an exploration of history painting in the Roman manner, see Marías F., "Joseph's Bloodied Coat Presented to Jacob. From Portrait to History: History at the Margins of the Human", in Knox – T.J. Tiffany (eds.), *Velázquez Re-Examined: Theory, History, Poetry, and Theatre* (Turnhout: 2017) 65–78.

FIGURE 1.9 Peter Paul Rubens, *The Negotiations at Angouleme*, 1622–1625. Oil on canvas, 394 × 295 cm. Musée du Louvre, Paris
PHOTO: ART RESOURCE

INTRODUCTION: *MOTUS MIXTI ET COMPOSITI* 25

FIGURE 1.10   *Veturia, Mother of Coriolanus* (also known as *Thusnelda*). Marble, over life size. Loggia dei Lanzi, Florence
PHOTO: ART RESOURCE

FIGURE 1.11 Diego Velázquez, *Joseph's Blooded Coat Presented to Jacob*, 1630. Oil on canvas, 213.5 × 284 cm. Nuevos Museos, El Escorial
PHOTO: ART RESOURCE

lost *Philip III and the Expulsion of the Moriscos*, Velázquez aimed to secure his reputation as a painter not just of *retratos* (portraits) and *bodegones* (paintings about the making, marketing, or eating of food), but also of *historias*.[56] Key to achieving this goal, as *Joseph's Bloodied Coat* makes clear, was the evocation of what one might best call emotional metacomplexity – the description of characters who express compound emotions in multiple ways, at once consciously but also unconsciously, naturally as well as performatively. In his important article on *Joseph's Bloodied Coat*, Fernando Marías points out that the painting operates simultaneously in several affective registers: the five young men before Jacob, identifiable as his sons, can be seen as epitomes of emotion, differentiated by temperament along the lines of the patriarch's characterisation of his sons in Genesis 49, known as the "Blessing of the Sons of Jacob": Reuben is a begetter of sorrow; Simeon and Levi are prone to wrath,

---

56 On Velázquez's *bodegones* as expressions of the *paragone* debate, see Knox G., "Eggs, Water, Metal: Velázquez, the *Paragone*, and the Products of *Practica*", in Knox – Tiffany (eds.), *Velázquez Re-Examined* 45–64.

INTRODUCTION: *MOTUS MIXTI ET COMPOSITI*

violence, and cruelty; Judah is as fierce as a lion, Issachar as stubborn and headstrong as an ass.

Onto these emotional ranges, Velázquez layers more specific emotions: shown from behind, plucking at his hair and twisting tormentedly, Reuben (who felt the most remorse at what he and his brothers had done to Joseph) expresses the greatest anguish, whereas Simeon and Levi, who tell the deceitful tale of Joseph's demise, show a less disconsolate sorrow, laced more with concern than desperation. Bearing false witness to their story, Judah and Issachar react less determinately: Judah, his face shaded by a wide-brimmed hat, appears to gaze with concern at Reuben, and Issachar, with cocked head, furrowed brow, and bent index finder pressed against his mouth, strikes a melancholy pose. But this conspicuous gesture, as Marías notes, also perfectly illustrates Lomazzo's word picture of an envious, disdainful person.[57] Marías further observes that it could just as well be taken for anxious remorse. Indeed, Velázquez leaves open the possibility that all five brothers express various kinds and degrees of remorse, either sincerely or feignedly. Indeed, as Friar Francisco de los Santos insisted in his *Descripción breve del Monasterio de S. Lorenzo del Escorial* (Madrid, Imprenta Real: 1668), the five men may depict not the sons of Jacob but the five shepherds whom they sent to apprise Jacob of Joseph's fate, and who did so, empathetically and painedly (Genesis 37:32).[58] The most affecting of these figures is the one sometimes called Reuben, whose attitude appears so out of the ordinary that it seems, by comparison with the nearby figures, to express an almost incalculable state of sadness:

> This last figure, in order to show his feeling, raises his nude right arm, in which we can count the veins; and he folds his arm so that his hand digs into his hair as if he were about to pull it out. The movement that he makes is unusual. Another figure has his fist to his mouth in sadness, while the others show their pain through various actions, their hoods and crooks thrown onto the floor.[59]

At the last, De los Santos hedged his bets, claiming that some of these men might be compassionate shepherds or, then again, the sons themselves who, seeing their father's reaction, felt truly moved to comfort him:

---

57 See ibid. 74, with reference to Lomazzo, *Trattato*, in *Scritti sulle arti*, ed. Ciardi 2:115.

58 De los Santos, *Descripción*, fol. 80r, as cited in Marías, "*Joseph's Bloodied Coat*" 72–73: 'The shepherds are also pained, and they and three others, who are seen at various distances [...] are painted with great skill and study'.

59 De los Santos, *Descripción*, fol. 80r, as cited in Marías, "*Joseph's Bloodied Coat*" 73.

Two or three of the shepherds shown here seem to indicate – in their manner as in their expression of pain and in their movement and actions – that, indeed, they are Joseph's brothers. To be sure, as they watch their father become heart-struck at what is happening, they show great feeling, albeit fabricated. [...] And so, it might be that the painter sought to bring the two things together in order to show at once the arrival of the shepherds sent with the coat and of the brothers trying to offer comfort to their father.[60]

In one scenario, these are shepherds who express compassionate sorrow; in another scenario, they are the brothers who either actually feel or merely simulate pity and remorse, to a greater or lesser extent admixed with their former hatred and contempt for Joseph and desire to be done with him; in a third scenario, explained by De los Santos as the painter's sleight of hand, they are shepherds, and they are the brothers, their respective affects discernible by the viewer in a palimpsest of mutual relation. As a matter of fact, the figure of Jacob, expressive of both anger and despair at the loss of his son, is equally a paragon of mixed emotion: 'and in [his eyes] is shown his entire heart, broken and enraged by the blood he sees and by the misfortune that is occurring'.[61] The central action of *Joseph's Bloodied Coat* stages a mise en abyme of the action of painting, since it depicts the showing of a read-stained white tunic and tan jerkin that are exhibited to tell a story. Within this context, mixed emotion becomes a principal attribute of the power of painting to seize the beholder, ensnaring her/him in a web of affects. The recursive exercise of reading Genesis 37 through the medium of painting, and thinking about painting by way of Genesis 37, inevitably raises questions about the seductive properties of pictorial images, and collaterally, about the presumption that such paintings, by spinning ostensibly truthful tales, both delight and instruct the viewer's eyes, mind, and heart.

If mixed emotion could function as a criterion of pictorial excellence, it was also a device crucial to defining and manipulating poetic genres and modes, and to enhancing their moral purposes. For brevity's sake, we will look at only two examples of this phenomenon. Raphaële Garrod, in an important article on Nicolas Caussin, s.j.'s martyr play *Felicitas*, one of five tragedies in his collection *Tragoediae sacrae* (Paris, Sebastian Chappelet: 1620), situates it in relation to Jesuit poetics of the 'pathetic tragedy', as discussed by Caussin in *Eloquentiae sacrae et humanae parallela, libri XVI* (Parallels of Sacred and

---

60   De los Santos, *Descripción*, fol. 80r, as cited in Marías, "*Joseph's Bloodied Coat*" 73–74.
61   De los Santos, *Descripción*, fol. 80r, as cited in Marías, "*Joseph's Bloodied Coat*" 72.

INTRODUCTION: *MOTUS MIXTI ET COMPOSITI*

Human Eloquence, 16 Books) (Paris, Sebastian Chappelet: 1619) and Martin Antonio Delrio, s.j. in *Syntagma tragoediae Latinae* (Doctrine of Latin Tragedy) (Antwerp, Ex officina Plantiniana, apud Viduam et Joannem Moretum: 1593).[62] Modeled on Senecan tragedy, pathetic tragedy, as evinced in martyr plays such as *Felicitas*, exemplify the Jesuit reading of Aristotelian catharsis as 'co-motion', or 'being moved with': on this view, rather than purging terror and pity, tragic drama instead aims to engender a 'commotion of pity and terror'. The pathetic tragedy abounds in moments of grief and fear, that put on show the *ethos* of its martyr heroes and heroines and educe the spectator's experience of *pathos*. These moments are staged recursively, each iteration serving gradually to teach the chief *dramatis personae*, e.g., Felicitas, and the audience not to jettison affect but to discipline it, so that its charge shifts or, rather, becomes mixed, the horror of bodily martyrdom shading into transcendent certainty of the soul's salvation. Through Felicity's hard-won realization that aggrieved maternal love can give access to exalted divine love, undergirded by her growing confidence in her martyred sons' transcendent heavenly glory, the spectator learns experientially, as if at first hand, how bodily *pathos*, based in corporeal pain and loss, can be sublimed into the higher, more refined *pathos* of willing martyrdom. Garrod refers to this ethical process as 'affective conditioning' or, alternatively, the 'affective reconfiguration of maternal love'. Act 5, scene 2 brilliantly distils this process of reconfiguration by exposing the juncture when Felicitas, qua mother, finally bids farewell to her sons' bodily remains (their mangled limbs strew the stage), now embracing her sons in spirit only. She imagines them as flowers turning away from their earthly roots and unfurling in the bright light of the sun, i.e., basking in Christ the Sun of Justice. On this account, martyrdom, though it cuts the maternal bond, physically severing Felicitas from her sons, is welcomed by her as a kind of growth, a spiritual efflorescence inspired by Christ:

> I acknowledge my entrails, and hold them against my bosom:
> The happy crown of martyrs? Shall I mourn you?
> [...]
> They called me mother, and as they grew up
> This golden youth of theirs unraveled from me,

---

62   See Garrod R., "Senecan Catharsis in Nicolas Caussin's *Felicitas* (1620): A Case Study in Jesuit Reconfiguration of Affects", in Haskell Y. – Garrod (eds.), *Changing Hearts: Performing Jesuit Emotions between Europe, Asia, and the Americas*, Jesuit Studies: Modernity through the Prism of Jesuit History 15 (Leiden – Boston: 2019) 23–42.

As the soft and delicate rose unfolds its opening petals
To the fiery light of the sun at the beginning of spring.[63]

Caussin's conception of affective conditioning – namely, the alteration of feeling instantiated by Felicitas in this passage – derives from Suárez's textbook commentary on the *Prima secundae*, in which, aligning virtue with pleasure, he argues that virtue does not destroy nature, but rather tempers it: 'Similarly, pleasure is the natural companion of virtue; finally, virtue does not destroy nature, just as health does not destroy either the humours or one's disposition, or as music does not destroy sound, but moderates it'.[64] So, the maternal sorrow and pain felt by Felicitas at the outrages committed against her sons (passions that Caussin considered natural and habitual, similar to the Stoic *propassiones*) are not so much erased as assuaged by the mounting conviction that her martyred sons live in/through Christ and by the virtuous joy that this brings her. Seen in this light, *Felicitas* exemplifies Caussin's argument, in *La cour sainte* (Paris, Sebastien Chappelet: 1624–1636), that the blood, tears, and fearful pain of martyrdom imbricate with and are moderated by the infinite joy that the martyr apprehends, even if distantly:

> Finally, I state that martyrdom strengthens our faith in the afterlife, as an obvious proof of beatitude […]. This brought solace to all martyrs in fearful pains, when their souls were torn out of their bodies with unprecedented violence. For, even if their mortal limbs succumbed to the iron of persecution yet they could see – although from behind a cloud of blood and tears – that beautiful glory that awaited them, and they could contemplate as if in a mirror, the thorns of these prodigious tortures, gathering to form crowns. […] There the Holy Felicity, mother of all glories and Trophies, could see her seven sons welcoming her with palms in their

---

63 Caussin Nicolas, S.J., *Felicitas*, in idem, *Tragoediae sacrae* (Paris, Sebastian Chappelet: 1620) 227–228:
   'Agnosco nostra viscera, et teneo sinu.
   Foelix corona martyrum! Vos lugeam?
   […]
   Matrem vocavit, et per aetatis gradus
   Haec se Juventus aurea explicuit mihi;
   Ut veris ortu solis ad tenera faces
   Sinus hiulcos mollis expandit rosa'.

64 Suárez Francisco, S.J., *Ad primam secundae D. Thomae tractatus quinque theologici* (Lyon, Jacobus Cardon: 1628) 331, as cited in Garrod, "Senecan Catharsis" 36.

INTRODUCTION: *MOTUS MIXTI ET COMPOSITI* 31

> hands into those beautiful pavilions of heaven, where all torments have come to an end and given way to infinite joys.[65]

The affects mingle in a cathartic mix that Garrod aptly describes as an eschatological compound of pain and loss, typical of the genre of 'pathetic tragedy'.

In Théodore Agrippa d'Aubigné's epic *Les Tragiques* (The Tragic Ones) (Geneva, L.B.D.D.: 1616), the display of mixed emotion goes hand in hand with the exploration of mixed genre, the two types of mixture working together to enhance the poem's affective charge. Written in the 1570s during the French Wars of Religion, *Les Tragiques*, recently elucidated by Kathleen Long in an invaluable article, contends with the morally dubious impulse of taking pleasure in the spectacle of violence, especially the crimes perpetrated by Catholics against Protestants.[66] To achieve this end, Agrippa d'Aubigné situates the reader as witness to unimaginable atrocities, deploying various poetic devices to refresh the experience of shock and horror, thus ensuring that anti-Protestant violence not be aestheticized or normalised. Mixed emotion is used to take the measure of extreme barbarity, as in the poet's remark that the poignant sight of wounded mothers struggling still to suckle their murdered babes terrified even their implacable murderers: 'There, I saw pitiless hearts astounded, I saw terror fall upon the terrifying. / What dry eye could observe these half-eaten members'?[67]

Book 5, "Les Fers" (The Iron Blades), focusing on bloody battles and massacres, repeatedly deploys the imagery of Petrarchan love poetry (itself awash with allusions to cruel beloveds and their mortally wounded would-be lovers)

---

65 Caussin, *Cour sainte*, 4 parts, 3:471–473, as cited in Garrod, "Senecan Catharsis" 38–39: 'Enfin je dis que la tribulation nous confirme en la foy des choses futures, comme estant une manifeste preuve de la beatitude [...]. C'est ce qui consoloit tous les Martyrs dans des peines effroyables, lorsqu'on leur arrachoit l'ame du corps avec des violences nompareilles. Car si bien les membres mortels succomboient au fer de la persecution, si est-ce qu'ils voyoient, quoyque d'un oeil trempé de sang et de larmes, cette belle gloire qui les attendoit, et contemploient comme dans un miroir, les espines de ces prodigieux travaux, qui se formoient toutes en couronnes. [...] Là saincte Felicité, la mere des gloires et des trophies, voyoit sept fils qui la recevoient les palmes en main dans ces beaux pavillons du Ciel, ou tous les tourmens prenoient fin pour donner commencement à des joys infinies'.

66 Long K., "Cruelty and Empathy in Théodore Agrippa d'Aubigné's *Les Tragiques*: The Gaze of and on the Reader", in Marculescu A. – Morand Métivier C.L. (eds.), *Affective and Emotional Economies in Medieval and Early Modern Europe* (Cham: 2018) 167–194.

67 Agrippa d'Aubigné T., "Misères", in *Oeuvres: Les Tragiques*, ed. H. Wéber (Paris: 1969) 31, v. 433–435, as cited in Long, "Cruelty and Empathy" 177. On Agrippa d'Aubigné's efforts to give the verb *esmouvoir* evidentiary force, see Frisch A., "Agrippa d'Aubigné's *Tragiques* as Testimony", in LaGuardia D.P. – Randell C. (eds.), *Memory and Community in Sixteenth-Century France* (Farnham: 2015) 97–111.

to unsettle the reader's expectations: tropes codified for rendering the *innamoramento*, the moment when the courtly lover first lays eyes on his beloved, are instead associated with heinous scenes of violence, with rapine, rape, and slaughter.[68] An expectation of love instilled by beauty is set up, its affiliated affects evoked, only to be despoiled and destroyed, as in the case of a preternaturally beautiful woman whose fine-complexioned face stops one murderer in his tracks, only to be ravaged by a second murderer unmoved by its ivory whiteness tinged with blushing crimson:

> These 'splitters' (*fendans*) having encountered a face which, being too beautiful, weakened their courage, a less hardened man let his arm drop, and then his sword. Another man picked it up, and full of hell, defying the power of pity over his sight, stripped the beauty so that he might tear it naked, and took pleasure in sullying the innocent colour, watching this living whiteness darken in death.[69]

Long observes that the many repetitions of variations on 'fendre' (cleave, pierce, split) call to mind previous scenes of brutes slicing open pregnant mothers, their own hearts utterly resistant to the cutting, penetrating power of love.[70] Whereas the disproportionate beauty of Laura assaults the Petrarchan persona in *Canzone* 23, disarming him so that he is left defenceless, overcome by love, here the woman's beauty overcomes one attacker, as if the Petrarchan scenario were being played out, before being violated by a second, immune to her charms. The power of the scene results from the layering of one affective scenario onto another, so that the lyric dynamic that locks lover and beloved in a *rencontre* (skirmish) wherein cruelty, pity, and desire oscillate, transforms into a more cruel, pitiless, impassible version of that encounter. The mixing of a generic allusion to erotic desire and its opposite, an anti-erotic (or perversely

---

68   On Agrippa d'Aubigné's deployments of the *innamoramento*, see Long, "Cruelty and Empathy" 184–185.

69   Agrippa d'Aubigné, "Les Fers", in *Oeuvres: Les Tragiques*, ed. Wéber 166, v. 637–644, as cited in Long, "Cruelty and Empathy" 185:
    'Ces fendans ayant fait recontre d'un visage
    Que de trop de beauté affligeoit leur courage,
    Un moins dur laissa choir son bras et puis son fer,
    Un autre le releve et, tout plein de l'enfer,
    Desfiant la pitié de pouvoir sur sa veuë,
    Despouilla la beauté pour la dechirer nuë,
    Print Plaisir à souiller la naïve blancheur'.

70   Ibid. 185–188.

INTRODUCTION: *MOTUS MIXTI ET COMPOSITI*

erotic) scene of violent fury, of hope that the woman may survive and despair at her atrocious end, heightens the reader's sense that mixed emotions are the wages of the collision between the sublimated, courtly pseudo-violence of Petrarchan lyric and the rawer, more explicitly martial violence of Agrippa d'Aubigné's epic about the Wars of Religion. The poet heightens the effect of lyric emotion adjured yet contravened, by linking the murdered woman's whiteness to the crimson dawn of Saint Bartholomew's Day: the ivory cum vermilion of the beloved's fine rosy complexion is displaced by the blood-red dawning of a day notorious for its massacres. This dawn, he declares earnestly, has lost every trace of the former floral hue for which he still pines: 'Dawn wishes to rise, the dawn which once had its dark complexion ornamented with flowers of paradise; when, through its trellis of gold, crimson red burst through [...]'.[71]

We have been considering some of the primary ways in which mixed emotions were used: to intensify mixed generic effects in poetry, to reconfigure affective experience, to advertise a painter's figural skills, to complicate the reader-viewer's sense of Marian virtue, or to enhance sacramental devotion to the *verum corpus*. The circumstances under which mixed emotions were displayed and the functions of such display, as we have tried to convey, were wide-ranging and multifaceted, ranging from exploration of tangled states of feeling to avowal of the metadiscursive capacities of painting and poetry. The essays that now follow, subdivided into three sections, extend our introductory discussion, offering collateral studies on the representation of mixed emotions. They interrogate the forms and functions of this ethopoetic/pathopoetic device that occurred frequently in literature and the visual arts, even though there was no specific term for it. The display of mixed emotions partook of the formal and functional characteristics of several tropes, figures of speech, and/or figures of thought, without fully aligning with any of them. For instance, apropos the definitions in one of the most popular rhetorical handbooks, Cyprian Soarez, S.J.'s *De arte rhetorica* (Paris, Dionisius a Prato: 1568), mixed emotional expression might be compared to such tropes as *catachresis*

---

71   Agrippa d'Aubigné, *Les Tragiques* 169, as cited in Long, "Cruelty and Empathy" 187:
      'L'aube se veut lever, aube qui eut jadix
      Son teint brunet orné des fleurs de paradis;
      Quand, par son trellis d'or, la rose carmoisie
      Eclatait [...]'.
      The verb *éclater*, as Long notes, recalls the *éclat* of the Petrarchan beauty's surpassingly lovely face.

('abusive use of a similar or related word, in place of using the right word'[72]),
as when a reference is made to joyful sorrow or sorrowful joy; *ironia* (antipodean usage that 'manifests something not only different but contrary to the meaning and the words'[73]), as when the melancholic declares her-/himself happy only to reveal that s/he is in fact sad; or *hyperbole* ('fabricated exaggeration, the nature of which is such that it can be used indifferently for exaggerating or minimizing'[74]), as when, in Agrippa d'Aubigné's "Les fers", pity collapses into inhumanity, or desire into rage. Amongst the figures of speech, the representation of mixed emotions conjures up *dissolutio* ('when several things are diffusely mentioned without conjunctions', to 'sharpen what is said and produce an impression of vehemence, such as might spring from more frequent outbursts of emotion'[75]), as when Lomazzo concatenates 'anxiety, heavines, sadnes, stubbournnes', then further parallels them to the cognate affects 'violence, rage, arrogancy, audacity, cruelty'; and *antitheton/contentio* ('when single words are contrasted with one another', e.g., 'Passion overcame shame, boldness, fear, madness, reason'[76]), as when De los Santos commends Velázquez for showing Jacob's heart 'broken and enraged by the blood he sees'. Amongst the figures of thought, there are analogies to *correctio* ('which by cancelling one notion, improves and amends it with another that appears more suitable'[77]), as when Felicitas, in Caussin's eponymous tragedy, superposes the experience of martyrdom as infinite joy onto the blood, tears, and fearful pain of martyrdom, subsuming one emotional range into another; and, of course, *ethopoeia* ('portraying the life and characteristics of others, a splendid ornament of discourse, especially suitable for winning over the mind and especially for often arousing the emotion'[78]), as when, in Felicity's heart and soul, maternal pain and loss are seen to accommodate to spiritual exaltation. (As will be

---

72 See Flynn L.J., s.J., *The 'De Arte Rhetorica' (1568) by Cypriano Soarez, s.J.* (Ann Arbor: 1955) 291. Cf. Soarez Cypriano, s.J., *De arte rhetorica libri tres ex Aristotele, Cicerone, et Quintiliano praecipua deprompti* (Paris, Thomas Brummenius: 1576), fol. 36v. On Soarez textbook, widely distributed throughout the Jesuit network of colleges and schools, see Flynn L.J., s.J., "The *De Arte Rhetorica* of Cyprian Soarez, s.J.", *Quarterly Journal of Speech* 42 (1956) 367–371; idem, "Sources and Influence of Soarez' *De Arte Rhetorica*", *Quarterly Journal of Speech* 43 (1957); and Mahlmann-Bauer B., *Jezuitische 'ars rhetorica' im Zeitalter der Glaubenskämpfe*, Mikrokosmos 18 (Frankfurt am Main – Bern: 1986) 138–140.

73 See Flynn, *'De Arte Rhetorica'* 298. Cf. Soarez, *De arte rhetorica libri tres*, fol. 37v.

74 See Flynn, *'De Arte Rhetorica'* 301. Cf. Soarez, *De arte rhetorica libri tres*, fol. 38r.

75 Flynn, *'De Arte Rhetorica'* 318–319. Cf. Soarez, *De arte rhetorica libri tres*, fol. 41r.

76 Flynn, *'De Arte Rhetorica'* 328–329. Cf. Soarez, *De arte rhetorica libri tres*, fol. 42v.

77 Flynn, *'De Arte Rhetorica'* 340. Cf. Soarez, *De arte rhetorica libri tres*, fol. 44v.

78 Flynn, *'De Arte Rhetorica'* 346–347. Cf. Soarez, *De arte rhetorica libri tres*, fol. 45v.

INTRODUCTION: *MOTUS MIXTI ET COMPOSITI*

evident from Soarez's references to seizing the mind and stirring emotion, his definition of *ethopoeia* shades into or even encompasses *pathopoeia*.)

The complex temporality of the pictorial image – the illusion of simultaneity it necessarily produces – which requires the painter to fold allusions to past and/or future experience into an expansive sensory and cognitive present of consciousness, easily comprehends, in the sense of comprises, the full spectrum of emotive effects induced more sequentially by rhetorical means. But mixed emotions or, in our neologist terminology, *motus mixti* were as ubiquitous in the telling and showing, not only in poetry and painting but also on stage, as they were, in a sense, undesignated, at least in rhetorical terms. Or, to put this another way, described in word and image, yet not strictly regulated on the authority of rhetorical or poetological precepts. What poets and playwrights and the more literate painters had to hand were ancient exempla of mixed emotion transmitted in Latin and the vernacular, and which likely circulated as commonplaces: amongst others, Aristotle's account of anger as a complex affect compounded of aggrieved pain tempered by the anticipated pleasure of revenge, in *Nicomachean Ethics* III.viii.12, and *Rhetoric* II.ii.2;[79] Achilles Tatius's novelistic exploration of the psyche and its by turns allied and combative emotions, in such passages of *Leucippe and Cleitophon* as 4.8.6, where Menelaus warns about a high-ranking man thwarted in love, 'If he has the power to act without fear of recrimination, the part of his soul uncurbed by timidity aggravates the part impelled by acerbity', or 6.14.2, where Cleitophon describes his vacillating emotions, 'My soul was poised between hope and fear: the part that hoped was fearing the part that feared was hoping';[80] or

---

79   See respectively, Aristotle, *Nicomachean Ethics*, trans. H. Rackham (Cambridge, MA – London: 1945) 168–169; and Aristotle, *The "Art" of Rhetoric*, trans. J.H. Freese (Cambridge, MA – London: 1939) 172–175. On anger's mixed constituent affects, see Enenkel K.A.E. – Traninger A., "Introduction: Discourse of Anger in the Early Modern Period", in eidem (eds.), *Discourses of Anger in the Early Modern Period*, Intersections 40 (Leiden – Boston: 2015) 1–15, esp. 2.

80   For/on both passages, which testify to Tatius's familiarity with the Platonic doctrine of the tripartite soul, see Repath I., "Emotional Conflict and Platonic Psychology in the Greek Novel", in Morgan J.R. – Jones M. (eds.), *Philosophical Presences in the Ancient Novel* (Groningen: 2007) 53–84, esp. 71–72. Also see ibid. 75 for a discussion of Ach. Tat. 7.1.1., in which Thersander is undone by a tidal wave of emotions: 'When Thersander heard this, he went through the full spectrum of reactions: he was distressed, he was furious, and he plotted. He was furious because he had been insulted, he was distressed due to his failure, and he plotted since he felt passionate desire. His soul was torn apart, and without a word to Leucippe he ran out. On the surface it was an exit in fury, but in fact he was giving his soul the opportunity to dissipate the threefold wave that had struck him'. The first Latin partial translation of *Leucippe and Cleitophon*, by Annibal della Croce (Crucejus), appeared in Lyon in 1544, followed by an Italian and French translations based on it,

Heliodorus's *Aethiopica* 10.16.2, where Hydaspes, having recognised a female sacrificial victim as his daughter, feels his soul 'buffeted by waves of fatherly love and manly resolve that fought for possession of his will, which was pulled in two directions by their opposing tide races', or 4.6.1, where 'the part of [Charicleia's] soul feeling shame' collides with her lovestruck feelings.[81]

In sum, *Motus mixti: The Portrayal of Mixed and Compound Emotions* examines deployments of mixed emotion in the literary and pictorial arts of early modern Europe. It consists of two parts, the first of which is variously subdivided by literary type. Part 1.A. focuses on theatre, 1.B. on poetry, and 1.C. on prose. In the theatre subsection, Bart Ramakers considers the performative functions of mixed emotion as an instrument of virtue ethics; and Lukas Reddemann examines selected plays by Dutch scholar-dramatists that stage the complex relation between spontaneous impulses and purposeful affects. In the poetry subsection, Ludovica Sasso provides a close reading of Georgius Sisgoreus's *Elegia de Sibenicensis agri vastatione* (Elegy on the Devastation of the Šibenik District), showing how righteous vengeance and regional pride are seen properly to emerge when the experience of anger stabilises the compound and shifting emotions provoked by the Ottoman invasion of the poet's homeland; Carolin Giere investigates the shared emotional economy of neo-Latin psalm poetry and erotic elegy; Aline Smeesters parses the emotional significance of the colour mixtures described by Jakob Balde, S.J. in his poetic ekphrases of paintings by Christoph Schwarz; and Tom Conley takes stock of the intricacies of emotion conveyed by the syntactic and graphic structures of Joachim Du Bellay's printed poetry. In the prose part, Anita Traninger elucidates the compound emotions generative of the pastoral culture of tears, with specific reference to Jorge de Montemayor's *Los siete libros de la Diana* (The Seven Books of the Diana); Paul Smith scrutinises the thematisation of mixed joy and sorrow in François Rabelais's *Gargantua et Pantagruel* and Michel de Montaigne's *Essais*; and Wietse de Boer explains how the purgation of mixed emotions enables both the application and relinquishment of the will in

---

respectively by Ludovico Dolce (Venice: 1546) and Philibert de Vienne (Paris: 1545), a full Italian translation from the Greek by Angelo Coccio (Venice: 1550), and Della Croce's full Latin translation (Basel: 1554). On the transmission history, see Gaselee S., "Introduction", in *Achilles Tatius*, trans. Gaselee (Cambridge, MA – London: 1947) vii–xvi, esp. xvi; and Ricquier K., "The Early Modern Transmission of the Ancient Greek Romances: A Bibliography Survey", *Ancient Narrative* 15 (2019) 1–34, esp. 6, 22–25.

81   For/on both passages, see Repath, "Emotional Conflict" 79–80. Stanisław Warszewicki's Latin translation of the *Aethiopica* appeared in 1551, followed by Jacques Amyot's French translation of 1547, Leonardo Ghini's Italian translation, published by Gabriele Giolito in Venice in 1556, 1560, and 1586, and Thomas Underdown's English translation of 1569; see Ricquier, "Early Modern Transmission" 8–9, 16–22.

INTRODUCTION: *MOTUS MIXTI ET COMPOSITI* 37

Achille Gagliardi's program of spiritual exercises, *Breve compendio intorno alla perfettione christiana* (Brief Summary concerning Christian Perfection).

Part 2.A. focuses on the forms and functions of mixed emotion in spiritual exercises centering on pictorial images. Mitch Merback explores the tragic emotional entanglements of Christ-recognition and self-recognition engendered by the passerby topos in late-medieval northern paintings of Christ in Misery; Walter Melion expounds the kinds and degrees of affective complexity put on view in Abraham Bloemaert's epitome of the eremitical life, *Sylva anachoretica* (1619), that jointly serves as an epitome of figural beauty; Raphaèle Presinger reveals how compound emotions were depicted in Jesuit and Franciscan propaganda to inspire reflection on the exemplary deaths of the earliest Christian martyrs in Japan; and Ruth Sargent Noyes recounts the material properties and multi-sensory address of the reliquary shrine of Saint Kazimierz Jagiellończyk, asking how, for the shrine's recipient, Cosimo III de' Medici, they might have served to enhance his mixed emotional experience of spiritual martyrdom. Part 2.B. focuses on the heuristic and/or restorative functions of portraying mixed emotion. Elliott Wise offers a Bonaventuran reading of Jan Provoost's Franciscan diptych *Christ Carrying the Cross*, showing how he invites meditation on the complex emotions of Christ in the Passion and then resolves these emotions into the certitude of divine constancy. Barbara Kaminska analyses the relation between mixed emotion and the representation of disability in the art of Hendrick Goltzius and the writings of his chief interpreter Karel van Mander. Graham Lea examines the narrative implications and moral impact of the complex, shifting emotions made intensely apparent by Pieter Lastman in his painting *Paul and Barnabas in Lystra* (1617). Finally, Stijn Bussels and Bram Van Oostveldt delve into the complex emotions stirred by Dutch marine paintings of storm and shipwreck, asking what sorts of consolation they afforded their viewers.

It should be noted that Intersections 91, *Theatre of Sexual Atraction and Psychological Destruction*, solely authored by Karl Enenkel, was originally conceived as a companion volume to *Motus mixti et compositi*. Now published as a freestanding monograph, it takes a close look at early modern depictions of the myth of Hercules and Omphale/Iole, which, following in the wake of Lukas Cranach's brilliant pictorial inventions of the 1530s, became a popular epitome for the skilful display of mixed emotions, not just in Germany but also Italy and elsewhere. Enenkel convincingly demonstrates that the popularity of this fable goes back to the mythopoetic writings of Boccaccio, *Genealogie deorum gentilium* (completed ca. 1361) and *De mulieribus claris* (dedicated 1362), in which the guileful Iole (whom Boccaccio purposely substitutes for Omphale) causes the lovestruck Hercules to succumb to the psychopathology of perfervid love. The shifting phases of Hercules's disordered emotions peak when, passion having overmastered his rational faculties, he enters a state of *furor mentis* (mental rage), raving uncontrollably; and, as he exhibits the symptoms of *furor*, so Iole/Omphale epitomises the performatively mixed emotional state of *affectus fictus* or *amor fictus* (feigned affect/affection or feigned love), her apparency of love masking hatred and contempt for Hercules (or, at the very least, indifference toward him). As Enenkel aptly observes, the shifting emotions of the textual tradition were for the most part transformed by painters and sculptors into compound, multilayered emotional effects. His monograph takes the soundings of the profoundly entangled emotions stirred and put on view by the encounter between Hercules and Iole/Omphale.

Bibliography

Agrippa d'Aubigné Théodore, *Les Tragiques* (Geneva, L.B.D.D.: 1616).

Agrippa d'Aubigné Théodore, *Oeuvres: Les Tragiques*, ed. H. Wéber (Paris: 1969).

Ampe A., "Naar een geschiedenis van de passie-beleving vanuit Marrows' *Passie-boek*", *Ons geestelijk erf* 58 (1984) 130–175.

Aristotle, *The "Art" of Rhetoric*, trans. J.H. Freese (Cambridge, MA – London: 1939).

Aristotle, *Nicomachean Ethics*, trans. H. Rackham (Cambridge, MA – London: 1945).

Baier W., *Untersuchungen zu den Passionsbetrachtungen in der 'Vita Christi' des Ludolfs von Sachsen: Ein Quellenkritischer Beitrag zu Leben und Werk Ludolfs und zur Geschichte des Passionstheologie*, Analecta Cartusiana 44, 3 vols. (Salzburg: 1977).

Broomhall S., *Emotions in the Household* (Basingstoke – New York: 2008).

Broomhall S., *Gender and Emotions in Medieval and Early Modern Europe* (Farnham: 2015).

Broomhall S., "Emotions of the Past in Catherine de Medici's Correspondence", in Marculescu A. – Moran Métivier C.-L. (eds.), *Affective and Emotional Economies in Medieval and Early Modern Europe*, Palgrave Studies in the History of Emotions (Cham: 2018) 87–104.

Burton Robert, *The Anatomy of Melancholy* (Oxford, J. Lichfield – J. Short: 1621).

Caussin Nicolas, S.J., *Felicitas*, in idem, *Tragoediae sacrae* (Paris, Sebastian Chappelet: 1620) 175–261.

Caussin Nicolas, S.J., *La cour sainte*, 4 parts (Paris, Sebastien Chappelet: 1624–1636).

Champion M. – Garrod R. – Ruys J., "But were they talking about emotions? *Affectus, affectio*, and the History of Emotions", *Rivista storica italiana* 128.2 (2016) 521–543.

Cotgrave Randle, *Dictionarie of the French and English Tongues* (London, Islip: 1611).

Cummings B. – Sierhuis F. (eds.), *Passion and Subjectivity in Early Modern Culture* (Farnham – Burlington, VT: 2013).

INTRODUCTION: *MOTUS MIXTI ET COMPOSITI* 39

David Jan, S.J., *Messis myrrhae et aromatum, ex instrumentis ac mysterijs Passionis Christi colligenda, ut ei commoriamur*, in *Paradisus Sponsi et Sponsae* (Antwerp, Balthasar and Jan Moretus: 1607).

David Jan, S.J., *Pancarpium Marianum, Septemplici Titulorum serie distinctum: ut in B. Virginis odorem curramus et Christus formetus in nobis*, in idem, *Paradisus Sponsi et Sponsae* (Antwerp, Balthasar and Jan Moretus: 1607).

Dekoninck R. – Delfosse A., "*Sacer Horror*: The Construction and Experience of the Sublime in the Jesuit Festivities of the Early Seventeenth-Century Southern Netherlands", *Journal of the Historians of Netherlandish Art* 8.2 (2016) 1–6, at https:// jhna.org/articles/sacer-horror-construction-experience-sublime-jesuit-festivities -early-seventeenth-century-southern-netherlands/ (accessed 26 September 2023).

Descartes René, *Les passions de l'âme* (Paris, Henry Le Gras: 1649).

Descartes René, *The passions of the soule in three books*, trans. s.n. (London, J. Martin – J. Ridley: 1650).

Deschamps J., "De 'Vita Christi' van Ludolf van Saksen in het Middelnederlands", in *Historia et spiritualitas cartusiensis. Colloquii quarti internationalis acta, Gandavi Antverpiae Brugis 16–10 Sept. 1982* (Destelbergen: 1983) 157–176.

Dickey S. – Roodenburg H. (eds.), *The Passions in the Arts of the Early Modern Netherlands*, Nederlands Kunsthistorisch Jaarboek 60 (Zwolle: 2010).

Filipczak Z.Z., "Rubens Adapts the Poses of Classical Sculptures for Deliberately Ambiguous and Other Emotions", in Dickey – Roodenburg (eds.), *Passions in the Arts* 125–149.

Flynn L.J., S.J., *The 'De Arte Rhetorica' (1568) by Cypriano Soarez, S.J.* (Ann Arbor: 1955).

Flynn L.J., S.J., "The *De Arte Rhetorica* of Cyprian Soarez, S.J.", *Quarterly Journal of Speech* 42 (1956) 367–371.

Flynn L.J., S.J., "Sources and Influence of Soarez' *De Arte Rhetorica*", *Quarterly Journal of Speech* 43 (1957).

Frisch A., "Agrippa d'Aubigné's *Tragiques* as Testimony", in LaGuardia D.P. – Randell C. (eds.), *Memory and Community in Sixteenth-Century France* (Farnham: 2015) 97–111.

Garrod R., "Senecan Catharsis in Nicolas Caussin's *Felicitas* (1620): A Case Study in Jesuit Reconfiguration of Affects", in Haskell Y. – Garrod (eds.), *Changing Hearts: Performing Jesuit Emotions between Europe, Asia, and the Americas*, Jesuit Studies: Modernity through the Prism of Jesuit History 15 (Leiden – Boston: 2019) 23–42.

Gaselee S., "Introduction", in *Achilles Tatius*, trans. Gaselee (Cambridge, MA – London: 1947) vii–xvi.

Gouk P. – Hills H. (eds.), *Representing Emotions: New Connections in the Histories of Art, Music, and Medicine* (Aldershot – Burlington, VT: 2005).

Groenendael Passion (Groenendael Priory, ca. 1480). Metropolitan Museum Album 2003.476.

Goudriaan K., "Middle Dutch Meditative *Lives of Jesus* on the Early Printing Press: An Exploration of the Field", in idem, *Piety in Practice and Print: Essays on the Late Medieval Religious Landscape*, ed. A. Dlabačová – A. Tervoort (Hilversum: 2016) 219–239.

Hoogstraten Samuel van, *Inleyding tot de hooge schoole der schilderkonst* (Rotterdam, Fransois van Hoogstraeten: 1678).

Houbraken Arnold, *De groote schouburgh der Nederlantsche konstschilders en schilderessen*, 2 vols. (The Hague, J. Swart – C. Boucquet – M. Gaillard: 1718).

James S., *Passion and Action: The Emotions in Seventeenth-Century Philosophy* (Oxford: 1997).

Junius Franciscus, *De pictura veterum libri 3* (Amsterdam, Johannes Blaeu: 1637).

Karant-Nunn S., *The Reformation of Feeling: Shaping the Religious Emotions in Early Modern Germany* (Oxford: 2010).

Kiliaen C., *Etymologicum teutonicae linguae*, ed. F. Claes, s.j. (Mouton – The Hague: 1972).

Kern Paster G., *Humoring the Body: Emotions and Shakespearean Stage* (Chicago: 2004).

Kern Paster G. – Rowe K. – Floyd-Wilson M. (eds.), *Reading the Early Modern Passions: Essays in the Cultural History of Emotion* (Philadelphia: 2004).

Knox G., "Eggs, Water, Metal: Velázquez, the *Paragone*, and the Products of *Practica*", in Knox – Tiffany (eds.), *Velázquez Re-Examined* 45–64.

Lomazzo Giovanni Paolo, *A Tracte containing the artes of curious Paintinge, Carvinge and Buildinge*, trans. Richard Haydocke (Oxford, Joseph Barnes for Richard Haydocke: 1598).

Lomazzo G.P., *Trattato dell'arte della pittura, sculture ed architettura*, in Ciardi R.P. (ed.), *Gian Paolo Lomazzo, Scritti sulle arti, vol. 2* (Florence: 1974).

Long K., "Cruelty and Empathy in Théodore Agrippa d'Aubigné's *Les Tragiques*: The Gaze of and on the Reader", in Marculescu A. – Morand Métivier C.L. (eds.), *Affective and Emotional Economies in Medieval and Early Modern Europe* (Cham: 2018) 167–194.

Lynch A., "Emotional Community", in Broomhall S. (ed.), *Early Modern Emotions: An Introduction* (Milton Park – Abingdon: 2017) 3–6.

Mahlmann-Bauer B., *Jezuitische 'ars rhetorica' im Zeitalter der Glaubenskämpfe*, Mikrokosmos 18 (Frankfurt am Main – Bern: 1986).

Mander Karel van, *Den Grondt der Edel vry Schilder-const*, Book 1 in idem, *Schilder-Boeck* (Haarlem, Paschier van Wesbusch: 1604).

Marías F., "Joseph's Bloodied Coat Presented to Jacob. From Portrait to History: History at the Margins of the Human", in Knox – T.J. Tiffany (eds.), *Velázquez Re-Examined: Theory, History, Poetry, and Theatre* (Turnhout: 2017) 65–78.

Marrow J.H., *Passion Iconography in Northern European Art of the Late Middle Ages and Early Renaissance*, Ars Neerlandica 1 (Kortrijk: 1979).

Meek R. – Sullivan E. (eds.), *The Renaissance of Emotion: Understanding Affect in Shakespeare and his Contemporaries* (Manchester: 2015).

Melion W.S., *Shaping the Netherlandish Canon: Karel van Mander's* Schilder-Boeck (Chicago: 1991).

Melion W.S., *Karel van Mander and his* Foundation of the Noble, Free Art of Painting (Leiden – Boston: 2022).

Melion W.S., "*De Virgine natalitia ad rapientem*: Marian Maternity, Militancy, and Mimesis in the First Marian Emblem Book – Jan David, s.j.'s *Pancarpium Marianum* of 1607", *Emblematica: Essays in Word and Image* 4 (2021) 139–209.

Melion W.S., "Meditating the Unbearable in a Fifteenth-Century Manuscript Prayerbook with Printed Images", in Dlabačová A. – Leerdam A. van – Thompson J. (eds.), *Vernacular Books and their Readers in the Early Age of Print (c. 1450–1600)*, Intersections 85 (Leiden – Boston: 2023) 328–393.

Montaigne Michel de, *The Essayes or Morall, Politike and Millitarie discourses of Lo: Michaell de Montaigne*, trans. John Florio (London: E. Blount, 1603).

Mullaney S., *The Reformation of Emotions in the Age of Shakespeare* (Chicago: 2015).

Quintilian, *The* Institutio oratoria, trans. H.E. Butler, 4 vols. (London – Cambridge, MA: 1939).

Repath I., "Emotional Conflict and Platonic Psychology in the Greek Novel", in Morgan J.R. – Jones M. (eds.), *Philosophical Presences in the Ancient Novel* (Groningen: 2007) 53–84.

Ricquier K., "The Early Modern Transmission of the Ancient Greek Romances: A Bibliography Survey", *Ancient Narrative* 15 (2019) 1–34.

Roodenburg H., "*Beweeghlijkheid* Embodied: On the Corporeal and Sensory Dimensions of a Famous Emotion Term", in Dickey – Roodenburg (eds.), *Passions in the Arts* 307–319.

Rosenwein B.H., *Anger's Past: The Social Uses of an Emotion in the Middle Ages* (Ithaca: 1998).

Rosenwein B.H., *Emotional Communities in the Early Middle Ages* (Ithaca: 2006).

Rosenwein B.H., "Problems and Methods in the History of Emotions", *Passions in Context: Journal of the History and Philosophy of the Emotions* 1.1 (2010), at www.passionsincontext.de/index.php/?id=557 (accessed 26 September 2023).

Rosenwein B.H., "Despair and Happiness", in eadem, *Generations of Feeling: A History of Emotions, 600–1700* (Cambridge: 2015) 248–287.

Santos Francisco de los, *Descripción breve del Monasterio de S. Lorenzo del Escorial* (Madrid, Imprenta Real: 1668).

Senault Jean François, *The Use of the Passions*, trans. Henry Earl of Monmouth (London, J.L. Moseley – Humphrey Moseley: 1649).

Sluijter E.J., "Rembrandt's Portrayal of the Passions and Vondel's *'staetverangeringe'*", in Dickey – Roodenburg (eds.), *Passions in the Arts* 285–306.

Soarez Cypriano, S.J., *De arte rhetorica libri tres ex Aristotele, Cicerone, et Quintiliano praecipua deprompti* (Paris, Thomas Brummenius: 1576).

Spinoza Benedictus de, *Ethica, ordine geometrico demonstrate*, in *Opera posthuman, quorum series post praefationem exhibetur* (Amsterdam, Jan Rieuwertsz.: 1677).

Spinoza Benedictus de, *Ethics Proved in Geometrical Order, Divided into Five Parts*, trans. A. Boyle (London: 1910; repr. ed., 1941).

Spiritual experiences, of sundry beleevers (London, n.p.: 1653).

Steiger J.A. (ed.), *Passion, Affekt, und Leidenschaft in der frühen Neuzeit*, Wolfenbütteler Arbeiten zur Barockforschung 43, 2 vols. (Wiesbaden: 2005).

Suárez Francisco, S.J., *Ad primam secundae D. Thomae tractatus quinque theologici* (Lyon, Jacobus Cardon: 1628).

Thorley D., "Towards a History of Emotion, 1562–1660", *The Seventeenth Century* 28.1 (2013) 3–19.

Tramelli B., *Giovanni Paolo Lomazzo's* Trattato dell'Arte della Pittura: *Color, Perspective, and Anatomy*, Nuncius Series 1 (Leiden – Boston: 2017).

PART 1

Portraying Mixed Emotions in the Literary Arts

∵

SECTION A

Mixed Emotions in Dutch and Latin Drama

∴

CHAPTER 2

All Motion Discovers Us: Moral Discernment and the Role of the Passions in Willem van Nieulandt's *Nero* (1618)

Bart Ramakers

Abstract

Late-sixteenth-century and early-seventeenth-century Netherlandish literature witnessed what may be called an ethical turn. In this essay, a tragedy by the Antwerp playwright Willem van Nieulandt (1584–1635), *Claudius Domitius Nero*, is being analysed as a spectacle of various emotions, to be perceived, processed, and evaluated for moral betterment. Although *Nero* is of the Neo-Senecan sort, meaning that several characters are driven by – and consequently exhibit – excessive emotions, it nevertheless advocates a conditionally positive attitude towards them, depending on their capacity to incite the characters – as well as the audience – to possess virtuous behaviour. A key quality in this respect was empathy and the ability to become empathically engaged. Tragedy was supposed to spark a process of moral discernment in the spectators.

Keywords

Willem van Nieulandt – tragedy – history painting – Antwerp – Aristotle – rhetoric – passions – ethics

Late-sixteenth-century and early-seventeenth-century Netherlandish literature witnessed what may be called an ethical turn. Moral plays, tragedies, emblem books, and mythological stories were used to instruct the reader or spectator in ethics. This involved not so much the formulation of rules of conduct but the creation or constitution – cognitively and emotionally – of a disposition or *habitus* that enabled man to act in an ethically sound manner in concrete circumstances.[1] The aforementioned genres confronted their

---

1 On habitus and disposition, primarily in relation to bodily behaviour, see, for example, Roodenburg H., *The Eloquence of the Body: Perspectives on Gesture in the Dutch Republic* (Zwolle: 2004) 9–25, esp. 19–21.

© BART RAMAKERS, 2025 | DOI:10.1163/9789004694613_003

readers, viewers, or spectators with paradigms, either positive or negative, of human behaviour. They functioned in the manner described by Neema Parvini for Shakespeare's plays, that is, 'as complex simulations of human thought processes in different situations'. To which she adds: 'And in considering the thought processes of Shakespeare's characters when they are deciding on their actions, we can in turn reflect on our own decision making'.[2]

Essential for our understanding of why during the early modern period Christ and other biblical personages and the vast array of classical and mythological figures kept being represented on stage is the inexhaustibility of their status as exemplars, as well as the need for spectators to be constantly exposed to them in order to succeed in their moral habituation. As theatrical characters they were meant to initiate a process of reflection on the circumstances and aspects – arguments as well as emotions – of their actions and the moral values that underlie them. As Michael Bristol cogently phrases it:

> There is no instruction manual for the characters, who have to operate in a fictional universe that requires them to find some kind of stable orientation to the unpredictable and often incomprehensible circumstances in which they place themselves. Most of the more interesting characters fail to maintain their integrity in one way or another. That's why they are interesting. That's why we care about them. That's why we recognize what it feels like to be in their predicament. And that is why, perforce, we pursue inquiry about their reasons, their motives, and their moral disposition.[3]

---

2   Parvini N., *Shakespeare and Cognition: Thinking Fast and Slow through Character* (Basingstoke – New York, NY: 2015) 10. See also Reynolds E., *A Treatise of the Passions and Faculties of the Soule of Man*, ed. Wiley M.E. (Gainesville, FL: 1971) 8, 19–20; Hampton T., *Writing from History: The Rhetoric of Exemplarity in Tasso, Montaigne and Cervantes* (Ph.D. dissertation, Princeton University: 1987) 6–8; Eagleton T., *Sweet Violence: The Idea of the Tragic* (Malden, MA: 2003) 78; Knapp J.A., *Image Ethics in Shakespeare and Spenser* (New York, NY: 2011) 19–22; and Berg J., "Moral Agency as Readerly Subjectivity: Shakespeare's Parolles and the Theophrastan Character Sketch", *Shakespeare Studies* 40 (2012) 36–43, esp. 36–37. For a philosophical perspective on exemplarity, see Adams R.M., *A Theory of Virtue: Excellence in Being for the Good* (Oxford: 2006) 14–15; Herman B., *Moral Literacy* (Harvard, MA – London: 2007) 1.

3   Bristol M.D., "Introduction", *Shakespeare Studies* 40 (2012) 19–25, at 20. See also Carroll N., "Theater and the Emotions", in Zunshine L. (ed.), *The Oxford Handbook of Cognitive Literary Studies* (Oxford: 2015) 313–326, esp. 319–321. On the classical (especially Aristotelian) concept of character, see Burns E., *Character: Acting and Being on the Pre-Modern Stage* (Basingstoke: 1990) 18–38. See also Kosman A., "Acting: Drama as the Mimēsis of Praxis", in Rorty A.O. (ed.), *Essays on Aristotle's Poetics* (Princeton, NJ: 1992) 51–72, esp. 64.

The process involves a weighing of circumstantial against dispositional conditions of moral behaviour.[4] The kind of ethics involved here is called situation ethics or moral contextualism.[5] It closely resembles – or coincides with – virtue ethics, whose main ancient proponent was Aristotle (384–322 BCE).[6]

Here the term "moral discernment" is used to describe this process. Consequently, reading and spectating are considered forms of ethical investigation. In this manner one learned to either bypass or imitate particular patterns of thought and behaviour in similar situations. By learning we mean internalizing or incorporating. A key quality in this respect was empathy and the ability to become empathically engaged.[7] Early modern authors were largely indebted to antiquity for both moral and philosophical ideas as well as literary forms

---

4 Walker L.J., "Moral Motivation through the Perspective of Exemplarity", in Heinrichs K. – Oser F. – Lovat T. (eds.), *Handbook of Moral Motivation: Theories, Models, Applications* (Rotterdam: 2013) 197–214, esp. 200–202. See also Gross D.M., *The Secret History of Emotion: From Aristotle's* Rhetoric *to Modern Brain Science* (Chicago, IL – London: 2006) 2–3; Grady H., "Moral Agency and Its Problems in *Julius Caesar*: Political Power, Choice, and History", in Bristol D. – Coodin S. – Fahmi M. – Finin K.R. (eds.), *Shakespeare and Moral Agency* (London: 2010) 15–28, esp. 17; and Critchley S., "Tragedy's Philosophy", in Fischer T. – Katsouraki E. (eds.), *Performing Antagonism* (Basingstoke – New York, NY: 2017) 25–42, esp. 27.

5 Langlands R., "Roman *Exempla* and Situation Ethics: Valerius Maximus and Cicero *de Officiis*", *Journal of Roman Studies* 100 (2011) 100–122, esp. 101.

6 MacIntyre A., *After Virtue: A Study in Moral Theory* (London – New York, NY: 2011 [1981]) 171–191; Sherman N., *The Fabric of Character: Aristotle's Theory of Virtue* (Oxford: 1989) 179–180, 157–183; Hursthouse R., *On Virtue Ethics* (Oxford: 1999) 8–16, 25–32, 35–36; Blackburn S., *Ruling Passions: A Theory of Practical Reasoning* (Oxford: 1998) 24–37. On Aristotle's ideas on virtuous living generally, see Cooper J.M., *Reason and Emotion: Essays on Ancient Moral Psychology and Ethical Theory* (Princeton, NJ: 1999) 253–280; Cooper J.M., *Pursuits of Wisdom: Six Ways of Life in Ancient Philosophy from Socrates to Plotinus* (Princeton, NJ – Oxford: 2012) 70–143. On early modern ideas in this respect, see Coodin S., "What's Virtue Ethics Got to Do With It? Shakespearean Character as Moral Character", in Bristol D. – Coodin S. – Fahmi M. – Finin K.R. (eds.), *Shakespeare and Moral Agency* (London: 2010) 184–199, esp. 188; Lyne R., *Shakespeare, Rhetoric and Cognition* (Cambridge: 2011) 2; Buys R., *Sparks of Reason: Vernacular Rationalism in the Low Countries 1550–1670* (Hilversum: 2015) 163–172, esp. 164–165; and Hellerstedt A., "Introduction", in Hellerstedt A. (ed.), *Virtue Ethics and Education from Late Antiquity to the Eighteenth Century* (Amsterdam: 2018) 9–36, esp. 17–19.

7 On the meaning of empathy generally, see, for example, Lanzoni S., "Introduction", in Lanzoni S., *Empathy: A History* (Princeton, NJ: 2018) 1–18; and Newton B.W., "Perspective Chapter: Having Heart – The Different Facets of Empathy", in Ventura S. (ed.), *Empathy – Advances Research and Applications* (London: 2023) 29–49. On emphatic engagement, especially in relation to the arts, see Coplan A., "Empathic Engagement with Narrative Fictions", *The Journal of Aesthetics and Art Criticism* 62.2 (2004) 141–152; Brinck I., "Empathy, Engagement, Entrainment: The Interaction Dynamics of Aesthetic Experience", *Cognitive Processing* 19 (2018) 201–213; and Kou X. – Konrath S. – Goldstein, T.R., "The Relationship among Different Types of Arts Engagement, Empathy, and Prosocial Behavior", *Psychology of Aesthetics, Creativity, and the Arts* 14.4 (2020) 481–492.

and techniques through which these ideas were transferred, including the narrative corpus – history, mythology – which served as a source for poetry and drama.

Aim and Setup

This essay primarily attempts to establish how tragedy, the dramatic genre that in the late sixteenth and early seventeenth centuries gained great prominence, was used as a tool for moral discernment. This approach amounts to what in modern literary criticism is called "ethical inquiry".[8] One Dutch tragedy in particular will be discussed: *Claudius Domitius Nero*, or *Nero* for short [Fig. 2.1], written by Willem van Nieulandt (1584–1635) [Fig. 2.2], a painter-poet from Antwerp, and performed and printed in 1618.[9] The aim is to ascertain how verbal and visual cues in this play may have been perceived and processed by their spectators. The contention is that Van Nieulandt's *Nero* was meant to be a spectacle of various emotions, to be perceived, processed, and evaluated for moral betterment. It was this variety of affects, singly or multiply expressed by one or more characters on stage, their mixed and compound character, so to speak, which may account for the genre's popularity among early modern audiences. Tragedy offered a sea of interrelated and mutually reinforcing emotions for the audience to navigate, and thus to train their discerning abilities, to discriminate between appropriate and inappropriate passions, between the acceptable and unacceptable causes spawning them, as well as between the defensible and indefensible actions they incited.

Thus, this essay is concerned with the agency of the historical audience in relation to the agency of the historical performance, especially the moral agency of the tragic characters. Perhaps it is better to speak of engagement,

---

8 Booth W.C., "Why Ethical Criticism Can Never Be Simple", in Davis T.F. – Womack K. (eds.), *Mapping the Ethical Turn: A Reader in Ethics, Culture, and Literary Theory* (Charlottesville, VA – London: 2001) 16–29, esp. 16–21.

9 Nieuwelandt Guilliam van, *Claudius Domitius Nero* (Antwerp, Guilliam van Tongheren: 1618). On Van Nieulandt's tragedies, see Keersmaekers A.A., *De dichter Guilliam van Nieuwelandt en de Senecaans-classieke tragedie in de Zuidelijke Nederlanden: Bijdrage tot de studie van de Zuidnederlandse literatuur der 17e eeuw* (Gent: 1957) 177–184; Ramakers B., "Sophonisba's Dress: Costume, Tragedy and Value on the Antwerp Stage (c. 1615–1630)", in Göttler C. – Ramakers B. – Woodall J. (eds.), *Trading Values in Early Modern Antwerp*, Netherlands Yearbook for History of Art 64 (Leiden – Boston, MA: 2014) 298–347. On Van Nieulandt as a painter, see Sluijter E.J., "Career Choices of Migrant Artists between Amsterdam and Antwerp: The Van Nieulandt Brothers", *De Zeventiende Eeuw* 31.1 (2015) 102–137.

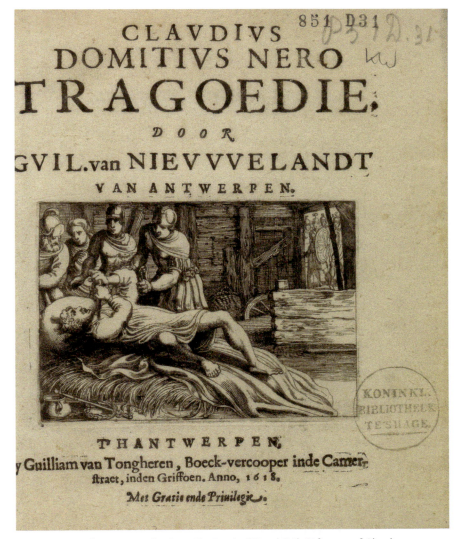

FIGURE 2.1 Willem van Nieulandt II, *The Death of Nero* (1618). Title page of *Claudius Domitius Nero* (Antwerp, Guilliam van Tongheren: 1618). The Hague, Koninklijke Bibliotheek, KW 851 D 31

FIGURE 2.2 Jean Meyssens, *Willem Nieulandt II* (1662). Engraving, 162 × 113 mm. Cornelis de Bie, *Het gulden cabinet vande edele vry schilder-const*, 3 vols. (Antwerp, Joannes Meyssens and Juliaen van Montfort, 1662), vol. 1, 63. Amsterdam, Rijksmuseum, RP-P-OB-23.603

involvement, or enticement, partly because performance and audience were interdependent, and partly because the aforementioned terms, more than agency, call to attention the role of viewers and spectators in the process of reception, and direct our attention towards what Caroline Lamb in relation to theatre calls 'engaged spectatorship'.[10] After all, it is the audience that makes a painting or play and the characters represented in them "work" or "act". In other words: Agency materialises in the act of viewing/watching. Ideally, this approach, besides 'the specifics of the media message' and the formal manner in which it is conveyed, should address the 'activities surrounding reception',[11] and takes into account the theatrical event as a whole.[12] As far as such engaged spectatorship involves the exerting of empathy it falls within the scope of emphatic engagement.[13] Research into engaged spectatorship calls for a phenomenological approach in which the 'lived experience' of the audience is reconstructed and interpreted through thick description of both the performance and the spectators' perception of it.[14]

This essay will position itself vis-à-vis two conflicting views on the passions current at the time – conflicting as to their suitability and appropriateness for moral reasoning, that is, as impetuses to virtuous behaviour. With these differing views on the passions concur two differing views on tragedy and the function of the characters' passions and the actions they incite, as well as on the spectators' preferred evaluation of these actions and passions, and the consequences to be drawn from them as regards their own behaviour.

---

10   Lamb C., *Corporeal Returns: Theatrical Embodiment and Spectator Response in Early Modern Drama* (Ph.D. dissertation, The University of Western Ontario: 2011) 37. See also Booth, "Why Ethical Criticism Can Never Be Simple" 18–19; Paster G.K., *Humoring the Body: Emotions and the Shakespearean Stage* (Chicago, IL – London: 2004) 20; Dickey S.S. – Roodenburg H., "Introduction: The Motions of the Mind", in Dickey S.S. – Roodenburg H. (eds.), *The Passions in the Arts of the Early Modern Netherlands* (Zwolle: 2010) 7–16, esp. 8–9; and Küpper J., *The Cultural Net: Early Modern Drama as a Paradigm* (Berlin – Boston: 2019) 168–169.

11   Bird S.E., "From Fan Practice to Mediated Moments: The Value of Practice Theory in the Understanding of Media audiences", in Bräuchler B. – Postill J. (eds.), *Theorising Media and Practice* (Oxford – New York: 2010) 85–104, esp. 87.

12   Sauter W., *The Theatrical Event: Dynamics of Performance and Perception* (Iowa City, IA, 2000).

13   See above and note 7.

14   For a short introduction to phenomenology, see Van Manen M., "Phenomenology of Practice", *Phenomenology & Practice* 1.1 (2007), 11–30, esp. 20–22; Langdridge D., "Phenomenology and Critical Social Psychology: Directions and Debates in Theory and Research", *Social and Personality Psychology Compass* 2.3 (2008) 1126–1142, esp. 1128, 1130, 1138; and Finlay L., "Debating Phenomenological Research Methods", *Phenomenology & Practice* 3.1 (2009) 6–25, esp. 8–13.

Whereas the one view on tragedy may be summarised as Senecan-Scaligerian, at the root of which lies a (Neo-)Stoic attitude towards the passions, the other may be characterised as Aristotelian, both as regards the function of tragedy and the role of the passions displayed in them. The Aristotelian character of the latter view on tragedy is related to the early modern concept of *catharsis* as it was adapted from Aristotle's definition in the *Poetics*. For his ideas on tragedy and the passions, however, one has to also look beyond the *Poetics* and take leads from his other works, foremost the *Art of Rhetoric* and the *Nicomachean Ethics*. A disclaimer should be added here: Quotations from or references to these treatises merely serve to explain the origin of what in early modern times was considered Aristotelian rather than to suggest any direct influence.

The argument boils down to the following: Although Van Nieulandt's *Nero*, like all of his tragedies, is of the Neo-Senecan sort, meaning that several characters are driven by – and consequently exhibit – excessive emotions, the play nevertheless advocates a conditionally positive attitude towards them, depending on their capacity to incite the characters – as well as the audience – to possess virtuous behaviour. *Nero* certainly does not propagate an attitude of unequivocal apathy (*apatheia*) towards the passions – the essentially Senecan-Scaligerian or (Neo-)Stoic position – but favours a more benevolent view of them, varying on a scale from Lipsian constancy (*constantia*) to Aristotelian metriopathy (*metriopatheia*). To better understand and explain this latter perspective, the medieval or wider Christian view on the passions, from Augustine, via Thomas, to sixteenth-century humanists such as Erasmus, Coornhert, Montaigne, and Lipsius himself, has to be placed into the equation. Behind the aforementioned conflicting views loom what William Bouwsma so fundamentally and famously called 'The Two Faces of Humanism'.[15]

The Senecan-Scaligerian view on tragedy is based on Julius Caesar Scaliger's (1484–1558) *Poetices libri septem* (Seven Books of Poetics) from 1561.[16] Scaliger's position can be critically challenged through a number of questions. How can the audience's required rejection of the passions be brought in line with the propagation of *movere*, that second of the three tasks of the orator (*officia oratoris*), which Scaliger expected the tragedian to exercise and which was deemed the most effective form of persuasion? How could tragedy move the spectators without agitating or provoking their emotions? In the same vein one may ask:

---

15   Bouwsma W.J., "The Two Faces of Humanism: Stoicism and Augustianism in Renaissance Thought", in Oberman H.O. – Brady T.A. (eds.), *Itinerarium Italicum: The Profile of the Italian Renaissance in the Mirror of its European Transformations* (Leiden: 1975) 3–60.

16   Scaliger Julius Caesar, *Poetices libri septem* (Lyon, Antonius Vincentius: 1561).

What other purpose could the characters' display of passions on stage possibly have or achieve than to emotionally stir or disturb the audience? To take the matter one step further: Does this emotive function not *a fortiori* apply to early modern tragedy, since Scaliger demanded the genre dramatise historical subject matter featuring high-placed personages, for whom he reserved treatment in the grand style, which was explicitly meant to engender passionate arousal? And finally: Is it not in line with expectations that early modern tragedians not only intended to trigger emotional responses in the audience – emotions triggered by the *atrocitates* (horrors) displayed on stage and the passions surrounding them – but that they expected spectators to constructively integrate these emotions, again both the characters' and their own, in a process of moral discernment?

The above reference was made to painting not only because the agency of works of art is currently a popular topic in art historical studies – in fact, the term has been significantly coined by art historians[17] – but also because it will be argued that both tragedy and painting, history painting in particular, functioned as instruments of moral discernment in the aforementioned manner, depicting and dramatising exemplary classical and biblical subject matter for ethical purposes. The contexts of production and reception of theatre and art were not only comparable but in many cases connected, even identical, especially in early modern Antwerp. Art and theatre in the Low Countries during this period generally were produced in close cooperation, and in social and professional contexts where poets and painters regularly met. The literary life in the vernacular took place within and outside chambers of rhetoric (*rederijkerskamers*), of which artists also were members. Willem van Nieulandt first practised his dramatic skills within The Olive Branch (*De Olyftack*), later becoming a prominent member of The Gillyflowers (*De Violieren*). The latter chamber formed a union with the painters' guild of St. Luke. We know about several artists who combined the skills of both poetry and painting. As noted, Van Nieulandt himself was such an all-around talent.

Towards the end of this essay, *Nero* will be linked to a painting by another artist from Antwerp, Frans Francken the Younger: *The Painter's Cabinet* [Fig. 2.6]. Art cabinets, like dining rooms and other domestic spaces, provided a social and spatial context for viewing and processing – either individually, through pondering, or convivially, through conversation – art shown in interior locations, which bears resemblance to what presumably happened during and after the performance of plays, particularly tragedies, which also took place

---

17   See seminally Bredekamp H., *Image Acts: A Systematic Approach to Visual Agency* (Berlin – Boston, MA: 2015).

indoors, in the meeting rooms of chambers of rhetoric or in public buildings such as town halls. Hence, not only were the mental dispositions of viewers of art and spectators of drama identical, so too were the social and spatial conditions under which their viewing/watching evolved.

Judging by Behaviour

In an engraving from 1596 by Johann Theodor de Bry after a print by Dirck Volckertszoon Coornhert and a design by Maarten van Heemskerck, we see a *globus cruciger* with a fool's cap lying on it [Fig. 2.3]. On either side stand the philosophers Democritus and Heraclitus. The first laughs, the second cries about what is happening in the world. Representations of the laughing and crying philosopher were very popular in the sixteenth and early seventeenth centuries. The philosophers' emotional expressions seem to be the outcome of a process of observing the world from some distance, as philosophers do. Although their emotions are opposites, both result from the same judgment, namely that the observed behaviour is foolish, immoral, or unvirtuous. It is this process of observation and judgment that makes the one cry and the other laugh.

In *Essai* (Essay) 50, Michel de Montaigne (1533–1592) provides us with insight into how this process works. It is Montaigne's aim 'to present an ethical way of living within the limits of the human',[18] taking human behaviour – his own and others', present as well as past – as the basis for moral discernment, applying reason, that distinctively human capacity, to analyse his thoughts and actions. His 'whole project is precisely to record the perpetual "vient en estre" of his mind's inwardness'.[19] He refers to Democritus and Heraclitus by way of illustration, preferring the former over the latter, that is, laughing over crying.[20]

---

18 Mack P., "Montaigne and Christian Humanism", in MacDonald A.A. – Martels Z.R.W.M. von – Veenstra J. (eds.), *Christian Humanism: Essays in Honour of Arjo Vanderjagt* (Leiden – Boston, MA: 2009) 199–209, esp. 208–209.

19 Tilmouth C., "Passion and Intersubjectivity in Early Modern Literature", in Cummings B. – Sierhuis F. (eds.), *Passions and Subjectivity in Early Modern Culture* (Abingdon – New York, NY: 2016) 13–32, esp. 14. See also Conley T., *An Errant Eye: Poetry and Topography in Early Modern France* (Minneapolis – London: 2011) 7.

20 It is from *Essai* 50 that the title of this essay was taken: 'All motion discovers us' – 'Tout mouvement nous descouvre'. Book I, Chapter 50; Montaigne Michel de, *Essays of Montaigne*, trans. Cotton C. – ed. Hazlitt W.C., 3 vols. (London: 1877), vol. 1, 401. French quotation taken from Montaigne Michel Eyquem de, *Les Essais*, eds. Villey P. – Saulnier V.-L. – online ed. Desan P. (Chicago, IL: n.d.) 302. See also Foglia M., "La question de l'interprétation chez Montaigne", *Cahiers philosophiques* 127.4 (2011) 81–96, esp. 86; Stock B., "Ethical

FIGURE 2.3   Johann Theodor de Bry after Dirck Volckertszoon Coornhert after Maarten van Heemskerck, *Democritus and Heraclites* (1596). Engraving, 100 × 100 mm. *Emblemata Saecularia* [...] (Frankfurt am Main, J.T. de Bry and J.I. de Bry: 1596). Amsterdam, Rijksmuseum, RP-P-BI-5187

What he means to say is that the observation of external behaviour provides insight into what is happening inside, in people's minds. He summarises this observation, both its process and its outcome, in the concept of judgment – 'le jugement'. This amounts to a kind of mind-reading[21] and can be applied any place, any time. All behaviour lends itself for analysis:

Values and the Literary Imagination in the Later Ancient World", *New Literary History* 29.1 (1998) 1–13, esp. 3.

21   Zunshine L., *Getting Inside Your Head: What Cognitive Science Can Tell Us about Popular Culture* (Baltimore, MD: 2012) 10; Beecher D., *Adapted Brains and Imaginary Worlds: Cognitive Science and the Literature of the Renaissance* (Montreal – Kingston – London: 2016) 26–32; Edinborough C., *Theatrical Reality: Space, Embodiment and Empathy in Performance* (Bristol – Chicago, IL: 2016) 48–49.

Each motion sheweth and discovereth what we are. The very same minde of *Cæsar* we see in directing, marshalling, and setting the battel of *Pharsalia*, is likewise seene to order, dispose, and contrive idle, trifling and amorous devices.[22]

To get to know Caesar's inner nature – to see or know his mind – one only needs to observe him in varying situations and moments, including trivial occasions.

Before proceeding, we should zoom out from Montaigne's words to the wider context of the humanist concern with reading another person's mind and mirroring it to one's own for reasons of character formation, since that is what the process of moral discernment or scrutiny was meant to accomplish. Besides man's thoughts, also his feelings – or whatever one likes to call them, affects, emotions, or passions[23] – attracted great attention. Although man's interior was deemed more important than his exterior, the latter nevertheless provided important clues to the former which were both prompted and registered with the help of observation, mainly through seeing and hearing,[24] but the other senses – taste, touch, and smell – could be involved as well. From this it followed that the body expressed what went on in the soul.

Montaigne considers body language an important complement of speech. Manfred Pfister draws on Montaigne when he writes:

> [I]t is to the extent that there is a natural tendency in body and soul towards congruence and that there is a conscious effort to realize this congruence, that the body becomes expressive of character, temperament, ideas and emotions and can be read in these terms.[25]

In short, 'man's body is as eloquent as his speech'.[26] The concept of bodily eloquence was rooted in contemporary rhetoric and theatre, including tragedy, 'in

---

22   Montaigne Michel de, *The Essays of Montaigne*, trans. Florio J. – intro. Saintsbury G., 3 vols. (London: 1892), vol. 1, 349.

23   Maus K.E., *Inwardness and Theater in the English Renaissance* (Chicago, IL – London: 1995) 11–12. On early modern English nomenclature, see, for example, Reynolds, *A Treatise of the Passions* 10.

24   Kambaskovic D., "'Among the Rest of the Senses ... Proved Most Sure': Ethics of the Senses in Pre-modern Europe", in Kambaskovic D. (ed.), *Conjunctions of Mind, Soul and Body from Plato to the Enlightenment* (Heidelberg: 2014) 337–370, esp. 338–351.

25   Pfister M., "Reading the Body: The Corporeality of Shakespeare's Text", in Scolnicow H. – Holland P. (eds.), *Reading Plays: Interpretation and Reception* (Cambridge et al.: 1991) 110–122, esp. 114.

26   Pfister, "Reading the Body" 115.

ALL MOTION DISCOVERS US: WILLEM VAN NIEULANDT'S *NERO* (1618)

which certain bodily features or actions are presented as decisively significant'
and 'which include a great number of explicit references in the dialogue to the
significance of this body language'.[27]

The belief that our actions reveal who we are, was seen as a stimulus to
role-playing, either to conceal our inner being or, more positively, to attain an
ethically grounded outer posture based on a corresponding inner composure.
Role-playing relates to the topic of the early modern formation of self, or *the
self*, and of self-fashioning.[28] As a figure of speech it is rooted in the broader
concept of the world-as-a-stage (*theatrum mundi*).[29] The latter metaphor
extended to the real theatre and the drama performed in it, inasmuch as tragedy presented to its spectators exemplary images of the world, of the "theatre"
beyond, and of the "personages" who "acted" in it, and who were seen as "theatres" too, both their bodies and their minds.

Passions from the Past

References to the expression of the passions rested on the early modern
belief in their physical materiality.[30] In medieval and early modern times it
was held that feelings were a product of the humoral body as described by the
Greco-Roman physician and physiologist Galen (129–216). They were thought
to play an important role in determining man's ethical disposition and ensuing
behaviour.[31] However subjective and personal man's inner musings might be,

---

27 Pfister, "Reading the Body" 118.

28 Tilmouth, "Passion and Intersubjectivity" 13. See also Stock, "Ethical Values" 4;
Schoenfeldt M.C., *Bodies and Selves in Early Modern England: Physiology and Inwardness
in Spenser, Shakespeare, Herbert, and Milton* (Cambridge – New York, NY: 1999) 17–18;
Steenbergh K., "Emotion, Performance and Gender in Shakespeare's Hamlet", in Ruberg
W.G. – Steenbergh K. (eds.), *Sexed Sentiments: Interdisciplinary Perspectives on Gender and
Emotion* (Amsterdam: 2011) 93–116, esp. 96–97; and Steenbergh K., "Emotions and Gender:
The Case of Anger in Early Modern English Revenge Tragedies", in Liliequist J. (ed.), *A
History of Emotions, 1200–1800* (London: 2012) 119–134, esp. 121–122.

29 For an introduction to the metaphor, see Quiring B., "Introduction", in Quiring B. (ed.), *"If
Then the World a Theatre Present ...": Revisions of the Theatrum Mundi Metaphor in Early
Modern England* (Berlin: 2014) 1–23. See also Plett H.F., *Rhetoric and Renaissance Culture*
(Berlin – New York, NY: 2004) 251–255, 272–277.

30 Paster, *Humoring the Body* 13–14, 22–24; Coodin S., "Fiction, Emotion, and Moral Agency",
Shakespeare Studies 40 (2012) 63–69, esp. 65; Craik K.A. – Pollard T., "Introduction:
Imagining Audiences", in Craik K.A. – Pollard T. (eds.), *Shakespearean Sensations:
Experiencing Literature in Early Modern England* (Cambridge: 2013) 1–25, esp. 5–8.

31 Schoenfeldt, *Bodies and Selves* 20. See also Pfister, "Reading the Body" 113; Roach J.R.,
The Player's Passion: Studies in the Science of Acting (Newark, NJ – London – Toronto:

these concerned thoughts and feelings which were universal or intersubjective in the sense that they related to the human condition. The same applied to the exterior symptoms that brought these thoughts and feelings to the fore. Both man's interior and exterior could thus be objectified and categorised. This intersubjectivity accounted for a process of exemplary mirroring, that is, reflecting on one's own actions and feelings by reflecting on those of others.

From the example of Caesar in *Essai* 50 it follows that as a source for moral discernment Montaigne considered not only his own and his fellow man's conduct but also that of people from the past, in this case from ancient history. Later he refers to Alexander the Great and cites the latter's obsession with chess as a key to understanding his mind. Montaigne recognises himself in the Macedonian ruler. He too is obsessed with the game of chess, and in practising it he is driven by various – negative – passions; he needs to overcome 'choller, spight, hatred, impatience, and vehement ambition'.[32] This makes abundantly clear what seeing or knowing other people's minds and his own comes down to: to determine the forces – passions, vices, and virtues – at play in governing human behaviour.[33]

It is also clear to which purpose that insight and knowledge serve: to reflect on one's own behaviour by analogy with that of others. The historical example was considered to have 'a performative force, in that it provokes a response with moral consequences. [...] In rhetorical terms, its effectiveness is in linking a *quaestio infinita* to a *quaestio finita*',[34] meaning that a general question was linked to a specific one concerning a particular person or case. Montaigne argues in favour of scrutinizing one's own and others' behaviour on every level of the soul, from the lowest, that of the vegetative soul, through the sensitive

---

1985) 38–46; Gowland A., "Melancholy, Passions and Identity in the Renaissance", in Cummings B. – Sierhuis F. (eds.), *Passions and Subjectivity in Early Modern Culture* (Abingdon – New York, NY: 2016) 75–93, esp. 79–81; and Marculescu A. – Morand Métivier C.L., "Introduction", in Marculescu A. – Morand Métivier C.L. (eds.), *Affective and Emotional Economies in Medieval and Early Modern Europe* (Cham: 2018) 1–16, esp. 1–2.

32 Book 1, Chapter 50; Montaigne, *The Essays of Montaigne*, vol. 1, 394.

33 On the virtues and vices, see, for example, Timpe K. – Boyd C.A. (eds.), *Virtues and Their Vices* (Oxford: 2014); Tucker S.R., *The Virtues and Vices in the Arts: A Sourcebook* (Eugene, OR: 2015).

34 Langer U., "The Ring of Gyges in Plato, Cicero, and Lorenzo Valla: The Moral Force of Fictional Examples", in Kessler E. – Maclean I. (eds.), *Res et verba in der Renaissance* (Wiesbaden: 2002) 131–145, esp. 139. See also Hampton, *Writing from History* 6–8; Syson L. – Thornton D., *Objects of Virtue: Art in Renaissance Italy* (Los Angeles, CA: 2001) 13; Zagzebski L., "The Admirable Life and the Desirable Life", in Chappel T. (ed.), *Values and Virtues: Aristotelianism in Contemporary Ethics* (Oxford: 2006) 53–66, esp. 56–65.

soul, where the passions arose, to the highest level, where they were assessed.[35] Every person reacted in a different way to what happened to him, and this is what made the moral discernment process necessary. He also resorts to allegory and personification to clarify how the soul or mind processed external matters and events.[36]

The complete and detailed mapping of the human mind through careful observation of behaviour in different situations – again, of one's own behaviour, that of one's fellow man, or that of past people – was a widespread endeavour in the early modern era. In the Netherlands, Desiderius Erasmus (1466/1469–1536) was (one of) the first to eloquently describe this phenomenon in the *Enchiridion Militis Christiani* (Manual of a Christian Knight) from 1501. The objective was the attainment of knowledge or wisdom needed to develop a virtuous character and to act virtuously. In the *Enchiridion* we come across the same insistence on scrutinizing the mind as in Montaigne's *Essai* 50. However, Erasmus describes the workings of the mind in much more detail, zooming in on the operation of its rational part, on reason, particularly on practical reason, which pertains to morals. This basically is an Aristotelian position: 'Aristotle tells us that virtuous action is the action that the person of practical wisdom (the *phronimos*) would choose [...]. To be wise is to know how to exercise those virtues as circumstances require'.[37]

Passing judgment, as Montaigne asks man to do, means making sense of events, which involves relating them intelligibly to human motivations and to the ways in which situations appear to agents. That will help us in our own

---

35   Book I, Chapter 50; Montaigne, *The Essays of Montaigne*, vol. 1, 393. On the vegetative soul and the passions, see Solomon J.R., "You've Got to Have Soul: Understanding the Passions in Early Modern Culture", in Pender S. – Struever N.S. (eds.), *Rhetoric and Medicine in Early Modern Europe* (Farnham – Burlington, VT: 2012) 195–228, esp. 200–201, 208–210. See also Reynolds, *A Treatise of the Passions* 17–18. On the rational soul and the intellect vis-à-vis the passions, see Gowland, "Melancholy, Passions and Identity" 83–85.

36   On the use of personification in (the representation of) thinking and contemplation, especially in Montaigne's *Essais*, see Lyons J.D., "Meditation and the Inner Voice", *New Literary History* 37.3 (2006) 525–538, esp. 527; Stock, "Ethical Values" 7.

37   Sherman N., "Character Development and Aristotelian Virtues", in Carr D. – Steutel J. (eds.), *Virtue Ethics and Moral Education* (London – New York, NY: 1999) 35–49, esp. 36 (italics added). See also Levi A., *French Moralists: The Theory of the Passions 1585 to 1649* (Oxford: 1964) 10; MacIntyre, *After Virtue* 180–181; Hursthouse, *On Virtue Ethics* 12; Sherman, *The Fabric of Character* 4–12, 87–88, 123; Broadie S., "Aristotle and Contemporary Ethics", in Kraut R. (ed.), *The Blackwell Guide to Aristotle's* Nicomachean Ethics (Oxford: 2006) 342–361, esp. 348, 353–354; Herdt J.A., *Putting On Virtue: The Legacy of the Splendid Vices* (Chicago, IL – London: 2008) 32–33; Gottlieb P., *The Virtue of Aristotle's Ethics* (Cambridge: 2009) 92–106, 151–156; Price A.W., *Virtue and Reason in Plato and Aristotle* (Oxford: 2011) 2–10; and Cooper, *Pursuits of Wisdom* 105–106.

situated decision-making.[38] To become discerning means to be able to scrutinise oneself: 'know thyself',[39] Erasmus repeatedly insists. Like Montaigne, he takes recourse to allegory and personification in order to envisage the mental procedures involved in ethical deliberation. The metaphor of struggle or battle so characteristic of the *Enchiridion* – which literally means "little dagger" – especially fits the moral discernment or scrutiny of one's inner self:

> But so it is that one Christian man hath not war with another but with himself, and verily a great host of adversaries spring out of our own flesh, out of the very bowels and inward part of us. [...] And there is so little difference between our enemy and our friend, and so hard to know the one from the other, that there is great jeopardy lest we somewhat recklessly or negligently defend our enemy instead of our friend, or hurt our friend instead of our enemy.[40]

Erasmus here is talking about the passions, which wage battle inside man and between which he has to discern who is enemy and friend, depending on the circumstances. He advises his readers to

> behold and consider diligently all the motions, movings or stirring of thy mind and have them surely known. Furthermore thou must understand no motions to be so violent but they may be either refrained of [that is, by] reason, or else turned to virtue.[41]

He implores them to 'do nothing after affections, but in all things after the judgment of reason'.[42] This is not to say that emotions have no positive role to play in human decision-making. As Erasmus himself indicates in the penultimate quotation: They should be refrained from with the assistance of reason or, alternatively, be employed to virtuous effect. Again, this basically is an

---

38 Coodin, "What's Virtue Ethics Got to Do With It?" 191.

39 Chapter 3; Erasmus Desiderius, *The Manual of a Christian Knight* (London: 1905) [after the edition London, Wynkyn de Worde for Johan Byddell: 1533] 79, passim. See also Kühlman W., "Wort, Geist und Macht – Unvorgreifliche Bemerkungen zu Formationen frühneuzeitlicher Intellektualität", in Held J. (ed.), *Intellektuelle in der Frühen Neuzeit* (München: 2002) 18–29, esp. 22–23; Ramakers B., "Embodied Wits: The Representation of Deliberative Thought in Rhetoricians' Drama", *Renaissance Studies* 32.1 (2018) 85–105, esp. 90–91.

40 Chapter 4; Erasmus, *The Manual of a Christian Knight* 80–81.

41 Chapter 5; Erasmus, *The Manual of a Christian Knight* 89–90.

42 Erasmus, *The Manual of a Christian Knight* 88.

ALL MOTION DISCOVERS US: WILLEM VAN NIEULANDT'S *NERO* (1618)   63

Aristotelian position, that is, a call for metriopathy, an approach towards the passions that will be discussed in more detail below.

Mimetic Virtue

How to deal with the passions and putting them to work in order to become virtuous or act virtuously was a matter of habituation through practice in concrete circumstances. As said in the beginning, this amounts to situation ethics or moral contextualism and can be related back to Aristotelian virtue ethics. In the *Nicomachean Ethics*, the Stagirite says:

> [M]oral or ethical virtue is the product of habit (*ethos*), and has indeed derived its name, with a slight variation of form, from that word. [...] [N]ature gives us the capacity to receive them [that is, the virtues], and this capacity is brought to maturity by habit.[43]

The acquisition of virtue is a matter of practice, like the learning of an art or craft:

> The virtues [...] we acquire by first having actually practised them, just as we do the arts. We learn an art or craft by doing the things that we shall have to do when we have learnt it [...]. Similarly we become just by doing just acts, temperate by doing temperate acts, brave by doing brave acts.[44]

It is not hard to imagine how such habituation to virtue, besides through individual practice, could be achieved by carefully observing the behaviour of others, morally discerning their actions as well as the emotions that motivated them.

Tragedy offered an experimental setting, so to speak, for what was earlier called exemplary mirroring, a process whereby the audience was supposed to go through – imitate – both the rational and emotional to-and-fro of the characters. Drama generally does not simply narrate or offer an argument, but dramatises and embodies human speech and action. 'The fabric of tragedy, or indeed

---

43   2.i, 1003a10–15, 22–26; Aristotle, *Nicomachean Ethics*, trans. Rackham H. (Cambridge, MA: 1934) 70–71 (italics added); Knapp J.A., "A Shakespearean Phenomenology of Moral Conviction", in Bristol D. – Coodin S. – Fahmi M. – Finin K.R. (eds.), *Shakespeare and Moral Agency* (London: 2010) 29–41, esp. 31.

44   2.i, 1003a30–1103b5; Aristotle, *Nicomachean Ethics* 72–73.

of all poetry, is the representation of human purpose striving for realisation, and therefore falls within the purview of "practical" or ethical philosophy'.[45] In Aristotelian tragedy the goals of the action are related to the supreme moral aim of *eudaimonia*, the state of human flourishing or happiness.[46] Action – or praxis, agency – is what counts, and it is the characters who perform these actions and express the emotions that motivate them:[47] 'As is well known, the relation between people's characters and their actions, in this order, was central to Aristotle's project in the *Ethics*'.[48] It is important to realise in this respect that the Greek word *ethos* roughly translates to "moral character", and that the use of the English word "characters" for stage personae stems from the belief that dramatic personages impersonated particular moral dispositions.[49]

The need for vivid representation of such characters follows from Aristotle's emphasis on enactment as the primary form of *mimesis*. In the *Poetics* he writes that 'the poet, like the painter or any other image-maker, is a mimetic artist'.[50] He distinguishes between two types of *mimesis*, that of image-making and that of impersonation, and frequently refers to the similarity between painting and poetry.[51] However, he does not place them on the same footing as far as their mimetic function is concerned. Although he compares the poet to a painter, he juxtaposes the 'enactive' – or dramatic – mode of mimesis over the 'imagistic' – or painterly – one, emphasizing the immediacy of the

---

45   Halliwell S., *Aristotle's Poetics* (Chapel Hill, NC: 1986) 140.

46   MacIntyre, *After Virtue* 174–175; Hursthouse, *On Virtue Ethics* 9–10; Bostock D., *Aristotle's Ethics* (Oxford: 2000) 11–13. On Aristotle's ideas on happiness, see Cooper, *Reason and Emotion* 212–236; Celano A., *Aristotle's* Ethics *and Medieval Philosophy: Moral Goodness and Practical Wisdom* (Cambridge: 2016) 14–22; and Hellerstedt, "Virtue Ethics" 12–13.

47   Nussbaum M.C., "Tragedy and Self-sufficiency: Plato and Aristotle on Fear and Pity", in Rorty (ed.), *Essays on Aristotle's Poetics* 264–265, 270–273; Bristol M., "Introduction: Is Shakespeare a Moral Philosopher", in Bristol M.D. – Coodin S. – Fahmi M. – Finin K.R. (eds.), *Shakespeare and Moral Agency* (London: 2010) 1–12, esp. 4; Schiaparelli A. – Crivelli P., "Aristotle on Poetry", in Shields C. (ed.), *The Oxford Handbook of Aristotle* (Oxford: 2012) 612–626, esp. 621. See also Halliwell, *Aristotle's Poetics* 138–167, esp. 158–163. On neuro-scientific evidence for the importance of emotions for human flourishing, see Kane R., *Ethics and the Quest for Wisdom* (Cambridge: 2010) 156–157.

48   Schiaparelli – Crivelli, "Aristotle on Poetry" 621.

49   Booth, "Why Ethical Criticism Can Never Be Simple" 18.

50   1460b5–10; Aristotle, *Poetics*, trans. Halliwell S. (Harvard, MA: 1995) 124–125. See also Woodruff P., "Aristotle on Mimēsis", in Rorty (ed.), *Essays on Aristotle's Poetics* 73–95, esp. 76–77; Warncke C.-P., *Sprechende Bilder – sichtbare Worte. Das Bildverständnis in der frühen Neuzeit* (Wiesbaden: 1987) 23–24.

51   Halliwell, *Aristotle's Poetics* 109–137, esp. 112–115.

ALL MOTION DISCOVERS US: WILLEM VAN NIEULANDT'S *NERO* (1618)

former, eventually denying the full status of mimesis to the latter where the representation of character and morals is concerned.[52]

The concept of mimetic virtue perfectly fits Aristotle's definition of *mimesis* in the *Poetics*, whereby he again draws a parallel with art:

> It can be seen that poetry was broadly engendered by a pair of causes, both natural. For it is an instinct of human beings, from childhood, to engage in mimesis [...]; and equally natural that everyone enjoys mimetic objects. [...] This is why people enjoy looking at images, because through contemplating them it comes about that they understand and infer what each element means, for instance that "this person is so-and-so".[53]

Erasmus explicitly refers to moral plays and tragedies as concrete embodiments of mimetic virtue.[54] In the *Enchiridion*, he presents Christ as the ultimate exemplum, the paradigmatic paradigm, so to speak, but he extends this moral exemplarity to the Bible as a whole and to classical history and mythology. In fact, he refers to classical theatre's function to morally instruct its audience:

> And also in comedies, tragedies, and other common plays of the gentiles a great clapping of hands and a shout was made for joy of the lay people, when vices were craftily and properly rebuked and checked.[55]

Emotions were displayed by characters in early modern theatre (or by the actors who impersonated them) with the express intention of making spectators experience these same emotions and express them in a like manner, for example, through weeping. Affect was thought to be transmittable or

---

52 Halliwell, *Aristotle's Poetics* 125. See also Zanker G., "Aristotle's *Poetics* and the Painters", *The American Journal of Philology* 121.2 (2000) 225–235, esp. 233; Roodenburg, *The Eloquence of the Body* 150.

53 1448b4–19; Aristotle, *Poetics* 36–39. On this passage, see Haskins E.V., "*Mimesis* Between Poetics and Rhetoric: Performance Culture and Civic Education in Plato, Isocrates, and Aristotle", *Rhetoric Society Quarterly* 30.3 (2000) 7–33, esp. 26–33; Fossheim H.J., "Habituation as *Mimesis*", in Chappel T. (ed.), *Values and Virtues: Aristotelianism in Contemporary Ethics* (Oxford: 2006) 105–112, esp. 109–112; and Herdt, *Putting On Virtue* 25–29. See also Halliwell S., "Pleasure, Understanding, and Emotion in Aristotle's *Poetics*", in Rorty (ed.), *Essays on Aristotle's Poetics* 241–260, esp. 247–248.

54 On the concept of mimetic virtue, especially from a Christian perspective, see Herdt, *Putting On Virtue* 6–9.

55 Chapter 14; Erasmus, *The Manual of a Christian Knight* 190.

contagious, like a disease.[56] The actors imitated the characters' passions, after which the audience imitated the actors.[57] And this was done for moral purposes: '[T]he movement of the emotions is a crucial step in clarifying the difference between virtue and vice: it is through emotional experience that the audience is able to draw lessons from a theatre performance'.[58] Theatre scholars nowadays provide experimental evidence from cognitive science to underscore this effect of theatrical performances, which they attribute to modes of perception specific to theatre as a mimetic genre, that is, seeing and hearing characters doing and expressing things, both verbally and physically, of which narrative (or diegetic) genres are not, or at least are less, capable.[59] This idea is similar to enactive perception, a concept coined by visual scholars, which is similarly based on insights from cognitive science.[60]

Movere

The early modern idea of tragedy as an instrument of moral discernment offering its spectators a chance to exercise mimetic virtue cannot be fully explained

---

56   Steggle M., *Laughing and Weeping in Early Modern Theatres* (Aldershot – Burlington, VT: 2007) 5; Steenbergh K., "Compassion and the Creation of an Affective Community in the Theatre: Vondel's *Mary Stuart, or Martyred Majesty* (1646)", *Low Countries Historical Review* 129.2 (2014) 90–112, esp. 99–100. See also Stolberg M., "'Zorn, Wein und Weiber verderben unsere Leiber': Affekt und Krankheit in der Frühen Neuzeit", in Steiger J.A. (ed.), *Passion, Affekt und Leidenschaft in der frühen Neuzeit* (Wiesbaden: 2005) 1051–1077, esp. 1053–1063.

57   Steenbergh, "Emotion, Performance and Gender" 99. See also Roach, *The Player's Passion* 27; Schiesaro A., *The Passions in Play*: Thyestes *and the Dynamics of Senecan Drama* (Cambridge: 2003) 229; Hobgood A.P., *Passionate Playgoing in Early Modern England* (Cambridge – New York, NY: 1977) 2–5; and Booth, "Why Ethical Criticism Can Never Be Simple" 26.

58   Steenbergh, "Emotion, Performance and Gender" 100.

59   Mancing H., "See the Play, Read the Book", in McConachie B. – Hart F.E. (eds.), *Performance and Cognition: Theatre Studies and the Cognitive Turn* (London – New York, NY: 2006) 189–206, esp. 193–195; Hart F.E., "Performance, Phenomenology, and the Cognitive Turn", in McConachie B. – Hart F.E. (eds.), *Performance and Cognition: Theatre Studies and the Cognitive Turn* (London – New York, NY: 2006) 29–51. See also Lamb, *Corporeal Returns* 38; Smith B.R., "Afterword: Senses of an Ending", in Craik – Pollard (eds.), *Shakespearean Sensation* 208–217, esp. 208–210.

60   Fingerhut J., "Das Bild, dein Freund. Der fühlende und der sehende Körper in der enaktiven Bildwahrnehmung", in Feist U. – Rath M. (eds.), *Et in imagine ego: Facetten von Bildakt und Verkörperung* (Berlin: 2012) 177–198, esp. 179–182. See also Freedberg D. – Gallese V., "Motion, Emotion and Empathy in Esthetic Experience", *Trends in Cognitive Sciences* 11.5 (2007) 197–203; Brinck, "Empathy, Engagement, Entrainment" 203–205.

without reference to rhetoric, both classical and humanist. Ancient but even more so early modern tragedy was written and performed under the aegis of the art of persuasion. Tragedy, like most literary genres, became rhetoricised.[61] As did many other authors of vernacular literature elsewhere in Europe, the Netherlandish rhetoricians regarded poetry, dramatic poetry in particular, as the contemporary equivalent of classical rhetoric, which they tried to emulate in terms of form, content, and function. Like the ancient orators, poets and playwrights were supposed to employ their rhetorical skills to better themselves as well as their fellow citizens. Orators were supposed to argue in such a manner that listeners – but one may expand this to viewers and spectators – were not only instructed in the virtues but also incited to performing virtuous acts. Describing in words, or visualizing in images, examples of both virtuous and vicious conduct counted as a demonstration of rhetorical *copia et varietas*.[62] Aristotle, in the *Art of Rhetoric*, says:

> The orator persuades by moral character when his speech is delivered in such a manner as to render him worthy of confidence; [...]. [M]oral character, so to say, constitutes the most effective means of proof. The orator persuades by means of his hearers, when they are roused to emotion by his speech; for the judgements we deliver are not the same when we are influenced by joy or sorrow, love or hate; [...].[63]

Quintilian, in the *Institutio Oratoria* (Institutes of Oratory), asserts:

> So, since the orator is a good man, and the concept of a good man is unintelligible apart from virtue, and since virtue, though it derives some impulses from nature, has none the less to be perfected by teaching, the orator must above all else develop his moral character by study, and undergo a thorough training in the honourable and the just, because without this no one can be either a good man or a skilled speaker.[64]

---

61   Plett, *Rhetoric and Renaissance Culture* 162–173.

62   Smits-Veldt M.B., *Samuel Coster, ethicus-didacticus: Een onderzoek naar dramatische opzet en morele instructie van Ithys, Polyxena en Iphegenia* (Groningen: 1986) 37–38, 40.

63   1356a4–5; Aristotle, *Art of Rhetoric*, trans. Freese J.H. – rev. Striker G. (Cambridge, MA – London: 2020) 16–17. On Aristotle's ideas on persuasion, see Allard-Nelson S.K., "Virtue in Aristotle's Rhetoric: A Metaphysical and Ethical Capacity", *Philosophy and Rhetoric* 34.3 (2001) 245–259, esp. 247–248.

64   12.2.1–2; Quintilian, *The Orator's Education*, vol. 5 (Books 11–12), ed. & trans. Russell D.A. (Cambridge, MA – London: 2001) 220–221.

The poet or playwright, like the orator, had to be a competent judge of virtue and character and had to have a thorough knowledge of the passions. What is more, as the opening lines of both previous quotations show, the orator had to be a good or virtuous person *himself*, lest he lose his moral persuasiveness.[65] Since they thought of themselves as orators, early modern poets and playwrights aimed, or were supposed to aim, for such personal virtue too. Like the orator they would also often deal with moral issues and present vivid examples of virtue and vice. Again, Quintilian:

> We are often obliged to speak of justice, courage, temperance, and the like – indeed, scarcely a Cause can be found in which some question relating to these is not involved – and all these topics have to be developed by Invention and Elocution: how then can there be any doubt that wherever intellectual power and fullness of diction are required, the orator has the leading role?[66]

Quintilian and other theorists of rhetoric customarily referred to the theatre as a venue for the practice of rhetoric and to the accomplished actor as a role model to the orator,[67] especially as regards the third and fifth of the five canons of rhetoric (*canones rhetoricae*), that of expression (*elocutio*) and delivery (*pronunciatio* or *actio*). Classical rhetoric advocated the use of figures of speech, such as the impersonation of an absent person (*sermonicatio*) or a thing or abstraction (*personificatio*). These devices fit another technique named *enargeia* (in Greek) or *evidentia/illustratio* (in Latin), that is, the enlivening of one's argument with a gripping account of events or a telling example, thus stimulating the audience's imagination.[68]

Obviously, the concept of *enargeia* perfectly suited that of *mimesis*, the basic principle of tragedy.[69] It was these telling examples, stories taken from

---

65   Hellerstedt, "Virtue Ethics" 14.

66   I.Pr.12–13; Quintilian, *The Orator's Education*, vol. 1 (Books 1–2), ed. & trans. Russell D.A. (Cambridge, MA – London: 2001) 56–57.

67   Plett, *Rhetoric and Renaissance Culture* 255–263.

68   Plett, *Rhetoric and Renaissance Culture* 278–282; Plett H.F., *Enargeia in Classical Antiquity and the Early Moderne Age: The Aesthetics of Evidence* (Leiden – Boston, MA: 2012) 23–28, 65–68, 168, 170–171, 177–178. See also Eck C. van, *Art, Agency and Living Presence: From the Animated Image to the Excessive Object* (Berlin – Leiden: 2015) 31–43.

69   Taylor P.A., "Sympathy and Insight in Aristotle's *Poetics*", *The Journal of Aesthetics and Art Criticism* 66.3 (2008) 265–280, esp. 273; Staley G.A., *Seneca and the Idea of Tragedy* (Oxford – New York, NY: 2009) 15–16, 56–60.

ALL MOTION DISCOVERS US: WILLEM VAN NIEULANDT'S *NERO* (1618)

history and mythology, that were to be employed for moral reasoning.[70] For the aforementioned elocutionary means to have a persuasive effect, they had to be delivered in a dramatic manner employing the full array of physical resources available to both the orator and the actor, that is, posture, gesture, and voice. These bodily means especially served the expression of emotions, which were deemed an effective – if not the most effective – means of persuasion.[71] In order for the orator or actor to be able to stimulate the audience's imagination, he had to spark his own imagination and elicit in himself the emotions related to recounted or dramatised events.[72] As a matter of fact, their expression was enshrined in the second of the three tasks of the orator, after teaching (*docere*/*probare*) and before delighting (*conciliare*/*delectare*), that is, moving (*movere*/*flectere*). Both in and outside the theatre, but especially in the theatre, the audience's imagination was to be stimulated to the extent that it would trigger a physical-emotional response.

Thus, it is not hard to fathom that theorists and practitioners of drama, as part of the early modern rhetoricisation of literature, conceived of tragedy as a genre of rhetoric, attributing to it purposes, means, and effects which were derived from the art of persuasion.[73] As a result, the actor came to be thought of as an orator.[74] Role-playing, both in the theatre and in real life, involved rhetoric and histrionics, and tragedy became a privileged medium for its practice.[75] Although the events in a tragedy were usually remote in time and place, and sometimes even improbable, the playwright's task was to present actions so vividly and credibly that the experiences and emotions of the characters, despite their remoteness and unfamiliarity, could be grasped imaginatively by the audience. In terms of rhetoric this meant that playwrights employed the grand style (*stilus magniloquens*), the highest among the three levels of stylistic espression (*genera elocutionis*), which befitted the rhetorical aim of *movere*.[76]

---

70 Skidmore C., *Practical Ethics for Roman Gentlemen: The Work of Valerius Maximus* (Exeter: 1996) 23. On the argumentative value of narrative, see Tindale C., "Narratives and the Concept of Argument", in Olmos P. (ed.), *Narration as Argument* (Cham: 2017) 11–30.

71 Roach, *The Player's Passion* 30–37.

72 Roach, *The Player's Passion* 24–29.

73 Lyne, *Shakespeare, Rhetoric and Cognition* 2–3.

74 Burns, *Character* 6–16, esp. 10; Plett, *Rhetoric and Renaissance Culture* 264–272; Lieblein L., "Embodied Intersubjectivity and the Creation of Early Modern Character", in Yachnin P. – Slights J. (eds.), *Shakespeare and Character: Theory, History, Performance and Theatrical Persons* (London: 2009) 117–135, esp. 125.

75 Lanham R.A., *The Motives of Eloquence: Literary Rhetoric in the Renaissance* (New Haven, CT – London: 1976) 4–5. See also Herdt, *Putting On Virtue* 5.

76 On the rhetoric of *movere* in Dutch tragedy, see Konst J.W.H., *Woedende wraakghierigheidt en vruchtelooze weeklachten: De hartstochten in de Nederlandse tragedie van de zeventiende eeuw* (Assen: 1993) 82–95.

Where drama is concerned, the application of rhetoric implied that the author should carefully choose, plan, and phrase a play's subject matter, its characters, and those characters' actions and speeches, and consider how to let them behave, speak, and feel in such a way that the audience might be emotionally affected and thus ethically formed or habituated. Characters in tragedy not only displayed a wide plethora of emotions but, like literary characters generally, were 'notorious for their moral reasoning prior to action'.[77] In other words, the emotions of the audience should be roused by the emotions and considerations expressed by the characters on stage.

Catharsis

There is ample evidence, especially from English theatre, of the emotive effect of performances of early tragedy in accordance with the rhetorical demand for *movere* as well as Aristotle's ideas on the passions and *catharsis*. These lay at the basis of early modern tragedians' intention to move the spectators as well as the latter's expectation to be moved as part of a process of moral reasoning.[78] Thus, tragedy became a means of what James Knapp calls *Image Ethics*,[79] or, analogous to what Katharine Craik and Tanya Pollard call 'passionate reading', a means of passionate viewing.[80] *Catharsis* – which literally means the purification or cleansing of emotions – was meant to elicit a transformation inside them.[81]

Although Aristotle allows for tragedy to have moral applications and effects, he does not attribute a moral purpose to the genre. Early modern theoreticians, however, did.[82] Chief among them was Julius Caesar Scaliger. In his *Poetices libri septem* he aligns key elements of Aristotle's tragedy definition with his.[83]

---

77   Knapp, "A Shakespearean Phenomenology" 33.
78   Craik – Pollard, "Introduction" 8–16.
79   Knapp, *Image Ethics* 2–4.
80   Craik – Pollard, "Introduction" 19.
81   Hobgood A.P., "Feeling fear in *Macbeth*", in Craik – Pollard (eds.), *Shakespearean Sensations* 29–46, esp. 38–42.
82   Pollard T., "Conceiving Tragedy", in Craik – Pollard (eds.), *Shakespearean Sensations* 85–100, esp. 87–90; Rist T., "Catharsis as 'Purgation' in Shakespearean Drama", in Clark – Pollard (eds.), *Shakespearean Sensations* 138–153, esp. 138–141; Rist T., "Miraculous Organ: Shakespeare and 'Catharsis'", *Skenè* 2.1 (2016) 133–150, esp. 134–138, 140–141; Kappl B., "Profit, Pleasure, and Purgation: Catharsis in Aristotle, Paolo Beni and Italian Late Renaissance Poetics", *Skenè* 2.1 (2016) 105–132, esp. 117–122. See also Eagleton, *Sweet Violence* 153–156.
83   Martinec T., "'Fürbild aller Tugenden': Rhetorik und Moral in der barocken Trauerspiel-poetik", *Daphnis* 35 (2006) 133–161, esp. 134–136, 139, 140–144, 150–152; Smits-Veldt, *Samuel Coster* 29–47.

ALL MOTION DISCOVERS US: WILLEM VAN NIEULANDT'S *NERO* (1618)

The most far-reaching of these modifications, instigating and impacting all the others, is that of assigning a moral purpose to the genre, which was causally linked to (the process of) *catharsis*.[84] Its context of use, in the *Poetics* as well as in the *Nicomachean Ethics*, the *Art of Rhetoric*, and the *Politics*, left ample space to develop the concept of *catharsis* in a moral-didactic direction.[85] Central to its meaning is Aristotle's definition of tragedy in the *Poetics*:

> Tragedy, then, is mimesis of an action which is elevated, complete, and of magnitude; in language embellished by distinct forms in its sections; employing the mode of enactment, not narrative; and through pity [*eleos*] and fear [*phobos*] accomplishing the *catharsis* of such emotion.[86]

Pity and fear were understood to cover a wide range of related emotional responses. According to the *Art of Rhetoric*

> [t]he emotions are all those affections that change men so as to influence their judgments, and are accompanied by pleasure and pain; such are anger, pity, fear, and all similar emotions and their contraries.[87]

---

84 Martinec, "'Fürbild aller Tugenden'" 136–138, 144–145; Halliwell, *Aristotle's Poetics* 168–201, esp. 173–175, 181–183, 195–197; Ford A., "*Katharsis*: The Ancient Problem", in Parker A. – Sedgwick E.K. (eds.), *Performativity and Performance* (New York, NY: 1995) 109–132, esp. 113–114; Ford A., "Catharsis: The Power of Music in Aristotle's *Politics*", in Murray P. – Wilson P. (eds.), *Music and the Muses: The Culture of Mousikê in the Classical Athenian City* (Oxford: 2004) 309–336, esp. 326; Orgel S., "The Play of Conscience", in Parker A. – Sedgwick E.K. (eds.), *Performativity and Performance* (New York, NY: 1995) 133–151, esp. 134–137.

85 Nussbaum, "Tragedy and Self-sufficiency" 273–276, 280–283; Curran A., "Brecht's Criticism of Aristotle's Aesthetics of Tragedy", *The Journal of Aesthetics and Art Criticism* 59.2 (2001) 167–184, esp. 168–170. See also Taylor, "Sympathy and Insight" 272–273; Beecher, *Adapted Brains and Imaginary Worlds* 32; and Steenbergh K. – Obbett K., "Introduction", in Steenbergh K. – Obbett K. (eds.), *Compassion in Early Modern Literature and Culture* (Cambridge: 2021) 1–21, esp. 3–11.

86 1449b 24–28; Aristotle, *Poetics* 46–47 (italics added). Several translations have the plural *emotions*. See also Kosman, "Acting" 57–58.

87 2.1 1378a9; Aristotle, *Art of Rhetoric* 168–169. On Aristotle's thinking about the passions, see James S., *Passion and Action: The Emotions in Seventeenth-Century Philosophy* (New York, NY: 1997) 57–64; Cates D.F., "Conceiving Emotions: Martha Nussbaum's *Upheavals of Thought*", *The Journal of Religious Ethics* 31.2 (2003) 325–341, esp. 332–333. See also Cummings B. – Sierhuis F., "Introduction", in Cummings B. – Sierhuis F. (eds.), *Passions and Subjectivity in Early Modern Culture* (London – New York, NY: 2016 [2013]) 1–9, esp. 3–4.

The following passage from the *Politics* clearly invites one to align tragedy with morality:

> And moreover everybody when listening to imitations is thrown into a corresponding state of feeling, even apart from the rhythms and tunes themselves. And since it is the case that music is one of the things that give pleasure, and that virtue has to do with feeling delight and love and hatred rightly, there is obviously nothing that it is more needful to learn and become habituated to than to judge correctly and to delight in virtuous characters and noble actions; [...].[88]

Spectators were supposed to feel pity with the fate of the characters and fear that they might suffer the same.[89]

The combined effect of these two emotions was that they might have less dread of fate and better endure it once it befell them.[90] This was the (Neo-)Stoic interpretation of the role of *catharsis*, that is, purgation in the sense of becoming apathetic or indifferent towards the passions. Ancient Greek tragedy, however, seems to have allowed for – if not to have intentionally triggered – emotional responses from its spectators, in much the same way as early modern tragedy did. Malcolm Heath, in his study of the genre, attributes great importance to the audience's emotional response – pity and fear, but also other emotions, such as grief, anger, and joy – 'drawn out by the condition and emotions of the characters',[91] a position he mainly arrives at by referencing the *Art of Rhetoric*. He adamantly affirms:

---

88   1340a14–20; Aristotle, *Politics*, trans. Rackham H. (Cambridge, MA – London: 1972) 656–657. See also Lear J., "Katharsis", in Rorty (ed.), *Essays on Aristotle's Poetics* 315–340, esp. 316.

89   'Let fear be defined as a painful or troubled feeling caused by the impression of an imminent evil that causes destruction or pain'; 2.5 1382a21; Aristotle, *Art of Rhetoric* 200–201; 'Let pity then be a kind of pain excited by the sight of evil, deadly or painful, which befalls one who does not deserve it; an evil which one might expect to come upon himself or one of his friends, and when it seems near'; 2.8 1385b2; ibidem 224–225. See also Halliwell, *Aristotle's Poetics* 163, 178; Kosman, "Acting" 68; Nehamas A., "Pity and Fear in the *Rhetoric* and the *Poetics*", in Rorty (ed.), *Essays on Aristotle's Poetics* 291–314, esp. 302–303; Lear, "Katharsis" 317–318, 328; Nussbaum M.C., *Upheavals of Thought: The Intelligence of Emotions* (Cambridge: 2001) 306–307, 314–316, 350–353; and Knuuttila S., *Emotions in Ancient and Medieval Philosophy* (Oxford: 2004) 24–47.

90   Martinec, "'Fürbild aller Tugenden'" 156–158.

91   Heath M., *The Poetics of Greek Tragedy* (Stanford, CA: 1987) 13–17. See also ibidem 87–88.

The point is not that the audience is made to undergo in imagination the experiences and emotions of the tragic characters, but that it is made to *respond* to those experiences and emotions: a distinction which does not, however, imply that the audience's response is in any sense muted or restrained; on the contrary, it is precisely on the readiness and intensity of the tragic audience's emotional response that I wish to insist.[92]

Although ancient Greek tragedy seems not to have provoked its spectators 'to undergo in imagination the experiences and emotions of the tragic characters', let alone – apparently – to physically reproduce them, it may justifiably be asked how the audience's emotional response to the characters' experiences and emotions could have been triggered other than by mimetically reliving them, whether physically, mentally, or both.[93]

Whatever the case may be, it is highly unlikely that tragedy, either ancient or early modern, ever intended to, or actually did, provoke only apathetic responses. It should also come as no surprise that Erasmus was critical of the Stoics' stance on the passions. In the *Enchiridion* he sides with the Peripatetics, Aristotle's followers. They

teach the affections not to be destroyed utterly, but to be refrained, and that the use of them is not utterly to be refused, for because they think them to be given of nature, as a prick or a spur to stir a man to virtue: as wrath maketh a man bold and hardy, and is a matter of fortitude. Envy is a great cause of policy, and in likewise of the other.[94]

Erasmus here advocates metriopathy. We come across the same positive attitude towards the passions in Dirk Volckertszoon Coornhert's (1522–1590) *Zedekunst, dat is wellevenskunste* (Ethics or the Art of Living Well) from 1586. They play a key role in his programme of human perfectibility with its characteristic 'emphasis on [...] self-knowledge and practical virtue':[95]

---

92   Heath, *The Poetics of Greek Tragedy* 15.

93   On this process and the role of memory in it, see Van Eck, *Art, Agency and Living Presence* 67–68, 71–72.

94   Chapter 5; Erasmus, *The Manual of a Christian Knight* 89. On Aristotle's view on the passions, see Sherman, *The Fabric of Character* 44–50; Hursthouse, *On Virtue Ethics* 108–111. On the emotions and their role in moral decision making, see generally Nussbaum, *Upheavals of Thought*, passim. On Aristotle's ideas on the passions, see Cooper, *Reason and Emotion* 406–423.

95   Mooij H. – Mooij-Valk S., "Coornhert on Virtue and Nobility", in MacDonald A.A. – Martels Z.R.W.M. von – Veenstra J. (eds.), *Christian Humanism: Essays in Honour of Arjo Vanderjagt* (Leiden – Boston, MA: 2009) 155–169, esp. 158.

It is of great importance to have a good understanding of these inferior powers of the soul [that is, the passions]. For they are instruments or tools, which if used correctly serve to bring their users virtue, joy, and salvation, but if they are abused they bring their abusers sin, sorrow, and perdition.[96]

Coornhert defines them as resulting from judgment:

The aforementioned four passions [that is, hope, joy, fear, and sorrow] in man stem from judgment – that is a judgment that either rightly judges the good to be good and the evil to be evil, or falsely judges the good to be evil and the evil to be good – it follows necessarily that each of the aforementioned four passions must be similar to the judgment from which they result, to wit sincere and good, or false and evil. Therefore, none of these is in itself either good or evil. They are intermediate.[97]

The faculty passing this judgment is reason – practical reason, to be sure.[98] After reason has passed its judgment, man's will sets to work:

After this judgment has been made, it brings forth volition [that is, will] being a determined intention to acquire what one has judged to be good or to flee from that which has been judged to be evil.[99]

That Coornhert calls the passions 'intermediate' means that they are not necessarily good or bad.[100] Their goodness or badness depends on reason's judgment, which in turn relies on the matters or things to which these emotions pertain. They are called intermediate too. These intermediate things (*res mediae*) either apply to the body (health, beauty) or manifest themselves outside man (wealth, power, reputation). They are ethically positioned between

---

96   Book I, Chapter 3; Coornhert Dirk Volckertszoon, *Ethics or the Art of Living Well*, trans., ed., and intro. Voogt G. (Hilversum 2015) 71.

97   Book I, Chapter 3; Coornhert, *Ethics or the Art of Living Well* 73; Ramakers, "Embodied Wits" 90.

98   See Book II, Chapter 2–4 on reason, deliberation, and judgment; Coornhert, *Ethics or the Art of Living Well* 157–171. On Coornhert and reason, see Buys, *Sparks of Reason* 31–54, 101–104. On the Aristotelian position in this respect, see Nehamas, "Pity and Fear" 296–300.

99   Book I, Chapter 3; Coornhert, *Ethics or the Art of Living Well* 72.

100   Konst, *Woedende wraakghierigheidt* 13–16, 36–40.

ALL MOTION DISCOVERS US: WILLEM VAN NIEULANDT'S *NERO* (1618)

good and evil things (*res bonae* and *res malea*), that is, things towards which one can always feel acceptable emotions.

Coornhert presents us with a detailed guideline for exercising Aristotelian virtue ethics, in which the passions are seen as essential symptoms of, and stimuli to, either virtuous or vicious behaviour. Whatever purgation meant and what passions were involved,[101] learning through tragedy can be described 'as a cathartic recognition of cause and effect of action mimetically reproduced by the plot'.[102] Among these causes and effects the passions reigned supreme. As Erasmus indicated prior to Coornhert, they should be refrained from with the assistance of reason, or alternatively be employed to virtuous effect.

Van Nieulandt's *Nero*

According to Scaliger, spectators of tragedy were supposed to suppress their emotions and take the Stoic attitude of apathy, emotions being considered dangerous perturbations, contrary to right reason.[103] Freya Sierhuis has contrasted this approach with the Aristotelian-Thomistic perspective on the passions – consonant with Augustine's (354–430) and Thomas Aquinas's (1225–1274) – 'which viewed the passions as natural impulses equipping us to pursue what is good, and shun what does us harm',[104] very much in line

---

101   Orgel, "The Play of Conscience" 137–140. See also ibidem 141–142.

102   Haskins, "*Mimesis* Between Poetics and Rhetoric" 27.

103   Inwood B. – Donini P., "Stoic Ethics", in Algra K. – Barnes J. – Mansfeld J. – Schofield M. (eds.), *The Cambridge History of Hellenistic Philosophy* (Cambridge: 1999) 675–738, esp. 699. See also Levi, *French Moralists* 29–46, esp. 30–31; Knuuttila, *Emotions in Ancient and Medieval Philosophy* 55–56; Staley, *Seneca and the Idea of Tragedy* 78–81; Cooper, *Pursuits of Wisdom* 165, 194; Konstan D., "Senecan Emotions", in Bartsch S. – Schiesaro A. (eds.), *The Cambridge Companion to Seneca* (Cambridge: 2015) 174–184, esp. 177, 197; and Buys, *Sparks of Reason* 172–181, esp. 173–174. Specifically with respect to Dutch tragedy, see Konst, *Woedende wraakghierigheidt* 127–127, 168–169.

104   Sierhuis F., "The Passions in the Literature of the Dutch Golden Age", *Tijdschrift voor Nederlandse Taal- en Letterkunde* 132.4 (2016) 333–365, esp. 334. On Augustine's ideas on the passions, see also Stock, "Ethical Values" 6; James, *Passion and Action* 8; Knuuttila, *Emotions in Ancient and Medieval Philosophy* 152–172; Cummings – Sierhuis, "Introduction" 3; and Levi, *French Moralists* 15, 17–18. On Thomas's view of the passions and their relation to Aristotle's, see James, *Passion and Action* 57–64; Knuuttila, *Emotions in Ancient and Medieval Philosophy* 139–255; Tilmouth C., *Passion's Triumph over Reason: A History of the Moral Imagination from Spenser to Rochester* (Oxford – New York, NY: 2007) 28; Herdt, *Putting On Virtue* 12; Levi, *French Moralists* 18–21; Cates D.F., *Aquinas on the Emotions: A Religious-Ethical Inquiry* (Washington, DC: 2009); Solomon J.R., "You've Got to Have Soul" 200–208; Pickavé M., "Emotion and Cognition in Later Medieval Philosophy: The Case of

with the ideas of Montaigne, Erasmus, and Coornhert, for that matter. Sierhuis speaks of 'sometimes incompatible paradigms [which] coexisted in uneasy equilibrium'.[105] She makes these observations in connection with the biblical tragedies by Joost van den Vondel (1587–1679) which date from the 1630s and after. However, they hold equally true for tragedies from the earlier decades of the seventeenth century, like Van Nieulandt's, that are said to conform to Senecan-Scaligerian principles. Sierhuis refers to Christian or sacred rhetoric, to preaching in particular, in which the grand style and *enargeia* were employed with the clear objective to move congregations towards emotions – pity, remorse, fear, blame, joy, affection, *et cetera* – that might cause a change of heart, directing their will to virtuous behaviour. Affects were seen as indispensable for moral development.[106] Sacred rhetoric even went beyond metriopathy to the extent that it fully and wholeheartedly displayed and propagated the passions.[107] Within the context of early modern Christianity, Aristotle's definition of *catharsis* became to mean 'a "cleansing" not *from*, but *of* pity, meaning: to a process of morally "refining" the emotion of pity'[108] – and other affects for that matter. Thus, by no means was (Neo-)Stoic apathy or suppression the most advocated or employed method of dealing with the passions.[109]

Adam Wodeham", in Pickavé – Shapiro L. (eds.), *Emotion and Cognitive Life in Medieval and Early Modern Philosophy* (Oxford: 2012) 94–115, esp. 95–99; and Rosenwein B.H., *Generations of Feeling: A History of Emotions, 600–1700* (Cambridge: 2016) 162–168.

105 Sierhuis, "The Passions" 334–335. See also Sierhuis F., "Therapeutic Tragedy: Compassion, Remorse, and Reconciliation in the Joseph Plays of Joost van den Vondel (1635–1640)", *European Review of History* 17.1 (2010) 31. On the important role of theology and devotion in the experience of emotions, see Meek R. – Sullivan E., "Introduction", in Meek R. – Sullivan E. (eds.), *The Renaissance of Emotion: Understanding Affect in Shakespeare and His Contemporaries* (Manchester: 2015) 1–22, esp. 7–8; James, *Passion and Action* 10–14. Even Stoic philosophers held that 'primal affect was a permanent feature of human life that sages, like the rest of us, would always have to cope with'; Becker L.C., "Stoic Emotion", in Strange S.K. – Zupko J.A. (eds.), *Stoicism: Traditions and Transformations* (Cambridge: 2004) 250–275, at 255. On emotions in Vondel's tragedies, see also Konst, *Woedende wraakghierigheidt*, passim; Konst J., "'Medoogen en schrick uit te wercken': Der emotionale Effekt von Vondels *Jephta* (1659)", in Steiger J.A. (ed.), *Passion, Affekt und Leidenschaft in der Frühen Neuzeit*, 2 vols. (Wiesbaden: 2005), vol. 2, 803–815.

106 See also Kehler T., *The Necessity of Affection: Shakespeare and the Politics of the Passions* (Ph.D. dissertation, McGill University: 2001) 36–50; Miles G., *Shakespeare and the Constant Romans* (Oxford – New York, NY: 1996) 64–66.

107 Sierhuis, "The Passions" 337, 339; Sierhuis, "Therapeutic Tragedy" 34–36. See also Levi, *French Moralists* 13; Craik – Pollard, "Introduction" 20–22.

108 Küpper, *The Cultural Net* 194.

109 Smith, "Afterword" 210–215. See also Hobgood, "Feeling fear in *Macbeth*" 45–46.

Willem van Nieulandt's *Nero*[110] is not an Aristotelian tragedy in the sense that the actions causally result from one another and centre on the activities of a 'flawed hero, neither purely virtuous nor wholly vicious, who commits an error (*hamartia*), suffers a reversal of fortune (*peripeteia*), and eventually gains insight into his fate (*anagnorisis/agnitio*)'.[111] Rather, this play contains a succession of unrelated scenes from the life of Nero as described by Tacitus and Suetonius, some of which lie far apart in time.[112] This fitted the Senecan-Scaligerian ideal of *copia et varietas*.[113] Nero is the main character for sure, but he is possessed by negative emotions which lead him to commit hideous deeds or force others to commit them in his name. He is being portrayed right from the start as a merciless tyrant,[114] a mirror of evil and vice. We also get to see much bloodshed. As a matter of fact, we witness the whole catalogue of horrors that Scaliger expected the tragedian to dramatise: the matricide of Nero's mother Agrippina and the violent end of his wife Octavia and of his stepbrother Britannicus (the latter in a dumb-show), but also Nero's suicide at the end, reproduced on the title page [Fig. 2.1], and, last but not least, the forced suicide of his teacher and counsellor Seneca. The ghost scenes form another typical element, of which we find two: one at the beginning, featuring Claudius, who had already been murdered before the opening of the play, and one almost at the end, prior to Nero's death scene, featuring the recently murdered Agrippina.

The question is whether *Nero* derived its moral-didactic effect exclusively from the representation, which was as graphic as possible, of the gruesome acts and violent negative passions of the characters who commissioned them, carried them out, or endured them. Certainly, these elements had an engaging

---

110 On *Nero*, see Keersmaekers, *De dichter Guilliam van Nieuwelandt* 82–85, 94–95, 102–105, 136, passim; Ramakers, "Sophonisba's Dress" 322–323, 324–325, 330.

111 Sierhuis, "The Passions" 346–347. See also Nussbaum, "Tragedy and Self-sufficiency" 276–278; Martinec, "Fürbild aller Tugenden'" 140, 142.

112 Keersmaekers, *De dichter Guilliam van Nieuwelandt* 102–105. On Senecan tragedy in the Low Countries, see Smits-Veldt, *Samuel Coster* 58–74; Bloemendal J., "Senecan Drama from the Northern and Southern Netherlands: Paganization and Christianization", *Dutch Review of Church History* 81.1 (2001) 38–45.

113 Smits-Veldt, *Samuel Coster* 37–38, 40. See also Van Gemert L., "The Politics of Visuality in Dutch Renaissance Tragedy", in Leuker M.-T. (ed.), *Die sichtbare Welt: Visualität in der niederländischen Literatur und Kunst des 17. Jahrhunderts* (Münster: 2012) 203–219, esp. 205–206.

114 On the representation of tyrants in early modern tragedy, see Ekstein N., "Staging the Tyrant on the Seventeenth-Century French Stage", *Papers on French Seventeenth Century Literature* 36 (1999) 111–129.

or enticing effect on their beholders.[115] But was the audience only supposed to take a non-emotional attitude towards these utterances and actions, focusing instead on a purely rational evaluation, as Scaliger would have it? Thomas Rosenmeyer remarks on the Stoic element in Senecan tragedy:

> In all endeavours to assess the nature of the Stoic share in the plays, the sights are trained on moral doctrines, the values that are most effectively communicated via *exempla*, the cautionary figures and actions of prominent men and women, and via precepts and *sententiae*, the often moving, but always safe, generalities offered by the characters and particularly by the chorus.[116]

This characterisation perfectly fits *Nero*. In addition, the first terzetto of the opening sonnet seems to call upon the audience to not react affectively to what it hears and sees happening on stage and accordingly to take an apathetic stance:

> Do not let this sorrowful play cause grief in you,
> Even if you witness matricide and other bloodshed;
> It is a mirror of evil, through which one recognises virtue.[117]

The second quatrain of the final sonnet appears to corroborate this:

> Even if the brute has frightened you with his curse,
> Do not let his words dishearten your soul;
> But remember that God will always make evil pay,
> And to our betterment retains it until the moment of retribution.[118]

One may rightly ask, though, whether the encouragement to not feel distressed or dismayed by the goings-on on stage only *confirms* that distress and dismay

---

115 Küpper, *The Cultural Net* 200–207.
116 Rosenmeyer T.C., *Senecan Drama and Stoic Cosmology* (Berkeley, CA – Los Angeles, CA – London: 1989) 12. On the *sententiae* and the chorus, see ibidem 29; Smits-Veldt, *Samuel Coster* 55–58. See also Küpper, *The Cultural Net* 188–189.
117 'Dit bloedigh droef tonneel en laet u niet verdrieten./ Al siet ghy moeders moordt en ander bloedt verghieten,/ 'T is spieghel van het quaet, waer door men kent de deught'; Van Nieuwelandt, *Nero* B 3 r.
118 'Al heeft den wreeden u door sijn ghevloeck vervaert;/ Laet in u siele doch sijn woorden gheenfins dalen./ Maer denckt dat Godt altijdt de boosheyt doet betalen,/ En dat hy tot ons leer haer tot haer straf bewaert'; Van Nieuwelandt, *Nero* 55.

ALL MOTION DISCOVERS US: WILLEM VAN NIEULANDT'S *NERO* (1618)   79

were precisely what the characters' words and deeds were expected to cause among the audience, either to be mitigated or to be experienced to the fullest.

Van Nieulandt does not refrain from impressing the sadness or poignancy of the play's action on the spectators, whether directly (as, for example, in the lines from the opening and closing sonnets quoted above) or indirectly (especially in the choruses spoken by Tiber and Rome). According to Seneca (*c.*4 BCE–65 CE), tragedy should confront its spectators with powerful, particularly frightening images (*species*), which hit them, so to speak, like a punch or blow (*ictus*).[119] These images literally left impressions on the soul or mind and consequently led to particular emotions or passions – 'as a prick or a spur to stir a man to virtue', to cite Erasmus anew (see above). *Nero* seems to have offered to the audience ample opportunities for *catharsis* by mirroring those of the characters on stage or by emotionally responding to their actions and motivations.[120] It is equally clear what purpose was served by such purgation: what was described earlier as the attainment of knowledge or wisdom needed to develop a virtuous character and to act virtuously.

Of all the characters, Nero and Agrippina prove to fall most acutely under the spell of the passions, expressing them in so-called passion portraits.[121] Agrippina is enraptured by anger on account of her declining power and influence at court. She feels that her honour is impugned and consequently she is intent upon revenge. Nero also shows himself to be angry and vengeful, but in addition he is also consumed by fear – in particular fear of loss of power and prestige. Early modern translations of Seneca's tragedies 'emphasize the pain of anger, and represent pain as a necessary step towards revenge'.[122] When one was truly wronged, it could even be seen as an expression of the virtue of justice.[123] Senecan tragedy is thought to have purposely aroused passions in the spectators and to have left considerable leeway for passing judgment

---

119   Schiesaro, *The Passions in Play* 232–233: Staley, *Seneca and the Idea of Tragedy* 63. See also Ramakers, "Sophonisba's Dress" 321.

120   Rist, "Catharsis as 'Purgation'" 152.

121   Konst, *Woedende wraakghierigheidt* 74–81.

122   Steenbergh, "Emotions and Gender" 125. See also Pollard, "Conceiving Tragedy" 90–93; Schoenfeldt M.C, "Shakespearean Pain", in Craik – Pollard (eds.), *Shakespearean Sensations* 191–207, esp. 193, 197–198, 204.

123   On the relation between passions and virtue generally and early modern thinking about this relation, see, for example, Taylor G. – Wolfram S., "Virtues and Passions", *Analysis* 31.3 (1971) 76–83; Roick M., "'Learn Virtue and Toil': Giovanni Pontano on Passion, Virtue and Arduousness", *History of Political Thought* 32.5 (2011) 732–750; and Sharpe K., "Virtues, Passions and Politics in Early Modern England", *History of Political Thought* 32.5 (2011) 773–798. On Aristotle's ideas on the relation between passions and virtue, see Sherman, *The Fabric of Character* 165–171.

on the characters and actions presented on stage.[124] As a Stoic philosopher, Seneca may have rejected anger, fear, and pity as emotions to act upon, but in the case of pity, for example, it remained 'possible to respond out of a settled disposition of kindliness or benevolence'.[125]

In the light of Sierhuis's observations concerning the importance of emotions as incentives for religious virtue, it may even be assumed that in early-seventeenth-century Antwerp, a hotbed indeed of Counter-Reformational fervour, spectators not only experienced but also expressed their emotions with barely restrained intensity – within the boundaries of decorum, naturally.[126] In any case, characters in *Nero* frequently express their affections, to which other characters repeatedly respond, both emotionally and intellectually. The spectators were supposedly incited to mimetically engage in this to-and-fro of action and reaction and make up their own minds about what was said, done, and experienced on stage, taking into consideration character and context.

Although *Nero* seems to be about suffering per se and about the violence causing it, the play is intent on clarifying lines of causation within the sphere of human agency. Among these are the objects to which the passions pertain, that is, *res bonae, res malae,* and *res mediae.* The passions had to be judged with the assistance of reason as to their suitability or appropriateness in relation to the matters to which they pertained. The resulting judgment determined the audience's overall assessment of the characters' behaviour and any conclusions drawn on their part as regards their own behaviour in like situations.

How this discerning process might have worked may be illustrated by a fragment from a dialogue between Nero and Seneca. In this scene they reflect on the passion which the latter unlike the former shows to have fully mastered: fear for loss of power and esteem. Seneca and Nero's other counsellor, Burrus, point out the importance of moderation, whilst referring to reason. In general, a call for moderation of the passions is repeatedly asserted, in particular by Tiber and Rome in the choruses, but Seneca and Burrus are the only characters who explicitly mention the importance of reason, especially where Nero's behaviour is concerned. The dialogue between Nero and Seneca is the only one which develops into a *stichomythia,* and therefore must have caught the

---

124 Schiesaro, *The Passions in Play* 234, 240, 244.

125 Konstan, "Senecan Emotions" 177. See also Sellars J., *Stoicism* (Chesham: 2006) 119.

126 Proof that spectators of Neo-Senecan tragedies became emotionally aroused is provided by Vondel. He recounts that the attendants of a performance of Samuel Coster's *Polyxena* from 1619 – the epitome, so to speak, of Dutch Neo-Senecan tragedy – broke down in tears at the moment when Astyanax, Polyxena's nephew and still a child, was thrown from a tower; Sierhuis, "Therapeutic Tragedy" 32.

audience's attention. Due to spatial constraints, only the beginning of their exchange is quoted here:

> NERO
> But Seneca, tell me, is there anyone
> Who fears loss of honour, but is still virtuous?
> SENECA
> He who can overcome fear through charity
> And allows his senses to be guided by reason.
> Virtue is more powerful than the sword that you carry,
> Because he who is righteous, has driven away all fear.
> NERO
> That's lunacy; fear triumphs reason.
> SENECA
> No, she produces virtue, and that gives us satisfaction.
> NERO
> So, if she produces virtue, will fear fade away?
> SENECA
> Yes, because virtue can quell fear.[127]

The passage describes the process of moral discernment in a nutshell. Agrippina's thirst for revenge has made Nero frightened of her. He will feasibly lose his power and consequently his honour, perhaps even his life. But is it possible to act virtuously in the face of this passion and its cause? Is it possible under these circumstances to act merciful instead of murderous, which is what Nero is inclined to do? Could the senses – both external and internal – be guided by reason in such a manner that the assessment of one's experiences or perceptions leads to an emotion different from fear, or to the moderation of fear? Seneca insists that justice can overcome fear. Fear, though, is stronger than reason, Nero retorts. No, Seneca replies, reason can get the better of fear and prompts us to act virtuously. As a result, one can achieve a state of contentment. Is Seneca here not referring to the state of human flourishing or happiness, that is, to *eudaimonia*? The following admonition, spoken by Burrus to Nero, seems to fit entirely within Aristotelian virtue ethics:

---

127 'N: Maer seght my, Seneca, wie isser die daer leeft,/ Die d'eer verliesingh vreest, en d'oude deugt noch heeft?/ S: Die door bermherticheyt de vreese can verwinnen,/ En door de reden laet gheleyden sijne sinnen/ De deught heeft meerder cracht dan 't ijser dat ghy draeght;/ Want die rechtveerdich is, heeft alle vrees' verjaeght./ N: Dat is al sotterny: de vrees' verwint de reden./ S: Niet, maer sy baert de deught, en die stelt ons te vreden./ N: Ghenomen sy baert deught, vergaet de vreese dan?/ S: Ja sy, door dat de deught de vreese dwinghen can'; Van Nieuwelandt, *Nero* 13.

No, Caesar, let reason conquer your heart;
Pay attention to the circumstances, necessity, and other matters.[128]

Ethical behaviour is dependent on context, and should be assessed as such. In the case of Nero, this means that he must moderate his fear because the matters to which it relates – power and honour – belong to the *res mediae*, the intermediate things, which should be treated phlegmatically, since they are subject to the vicissitudes of fortune, that is, we have (almost) no power over them. Thus, the affects were to be conditionally rejected, not categorically. The aforementioned dialogue was meant to stimulate the audience's own moral discernment of Nero's behaviour, a process of which the mirroring of the latter's emotions, *in casu* his fear, might well have been an intended and effective part.

Constancy, Fortune, and Choice

Nero invited its spectators to engage in a process of moral discernment that conformed to metriopathy. The mitigation of passions closely resembles the attitude of constancy as it was advocated by Justus Lipsius (1547–1606) in his *De Constantia* (On Constancy) from 1583. Lipsius departed from Stoicism in that he firmly believed in free will and the subjection of fate to God.[129] In *Nero* fortune's fickle nature is repeatedly emphasised. Agrippina and Nero express this sentiment towards the moment when their cause is definitively and irreversibly lost. Seneca also complains about his fate, but he declares that he will accept it and resolves to demonstrate 'that one can endure adversity without fear'.[130] It is clear from his attitude that he serves as Nero's opposite in this respect, exemplifying the virtue of constancy.

---

128 'Neen, Caesar, u ghemoet laet dat met reden dwinghen;/ Let op d'omstandicheyt, den noodt, en ander dinghen'; Van Nieuwelandt, *Nero* 16.

129 Miles, *Shakespeare and the Constant Romans* 70–75; Papy J., "Lipsius' (Neo-)Stoicism: Constancy between Christian Faith and Stoic Virtue", *Grotiana* 22.1 (2001) 47–71, esp. 54–56; Schmidt J., "Grundlagen, Kontinuität und geschichtlicher Wandel des Stoizismus", in Neymeyr B. – Schmidt J. – Zimmermann B. (eds.), *Stoizismus in der europäischen Philosophie, Literatur, Kunst und Politik*, 2 vols. (Berlin – New York, NY: 2008), vol. 1, 3–133, esp. 70–75, 84–85, 90; Grätz K., "Seneca christianus: Transformationen stoischer Vorstellungen in Andreas Gryphius' Märtyrerdramen *Catharina von Georgien* und *Papinian*", in Neymeyr B. – Schmidt J. – Zimmermann B. (eds.), *Stoizismus in der europäischen Philosophie, Literatur, Kunst und Politik*, 2 vols. (Berlin – New York, NY: 2008), vol. 2, 731–770, esp. 732–734. See also Taylor C., *A Secular Age* (Cambridge, MA – London: 2007) 115–116.

130 'datmen teghenspoet can sonder vreese lijden'; Van Nieuwelandt, *Nero* 43.

Being an Antwerp tragedy written and performed in the second decade of the seventeenth century, referencing *De Constantia* makes sense. At the time Lipsius's Neo-Stocism was very much alive in the city, as is evidenced by, among other things, Peter Paul Rubens's (1577–1640) painting *The Four Philosophers* from 1611/1612 [Fig. 2.4], in which Lipsius prominently features together with Rubens himself, the antiquarian and philologist Philip Rubens, the artist's brother, who until his death in 1611 had been the city's secretary, and Joannes Woverius, one of the city's alderman.[131] Woverius ensured the posthumous publication of some of Lipsius's works. Notably, Rubens in this painting also included a bust of Seneca.

Lipsius defines constancy as 'a right and immovable strength of the mind, neither lifted up nor pressed down with external or casual accidents'.[132] He relates these external and casual accidents to the intermediate things discussed before. By 'strength' he understands 'a steadfastness' coming 'from judgment and sound Reason'.[133] Thus, constancy is the outcome of a process of moral discernment with reason as principal mental tool. That constancy is not the same as apathy becomes clear when he calls for passion-driven virtuous behaviour. One should 'behold men's miseries with the eye of compassion, yet ruled and guided by reason'.[134] The 'casual and inconstant variableness of all things'[135] does not imply that man should not act on them. The changes of fortune are all foreseen by God. They are subject to divine providence: 'If you look at God and his providence, all things succeed in a steady and immovable order'.[136] But it is exactly this providence which allows man to act according to reason and free will.

Lipsius explicitly distances himself from the Stoic concept of destiny by stating that those who follow him 'do both allow Fate or Destiny, and also join hands with liberty or freedom of will'.[137] God, he writes, 'wishes that men should use deliberation and choice'.[138] From a Christian perspective, to have a choice and make one was a confirmation of the existence and importance

---

131   Prinz W., "The Four Philosophers by Rubens and the Pseudo-Seneca in Seventeenth-Century Painting", *The Art Bulletin* 55.3 (1973) 410–428, esp. 418–422. See also Schmidt, "Grundlagen" 72; Ramakers, "Sophonisba's Dress" 319.

132   Lipsius J., *On Constancy: De Constantia translated by Sir John Stradling (1595)*, ed. Sellars J. (Exeter: 2006) 37. See also Lagrée J., "Constancy and Coherence", in Strange S.K. – Zupko J.A. (eds.), *Stoicism: Traditions and Transformations* (Cambridge: 2004) 148–176, esp. 153–159; Levi, *French Moralists* 57–58.

133   Lipsius, *On Constancy* 37.

134   Lipsius, *On Constancy* 53.

135   Lipsius, *On Constancy* 62.

136   Lipsius, *On Constancy* 62.

137   Lipsius, *On Constancy* 69.

138   Lipsius, *On Constancy* 69.

FIGURE 2.4 Peter Paul Rubens, *The Four Philosophers* (1611–1612). Oil on panel, 167 × 143 cm. Florence, Galleria Palatina
IMAGE © SCALA, FLORENCE; MINISTERO BENI E ATT. CULTURALI

of free will.[139] Montaigne too asserts that the soul or mind possesses so much independent, individual potency that man to a large extent is responsible for his own fate:

139   Dewan L., *Wisdom, Law, and Virtue: Essays in Thomistic Ethics* (Bronx, NY: 2007) 18–20; Perkams M., "Aquinas on Choice, Will, and Voluntary Action", in Hoffmann T. – Müller J. – Perkams M. (eds.), *Aquinas and the* Nicomachean Ethics (New York, NY: 2013) 72–89.

Therefore let us take no more excuses from externall qualities of things. To us it belongeth to give our selves accoumpt of it. Our good and our evil hath no dependancy but from our selves. Let us offer our vowes and offerings unto it, and not to fortune. She hath no power over our manners.[140]

For the last time, we may reference Aristotle for context here. He uses the term *prohairesis* for choice or moral choice. In the *Poetics* it says:

Character is that which reveals moral choice – that is, when otherwise unclear, what kinds of thing an agent chooses or rejects (which is why speeches in which there is nothing at all the speaker chooses or rejects contain no character); [...].[141]

And in the *Nicomachean Ethics*:

Now the cause of action [...] is choice, and the cause of choice is desire and reasoning directed to some end. Hence choice necessarily involves both intellect or thought and a certain disposition of character [for doing well and the reverse in the sphere of action necessarily involve thought and character].[142]

In the words of Polish sociologist and philosopher Zygmunt Bauman: 'Morality, after all (perhaps rather *first of all*) is about *choice*. No choice, no morality'.[143]

Frans Francken's *The Painter's Cabinet*

In *Nero*, Seneca's suicide is portrayed in great detail. It also was a popular theme in Antwerp painting at the time, which is not surprising given the scene's significance as an example of constancy. After all, by calmly and deliberately taking his own life, accepting its fatal inevitability, Seneca had exemplified

---

140 Book I, Chapter 50; Montaigne, *The Essays of Montaigne*, vol. 1, 394.
141 1450b7–11; Aristotle, *Poetics* 52–53. See also Halliwell, *Aristotle's Poetics* 151–152; Sherman, *The Fabric of Character* 79–80; Hursthouse, *On Virtue Ethics* 16; and Nussbaum, "Tragedy and Self-sufficiency" 264–265.
142 6.ii, 1139a30–35; Aristotle, *Nicomachean Ethics* 328–331.
143 Bauman Z. – Tester K., *Conversations with Zygmunt Bauman* (Cambridge: 2001) 44.

the ultimate essence of his own philosophy.[144] Rubens's *The Death of Seneca* (1610) [Fig. 2.5] offers by far the best-known rendering of the theme.[145] It is also depicted in one of the paintings hanging from the wall of an art cabinet by Frans Francken the Younger (1581–1642), a contemporary of Van Nieulandt and fellow resident of Antwerp. Francken was a prolific painter of cabinet paintings – and a theatre lover at that. As a matter of fact, he donated a costume of Pictura to The Gillyflowers.[146] The painting bears the title *The Painter's Cabinet* [Fig. 2.6], since in it we see a painter – probably Francken himself – at work. Thus, the depicted space holds the middle between an art cabinet or *constkamer* and a studio. It is dated approximately 1627.

The painting-in-a-painting of Seneca's death is visible right above the artist and the obviously high-class couple standing behind him. It is flanked on the left by a Crucifixion and on the right by an Adoration of the Magi. The painting over the mantel piece depicts Croesus showing Solon his wealth. According to Lisa Rosenthal all these images 'coalesce around the theme of a virtuous death and Christian salvation'.[147] They provide a context, a frame as it were, for the interpretation of the scene they surround, that is, of the painter painting Fortuna, the female personification of fortune, after the model before him, who is balancing on a globe, that is, the world, whose unsteady luck she determines. Rosenthal affirms that in this painting

> the Neostoic program [of the surrounding paintings] appears to complete and resolve Fortuna's meaning: she is the erratic force against which *tranquillitas* and *Constantia* must be won through the exercise of intellectual rationality and Catholic faith.[148]

---

144   Zimmermann B., "Der Tod des Philosophen Seneca. Stoische probatio in Literatur, Kunst und Musik", in Neymeyr B. – Schmidt J. – Zimmermann B. (eds.), *Stoizismus in der europäischen Philosophie, Literatur, Kunst und Politik. Eine Kulturgeschichte von der Antike bis zur Moderne*, 2 vols. (Berlin – New York, NY: 2008), vol. 1, 393–422, esp. 398–403, 410–415; Ker J., *The Deaths of Seneca* (Oxford: 2009) 140–143.

145   Noll T., "'Der sterbende Seneca' des Peter Paul Rubens: Kunsttheoretisches und weltanschauliches Programmbild", *Münchner Jahrbuch der bildenden Kunst* 52 (2001) 89–158. See also Prinz, "The Four Philosophers" 417–418; Zimmermann, "Der Tod des Philosophen Seneca" 411–412.

146   Ramakers, "Sophonisba's Dress" 314, 317–318, 332, 334.

147   Rosenthal L., "Precarious Personification: Fortuna in the Artist's Cabinet", in Melion W.S. – Ramakers B. (eds.), *Personification: Embodying Meaning and Emotion* (Leiden – Boston, MA: 2016) 629–654, at 632.

148   Rosenthal, "Precarious Personification" 633.

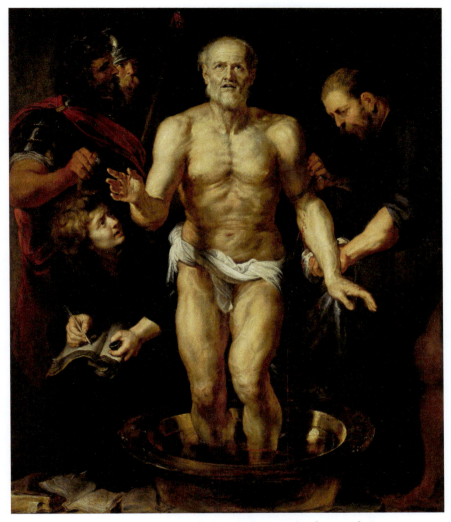

FIGURE 2.5 Peter Paul Rubens, *The Death of Seneca* (1612–1613). Oil on panel, 185 × 154,7 cm. Münich, Bayerische Staatsgemäldesammlungen – Alte Pinakothek

By means of a number of other images she then reaches the interpretation that the painter 'tames and contains Fortuna's powers by transforming her into an image'.[149] For this to succeed, he needs to master or balance his own passions –

---

149 Rosenthal, "Precarious Personification" 638.

FIGURE 2.6 Frans Francken the Younger, *The Painter's Cabinet* (c.1627). Oil on panel, 54 × 69 cm. Private collection, Las Arenas, Getxo, Spain

his lust or desire to paint – 'by proper training and knowledge'.[150] She then connects the importance of knowledge in art to that of reason in ethics.

One of the images she uses to establish this connection is a drawing, also by Francken, representing *The Painter and the Poet*, dated 1618 [Fig. 2.7]. In it we see an artist painting geography. The translation of the two-line Dutch verse underneath reads: 'While you are young learn good art; many who made a fervent beginning have stopped along the way'. '"Good art", according to Rosenthal, '[…] refers in this context to geometry as the scientific grounding of artistic practice that establishes the painter as the intellectual equal of the poet'.[151] This may be true, but is not the poet – and, thus, is not poetry – represented here as the provider or source of knowledge? The 'good art' referred to in the poem underneath is called *goede conste* in Dutch. The word *conste* could refer to all kinds of practical and theoretical knowledge, including the

---

150 Rosenthal, "Precarious Personification" 636.
151 Rosenthal, "Precarious Personification" 636.

ALL MOTION DISCOVERS US: WILLEM VAN NIEULANDT'S *NERO* (1618)   89

FIGURE 2.7   Frans Francken the Younger, *The Painter and the Poet* (1618). Pen with brown and blue ink, brown wash on paper, 29.1 × 19.8 cm. Paris, Musée du Louvre, inv. no. 19981
IMAGE © RMN-GRAND PALAIS/ART RESOURCE, NEW YORK

liberal arts, among which was geometry. But in the context of a poem it most likely refers to the *conste* or art of rhetoric as it was practiced by the vernacular rhetoricians. If the person instructing the painter from a book is indeed a poet, could he not be quoting poetry?

This raises the question of whether rhetoric in its sixteenth- and early-seventeenth-century manifestation as poetry, especially dramatic poetry, should not be taken into account when trying to establish how paintings like *The Painter's Cabinet* were not only *conceived* by their makers but also *perceived* by their viewers. Is it possible that this and other paintings of art cabinets, but also separate history paintings, of which Francken and his contemporaries produced so many, engaged their viewers in a process of moral discernment comparable to that supposedly triggered by contemporary tragedies? And could Franken and the bourgeois couple looking over his shoulder in their appreciation of art cabinets and history paintings not have been influenced by their familiarity with tragedies? This seems all the more likely given the process of rhetoricization which during the early modern period effected both the literary and the visual arts, and ultimately served moral-didactic purposes.[152]

Rosenthal links the personification of Fortuna to the vicissitudes of fortune in economic affairs, pointing to 'Mercury, god of eloquence and commerce'.[153] Mercury, according to her, 'also was the particular patron of painters, as is celebrated in Jan Saenredam's engraving after a design by Hendrick Goltzius' [Fig. 2.8]. Certainly, but first and foremost he was the god of eloquence, that is, of rhetoric and poetry, again especially dramatic poetry, at which the stage towards the centre back is a subtle hint.[154] Rosenthal identifies the bourgeois couple as 'sophisticated connoisseurs equipped to exercise their good judgment' on the painter's skill and expertise,[155] but also, one should add, on the paintings that are on display, not only that of Pictura, but also of those paintings hanging on the wall and the very kind of paintings in which they themselves occur, that is, in art cabinets. Their connoisseurship of, and interest in, these paintings extended beyond their artistic and commercial value. They also appreciated – or prized – them for their moral-didactic content and the opportunity they offered to engage in a process of moral discernment, when viewed

---

152 Warncke, *Sprechende Bilder – sichtbare Worte*, 25–26, 217, 246–247.

153 Rosenthal, "Precarious Personification" 645.

154 Ramakers B., "Voor stad en stadgenoten: Rederijkers, kamers en toneel in Haarlem in de tweede helft van de zestiende eeuw", in Ramakers B. (ed.) *Conformisten en rebellen: Rederijkerscultuur in de Nederlanden (1400–1650)* (Amsterdam: 2003) 109–123, esp. 121.

155 Rosenthal, "Precarious Personification" 641.

ALL MOTION DISCOVERS US: WILLEM VAN NIEULANDT'S *NERO* (1618) 91

FIGURE 2.8 Jan Saenredam after Hendrick Goltzius, *Mercury* (1596). Engraving, 257 × 180 mm. Amsterdam, Rijksmusueum, RP-P-OB-10.599

in their own homes or in those of family members, friends, and acquaintances, especially when these paintings depicted historical subject matter involving the impassioned behaviour of virtuous or vicious characters.

Concluding Remarks

Just as Aristotle aimed to morally educate the citizens of the Greek *polis*,[156] so too did early modern tragedians seek to stimulate virtuous behaviour in the middle and upper classes that came to watch their plays.[157] They aimed to create an affective or emotional community in the theatre.[158] The Antwerp chamber of rhetoric The Gillyflowers, which, as mentioned before, formed a union with the painters' guild of St. Luke, knew a category of members referred to as lovers or amateurs: the so-called *liefhebbers*.[159] Among them were civic officials and merchants who attended performances of tragedies. These were the same burghers that collected paintings and enjoyed talking about them as is witnessed by cabinet paintings. 'Fundamental to the practice of connoisseurship is the discourse regarding attributing works of art and sharing judgments about them'.[160] Conversations about history paintings like those represented in *The Painter's Cabinet* likely extended to the emotions expressed by the personages figuring in them. According to Stephanie Dickey, '[i]t has become an accepted principle that early modern connoisseurs expected paintings to

---

156   Cooper, *Pursuits of Wisdom* 112–113, 139–140, passim.

157   Steenbergh, "Compassion" 96–97; McCloskey D.N., *The Bourgeois Virtues: Ethics for an Age of Commerce* (Chicago, IL – London: 2006) 85. See also Reynolds, *A Treatise of the Passions* 7; Martinec, "Fürbild aller Tugenden'" 154–157; and Orgel, "The Play of Conscience" 143.

158   Steenbergh, "Compassion" 102, 112. See also Marion O. van – Vergeer T., "Gezongen emoties: Toneelliederen in Rodenburghs *Vrou Iacoba* bij de opening van de nieuwe Schouwburg", *De Zeventiende Eeuw* 30.2 (2014) 168–184, esp. 171.

159   Ramakers, "Sophonisba's Dress" 303, 310.

160   Doherty T., "Painting Connoisseurship: *Liefhebbers* in the Studio", in Chapman H.P. – Weststeijn T. – Meijers D. (eds.), *Connoisseurship and the Knowledge of Art* (Leiden – Boston, MA: 2019) 146–173, at 154. See also Marr A., "Ingenuity and Discernment in *The Cabinet of Cornelis van der Geest* (1628)", in Chapman H.P. – Weststeijn T. – Meijers D. (eds.), *Connoisseurship and the Knowledge of Art*, Netherlands Yearbook for History of Art 69 (Leiden – Boston, MA: 2019) 106–145, esp. 112.

provoke emotional responses'.[161] In this respect she also refers to contemporary ideas on tragedy.[162]

We may therefore safely assume that expert and accomplished viewers in their perception and evaluation of paintings – history paintings and otherwise – incorporated their experiences as spectators of tragedies like Van Nieulandt's.[163] He wrote *Nero* when he was still a member of The Olive Branch, before switching to The Gillyflowers. The Antwerp magistrates paid a large sum to have it performed at Town Hall.[164] We also know that the chamber's dean, Jan van der Ast, paid 66 florins for a flowered gown.[165] The chamber's accounts explicitly state that it was made for the staging of *Nero*, which Van Nieulandt dedicated to Van Ast. It is unknown who wore the gown. But we do know that Nero wore a waistcoat made out of 3.5 ells of black brocade with gold threads woven into it, costing no less than 18 florins. Such conspicuous apparel, which can equally be seen in contemporary history paintings, must have enhanced the energetic effect of the deeds, words, and passions displayed on stage, which reveal the minds or souls of the characters, as well as – through mirroring and reflection – those of the spectators who observed them, and who, borrowing two lines from Michael Bristol's earlier quotation, recognised what it felt like to be in their predicament and who perforce pursued inquiry about their reasons, their motives, and their moral disposition.

161 Dickey S.S., "Damsels in Distress: Gender and Emotion in Seventeenth-Century Netherlandish Art", in Dickey S.S. – Roodenburg H. (eds.), *The Passions in the Arts of the Early Modern Netherlands*, Netherlands Yearbook for History of Art 60 (Zwolle: 2010) 53–81, esp. 53.

162 Dickey, "Damsels in Distress" 54, 63, 69.

163 Ramakers, "Sophonisba's Dress" 314–318. Van Nieulandt's tragedies by no means are the only rhetoricians' plays that lend themselves to such an approach. The tragic oeuvre of Abraham de Koning (1588–1619), among others, presents a similar opportunity for a contrastive analysis of history painting and tragedy. On De Koning's tragedies, see Van Gemert, "The Politics of Visuality in Dutch Renaissance Tragedy". A recent monograph taking this approach is Lea G.R., *Silent Eloquence: The Rhetorical Pictures of Biblical History by Hendrick Goltzius and Pieter Lastman* (Ph.D. dissertation, Emory University – University of Groningen: 2022). See also his essay elsewhere in this volume.

164 Ramakers, "Sophonisba's Dress" 322.

165 Ramakers, "Sophonisba's Dress" 330.

Bibliography

Adams R.M., *A Theory of Virtue: Excellence in Being for the Good* (Oxford: 2006).

Allard-Nelson S.K., "Virtue in Aristotle's Rhetoric: A Metaphysical and Ethical Capacity", *Philosophy and Rhetoric* 34.3 (2001) 245–259.

Aristotle, *Art of Rhetoric*, trans. Freese J.H. – rev. Striker G. (Cambridge, MA – London: 2020).

Aristotle, *Nicomachean Ethics*, trans. Rackham H. (Cambridge, MA: 1934).

Aristotle, *Poetics*, trans. Halliwell S. (Cambridge, MA: 1995).

Aristotle, *Politics*, trans. Rackham H. (Cambridge, MA: 1972).

Bauman Z. – Tester K., *Conversations with Zygmunt Bauman* (Cambridge: 2001).

Becker L.C., "Stoic Emotion", in Strange S.K. – Zupko J.A. (eds.), *Stoicism: Traditions and Transformations* (Cambridge: 2004) 250–275.

Beecher D., *Adapted Brains and Imaginary Worlds: Cognitive Science and the Literature of the Renaissance* (Montreal – Kingston, ON – London: 2016).

Berg J., "Moral Agency as Readerly Subjectivity: Shakespeare's Parolles and the Theophrastan Character Sketch", *Shakespeare Studies* 40 (2012) 36–43.

Bird S.E., "From Fan Practice to Mediated Moments: The Value of Practice Theory in the Understanding of Media audiences", in Bräuchler B. – Postill J. (eds.), *Theorising Media and Practice* (Oxford – New York: 2010) 85–104.

Blackburn S., *Ruling Passions: A Theory of Practical Reasoning* (Oxford: 1998).

Bloemendal J., "Senecan Drama from the Northern and Southern Netherlands: Paganization and Christianization", *Dutch Review of Church History* 81.1 (2001) 38–45.

Booth W.C., "Why Ethical Criticism Can Never Be Simple", in Davis T.F. – Womack K. (eds.), *Mapping the Ethical Turn: A Reader in Ethics, Culture, and Literary Theory* (Charlottesville, VA – London: 2001) 16–29.

Bostock D., *Aristotle's Ethics* (Oxford: 2000).

Bouwsma W.J., "The Two Faces of Humanism: Stoicism and Augustianism in Renaissance Thought", in Oberman H.O. – Brady T.A. (eds.), *Itinerarium Italicum: The Profile of the Italian Renaissance in the Mirror of its European Transformations* (Leiden: 1975) 3–60.

Bredekamp H., *Image Acts: A Systematic Approach to Visual Agency* (Berlin – Boston, MA: 2015).

Brinck I., "Empathy, Engagement, Entrainment: The Interaction Dynamics of Aesthetic Experience", *Cognitive Processing* 19 (2018) 201–213.

Bristol M., "Introduction: Is Shakespeare a Moral Philosopher", in Bristol D. – Coodin S. – Fahmi M. – Finin K.R. (eds.), *Shakespeare and Moral Agency* (London: 2010) 1–12.

Bristol M.D., "Introduction", *Shakespeare Studies* 40 (2012) 19–25.

Broadie S., "Aristotle and Contemporary Ethics", in Kraut R. (ed.), *The Blackwell Guide to Aristotle's* Nicomachean Ethics (Oxford: 2006) 342–361.

Burns E., *Character: Acting and Being on the Pre-Modern Stage* (Basingstoke: 1990).

Buys R., *Sparks of Reason: Vernacular Rationalism in the Low Countries 1550–1670* (Hilversum: 2015).

Carroll N., "Theater and the Emotions", in Zunshine L. (ed.), *The Oxford Handbook of Cognitive Literary Studies* (Oxford: 2015) 313–326.

Cates D.F., "Conceiving Emotions: Martha Nussbaum's *Upheavals of Thought*", *The Journal of Religious Ethics* 31.2 (2003) 325–341.

Cates D.F., *Aquinas on the Emotions: A Religious-Ethical Inquiry* (Washington, DC: 2009).

Celano A., *Aristotle's* Ethics *and Medieval Philosophy: Moral Goodness and Practical Wisdom* (Cambridge: 2016).

Conley T., *An Errant Eye: Poetry and Topography in Early Modern France* (Minneapolis, MN – London: 2011).

Coodin S., "What's Virtue Ethics Got to Do With It? Shakespearean Character as Moral Character", in Bristol D. – Coodin S. – Fahmi M. – Finin K.R. (eds.), *Shakespeare and Moral Agency* (London: 2010) 184–199.

Coodin S., "Fiction, Emotion, and Moral Agency", *Shakespeare Studies* 40 (2012) 63–69.

Cooper J.M., *Reason and Emotion: Essays on Ancient Moral Psychology and Ethical Theory* (Princeton, NJ: 1999).

Cooper J.M., *Pursuits of Wisdom: Six Ways of Life in Ancient Philosophy from Socrates to Plotinus* (Princeton, NJ – Oxford: 2012).

Coornhert Dirk Volckertszoon, *Ethics or the Art of Living Well*, trans., ed., and intro. Voogt G. (Hilversum 2015).

Coplan A., "Empathic Engagement with Narrative Fictions", *The Journal of Aesthetics and Art Criticism* 62.2 (2004) 141–152.

Craik K.A. – Pollard T., "Introduction: Imagining Audiences", in Craik – Pollard (eds.), *Shakespearean Sensations* 1–25.

Craik K.A. – Pollard T. (eds.), *Shakespearean Sensations: Experiencing Literature in Early Modern England* (Cambridge: 2013).

Critchley S., "Tragedy's Philosophy", in Fischer T. – Katsouraki E. (eds.), *Performing Antagonism* (Basingstoke – New York, NY: 2017) 25–42.

Cummings B. – Sierhuis F., "Introduction", in Cummings B. – Sierhuis F. (eds.), *Passions and Subjectivity in Early Modern Culture* (London – New York, NY: 2016 [2013]) 1–9.

Curran A., "Brecht's Criticism of Aristotle's Aesthetics of Tragedy", *The Journal of Aesthetics and Art Criticism* 59.2 (2001) 167–184.

Dewan L., *Wisdom, Law, and Virtue: Essays in Thomistic Ethics* (Bronx, NY: 2007).

Dickey S.S., "Damsels in Distress: Gender and Emotion in Seventeenth-Century Netherlandish Art", in Dickey S.S. – Roodenburg H. (eds.), *The Passions in the Arts of the Early Modern Netherlands*, Netherlands Yearbook for History of Art 60 (Zwolle: 2010) 53–81.

Dickey S.S. – Roodenburg H., "Introduction: The Motions of the Mind", in Dickey S.S. – Roodenburg H. (eds.), *The Passions in the Arts of the Early Modern Netherlands*, Netherlands Yearbook for History of Art 60 (Zwolle: 2010) 7–16.

Doherty T., "Painting Connoisseurship: *Liefhebbers* in the Studio", in Chapman H.P. – Weststeijn T. – Meijers D. (eds.), *Connoisseurship and the Knowledge of Art*, Netherlands Yearbook for History of Art 69 (Leiden – Boston, MA: 2019) 146–173.

Eagleton T., *Sweet Violence: The Idea of the Tragic* (Malden, MA: 2003).

Eck C. van, *Art, Agency and Living Presence: From the Animated Image to the Excessive Object* (Berlin – Leiden: 2015).

Edinborough C., *Theatrical Reality: Space, Embodiment and Empathy in Performance* (Bristol – Chicago, IL: 2016).

Ekstein N., "Staging the Tyrant on the Seventeenth-Century French Stage", *Papers on French Seventeenth Century Literature* 36 (1999) 111–129.

Erasmus Desiderius, *The Manual of a Christian Knight* (London: 1905) [after the edition London, Wynkyn de Worde for Johan Byddell: 1533].

Fingerhut J., "Das Bild, dein Freund. Der fühlende und der sehende Körper in der enaktiven Bildwahrnehmung", in Feist U. – Rath M. (eds.), *Et in imagine ego: Facetten von Bildakt und Verkörperung* (Berlin: 2012) 177–198.

Finlay L., "Debating Phenomenological Research Methods", *Phenomenology & Practice* 3.1 (2009) 6–25.

Foglia M., "La question de l'interprétation chez Montaigne", *Cahiers philosophiques* 127.4 (2011) 81–96.

Ford A., "*Katharsis*: The Ancient Problem", in Parker A. – Sedgwick E.K. (eds.), *Performativity and Performance* (New York, NY: 1995) 109–132.

Ford A., "Catharsis: The Power of Music in Aristotle's *Politics*", in Murray P. – Wilson P. (eds.), *Music and the Muses: The Culture of Mousikê in the Classical Athenian City* (Oxford: 2004) 309–336.

Fossheim H.J., "Habituation as *Mimesis*", in Chappel T. (ed.), *Values and Virtues: Aristotelianism in Contemporary Ethics* (Oxford: 2006) 105–112.

Freedberg D. – Gallese V., "Motion, Emotion and Empathy in Esthetic Experience", *Trends in Cognitive Sciences* 11.5 (2007) 197–203.

Gemert L. van, "The Politics of Visuality in Dutch Renaissance Tragedy", in Leuker M.-T. (ed.), *Die sichtbare Welt: Visualität in der niederländischen Literatur und Kunst des 17. Jahrhunderts* (Münster: 2012) 203–219.

Gottlieb P., *The Virtue of Aristotle's Ethics* (Cambridge: 2009).

Gowland A., "Melancholy, Passions and Identity in the Renaissance", in Cummings B. – Sierhuis F. (eds.), *Passions and Subjectivity in Early Modern Culture* (Abingdon – New York, NY: 2016) 75–93.

Grady H., "Moral Agency and Its Problems in *Julius Caesar*: Political Power, Choice, and History", in Bristol D. – Coodin S. – Fahmi M. – Finin K.R. (eds.), *Shakespeare and Moral Agency* (London: 2010) 15–28.

Grätz K., "Seneca christianus: Transformationen stoischer Vorstellungen in Andreas Gryphius' Märtyrerdramen *Catharina von Georgien* und *Papinian*", in Neymeyr B. – Schmidt J. – Zimmermann B. (eds.), *Stoizismus in der europäischen Philosophie, Literatur, Kunst und Politik*, 2 vols. (Berlin – New York, NY: 2008), vol. 2, 731–770.

Gross D.M., *The Secret History of Emotion: From Aristotle's* Rhetoric *to Modern Brain Science* (Chicago, IL – London: 2006) 2–3.

Halliwell S., *Aristotle's Poetics* (Chapel Hill, NC: 1986).

Halliwell S., "Pleasure, Understanding, and Emotion in Aristotle's *Poetics*", in Rorty (ed.), *Essays on Aristotle's Poetics* 241–260.

Hampton T., *Writing from History: The Rhetoric of Exemplarity in Tasso, Montaigne and Cervantes* (Ph.D. dissertation, Princeton University: 1987).

Hart F.E., "Performance, Phenomenology, and the Cognitive Turn", in McConachie B. – Hart F.E. (eds.), *Performance and Cognition: Theatre Studies and the Cognitive Turn* (London – New York, NY: 2006) 29–51.

Haskins E.V., "*Mimesis* Between Poetics and Rhetoric: Performance Culture and Civic Education in Plato, Isocrates, and Aristotle", *Rhetoric Society Quarterly* 30.3 (2000) 7–33.

Heath M., *The Poetics of Greek Tragedy* (Stanford, CA: 1987).

Hellerstedt A., "Introduction", in Hellerstedt A. (ed.), *Virtue Ethics and Education from Late Antiquity to the Eighteenth Century* (Amsterdam: 2018) 9–36.

Herdt J.A., *Putting On Virtue: The Legacy of the Splendid Vices* (Chicago, IL – London: 2008).

Herman B., *Moral Literacy* (Harvard, MA – London: 2007).

Hobgood A.P., *Passionate Playgoing in Early Modern England* (Cambridge – New York, NY: 1977).

Hobgood A.P., "Feeling fear in *Macbeth*", in Craik – Pollard (eds.), *Shakespearean Sensations* 29–46.

Hursthouse R., *On Virtue Ethics* (Oxford: 1999).

Inwood B. – Donini P., "Stoic Ethics", in Algra K. – Barnes J. – Mansfeld J. – Schofield M. (eds.), *The Cambridge History of Hellenistic Philosophy* (Cambridge: 1999) 675–738.

James S., *Passion and Action: The Emotions in Seventeenth-Century Philosophy* (New York, NY: 1997).

Kambaskovic D., "'Among the Rest of the Senses ... Proved Most Sure': Ethics of the Senses in Pre-modern Europe", in Kambaskovic D. (ed.), *Conjunctions of Mind, Soul and Body from Plato to the Enlightenment* (Heidelberg: 2014) 337–370.

Kane R., *Ethics and the Quest for Wisdom* (Cambridge: 2010).

Kappl B., "Profit, Pleasure, and Purgation: Catharsis in Aristotle, Paolo Beni and Italian Late Renaissance Poetics", *Skenè* 2.1 (2016) 105–132.

Keersmaekers A.A., *De dichter Guilliam van Nieuwelandt en de Senecaans-classieke tragedie in de Zuidelijke Nederlanden: Bijdrage tot de studie van de Zuidnederlandse literatuur der 17e eeuw* (Ghent: 1957).

Kehler T., *The Necessity of Affection: Shakespeare and the Politics of the Passions* (Ph.D. dissertation, McGill University: 2001).

Ker J., *The Deaths of Seneca* (Oxford: 2009).

Knapp J.A., "A Shakespearean Phenomenology of Moral Conviction", in Bristol D. – Coodin S. – Fahmi M. – Finin K.R. (eds.), *Shakespeare and Moral Agency* (London: 2010) 29–41.

Knapp J.A., *Image Ethics in Shakespeare and Spenser* (New York, NY: 2011).

Knuuttila S., *Emotions in Ancient and Medieval Philosophy* (Oxford: 2004).

Konst J.W.H., *Woedende wraakghierigheidt en vruchtelooze weeklachten: De hartstochten in de Nederlandse tragedie van de zeventiende eeuw* (Assen: 1993).

Konst J., "'Medoogen en schrick uit te wercken': Der emotionale Effekt von Vondels *Jephta* (1659)", in Steiger J.A. (ed.), *Passion, Affekt und Leidenschaft in der Frühen Neuzeit*, 2 vols. (Wiesbaden: 2005), vol. 2, 803–815.

Konstan D., "Senecan Emotions", in Bartsch S. – Schiesaro A. (eds.), *The Cambridge Companion to Seneca* (Cambridge: 2015) 174–184.

Kosman A., "Acting: Drama as the Mimēsis of Praxis", in Rorty (ed.), *Essays on Aristotle's Poetics* 51–72.

Kou X. – Konrath S. – Goldstein, T.R., "The Relationship among Different Types of Arts Engagement, Empathy, and Prosocial Behavior", *Psychology of Aesthetics, Creativity, and the Arts* 14.4 (2020) 481–492.

Kühlman W., "Wort, Geist und Macht – Unvorgreifliche Bemerkungen zu Formationen frühneuzeitlicher Intellektualität", in Held J. (ed.), *Intellektuelle in der Frühen Neuzeit* (München: 2002) 18–29.

Küpper J., *The Cultural Net: Early Modern Drama as a Paradigm* (Berlin – Boston: 2019).

Lagrée J., "Constancy and Coherence", in Strange S.K. – Zupko J.A. (eds.), *Stoicism: Traditions and Transformations* (Cambridge: 2004) 148–176.

Lamb C., *Corporeal Returns: Theatrical Embodiment and Spectator Response in Early Modern Drama* (Ph.D. dissertation, The University of Western Ontario: 2011).

Langdridge D., "Phenomenology and Critical Social Psychology: Directions and Debates in Theory and Research", *Social and Personality Psychology Compass* 2.3 (2008) 1126–1142.

Langer U., "The Ring of Gyges in Plato, Cicero, and Lorenzo Valla: The Moral Force of Fictional Examples", in Kessler E. – Maclean I. (eds.), *Res et verba in der Renaissance* (Wiesbaden: 2002) 131–145.

Langlands R., "Roman *Exempla* and Situation Ethics: Valerius Maximus and Cicero *de Officiis*", *Journal of Roman Studies* 100 (2011) 100–122.

Lanham R.A., *The Motives of Eloquence: Literary Rhetoric in the Renaissance* (New Haven, CT – London: 1976).

Lanzoni S., "Introduction", in Lanzoni S., *Empathy: A History* (Princeton, NJ: 2018) 1–18.

Lea G.R., *Silent Eloquence: The Rhetorical Pictures of Biblical History by Hendrick Goltzius and Pieter Lastman* (Ph.D. dissertation, Emory University – University of Groningen: 2022).

Lear J., "Katharsis", in Rorty (ed.), *Essays on Aristotle's Poetics* 315–340.

Levi A., *French Moralists: The Theory of the Passions 1585 to 1649* (Oxford: 1964).

Lieblein L., "Embodied Intersubjectivity and the Creation of Early Modern Character", in Yachnin P. – Slights J. (eds.), *Shakespeare and Character: Theory, History, Performance and Theatrical Persons* (London: 2009) 117–135.

Lipsius J., *On Constancy:* De Constantia *translated by Sir John Stradling (1595)*, ed. Sellard J. (Exeter: 2006).

Lyne R., *Shakespeare, Rhetoric and Cognition* (Cambridge: 2011).

Lyons J.D., "Meditation and the Inner Voice", *New Literary History* 37.3 (2006) 525–538.

McCloskey D.N., *The Bourgeois Virtues: Ethics for an Age of Commerce* (Chicago, IL – London: 2006).

MacIntyre A., *After Virtue: A Study in Moral Theory* (London – New York, NY: 2011 [1981]).

Mack P., "Montaigne and Christian Humanism", in MacDonald A.A. – Martels Z.R.W.M. von – Veenstra J. (eds.), *Christian Humanism: Essays in Honour of Arjo Vanderjagt* (Leiden – Boston, MA: 2009) 199–209.

Mancing H., "See the Play, Read the Book", in McConachie B. – Hart F.E. (eds.), *Performance and Cognition: Theatre Studies and the Cognitive Turn* (London – New York, NY: 2006) 189–206.

Manen M. van, "Phenomenology of Practice", *Phenomenology & Practice* 1.1 (2007) 11–30.

Marculescu A. – Morand Métivier C.L., "Introduction", in Marculescu A. – Morand Métivier C.L. (eds.), *Affective and Emotional Economies in Medieval and Early Modern Europe* (Cham: 2018) 1–16.

Marion O. van – Vergeer T., "Gezongen emoties: Toneelliederen in Rodenburghs *Vrou Iacoba* bij de opening van de nieuwe Schouwburg", *De Zeventiende Eeuw* 30.2 (2014) 168–184.

Marr A., "Ingenuity and discernment in *The Cabinet of Cornelis van der Geest* (1628)", in Chapman H.P. – Weststeijn T. – Meijers D. (eds.), *Connoisseurship and the Knowledge of Art*, Netherlands Yearbook for History of Art 69 (Leiden – Boston, MA: 2019) 106–145.

Martinec T., "'Fürbild aller Tugenden': Rhetorik und Moral in der barocken Trauerspielpoetik", *Daphnis* 35 (2006) 133–161.

Maus K.E., *Inwardness and Theater in the English Renaissance* (Chicago, IL – London: 1995).

Meek R. – Sullivan E., "Introduction", in Meek R. – Sullivan E. (eds.), *The Renaissance of Emotion: Understanding Affect in Shakespeare and His Contemporaries* (Manchester: 2015) 1–22.

Miles G., *Shakespeare and the Constant Romans* (Oxford – New York, NY: 1996).

Montaigne Michel de, *Essays of Montaigne*, trans. Cotton C. – ed. Hazlitt W.C., 3 vols. (London: 1877). https://openlibrary.org/books/OL23410802M/Essays_of_Montaigne.

Montaigne Michel de, *The Essays of Montaigne*, trans. Florio J. – intro. Saintsbury G., 3 vols. (London: 1892).

Montaigne Michel Eyquem de, *Les Essais*, eds. Villey P. – Saulnier V.-L. – online ed. Desan P. (Chicago, IL: n.d.). https://www.lib.uchicago.edu/efts/ARTFL/projects/montaigne/.

Mooij H. – Mooij-Valk S., "Coornhert on Virtue and Nobility", in MacDonald A.A. – Martels Z.R.W.M. von – Veenstra J. (eds.), *Christian Humanism: Essays in Honour of Arjo Vanderjagt* (Leiden – Boston, MA: 2009) 155–169.

Nehamas A., "Pity and Fear in the *Rhetoric* and the *Poetics*", in Rorty (ed.), *Essays on Aristotle's Poetics* 291–314.

Newton B.W., "Perspective Chapter: Having Heart – The Different Facets of Empathy", in Ventura S. (ed.), *Empathy – Advances Research and Applications* (London: 2023) 29–49.

Nieuwelandt Guilliam van, *Claudius Domitius Nero* (Antwerp, Guilliam van Tongheren: 1618).

Noll T., "'Der sterbende Seneca' des Peter Paul Rubens: Kunsttheoretisches und weltanschauliches Programmbild", *Münchner Jahrbuch der bildenden Kunst* 52 (2001) 89–158.

Nussbaum M.C., "Tragedy and Self-sufficiency: Plato and Aristotle on Fear and Pity", in Rorty (ed.), *Essays on Aristotle's Poetics* 261–290.

Nussbaum M.C., *Upheavals of Thought: The Intelligence of Emotions* (Cambridge: 2001).

Orgel S., "The Play of Conscience", in Parker A. – Sedgwick E.K. (eds.), *Performativity and Performance* (New York, NY: 1995) 133–151.

Papy J., "Lipsius' (Neo-)Stoicism: Constancy between Christian Faith and Stoic Virtue", *Grotiana* 22.1 (2001) 47–71.

Parvini N., *Shakespeare and Cognition: Thinking Fast and Slow through Character* (Basingstoke – New York, NY: 2015).

Paster G.K., *Humoring the Body: Emotions and the Shakespearean Stage* (Chicago, IL – London: 2004).

Perkams M., "Aquinas on Choice, Will, and Voluntary Action", in Hoffmann T. – Müller J. – Perkams M. (eds.), *Aquinas and the* Nicomachean Ethics (New York, NY: 2013) 72–89.

Pfister M., "Reading the Body: The Corporeality of Shakespeare's Text", in Scolnicow H. – Holland P. (eds.), *Reading Plays: Interpretation and Reception* (Cambridge et al.: 1991) 110–122.

Pickavé M., "Emotion and Cognition in Later Medieval Philosophy: The Case of Adam Wodeham", in Pickavé M. – Shapiro L. (eds.), *Emotion and Cognitive Life in Medieval and Early Modern Philosophy* (Oxford: 2012) 94–115.

Plett H.F., *Rhetoric and Renaissance Culture* (Berlin – New York, NY: 2004).

Plett H.F., *Enargeia in Classical Antiquity and the Early Moderne Age: The Aesthetics of Evidence* (Leiden – Boston, MA: 2012).

Pollard T., "Conceiving Tragedy", in Craik – Pollard (eds.), *Shakespearean Sensations* 85–100.

Price A.W., *Virtue and Reason in Plato and Aristotle* (Oxford: 2011).

Prinz W., "The Four Philosophers by Rubens and the Pseudo-Seneca in Seventeenth-Century Painting", *The Art Bulletin* 55.3 (1973) 410–428.

Quintilian, *The Orator's Education*, vol. 1 (Books I–II), ed. and trans. Russell D.A. (Cambridge, MA – London: 2001).

Quintilian, *The Orator's Education*, vol. 5 (Books 11–12), ed. and trans. Russell D.A. (Cambridge, MA – London: 2001).

Quiring B., "Introduction", in Quiring B. (ed.), *"If Then the World a Theatre Present ...": Revisions of the Theatrum Mundi Metaphor in Early Modern England* (Berlin: 2014) 1–23.

Ramakers B., "Voor stad en stadgenoten: Rederijkers, kamers en toneel in Haarlem in de tweede helft van de zestiende eeuw", in Ramakers B. (ed.) *Conformisten en rebellen: Rederijkerscultuur in de Nederlanden (1400–1650)* (Amsterdam: 2003) 109–123.

Ramakers B., "Sophonisba's Dress: Costume, Tragedy and Value on the Antwerp Stage (c. 1615–1630)", in Göttler C. – Ramakers B. – Woodall J. (eds.), *Trading Values in Early Modern Antwerp*, Netherlands Yearbook for History of Art 64 (Leiden – Boston, MA: 2014) 298–347.

Ramakers B., "Embodied Wits: The Representation of Deliberative Thought in Rhetoricians' Drama", *Renaissance Studies* 32.1 (2018) 85–105.

Reynolds E., *A Treatise of the Passions and Faculties of the Soule of Man*, ed. Wiley M.E. (Gainesville, FL: 1971).

Rist T., "Catharsis as 'Purgation' in Shakespearean Drama", in Clark – Pollard (eds.) *Shakespearean Sensations* 138–153.

Rist T., "Miraculous Organ: Shakespeare and 'Catharsis'", *Skenè* 2.1 (2016) 133–150.

Roach J.R., *The Player's Passion: Studies in the Science of Acting* (Newark, NJ – London – Toronto: 1985).

Roick M., "'Learn Virtue and Toil': Giovanni Pontano on Passion, Virtue and Arduousness", *History of Political Thought* 32.5 (2011) 732–750.

Roodenburg H., *The Eloquence of the Body: Perspectives on Gesture in the Dutch Republic* (Zwolle: 2004).

Rorty A.O. (ed.), *Essays on Aristotle's Poetics* (Princeton, NJ: 1992).

Rosenmeyer T.C., *Senecan Drama and Stoic Cosmology* (Berkeley, CA – Los Angeles, CA – London: 1989).

Rosenthal L., "Precarious Personification: Fortuna in the Artist's Cabinet", in Melion W.S. – Ramakers B. (eds.), *Personification: Embodying Meaning and Emotion* (Leiden – Boston, MA: 2016) 629–654.

Rosenwein B.H., *Generations of Feeling: A History of Emotions, 600–1700* (Cambridge: 2016).

Sauter W., *The Theatrical Event: Dynamics of Performance and Perception* (Iowa City, IA, 2000).

Scaliger Julius Caesar, *Poetices libri septem* (Lyon, Antonius Vincentius: 1561).

Schiaparelli A. – Crivelli P., "Aristotle on Poetry", in Shields C. (ed.), *The Oxford Handbook of Aristotle* (Oxford: 2012) 612–626.

Schiesaro A., *The Passions in Play:* Thyestes *and the Dynamics of Senecan Drama* (Cambridge: 2003).

Schmidt J., "Grundlagen, Kontinuität und geschichtlicher Wandel des Stoizismus", in Neymeyr B. – Schmidt J. – Zimmermann B. (eds.), *Stoizismus in der europäischen Philosophie, Literatur, Kunst und Politik*, 2 vols. (Berlin – New York, NY: 2008), vol. 1, 3–133.

Schoenfeldt M.C., *Bodies and Selves in Early Modern England: Physiology and Inwardness in Spenser, Shakespeare, Herbert, and Milton* (Cambridge – New York, NY: 1999).

Schoenfeldt M., "Shakespearean Pain", in Craik – Pollard (eds.), *Shakespearean Sensations* 191–207.

Sellars J., *Stoicism* (Chesham: 2006).

Sharpe K., "Virtues, Passions and Politics in Early Modern England", *History of Political Thought* 32.5 (2011) 773–798.

Sherman N., *The Fabric of Character: Aristotle's Theory of Virtue* (Oxford: 1989).

Sherman N., "Character Development and Aristotelian Virtues", in Carr D. – Steutel J. (eds.), *Virtue Ethics and Moral Education* (London – New York, NY: 1999) 35–49.

Sierhuis F., "Therapeutic Tragedy: Compassion, Remorse, and Reconciliation in the Joseph Plays of Joost van den Vondel (1635–1640)", *European Review of History* 17.1 (2010) 27–51.

Sierhuis F., "The Passions in the Literature of the Dutch Golden Age", *Tijdschrift voor Nederlandse Taal- en Letterkunde* 132.4 (2016) 333–365.

Skidmore C., *Practical Ethics for Roman Gentlemen: The Work of Valerius Maximus* (Exeter: 1996).

Sluijter E.J., "Career Choices of Migrant Artists between Amsterdam and Antwerp: The Van Nieulandt Brothers", *De Zeventiende Eeuw* 31.1 (2015) 102–137.

Smith B.R., "Afterword: Senses of an Ending", in Craik – Pollard (eds.), *Shakespearean Sensations* 208–217.

Smits-Veldt M.B., *Samuel Coster, ethicus-didacticus: Een onderzoek naar dramatische opzet en morele instructie van Ithys, Polyxena en Iphegenia* (Groningen: 1986).

Solomon J.R., "You've Got to Have Soul: Understanding the Passions in Early Modern Culture", in Pender S. – Struever N.S. (eds.), *Rhetoric and Medicine in Early Modern Europe* (Farnham – Burlington, VT: 2012) 195–228.

Staley G.A., *Seneca and the Idea of Tragedy* (Oxford – New York, NY: 2009).

Steenbergh K., "Emotion, Performance and Gender in Shakespeare's Hamlet", in Ruberg W.G. – Steenbergh K. (eds.), *Sexed Sentiments: Interdisciplinary Perspectives on Gender and Emotion* (Amsterdam: 2011) 93–116.

Steenbergh K., "Emotions and Gender: The Case of Anger in Early Modern English Revenge Tragedies", in Liliequist J. (ed.), *A History of Emotions, 1200–1800* (London: 2012) 119–134.

Steenbergh K., "Compassion and the Creation of an Affective Community in the Theatre: Vondel's *Mary Stuart, or Martyred Majesty* (1646)", *Low Countries Historical Review* 129.2 (2014) 90–112.

Steenbergh K. – Obbett K., "Introduction", in Steenbergh K. – Obbett K. (eds.), *Compassion in Early Modern Literature and Culture* (Cambridge: 2021) 1–21.

Steggle M., *Laughing and Weeping in Early Modern Theatres* (Aldershot – Burlington, VT: 2007).

Stock B., "Ethical Values and the Literary Imagination in the Later Ancient World", *New Literary History* 29.1 (1998) 1–13.

Stolberg M., "'Zorn, Wein und Weiber verderben unsere Leiber': Affekt und Krankheit in der Frühen Neuzeit", in Steiger J.A. (ed.), *Passion, Affekt und Leidenschaft in der frühen Neuzeit* (Wiesbaden: 2005) 1051–1077.

Syson L. – Thornton D., *Objects of Virtue: Art in Renaissance Italy* (Los Angeles, CA: 2001).

Taylor C., *A Secular Age* (Cambridge, MA – London: 2007).

Taylor G. – Wolfram S., "Virtues and Passions", *Analysis* 31.3 (1971) 76–83.

Taylor P.A., "Sympathy and Insight in Aristotle's *Poetics*", *The Journal of Aesthetics and Art Criticism* 66.3 (2008) 265–280.

Tilmouth C., *Passion's Triumph over Reason: A History of the Moral Imagination from Spenser to Rochester* (Oxford – New York, NY: 2007).

Tilmouth C., "Passion and Intersubjectivity in Early Modern Literature", in Cummings B. – Sierhuis F. (eds.), *Passions and Subjectivity in Early Modern Culture* (Abingdon – New York, NY: 2016) 13–32.

Timpe K. – Boyd C.A. (eds.), *Virtues and Their Vices* (Oxford: 2014).

Tindale C., "Narratives and the Concept of Argument", in Olmos P. (ed.), *Narration as Argument* (Cham: 2017) 11–30.

Tucker S.R., *The Virtues and Vices in the Arts: A Sourcebook* (Eugene, OR: 2015).

Walker L.J., "Moral Motivation through the Perspective of Exemplarity", in Heinrichs K. – Oser F. – Lovat T. (eds.), *Handbook of Moral Motivation: Theories, Models, Applications* (Rotterdam: 2013) 197–214.

Warncke C.-P., *Sprechende Bilder – sichtbare Worte. Das Bildverständnis in der frühen Neuzeit* (Wiesbaden: 1987).

Woodruff P., "Aristotle on Mimēsis", in Rorty (ed.), *Essays on Aristotle's Poetics* 73–95.

Zagzebski L., "The Admirable Life and the Desirable Life", in Chappel T. (ed.), *Values and Virtues: Aristotelianism in Contemporary Ethics* (Oxford: 2006) 53–66.

Zanker G., "Aristotle's *Poetics* and the Painters", *The American Journal of Philology* 121.2 (2000) 225–235.

Zimmermann B., "Der Tod des Philosophen Seneca: Stoische probatio in Literatur, Kunst und Musik", in Neymeyr B. – Schmidt J. – Zimmermann B. (eds.), *Stoizismus in der europäischen Philosophie, Literatur, Kunst und Politik*, 2 vols. (Berlin – New York, NY: 2008), vol. 1, 393–422.

Zunshine L., *Getting Inside Your Head: What Cognitive Science Can Tell Us about Popular Culture* (Baltimore, MD: 2012).

CHAPTER 3

Staging the In-Between: Compound, Conflicting and Shifting Emotions in Seventeenth-Century Neo-Latin Drama from the Dutch Republic

Lukas Reddemann

Abstract

This chapter explores the complex relationship between mixed and transitional passions and emotions, theoretical and philosophical approaches to affects, and visual representations of emotions in Neo-Latin drama. After a brief outline of Neo-Stoic and Aristotelian theories of affects and their reception in Neo-Latin Drama, it examines selected exemplary scenes from three Latin tragedies from the early 17th-ct. Dutch Republic (Jacob van Zevecote, *Rosimunda*; Rochus van den Honert, *Thamara*; Daniel Heinsius, *Auriacus*). These case studies show that scenes involving mixed emotions heavily draw on Stoic and Neo-Stoic terminology and theories of affects (e.g. the subtle distinction between *impetus* and *affectus*). The concept of *apatheia* can serve as an ideal against which single characters and their actions can be morally measured. The Stoic theory also involves precise concepts of physical representations of affects, which, in turn, has important consequences on their visual representation on stage during performances. This chapter argues that descriptions of corporeal appearances, facial expressions, and movements in dialogues on stage serve as implicit stage directions, i.e. hints on how actors should move and act on stage.

Keywords

Neostoicism – Aristotelianism – Seneca – Performativity – Chambers of Rhetoric – Biblical drama

1 Introduction

Neo-Latin drama was a core element of public and intellectual life in the early modern Low Countries. Schoolmasters and scholars in the 16th and 17th centuries produced numerous comedies and tragedies about episodes from ancient

© LUKAS REDDEMANN, 2025 | DOI:10.1163/9789004694613_004

mythology, contemporary history, and, above all, the Bible.[1] Such plays were often modelled after examples from Roman antiquity, especially Terence's comedies and the Senecan tragedies.[2] There are few literary genres in which the power, layers, thresholds, and abysses of human emotions can be so extensively scrutinised, dissected and explored by both dramatists and their audiences. By visualizing love, rage, sorrow, and fear on stage, Neo-Latin drama also reacts and contributes to contemporary theoretical and philosophical debates on passions and affects (in Latin: *affectus*) and is relevant to two key discourses in particular: the revival of Aristotle's theory of tragedy in poetics from the early 16th century onward and the emergence of Neostoicism as a philosophical movement in the late 16th century. It has long been established that, in the early modern period, drama not only reflected contemporary theological and philosophical discourses, it actively and energetically participated in them.[3]

In the Dutch Republic, especially within the grounds of the University of Leiden, the production of academic Latin drama went hand in hand with researching its literary and philosophical traditions. The philologist Daniel Heinsius (1580–1655), for instance, published two Latin tragedies, on the

---

1 For a concise overview of Neo-Latin drama in the Low Countries, see Bloemendal J., "Neo-Latin Drama in the Low Countries", in Bloemendal J. – Norland H. (eds.), *Neo-Latin Drama and Theatre in Early Modern Europe*, Drama and Theatre in Early Modern Europe 3 (Leiden – Boston: 2013) 293–364. Furthermore: IJsewijn J., "Annales Theatri Belgico-Latini. Inventory of Latin Theatre from the Low Countries", in Tournoy G. (ed.), *Humanism in the Low Countries. Jozef IJsewijn*, Supplementa Humanistica Lovaniensia 40 (Leuven: 2015), 221–285. Idem, "Theatrum Belgo-Latinum. Het neolatijns toneel in de Nederlanden", *Mededelingen van de koninklijke academie voor wetenschappen, letteren en schone kunsten van België. Klasse der letteren* 43 (1981) 69–114. Parente J.A., *Religious Drama and the Humanist Tradition. Christian Theater in Germany and in the Netherlands 1500–1680*, Studies in the History of Christian Thought 39 (Leiden et al.: 1987). Bloemendal J., *Spiegel van het dagelijks leven? Latijnse school en toneel in de noorderlijke Nederlanden in de zestiende en de zeventiende eeuw*, Zeven Provinciënreeks 22 (Hilversum: 2003). Idem, "Receptions and Impact: Early Modern Latin Drama, its Effect on the Audience and its Role in Forming Public Opinion", in Idem – Ford P. (eds.), *Neo-Latin Drama. Forms, Functions, Receptions*, Noctes Neolatinae. Neo-Latin Texts and Studies 9 (Hildesheim – Zürich – New York: 2008), 7–22. Idem, "Similarities, Dissimilarities and Possible Relations Between Early Modern Latin Drama and Drama in the Vernacular", in Ford P. – Taylor A (eds.), *The Early Modern Cultures of Neo-Latin Drama*, Supplementa Humanistica Lovaniensia 32 (Leuven: 2013), 141–157.

2 Cf. e.g. Harst J., "Germany and the Netherlands: Tragic Seneca in Scholarship and on Stage", in Dodson-Robinson E. (ed.), *Brill's Companion to the Reception of Senecan Tragedy. Scholarly, Theatrical and Literary Receptions*, Brill's Companions to Classical Reception 5 (Leiden – Boston: 2016), 149–173.

3 Cf. e.g. Leo R., *Tragedy as Philosophy in the Reformation World* (Oxford: 2019). Kemper A., "Anger in the Jesuit Theatre of the 16th Century Discussions of affect in the tension between Christianity, Neo-Stoicism and Aristotelianism", *Daphnis* 43 (2015) 97–124.

assassination of William the Silent (*Auriacus sive libertas saucia*, 1602) and the Massacre of the Innocents (*Herodes infanticida*, 1632), in addition to an edition of Aristotle's *Poetics* together with his treatise *De tragoediae constitutione* (1611; 1643) on the theory of tragedy, and, finally, an edition of Seneca's tragedies (1611).[4] Heinsius' work resulted from a fruitful exchange with other Dutch dramatists in the first years of the 17th century. Almost all of them were acquainted and corresponded with each other and, above all, were very familiar with Aristotelian poetics and Neostoic philosophy. Heinsius and Hugo Grotius (1583–1645), for example, knew each other well from their time studying in Leiden, and regularly exchanged drafts of their Latin tragedies for feedback before having them printed.[5] In 1608, when Grotius published his passion play *Christus patiens*, Heinsius was busy writing his *Herodes infanticida* and preparing the edition of Seneca's dramas.[6] Heinsius also dedicated his *De tragoediae constitutione* to Rochus van den Honert (1572–1638), a Latin poet and public official from The Hague, who, for his part, dedicated his biblical tragedy *Thamara* to Heinsius and Grotius in the same year.[7] Jacob van Zevecote (Zevecotius, 1590–1642), the author of the tragedy *Rosimunda* (1621) about the Gepid princess Rosamund.[8] Van Zevecote, who was related to Heinsius and moved to Leiden in the 1620s, translated Heinsius' philosophical didactic poem *De contemptu mortis* (1621) into Dutch (*Verachtinge des doots*, 1625)

---

4 Heinsius Daniel, *Auriacus sive libertas saucia, accedunt eiusdem Iambi partim morales, partim ad amicos, partim amicorum causa scripti* (Leiden, Andries Cloucq: 1602). Quoted after the critical edition *Auriacus, sive Libertas saucia* (*Orange, or Liberty Wounded*), ed. J. Bloemendal (Leiden – Boston: 2020). Idem, *Herodes infanticida, tragoedia* (Leiden, Elzevir: 1632). Idem, *De tragoediae constitutione liber, in quo inter caetera tota de hac Aristotelis sententia dilucide explicatur* (Leiden, Ioannes Balduinus: 1611). Second edition: *De tragoediae constitutione liber, in quo inter caetera tota de hac Aristotelis sententia dilucide explicatur. Editio auctior multo, cui et Aristotelis de poetica libellus cum eiusdem notis et interpretatione accedit* (Leiden, Elzevir: 1643). *L. Annaei Senecae et aliorum tragoediae serio emendatae, cum Iosephi Scaligeri nunc primum ex autographo auctoris editis et Danielis Heinsii animadversionibus et notis* (Leiden, Hendrik van Haestens: 1611).

5 Cf. Bloemendal, "Neo-Latin Drama in the Low Countries" 348.

6 Grotius Hugo, *Tragoedia Christus patiens* (Leiden, Thomas Basson: 1608). He also published two other biblical tragedies: Grotius Hugo, *Sacra in quibus Adamus exul tragoedia aliorumque eiusdem generis carminum cumulus consecrata Franciae principi* (The Hague, Aelbrecht Hendricksz: 1601). Idem, *Tragoedia Sophompaneas, accesserunt tragoedia eiusdem Christus patiens et sacri argumenti alia, editio nova* (Amsterdam, Willem Blaeu: 1635). For an overview, see Eyffinger A., "Literary Writings", in Lesaffer R. – Nijman J.E. (eds.), *The Cambridge Companion to Hugo Grotius* (Cambridge: 2021), 293–314.

7 Honerdus Rochus, *Thamara, tragoedia* (Leiden, Joannes Patius: 1611).

8 *Rosimunda* was first published in 1621 but is henceforth cited from *Poematum editio nova* (Leiden, Andries Cloucq: 1625), 123–157. See below for more on the play.

and dedicated an edition of another Latin tragedy, *Maria Graeca* (1623), to Rochus van den Honert.[9] The tragedies in question here were all produced within this 'Leiden circle', a relatively close personal network centred around Heinsius.[10]

Although the full range of human emotions is staged both in classical and Neo-Latin tragedy, affects do not always manifest themselves in a clear and unambiguous form. Instead, they merge, blend, and come into conflict with one another. Thus, scholarly interest in ancient drama and the theory of affects also stimulated Dutch Neo-Latin dramatists to explore the scope and potential of such dubious, mixed, and transitional passions and emotions, as well as how they were visually represented on stage. This chapter examines these representations and their interrelations with the philosophical conceptions of affects based on several exemplary scenes from early 17th-century academic Latin tragedies. The first part of the chapter provides a brief overview of the (Neo-)Stoic theory of affects, the Aristotelian and Heinsian conceptions of affects in tragedy, and their interdependencies with Neo-Latin drama. This is followed by some case studies from van Zevecoten's *Rosimunda*, Honerdus' *Thamara*, and Heinsius' *Auriacus*. In my discussion, I highlight the significance of *motus mixti* in Neo-Latin drama regarding the poetic and philosophical conceptions of affects and their traditions. Furthermore, considering the close connection between motions of the body and inner affects sheds further light on the question of how mixed emotions were visualised on stage.

2 Neo-Stoic and Aristotelian Theories of Affects in Neo-Latin Drama

In Neo-Latin drama, the theoretical notion of affects is particularly relevant in two contexts. The first is the revival of the classical philosophical tradition of Stoicism during the late 16th century, a development usually described as

---

9   Heinsius Daniel, *De contemptu mortis libri IV ad nobilissimum amplissimumque virum Ianum Rutgersium* (Leiden, Elzevir: 1621). Zevecote Jacob van, *Verachtinge des doots int Latijn beschreven door den ed. ende wijtvermaerden Daniel Heinsius. Overgeset door Jacobus Zevecotius* (Leiden, Andries Cloucq: 1625). Cf. Becker-Contarino B., "Daniel Heinsius' *De contemptu mortis* und Opitz' *Trostgedichte*" in Becker-Contarino B. – Fechner J.-U. (eds.), *Opitz und seine Welt. Festschrift für George Schulz-Behrend zum 12. Februar 1988*, Chloe 10 (Amsterdam – Atlanta: 1990), 37–56, here 37–45. Dedication to van den Honert in Zevecote, *Poematum editio nova* 84. On the complex editing history of *Maria Graeca* see IJsewijn J., "Jacobus Zevecotius. Maria Stuarta / Maria Graeca, tragoedia. A Synoptic Edition of the Five Extant Versions", *Humanistica Lovaniensia* 22 (1973) 256–319.

10   Cf. Bloemendal, "Neo-Latin Drama in the Low Countries" 348.

'Neo-Stoicism'. Like its ancient precursor, Neo-Stoicism generally regarded virtue (*virtus/honestum*) as the supreme and only moral good that can be attained through reason (*ratio*). For the Stoics, it is reason that enables the wise man to conduct a good life not only by enabling him to comprehend true virtue, but also by empowering him to dismiss emotional affects and, thus, control his passions.[11] The turbulent times of the French Wars of Religion and the Dutch Revolt prompted general interest in a philosophical teaching that promised to give the individual independence from challenging external conditions. Two key writings in this regard were *De constantia* (1584) by the Flemish humanist Justus Lipsius (1547–1606) and *De la constance et consolation* by the French lawyer Guillaume du Vair (1556–1621).[12] Both works were closely associated with the contemporary political and military troubles. The setting of *De constantia* is based on Lipsius' actual journey to Vienna in 1572 when he fled from the Netherlands during the beginning of the Dutch Revolt. He presents himself during a visit to Carolus Langius (Karel de Langhe, 1521–1573) in Liège where the two men hold a conversation on Stoic values. Du Vair actually wrote his *De la constance* during the devastating Siege of Paris in 1590.

When it comes to the reception and adaptation of the ancient Stoic tradition, Neo-Stoicism focuses on some aspects more than others. In general, of the three fields that the ancient Stoic tradition developed theoretical approaches on – logic, physics, and ethics – Neo-Stoic writers set a clear focus on the latter. In terms of influential texts, Neo-Stoicism concentrates on the so-called 'Later Stoicism' (1st and 2nd centuries), represented by works such as the *Discourses* and the *Enchiridion*, which are, in turn, based on the teachings of the Greek Stoic Epictetus (1st/2nd century) and, above all, the *Epistulae morales* and the *Dialogi* by the Roman philosopher Seneca.[13] Neo-Stoics committed themselves

---

11 Abel G., *Stoizismus und Frühe Neuzeit. Zur Entstehungsgeschichte modernen Denkens im Felde von Ethik und Politik* (Berlin – New York: 1978), 7–42 provides a concise overview of Stoic teachings in early modern times. For an extensive overview of Stoic moral philosophy and the Stoic theory of emotions, see Graver M., *Stoicism and Emotion* (Chicago – London: 2007), for a shorter overview see e.g. Kraye J., "Moral Philosophy", in Schmitt C.B. et al. (eds.), *The Cambridge History of Renaissance Philosophy* (Cambridge: 1988), 303–386, here 360–367.

12 Lipsius Justus, *De constantia libri duo, qui alloquium praecipue continent in publicis malis* (Antwerp, Christoffel Plantijn: 1584). On the work, see Oestreich G., *Neostoicism and the Early Modern State* (Cambridge et al.: 1982), 13–27. Vair Guillaume du, *De la constance et consolation és calamitez publiques* (Paris, Mamert Patisson: 1594). On du Vair's stoicism see Radouant R., *Guillaume du Vair. L'homme et l'orateur jusqu'à la fin des troubles de la Ligue (1556–1596)* (Paris: 1907) and Abel, *Stoizismus und Frühe Neuzeit* 114–152.

13 The *Discourses* were not written by Epictetus, but are transcripts of his lectures given in Nicopolis, made by his pupil Arrianus. The *Enchiridion* is an epitome of the *Discourses* but

to making such works widely accessible and outlining them: Lipsius published a complete edition of the philosophical works of Seneca (1605), as well as two introductory treatises on Stoic philosophy based on the Senecan writings, the *Manductio ad Stoicam philosophiam* and the *Physiologia Stoicorum* (both 1604).[14] Guillaume du Vair published the treatise *La philosophie morale des Stoiques* and a translation of Epictetus' *Enchiridion* (*Le Manuel d'Épictète*).[15] Although ties and distinctions between the Stoic and Christian traditions have been regularly discussed since the time of the Church fathers (such as St. Augustine), Neo-Stoic authors made fresh attempts to reconcile both, especially as Stoic teachings were by no means unchallenged during the 16th century.[16]

The Stoic and Neo-Stoic theory of passion and emotions, a core element of Stoic moral philosophy, is based on the concept of affects. Latin texts use either the term *affectus* or, in the Ciceronian tradition, *perturbationes animi*.[17] Early modern readers became acquainted with the concepts not only through the *Epistulae morales* and the *Dialogues* by Seneca, but also through the accounts of Stoic teachings in Cicero's *De finibus bonorum et malorum* and, in particular, the *Tusculanae disputationes*.[18] Stoics considered affects to be excessive movements of the soul which are not controlled by *ratio* and therefore take control over a person or, as Langius puts it in Lipsius' *De constantia*, "Your affects won't

---

    turned out to be by far more influential in the reception of Epictetus. For an overview of his works and their reception, see Boter G., "Epictetus", in Brown V. – Hankins J. – Kaster R.A. (eds.), *Catalogus Translationum et Commentariorum: Mediaeval and Renaissance Latin Translations and Commentaries vol. IX* (Washington: 2019), 1–54.

14   *L. Annaei Senecae philosophi opera quae exstant omnia a Justo Lipsio emendata et scholiis illustrata* (Antwerp, Jan Moretus: 1605). *Manductionis ad Stoicam philosophiam libri tres L. Annaeo Senecae aliisque scriptoribus illustrandis* (Paris, Hadrian Perier: 1604). *Physiologiae Stoicorum libri tres L. Annaeo Senecae aliisque scriptoribus illustrandis* (Antwerp, Jan Moretus: 1604).

15   The early printing history of du Vair's writings is not entirely clear. The *Manuel d'Épictète* was often printed together with *La philosophie morale des Stoiques*. With the exception of *De la constance*, his works seem to have been written prior to April 1584 (cf. Abel, *Stoizismus und Frühe Neuzeit* 114), although printed later, most probably during the second half of the 1580s. There was a bibliographic discussion about the first printing dates of the *Manuel d'Épictète* in particular, however, there were no clear results, cf. Radouant R., "Recherches bibliographiques sur Guillaume Du Vair et correspondance inédite", *Revue d'Histoire littéraire de la France* 6.2 (1899) 253–266. Giraud V., "Sur Guillaume du Vair. Notes bibliographiques", *Revue d'Histoire littéraire de la France* 13.2 (1906) 317–321. Radouant, *Guillaume du Vair* 130–131; 144.

16   Cf. Kraye, "Moral Philosophy" 367–370.

17   Cf. Cicero, *Tusculanae disputationes*, III, 7.

18   Idem, *De finibus bonorum et malorum*, III, 35 and *Tusculanae disputationes*, III.

EMOTIONS IN 17TH-CENTURY NEO-LATIN DRAMA 111

follow your lead, but rather drag you away".[19] Pleasure (*voluptas/gaudium*), desire (*cupiditas/libido*), fear (*metus*), and grief (*aegritudo/dolor*) are usually the four main classes into which other affects are then classified.[20] Anger, for instance, is merely a variant of *libido*, as, according to Aristotle and Cicero, anger is ultimately a desire for revenge (*ulciscendi libido*).[21] According to the Stoics, the best way to handle passions and emotions is to fully eliminate affects altogether. The ideal Stoic sage is therefore a person who achieved *apatheia*, a state of mind rendering the person completely untouched by affects and who is, therefore, independent of any form of disturbance caused by them, and free from unfavourable external circumstances that may give rise to affects. This aspect constitutes an important connection between the Neo-Stoic theory of affect and the political troubles of the late 16th century and is also prominently expressed in Lipsius' *De constantia*: "We should not escape from our home country, but rather from our affects. We should strengthen and prepare our mind in a way that we find rest amidst troubles and peace amidst war".[22]

It is on the proper handling of affects that the Stoics are fundamentally different from the Peripatetic school. According to Aristotle, passions should merely be contained, not avoided altogether and, if necessary, reduced to a level that is appropriate to the cause and the circumstances.[23] One of the Stoics's and Neo-Stoics's most effective rhetorical instruments to defend their conception was the imagery of affects as mental diseases (*morbus/aegritudo animi*).[24] In his famous *Epistle* 116, for instance, Seneca argues, "The question has often been raised whether it is better to have moderate emotions, or none at all. Philosophers of our school reject the emotions; the Peripatetics keep

---

19   Lipsius, *De constantia* 7: "non sequentur te adfectus tui, sed trahent".

20   Cf. Cicero, *Tusculanae disputationes*, III, 24–25 and Lipsius, *De constantia* 19.

21   Cicero, *Tusculanae disputationes*, III, 11. Aristotle, *Rhetoric*, II, 2. For on instructive overview of the single affects grouped under these four n the Stoic tradition, see Graver, *Stoicism and Emotion* 55–59.

22   Lipsius, *De constantia* 3: "Itaque non patria fugienda, Lipsi, sed adfectus sunt, et firmandus ita formandusque hic animus, ut quies nobis in turbis sit et pax inter media arma".

23   Cf. Aristotle, *Nicomachean Ethics*, II, 2–4.

24   Cf. e.g. Cicero, *De finibus bonorum et malorum*, I, 59 ("animi morbi sunt cupiditates inmensae et inanes"), quoted after Cicero, *On Ends*, Loeb Classical Library 40, ed. H. Rackham (Cambridge: 1914). Idem, *Tusculanae disputationes*, III, 7–8 ("Num reliquae quoque perturbationes animi, formidines, libidines, iracundiae? Haec enim fere sunt eius modi, quae Graeci πάθη appellant; ego poteram morbos et id verbum esset e verbo, sed in consuetudinem nostram non caderet: nam misereri, invidere, gestire, laetari, haec omnia morbos Graeci appellant, motus animi rationi non obtemperantes; nos autem hos eosdem motus concitati animi recte, ut opinor, perturbationes dixerimus, morbos autem non satis usitate, nisi quid aliud tibi videtur"). Quoted after Cicero, *Tusculan Disputations*, Loeb Classical Library 141, ed. J.E. King (Cambridge: 1927).

them in check. I, however, do not understand how any half-way disease can be either wholesome or helpful".[25] This imagery remained significant in Neo-Stoic writings and may have been represented best by the title and scope of Johann Weyer's (1515/16–1588) *De ira morbo* (1577), an early Neo-Stoic treatise on the affect of anger and its therapy.[26] Adhering to this imagery, philosophy in general and Stoicism, in particular, can be depicted as "remedy" for affects, as is done, by Petrarch in his *De remediis* and Lipsius in *De constantia*.[27]

This conception, however, does not mean that the ideal Stoic sage is devoid of any form of emotion at all. In a key passage at the beginning of the second book of his *De ira*, Seneca differentiates between affects and "sensations that do not result from our own volition" (*motus, qui non voluntate nostra fiunt*) or "things which move the mind through the agency of chance" (*quae animum fortuito impellunt*).[28] All humans experience spontaneous sensations that are beyond their control, including goosebumps, impulses of sorrow after being insulted, and spontaneous compassion. However, these reactions are not affects but merely "the beginnings that are preliminary to passions" (*principia*

---

25 Seneca, *Epistle* 116, 1: "Utrum satius sit modicos habere adfectus an nullos, saepe quaesitum est. Nostri illos expellunt, Peripatetici temperant. Ego non video, quomodo salubris esse aut utilis possit ulla mediocritas morbi". Text and translation here and henceforth quoted after Seneca, *Epistles, Volume III: Epistles 93–124*, Loeb Classical Library 77, ed. R.M. Gummere (Cambridge: 1925). Cf. also Seneca, *De ira*, I, 10: "modicus affectus nihil aliud quam malum modicum est". Here and henceforth quoted after Seneca, *Moral Essays, Vol. I: De Providentia. De Constantia. De Ira. De Clementia*, Loeb Classical Library 214, ed. J.W. Basore (Cambridge: 1928).

26 Weyer Johann, *De ira morbo, eiusdem curatione philosophica, medica et theologica liber* (Basel, Johannes Oporinus: 1577). On the work and its contexts, see Enenkel K.A.E., "Neo-Stoicism as an Antidote to Public Violence before Lipsius's *De constantia*: Johann Weyer's (Wier's) Anger Therapy, *De ira morbo* (1577)", in Enenkel K.A.E. – Traninger A. (eds.), *Discourses of Anger in the Early Modern Period*, Intersections 40 (Leiden – Boston: 2015), 49–96. Idem, "Neo-Stoicism before Lipsius: Johann Weyer's *De ira morbo* (1577)", *Neulateinisches Jahrbuch* 19 (2017) 125–155.

27 For *De remediis* and Neo-Stoicism, cf. e.g. Kraye J., "Stoicism in the Renaissance from Petrarch to Lipsius", *Grotiana* 22–23 (2001) 21–45, here 23–25. Examples for the imagery of "sickness" and "remedy" in *De constantia* include 4 ("Ut ii, qui febriunt, iactant se inquiete et versant et lectum subinde mutant vana spe lenamenti, in eadem causa nos, qui terram e terra frustra mutamus, aegri scilicet mentis. Aperire enim hoc est morbum, non tollere, fateri internum hunc calorem, non mederi").

28 Seneca, *De ira*, II, 2–3. Cf. e.g. Konstan D., "Senecan Emotions", in Bartsch S. – Schiesaro A. (eds.), *The Cambridge Companion to Seneca* (Cambridge: 2015), 174–184, esp. 174–179. Graver, *Stoicism and Emotion* 93–99. For Seneca's model and Lipsius' reception of it, see Papy J., "Neostoic Anger: Lipsius's Reading and Use of Seneca's Tragedies and *De ira*", in Enenkel K.A.E. – Traninger A. (eds.), *Discourses of Anger in the Early Modern Period*, Intersections 40 (Leiden – Boston: 2015), 126–142, esp. 131–138.

EMOTIONS IN 17TH-CENTURY NEO-LATIN DRAMA

proludentia adfectibus).[29] Lipsius, for instance, adopted the concept in his *De constantia* and distinguishes affects from the "small first movements" (*commotiunculae*) that are physical rather than affective reactions.[30] As is shown below, the distinction between a first impulse (*impetus, commotiuncula*) and fully developed affect (*affectus*) is paramount and repeatedly referred to in classical as well as Neo-Latin drama. An affect in the proper sense "does not consist in being moved by the impressions that are presented to the mind, but in surrendering to these and following up such a chance prompting".[31] According to Seneca, anger, for instance, is thus "a weakness of the mind" (*animi vitium*) and can be "aroused only with the assent of the mind" (*animo ... adsentiente*).[32] This specification is crucial for the Stoic conception of passions as they believe that affects do not just befall humans but are the result of a conscious (albeit imprudent) decision to surrender to natural impulses and therefore allow excessive passions to take control.[33] Early modern readers were perfectly acquainted with this conception, not least because of writings such as Lipsius' *Manductio*, which quotes, among others, Seneca's *Epistle* 116 and the second book of *De ira* to elucidate the notion of affect and the concept of *apatheia*.[34]

In his *De ira*, Seneca also addresses the question of contrasting and conflicting affects in the context of the Stoic theory of emotions. Based again on the distinction between a first impulse and a full affect, he argues that the best way to deal with anger is to resist its very first impulse (*primum irritamentum irae protinus spernere*) and not let it develop to the point that the affect takes full control and reason has no effect.[35] It is true, he continues, that sometimes, people do not follow their first impulse and retaliate against their opponents, not because reason prevails but because conflicting affects, such as fear or desire, push the anger back. If anger does not lead to immediate action in such cases, it is not due to the power of reason, but because one affect is fighting

---

29   Seneca, *De ira*, II, 2.

30   Lipsius, *De constantia* 6.

31   Seneca, *De ira*, II, 3: "Nihil ex his, quae animum fortuito impellunt, adfectus vocari debet; ista, ut ita dicam, patitur magis animus quam facit. Ergo adfectus est non ad oblatas rerum species moveri, sed permittere se illis et hunc fortuitum motum prosequi".

32   Ibidem, II, 1–2.

33   For a stimulating modern approach to this point of view, see Nussbaum M.C., *Upheavals of Thought. The Intelligence of Emotions* (Cambridge: 2001), 19–88.

34   Cf. Lipsius, *Manductio* 121–130.

35   Seneca, *De ira*, I, 8: "Optimum est primum irritamentum irae protinus spernere ipsisque repugnare seminibus et dare operam, ne incidamus in iram. Nam si coepit ferre transversos, difficilis ad salutem recursus est, quoniam nihil rationis est, ubi semel adfectus inductus est iusque illi aliquod voluntate nostra datum est; faciet de cetero quantum volet, non quantum permiseris".

against another (*affectus repercussit affectum*), a situation which Seneca calls "a treacherous and evil agreement between the passions".[36] This statement is remarkable as it makes it clear that, according to the Stoic theory of emotions, people are not primarily judged on their actions, but on their affective attitude towards their actions. According to the Stoic conception, conflicting affects are just another state in which *ratio* no longer prevails and which is to be rejected, regardless of the actions the state might result in.

Neo-Latin drama referenced the Stoic theory of emotions time and again. For example, the Stoic metaphor of affects as illnesses of the mind was already omnipresent in Latin school comedies in the 16th century. In later tragedies, single scenes are often designed as philosophical dialogues about affects and their significance. Even more importantly, the Stoic sage served as an ideal against which characters could be morally measured. For the dramatists discussed in this chapter, the theoretical approach to emotions takes the Stoic concept of *affects* as it was outlined in the works of Cicero, Seneca, Epictetus, and Lipsius as its starting point.[37] The different branches of the reception of Seneca during the 16th century and their interdependencies stimulated the discussion of (Neo-)Stoic concepts in Neo-Latin drama in particular. It was only during the revival of philological interest in the Senecan works during the 16th century that it was acknowledged that the author who wrote the corpus of tragedies (*Seneca tragicus*) was actually the same person who authored the philosophical treatises (*Seneca philosophus*).[38]

The second theoretical framework in which affects play a vital role is the Aristotelian theory of tragedy. Above all, Aristotle's concept of *katharsis*, first outlined in his *Poetics*, still stimulates and fascinates commentators and theorists today. *Katharsis* is usually understood as a process in which spectators of

---

36 Ibidem: "'Quid ergo? Non aliquando in ira quoque et dimittunt incolumes intactosque quos oderunt et a nocendo abstinent?' Faciunt. Quando? Cum adfectus repercussit adfectum et aut metus aut cupiditas aliquid impetravit. Non rationis tunc beneficio quievit, sed affectuum infida et mala pace". Cf. Wiener C., *Stoische Doktrin in römischer Belletristik. Das Problem von Entscheidungsfreiheit und Determinismus in Senecas Tragödien und Lucans Pharsalia*, Beiträge zur Altertumskunde 226 (München – Leipzig: 2006), 36–37.

37 In contrast to more recent interpretations of the affects, cf. e.g. Trigg S., "Affect Theory", in Broomhall S. (ed.), *Early Modern Emotions. An Introduction* (London – New York: 2017), 10–13.

38 For an overview of the debate on *Seneca philosophus* and *Seneca tragicus*, see Mayer R., "Personata Stoa. Neostoicism and Senecan Tragedy", *Journal of the Warburg and Courtauld Institutes* 57 (1994) 151–174. For an overview of relations between Seneca's tragic and philosophical work, see Trinacty C., "Senecan Tragedy", in Bartsch S. – Schiesaro A. (edd.), *The Cambridge Companion to Seneca* (Cambridge: 2015), 29–40, here 36–38.

EMOTIONS IN 17TH-CENTURY NEO-LATIN DRAMA 115

tragedy are purified of emotions by watching tragic events on stage that arouse those emotions, in particular, pity (ἔλεος/eleos) and fear (φόβος/phobos).[39] However, there is a fundamental problem in that, despite its remarkable later popularity, Aristotle never explicitly defined the term *katharsis* meaning that the term remains open to interpretation. Thus, the question of what "purification" actually involved led to a lively debate among 16th century-commentators on Aristotle.[40] The central question was whether *katharsis* purifies the affects by reducing them to an appropriate level or whether it purifies the audience from certain affects altogether.[41] What is most important in our context is that the idea of *katharsis* not only presupposes the affective involvement of the audience, but also that the very act of watching tragic events is capable of arousing and, in a sense, modifying affects.

The most important stimulus for the reception of Aristotelian poetics in the Dutch Republic and soon in the whole of Northern Europe was Daniel Heinsius' treatise *De tragoediae constitutione*, published in Leiden in 1611.[42] Heinsius did not write a commentary on Aristotle's *Poetics*, rather he gave a continuous account of its main ideas, often with additional explanations or clarifications. In the second chapter, he turns to the concept of *katharsis*. For Heinsius, the purpose of tragedy is to arouse affects, then moderate and settle them. In accordance with Aristotle, he names two primary affects: fear and pity, which he translates as *horror* and *misericordia*. It becomes clear that Heinsius' understanding of this process is closely connected to the Peripatetic theory of emotions. The objective of *katharsis* is not to avoid or even eliminate

---

39   Cf. Aristotle, *Poetics*, 6. Among the numerous research contributions on the Aristotelian *katharsis* and its interpretations, see e.g. Halliwell S., *Between Ecstasy and Truth. Interpretations of Greek Poetics from Homer to Longinus* (Oxford: 2012), 208–265.

40   See Kappl B., *Die Poetik des Aristoteles in der Dichtungstheorie des Cinquecento*, Untersuchungen zur antiken Literatur und Geschichte 83 (Berlin – New York: 2006), 266–311. Lohse R., "The Early Reception of Aristotelian Poetics", *Horizonte. Neue Serie* 2 (2017) 38–58. Brazeau B., "Emotional History and Early Modern Readings of Aristotle's Poetics", in Idem, *The Reception of Aristotle's Poetics in the Italian Renaissance and Beyond: New Directions in Criticism* (London: 2020), 201–226.

41   Cf. Kappl, *Poetik des Aristoteles* 266–311.

42   On the work, see Meter J.H., *Literary Theories of Daniel Heinsius. A Study of the Development and Background of his Views on Literary Theory and Criticism During the Period from 1602 to 1612*, Republica Literaria Neerlandica 6 (Assen: 1984), 137–270. Somos M., *Secularisation and the Leiden Circle* (Leiden – Boston: 2011), 104–150. Russ, *Tragedy as Philosophy* 167–206. On affects in theoretical approaches to tragedy in the 17th century in general, see Zeller R., "Tragödientheorie, Tragödienpraxis und Leidenschaften", in Steiger J.A. (ed.), *Passion, Affekt und Leidenschaft in der Frühen Neuzeit*, Wolfenbütteler Arbeiten zur Barockforschung 43, 2 vols. (Wiesbaden: 2005), vol. II, 691–704, here 693–699.

affects altogether but to reduce their intensity to a reasonable level.[43] This interpretation is most like the approach followed by the Italian humanist Francesco Robortello (1516–1567) in his commentary on Aristotle (1548), as others construed some kind of Stoic *katharsis* more as a means to avert affects.[44] Therefore, in accordance with Robortello, Heinsius presents the idea of a habituation effect. By watching things on stage that arouse certain affects, a spectator can become increasingly accustomed to them and, thus, exercise. Heinsius gives the example of a person heavily injured in a war. Seeing such wounds would normally cause shock and compassion in others, whereas a surgeon, who would be used to seeing such things, is affected to a far lesser extent. Therefore, employing the metaphor of physical training, Heinsius refers to theatre as a "training ground of human affects" (*affectuum humanorum palaestra*).[45]

The Dutch scholar-dramatists reflected Stoic and Aristotelian conceptions of passions and emotions in their tragedies in multiple ways and applied them to situations that involved *motus mixti*. As will be seen, this holds true for all kinds of tragic subject-matter, whether it be biblical, mythological, or historical. The following case studies clarify how dramatists referred to particular theories of affects, how their application helped to interpret a character's situation, and how affects – both individual and mixed – were visualised in texts and on stage.

---

43 Heinsius, *De tragoediae constitutione* 20–21: "Sequitur usus tragoediae et finis. Quippe in concitandis affectibus cum maxime versetur haec Musa, finem eius esse, hos ipsos ut temperet iterumque componat, Aristoteles putavit. Affectus propria illius sunt duo, misericordia et horror. Quos cum excitet in animo, paulatim quoque efferentes sese, deprimit, quemadmodum oportet, et in ordinem cogit. Hoc vero expiationem affectuum sive perturbationum Aristoteles vocavit".

44 Robortello Francesco, *In librum Aristotelis de arte poetica explicationes* (Florence, Lorenzo Torrentino: 1548). Cf. Kappl, *Poetik des Aristoteles* 269–274. Meter, *Literary Theories* 170–174.

45 Heinsius, *De tragoediae constitutione* 22–23: "Nam ut artem quandam perficit quemadmodum oportet, qui illius usum longa sibi actione comparavit, ita obiectorum quibus excitari in animo affectus solent, assuetudine quadam mediocritatem eorum induci. Hominem crudeliter in bello vulneratum qui videt, horret, miseret, sui vix est compos. Accedat chirurgus longo usu non modo ut oportet admovet manum, sed nec magis commovetur, quam oportet. Medicus aegrum primo cum accedit, vehementer tangitur, donec habitus affectum temperat et artem. Tyro hostem metuit ac horret, donec veteranus animo et affectu consistit. Ita qui miserias frequenter spectat, miseratur, et quidem ut oportet. Qui frequenter ea quae horrorem movent intuetur, minus tandem horret et ut decet. Talia autem in theatro exhibentur, quod affectuum humanorum quaedam quasi est palaestra".

3   Applying the Stoic Analysis of Affects: Zevecotius, *Rosimunda*

Neo-Latin dramatists frequently applied the Stoic theory of affects and its terminology as an analytic tool to explore separate, shifting, and conflicting emotions of individual characters. The work of Jacob van Zevecote is interesting in this regard and, therefore, is our first case study. Born in Gent in the Southern Netherlands, he studied law in Leuven and also lived in Rome for a time. In the early 1620s, however, he moved to the Dutch Republic, where he visited his relative Daniel Heinsius in Leiden, converted to Protestantism, and then became a professor at the academy of Harderwijk.[46] Zevecotius was a prolific writer: In addition to volumes of poems in Dutch and in Latin, he published an emblem book (*Emblemata ofte Sinnebeelden*, 1626), two political commentaries on the works of the Roman historians Suetonius and Florus, two tragedies on the Spanish siege of Leiden in Dutch (*Belegh van Leyden*, 1626; *Ontset van Leyden*, 1630), and three Latin dramas: A tragedy on the wife of the Byzantine Emperor Constantine VII (*Maria Graeca*, 1623), a tragicomedy on the Jewish queen Esther (*Esther*, 1621 or 1623), and his tragedy *Rosimunda* (1621).[47] In the case of *Rosimunda*, van Zevevote presented the story of the Gepid princess Rosamund, which emerged in late antiquity but was mainly known from medieval chronicles.[48] Rosamund's father Cunimund, King of the Gepids, was

---

46   For overviews of van Zevecote's biography and works, see IJsewijn, "Jacobus Zevecotius" 258–264. Parente J.A., "Latin and the Transmission of the Vernacular. Multilingualism and Interculturality in the Tragedies of Jacob Zevecotius", *Renaissance Studies* 36.1 (2022) 104–121, here 104–116.

47   Zevecote Jacob van, *Emblemata ofte sinnebeelden met dichten verciert, door Jacobus Zevecotius. Item noch andere dichten van den selven* (Leiden, Bonaventura and Abraham Elzevir: 1626). Repr. Amsterdam, Johannes Janssonius: 1638. Idem, *Observata politica ad C. Suetonii Tranquilli Iulium Caesarem* (Amsterdam, Johannes Janssonius: 1630). Repr. 1637. Idem, *Lucii Annaei Flori rerum Romanarum libri IV, accedunt Jacobi Zevecotii observationes maxime politicae* (Amsterdam, Nicolaes van Wieringen: 1633). Idem, *Belegh van Leyden. Treur-spel* (Leiden, Bonaventura and Abraham Elzevir: 1626). Repr. 1632. Idem, *Ontset van Leyden. Bly-eindich spel* (Harderwijck, Nicolaes van Wieringen: 1630). Copies of this play are rare, but it is edited in Idem, *Gedichten van Jacob van Zevecote*, ed. J.P. Blommaert (Gent – Rotterdam: 1840), 279–337. IJsewijn, "Jacobus Zevecotius" 264 mentions a second edition of *Rosimunda* that also included *Esther*, however, no copies of this version are known. The first verifiable print is the third edition of van Zevecote's *Poemata* (Antwerp, Gerardus Wolfschatius: 1623).

48   Gregory of Tours, *Historiae*, IV, 41 (in this account, Rosamund remains nameless). Edited as Gregory of Tours, *Libri historiarum X*, Monumenta Germaniae historica. Scriptores rerum Merovingicarum 1.1, ed. B. Krusch – Levison W. (Hannover: 1951). Peter the Deacon, *Historia Langobardorum*, II, 28. Edited as Paul the Deacon, *Pauli historia Langobardorum*, Monumenta Germaniae historica. Scriptores rerum Germanicarum 48, ed. L. Bethmann – G. Waitz (Hannover: 1878). Van Zevecote probably became acquainted with the topic

FIGURE 3.1 Peter Paul Rubens (workshop of), *Alboin and Rosamund*, painted ca. 1615. Oil on canvas, 202 × 132 cm. Vienna, Kunsthistorisches Museum. Public Domain

killed by Alboin, King of the Lombards. Alboin then forced Rosamund to marry him, had her dead father's skull reworked into a chalice, and ultimately forced Rosamund to drink from it. The scene in which she drinks from the skull was also depicted in a painting from the workshop of Peter Paul Rubens a few years before van Zevecote's tragedy was published in 1621 [Fig. 3.1]. In response, Rosamund takes revenge by allying herself with Alboin's servant Helmiges and having him kill her husband.

Although the scene in which Rosamund drinks from the skull is the most famous episode of the story, van Zevecote also includes the events that followed. Rosamund and Helmiges marry and flee to the court of the Byzantine exarch Longinus who also wants to take Rosamund as his wife and successfully wins her over. However, when she attempted to kill Helmiges by poisoning

through a work on early medieval kingdoms in Italy, Puteanus Erycius, *Historiae insubricae libri VI, qui irruptiones Barbarorum in Italiam continent. Rerum ab origine gentis ad Othonem M. epitome* (Louvain, Jean Christophe Flavius: 1614). Cf. Parente, "Transmission of the Vernacular" 112. On the Rosamund story in French drama in the 17th century, see Ding R., "Les quatre *Rosemonde* du XVIIe siècle, ou le tyrannicide châtié: évolution et impasse d'un sujet", *Dix-septième siècle* 284 (2019) 515–532. Meere M., "On Specters and Skulls: Rosamund and Alboin in Seventeenth-Century French Tragedy", in Lyons J.D. (ed.), *The Dark Thread. From Tragical Histories to Gothic Tales* (Newark: 2019), 129–148.

EMOTIONS IN 17TH-CENTURY NEO-LATIN DRAMA

him, he saw through her and made her drink from the poisoned wine as well, and both eventually died. Even if it provides suitable material, the plot's structure does not actually fit the criteria of unity within a tragedy in terms of actions and time outlined by Aristotle and Heinsius. There is not only a time gap between Rosamund's two crimes, they also lack a direct causal link – therefore, strictly speaking, van Zevecote includes two tragic plots in one tragedy. He is, however, perfectly aware of this and states in a 1625 edition of the play, "Dear reader, a warning in advance: the laws of tragedy are not always obeyed within the *Rosimunda*".[49] He then explains that those who encouraged him to write the play also urged him to include both crimes, "To satisfy them, I decided to depart from the Aristotelian norm in this case".[50] There is, therefore, little doubt that van Zevecote had Heinsius and his *De tragoediae constitutione* in mind. His statement is also evidence that works on the Aristotelian theory of tragedy circulated within the network of Dutch scholar-dramatists and that they also assumed their readers would be familiar with it.

Rosimunda contains numerous scenes in which mixed emotions come into play, featuring the protagonist herself in particular. For example, van Zevecote focusses on Rosamund's affective involvement when she plans to take revenge upon Alboin after he killed her father. Thus, it comes as no surprise that she is furious at her husband but her fury is intertwined with affection for her deceased father. In the very first scene of the play, her father Cunimund appears to her as a ghost, seeking retribution. After directly addressing Alboin and announcing Rosamund's imminent vengeance, he turns to his daughter:

> Perge genitoris sui,
> Rosimunda, vindex, crimini tanto parem
> Concipe dolorem, coniugem totam exue
> Et si quis usquam patris occisi tuis
> Amor medullis restat et pie furit,
> Succedat orbae convenit natae furor.

You, Rosamund, go forward as your father's avenger, suffer a pain equal to this enormous crime and give up your role as a wife. And if there is still

---

49   Van Zevecote, *Rosimunda* 124: "Praemoneo te, amice lector, in Rosimunda tragoediae leges servatas non esse".

50   Ibidem: "Cum enim illi, quorum impulsu et primum hoc meum opus et poeticam suscepi, utrumque Rosimundae scelus in scena exprimi vellent, malui ab Aristotelica norma ea vice deflectere, ut iis satisfacerem, a quorum iudicio tunc pendere videbar".

any affection for your slain father in your heart, which rages justly, it shall rightly be followed by an orphaned daughter's rage.[51]

His argument spans several affective levels. He urges her to feel a sorrow (*concipe dolorem*) intense enough that it was appropriate to the heinous crime that Alboin committed against her father and herself. Therefore, it is necessary that Rosamund responds in her role as his daughter, rather than as Alboin's wife (*coniugem totam exue*).[52] He then concludes that her affection (*amor*) for him rightly leads to fury and rage (*pie furit* and *succedat furor*). For Cunimund, the link between *amor* and the desire for revenge is inherent in the relationship between father and daughter as he makes clear in his conclusive appeal: "Prove yourself as avenger and daughter of your father".[53] Within the interplay of different emotions that Cunimund refers to, *furor* is doubtlessly the privileged one while sorrow and affection are supposed to intensify Rosamund's rage and, ultimately, make her take her revenge.

Later, in a conversation with her maid Diletta, Rosamund confesses her murder plot. Although Diletta at least tries to dissuade her from carrying out the plan, Rosamund insists:

> *Rosimunda*: Nil humile tot sceleribus offensam decet
> Agitare natam, totus armetur dolor,
> Tuoque cuncta secula exemplo sciant
> Quid possit orbae strenuus natae furor,
> Quid laesa coniux. *Diletta*: Siste furialem impetum
> Tibique frenos iniice. *Rosimunda*: Invisum caput.
> Vah Alboine! *Diletta*: Nimius expiret dolor.
> *Rosimunda*: Expiret Alboinus. *Diletta*: At primum dolor,
> Dum saniora ratio consilia ingerat
> Et aliqua luctum minuat immensum dies.
> *Rosimunda*: Diletta, tu dolere Rosimundam vetas?
> Non tardus adeo concitat fibras amor
> Caesi parentis.

---

51 Ibidem, 129.

52 For *exuere* in the sense of "cease to act as", cf. Seneca, *Epistulae morales*, 95, 21 ("Beneficium sexus sui vitiis perdiderunt et, quia feminam exuerant, damnatae sunt morbis virilibus") and Valerius Maximus, *Dicta et facta memorabilia*, V, 8, 1 ("exuit patrem, ut consulem ageret"). Quoted after Valerius Maximus, *Memorable Doings and Sayings*, Loeb Classical Library 492–493, ed. D.R. Shackleton Bailey, 2 vols. (Cambridge: 2000).

53 Van Zevecote, *Rosimunda* 129: "Tu te parentis vindicem et natam proba".

Rosamund: When a daughter has to suffer so many atrocities, it is fitting for her to set something significant in motion. All your sorrow will equip you to do so and through your example, all subsequent generations shall understand what an orphaned daughter's, what an offended wife's turbulent rage is capable of. *Diletta*: Stop this impulse of rage and rein yourself in. *Rosamund*: This hateful face! Ah, Alboin! *Diletta*: Your excessive sorrow ought to perish. *Rosamund*: It is Alboin who ought to perish! *Diletta*: But first your sorrow. Meanwhile, reason will come up with better advice and someday, your grief might be alleviated. *Rosamund*: Diletta, do you really forbid me, Rosamund, to feel sorrow? As my affection for my slain father sets me in heavy motion deep inside.[54]

Throughout the dialogue, we observe the same intertwining of sorrow (*dolor*), rage (*furor*), and affection (*amor*) that characterised Cunimund's speech to his daughter. In the meantime, however, Alboin had forced her to drink from her dead father's skull and thus offended her as both Cunimund's daughter and as his own wife. Therefore, there is no longer any need to differentiate between the two roles: The upcoming *furor* is the reaction to both of Alboin's insults. Moreover, the dialogue between Rosamund and Diletta makes a textbook example of the attempt for Stoic guidance in a confrontation over whether to follow reason or indulge affects. Diletta advises her mistress to contain her rage and to listen to *ratio*, the supreme Stoic good. Furthermore, Diletta does not talk of rage, but only an "impulse to rage" which is a reference to the Senecan distinction between spontaneous emotional impulses that befall every human being and true affects that require active assent to indulge in such impulses. According to the Stoic conception, Rosamund does not find herself at the mercy of her passions but is certainly able to prevent her impulse from becoming a proper affect through her reason.

However, the dialogue not only draws on Seneca *philosophus*, it also refers to two scenes from his tragedies, both of which are also modelled after the standard pattern of *nutrix*-scenes, namely, the conversations between a mistress and her maid. Diletta's recommendation to "stop this impulse of rage and rein yourself in" (*siste furialem impetum/ Tibique frenos iniice*) quotes two scenes from Senecan dramas. In both cases, the maid tries to dissuade her mistress from taking revenge and prevent her from allowing her affects to take over. In the second act of *Agamemnon*, Clytemestra confided in her maid, telling her of her desire to retaliate against her husband Agamemnon who, upon returning from

---

54   Ibidem, 133.

the Trojan War, took the Trojan princess Cassandra as his hostage and concubine. Clytemnestra's nameless maid then advises her to "rein yourself in, control your impulses" (*frena temet et siste impetus*).[55] In the second act of *Medea*, the protagonist is furious at her husband Jason for taking Creusa, princess of Corinth, as his new wife, and at Creon, Creusa's father, for arranging it. After telling her maid about her plan to take revenge, the maid tells her to "control your impulsive rage" (*siste furialem impetum*).[56] Although each of the maids take the role of a Stoic consultant and urge their mistresses not to succumb to their impulses and let affects take over, they do not succeed: Rosamund, Clytemnestra, and Medea all ultimately indulge their desire for revenge.

According to the Senecan model, Rosamund decisively takes the step from a first *impetus* to an unmanageable *affectus* as she does not apply *ratio*. When she finally decides the murder to be carried out, the chorus observes her emotions shift from the established puzzle of sorrow, affection, and fury to a state in which anger and fury become dominant.[57] Towards the end of the third act, the chorus describes her physical appearance:

> Quo tam celeri concita gressu
> Rosimunda ruit? Quo se rapient
> Tam praecipitis monstra furoris?
> Vultus nimia flammeus ira,
> scintillanti fulgurit oculo.
> Et modo totum pallida corpus
> Et modo multo tincta rubore.
> Cuncta minaci pectore versat,
> Per diversos acta colores
> Nusquam stabilis forma vagatur
> Et se species mutat in omnes.
> Quid non audes, animose dolor,
> Dum defuncti funera patris
> Filia toto concipit animo?

---

55 Seneca, *Agamemnon*, 203. Text and translation quoted from Seneca, *Tragedies, Volume II: Oedipus. Agamemnon. Thyestes. Hercules on Oeta. Octavia*, Loeb Classical Library 78, ed. J.G. Fitch (Cambridge: 2018).

56 Seneca, *Medea*, 157. Text and translation henceforth quoted after Seneca, *Tragedies, Volume I: Hercules. Trojan Women. Phoenician Women. Medea. Phaedra*, Loeb Classical Library 62, ed. J.G. Fitch (Cambridge: 2018). For an examination of the Senecan model of anger in *Medea*, see Wiener, *Stoische Doktrin* 36–46.

57 On the chorus in Neo-Latin drama, see Janning V., *Der Chor im neulateinischen Drama. Formen und Funktionen* (Münster: 2005).

EMOTIONS IN 17TH-CENTURY NEO-LATIN DRAMA

Postquam miseros praefica lessus
Fessa dolendi rupit et omni
Exhausta stupent lumina fletu
Colligit aegro corde furorem
Et crescentes incitat iras.

Where is Rosamund rushing with such quick steps? Where do the monsters of rash fury tear themselves? Her face is fiery red with immoderate anger and her eyes are flickering. First, she is pale all over, then, she is imbued with red. In her intimidating heart, she turns everything over. Her look changes its colour several times and does not stay the same. What do you not venture, violent sorrow, when a daughter sees her father's dead before her inner eye? After the mourner, exhausted by her sorrow, stopped her funeral lamentation, her eyes being tired from all the crying, she accumulates rage in her troubled heart and rouses growing anger.[58]

In many respects, the description of Rosamund's appearance is modelled after a chorus section in Seneca's *Medea*, again drawing a parallel between the two protagonists who both face *motus mixti* and whose bodies mirror their emotional states. While Medea is torn between rage (*ira*) and affection (*amor*) before she decides to retaliate against Jason by sacrificing her own children, Rosamund's body visualises the transition from a mix of sorrow, rage and affection to pure anger.[59] The chorus of the tragedy expresses the general physical shift through the image of a *praefica*, a professional funeral mourner. During this transition, Rosamund's appearance never stays the same, it changes constantly (*nusquam stabilis forma*). The chorus also reports that Rosamund's general external appearance alters considerably. She quickens her pace, her eyes flicker, her face is fiery red, and her whole body turns from white to red. As is not atypical for classical drama, the chorus performs the role of an observer describing Rosamund's physical appearance and interpreting it with regard to emotions. They read certain external physical reactions as unambiguous

---

58   Van Zevecote, *Rosimunda* 143.

59   Seneca, *Medea*, 849–873: "Quonam cruenta maenas/ praeceps amore saevo/ rapitur? quod impotenti/ facinus parat furore?/ vultus citatus ira/ riget, et caput feroci/ quatiens superba motu/ regi minatur ultro./ quis credat exulem?/ Flagrant genae rubentes,/ pallor fugat ruborem./ nullum vagante forma/ servat diu colorem/ huc fert pedes et illuc,/ ut tigris orba natis/ cursu furente lustrat/ Gangeticum nemus./ Frenare nescit iras/ Medea, non amores;/ nunc ira amorque causam/ iunxere: quid sequetur?/ quando efferet Pelasgis/ nefanda Colchis arvis/ gressum, metuque solvet/ regnum simulque reges?"

indicators of certain affects. For instance, "the monsters of rash fury" (*praecipitis monstra furoris*) make Rosamund quicken her pace and her face becomes red because of "immoderate anger" (*vultus nimia flammeus ira*). The presumed linkage between Rosamund's bodily reactions and the development of her affects culminates in a simile presented at the end of the chorus's part, another imitation of the Senecan model. Here, she is likened to a tigress whose cubs were stolen from her, revealing her anger showing over her entire body (*toto corpore ... indicat iram*).[60]

The observations made by the chorus in sections such as this reflect another Stoic key feature in Neo-Latin drama, namely the idea that certain facial expressions and physical motions are clear outer signs of certain inner affects. Both Stoic writings from antiquity and Neo-Stoic treatises from the end of the 16th century reflect extensively on the ways in which certain affects changes a person's physical appearance. For example, in a famous section at the beginning of *De ira*, Seneca explains that anger causes red cheeks due to an accelerated pulse, the eyes to start to flicker and people to usually quicken their pace.[61] In his *De ira morbo*, Johann Weyer elaborates further on this and includes an entire chapter on the "indications of anger" (*De signis irae*), which he subdivides into several groups.[62] He lists, among others, an accelerated pulse, shallow breathing and certain eye movements as general signs of anger (*communia irae signa*), a flushed and sometimes swollen face as signs in terms of facial expressions (*signa ex facie*) or a stretched neck with regard to gestures (*signa a gestibus*). Thus, Rosamund not only shows classic signs of anger, her body also reflects the change from mixed emotions to pure anger, as her appearance and her colour fluctuate. This physical aspect of the Stoic and Neo-Stoic theory of emotions provides the chorus of the tragedy with a distinct system of signs

---

60 Van Zevecote, *Rosimunda* 143: "Non sic catulis tigris ademptis/ fremit et toto corpore sparsam/ centum maculis indicat iram". Cf. Seneca, *Medea*, 862–865.

61 Seneca, *De ira*, I, 1: "Ut scias autem non esse sanos quos ira possedit, ipsum illorum habitum intuere; nam ut furentium certa indicia sunt audax et minax vultus, tristis frons, torva facies, citatus gradus, inquietae manus, color versus, crebra et vehementius acta suspiria, ita irascentium eadem signa sunt: flagrant ac micant oculi, multus ore toto rubor exaestuante ab imis praecordiis sanguine, labra quatiuntur, dentes comprimuntur, horrent ac surriguntur capilli, spiritus coactus ac stridens, articulorum se ipsos torquentium sonus, gemitus mugitusque et parum explanatis vocibus sermo praeruptus et conplosae saepius manus et pulsata humus pedibus et totum concitum corpus 'magnasque irae minasagens,' foeda visu et horrenda facies depravantium se atque intumescentium – nescias utrum magis detestabile vitium sit an deforme. Cetera licet abscondere et in abdito alere; ira se profert et in faciem exit, quantoque maior, hoc effervescit manifestius".

62 Weyer, *De ira morbo* 33–42.

EMOTIONS IN 17TH-CENTURY NEO-LATIN DRAMA 125

that makes it possible to "translate" specific corporeal reactions and appearances into affects.

4 Unfinished Anger: Rochus Honerdus, *Thamara*

Whereas Rosamund's affective status shifts from mixed emotions to unblended anger, other dramas portray individual characters as being trapped between different affects and not solving the situation in favour of one of them. For instance, Rochus van den Honert's biblical tragedy *Thamara* (1611) was modelled after the episode in the second book of Samuel. As Amnon, the eldest son of king David, is attracted to his own half-sister Tamar, he makes a plan with the help of his companion Jonadab. Amnon pretends to be sick and to need nursing and then asks his father David to send Tamar to prepare him a meal and to take care of him. After she prepared the meal, he takes advantage of the situation and rapes her. Thereafter, Tamar tells her brother Absalom about the incident.[63] Numerous visual artworks depicted the story in the 16th and 17th centuries, usually with a focus on Amnon, Tamar, and the crime itself [Figs. 3.2–3]. However, van den Honert focuses on the figure of David and his delicate role in the situation: While in the book of Samuel, we only learn that the king becomes furious after hearing what happened, van den Honert's tragedy explores his emotional status in much more nuanced detail.[64] David is thrown into a tragic situation in the proper sense. In his *De tragoediae constitutione*, for example, Heinsius explains that, for the affects of *horror* or *misericordia* to be aroused, a crime must be committed between close friends or relatives.[65] David, however, is the father of both the perpetrator and the victim of this particular crime which makes it extremely difficult for him to take action and adopt an unambiguous affective attitude.

---

63 2 *Samuel* 13.
64 Bloemendal, "Similarities, Dissimilarities" 156. There were two other dramas on the subject, Chrétien Nicolas, *Tragédie d'Amnon et Thamar* (Rouen, Theodore Reinsart: 1608) and Lummenaeus a Marca Jacobus Cornelius, *Amnon tragoedia sacra* (Ghent, Cornelius Marius: 1617), but Honerdus's comprehensive treatment of David's emotional status seems to be rather a unique feature of his *Thamara*. For some observations on the differences between the versions, see Parente J.A., "The Paganization of Biblical Tragedy: The Dramas of Jacob Cornelius Lummenaeus a Marca (1570–1629)", *Humanistica Lovaniensia* 38 (1989) 209–237.
65 On the tragic situation, see Aristotle, *Poetics*, chapter 14 and Heinsius, *De tragoediae constitutione*, chapter 9. On the aspect of crimes among friends and relatives, see ibidem, 104–105. Cf. Meter, *Literary Theories* 203–213.

FIGURE 3.2 Philips Galle after Maarten van Heemskerck, *Amnon rapes Tamar* from the series *Geschiedenis van Tamar en Amnon*, 1559. Engraving, 24,5 × 20,3 cm. Public Domain

Van den Honert is particularly interested in exploring David's emotional state after hearing about the crime in a dialogue with Tamar's brother Absalom in the fifth act of the drama. David finds himself forced to choose between two unacceptable options: to either avenge his daughter and have his own son murdered or forgive his son and leave the horrific crime against his daughter unavenged. However, David is undecided about what to do and is, therefore, unable to completely indulge in one emotion. At the beginning of the dialogue, he speaks of a wavering outbreak (*anceps doloris aestus*) and a baffling sorrow (*perplexus dolor*).[66] The situation is even more complicated by the fact that David then interprets this family's present calamity as a just punishment for his act of adultery with Batseba.[67]

---

66   Honerdus, *Thamara* 47.
67   Cf. 2 *Samuel* 11. Honerdus, *Thamara* 49: "Accipio nostri generis haud vanam indolem/ moechum parentem natus incestus decet./ Proles Iudae nuptiis claris fave./ Firmantur

FIGURE 3.3 Eustache Le Sueur, *The Rape of Tamar*, painted ca. 1640. Oil on canvas, 189.2 × 161.3 cm. New York, Metropolitan Museum of Art. Public Domain

In the dialogue, he hesitates to choose a course of action. Absalom tries to urge his father to decide based on his anger (*ira*) but observes that David is not fully taken by this affect and that the impulse of anger may, therefore, not

ecce fata regalis domus,/ avo nepotes stirpe sincera soror/ ex fratre spondet. Certior sceptris nequit/ haeres parari".

be strong enough to lead to revenge. He complains, "Oh, slow anger! Whoever takes hesitating steps in seeking punishment [...], is a cowardly avenger, as he spares the accused a lot".[68] Even after David has seemingly decided to have Amnon arrested, Absalom realises that his father is still unsure, which is apparent from his outward appearance:

> Sed quid? Quid iste mentis incertae status,
> Variusque trepidis vultus ostentat notis?
> Luctatur animus secum et haerentis movet
> non una ratio pectus. Intendit minas,
> rursum remittit, ira pietatem excutit,
> iramque pietas. Pendet alternus polo
> soloque vultus. Solvit in vocem dolor,
> constringit idem verba. Num dubitas, pater?
> Absolvere est damnare tam tarde nefas.
> Erumpit ecce flumen et multo natat
> humore barba. Segnius dudum dolet
> pulsoque primus impetu languet furor.

What? Why this ambiguous state of mind, why does his inconstant facial expression show these unsteady signs? He is in the middle of an inner struggle, at a standstill, and there is surely more than one concern afflicting his heart. He's making threats and taking them back, his anger supersedes his sense of duty and his sense of duty his anger again. His face turns, alternating between to the sky and the ground. His sorrow shows itself in his voice and, at the same time, renders him speechless. Do you really hesitate, father? To condemn a crime so haltingly means to pardon it. Look at this flood of tears wetting your beard. For a long time now, he has felt a slow kind of sorrow, but when the first impulse is over, fury lacks its vigour.[69]

Absalom observes David's changing, trembling facial expressions (*varius trepidis vultus notis*), how his face turns from the sky to the ground and back again

---

68 Ibidem, 50: "Pro segnis ira! Quisquis ad poenam gradu/ cunctante pergit inque vindictam Deum/ votis ab ipso lentus abducit polo,/ quantum remittit ultor ignavus reo!" Cf. Ps.-Seneca, *Hercules Oetaeus*, 434–435: "quid stupes segnis, furor?/ scelus occupandum est: perge, dum fervet manus". Here and henceforth quoted after Seneca, *Tragedies, Volume II: Oedipus. Agamemnon. Thyestes. Hercules on Oeta. Octavia*, Loeb Classical Library 78, ed. J.G. Fitch (Cambridge: 2018).

69 Honerdus, *Thamara* 51.

EMOTIONS IN 17TH-CENTURY NEO-LATIN DRAMA   129

and again (*Pendet alternus polo soloque vultus*), and that he cries. He concludes
that his father finds himself caught in an internal struggle and notes that certain affects are present, that have not reached their full expressions. His rage
(*ira*) is in conflict with his sense of duty (to protect his son) and his sorrow
(*dolor*) can be recognised in his voice and lets him speechless at the same time.
His fury (*furor*), finally, gradually fades. During the dialogue, all of the affects in
play turn out to be volatile, shifting and transforming into each other. David's
shame (*pudor*) turns into sorrow (*dolor*) which then renders him less ferocious
and eventually puts him in a state of grief.[70] Absalom interprets David's inca-
pacity to hold Amnon accountable as a result of unarticulated, incompletely
formed, and easily shifting emotions. By speaking of an *impetus*, he even technically refers to the Stoic theory of emotions. In this view, David is to blame not
so much because of his tragic situation, but because he did not indulge in his
first affective impulse of anger (*pulsoque primus impetu languet furor*).

It is interesting to observe that, in van Zevecoten's *Rosimunda*, we encounter the reverse situation. Whereas Rosamund's maid advises her not to succumb to the impulse of anger, Absalom reproaches his father for his *impetus*,
for being too half-hearted and not taking action. Even though the two advisers
are pursuing opposite goals – one to prevent and the other to provoke acts of
revenge – both make their arguments on the level of affects and refer to the
Stoic theory of emotions, in particular, the phase when a first impulse may or
may not turn into a proper affect. Furthermore, in both cases, facial expressions
and bodily movements are not only interpreted as signs of affects as such, but
as indicators of affective shifts – either from *impetus* to an ambiguous *affectus*
or from *impetus* back to a vague mixture of emotions.

5   Conflicting Emotions and Implicit Stage Directions: Daniel
Heinsius, *Auriacus*

As we can see, the physical externalisation of changing and mixed emotions
is paramount for Neo-Latin drama. This is also true of one of the most widely
known Latin tragedies ever written in the Dutch Republic: Daniel Heinsius'
Auriacus (1602) on the assassination of William of Orange in 1584. As previously mentioned, Heinsius was an important exponent of Neo-Latin drama
in the Dutch Republic and, in addition to *De tragoediae constitutione*, he composed two dramas himself, namely the *Auriacus* and a biblical play on the

---

70   Ibidem, 52: "Iamque in dolorem erumpat ut verum dolor". Ibidem, 53: "Quam cito ferocem
vanus infregit dolor,/ facilemque mollis cessit in luctum pater".

Massacre of the Innocents, called *Herodes infanticida* from 1611. He was also a key figure in the extensive network of Latin dramatists. In the *Auriacus*, he turned his attention to a topic of contemporary history that was not only central to the political development of the Dutch provinces but also important as a cultural icon for the Dutch revolt as such. The assassination was represented countless times in different media in the late 16th and early 17th centuries.

Heinsius was neither the first nor the only writer to convert the dreadful event into a Latin tragedy. In 1589, Toussaint du Sel (Panagius Salius), a poet from the Southern Netherlands, published his *Nassovius*, followed by Kaspar Ens' (Casparus Casparius) *Princeps Auriacus sive libertas defensa* from 1599.[71] Whereas du Sel conveys a pro-Spanish position and depicts William of Orange as a seditious rebel, Ens writes from the perspective of the Dutch provinces and portrays the protagonist as an important political figure in the Dutch Revolt. The *Auriacus* was quickly followed by a vernacular adaptation in the tradition of Dutch rhetorician drama, *Het moordadich stuck van Balthasar Gerards* (1606), which was written by the playwright and member of the Leiden Chamber of Rhetoric "De Witte Acoleyen" Jacob Duym (born 1547).[72] Whereas Duym takes Heinsius' *Auriacus* as the textual model for his Orange play, he certainly does not provide a word-for-word translation. The *Moordadich stuck* is clearly shorter than the *Auriacus* (2171 vs. 1342 verses) and

---

71 Salius Panagius, *Nassovius tragoedia*, in *Panagii Salii Audomarensis varia poemata ad illustrissimum principem ducemque invictissimum Alexandrum Farnezium ducem Parmae et Placentiae etc. Philippi regis Catholici in Belgio praefectum* (Paris, Denis du Pré: 1599), 86–115. Casparius Caspar, *Princeps Auriacus sive libertas defensa, tragoedia nova* (Delft, Bruno Schinckel: 1599). Cf. Bloemendal J., "De dramatische moord op de Vader des Vaderlands. De verhouding tussen vier typen toneel in de vroegmoderne Nederlanden", *Zeventiende Eeuw* 23 (2007) 99–117. Idem, "Introduction" 28–30. Becker-Contarino B., "Das Literaturprogramm des Daniel Heinsius in der jungen Republik der Vereinigten Niederlande", in Garber K. (ed.), *Nation und Literatur im Europa der Frühen Neuzeit. Akten des ersten Internationalen Osnabrücker Kongresses zur Kulturgeschichte der Frühen Neuzeit*, Frühe Neuzeit 1 (Tübingen: 1989), 595–626, here 610–613.

72 Duym Jacob, *Het moordadich stuck van Balthasar Gerards, begaen aen den Doorluchtighen Prince van Oraingnen 1584* (Leiden, Henrick Lodewijcxsoon van Haestens: 1606). Cf. Becker-Contarino, "Literaturprogramm des Daniel Heinsius" 614–615. Groenland J., "Playing to the Public, Playing with Opinion. Latin and Vernacular Dutch History Drama by Heinsius and Duym", in Bloemendal J. – Dixhoorn A. van – Strietman E. (edd.), *Literary Cultures and Public Opinion in the Low Countries, 1450–1650*, Brill's Studies in Intellectual History 197 (Leiden – Boston: 2011), 121–150. For the chamber of rhetoric, see Boheemen F.C. van – Heijden Th.C.J. van der, *Retoricaal memorial. Bronnen voor de geschiedenis van de Hollandse rederijkskamers van de middeleeuwen tot het begin van de achttiende eeuw* (Delft: 1999), 492–603 and Koppenol J., "Jacob Duym en de Leidse rederijkers", *Neerlandistiek.nl* 1 (2001) 1–23.

EMOTIONS IN 17TH-CENTURY NEO-LATIN DRAMA 131

includes, for example, a supplementary prologue and an epilogue spoken by the poet ('dichtstelder').[73] Furthermore, Duym's play was often interpreted as a contribution to the public political debate on whether the Dutch Republic should continue the war against Spain or attempt to negotiate peace. It was clearly possible to understand the *Moordadich stuck* as a plea for the retention of military efforts.[74]

Duym's *Moordadich stuck* provides a useful object of comparison which helps to identify what is specific about Heinsius' Orange play. Having said that, it is important to differentiate between various performance conditions and audiences. While Heinsius was writing for a well-educated humanist audience that was trained in the Latin language and familiar with the tradition of classical drama, Duym's vernacular adaptation addresses a wider target group more accustomed to the characteristics of Dutch rhetorician drama.[75] Nevertheless, whereas the *Auriacus* was performed several times in the immediate vicinity of the university library, we do not know whether and, if so, how often the *Moordadich stuck* was actually performed.[76] In contrast, Heinsius's *Auriacus* not only matched the popularity of historical subjects in dramas that had continually increased in the 1580s and 1590s, it also played an important role in theatre life in Leiden. Although Greek and Roman plays had been performed frequently at the university, a general prohibition of theatre performances was imposed between 1595 and 1601 at the behest of Calvinist priests.[77] Just as Grotius with his *Adamus exul*, for instance, Heinsius attempted to influence the debate about theatre in Leiden in the *Auriacus*, and he had some success. The university curators made an exception for the tragedy about the great hero of the Dutch Revolt, and Heinsius' *Auriacus* was performed repeatedly, even before it was published in print.[78]

In contrast to his fellow playwrights, Heinsius takes a particular angle that allows him to discuss passions, affects, and how they should be handled in detail. In his Orange play, he does not so much focus on the act of murder itself,

---

73   Cf. Groenland, "Playing to the Public" 136–138.
74   Cf. Ibidem, 137–139. Bloemendal, "De dramatische moord" 125.
75   Cf. Groenland, "Playing to the Public".
76   Cf. Bloemendal, "Introduction" 12; Groenland, "Playing to the Public" 141.
77   On historical drama, see Parente J.A., "Historical Tragedy and the End of Christian Humanism. Nicolaus Vernulaeus (1583–1649)", in Bloemendal J. – Smith N. (eds.), *Politics and Aesthetics in European Baroque and Classicist Tragedy*, Drama and Theatre in Early Modern Europe 5 (Leiden – Boston: 2016), 152–181, here 161–162. Groenland, "Playing to the Public" 124–126. On the prohibition, see Bloemendal, "Introduction" 10–12. Meter, *Literary Theories* 36–38. Groenland, "Playing to the Public" 129.
78   Cf. Meter, *Literary Theories* 24.

rather on how the characters prepare for it. In this, William of Orange himself functions as prototypical Stoic sage. From his first monologue to his last words in the tragedy, he embodies the Stoic quality of constancy (*constantia*) and is ready to equanimously endure whatever fate may bring.[79] Furthermore, in regard to his emotions, he aligns with the Stoic ideal as he 'subjected the ineffective emotions' which, according to Heinsius, makes him a capable political leader who does not put his homeland at risk.[80] William's wife, Louise de Coligny, is scared because her husband's impending death was revealed to her in a dream. Her consequential fear and sorrow, for example, provide an opportunity for a discussion between her and an old wise man about the insignificance of affects in general.[81] The most interesting character for our context, however, is Balthasar Gerards, the assassin himself, as Heinsius puts a particular emphasis on his emotions. From his first appearance until the very last moment before the crime is committed, Gerards is unsure of what to do as he is trapped between two affects: fear and rage (*metus* and *furor*). He explains this state at the beginning of his first scene in the third act:

> Exaestuatque mens; et incertus ferit
> Ardens tremensque pectoris votum tumor,
> Sedemque mentis hinc et hinc pessum trahit
> Metus, tenaxque consili ingentis furor,
> Cordisque caecis impetita fluctibus
> Casura nutat vis, retroque corruit,
> Incerta quonam, quodque factura annuit
> Fecisse nondum luget, insultans sibi,
> Praeponderatque utroque et utroque imminet,
> Inobsequensque pectoris magni ciet
> Motum reluctans fervor, et premi negat,
> Redireque ardet rursus, et rursus nequit.

My spirit is in a violent wavering: an ambiguous impulse, of fervent desire and fear, meets the vow of my heart. On the one hand, it is fear that

---

79 See Bloemendal J., "Willem van Oranje: een Hercules op Leidse planken", *De Zeventiende Eeuw* 10 (1994) 159–164. Idem, "De dramatische moord" 124–126.

80 Heinsius, *Auriacus*, ll. 113–116: "Motusque vanos pectoris molem mei,/ aestusque et iras impetusque subdidi/ Deo mihique. Latius virtus nequit/ efferre gressus". Cf. Heinsius, *Auriacus* ed. Bloemendal, 376–377.

81 Heinsius, *Auriacus*, act II, scene 2. Cf. also van Gemert L., "'Hoe dreef ick in myn sweet'. De rol van Louise de Coligny in de Oranje-drama's", *De Zeventiende Eeuw* 10 (1994) 169–178, esp. 172–173.

EMOTIONS IN 17TH-CENTURY NEO-LATIN DRAMA

confuses my mind, on the other, a desire that holds on to the enormous plan. My heart, otherwise so steadfast, attacked by blind turmoil, waves, about to fall, and falls backwards. Insecure what to do, it repents that it has not yet done what it promised, and curses itself. It tilts its weight to both sides and longs for both: there is an irrepressible drive in my big heart, impetuous, indomitable, and then it burns again with desire to return, but cannot do that either.[82]

Gerards is subject to an "ambiguous impulse" (*incertus tumor*) that actually includes two affective impulses, both tied to different choices of action. On the one hand, Gerards is scared (*metus*) about the enormous crime he is planning and would therefore refrain from it. On the other hand, he is furious (*furor*) because he wants to take revenge for his father's death. In the course of the dialogue, he reports that his father's cruel execution came about for religious and political reasons during the troubled times of the revolt. Even though the story does not match the historical facts, it provides a rationale for Gerards fatal rage within the plot.[83] He describes himself as being fully caught between fear (*metus*) and fury (*furor*) and, therefore, undecided about how to act, a situation also frequently encountered in the Senecan dramas. However, Gerards' affective status is complicated further still. The very fact that, being stuck between *furor* and *metus*, he is not able to decide how to act leads to further emotions, and makes him feel a kind of sorrow (*quodque factura annuit/ fecisse nondum luget*). He blames himself (*insultans sibi*) for being too indecisive and, therefore, feels ashamed.

His affective status makes Gerards some kind of 'Stoic anti-hero' and a counterpart of the protagonist of the *Auriacus*. It is clear that Gerards is already beyond his first impulse, and that the fully realised affect has taken him to the extent that his mind is swept away by his fear (*sedemque mentis hinc et hinc pessum trahit/ metus*) and there is no chance reason will regain control. Furthermore, both options for action would be failures in the Stoic sense: Gerards could avenge his father, as according to Seneca, for instance, Stoicism does not completely reject the idea of revenge, but only if it is done to fulfil a moral requirement (*quia oportet*), rather than as a consequence of rage or sorrow – as is the case with Rosamund and Gerards.[84] However, Gerards could also refrain from killing William of Orange but, if he did, it would not

---

82   Heisnius, *Auriacus*, ll. 741–752.

83   Heisnius, *Auriacus*, ll. 867–947. Cf. Heinsius, *Auriacus* ed. Bloemedal, 445–446.

84   Seneca, *De ira*, I, 12: "Pater caedetur, defendam; caesus est, exsequar, quia oportet, non quia dolet".

be considered the result of a reasonable decision-making process, it would be attributed to the notion that his fear had surpassed his rage. In this case, it would be nothing more than one affect defeating another (*affectus repercussit affectum*) and, therefore, what Seneca referred to as "a treacherous and evil agreement between the passions".[85] Thus, the monologue outlining Gerards' affective status at the beginning of the scene highlights that it is highly unlikely the situation will have a positive outcome.

After Gerards outlines his conflicted state at the beginning of the scene, Heinsius introduces another character, a commander near William's house. As is the case with the chorus in van Zevecote's *Rosimunda*, the commander describes Gerards' physical appearance:

> Quo fluctuantes insolens gressus refert
> Titubante passu temere, et incerto pede
> Ambiguus hospes? Creperus haud quaquam color,
> Exanguis, amens, et profundi luminum
> Placent recessus, et supercilii tremor,
> Nimioque ceu furore labentes genae,
> Vecordiaeque proditor, vanus timor.
> En metuit, en, trepidatque, maestaque huc et huc
> Flectit reflectitque ora, nec satis sibi
> Lucique credit; maximum hoc pectus scelus
> Metuit paratve.

> Why does this unusual guest indecisively, with hesitating step and uncertain foot wander aimlessly back and forth? His undefined colour, white and mad, his deeply receding eyes, the vibration of his eyebrow, his cheeks collapsed by violent rage and his senseless fear, which betrays insanity, do not please me at all. Look, he is afraid, he is trembling and turns his sad face now here, now back again, and he does not trust himself and the daylight: this person is either fearing or planning a very great crime.[86]

Heinsius here visualises the conflicting affects of fear and rage with regard to body movement and facial expressions. The fact that Gerards steps back and forth nervously is expressed in three variants in the Latin text (*fluctuantes gressus*; *titubante passu*; *incerto pede*). The colour of his skin is bloodless and dubious, he has sunken eyes and cheeks, his eyebrows are quivering and his

---

85   Cf. above.
86   Heinsius, *Auriacus*, ll. 800–810.

face turns here and there. The commander interprets these physical signs in relation to affects, mainly noticing fear (*vanus timor*; *en metuit*), but also rage (*furor*). The fact that the commander's affective interpretation of Gerards' physical signs is correct again corresponds to the Stoic theory of inner affects as being embodied: However, what is particularly interesting about this scene is that this concept also applies to mixed and conflicting affects. The commander is, here, perfectly able to recognise fear and rage at the same time.

The special focus on Gerards and the presentation of the characters through the lens of the Stoic theory of affects is by no means typical of dramatic adaptations of William's assassination, rather it is something particularly Heinsian. In Casparius' *Auriacus*, for instance, Gerards is not even included as a character, whereas in Duym's *Moordadich stuck*, the assassin appears in the title of the work. However, as he mentions in the preface, Duym applied changes to some of the characters in his model.[87] This becomes particularly clear regarding Heinsius' Stoic conception of the emotional states of the characters. In his version of the opening monologue, for instance, Duym does not present William as a Stoic hero, a victor over his own passions and, therefore, a competent political leader, rather he focuses on the political conflict with the Spanish king.[88] When it comes to Gerards himself, Duym includes his indecisiveness and his doubts but does not stage this situation as a conflict between affects. Rather, Gerards is sure that he will eventually commit the crime from the very beginning, even though the fear of his own death initially inhibits him from doing so.[89] Two key elements of Heinsius' Stoic perspective on Gerards's emotional state do not reappear in Duym's versions. First, Gerards' initial hesitation does not render him ashamed of himself in the sense that two conflicting affects produce further ones. Second, Duym does not adopt Heinsius' focus on the verbalisation of physical representations of emotions. In Duym's remake of the scene between Gerards and the commander, for example, the latter does not describe Gerards's gestures, movements, or facial expressions at all. He merely states that this person seems 'confused and perplexed' ('verstoort en beroerd') without linking this interpretation to Gerards's physical appearance.[90]

Over the course of the *Auriacus*, Gerards continues to fluctuate between *metus* and *furor* and describes himself as a victim, fully overcome by his own

---

87   Duym, *Moordadich stuck*, fol. Aiii v: "soo hebben wij hem ter eeren nochtans den selven Auriacum ghevolght, ende sommighe Personagien ghevoechelick naer onsen sin verandert". Cf. Groenland, "Playing to the Public" 141–143.

88   Cf. Duym, *Moordadich stuck*, fol. Bii r–<Biv> r.

89   Cf. ibidem, fol. <D iiii> r–<D iiii> v.

90   Ibidem, fol. <D iiii> v.

affects several times.[91] He seems to recognise that he has failed to comply with the ideal of the Stoic management of affects but is already at a point where reason can no longer regain control. Thus, Gerards is confronted with a third affect: the shame (*pudor*) of being indecisive and incapable of controlling himself. As he is not able to act, Megaera, one of the three Erinyes, the Greek goddesses of fury, attempts to incite him to act, to make his *furor* superior to his *metus* and, thus, to solve the conflict between the affects.[92] However, even in the very last moment before committing the crime, Gerards is still indecisive and ashamed about it:

> Pudet fateri, pudet, at intremui tamen,
> Nec lingua sequitur. Deseror rursus Dei,
> Et me reliqui. Genua trepidanti labant,
> Quotiesque gressum protuli, retro feror.

> I am ashamed to admit it, really, but still I fear and my tongue fails to speak. Again I do not control myself, gods, and am outside of myself. I shake, my knees shake and every time I have made a step forward, I retire.[93]

Such descriptions of corporeal appearances, facial expressions, gestures, and movements perform three basic functions in tragedies and their interpretations. Firstly, they create a physical expression of emotions – both 'pure' and mixed – and thus help explore the characters' affective states and shifts by

---

91 For example see ibidem, 1406–1415: "Ignosce victo Roma: cor retro salit/ Fugamque versat intus. O sacerrimi/ Tutela patris, votaque, et fides mea,/ Et fibulati curiae sanctae patres,/ Superatus adsto: victus, ignauus feror,/ Mihique cessi; pectus imbellis ferit/ Tremor, quatitque, faedus, ignauus timor/ Inuicta mentis maenia obsedit meae,/ Et iam triumphum ducit: en victus trahor,/ Sed ante pugnam". Ibidem, 1450–1458: "Quo voluor amens? Vela mens impos tua/ Lege, et furoris dirigas clauum tui./ Tun' ora ut illa et frontis augustae decus/ Vultusque tantae conscius fraudis feras?/ Nec victus ibis? Linguaque et vocis via/ Potentiori vincta torpebit metu?/ Et inter ipsae facinus horrebunt manus?/ Sudor trementes imbre pertentans graui/ Dissoluit artus. Iunge, iunge et hunc tuis/ Batauia titulis: victus accedo tibi".

92 Cf. ibidem, 1460–1502. The three furies Alecto, Megaera, and Tisiphone also appeared in Heinsius' *Herodes infanticida* which led to a famous controversy as the French author Jean-Louis Guez de Balzac (1597–1654) criticised Heinsius for using both biblical and pagan figures in a biblical tragedy, cf. Leo R., "Herod and the Furies: Daniel Heinsius and the Representation of Affect in Tragedy", *Journal of Medieval and Early Modern Studies* 49.1 (2019) 137–167.

93 Heinsius, *Auriacus*, ll. 1720–1729.

EMOTIONS IN 17TH-CENTURY NEO-LATIN DRAMA   137

rendering them observable. Therefore, we are often presented with descriptions given by observers, such as the chorus in *Rosimunda*, David's son Absalom in *Thamara*, and the commander in the *Auriacus*. As has been shown, the semiotic code that links certain affects to specific physical expressions is derived, to a great extent, from the Stoic theory of affects. Secondly, these descriptions are often modelled after certain passages from Senecan tragedies and, hence, point to the literary tradition of Roman drama that the plays see themselves located within. The commander's description of Gerards, for instance, refers to two particular Senecan passages: In *Phaedra*, the protagonist falls in love with her stepson Hippolytus, is rejected by him, and then trapped between sorrow (*dolor*) and rage or madness (*furor*). Similarly, in *Hercules Oetaeus*, Heracles' wife Deianira finds herself experiencing a mixture of sorrow (*dolor*) and rage (*furor*) stemming from the jealousy she feels after finding out that her husband took the young princess Iole captive.[94] Balthasar Gerards shares, with both these characters, certain physical expressions of mixed emotions which

---

94   Seneca, *Phaedra*, 360–383: "Spes nulla tantum posse leniri malum,/ finisque flammis nullus insanis erit./ torretur aestu tacito et inclusus quoque,/ quamvis tegatur, proditur vultu furor;/ erumpit oculis ignis et lassae genae/ lucem recusant; nil idem dubiae placet,/ artusque varie iactat incertus dolor:/ nunc ut soluto labitur marcens gradu/ et vix labante sustinet collo caput,/ nunc se quieti reddit et, somni immemor,/ noctem querelis ducit; attolli iubet/ iterumque poni corpus et solvi comas/ rursusque fingi; semper impatiens sui/ mutatur habitus. nulla iam Cereris submit/ cura aut salutis. vadit incerto pede,/ iam viribus defecta: non idem vigor,/ non ora tinguens nitida purpureus rubor;/ [populatur artus cura, iam gressus tremunt,/ tenerque nitidi corporis cecidit decor]/ et qui ferebant signa Phoebeae facis/ oculi nihil gentile nec patrium micant./ lacrimae cadunt per ora et assiduo genae/ rore irrigantur, qualiter Tauri iugis/ tepido madescunt imbre percussae nives". Quoted after Seneca, *Tragedies, Volume 1: Hercules. Trojan Women. Phoenician Women. Medea. Phaedra*, Loeb Classical Library 62, ed. J.G. Fitch (Cambridge: 2018). Ps.-Seneca, *Hercules Oetaeus*, 233–253: "O quam cruentus feminas stimulat furor,/ cum patuit una paelici et nuptae domus!/ Scylla et Charybdis Sicula contorquens freta/ minus est timenda, nulla non melior fera est./ namque ut reluxit paelicis captae decus/ et fulsit Iole qualis innubis dies/ purisve clarum noctibus sidus micat,/ stetit furenti similis ac torvum intuens/ Herculea coniunx, feta ut Armenia iacens/ sub rupe tigris hoste conspecto exilit,/ aut iussa thyrsum quatere conceptum ferens/ Maenas Lyaeum dubia quo gressus agat./ haesit parumper; tum per Herculeos lares/ attonita fertur, tota vix satis est domus;/ incurrit, errat, sistit, in vultus dolor/ processit omnis, pectori paene intimo/ nihil est relictum; fletus insequitur minas./ nec unus habitus durat aut uno furit/ contenta vultu: nunc inardescunt genae,/ pallor ruborem pellit et formas dolor/ errat per omnes; queritur implorat gemit". The *Hercules Oetaeus* had long been attributed to Seneca, but was probably written later (possibly early 2nd century) by an imitator, cf. Marshall C.W., "The Works of Seneca the Younger and their Dates", in Heil A. – Damschen G. (edd.), *Brill's Companion to Seneca. Philosopher and Dramatist* (Leiden – Boston: 2013), 33–44. Heinsius himself rejected Seneca's authorship but included the play in his 1611 edition of the Senecan tragedies, cf. Meyer, *Literary Theories* 235.

act as markers for literary references. For instance, all three characters constantly walk back and forth with uncertain steps, the colouring of their faces alters, and both Phaedra and Gerards are described as trembling and having sunken cheeks.[95] In that sense, the bodily expressions of mixed emotions in tragedy remain strikingly consistent.

The third function of such descriptions relates to the practical side of Neo-Latin drama, to its performance and the question of how mixed emotions might have looked on stage. Compared to early modern English drama, for instance, relatively little is known about specific acting practices in performances of Neo-Latin plays. Daniel Heinsius takes an unequivocal stand on the theoretical aspect of acting and affects in *De tragoediae constitutione*. According to him, a tragedy is supposed to arouse the affects of commiseration and horror solely through the structure of its plot and the tragic situation it presents, rather than through the actors' skill or talent.[96] However, there are also many indications that performances of Neo-Latin tragedies were not mere recitations but, to a certain degree, included acting on stage.[97] Recent research has demonstrated that, although Neo-Latin tragedies were usually printed without stage directions, plays preserved in manuscripts or prints with handwritten additions are sometimes full of detailed stage directions.[98] A particular passage from Heinsius' laudatory poem for Duym's *Moordadich stuck* suggests that physical acting was also part of the performances of Orange plays. He states that a Dutch version of the play is particularly useful as people

---

95 Uncertain steps: Cf. Seneca, *Phaedra* 374 ("vadit incerto pede"), Ps.-Seneca, *Hercules Oetaeus* 244–245 ("dubia quo gressus agat./ haesit parumper"), and Heinsius, *Auriacus* 800–801 ("Quo fluctuantes insolens gressus refert/ titubante passu temere, et incerto pede"). Face colouring: Cf. Seneca, *Phaedra* 375–367 ("non idem vigor,/ non ora tinguens nitida purpureus rubor"), Ps.-Seneca, *Hercules Oetaeus* 250–253("nec unus habitus durat aut uno furit/ contenta vultu: nunc inardescunt genae,/ pallor ruborem pellit et formas dolor/ errat per omnes"), and Heinsius, *Auriacus* 802–803 ("creperus haud quaquam color,/ exanguis, amens"). Trembling: Cf. Seneca, *Phaedra* 367–368 ("nunc ut soluto labitur marcens gradu/ et vix labante sustinet collo caput") and Heinsius, *Auriacus* 807–808 ("trepidatque maestaque huc et huc/ flectit reflectitque ora"). Sunken cheeks: Cf. Seneca, *Phaedra* 364 ("lassae genae") and Heinsius, *Auriacus* 805 ("labentes genae").

96 Heinsius, *De tragoediae constitutione* 92: "Praeclare autem praecipit philosophus ita constitutam absque ullo histrionis artificio aut ope debere esse fabulam, ut, qui audiat solummodo aut legat, miseratione perfundatur et horrore".

97 Cf. Heinsius, *Auriacus* ed. Bloemedal, 12.

98 Cf. e.g. Norland H.B., "Neo-Latin Drama in Britain", in Bloemendal – Norland (eds.), *Neo-Latin Drama* 471–544, here 515–516. Rädle F., "Jesuit Theatre in Germany, Austria, and Switzerland", ibidem, 185–292.

EMOTIONS IN 17TH-CENTURY NEO-LATIN DRAMA

who do not know Latin "are not able to understand the play only on the basis of gestures".[99]

For the *Auriacus*, the question is all the more crucial in two respects. The assassination of William of Orange as the central crime in the *Auriacus* does not happen off stage and is retold by a messenger as, for instance, in Casparius' *Auriacus*, but forms part of a scene in which both Gerards and William find themselves on stage.[100] Moreover, we know that there were several public performances of the Latin version and possibly also of Jacob Duym's Dutch adaptation. This underlines the fact that the play was physically performed on stage rather than merely read. In contrast to the *Auriacus*, however, the printed version of Duym's *Moordadich stuck van Balthasar Gerards* does contain some basic stage directions in the page margins [Fig. 3.4]. They do not usually go into detail about gestures or facial expressions but clearly testify to the fact that physical acting was an integral part of the performance and give an impression of how actors actually moved on the stage. In the murder scene of the *Moordadich stuck*, for instance, Gerards is instructed to come closer to William, speak directly to him, and fire the weapon while speaking, which even points to the intention to use props in the performances.[101] While uttering his last words, William himself is supposed to lie on the ground before the guards carry away his dead body.[102] There is no need to assume fundamental differences between plays in Latin and in Dutch. Public performances of tragedies about the assassination of William of Orange apparently generally included such forms of acting.

The physical expressions of affects and affective states that are verbalised by observing figures in the *Auriacus* can, therefore, be understood as 'implicit stage directions'.[103] Such descriptions could have been interpreted as guidance

---

99   The poem was included in Duym Jacob, *Een Ghedenck-Boeck het welck ons leert aen al het quaet en den grooten moetwil van de Spaingnaerden en haren aenhanck ons aen-ghedaen te ghedencken* (Leiden, Henrick Lodewijcxsoon van Haestens: 1606), of which *Het moordadich stuck* formed one part, fol. **ii v.: "Muto caetera gens stetit theatro/ solis nescia gestibus doceri". Cf. Groenland, "Playing to the Public" 130–131.

100   Heinsius, *Auriacus*, act IV, scene 3.

101   On stage costumes and props owned by the chambers of rhetoric, see Heijden Th.C.J. van der – Boheemen F.C. van, "Accomodation and Possession of Chambers of Rhetoric in the Province of Holland", in Strietman E. – Happé P. (eds.), *Urban Theatre in the Low Countries, 1400–1625*, Medieval Texts and Cultures of Northern Europe 22 (Turnhout: 2006) 253–281, esp. 269–274.

102   Duym, *Het moordadich stuck* fols. G iii r–G iii v in marg.

103   Heinsius, *Auriacus* ed. Bloemedal, 12. The concept of implicit stage directions was applied to classical Greek and Roman drama, cf. Chancellor G., "Implicit Stage Directions in Ancient Greek Drama. Critical Assumptions and the Reading Public", *Arethusa* 12.2 (1979)

on how actors should move and act on stage and, therefore, provide indications of how mixed emotions were visualised on the stage. This is all the more plausible given such accounts include a large variety of different gestures, facial expressions, and movements. While actors cannot be expected to have influenced certain aspects, such as the colour of their face to express their character's feeling of rage, fear, or both, the descriptions discussed above include physical movements that could easily be performed on stage and recognised by the audience. In most cases, such movements come into play to express compound and conflicting emotions and the resulting doubt. For example, Gerards in the *Auriacus* and King David in Honerdus' *Thamara* both consistently turn their heads in different directions. Gerards' knees tremble and he walks back and forth undecidedly. This last detail, in particular, is already observed by the commander during Gerards' very first appearance on stage and reoccurs in his description of himself in the moments before the assassination.

Interpreting the physical expressions of affects as implicit stage directions is all the more feasible given we can observe that, in his *Moordadich stuck*, Duym transformed some of the implied directions in Heinsius' *Auriacus* into explicit ones. For example, in the murder scene in Heinsius' version, William of Orange shouts "I fall, I fall down" several times (*en praeceps fluo,/ fluo, fluo, fluo*) before speaking his last words.[104] In this case, to fall and lie down is the obvious thing for the actor to do on stage when the fatal shot is fired. In Duym's *Moordadich stuck*, William does not verbalise his fall, but there is a stage direction on the page margin instructing the actor to lie down on the ground during William's final words ('Ter aerden ligghende') [Fig. 3.4a]. Regarding affects and their physical indications, it seems instructive to examine the scene of Gerards first appearance on stage again. As we have seen, Duym does not adopt the detailed description given by the commander. However, there is a direct stage direction that instructs Gerards to enter the stage in a rather 'bewildered' manner ('hy comt uyt seer verbaest') [Fig. 3.4b].[105] Thus, Heinsius and Duym both highlight that Gerards's indecisiveness is reflected in his physical behaviour. Heinsius draws on a literary technique well known from classical drama (a third character giving a verbal description) and the Stoic concept that certain physical reactions indicate specific affects. Duym also emphasises Gerards doubts but

---

133–152 and Sutton D.F., *Seneca on the Stage*, Mnemosyne Supplementa 96 (Leiden: 1986). Regarding early modern drama, most of the research on implicit stage directions focusses on the Shakespearean corpus, cf. e.g. Banham M., "'The Merchant of Venice' and the Implicit Stage Direction", *Critical Survey* 3.3 (1991) 269–274 and West C., "Implied Stage Directions in Shakespeare: A Workshop Approach", *Metaphor* 2 (2021) 24–28.

104   Heinsius, *Auriacus*, ll. 1735–1736.

105   Duym, *Het moordadich stuck* fol. <D iiii> r.

EMOTIONS IN 17TH-CENTURY NEO-LATIN DRAMA

En my met eenich vverck so ick best kan daer gheneeren,

Met dat hy dit spreeckt geeft hy de scheut.

Des soud' ick eenen brieff van u Ghenaed' begeeren.
Sa,Sa,hy leyter al,ick heb hem vvel ghetreft,
Sa,nu loop ick ras vvegh,dit is al vvel beseft,
Och mocht ick doch nu noch gheraken uyt de Landen.

De Prins.

Ter aerde ligghende.

O God,miin arme siel beveel ick in u handen,
En aen de Staten s'Lands miin kinders groot en cleyn,
O Heer u beveel ick dees Landen int ghemeyn,
Het gheen dat gheschied is,laet ick o Heer u vvreken.

d'Ouerste vande VVacht.

De wacht van de Hellebar-diers comt uyt met eenen Be-vel-hebber en somni-ghe Edel-lieden.

Och,och,miin Heer die sterft,hy en can niet meer spreken,
Och,och, barmhertich God,dit is een arme saeck:
Och vvaer is den rabaut? dat hem den helschen Draeck
Hals en neck breken moet,laet hem al om naer loopen:
Sa,sa,loopt als ras uyt,bedeylt u in vier hoopen:
Laet oock de poorten al vast sluyten van der Stat,
Laet oock vvel gaede slaen, dat daer niet anders vvat
En schuyl,tsy eenich quaet,oft oock verraet van binnen:
Den moordenaer tast aen,maer vanght hem doch met sinne
Brengt hem niet om den hals,en vvel voordachtich leeft,
En hem dan terstont in der Staten handen gheeft:
vvaer hy in handen doch,mocht sulcx voor ons gheschieden,
Slaet doch nu al hand aen,en meest ghy Edel-lieden:
Och hem doch met ghemack,al stil daer binnen draeght,
Hoe vverd doch dese dood van allen man beclaeght,
T'heel Land mach voorvvaer vvel dees dood hier bevvee-
nen,,nu,

Sy draghe t'lichaem in.

Elck een die vroom is,salt van herten oock meenen,,nu.

Vande

Vande derde Gheschiedenis, de eerste uytcomst.

Baltazar Gherards , den Hoofmeester.

Gherards.

Hy comt uyt seer verbaest.

SAl ick,neen ick, jae ick,het moet doch zijn ghevvaegt,
vvil ick voortgaë,neen ick,vvaerom is t'hert vertzaegt?
Ick hebt doch vast belooft,d'uytstelle ziin maer drome,
Maer als ick om de daet peys', t'hert begint te schromen,
Den moed vvord cleyn,en hy valt my in mynen schoen,
Maer vvat helpt dit,ick moet dats claer miin beste doen:
Die belooft,die maeckt schult,ick moet het oock aenvange,
Sa,Sa,met cloecken moed,ick neem daer toe miin gangen,
Maer hoe sal ickt oock doen,strijd teghen mijnen sin,
Hy en deed' my noyt quaet,ick sulcx recht uyt bekin,
vvat pas ick daer op,hy,oft ick,sal sulcx beturen,
Oft alle beyde oock,ick sal het stuck uytvuren,
Nochtans t'hert my int lijf,als een broos riet nu beeft,
Vrees benout my,en hoop my vvederom troost gheeft,
Des ben ick tusschen beyd'hanghen en vervvorghen,
Maer laet loopen den bras,vvaer voor vvil ick doch sorghen,

Het

FIGURES 3.4A–B
Duym, *Het moordadich stuck*, fols. G iii v. and <D iiii> r

leaves the specifics of their staging to the actor. When he uses an explicit stage direction instead of including a verbal description, he closely follows his textual model by including a physical visualisation of Gerards's state of mind.

As demonstrated through the comparison with Duym's *Moordadich stuck*, the Stoic conception of the characters and their affective states is a particular feature of Heinsius's *Auriacus*. However, stating that it is more nuanced regarding philosophical theory is not to say that Heinsius's Orange play is less explicit in its political message. Heinsius's concentration on the affects, their conflicts, and bodily indices reverses the roles of William and his assassin in a sense. Although Gerards eventually does assassinate the Prince of Orange, the physical externalisation of conflicting affects and the resulting indecisiveness is a key element of the overall strategy to depict his failure. Heinsius presents him as a victim of his own affects without the slightest chance of defying their power and returning to *ratio*. From the very beginning, his affects have control over him and, from the Stoic point of view, the boundary between *impetus* and *affectus* had already been crossed. Conflicting emotions, then, lead to other emotions. The confrontation between rage and fear produces and intensifies shame, rendering Gerards even more indecisive. His reluctant steps back and forth and his shaking head visualise the conflict of affects and his resulting desperation. Conversely, although William of Orange is the victim of the crime, he controls his emotions fully and is, therefore, a representation of a Stoic sage and victor over his affects. Gerards political crime is therefore aggravated by his failure to aspire to the Stoic way of managing affects as so brilliantly exemplified by William, both a political hero of the Dutch revolt and an ideal Stoic.

6 Conclusion

The exploration of compound, conflicting and shifting emotions in Neo-Latin drama is very closely linked to Aristotelian dramatic theory, the Stoic theory of affects, Senecan tragedy, and early modern receptions and adaptations of these backgrounds. The example of the early 17th-century Dutch Republic demonstrates that the texts that were relevant in that regard – poetical and philosophical treatises, text editions and commentaries, and Neo-Latin themselves – circulated within a confined personal network around Daniel Heinsius.

A closer look at some exemplary scenes could illustrate that the Stoic and Neo-Stoic theory of affects provided dramatists with a powerful tool to delve into their characters' affective states. Sometimes, the ideal of *apatheia*, the individual's victory over affects, is referred to as an example, as is the case with William of Orange in Heinsius's *Auriacus*. However, when it comes to conflicting and shifting emotions, the Stoic concept is often used in a more analytical way. Dramatists focus on the formation of affects and, in particular, the distinction between spontaneous, unintentional impulses (*impetus*) and actual affects that require deliberate consent of *ratio*. The relationship between both is by no means determined in advance, therefore, it can vary. Whereas the protagonist in van Zevecote's *Rosimunda* is warned to stop her angry impulse, in Honerdus' *Thamara*, David is criticised for not succumbing to the full extent of his anger. Both examples are premised on the Stoic notion that affects are the result of conscious choice. Furthermore, the comparison between Heinsius' *Auriacus* and Duym's *Moordadich stuck* pointed out that this very theoretical approach to emotions is more typical for the Neo-Latin than for the vernacular tradition of drama.

An integral part of performing mixed emotions on stage consisted in externalizing the affects through body movements and facial expressions. Again, it was the Stoic and Neo-Stoic traditions that provided the idea that physical reactions correlate with specific affects. The examples discussed above demonstrate that verbal descriptions of a character's physical appearance often occur when they find themselves in a state of transitioning or conflicting affects. Thus, as Duym's *Moordadich stuck*, the vernacular adaptation of Heinsius' *Auriacus*, transforms some of Heinsius' descriptions into explicit stage directions, it is plausible to interpret such accounts as implicit stage directions offering insight into how actors may have conveyed mixed emotions on stage. In that sense, the Stoic concept of affects and their externalisation is not merely an important element of the intellectual background of Neo-Latin drama, it has a significant impact on performance practices and, therefore, plays a critical role in effectively staging compound, conflicting and shifting emotions.

Select Bibliography

Abel G., *Stoizismus und Frühe Neuzeit. Zur Entstehungsgeschichte modernen Denkens im Felde von Ethik und Politik* (Berlin – New York: 1978).

Banham M., "'The Merchant of Venice' and the Implicit Stage Direction", *Critical Survey* 3.3 (1991) 269–274.

Becker-Contarino B., "Das Literaturprogramm des Daniel Heinsius in der jungen Republik der Vereinigten Niederlande", in Garber K. (ed.), *Nation und Literatur im*

Europa der Frühen Neuzeit. Akten des ersten Internationalen Osnabrücker Kongresses zur Kulturgeschichte der Frühen Neuzeit, Frühe Neuzeit 1 (Tübingen: 1989) 595–626.

Bloemendal J., "Willem van Oranje: een Hercules op Leidse planken", *De Zeventiende Eeuw* 10 (1994) 159–164.

Bloemendal J., "Receptions and Impact: Early Modern Latin Drama, its Effect on the Audience and its Role in Forming Public Opinion", in Idem – Ford P. (eds.), *Neo-Latin Drama. Forms, Functions, Receptions*, Noctes Neolatinae. Neo-Latin Texts and Studies 9 (Hildesheim – Zürich – New York: 2008) 7–22.

Bloemendal J. – Norland H. (eds.), *Neo-Latin Drama and Theatre in Early Modern Europe*, Drama and Theatre in Early Modern Europe 3 (Leiden – Boston: 2013).

Bloemendal J., "Neo-Latin Drama in the Low Countries", in Bloemendal – Norland (eds.), *Neo-Latin Drama* 293–364.

Bloemendal J. "Similarities, Dissimilarities and Possible Relations Between Early Modern Latin Drama and Drama in the Vernacular", in Ford P. – Taylor A (eds.), *The Early Modern Cultures of Neo-Latin Drama*, Supplementa Humanistica Lovaniensia 32 (Leuven: 2013) 141–157.

Brazeau B., "Emotional History and Early Modern Readings of Aristotle's Poetics", in Idem, *The Reception of Aristotle's Poetics in the Italian Renaissance and Beyond: New Directions in Criticism* (London: 2020) 201–226.

Casparius Caspar, *Princeps Auriacus sive libertas defensa, tragoedia nova* (Delft, Bruno Schinckel: 1599).

Chancellor G., "Implicit Stage Directions in Ancient Greek Drama. Critical Assumptions and the Reading Public", *Arethusa* 12.2 (1979) 133–152.

Chrétien Nicolas, *Tragédie d'Amnon et Thamar* (Rouen, Theodore Reinsart: 1608).

Ding R., "Les quatre *Rosemonde* du XVIIᵉ siècle, ou le tyrannicide châtié: évolution et impasse d'un sujet", *Dix-septième siècle* 284 (2019) 515–532.

Duym Jacob, *Het moordadich stuck van Balthasar Gerards, begaen aen den Doorluchtighen Prince van Oraingnen 1584* (Leiden, Henrick Lodewijcxsoon van Haestens: 1606).

Enenkel K.A.E., "Neo-Stoicism as an Antidote to Public Violence before Lipsius's *De constantia*: Johann Weyer's (Wier's) Anger Therapy, *De ira morbo* (1577)", in Enenkel K.A.E. – Traninger A. (eds.), *Discourses of Anger in the Early Modern Period*, Intersections 40 (Leiden – Boston: 2015) 49–96.

Enenkel K.A.E., "Neo-Stoicism before Lipsius: Johann Weyer's *De ira morbo* (1577)", *Neulateinisches Jahrbuch* 19 (2017) 125–155.

Ens Kaspar, *Princeps Auriacus sive libertas defensa, tragoedia nova* (Delft, Bruno Schinckel: 1599).

Gemert L., "'Hoe dreef ick in myn sweet'. De rol van Louise de Coligny in de Oranje-drama's", *De Zeventiende Eeuw* 10 (1994) 169–178.

Graver M., *Stoicism and Emotion* (Chicago – London: 2007).

Groenland J., "Playing to the Public, Playing with Opinion. Latin and Vernacular Dutch History Drama by Heinsius and Duym", in Bloemendal J. – Dixhoorn A. van – Strietman E. (edd.), *Literary Cultures and Public Opinion in the Low Countries, 1450–1650*, Brill's Studies in Intellectual History 197 (Leiden – Boston: 2011) 121–150.

Grotius Hugo, *Tragoedia Christus patiens* (Leiden, Thomas Basson: 1608).

Halliwell S., *Between Ecstasy and Truth. Interpretations of Greek Poetics from Homer to Longinus* (Oxford: 2012).

Harst J., "Germany and the Netherlands: Tragic Seneca in Scholarship and on Stage", in Dodson-Robinson E. (ed.), *Brill's Companion to the Reception of Senecan Tragedy. Scholarly, Theatrical and Literary Receptions*, Brill's Companions to Classical Reception 5 (Leiden – Boston: 2016) 149–173.

Heinsius Daniel, *Auriacus sive libertas saucia, accedunt eiusdem Iambi partim morales, partim ad amicos, partim amicorum causa scripti* (Leiden, Andries Cloucq: 1602).

Heinsius Daniel, *De tragoediae constitutione liber, in quo inter caetera tota de hac Aristotelis sententia dilucide explicatur* (Leiden, Ioannes Balduinus: 1611).

Heinsius Daniel, *Herodes infanticida, tragoedia* (Leiden, Elzevir: 1632).

Heinsius Daniel, *Auriacus, sive Libertas saucia (Orange, or Liberty Wounded)*, ed. J. Bloemendal (Leiden – Boston: 2020).

Honerdus Rochus, *Thamara, tragoedia* (Leiden, Joannes Patius: 1611).

IJsewijn J., "Jacobus Zevecotius. Maria Stuarta / Maria Graeca, tragoedia. A Synoptic Edition of the Five Extant Versions", *Humanistica Lovaniensia* 22 (1973) 256–319.

Kappl B., *Die Poetik des Aristoteles in der Dichtungstheorie des Cinquecento*, Untersuchungen zur antiken Literatur und Geschichte 83 (Berlin – New York: 2006).

Lummenaeus a Marca Jacobus Cornelius, *Amnon tragoedia sacra* (Ghent, Cornelius Marius: 1617).

Kemper A., "Anger in the Jesuit Theatre of the 16th Century Discussions of Affect in the Tension between Christianity, Neo-Stoicism and Aristotelianism", *Daphnis* 43 (2015) 97–124.

Konstan D., "Senecan Emotions", in Bartsch S. – Schiesaro A. (eds.), *The Cambridge Companion to Seneca* (Cambridge: 2015) 174–184.

Koppenol J., "Jacob Duym en de Leidse rederijkers", *Neerlandistiek.nl* 1 (2001) 1–23.

Kraye J., "Moral Philosophy", in Schmitt C.B. et al. (eds.), *The Cambridge History of Renaissance Philosophy* (Cambridge: 1988) 303–386.

Kraye J., "Stoicism in the Renaissance from Petrarch to Lipsius", *Grotiana* 22–23 (2001) 21–45.

Leo R., *Tragedy as Philosophy in the Reformation World* (Oxford: 2019).

Leo R., "Herod and the Furies: Daniel Heinsius and the Representation of Affect in Tragedy", *Journal of Medieval and Early Modern Studies* 49.1 (2019) 137–167.

Lipsius Justus, *De constantia libri duo, qui alloquium praecipue continent in publicis malis* (Antwerp, Christoffel Plantijn: 1584).

Lipsius Justus, *Manductionis ad Stoicam philosophiam libri tres L. Annaeo Senecae aliisque scriptoribus illustrandis* (Paris, Hadrian Perier: 1604).

Lipsius Justus, *Physiologiae Stoicorum libri tres L. Annaeo Senecae aliisque scriptoribus illustrandis* (Antwerp, Jan Moretus: 1604).

Mayer R., "Personata Stoa. Neostoicism and Senecan Tragedy", *Journal of the Warburg and Courtauld Institutes* 57 (1994) 151–174.

Meere M., "On Specters and Skulls: Rosamund and Alboin in Seventeenth-Century French Tragedy", in Lyons J.D. (ed.), *The Dark Thread. From Tragical Histories to Gothic Tales* (Newark: 2019) 129–148.

Meter J.H., *Literary Theories of Daniel Heinsius. A Study of the Development and Background of his Views on Literary Theory and Criticism During the Period from 1602 to 1612*, Respublica Literaria Neerlandica 6 (Assen: 1984).

Nussbaum M.C., *Upheavals of Thought. The Intelligence of Emotions* (Cambridge: 2001).

Papy J., "Neostoic Anger: Lipsius's Reading and Use of Seneca's Tragedies and De ira", in Enenkel K.A.E. – Traninger A. (eds.), *Discourses of Anger in the Early Modern Period*, Intersections 40 (Leiden – Boston: 2015) 126–142.

Parente J.A., *Religious Drama and the Humanist Tradition. Christian Theater in Germany and in the Netherlands 1500–1680*, Studies in the History of Christian Thought 39 (Leiden et al.: 1987).

Parente J.A., "Historical Tragedy and the End of Christian Humanism. Nicolaus Vernulaeus (1583–1649)", in Bloemendal J. – Smith N. (eds.), *Politics and Aesthetics in European Baroque and Classicist Tragedy*, Drama and Theatre in Early Modern Europe 5 (Leiden – Boston: 2016) 152–181.

Parente J.A., "Latin and the Transmission of the Vernacular. Multilingualism and Interculturality in the Tragedies of Jacob Zevecotius", *Renaissance Studies* 36.1 (2022) 104–121.

Radouant R., *Guillaume du Vair. L'homme et l'orateur jusqu'à la fin des troubles de la Ligue (1556–1596)* (Paris: 1907).

Robortello Francesco, *In librum Aristotelis de arte poetica explicationes* (Florence, Lorenzo Torrentino: 1548).

Sel Toussaint du, *Panagii Salii Audomarensis varia poemata ad illustrissimum principem ducemque invictissimum Alexandrum Farnezium ducem Parmae et Placentiae etc. Philippi regis Catholici in Belgio praefectum* (Paris, Denis du Pré: 1599).

Somos M., *Secularisation and the Leiden Circle* (Leiden – Boston: 2011).

Sutton D.F., *Seneca on the Stage*, Mnemosyne Supplementa 96 (Leiden: 1986).

Trigg S., "Affect Theory", in Broomhall S. (ed.), *Early Modern Emotions. An Introduction* (London – New York: 2017).

Trinacty C., "Senecan Tragedy", in Bartsch S. – Schiesaro A. (edd.), *The Cambridge Companion to Seneca* (Cambridge: 2015) 29–40.

Vair Guillaume du, *De la constance et consolation és calamitez publiques* (Paris, Mamert Patisson: 1594).

Wiener C., *Stoische Doktrin in römischer Belletristik. Das Problem von Entscheidungsfreiheit und Determinismus in Senecas Tragödien und Lucans Pharsalia*, Beiträge zur Altertumskunde 226 (München – Leipzig: 2006).

Zevecote Jacob van, *Poematum editio nova* (Leiden, Andries Cloucq: 1625).

SECTION B

Mixed Emotions in Neo-Latin and French Poetry

∵

CHAPTER 4

Between Fleeting and Compound Emotions in Neo-Latin Lyric Poetry on 'Turks': Georgius Sisgoreus' *Elegia de Sibenicensis agri vastatione*

Ludovica Sasso

Abstract

Especially from the second half of the 15th century the Croatians experienced the constant Ottoman attacks at first hand. For this reason, the intensity and the pathos of Croatian poetry on the 'Turks' appear with special vividness to register a sense of menace and shock, and it offers an important field for the investigation of complex, unstable and shifting emotions. In this essay special attention will be paid to the earliest poetic response to the Ottoman attacks published in Croatia, the *Elegia de Sibenicensis agri vastatione* (Elegy on the devastation of the district of Šibenik) of Georgius Sisgoreus. Through this example it will be demonstrated how conflicting or compound emotions, as well as ambiguous emotional states can be present in lyric poetry, and how the expressions of emotion can shift, one into another, although specific literary genres can theoretically represent a medium of basal emotions, which are codified as the core of the genre itself.

Keywords

Türkenlyrik – *'Türkenfurcht'* – Sisgoreus – elegy-lamentation, – Renaissance-Dalmatia – Ottoman Empire – Croatian Humanism

1 Introduction

The Ottoman advance to the West and the fall of Constantinople in 1453 represented the 'great drama' for early modern Europe and its perception of itself as a *unitas christiana*.[1] The loss of a symbolic place like Constantinople, the

---

1 Cf. Hanß S., *Lepanto als Ereignis. Dezentrierende Geschichte(n) der Seeschlacht von Lepanto (1571)* (Goettingen: 2017) 28.

© LUDOVICA SASSO, 2025 | DOI:10.1163/9789004694613_005

former capital of the Eastern Roman Empire, initiated the rise of the Ottoman Empire from being a local power in Near East and Southeast Europe to becoming a major and dangerous force.[2] By the early 1460s all political leaders in Eastern, Central and Southern Europe had realised that the Ottomans' advance represented a tangible danger which they would have to face head on, either on the battlefield or through diplomacy.

The shocking announcement of the Ottoman's conquest of Constantinople and their subsequent military campaigns, however, not only impacted European politics but also prompted a vast number of literary texts. In these works, the catastrophic fall and related events were not only described but above all mourned, commented upon, and used as a Christian cue for a common call to arms. Often the Christians viewed the struggle against the 'Turks' as a punishment for sins against God and an opportunity to redeem these transgressions.[3] In humanistic literature written between 1450 and 1620, the Turkish question was the topic most frequently and intensively discussed.[4]

Between the second halves of the fifteenth and sixteenth centuries, the construction of the image of the 'Turks' mainly took place in the widespread genres of anti-Turkish speeches and epistles, but also in travel reports, historiographical works, and *Flugblätter* or *Flugschriften* (polemical flyers or pamphlets).[5] Written exclusively in Latin, these texts were addressed to popes, European kings or emperors, and the Venetian Doges. Numerous and varied, they differed in expressive usage and the stress placed on the representation of emotion, especially as respects what scholars call *Türkenfurcht* (fear of the Turks) and *Türkengefahr* (the Turkish danger).[6]

---

2   Bisaha N., *Creating East and West. Renaissance Humanists and the Ottoman Turks* (Philadelphia: 2010) 1–12.

3   Bisaha, *Creating East and West* 143–161.

4   According to Hankins J., "Renaissance Crusaders: Humanist Crusade Literature in the Age of Mehmed II.", *Dumbarton Oaks Papers* 49 (1995) 111–207, 112: 'The humanists wrote far more often and at far greater length about the Turkish menace and the need for crusade than they did about such better-known humanist themes as true nobility, liberal education, the dignity of man, or the immortality of the soul'.

5   Göllner C., *Turcica. Die europäischen Türkendrucke des XVI. Jahrhunderts*, 3 vols. (Bucharest – Berlin – Baden-Baden: 1961–1968).

6   Ebermann R., *Die Türkenfurcht, ein Beitrag zur Geschichte der öffentlichen Meinung in Deutschland während der Reformationszeit* (Halle: 1904); Kissling H.J., "Türkenfurcht und Türkenhoffnung im 15./16. Jahrhundert. Zur Geschichte eines 'Komplexes'", *Südost-Forschungen* 23 (1964) 1–18, esp. 2; Höfert H., *Den Feind beschreiben. "Türkengefahr" und europäisches Wissen über das Osmanische Reich 1450–1600* (Frankfurt: 2003); and Hanß, *Lepanto als Ereignis* 27–42.

Most authors settled on a limited canon of more or less entrenched stereotypes and generalities. The Turkish conquerors are generally portrayed as violent: they destroy towns and villages, set fields on fire, capture and rape Christians, violate nuns, and turn churches into stables; this final desecration is repeatedly invoked as a symbol of extreme anti-Christianity.[7] These same authors handle emotional representation similarly: the trade constantly in sentiments of fear and anger against the cruel, brutal and bestial 'Turks', or express joy and enthusiasm for a Christian victory, or steadfastly place their hope in God's support for the Christian forces.

Previous research on this anti-Turkish discourse, on the construction, dissemination and consolidation of stereotypes, and on conventional emotional representations of these prototypical enemies, has focused almost exclusively on prose.[8] Poetic texts in Latin have largely been excluded from consideration, even though they constitute a specific tradition of occasional poetry which might justly be designated *Türkenlyrik*, i.e., Neo-Latin poetry on the 'Turks'.[9] A peculiarity common to most of these poetic texts is that they re-functionalised ancient genres devoted to themes of love, grief and mourning (such as the elegy), or mockery, contempt, hatred and derision (such as the epigram), and adapted them to the new theme of the Ottoman expansion in Western Europe. In this concert of outrage, lamentation, despair, or joy for a Christians victory

---

7   See, above all, Höfert, *Den Feind bescreiben* 201; and Helmrath J., "Pius II. und die Türken", in Guthmüller B. – Kühlmann W. (eds.), *Europa und die Türken in der Renaissance* (Tübingen: 2000) 79–137, esp. 104–117.

8   See, among other publications, Schwoebel R., *The Shadow of the Crescent. The Renaissance Image of the Turk (1453–1517)* (Nieuwkoop: 1967); Schmugge L., *Die Kreuzzüge aus der Sicht humanistischer Geschichtschreiber* (Basel – Frankfurt: 1987); Höfert, *Den Feind beschreiben*; Döring K.D., *Türkenkrieg und Medienwandel im 15. Jahrhundert (mit einem Katalog der europäischen Türkendrucke bis 1500)* (Munich: 2013); Guthmüller – Kühlmann, *Europa und die Türken in der Renaissance*; Bisaha N., *Creating East and West*; and Hankins, "Renaissance Crusaders" 111–207. On the poetry on Turks, see Schindler C., "'Barbarico tingi sanguine vidit aquas'. Die Sclacht von Lepanto in der neulateinischen Dichtung", in Föking M. – Schindler C. (eds.), *Der Krieg hat kein Loch. Friedenssehnsucht und Kriegsapologie in der Frühen Neuzeit* (Heidelberg: 2014) 111–140; Wright E. et al., *The battle of Lepanto* (Harvard: 2014); Laureys M., "Poetic crisis talks between Constantinople and Rome", *Nordic Journal of Renaissance Studies. Studia Humanitatis: Essays in Honour of Marianne Pade on the Occasion of her Sixty-Fifth Birthday* 18 (2022) 277–292.

9   The term *Türkenlyrik* comes from Kühlmann W., "Der Poet und das Reich – Politische, kontektuelle und ästetische Dimension der humanistischen Türkenlyrik in Deutschland", in Guthmüller B. – Kühlmann W. (eds.), *Europa und die Türken in der Renaissance* (Tübingen: 2000) 193–247. As part of a scholarly project co-hosted by the Universities of Göttingen and Münster (Germany), two monographs on early modern occasional *Türkenlyrik* in Italy and Germany are currently being written. I am author of the monograph on *Türkenlyrik* in the Italian context.

over the Ottomans, humanists in Eastern, Central and Southern Europe – some well known, such as Enea Silvio Piccolomini and Giovanni Gioviano Pontano, others anonymous or nearly unknown – raised their voices as well. Poets of Balkan origin, especially Dalmatians, built over time a specifically Croatian anti-Turkish literary movement.

2 Croatians against the "Turks"

New Mediterranean conquests rapidly followed the fall of Constantinople, especially in Greece and the Balkan peninsula. Indeed, from the early years of the 15th century, the Ottomans had been making incursions into Croatia.[10] For example, they attacked Zadar in 1432. Between 1450 and 1500, the raids intensified due to the fact that nearby Hungary was well defended during the reign of Mathias Corvinus. The Ottomans fell back onto the Adriatic coast and Istria, and penetrated as far as the duchies of Carniola, Styria, and Carinthia.[11] Moreover, since Serbia had already fallen in 1459, and Bosnia in 1463, Croatia became more directly exposed to Ottoman attacks. Split and many other important Dalmatian towns, including Dubrovnik, suffered greatly, particularly during the Venetian-Turkish War of the years 1499–1503.[12]

According to Davor Dukić, in Croatian pre-modern culture the 'Turks' dominate the image spectrum for the representation of enemies; over time, Turkish imagery evolved into a complex and dynamic construction encompassing contradictory ideas.[13] The most important genre for the construction of the image of the 'Turks' in early modern Croatia were anti-Turkish speeches and epistles, written in Latin and mainly addressed to the popes, the Hungarian, and the Polish kings, the Habsburg emperors, and the Venetian Doges. In this communication network, strong expressions of *Türkenfurcht* and stereotypical

---

10 Hrabak B., "Turske provale i osvajanja na području današnje severne Dalmacije do sredine XVI stoleća, Radovi, Sveučilište u Zagrebu" ["Turkish raids and conquests in the area of today's northern Dalmatia until the middle of the 16th century, Papers, University of Zagreb"], *Centar za povijesne znanosti* 19 (1986) 69–100; and Pust K., "'Le genti della citta, delle isole e del contado, le quale al tutto volevano partirsi'. Migrations from the Venetian to the Ottoman Territory and Conversions of Venetian Subjects to Islam in the Eastern Adriatic in the Sixteenth Century", *Povijesni prilozi* 40 (2011) 121–159.

11 Pitcher D.E., *An Historical Geography of the Ottoman Empire* (Leiden: 1968) 92.

12 Posset F., *Catholic Advocate of the Evangelical Truth: Marcus Marullus (Marko Marulić) of Split (1450–1524)*, (Eugene, OR: 2021) 150.

13 Dukić D., "Das Türkenbild in der kroatischen literarischen Kultur vom 15. bis zur Mitte des 19. Jahrhunderts", in Lauer R. – Majer H.G. (eds.), *Osmanen und Islam in Südosteuropa* (Berlin: 2013) 157–191.

satanisation of 'Turks' functioned also as pragmatic means of achieving key political goals, above all, financial and military backing for the fight against the Ottomans. Because of the prevailing tone created by the repeated portrayal of Christian suffering at the hands of the Ottoman conquerors, Davor Dukić has identified the first period of literary representation of the 'Turks' in Croatian culture (from about the mid-fifteenth to the first quarter of the sixteenth century) as 'die Zeit der Klagelieder' (time of lamentations).[14] Since these works formed part a wave of anti-Turkish literature that arose in central and southeastern Europe at this time, and given that fear of the 'Turks' was ubiquitous in Europe, also among populations not directly threatened (a sense of imminent threat that Jean Delumeau characterises as fear 'venue d'en haut', i.e., from the papacy),[15] it could be claimed that the search for anything regionally or culturally Croatian about this literature is likely to prove futile. But it is a fact that the Croatians experienced the constant Ottoman attacks at first hand. For this reason, the intensity and the pathos of Croatian poetry on the 'Turks' appear with special vividness to register a sense of menace and shock. This poetry offers a field for the investigation of complex, unstable, and shifting emotions and ambiguities of expression as responses to the experience of social and cultural disruption. This is evident, for example, in the poetic production (both in Latin and Croatian) of Marco Marulić, whom the Croatian literary historiography has styled a symbol of literary resistance to Turkish conquest within the context of the *Türkendiskurs* (the discourse about the 'Turks').[16] The Latin section of his *Judita*, the first Croatian epic,[17] contains a famous anti-Turkish epistle written

---

14   Ibidem.

15   Delumeau J., *La peur en Occident* (Paris: 1978) 347.

16   See Lučin B., "Marko Marulić – kroatischer Dichter und europäischer Humanist", *Colloquia Maruliana* 18 (2009) 349–355.

17   Written in 1501, during the war between Venice and the Turks, *Judita* was printed in Venice two decades later, first in 1521, when the war was raging again, and then in 1522 and 1523. No early manuscripts of *Judita* are extant; see MS Zagreb, National and University Library – R 3642, 6 fasc. fols. 1–85 (19th-century transcription of the first printed edition by F. Kurelac [1811–74]). For a contemporary translation of the poem see Marulić M., *Judita, selections*, Croatian trans. B. Lučin – French trans. L. Gordiani – English trans. J. Tyler Tuttle, in Livljanić K., *Judith. Une histoire biblique de la Croatie renaissante* (Paris: 2013) 38–59. For further bibliography, see Tomasović M. – Novaković D., *Judita Marka Marulića. Latinsko pjesništvo hrvatskoga humanizma* [Marko Marulić's Judita. Latin poetry of Croatian humanism] (Zagreb: 1994) 86–87, and Posset F. – Lučin B., "Marcus Marulus", in Thomas, D. – Chesworth, J. (eds.), *Christian-Muslim Relations, a Bibliographical History, Vol. 6: Western Europe (1500–1600)* 99–107. Also see issue 11 (2002) of the journal *Colloquia Maruliana*, which contains numerous studies on *Judita*: http://hrcak .srce.hr/index.php?show=toc&id_broj=30.

in 1522 and addressed to Pope Adrian VI.[18] Two Croatian poems are even more important for their special place in the history of Croatian Ottomanism:

a. *Tuženje grada Hjerozolima* ("Lamentation of the City of Jerusalem", approximately 1516–1517),[19] a poetic call to the Pope and European rulers to engage in a 'holy war' against the Ottomans, which features a prosopopeia of the city of Jerusalem;

b. *Molitva suprotiva Turkom* ("Prayer against the Turks", between 1493 and probably 1500),[20] in which the suffering of Christians is described in great detail and with great pathos. In this Prayer, the narrator is Marulić himself, and he includes himself among the victims of the Ottomans. This was no mere rhetorical device, since the author had lived constantly under Turkish threat and seems entirely credible when he writes 'nas je strah ubil' (v. 31) – 'we were killed by fear'.[21]

This last poem in particular, considered a model of patriotic poetry, epistomises the construction of a Croatian *imago patriae*.[22] This image originates in the Turkish invasion and the need to defend the homeland. Marulić, 'Father of the Renaissance in Croatia', attended a school run in Split by the Italian Renaissance scholar Tideo Acciarini (*1430–†1490); he probably studied law

---

18   *Epistola Domini Marci Maruli Spalatensis ad Adrianum VI. Pontificem Maximum de calamitatibus occurrentibus et exhortatio ad communem omnium christianorum unionem et pacem* (Romæ: Anno D. MDXXII pridie kalendas maii feliciter explicit); on which, see Cattaneo R., "L'epistola a papa Adriano VI di Marco Marulić in Italiano: versione e nota traduttologica", *Colloquia Maruliana* 22 (2013) 145–149. Walser-Bülger, I., "Europe under Attack: Some Thoughts on the Continental Dimension of Marko Marulić's *Epistola ad Adrianum VI. Pontificem Maximum*", *Colloquia Maruliana* 31 (2022) 125–152. For further information and bibliography, see Posset – Lučin, "Marcus Marulus", 118–123.

19   Marco Marulić, *Pisni razlike, priredio i popratio bilješkama Josip Vončina, rječnik sastavio Milan Moguš* [Various poems, prepared and annotated by Josip Vončina, with a dictionary prepared by Milan Moguš], in *Opera omnia* II (Split: 1993) 144–147. For an English translation, see Lučin B. (ed.), *The Marulić reader*, trans. M. Kovačićek (Split: 2007) 246–253.

20   Marulić, *Pisni razlike* 148–152. For an English translation, see Lučin (ed.), *The Marulić Reader* 236–45. On the "Prayer", see Paljetak L., "Molitva suprotiva Turkom u kontekstu protuturskog otpora u Europi Marulićeva vremena i poslije njega" ["Prayer against the Turks in the context of the anti-Turkish resistance in Europe during and after Marulić's time"], *Colloquia Maruliana* 11 (2002) 333–362.

21   See Kraljic I., "'Nous sommes morts de peur': considérations pathémiques sur les opuscules antiturcs de Marko Marulić de Split", *Renaissance et Réforme* 42.2 (2019) 105–140.

22   Dukić D., "Das Türkenbild in der kroatischen literarischen Kultur vom 15. bis zur Mitte des 19. Jahrhunderts", 157–191; Dukić D., *Sultanova djeca. Predodžbe Turaka u hrvatskoj književnosti ranog novovjekovlja* [Sultan's children. Images of Turks in Croatian Literature of the Early modern Period] (Zadar: 2004) 245–253; and Lučin B. (ed.), *The Marulić reader* 246–253.

at Padua University,[23] and created in his hometown, Split, an intellectual circle that might be described as a *Sodalitas Spalatensis*. The *Türkendiskurs* was of key interest to intellectuals in the Marulian circle, and the influence of the 'Croatian Dante'[24] on their literary and poetic production was intense and very extensive.[25]

The corpus of Croatian anti-Turkish writings consists of about 70 works of prose and poetry written between 1448 and 1600 by at least 39 authors, urging Christian action against the 'Turks' in defence of Dalmatia, Croatia, Hungary, and Europe as a whole.[26] This corpus of anti-Turkish texts expresses and reinforces over time the ideology of Croatia as an *antemurale Christianitatis*, 'a bulwark of Christianity', a borderland defence zone where, over centuries, the people have selflessly held back the much stronger enemy.[27] This ideology also pervades some important and well-known examples of Neo-Latin poetry from the Dalmatian area on the 'Turks', for example, *Ad sanctissimum dominum d. Paulum tertium, totius Christianae rei publicae diuino nutu pontificem maximum, quod oppidum Chlissae conseruando plurimae sacrosanctae fidei nationes saluabuntur elegia* (Elegy to the most holy lord Paul III, by God's will pope of the whole Christian estate: by supporting the town of Klis, many nations of the holy faith will be saved, 1535), actually addressed to Pope Pius III, written by Frano Božićević (Split, 1469–1542), better known as Franciscus Natalis, friend of Marko Marulić and author of his biography (*Vita Marci Maruli Spalatensis*).[28] Božićević prophesies the happy outcome of an anti-Turkish mission sent by the Pope in response to the Ottoman siege of the Dalmatian town of Clissa (Klis, a strategically important fortress near Split), which the author portrays as stronghold from which the Ottomans could easily reach Ancona, Quarnero and Istria, as well as Croatia. The elegiac narrator not only describes the unbearable

---

23   Praga G., "Acciarini, Tideo", in *Dizionario Biografico degli Italiani*, vol. 1 (Rome: 1960): https://www.treccani.it/enciclopedia/tideo-acciarini_%28Dizionario-Biografico%29/. However, there is no consistent evidence to confirm his stay in Padua; see Fiaschi S. (ed.), *Tideo Acciarini maestro e umanista fra Italia e Dalmazia. Atti del Convegno internazionale di studi, Macerata, 21 ottobre 2011* (Macerata: 2014).

24   Gutsche G.J., "Classical Antiquity in Marulić's Judita", in *Slavic and East European Journal* 19 (1975) 310–321, esp. 310.

25   Posset – Lučin, "Marcus Marulus" 90–95.

26   Jovanović N., "Croatian anti-Turkish writings during the Renaissance", in Thomas – Chesworth (eds.), *Christian-Muslim Relations* 491–515.

27   Hopp L., *Az 'antemurale' és 'conformitas' humanista eszméje a magyarlengyel hagyományban* [The humanist Ideas of 'antemurale' and 'conformitas' in the Hungarian and Polish Tradition] (Budapest: 1992) 80–81.

28   Ferrari-Cupilli S., *Cenni biografici di alcuni uomini illustri della Dalmazia* (Zara: 1887) 113–114.

158

fate that would befall Dalmatia and Italy – as the center of Christianity and the West – if Clissa were conquered by the 'Turks', but also asserts that if Clissa were to remain free, all the West would be saved from the infidels.[29]

The figure of Marulić has become a sort of temporal marker, and scholars often distinguish between the pre- and post-Marulić production of anti-Turkish texts in Croatia. In this essay special attention will be paid to the earliest poetic response to the Ottoman attacks published in Croatia, the *Elegia de Sibenicensis agri vastatione* (Elegy on the devastation of the district of Šibenik) of Georgius Sisgoreus (after 1470).[30] The aim is to demonstrate how conflicting or compound emotions, as well as ambiguous emotional states are present in this elegy, and how the expressions of emotion shift, one into another.

3 Methodological Issues

The fraught context of the Ottoman invasion did not produce a homogeneous poetic representation of the emotions. This is due to the fact that the communities which suffered grave losses were divided by political and religious differences. Exposure to the Turkish advance could be direct or indirect, since not all areas of Europe, either continental or Mediterranean, were directly affected by the Ottoman conquests. For this reason, poets' responses to the emotional experience of invasion varied.

Moreover, as the ancient author of the Greek treatise *On the Sublime* put it: "there is an indefinite multiplicity of emotions and no one can even say how many they are".[31] The emotions in the poems almost never manifest in a monolithic or even a patently clear form; rather, as a famous Quattrocento humanist, Francesco Filelfo, states: 'Nam et faciles sunt [scil., affectiones] et celeriter moventur transmutanturque'.[32] They emerge through ambiguous expressions or representations; one emotion mixes with or transitions into another, or they come into conflict, or again, are comprised by compounds of more than one emotion.

---

29   Marković M. (ed.), *Pesme Franja Božičevića Natalisa* [Poems by Franjo Božičević Natalis] (Belgrade: 1958), poem n. 79. See also MS Split, Gradska knjižnica [City library] – M-35 (Frano Božićević Natalis, autograph).

30   Bettarini F., "Sisgoreo, Giorgio", in *Dizionario Biografico degli Italiani*, vol. 92 (Rome: 2018): https://www.treccani.it/enciclopedia/giorgio-sisgoreo_%28Dizionario-Biografico%29/.

31   Cf. Περὶ ὕψους (On the Sublime) 22.1: πολλὰ γὰρ καὶ ἀναρίθμητα πάθη καὶ οὐδ' ἂν εἰπεῖν τις ὁπόσα δύναιτο.

32   Filelfo F., *De Morali Disciplina*, in Robin D., *Filelfo in Milan* (Princeton: 1991) 230.

The Neo-Latin poetry on the Turkish threat finds expression above all in elegies and epigrams, the forms most favoured by early modern poets of occasional poetry in Neo-Latin.[33] The elegy as genre requires some preliminary observations. It is not easy to give an unambiguous and universal definition of elegy as a genre, but already in Horace's *Ars poetica* (75–76) the function of elegy as *querimonia* ('complaint', 'lamentation') can be found. Iulius Caesar Scaliger, in the sections on elegy in his famous *Poetices libri septem* (published posthumously in 1561), recognises the adaptable character of the elegiac couplet, despite the primary associations of the genre with amatory topics: 'Epicedia quoque et epitaphia et epistolae hoc genere poematis recte conficiuntur' (Eulogies too, and epitaphs and letters, are properly executed in this kind of poem).[34] According to Jozef Ijsewijn: "generally speaking, [the elegy] is a poem in elegiac distichs dealing with passionate love (*Amores*) or deep sorrow (*Querelae, querimoniae, threnodiae*)".[35] Not all elegies have the same fixed characteristics, and since ancient times there have been different elegiac 'sub-genres'. Neo-Latin poems on the Turks respond to the specific occasions for which they were composed in a great variety of lyrical sub-genres, e.g., paraeneses, eulogies, panegyrics, lamentations, prophecies, prayers, and epitaphs. Each of these corresponds in turn to specific and prevailing speech acts, respectively, exhortation, praises lamentation, supplication, and so on.[36] According to Ijsewijn and the *Oxford Handbook of Neo-Latin*, elegies deal in general with strong emotions and, in particular, with such emotions as love, grief, and pain,[37] which can be identified as the encoded basal emotions of this specific genre.

---

33   See de Beer S., "Poetics Genres – Occasional Poetry: Practice", in Ford P. – Bloemendal P. – Fantazzi C. (eds.), *Brill's Encyclopaedia of the Neo-Latin World. Micropaedia* (Leiden – Boston: 2014) 1142–1144.

34   Iulius Caesar Scaliger, *Poetices libri septem. Sieben Bücher über die Dichtkunst*, ed. L. Deitz – G. Vogt-Spira (Stuttgart: 1994–2011) 3. 202; on elegy see also 1.414–16.

35   Ijsewijn J., "Elegiac Poetry", in Ijsewijn J. – Sacré D. (eds.), *Companion to Neo-Latin Studies, Part II* (Leuven 1998) 80–85, esp. 80.

36   An important influence on this textual range was the variety of genres in which Ovid wrote in elegiac couplets, including the verse letters of the *Heroides* (Heroines) and *Tristia* (Sorrows), and the comic didactic ones of the *Ars Amatoria* (Art of Love) and *Remedia amoris* (Remedies for Love), as well as the books of love elegies, *Amores* (Loves). See Moul V., "Lyric poetry", in Knight S. – Tilg S. (eds.), *The Oxford Handbook of Neo-Latin* (Oxford: 2015) 41–56.

37   Neo-Latin elegiac poems in general are not confined to love poetry: often poems of mourning or political praise are included (influenced perhaps by the varied components of Propertius's fourth book), and many Neo-Latin poets composed religious elegies or exile-poems, in which the poet mourns for himself, on the model of Ovid's exile verse.

Depending on the genre to which the single poetic composition belongs, a prevailing basal emotion tends to subsist, for example, pain, sadness, and mourning in the elegy.[38] Although it is possible to assign core emotions to specific literary genres, this does not imply the existence of definite relational classifications, such as elegy-pain or hymn-enthusiasm. Indeed, as variously claimed, emotions, even in their literary display and thematisation, usually appear neither immovable nor constant in the poetic texts that are my concern here. Such occasional poetry could derive from and/or combine different ancient models, or be couched in a new poetic format, but above all, they relied on the *modi* of certain speech acts (reproaches, threats, repeated requests, supplications, and so forth), which could be distributed among different sections of a single poem and also affect the manner and mode of emotional expression.[39] This is particularly evident in lamentations, which can contain elements of entreaty or of recrimination, or in prophecies with paraenetic elements, or in panegyrics in honor and praise of Christian princes distinguished by their military activity against the Ottomans. Conversely, panegyrics can contain insults directed against one's enemies. In these cases, the speech-act of entreaty intersects with the speech-act of complaint, or the speech-act of prophecy with the speech-act admonition, or praise joins with insult. Complaining, entreating, praising, wishing, blessing, banning, thanking can be the component parts of an overall communicative strategy of address that incorporates various emotions: the speech-acts correspond to different types of emotional expression, complementing or contrasting with the ones that come before of after; they can also be layered or compounded within a single poem.

Indeed, neither poetic texts nor the emotions they convey should be construed as immovable monolithic blocks: an elegy on an irretrievable loss need not be pervaded *exclusively* by pain and suffering. Different themes can be felt to evoke specific emotions: a loss or bereavement, the memory of a person now lost to time or of years lived at home before exile abroad or occupation by a foreign power can offer specific relational emotions; they can shift or fluctuate from one verse to the next, or mixed feelings and conflicting or contrasting emotions can co-exist in a single verse.

See Moul, "Lyric poetry" 41–56, and Houghton L.B.T., "Elegy", in Moul V. (ed.), *A Guide to Neo-Latin Literature* (Cambridge: 2017) 98–112.

38   See Winko S., *Kodierte Gefühle. Zu einer Poetik der Emotionen in lyrischen und poetologischen Texten um 1900* (Berlin: 2003), and Meyer-Sickendiek B., *Affektpoetik: eine Kulturgeschichte literarischer Emotionen* (Würzburg: 2005) 45–48.

39   Schiewer G.L., "Sprache und Emotion in der literarischen Kommunikation. Ein integratives Forschungsfeld der Textanalyse", *Mitteilungen des Deutschen Germanistenverbandes* 2 (2007) 346–361.

Emotions can be defined lexically, and certain words, such as the interjections *Oh* or *Alas*, have a strong emotional valence, but there are also sentiments, by which I mean ambiguous or fluctuating emotional states, that either cannot or need not be semantically fixed: their presence can instead be inferred from such specific devices as rhetorical figures (rhetorical questions, anaphoras, asyndeta, similitudes, hyperboles, metaphors, and so forth), *exempla* or comparisons, the affective application of demonstrative or personal pronouns, and of morphological tools (prefixes, suffixes, diminutives), or the use of words connotative of emotions in specific cultural and communicative contexts, e.g., homeland, honour, pride, progress, etc.[40] Be that as it may, in studying the literary expression and flexible representation of the emotions in poetry, it is useful to start with lexical analysis. Indeed, the use of lexems that explicitly refer to the semantics of emotion itself constitutes an emotional practice.[41] The production of emotion is integral to rhetorical communication and, even more, to poetic forms of language designed to represent emotions either explicitly or implicitly, and also to thematise their presence and effects. Texts, in their constitutive structure, can incorporate marks of emotional expression,[42] but as already noted, emotions are not fixed or immovable entities and consequently, neither is their literary representation.

The ambiguity and discontinuity of certain kinds of emotional experience can cause discontinuities and distortions of/in speech: these discontinuities and the emotional shifts they represent can be enhanced through rhetorical devices premised on the possibility of externalising the emotions. Thus, even if one were to agree with Angelos Chaniotis that the historian cannot study what 'ancient' people *really* felt,[43] it would still be possible to claim that the ancients' experience of emotion is not completely inaccessible to us.

Occasional poetry in general and Neo-Latin poetry on the Turks in particular provided poets with an opportunity to display their erudition and *labor*: a noteworthy event could give rise to poems in Latin or ancient Greek, or other scholarly languages, such as Hebrew.[44] In displaying his knowledge of ancient

---

40   Winko, *Kodierte Gefühle* 102–105 and 132–136.

41   Scheer M., "Are Emotions a Kind of Practice (and is that what makes them have a History)? A Bourdieuian Approach to understanding Emotions", *History and Theory* 51/2 (2012) 193–220.

42   See for example Demetrius, *De Elocutione* 57 on the use of the particle *indeed* in Homerus, *Od.* 5. 203.

43   Chaniotis A., "Moving Stones: The Study of Emotions in Greek Inscriptions", in Chaniotis A. (ed.), *Unveiling Emotions: Sources and Methods for the Study of Emotions in the Greek World* (Stuttgart: 2012) 91–130, esp. 94.

44   de Beer S., "Poetics Genres – Occasional Poetry: Practice" 1142–1144.

rhetorical treatises, choosing the appropriate genre for a given topic or theme, and using specific emotional expressions, he could exhibit his scholarly *discrimen* and affirm his participation in a European-wide intellectual community. The humanists of the early *Quattrocento* did not distinguish themselves as treatise writers on the rhetoric of emotions, nor as authors of theories on poetry or experts in the lyric portrayal of the emotion.[45] In addition to the humanist interest in Horace's *Ars Poetica*,[46] the most striking feature of early Renaissance poetics was its close connection with Rhetoric. The first Renaissance commentaries on the *Ars Poetica* date back only to the end of the 15th century. They, far from focusing exclusively on a particular approach, favoured the guiding principles appropriateness (*convenientia*) and consideration for the audience.[47] Cristoforo Landino, for example, whose text probably first appeared in 1482, tried to classify the teachings of Horace, placing them under the guiding concept of *decorum* and showing that each subject had an appropriate style and genre.[48] Diction, as the style of enunciation, had to be appropriate to the emotion to be elicited and portrayed, as well as to character and circumstance.[49]

Another important point is the difficulty of separating the 'emotional' analysis of a particular genre, especially one that refers to a traumatic event such as the Ottoman's advance in Europe, from the lived experience of the same epoch. According to Douglas Cairns, who has devoted many years to the study of emotions in ancient literature, 'the experiences we pick out and label as emotions or emotional episodes are just the peaks and troughs in a continuous affective landscape; not only individuals, but also cultures will differ in the

---

45 This only happened at a late stage, at a time when the epoch had become fully aware of itself and its achievements. The half-century from 1520 to 1570 can be seen as the heyday of Italian poetry theory: during this period, in 1520, Marco Girolamo Vida wrote the first Renaissance Poetics; at its end, in 1570, the last significant commentary on Aristotelian Poetics appeared, a work by Lodovico Castelvetro; see Fuhrmann M., *Einführung in die antike Dichtungstheorie* (Darmstadt: 1973) 185–211.

46 See Laureys, M. – Dauvois, N. – Coppini, D., *Non omnis moriar. Die Horaz-Rezeption in der neulateinischen Literatur vom 15. Bis zum 17. Jahrhundert* (Hildesheim – Zürich – New York: 2020), and Enenkel K. – Laureys M., *Horace across the Media. Textual, Visual and Musical Receptions of Horace from the 15th to the 18th Century* (Leiden – Boston: 2022).

47 Hor. *Ars* 105–111.

48 *Opera Horatii cum commentario Christophori Landini*, Florence 1482, CLVIv–CLXXIv. Also see Weinberg B., *A History of Literary Criticism in the Renaissance* 1 (Chicago: 1961) 79–81.

49 Of course, this had already been stated by Aristotle: Arist. *Rhet.* 3.7.1–11. Also the most recent socio-linguistic studies, according to which a wealth of display rules tends to be found in the representation of emotions in literary texts, which vary according to cultural conditions and are transmitted and mediated through social learning processes. See Winko, *Kodierte Gefühle* 31–145.

experiences they label and the categories into which they organize them'.[50] The norms and ideologies of the societies in which the emotions originate are always very important, because emotions and their interpretation, especially wherever there is ambiguity of expression, are inextricable from the dynamic social relations and the historical and cultural contexts in which such relations play out. The humanist poets who explored emotional expression in their poetry operated within peer groups that shared common values vis-à-vis the world of felt experience.[51]

For this reason, the true focus of the scholarly analysis of emotion cannot be the subjective inner life of psychological experience, but merely the representation of such experience in the form of concepts, expressions, and evaluative standards of behaviour, what Rüdiger Schnell calls 'signs' (*Zeichen*) of emotions.[52] These forms of lyrical representation reflect the paradigmatic affective scenarios licensed by a particular 'emotional communities' for performance within literary, virtual spaces where emotions such as fear, hope, anger, shame, wonder, pride, etc. can be enacted and ambiguous mixtures of the same expressed and explored. Emotional communities supply the communicative context in/through which the lyrical subjects narrate their emotional states or describe those of others. It goes without saying that they do not necessarily correspond to modern criteria: anger, shame or pride could have different meanings and values in the Renaissance, and they were performed in accord with the communicative expectations of their respective emotional communities. Only with these principles in mind will it prove possible to analyse the emotions bodied forth in the poem to which I now turn, with a view to interpreting the ambiguous emotional states it evokes.

4 Georgius Sisgoreus (1445–1509): from Anger and Pain to Pride and Bravery

Juraj Šižgorić, better known as Georgius Sisgoreus, was the author of the first Croatian *Incunabulum* containing poetry, the *Elegiarum et carminum libri tres*,

---

50 Cairns D., "Introduction. Emotion History and the Classics", in Cairns D. (ed.), *A Cultural History of the Emotions in Antiquity* (1) (London: 2021) 1–16, esp. 1.

51 Among the wide bibliography on the subject, see the most recent publication Enenkel K., "'Identities' in Humanist Autobiographies and related Self-Presentations", in Scholten K. – Enenkel K. (eds.), *Memory and Identity in the Learned World. Community Formation in the Early Modern World of Learning and Science* (Leiden – Boston: 2022) 31–80.

52 Schnell R., *Haben Gefühle eine Geschichte? Aporien einer History of Emotions* (Göttingen: 2015) 17–20.

which was published during his lifetime, in 1477.[53] He was born to a noble family from Luka County in neighboring Croatia around 1445, in Šibenik (Sebenico), Dalmatia, part of the Venetian domain on the east coast of the Adriatic Sea. In 1465, Sisgoreus completed his studies at the University of Padua, where he obtained a degree in canon law in February 1471.[54] At this celebrated institution, which in the fifteenth century was a breeding ground for encounters between humanists and jurists from all over Europe and a place where the foremost intellectuals of the time studied and sojourned, Sisgoreus had the opportunity to meet distinguished professors and students and build lasting friendships. He befriended the aforementioned Tideo Acciarini, author of the *Cohortatio in Turcos ad Sixtum IV* (Exhortation for Sixtus IV to wage war against the Turks, approximately 1471), a paraenetic elegy calling for a crusade against the 'Turks'.[55] Acciarini, as mentioned above, became teacher to the young Marulić. He also became close to Raffaele Zovenzoni (1431–1480), well-known author of the *Istrias*, a poetic collection (divided into three books) that paid homage to his homeland, and also of Neo-Latin lyric poems on the Turks, above all the *Carmen concitatorium ad principes Christianos in Turcum* (Exhortation for Christian sovereign against the Turks), another call to engage in a common war against the Ottomans.[56] Zovenzoni was also one of the main exponents of Friulian humanism (based in Istria), closely associated with literature on the *Türkengefahr*; indeed like Dalmatia and the Balkans, Friuli was constantly under attack by the Ottoman Empire.[57]

The Ottoman Empire began threatening Šibenik during its struggle against Venice in the late fifteenth century: in 1467, 1468, and 1469 the Ottoman

---

53 Jovanović N., "Šižgorić, Juraj" 31–35.

54 See Bettarini, "Sisgoreo, Giorgio".

55 For the biography see Praga, "Acciarini, Tideo", and Fiaschi (ed.), *Tideo Acciarini*. For the *Cohortatio in Turcos* see Lučin B., "An Unpublished Poem of Tideo Acciarini to Pope Sixtus IV", *Colloquia Maruliana* 24 (2015) 65–114. Sisgoreus also wrote an epigram for his friend Acciarini, the *Ad Tydeum Acciarinum poetam* (poem n. III 2 in his *Elegiarum et carminum libri*), a *propemptikon* wishing of a good and prosperous navigation.

56 Vinco M., "Zovenzoni, Raffaele", in *Dizionario Biografico degli Italiani*, vol. 94 (Rome: 2020): https://www.treccani.it/enciclopedia/raffaele-zovenzoni_%28Dizionario-Biografico%29/.

57 On the literary friendship between Šižgorić and Zovenzoni, see Čvrljak K., "Tršćanski humanist Raffaele Zovenzoni (1434–1485?) u Istri i Dalmaciji: s posebnim osvrtom na Kopar i Šibenik te Jurja Šižgorića" ["Humanist of Trieste Raffaele Zovenzoni (1434–1485?) in Istria and Dalmatia: with special reference to Kopar and Šibenik and Juraj Šižgorić"], *Mogućnosti* 39 (1992) 890–915. As he did for Acciarini, Sisgoreus also wrote an epigram for Zovenzoni, the *Raphael Zovenzonius poeta* (poem n. III 3 in his *Elegiarum et carminum libri*).

EMOTIONS IN NEO-LATIN LYRIC POETRY ON TURKS   165

incursions reached the city, and the raids were repeated in 1471 and 1472,[58] extending to the hinterland of Split. Around this time, probably after the raid of 1469, Sisgoreus composed what is perhaps his best known text, the *Elegia de Sibenicensis agri vastatione*.[59] Although the name of Sisgoreus is remembered mostly for this elegy, the Ottomans, always labelled as *Turcae*, are not a usual theme in his oeuvre; according to Dukić-Grgin, among his 88 poems, only two mention the 'Turks'.[60] Beyond the elegy on the devastation of Sebenico, at the beginning of the verse epistle *Ad Symonem Diphnycum theologum* the poet recalls the death of his brothers (one of whom died during a battle against the Turks);[61] he also recounts the Turkish attacks on his homeland: 'Et solitus Turcus nostris accurrere campis/ turbavit querulo carmina nostra sono' (And the Turk accustomed to assaulting our fields/ irked the sound of my song with their howls).[62] In his geographic-historical work in prose, *De situ Illyriae et civitate Sibenici* (1487),[63] there is no mention of the Ottoman-Venetian wars.[64]

The elegy for Sebenico, an exceptional subject in this poet's oeuvre, nevertheless enjoys canonical status as one of the 'most exciting' and 'certainly the oldest poetic testimonies on the Turkish invasions in European literature'.[65] The elegy for Sebenico is more than an individual response to a dramatic historical

---

58   As Sisgoreus attests in his Elegy for Sebenico: 'Ter conatus erat nostras invadere turmas,/ Ter nostris Turcus Martia terga dedit' (vv. 67–8).

59   Raukar T., *Hrvatsko srednjovjekovlje. Prostor, ljudi, ideje* [Croatian Middle Ages. Space, People, Ideas] (Zagreb: 1997) 407–408.

60   Dukić D. – Grgin B., "Juraj Šižgorić and the Ottomans. The image of the other in a late medieval Dalmatian commune", *Association Internationale d'Études du Sud-Est Européen – Revue* (2014) 97–112.

61   *Elegia de duorum obitu fratrum*: 'Infoelix cecidit crudele vulnere maior/ pro patria pugnans, pro laboribusque suis'. Cfr. Šigžorić, J., *Elegiarum et carminum libri III* ed. by Gortan, V. (Zagreb: 1966) 83.

62   Ibidem 115.

63   *De situ Illyriae et civitate Sibenici* remained unpublished until the end of the 19th century (1899); the 2nd improved edition with translation in Croatian (1981) includes 17 chapters dealing with the etymology of the Illyrian name, the borders of Illyria, and the history and geography of Dalmatia and Sebenico. See Šigžorić J., *O smještaju Ilirje i o gradu Šibeniku, Muzej grada Šibenika. Priredio i preveo Veljko Gortan* [About the accommodation of Ilirje and the city of Šibenik, Museum of the City of Šibenik, edited and translated by Veljko Gortan] (Sebenico: 1981) 103.

64   This could be explained by the fact that a geographical treatise containing information on the origins of the inhabitants of Sebenico and their customs, unlike an elegy, was not an appropriate literary genre for staging and sharing such an intimate experience such as the advance of the Turks; it was more a real homage to one's homeland and its history.

65   Novak S.P., *Povijest hrvatske književnosti* [History of Croatian Literature], 2 vols. (Zagreb: 1997) 118.

166   SASSO

event,[66] and it shares many features typical early Renaissance Latin poetry and poetics. The poem marshals all the stereotypical attributes ascribed to the 'Turks' until the seventeenth century: cruelty, brutality, sexual lust, barbarism. It also codified the lyrical representation of patriotic feelings that would continue to characterise Croatian literature at least until the nineteenth century.[67]

The poem is clearly structured in three parts:

1.   In verses 1–28, the elegiac narrator introduces the event as one of a series of torments that have plagued him throughout his life.

2.   The central section of the poem, verses 29–86, can be subdivided into three sections: first, Šižgorić, as already mentioned, describes the enemies, using anti-Ottoman stereotypes that emphasise religious difference; then he refers current military events, such as the conquests of Costantinople (1453), Lesbos (1462) and Negroponte (1470). Finally, he describes the three attacks on Šibenik: skirmishes between 'Turks' and the local population that occurred in front of the city walls, before the 'narrator's eyes'.

3.   In conclusion, the poem reaches its emotional *climax*, at verses 87–98, where the narrator declares that – ready to die for his faith and homeland – he has been forced to lay down Apollo's lyre and books of law, and take up arms.[68]

Sisgoreus' poem, titled an elegy, develops as a complaint in elegiac couplets against the devastation of the poet's homeland by the 'Turks'. Since it is both an elegy and a lamentation, the prevailing emotion, as codified for the literary genre to which the poem belongs, is pain. However, the poem begins with the clear thematisation of other emotions – disappointment and resignation – and the three narrative macro-sections enumerated above do not correspond to the same number of displayed emotions.

> 'Credebam post multa mei mala fata vigoris/
>   Denique iam fatis vivere posse bonis./
> Interdum celum nimbis agitatur et auris,/
>   Interdum radiis ornat Apollo suis./
> 5   Non mutat scaevas in me fortuna sagittas;/

---

66   For this interpretation (the elegy for Sebenico as a 'picture taken from life') see Kombol M., *Povijest hrvatske književnosti do narodnog preporoda* [History of Croatian Literature until the national Revival] (Zagreb: 1961) 65, and Novak, *Povijest hrvatske književnosti*, 118–119, which sets the poem within a history of Croatian Renaissance literature.

67   Dukić, *Sultanova djeca*, 11–12.

68   See Jovanović, "Šižgorić, Juraj" 31–35.

EMOTIONS IN NEO-LATIN LYRIC POETRY ON TURKS

> Me miserum semper, fors mala, quid crucias?/
> Sapphica credebam iam leto condere cantu/
> Te, pulcher, Musis, Phoebe, favente meis./
> Nunc elegos iterum cogor cantare dolentes/
> Et premor a lacrimis protinus ipse meis'.

'I believed that after many unfortunate effort/ finally now I could experience good fortune./ Sometimes the sky is agitated by clouds and mists,/ sometimes Apollo adorns it with his rays./ But fortune does not stop hurling its arrows against me;/ I [who am] always unhappy, oh evil fate, why do you torment me?/ Ere now I thought I could compose a happy song in Sapphic stanzas,/ You, beautiful Phoebe, with the Muses, favoring me./ Now I am forced again to sing verses that cause pain/ and I am urged to do it immediately by my own tears'.

From line 1 to line 10, the poet expresses profound disillusionment as respects his expectations and hopes of living peacefully and practising his poetic art in a *laeto cantu*: this is evident especially from the use of the verb *credo* in the imperfect tense and from the explicit observation that fortune instead continues to shoot arrows against him; this brings out resignation about the impossibility of changing destiny, but also a feeling of betrayed hope and therefore disappointment. These verses of resignation are temporarily interrupted by verse 6 ('Me miserum semper, fors mala, quid crucias?'), where the elements which display pain multiply:

a. the sentence is a direct question;
b. the poet addresses fate directly, through the vocative *fors mala*, and the use of the *Du-Stil*;
c. he uses the adjective *miserum* – 'who suffers disaster', which alludes to the experience of pain suffered from external forces, due to events that cannot be controlled by the ego;
d. the position of the object pronoun *me* in the first foot of the verse, followed by the adjective *miserum*, attributes pathos to the protagonist who is the object of misfortune and therefore suffers;
e. according to the same mechanism, the verb *crucio*, i.e., 'to torment', is positioned at the end of the same verse.

After verse 6 disappointment and delusion return as prominent themes, and this is linguistically traceable in the repetition of the verb *credebam*. Then vv. 9–10 ('Nunc elegos iterum cogor cantare dolentes/ et premor a lacrimis protinus ipse meis') present the first occurrence of the explanatory verb linked to the basal emotion typical of the poem's genre, i.e., pain; this receives support from the use in two consecutive verses of the verbs *cogor* and *premor* – 'to be obliged, forced' (both in passive diathesis, to indicate suffering from an external source): the poet seems to express his compulsion to sing a poem about pain and the urgency with which he sings. Here the verses (*elegos*) are described as *dolentes*; the verb *doleo* is ambivalent in meaning,[69] because in some cases it can be translated as 'to feel pain', 'to suffer', and in other cases as 'to cause pain'. In v. 9, the interpretation of the participle *dolentes* is not immediately apparent: here *elegos dolentes* could mean both 'verses of pain', since Sisgoreus's poem represents a complaint, and 'verses that cause or bring about pain'. The presence of the passive diathesis (*cogor*), whereby the poet declares that external events have forced him to compose an elegy, suggests that the line might best be translated 'I am forced again to compose verses that cause pain'. This would best express the poet's feeling of having greatly suffered: Sisgoreus would thus not only avow that he has been compelled to compose elegiac verses (of mourning and lamentation), but also that composing these verses have caused him further pain. However, the other interpretation also remains valid: the verse is thus exemplary, for it shows how a single word can carry the weight of expressive ambiguity.

The theme of pain is introduced by feelings of constraint and obligation, and then through a comparison; the poet refers to the analogous grief to be found in Latin elegiac models, such as Tibullus and Ovid:

> 'Non fato similes habeo, fortuna, poetas,/
> Qui cecinere elegos corde gemente malos./
> Delia, te cultus cantat, formosa, Tibullus/
> Et dolet ingratas semper habere faces./
> 15 Non erat ille dolor vatis sine vulnere ceco,/
> Attamen ille dolor plenus amoris erat'.

> 'I do not share the same fate, oh luck, as the poets,/ who sang sorrowful poems with a groaning heart./ Beautiful Delia, the cultured Tibullo celebrates you/ and he suffers always from possessing thankless passions./ That pain of the poet was not free from wounds,/ however, that pain was filled full with love'.

Sisgoreus declares that he does not have the same happiness as Tibullus who could sing of the beauty of his *puella*. What is particularly interesting is the

---

69   ThLL *doleo, 5, 1: 1819.

EMOTIONS IN NEO-LATIN LYRIC POETRY ON TURKS

contradictory emotional picture of a 'Tibullian' (typically elegiac) love's pain that may be viewed as desirous and desired pain, as in the canonical elegiac depiction of love as *dolor cupitus*. A comparison is immediately set up with a well-known exponent of ancient poetry. This is further supported by the use of the conjunction *attamen*: Sisgoreus does not deny that Tibullus suffered for the woman celebrated in his poems; he speaks explicitly of their groaning hearts (*corde gemente*). However, the pain of the ancient poet was the pain of love, in this sense desired, and not comparable to the pain felt by the Dalmatian poet whose *lamentatio* arises from the destruction of his homeland. This comparison also emerges from the following verses, where Ovid is mentioned, the paradigmatic author of poems of sad exile.

> 'Naso, pulsus eras patria cariturus, amicis,/
>   Sollatio multo, coniuge et ipse tua./
> Ille dolor cunctos vincebat, Naso, dolores,/
> 20   Quem vincit certe nunc meus iste dolor'.

> 'Ovid, you were expelled from your homeland, separated from your friends,/ from great relief, your wife and yourself./ That pain overcomes all pains, Ovid,/ but certainly now this pain of mine surpasses your pain'.

Sisgoreus declares that his suffering and the Ovid's pain of exile are not commensurate, even if the ancient poet claims his pain exceeds any other: the *cunctos dolores* to which he refers implicitly encompasses every type of suffering expressed in verse, including that of Tibullus; but if Ovid's pain, by his own admission, surpasses every other, Sisgoreus' suffering for the devastation of his homeland surpasses even Ovid's misery, and by extension that of every other person.

This reading is confirmed on four counts. First, by what the poet says before and after these verses. In lines 1–10, Sisgoreus confesses profound disappointment in his unmet expectations, his hopes of living peacefully and writing poetry.

Second, at line 23, after the comparison with Ovid's pain, he says: 'Et taceo multos, qui me presseres, dolores' (And I keep silent about many [other] pains that oppress my soul). The poet implies that the pains about which he sings represent only a small part of misfortune he bears; this sharpens his suffering, making it more acute than Ovid's. Sisgoreus thereby presents himself as *primus inter pares* among the poets of sorrow, more exceptional than any disappointed lover or hapless exile, in that he must behold the tragic spectacle of his devastated homeland.

Third is the anaphora of the lexeme *dolor* in both verses, placed respectively in the last two feet of the hexameter and the pentameter. The end placement, along with the repeated emphasis on the theme of pain, ramps up the emotional tension and concentrates attention on the comparison between Sisgoreus and his illustrious predecessors. He also uses the demonstrative pronoun *ille* at the start of the verse to indicate Ovid's exilic suffering, and counterposes it to *iste* (supported by the possessive pronoun *meus*) at the end of the following verse to indicate the pain of the Dalmatian poet. Rhetorically this usage positions the two verses in an implied chiastic structure, with the pronoun *ille* making Ovid's pain appear more distant, and the pronounon *iste* Sisgoreus's pain more proximate.

Fourth, at line 28 which concludes the first section of the elegy, asserts: 'Et superat querulos nostra querella modos' (Our lament [scil., this elegy, these verses] goes beyond the plaintive genres). In using the verb *supero* (to overcome), the poet intensifies his emphasis on the felt pain he at the same time celebrates. Only at line 20 does Sisgoreus refer to his own suffering: the emotional flow shifts from disillusion to disappointment, and the concentration on grief increases as the semantics of pain and suffering come uninterruptedly to dominate the following verses until they collide with the description of the malevolent Turkish enemy (vv. 30–50).

The 'Turks', despite multiple campaigns, never managed to conquer Šibenik, but they caused losses, grief and great devastation, about which Sisgoreus sings about with great pathos. For example, in the vv. 21–28:

> 'Praetereo fratres crudeli morte peremptos,/
> Quos flevit misero nostra querella sono,/
> Et taceo multos, qui me pressere, dolores;/
> Me miserum semper, fors mala, quid crucias?/
> 25 Hei mihi, nunc doleo patrios vastarier agros/
> Factaque Christicolis maxima probra viris./
> Ista mei luctus et magni causa doloris,/
> Et superat querulos nostra querella modos'.

'I leave aside the brothers killed by a cruel death,/ for whom our laments have wept with pitiable sound,/ and I am silent about the many sorrows that oppress me;/ poor me, bad luck, why do you torment me always?/ Woe is me, now I suffer for paternal fields more than devastated / and because they [the Turks] have committed the greatest injury against Christians./ This is the cause of my grief and utmost pain,/ and our complaining surpasses plaintive bounds'.

EMOTIONS IN NEO-LATIN LYRIC POETRY ON TURKS 171

Pain, tears, wailing, sorrow: here the insistence on the emotional semantics of pain is evident. The poet concludes this section with an explicit declaration of extreme grief and mourning: 'Ista [scil., the devastation of his homeland by the Turks] mei luctus et magni causa doloris'.

The verses on the 'Turks' that follow refer to Islam's ban on alcohol and eating pork, even while comparing the Turks themselves to pigs. The Turkish enemy is conventionalised as a *perfida turba*;[70] dedicated only to nefarious wars, they portend nothing good for anyone who meets them on the battlefield (*scevo bello*). Despite the conventional character of these descriptions, which can easily be situated within the literary tradition of anti-Ottoman propaganda, the poet's feelings of contempt and outrage, his indignant awareness of the Turkish depredation of his homeland, are readily discernible.[71]

Sisgoreus now expresses a further emotion, quite unexpected in the register of elegy: elements of fascination and esteem for the enemy (vv. 55–60). Up to now, a sequence of interlinked negative emotions has predominated, underscored by mourning; at this point, for the first time, a form of 'positive' emotion – admiration – emerges:

55   'Cernebam Turcos alta de turre furentes/
      In patrios iuvenes in patriosque viros./
     Certe ego veloces cursus mirabar equorum/
      Hastarumque minas barbaricumque dolum/
     Motaque per varios vexilla rubentia ventos/
60   Saepius et vidi candida signa trahi'.

'I saw the Turks raging from the top of the tower/ against the youth of the country, against the homeland's men./ Certainly I marveled at the swift coursing of the horses, the threat of spears and barbaric deception/ and

---

70   See, for example, Helmrath, "Pius II. und die Türken" 104–117, and Höfert, *Den Feind beschreiben* 51–87.

71   Indeed, after mentioning some famous cities or regions conquered by the Turks (such as Constantinople and Negroponte) and stating that not even Xerxes had managed to conquer so many territories (vv. 44–50), the poet says: 'Dicere si vellem, quot vicit regna, quot urbes,/ Deficeret carmen deficerentque dies' (If I should wish to relate how many reigns, how many cities [they conquered],/ the poem would weaken and my days forsake me). If as Horace writes, each genre has its own subject and style, Sisgoreus's elegy requires appropriateness and cannot be reduced to a list of names and events, but the absence of surprise also emerges with respect to the fact that his homeland too had been so severely hit: *Turcus adest patriae* (v. 53: 'the Turk is in the homeland') and this is and could be the only theme of the mourning.

the banners stirred by the changeable winds,/ more often did I see white banners being dragged along'.

According to Dukić-Grgin, 'the narrator appears as a witness of the Turkish attack on his homeland';[72] this is confirmed above all by the use of the verbs *cerno* (to distinguish, to recognize clearly) and *video* (to see), although this section of the poem appears to be anything but an 'eyewitness account' of the events described and narrated. In v. 27, having recalled the destruction of his homeland territories and the injuries suffered by his fellow Christians as the chief causes of his own suffering ('Ista mei luctus et magni causa doloris'), and expressed great indignation at the behaviour of the invaders, he then uses a verb belonging to the sphere of emotional semantics – *miro* (to admire). Moreover, he uses it in passive diathesis (*miror*), fully expressing the violent, impetuous character of this emotion: fascinated by the enemy, he is struck with admiration for his destructive adversaries.

Expressing fascination with the Turkish military and their readiness to fight for their imperial homeland is unusual in the tradition of Turkish-centered poetry that usually directs the admiration and the praise solely toward the Christian troops.[73] This phenomenon complicates the analysis of elegiac emotion: what surfaces here is a clear *motus animi* of the poet who, though saddened by the Turkish advance, does not shy away from admiring the formidable foe. Pain and inner conflict arising from disappointment and suffering lead to indignation, which then develops into a form of admiration: the emotions shift from loathing to guarded esteem before reverting to their prior state. This recognition of the enemy is fraught with ambivalence since the poet is also justifying Sebenico's youth by acknowledging their foe's superior military preparedness and efficacy.

Moreover, the poet uses the adjective *furens* to describe the 'Turks' (*Turcos furentes*), a participle that invites a mixed or ambiguous reading of the emotions. With regard to the semantics of anger in Turkish poetry, two moments must be distinguished: on the one hand, anger ascribed to the enemy underlines their barbarism, almost in a canonical way. On the other hand, when anger is ascribed to Christian figures – for example, a leader of locals defending

---

72   Dukić D. – Grgin B., "Juraj Šižgorić and the Ottomans" 102.

73   Only at the end of the 16th century did the standard hostile view of the Turks begin to alter, due in part to the religious wars then raging in Europe. Two other important factors contributed to the more nuanced appreciation of the Turks: first, the alliance between France and the Sultan; second, the decision of the Habsburg King Ferdinand I to send permanent envoys to Constantinople (1554–1562). See von Martels Z., "Neo-Latin Literature – The Ottoman Empire", in Ford P. – Bloemendal J. – Fantazzi C. (eds.), *Brill's Encyclopaedia of the Neo-Latin World. Micropaedia* (Leiden – Boston: 2014) 1101–1103.

EMOTIONS IN NEO-LATIN LYRIC POETRY ON TURKS

their homeland – it becomes a positive attribute of righteous men (*iusta ira*).[74] Sisgoreus, in applying *furens* to the 'Turks' and then expressing a kind of admiration for their military might, allows the term to carry both positive and negative connotations. His ambivalent usage can be analysed by reference to adjacent verses. First, he again uses the adjective *furens* to describe Sebenico's youth fighting for their people (vv. 61–62: 'Pulchra iuventa furens scutum portabat et ensem/ Pro patria pugnans pro domibusque suis');[75] here the usage of *iusta ira*, expressing admiration for compatriots, is conventional. But the poet then utilises the same adjective for the 'Turks' (vv. 70–71): 'Noster ager Turco milite plenus erat./ Impius ille furens villas dedit ignibus omnes' ('Our fields were full of Turkish soldiers./ Angry, sacrilegious, they set fire to all the villages'). The presence of a further adjective, *impius*, typically applied to the 'infidel Turks' in *Türkenlyrik*, insists on a negative reading, in contrast to the characterisation of the Christians as *pia gens*.[76] Furthermore, the demonstrative pronoun *ille* indicates moral distance and expresses scorn. In compressed form, *impius ille furens* alludes to the Turks' cruelty, savagery and barbarism. Two contrasting if not conflicting emotions thus emerge: the 'Turks' may be cruel and ferocious, animated by negative anger and worthy of scorn, but still they are in certain respects admirable.

In a recursive movement, indignation and the anger against the enemy pervades the subsequent section of the poem, where Sisgoreus circles back to describe Turkish barbarism and cruelty, again in canonical images. The Turks captured the youth of Sebenico, desecrated sacred sites, burned Christian 'temples': indignation and contempt for the enemy mix with emotions issuing from pain, that felt experience thoroughly encoded in the elegiac genre. This becomes particularly evident when the interjection *Hei* (Alas) registers both grief and anguish (v. 85: 'Hei mihi, nec sacre numina fixa cruci'). The invocation of pain prefaces the final section of the poem, which from the point of view of 'emotional' analysis can be divided into two parts:

1. vv. 87–90, where inconsolable suffering meaningfully emerges;
2. vv. 91–98, where the events caused by the Turkish advance incite prideful anger, and where angry pride saturates the poet's promise himself to fight in defense of Sebenico.

---

74 On the concept of *iusta ira*, see Peters C., "*iustas in iras*? Perspectives on Anger as a Driving Force in Neo-Latin Epic", in Enenkel K. – Traninger A., *Discourses of Anger in the Early Modern Period* (Leiden – Boston: 2015) 261–287.

75 'The furious beautiful youth (from Šibenik) carried the shield and the sword/ fighting for the country and for his compatriots'.

76 Helmrath, "Pius II. und die Türken" 104–117.

'Carmine quo flebo? Faciam quid, patria dulcis?/
    Quidve miser faciam, tuque sacrata fides?/
Est mea mens tanto nimium, queror, egra dolore,/
90   Rumpuntur fletu pectora nostra gravi./
Cogor Apollineum vates deponere plectrum/
    Et gladium nostra stringere posse manu./
Consultus ponam numerosa volumina iuris/
    Et clypeum capiam Marte favente mihi./
95   Pro te, sacra fides, et, dulcis patria, pro te/
    Sit mea barbaricis dedita vita viris!/
Pro te me voveo, pro te mea pectora trado/
    Et morior pro te vulnera sceva ferens'.

'In what poem shall I weep? What shall I do, sweet homeland?/ What
should I, a miserable wretch, do, and what of you, sacred faith?/ My ach-
ing mind takes on too much pain, I moan, our hearts burst with profound
weeping./ Poets, I am forced to lay down the Apollonian pen/ that we
be able with our hand to draw the sword./ As a jurist, I should ponder
numerous volumes of the law/ and I should take up the shield by favour
of Mars./ For you, holy faith, and for you, my sweet homeland/ may my
life be consecrated to the barbarians./ For you I vow, for you I deliver my
heart/ and I die for you, enduring outrageous wounds'.

The first part of this poetic peroration poses three *Du-Stil* questions, the first
addressed by the poet to himself, asking in what (other) poem he should be
able to weep; then despairingly calling upon his homeland, he asks what should
he do; and finally, he appealing to his religion, he identifies himself as *miser*
(a miserable, unfortunate wretch). The recourse to the direct discourse and
the anaphora of the verb *faciam*, used to underscore his doubts about a future
plan of action, give these verses a nervous energy, bringing out the anguish,
disorientation and despair that inform them. This is followed by another clear
affirmation of pain, entirely concentrated v. 90, where the semantics of suffering emerges (for example, in the poet's description of his burdened mind,
afflicted by pain); the final position of the word *dolor* assigns a leading role to
the lexeme and to the emotion it carries, amplified by the adjective *tantus* (so
big, so intense), and accompanied by *nimium* (too great), an evident pleonasm.
In declaring that he will exchange poetry for the sword in defense of his homeland, Sisgoreus deploys the verb *cogor*, which refers back to the initial section
of the poem, where he averred that he has been forced once again to write
about sad events. The passive diathesis of the verb *cogo* clearly indicates that a

EMOTIONS IN NEO-LATIN LYRIC POETRY ON TURKS 175

decision has been taken reluctantly, under the duress of external events. This connects to the sense of desperation expressed above, in the initial questions, where the abandonment of poetry evinces both anguish and sorrow. The poem concludes with a sense of duty and surge of pride: in answer to the questions posed earlier, Sisgoreus answers to religion and the homeland ('sacra fides et dulcis patria') that he is ready to die for them. The five-fold occurrence of the anaphora *pro te* reveals how emphatic his decision to abandon himself to love of country has become; the steady beat of anaphorae concludes this elegy of pained lament in a movement of courage and pride.

The lyrical tension and grief engendered by the expressive oscillation of emotion, from resignation to pain, fascination to indignation, lead to the declaration of *amor patriae*.[77] Apropos the love of country, Sisgoreus adduces Tibullus and Ovid, positioning himself within a poetic *continuum* anchored to the greatest representatives of Latin elegiac poetry; at line 28, as already noted, he says: 'Et superat querulos nostra querella modos' ('our lament [scil., this elegy, these verses] goes beyond the plaintive genres'). The use of the verb *supero* (to overcome) already interpreted as an accentuator of felt pain, also adverts to the agonal triad *imitari-aemulari-superare*; as such, it function as a coded allusion to the poet's superiority in the elegiac tradition, as compared to other ancient paragons of *lamentatio*.[78] Despite this, the poet ends by declaring his intention of putting aside his art in defense of the fatherland: the honorable exercise of patriotic fervor in face of the Ottoman threat brings the elegy's emotional journey to its close.

5   **The Lament for Sebenico: a Poem of Compound Emotion**

Sisgoreus' poem, titled an elegy, is, as we have seen, a lament; it inaugurated the *Türkendiskurs* in the Croatian poetic sphere, as the threshold poem of the so-called *Zeit der Klagelieder* (the time of lamentations) in the Croatian-Dalmatian area. The elegy for Sebenico, a lament in the sense of the Latin word *querimonia* (complaint), accords with Horace's functional definition of elegy. On the other hand, it does not belong to the biblical genre of lamentation, unlike other important poems from the Croatian area, for example, Marco Marulić's aforementioned *Lamentation of the City of Jerusalem*. Missing from the poem is the idea that the 'Turks' are God's punishment for the sins

---

77   See (also for further informations) McClure G., *Sorrow and Consolation in Italian Humanism* (Princeton: 1990).

78   Burke P., *Die europäische Renaissance. Zentren und Peripherien* (Munich: 2012²) 92–133.

committed by wayward Christians, and nor does Sisgoreus demand that a Christian Holy War be waged against the 'Turks', core themes of anti-Turkish *lamentationes* on the model of the *Lamentations of Jeremiah*. Also lacking is any prophecy of an apocalyptic scenario.[79] Sisgoreus, in focusing on cruelty and fury of the 'Turks' and the suffering they have caused, neither brings up the promise of redemption nor makes an accusation of spiritual poverty, and nor does he admonish his compatriots in a censorious tone.[80] His elegy is a real complaint, a sorrowful elegy, in which the influence of classical authors such as Virgil and especially Ovid is quite apparent. Indeed his portrayal of the 'Turks' shows a certain affinity with that of the *Getae* in Ovid's *Tristia* 5.7.[81]

The prevailing emotion codified in the relevant poetic genre should therefore be grief, which traditionally plays a leading role in elegy, but in the two long sections describing the customs and mores of the 'Turks', other emotions prevail, namely, indignation and scorn combined with anger against the enemy for their misdeeds. The cause of his complaint is revealed in the central section of the elegy (vv. 29–86), where grief shifts into anger against the Turks. Anger manifests as a compound emotion, something between the pain of a suffered slight and the desire for revenge, along with longing for the rehabilitation of honor lost to an offending enemy. Anger is defined through the formula 'pain-revenge', which goes at least as far back as Aristotle.[82]

In this meaning the emotion of anger could also be interpreted as a virtue: whoever fails to get angry when he or his family or country is insulted, is defenseless rather than virtuous, whereas one *should* defend oneself against anyone who hurls insults. Thus interpreted, anger emerges as a compound emotion of at least two others: it mixes pain with the desire for revenge against

---

79 The anti-Turkish *Lamentations* form part of the more recent tradition of the Italian *lamenti* and the French *laments*. They include the *Lamenti di Costantinopoli* of 1453 and the *Lamenti di Negroponte* of 1470. See *Lamenti storici dei secoli XIV, XV e XVI raccolti e ordinati a cura di Antonio Medin e Ludovico Frati*, 4 vols. (Bologna: 1887–1894) 2:121–229, 249–320.

80 See Höfert, *Den Feind beschreiben* 201.

81 The allusion to Ovid's *Tristia* 5.7 remains irrefutable and is already hint, but the similarities do not go beyond common themes and motifs, such as an intimidating appearance and barbaric cruelty; see Dukić – Grgin, "Juraj Šižgorić and the Ottomans" 104.

82 See Engelen E.M., "Eine kurze Geschichte von 'Zorn' und 'Scham'", in *Archiv für Begriffsgeschichte* 50 (2008) 41–73, and Enenkel K. – Traninger A., *Discourses of Anger in the Early Modern Period* (Leiden – Boston: 2015) 2–5. With reference to Aristotle, mainly see *Art of Rhetoric*, 1378a 31–33, and *Nicomachean Ethics*, VII 7, 1149a 32–34. Regarding the formula 'pain-revenge', it is not possible to state with absolute certainty that Sisgoreus had read Aristotle's *Rhetorica*, or that he knew it so thoroughly as to have based the development of his own poem about it.

EMOTIONS IN NEO-LATIN LYRIC POETRY ON TURKS   177

one or more individuals whose hostility makes them enemies; the offensive act they have perpetrated, the injury they inflict demands revenge, and just revenge can alone provide satisfaction and rehabilitate personal pride and honour. The principle that pain necessarily begets the desire for vengeance comes close to the notion or, better, doctrine of societal destiny: on this view, anger always arises from a sense of superiority over an enemy; it can be understood as a projection of this feeling of supremacy.[83] The pleasure that results from the hope of being able to exact revenge 'is not limited to personal satisfaction, but rather serves a greater good'.[84] According to this definition, anger joins pain and pleasure together and above all it combines with a complex model of social roles: 'when anger was regarded as a social emotion, [...] one that consisted of conscious action as much as spontaneous reaction'.[85] Therefore, as Barbara Rosenwein states: 'Thus Anger in the Latin West had a privileged place: it was a sin, but a sin that could be turned into a virtue, monopolized by an aristocracy'.[86]

Sisgoreus's poem assigns a strong leading role to indignation and anger against the 'Turks', undoubtedly in line with the Dalmatian social elite's shared response to the wartime situation in the second half of the fifteenth century; indignation combines with feelings of intense sorrow and pain, since suffering inflicted on the homeland is experienced as a personal slight. This causal chain then leads to the expression of pride and patriotism, attested by the poet's willingness to abandon every other activity and take up arms to defend his homeland. Intermixed with these emotions is the hope for revenge, upon which the rehabilitation of honour depends. Pain, although it is the basal emotion in the genre to which the poem belongs (elegy in the form of a lament), emerges as a component of righteous anger against the 'Turks' for atrocities committed against the city of Sebenico and the entire Christian world. The formula 'pain-revenge' appears explicitly in the aforementioned use of the adjective *furens*, which belongs to the semantics of anger: driven by pain, the enraged youth of Sebenico, through the exercise of martial virtue, avenge themselves upon Turkish enemy, who are also *furens* in another sense, moved not by any pain for a suffered injury but only by bestial cruelty. If anger arises for Christians as a compound emotion between suffered pain and longing for

---

83   See Rapp C., *Aristoteles, Rhetorik* (übers. und erl. von C. Rapp) (Darmstadt: 2002) 543–583.

84   Enenkel – Traninger, *Discourses of Anger* 2; see also Konstan D., *The Emotions of the Ancient Greeks. Studies in Aristotle and Classical Literatur* (Toronto – Buffalo – London: 2006) 99–119.

85   Enenkel – Traninger, *Discourses of Anger* 1.

86   Rosenwein B., *Anger's Past. The social Uses of an Emotion in the Middle Ages* (Ithaca – London: 1998) 5.

a restoration of slighted honour, this definition of anger cannot pertain to the 'Turks', whose fury is one-dimensional. On this account, Christian anger is the attribute of a higher ranking people treated insolently by people of lower rank; such anger therefore originates in a presumed, instantaneous judgement of one's moral superiority over the 'Turks'. So too, the anger displayed by the poet Sisgoreus, as elegiac narrator and lyrical subject, arises from the pain of a perceived injury which fuels the desire for revenge as a therapeutic to damaged pride. The poet's display of compound emotion binds him to the elite Dalmatian community from which he draws emotional support.

6 Conclusion

As it has been demonstrated, if Sisgoreus's poem can be divided thematically into three large sections, from the point of view of the investigation of emotion, several constituent parts can be found:

1. vv. 1–5: disappointment and disillusion;
2. v. 6: pain;
3. vv. 7–8: disappointment and disillusion;
4. vv. 9–10: feeling of compulsion and pain;
5. vv. 11–28: sadness and pain;
6. vv. 29–54: indignation and anger (against the 'Turks');
7. vv. 55–60: admiration for the 'Turks' and their military art;
8. vv. 61–69: indignation against the 'Turks' and admiration for the *amor patriae* of his compatriots;
9. vv. 70–83: indignation and anger against the 'Turks';
10. v. 84: pain;
11. vv. 85–86: indignation;
12. vv. 87–90: anguish, feeling of desorientation and pain;
13. vv. 91–94: feeling of compulsion and sadness;
14. vv. 95–98: pride and bravery.

From lines 1–86 there is an almost constantly fleeting movement from emotion to emotion; a pattern prevails, however: after diverging from the previous emotion, the succeeding one circles back from whence it came. For example, disappointment and the sad disillusion at vv. 1–5 turn into painful suffering (v. 6), and then return to in their originary state (vv. 7–8); or indignation and anger against the enemy at vv. 29–54 turn into guarded admiration for them (vv. 55–60, esp. 57), and then resurface (vv. 61–69), now admixed with admiration for Christian *amor patriae*. These emotions and the recursive pattern of shifting emotion can be verified not only through an analysis of terms relating to the semantics of emotions, such as interjections, but also through a rhetorical-stylistic interpretation. This brings out in the emotional economy of Sisgoreus's verses: v. 6 emerges as a transitory movement of pain that interrupts the predominant emotions expressed in vv. 1–10; and this occurs in that single verse as already in v. 7, the previous emotional range, anchored in disappointment, returns. In this emotional 'micro-perspective', as evident from lexical and rhetorical analysis of the verses and words, a lyrical trend can be discerned: the emotional movement is often sudden, abrupt, and fleeting, characterised by incursions into the emotion(s) that prevail in the immediately prior verses. Emotions seem to arise in the 'storm' of an intense passion, in the form of brief, intense impulses of the soul, not really as sustained feelings that arise gradually or pervade the entire poem. Conversely in the emotional 'macro-perspective' is the poet's prevalent feeling the anger against the 'Turks', from which issue pain (for the suffered injury) and the desire of revenge. It may thus be no coincidence that the most explicit expression of anger takes place at the centre of the poem, where it functions as a pivot for the poem's other emotional swings. If anger underlies the whole of the poem, then the other emotions – pain, vengefulness, and the pride featured at the conclusion – can be seen as inflections of it. Viewed through this lens, these emotions would then seem to emerge gradually, not in a storm of violent passion. As the poem develops, anger against the Ottoman enemy, compounded by pain and the desire of revenge, comes increasingly to be expressed as a conscious action, staged duly as the justified reaction of a virtuous man against a perceived slight. Through analysis of the poem's emotional fluctuations, it becomes clear that specific literary genres – here the elegy – can theoretically represent a medium of basal emotions, which are codified as the core of the genre itself. In the case of the elegy, this emotion would be pain, which however Sisgoreus describes as flowing from anger and fluctuating in a movement of mixed emotions.

Bibliography

Bettarini F., "Sisgoreo, Giorgio", *Dizionario Biografico degli Italiani* 92 (Rome: 2018), available from https://www.treccani.it/enciclopedia/giorgio-sisgoreo_%28Diziona rio-Biografico%29/ (accessed 31.01.2023).

Bisaha N., *Creating East and West. Renaissance Humanists and the Ottoman Turks* (Philadelphia: 2010).

Burke P., *Die europäische Renaissance. Zentren und Peripherien* (Munich: 2012[2]).

Cairns D., "Introduction. Emotion History and the Classics", in Cairns D. (ed.), *A Cultural History of the Emotions in Antiquity* (1) (London: 2021) 1–16.

Cattaneo R., "L'epistola a papa Adriano VI di Marco Marulić in Italiano: versione e nota traduttologica", *Colloquia Maruliana* 22 (2013) 145–149.

Chaniotis A., "Moving Stones: The Study of Emotions in Greek Inscriptions", in Chaniotis A. (ed.), *Unveiling Emotions: Sources and Methods for the Study of Emotions in the Greek World* (Stuttgart: 2012) 91–130.

Čvrljak K., "Tršćanski humanist Raffaele Zovenzoni (1434–1485?) u Istri i Dalmaciji: s posebnim osvrtom na Kopar i Šibenik te Jurja Šižgorića", *Mogućnosti* 39 (1992) 890–915.

de Beer S., "Poetics Genres – Occasional Poetry: Practice", in Ford P. – Bloemendal P. – Fantazzi C. (eds.), *Brill's Encyclopaedia of the Neo-Latin World. Micropaedia* (Leiden – Boston: 2014) 1142–1144.

Delumeau J., *La peur en Occident* (Paris: 1978).

Döring K.D., *Türkenkrieg und Medienwandel im 15. Jahrhundert (mit einem Katalog der europäischen Türkendrucke bis 1500)* (Munich: 2013).

Dukić D. – Grgin B., "Juraj Šižgorić and the Ottomans. The image of the other in a late medieval Dalmatian commune", *Association Internationale d'Études du Sud-Est Européen – Revue* (2014) 97–112.

Dukić D., "Das Türkenbild in der kroatischen literarischen Kultur vom 15. bis zur Mitte des 19. Jahrhunderts", in Lauer R. – Majer H.G. (eds.), *Osmanen und Islam in Südosteuropa* (Berlin: 2013) 157–191.

Dukić D., *Sultanova djeca. Predodžbe Turaka u hrvatskoj književnosti ranog novovjekovlja* (Zadar: 2004).

Ebermann R., *Die Türkenfurcht, ein Beitrag zur Geschichte der öffentlichen Meinung in Deutschland während der Reformationszeit* (Halle: 1904).

Enenkel K. – Laureys M., *Horace across the Media. Textual, Visual and Musical Receptions of Horace from the 15th to the 18th Century* (Leiden – Boston: 2022).

Enenkel K. – Traninger A., *Discourses of Anger in the Early Modern Period* (Leiden – Boston: 2015).

Enenkel K.A.E., "'Identities' in Humanist Autobiographies and Related Self-Presentations", in Scholten K. – Enenkel K.A.E. (eds.), *Memory and Identity in the Learned World. Community Formation in the Early Modern World of Learning and Science*, Intersections 81 (Leiden – Boston: 2022) 31–80.

Engelen E.M., "Eine kurze Geschichte von 'Zorn' und 'Scham'", *Archiv für Begriffsgeschichte* 50 (2008) 47–73.

Ferrari-Cupilli S., *Cenni biografici di alcuni uomini illustri della Dalmazia* (Zadar: 1887).

Fiaschi S. (ed.), *Tideo Acciarini maestro e umanista fra Italia e Dalmazia. Atti del Convegno internazionale di studi, Macerata, 21 ottobre 2011* (Macerata: 2014).

Fuhrmann M., *Einführung in die antike Dichtungstheorie* (Darmstadt: 1973).

Göllner C., *Turcica. Die europäischen Türkendrucke des XVI. Jahrhunderts*, 3 vols. (Bucharest – Berlin – Baden-Baden: 1961–1968).

Guthmüller B. – Kühlmann W. (eds.), *Europa und die Türken in der Renaissance* (Tübingen: 2000).

Gutsche G.J., "Classical Antiquity in Marulić's Judita", *Slavic and East European Journal* 19 (1975) 310–321.

Hankins J., "Renaissance Crusaders: Humanist Crusade Literature in the Age of Mehmed II.", *Dumbarton Oaks Papers* 49 (1995) 111–207.

Hanß S., *Lepanto als Ereignis. Dezentrierende Geschichte(n) der Seeschlacht von Lepanto (1571)* (Göttingen: 2017).

Helmrath J., "Pius II. und die Türken", in Guthmüller B. – Kühlmann W. (eds.), *Europa und die Türken in der Renaissance* (Tübingen: 2000) 79–137.

Höfert H., *Den Feind beschreiben. "Türkengefahr" und europäisches Wissen über das Osmanische Reich 1450–1600* (Frankfurt: 2003).

Hopp L., *Az 'antemurale' és 'conformitas' humanista eszméje a magyarlengyel hagyományban* (Budapest: 1992).

Houghton L.B.T., "Elegy", in Moul V. (ed.), *A Guide to Neo-Latin Literature* (Cambridge: 2017) 98–112.

Hrabak B., "Turske provale i osvajanja na području današnje severne Dalmacije do sredine XVI stoleća, Radovi, Sveučilište u Zagrebu", *Centar za povijesne znanosti* 19 (1986) 69–100.

Ijsewijn J., "Elegiac Poetry", in Ijsewijn J. – Sacré D. (eds.), *Companion to Neo-Latin Studies, Part II* (Leuven: 1998) 80–85.

Iulius Caesar Scaliger, *Poetices libri septem. Sieben Bücher über die Dichtkunst*, ed. L. Deitz – G. Vogt-Spira (Stuttgart: 1994–2011).

Jovanović N., "Croatian anti-Turkish writings during the Renaissance", in Thomas D. – Chesworth J.A. (eds.), *Christian-Muslim Relations. A Bibliographical History, 7. Central and Eastern Europe, Asia, Africa and South America (1500–1600)* (Leiden – Boston: 2015) 491–515.

Kissling H.J., "Türkenfurcht und Türkenhoffnung im 15./16. Jahrhundert. Zur Geschichte eines 'Komplexes'", *Südost-Forschungen* 23 (1964) 1–18.

Kombol M., *Povijest hrvatske književnosti do narodnog preporoda* (Zagreb: 1961).

Konstan D., *The Emotions of the Ancient Greeks. Studies in Aristotle and Classical Literature* (Toronto – Buffalo – London: 2006).

Kraljic I., "'Nous sommes morts de peur': considérations pathémiques sur les opuscules antiturcs de Marko Marulić de Split", *Renaissance et Réforme* 42.2 (2019) 105–140.

Laureys M. – Dauvois N. – Coppini N., *Non omnis moriar. Die Horaz-Rezeption in der neulateinischen Literatur vom 15. Bis zum 17. Jahrhundert* (Hildesheim – Zürich – New York: 2020).

Laureys M., "Poetic crisis talks between Constantinople and Rome", *Nordic Journal of Renaissance Studies. Studia Humanitatis: Essays in Honour of Marianne Pade on the Occasion of her Sixty-Fifth Birthday* 18 (2022) 277–292.

Livljanić K., *Judith. Une histoire biblique de la Croatie renaissante* (Paris: 2013).

Lučin B. (ed.), *The Marulić reader* (Split: 2007).

Lučin B., "An Unpublished Poem of Tideo Acciarini to Pope Sixtus IV", *Colloquia Maruliana* 24 (2015) 65–114.

Lučin B., "Marko Marulić – kroatischer Dichter und europäischer Humanist", *Colloquia Maruliana* 18 (2009) 349–355.

Marković M. (ed.), *Pesme Franja Božičevića Natalisa* (Belgrade: 1958).

Marulić M., *Pisni razlike*, priredio i popratio bilješkama Josip Vončina, rječnik sastavio Milan Moguš, *Opera omnia* II (Split: 1993).

McClure G., *Sorrow and Consolation in Italian Humanism* (Princeton: 1990).

Meyer-Sickendiek B., *Affektpoetik: eine Kulturgeschichte literarischer Emotionen* (Würzburg: 2005).

Moul V., "Lyric poetry", in Knight S. – Tilg S. (eds.), *The Oxford Handbook of Neo-Latin* (Oxford: 2015) 41–56.

Novak S.P., *Povijest hrvatske književnosti.* 2 vols. (Zagreb: 1997).

Paljetak L., "Molitva suprotiva Turkom u kontekstu protuturskog otpora u Europi Marulićeva vremena i poslije njega", *Colloquia Maruliana* 11 (2002) 333–362.

Peters C., "*iustas in iras*? Perspectives on Anger as a Driving Force in Neo-Latin Epic", in Enenkel K.A.E. – Traninger A. (eds.), *Discourses of Anger in the Early Modern Period* (Leiden – Boston: 2015) 261–287.

Pitcher D.E., *An Historical Geography of the Ottoman Empire* (Leiden: 1968).

Posset F. – Lučin B., "Marcus Marulus", in Thomas, D. – Chesworth, J. (eds.), *Christian-Muslim Relations. A Bibliographical History, 6. Western Europe (1500–1600)* (Leiden – Boston: 2014) 99–107.

Posset F., *Catholic Advocate of the Evangelical Truth: Marcus Marullus (Marko Marulić) of Split (1450–1524)*, (Eugene, Oregon: 2021).

Praga G., "Acciarini, Tideo", *Dizionario Biografico degli Italiani* 1 (Rome: 1960) https://www.treccani.it/enciclopedia/tideo-acciarini_%28Dizionario-Biografico%29/ (accessed 31.01.2023).

Pust K., "'Le genti della citta, delle isole e del contado, le quale al tutto volevano partirsi'. Migrations from the Venetian to the Ottoman Territory and Conversions of Venetian Subjects to Islam in the Eastern Adriatic in the Sixteenth Century", *Povijesni prilozi* 40 (2011) 121–129.

Rapp C., *Aristoteles, Rhetorik* (übers. und erl. von C. Rapp) (Darmstadt: 2002).

Raukar T., *Hrvatsko srednjovjekovlje. Prostor, ljudi, ideje* (Zagreb: 1997).

Robin D., *Filelfo in Milan. Writings 1451–1477* (Princeton: 1991).

Rosenwein B., *Anger's Past. The social Uses of an Emotion in the Middle Ages* (Ithaca – London 1998).

Scheer M., "Are Emotions a Kind of Practice (and is that what makes them have a History)? A Bourdieuian Approach to understanding Emotions", *History and Theory* 51/2 (2012) 193–220.

Schiewer G.L., "Sprache und Emotion in der literarischen Kommunikation. Ein integratives Forschungsfeld der Textanalyse", *Mitteilungen des Deutschen Germanistenverbandes* 2 (2007) 346–361.

Schindler C., "'Barbarico tingi sanguine vidit aquas'. Die Schlacht von Lepanto in der neulateinischen Dichtung", in Föking M. – Schindler C. (eds.), *Der Krieg hat kein Loch. Friedenssehnsucht und Kriegsapologie in der Frühen Neuzeit* (Heidelberg: 2014) 111–140.

Schmugge L., *Die Kreuzzüge aus der Sicht humanistischer Geschichtschreiber* (Basel – Frankfurt: 1987).

Schnell R., *Haben Gefühle eine Geschichte? Aporien einer History of Emotions* (Göttingen: 2015).

Schwoebel R., *The Shadow of the Crescent. The Renaissance Image of the Turk (1453–1517)* (Nieuwkoop: 1967).

Šigžorić J., *Elegiarum et carminum libri III* ed. by V. Gortan (Zagreb: 1966).

Šigžorić J., *O smještaju Illirje i o gradu Šibeniku, Muzej grada Šibenika. Priredio i preveo Veljko Gortan* (Sebenico: 1981).

Tomasović M. – Novaković D., *Judita Marka Marulića. Latinsko pjesništvo hrvatskoga humanizma* (Zagreb: 1994).

Vinco M., "Zovenzoni, Raffaele", *Dizionario Biografico degli Italiani*, 94 (Rome: 2020) https://www.treccani.it/enciclopedia/raffaele-zovenzoni_%28Dizionario-Biografico %29/ (accessed 31.01.2023).

von Martels Z., "Neo-Latin Literature. The Ottoman Empire", in Ford P. – Bloemendal J. – Fantazzi C. (eds.), *Brill's Encyclopaedia of the Neo-Latin World (Micropaedia)* (Leiden – Boston: 2014) 1101–1103.

Walser-Bülger I., "Europe under Attack: Some Thoughts on the Continental Dimension of Marko Marulić's *Epistola ad Adrianum VI. Pontificem Maximum*", *Colloquia Maruliana* 31 (2022) 125–152.

Weinberg B., *A History of Literary Criticism in the Renaissance* 1 (Chicago: 1961).

Winko S., *Kodierte Gefühle. Zu einer Poetik der Emotionen in lyrischen und poetologischen Texten um 1900* (Berlin: 2003).

Wright E. – Spence S. – Lemons A. (eds.), *The battle of Lepanto* (Cambridge – Massachusetts – London: 2014).

CHAPTER 5

Shifting Emotions in Neo-Latin Psalm Poetry and Erotic Elegy: George Buchanan and Janus Lernutius

Carolin A. Giere

Abstract

This paper deals with the poetic processing of opposing, mixed and shifting emotions in 16th century psalm poetry and erotic love elegy. Despite the fundamentally different subject matter, both genres have many overlaps and similar strategies. On the basis of communicative codes and rhetorical-stylistic techniques, the concept of emotion used will be identified. To this end, poems by two well-known poets, George Buchanan and Janus Lernutius, will be examined, both of whom placed importance on demonstrating their literary humanistic skills and had a (different) religious background.

The paper retraces the historical bond of psalm poetry and erotic elegy to the lyric genre, examines their common emotional characteristics in light of genre-specific and methodological considerations and takes into account fundamental socio-psychological and poetological criteria that provide information about the way feelings were dealt with in this literary period.

Keyword

16th century Neo-Latin humanism – psalm paraphrase – love elegy – lyric genre – rhetorical strategies – multi-perspectival emotions – religious transcendence – erotic connotation

1 Introduction

Composing lyric poems became part of social life during the Renaissance of the sixteenth century, especially in courtly and educated circles. After printing had largely replaced handwritten manuscripts as the predominant literary medium, it was no longer just a matter of passing on manuscripts from hand

© CAROLIN A. GIERE, 2025 | DOI:10.1163/9789004694613_006

to hand or reading them aloud to an audience.[1] A thriving book market had emerged that, while still presenting handwritten small pamphlets and quarto books, was also filled with printed volumes that brought with them new economic and social conditions.

In this present situation, sixteenth-century poets faced a specific challenge: They had to enrol in the humanistic *Respublica litteraria* by introducing themselves to a readership interested primarily in modes of human thought, feeling, and self-expression. The (semi-) autobiographical erotic poem seemed to offer one of the best answers to this requirement, and it soon became one of the most appreciated genres of the time. Short poems, occasional and especially erotic poetry, were often used by aspiring young poets to demonstrate their classical education and literary skills, which were modelled on the ancient authors. The conception of texts as "social ephemera", intended for circulation and collection, was typical of the time and can best be understood from its social context.[2] Since Italy was the source of much new scholarship, imitators beyond the Alps had to follow the example of Italian scholars. The trend of writing these erotic verses, therefore, became almost universal in all countries where Latin verse was cultivated. However, there was another, thematically quite different and important poetic exercise for humanists, which originally had nothing to do with the preferred erotic verse, but also aimed at a demonstration of their Latinity: the metrical translation of the biblical Psalms into Latin.

For many humanists, however, whether Catholics, Lutherans or Calvinists, it was more an exercise they took up in old age.[3] Marcantonio Flaminio as well as the Scottish writer George Buchanan changed their poetic interest – having previously been very well known for their erotic *Iuvenilia* – and devoted themselves exclusively to psalm paraphrases. They even showed a sense of remorse by apologizing for their *Iuvenilia* and calling them a mistake of their youth.[4] It goes without saying that both genres, love elegy and psalm poetry, are about love, but that the object of desire is different and modifies the principles: Love elegy is the poetic play with erotic-secular love for a *puella* in the style of

---

1   For oral performance of literature in Early Modern Europe see: Chartier R., "Leisure and Sociability: Reading Aloud in Modem Europe", in Zimmerman S. – Weissman R.F.E. (eds.), *Urban Life in the Renaissance* (Newark: 1989) 103–120.
2   Marotti A.F., *Manuscript, Print and the English Renaissance Lyric* (Ithaca: 1995) 2–3.
3   On psalm paraphrases as part of Neo-Latin lyric poetry see Moul V., "Lyric Poetry", in Knight S. – Tilg S. (eds.), *The Oxford Handbook of Neo-Latin* (Oxford 2015) 45.
4   Brown P.H., *George Buchanan: Humanist and Reformer, a Biography* (Michigan: 1890) 139–140.

classical Roman poetry. Psalm poetry[5] is an expression of praise for God and an interpretation of the Psalms; it centres on the religious love for God. But what was the special interest of humanist poets in both genres? What special connections are there between psalm poetry and love elegy, given their very different themes?

A fundamental connection arises from the difference in content mentioned above: both genres, psalm poetry and love elegy, have comparable perspectives on their specific topic, that is, a very personal approach expressing deep and intimate emotions. Humanism's focus on the individual, in contrast to the previous ethos of the Middle Ages, is certainly one of the most important reasons why both forms of poetic expression gained popularity.

In this paper, I give attention to the very particular expression of *mixed emotions*, which – and this will be the thesis of my remarks – are a phenomenon of both humanist psalm poetry and love elegies in the sixteenth century. The questions will be: What kinds of emotions are expressed and how? Which genre-specific and independent strategies can be identified in their modes of expression? Are there stylistic overlaps in form, meter and mode that confirm the theoretical connection between the two different genres?

In order to gain an understanding of the two complementary yet distinct genres, I will retrace their historical bond to the lyric genre, assuming a mutual dependence. Secondly, I examine their common emotional characteristics in light of genre-specific and methodological considerations. For the emotion-based strategies of sixteenth-century poems, it is illuminating to consider basic socio-psychological and poetological criteria. The treatment of emotions in love elegies is widely documented; Petrarch, in particular, with his bittersweet love for the hard-hearted Donna Laura, has often been discussed as a model for Neo-Latin literature. Of interest to this paper is the connection between psalm poetry and the elegiac moment with its stylistic characteristics of emotional expression, on the one hand, and love poetry integrating religious and psalm poetic criteria, on the other. Before concluding by discussing some poems and their emotional expression, I will briefly outline the situation of psalm poetry in the sixteenth century in contrast to the Middle Ages. In view of the large number of psalm-poetic and love-elegiac works, the present study has to be restricted to only a few exemplary passages; I will draw on George Buchanan, who was one of the best-known psalm poets of his time throughout

---

5   The term "psalm poetry" is used here to refer to the free translation or paraphrase of an originally Hebrew psalm. The paraphrase is an expanding and explanatory transliteration that might change both the external form of a text and its appearance, such as the form of speech, e.g., from prose to verse.

SHIFTING EMOTIONS IN NEO-LATIN PSALM POETRY AND EROTIC ELEGY   187

Europe, and on some relatively well-known Dutch poets of the sixteenth century who composed love elegiac cycles and may have known Buchanan's poetry well.

2   The "Defense of the Poetry" as a Link between Psalm Poetry and Love Elegy

The common idea of emphasising emotions in both psalm poetry and love elegies is related to another shared characteristic: the conceptual aspect of genre-specific characteristics. The poetic motivations of both genres are linked to each other and each justifies itself to the other as an important component of the lyric genre. Whereas Jerome argued against the enemies of paganism in late antiquity that the Bible itself was linguistically sophisticated poetry and thus comparable to ancient poetry, Petrarch turned the argument around, defending pagan poetry against theological rigorists of his time. One might almost say that the two genres, with their opposing purposes and argumentation, helped each other succeed in having a place in the lyric genre, since both emphasise the poetic aspect of the Bible:

From Jerome onwards (347–420), the harmonisation of pagan and Christian culture gained traction.[6] Through the Psalms, he argued, the Holy Bible as a literary work of art meets the standards of ancient rhetoric and poetry.[7] In making his case, he highlighted the psalms themselves as poetry. Apart from that, he described the Bible as the oldest document in the world, predating even pagan philosophers and authors. His contradictory argumentation, which at times identifies Moses as an acquaintance of the ancient pagan writers and at other times presents him as the first poet, can be traced back to his own ambivalence about reconciling the Christian ascetic ideal and the *sapientia mundi*.[8] Despite all the inherent contradictions, however, the Psalms have been considered poetry since Jerome, whether on the grounds that the Bible is older than ancient literature, or that its linguistic form can be compared with the works of the Greeks and Romans.[9] Isidore of Seville (560–636) juxtaposes the sacred

---

6   Eiswirth R., *Hieronymus' Stellung zu Literatur und Kunst* (Wiesbaden 1955).

7   Curtius E.R., *Europäische Literatur und lateinisches Mittelalter* (Tübingen – Basel: 1993) 44.

8   Dyck J., *Athen und Jerusalem: Die Tradition der argumentativen Verknüpfung von Bibel und Poesie im 17. und 18. Jahrhundert* (München 1977) 28.

9   Thus, Augustine (354–430) argues that the words of the Bible are "*divina mente fusa et sapienter et eloquenter ... Quod mirum si et in istis inveniuntur, quos ille misit, qui fecit ingenia?*" (*De doctr. chr.* IV. 7, 21; CC Ser Lat XXXII 131.) The authors of the Bible were not only wise but also eloquent in the sense of Roman rhetoric: "*Nam ubi eos* [*sc. auctores*] *intellego, non solum nihil*

and secular writings without calling undue attention to their distinctive characteristics or addressing the gap between ancient culture and Christian faith.[10] Interesting in this context is his *De metris*: he reports that Moses was the first to use hexameter; thus the Hebrews were the first to write poetry. Hymns, he states, had first been written by David in praise of God, while the Greeks had used the genre *'longe post David'*.[11] This reasoning for the poetic status of the psalms is closely related to a fundamental question that had long been debated: *Did the prophets write in verse?* Jerome himself, who clearly admired the Hebrew verses and tried to adapt them to the standard classical meters, had written:

> Denique quid Psalterio canorius? quod in morem nostri Flacci, et Graeci Pindari, nunc iambo currit, nunc alcaico personat, nunc Sapphico tumet, nunc semipede ingreditur. Quid Deuteronomii et Isaiae Cantico pulchrius? quid Salomone gravius? quid perfectius Iob? Quae omnia hexametris et pentametris versibus ut Iosephus et Origenes scribunt, apud suos composita decurrunt.[12]

> What is more musical than the Psalter, which, in the manner of Flaccus or of the Greek Pindar, now flows in iambs, now rings with Alcaics, swells to a Sapphic measure or moves along with a half-foot? What is fairer than the hymns of Deuteronomy or Isaiah? What is more solemn than Solomon, what more polished than Job? All of which books, as Josephus and Origen write, flow in the original in hexameter and pentameter verse.[13]

Jerome does not say precisely where in Scripture these iambs, alcaics, hexameters or pentameters are to be found, but his comments and translations were accepted as sufficient evidence that the psalms, like Greek and Latin poetry, were constructed in meters.

---

       eius sapientius, verum etiam nihil eloquentius mihi videri potest' (*De doctr. chr.* IV. 6,9; CC Ser Lat XXXII 122.). Later on, Beda Venerabilis (672–735) even argues for the Bible's own rhetoric, taking up the arguments for the document's age and poetic style. See *De schematibus et tropis sacrae scripturae*, Migne Patrologia Latina 90, 175 B.

10   Curtius, *Europäische Literatur* 451.

11   Isidore, *Etymologiae* 1,39,11 ff.

12   Jerome, *Praefatio in Librum II Chronicorum Eusebii*, Migne Patrologia Latina 27, 223–224, Praefatio 12–13.

13   Kugel J.L., *The Idea of Biblical Poetry: Parallelism and its History* (New Haven: 1981) 159–60.

SHIFTING EMOTIONS IN NEO-LATIN PSALM POETRY AND EROTIC ELEGY 189

Probably the best-known modern theory dealing with the question of Hebrew prosody is Robert Lowth's concept of *parallelismus membrorum*, the 'parallelism of the members' (parts of the verse).[14] The eighteenth-century English Hebraist is said to have been the discoverer of biblical parallelism, which defines scriptural poetry according to this systematic feature:[15] The theory is based on the assumption that the original Hebrew had some sort of meter, now difficult to recover. The Hebrew, passed down from generation to generation, became susceptible to errors of transmission with regard to poetic structure.[16] Nevertheless, from the Middle Ages to the Early Modern Period, the consensus always prevailed: the original Hebrew texts of the Psalms were already metrical and thus poetic. This idea of Jerome and Isidore of Seville (ca. 560–636) found a later advocate in Petrarch (1304–1374).[17] He refers appreciatively to Jerome's translation of the Bible, which, although it could not preserve the original verse form of the Psalms alongside the content, did to some extent preserve their poetic structure, translating the Psalms into verse.[18]

Even though Petrarch quotes the Church Fathers and uses the same arguments as Jerome, this does not change the fact that he pursues completely different, even opposite goals to Jerome. Almost 700 centuries later, he is not faced with the problem of justifying the Bible as a poetic text, but aims rather

---

14 Lowth R., *Lectures on the Sacred Poetry of the Hebrews*, trans. G. Gregory, 2 vols. (London: 1787) II:34.

15 See Harris R.A., *Discerning Parallelism: A Study in Northern French Medieval Jewish Biblical Exegesis* (Providence 2004) 55–73. Kugel states that Lowth's argument was not a new one ("Poets and Prophets: An Overview", in Kugel J.L. (ed.), *Poetry and Prophecy: The Beginnings of a Literary Tradition* (New York: 1990) 23) and argues for an alternative literary perspective of Lowth's analysis: Kugel, *The Idea of Biblical Poetry* 12–85.

16 See Kugel, "Poets and Prophets" 23.

17 Petrarch, *Familiaria* X,4,6. [...] *et Veteris Testamenti Patres heroyco atque aliis carminum generibus usi sunt: Moyses Iob David Salomon Ieremias; Psalterium ipsum daviticum, quod die noctuque canitis, apud Hebreos metro constat, ut non immerito neque ineleganter hunc Christianorum poetam nuncupare ausim* [...]. – "The patriarchs in the Old Testament used heroic and other forms of poetry, as well, for example Moses, Job, David, Solomon and Jeremiah. And the Psalter of David, which you sing day and night, is written in Hebrew in a specific meter, so it is not incorrect or misleading if I dare to call David a poet of the Christians." (Unless otherwise indicated, translations are mine.)

18 Petrarch, *Familiaria* X,4,6–7: [...] *idem video sensisse Ieronimum, quamvis sacrum illud poema quod beatum virum, scilicet Cristum,* [...] *in aliam linguam simul sententia numerisque servatis transire nequiverit. Itaque sententie inservitum est, et tamen adhuc nescio quid metrice legis inest et Psalmorum particulas ut sunt, sic versus vulgo dicimus.* – "Jerome also seems to have been aware of this. He was not able to translate the consecrated chant into Latin, both according to the content and while preserving the rhythms, and therefore paid attention to the content; but until today a certain metrical system is inherent in the Holy Scriptures, and we usually call the passages of the Psalms verses."

to defend secular poetry from strict theologians who feared the influence of pagan thought. Petrarch refutes their attacks by positing a 'defence of biblical poetry'. He points out that the first poets were prophets. Theology and poetry are not as a rule automatically opposed to each other;[19] secular and religious poetry, meanwhile, differ only in their content: 'illic de Deo deque divinis, hic de diis hominibusque tractatur' (*Fam.* x, 4, 2.), one concerns solely God himself and all divine things, the other concerns the divine and the human equally. The argument that 'the Bible contains poetry' thus becomes a strategy for defending both Renaissance poets and the Bible as poetry. The topos of poetry as 'concealed theology'[20] extends from Coluccio Salutati (1331–1406) to Julius Caesar Scaliger's defence of poetry[21] (approx. 1550) and Philip Sidney's *Defense of Poesy* (1580).[22] This legitimation of poetry has been firmly anchored in the European literary tradition at least since Petrarch and his adoption of Jerome's arguments. The connection between psalm poetry and secular poetry through the mutual recourse to the Bible as poetry 'appealed to the syncretic tendencies of readers and writers eager to connect the two ancient streams that flowed together into the turbulent cultural pool of Renaissance and Reformation England',[23] an era of particular interest in this case study because of Buchanan, and which was closely associated with Dutch writers of the period, as will be shown with reference to Lernutius.

The basic element here was the contemporary desire to express one's emotions and feelings through culture. This was reflected in an increased interest

---

19   Petrarch, *Familiaria* x,4,6: *theologie quidem minime adversa poetica est.*

20   Bachem R.: *Dichtung als verborgene Theologie. Ein dichtungstheoretischer Topos vom Barock bis zur Goethezeit und seine Vorbilder* (Bonn: 1955).

21   For Scaliger's *Contra poetices calumniatores declamatio* see Julius Caesar Scaliger, *Iulii Caesaris Scaligeri Epistolae et orations nunquam ante hac excusae* (Leyden, Franciscus Dousa: 1600), 409–413.

22   In his *Defense of Poesy* Sir Philip Sidney describes divine poetry as the earliest and preeminent literary kind; he enunciates "Poetics of Psalm translation": Niefer J. *Inspiration and utmost art: the poetics of early modern English psalm translations* (Wien – Zürich: 2018) 228–236. By praising the biblical *vates*, Sidney highlights the Psalms as outstanding poetry: "And may not I presume a little further to show the reasonableness of this word *vates*, and say that the holy David's Psalms are a divine poem? If I do, I shall not do it without the testimony of great learned men, both ancient and modern. But even the name of Psalms will speak for me, which, being interpreted, is nothing but Songs; then, that it is fully written in metre, as all learned Hebricians agree, although the rules be not yet fully found; lastly and principally, his handling his prophecy, which is merely poetical." Sir Philip Sidney, *An apology of poetry or the defense of poesy* ed. R.W. Maslen – G. Shepherd (Manchester – New York: 2002) 84.

23   Hamlin H., *Psalm Culture and Early Modern English Literature* (Cambridge: 2006) 87.

SHIFTING EMOTIONS IN NEO-LATIN PSALM POETRY AND EROTIC ELEGY   191

in devotional poetry, more precisely psalm poetry, even though the humanists did not neglect their affection for pagan poetry.

3   Questions of Genre and Theoretical Aspects of the Emotions

Strictly speaking, the lyric genre of Roman and Greek antiquity comprises those poems written 'in the collection of meters designed for songs accompanied by the lyre'.[24] The Greek lyric tradition, with its most influential poet Pindar, influenced Roman lyric poetry, especially the major lyric poet Horace. Their lyric stanza forms were sapphics, alcaics and the Asclepiad meter, but not primarily elegiac couplets or epodic meters. However, because elegy in particular had been used since Roman antiquity for themes that were common to ancient Greek poetry, such as love or political praise, a blurred or permeable boundary emerged between lyric and elegy, which Neo-Latin poets took up with great abandon. For Neo-Latin poetry, elegiac couplets were the most popular meter. Since the ancient poets, the elegiac couplet, associated with a variety of topics, was preferred for the expression of 'strong emotions, whether of love (as in Ovid's *Amores*, but also in those of Propertius and Tibullus), grief or praise'.[25] The expression of feelings was thus one of the lyrical devices of elegy. It is worth mentioning that the elegies were originally songs of lament; also, the medieval elegy was firmly linked to this gesture of mourning and lament. The emotion of grief and the mood of sadness are thus also fundamental for elegy.

In emotion theory, grief is considered particularly complex and associated with other emotions: In 'attempting to cope with loss, [...] several emotions are involved, typically grief, anger, fear, and guilt'.[26] Just as complex as the emotions associated with lament are the phases of the grieving process, which after the initial numbing may turn into longing or the pleasant memory of shared experiences.[27] This basic multiformity of grief and its phases, already handed down in the ancient lament, was less associated with the soft tone that later traditions would consider characteristic. Rather, it took the form of wild, orgiastic lamentation. As was common in the cult of Attis and Adonis, it could turn into unbridled and dissolute lust. Thus, already in the origins of mourning, joy and sorrow are connected: the opposing basic emotions become one in the

---

24   Moul, "Lyric Poetry" 41.
25   Ibidim, 45.
26   Lazarus, *Emotion and adaption* 248.
27   Meyer-Sickendiek B., *Affektpoetik: Eine Kulturgeschichte literarischer Emotionen* (Würzburg: 2005) 120.

lament. Beissner sees this characteristic in the different varieties of elegy and occasional poetry in general, from lament to love song, from hymn-psalm to lament song.[28] This is what intimately connects the two genres of love elegy and psalm poetry. Both make use of the varieties of elegy and thus deviate from a prevailing basic emotion:[29] in elegy, grief becomes joy, joy is mixed with lament; in the Psalms, hymnic enthusiasm turns into lament, one of the most frequent figurations of Psalm poetry. Indeed, comparison of the two genres clearly shows how both utilise similar combinations of basic emotions to deal with different topoi.

This fact is also relevant for the occurrence of various affective speech-acts which are characteristic for the genre of elegy: begging, praises, compliments, complaints, accusations, blessings, laments; these speech-acts often appear in one and the same poem, alternately or intertwined.[30] This is why in love elegy – both Roman and Neo-Latin – the complaint about the unattainability of the beloved is followed by a supplication or praise of the beloved as an attribute of the genus. Likewise in Psalm poetry, praise, prayer and lament alternate.

On the basis of two exemplary case studies of Buchanan and Lernutius respectively, I will examine both Neo-Latin psalm poetry and love elegy to investigate to what extent the parallel poetic representation of centrifugally-oriented basic emotions results in emotional fluctuations, shifts or blends.[31] I submit the hypothesis that such shifts of emotions (e.g., from joy or enthusiasm to grief, and vice versa) are meant as artful imitations of the changeable character of natural feelings. In this context my paper focusses on the occurrence of conflicting or opposite emotions in one and the same poem, and tries to map their various combinations and compounds, and the shifts and turns from one emotion to the other. To identify similarities and differences for love elegy and psalm poetry, I shall base my examination on the following four questions: How are the various emotions rendered and defined? How are the various shifts poetically expressed? How do they function in the poems? In what way do they affect the structure of the poems?

---

28 Beissner F., *Geschichte der deutschen Elegie* (Berlin: 1961) 6.

29 Meyer-Sickendiek, *Affektpoetik* 118–127.

30 Ochs E. – Schieffelin B., "Language has a heart", in *Text: Interdisciplinary Journal for the Study of Discourse* 9.1, (1989) 7–25, 14.

31 Meyer-Sickendiek emphasizes for both, the elegiac grief and hymnal enthusiasm, the centrifugal character as an outpouring in all directions from the affected (= grieving and lamenting singer of the poem), *Affektpoetik* 57.

SHIFTING EMOTIONS IN NEO-LATIN PSALM POETRY AND EROTIC ELEGY 193

4 Devotional Poetry in the Sixteenth Century: Psalm Poetry beyond the Alps

The Psalter has always been the most intensely used of all biblical books. In number the Psalms far exceed the books of the New Testament. The genre of metrical Bible translations into Latin or, equivalently, the genre of the psalm paraphrases, existed in the Middle Ages but had little or no major significance. There were some psalm versifications by Paulinus of Nola and Florus of Lyon, but overall the Middle Ages produced surprisingly little psalm poetry.[32] Starting in the twelfth century, rhythmic and rhymed psalters were written, especially prayers and invocations to Mary or Christ, as published in the *Analecta hymnica*[33] and a few years ago by Colker.[34] These incorporate individual verses or key words from the Psalms instead of paraphrasing the entire Book of Psalms.

It was not until the sixteenth century that the genre of Psalm poetry developed into a medium of expression that flourished throughout Europe. It seems to have become a humanistic exercise to paraphrase the psalms, showing off one's own literary skills in stylistic translations of the originals. Johannes Gaertner describes the phenomenon, referring to the 'particular shock of recognition' which educated readers who consumed Latin metrical translations would have experienced: 'The Psalms were well known to everyone through liturgical use, through responsive reading or chanting, through musical versions used in school, church and home, through the prayer books and books of hours; any new version of the old familiar text therefore must have given both Catholics and Protestants the same curious delight [...]'.[35]

Readers familiar with classical poetry in addition to the Psalms would have been particularly impressed by the poets' diverse paraphrases of the Psalms and their 'renegotiation of the genre's demands'.[36] Considerable attention was paid to psalm paraphrases, some of which were published in anthologies.[37]

---

32 Orth P., "Metrische Paraphrase als Kommentar: Zwei unedierte mittelalterliche Verifikationen der Psalmen im Vergleich", *The Journal of Medieval Latin* 17 (2007) 189–209, 192.

33 *Analecta hymnica medii aevi*, ed C. Blume – G.M. Dreves, (Leipzig: 1886–1922), vol 35–38.

34 Colker M.L., "A Christianized Latin Psalter in Rhythmic Verse", *Sacris erudiri* 30 (1987–1988) 329–408.

35 Gaertner J.A., "Latin Verse Translations of the Psalms, 1500–1620", *Harvard Theological Review* 49 (1956) 271–305, 274.

36 Green R.P.H., "George Buchanan's Psalm Paraphrases in a European Context", in Hubbard T. – Jack R.D.S. (eds.), *Scotland in Europe* (Scottish Cultural Review of Language and Literature 7) 25–38, 27.

37 Gaertner, "Latin Verse Translations of the Psalms" 275.

The end came as quickly as the beginning: after a peak at the end of the six-teenth century, the genre disappeared abruptly at the beginning of the seven-teenth century. Vernacular psalm songs and Latin psalm poems emerged side by side in the sixteenth century,[38] but vernacular psalm poetry almost com-pletely replaced Latin paraphrases in the seventeenth century among poetry reformers such as Martin Opitz.[39]

Two of the most famous psalm paraphrases of the sixteenth century were written by Marcantonio Flaminio and George Buchanan, the latter of whom was known as the 'chieftain of neo-Latin poets'.[40] As was customary at that time, their first editions incorporated supplementary translations by another author or additional biblical texts:[41] for example, texts by Franciscus Spinula completed one of Flaminio's earlier editions (T. I, 1558), and texts by Theodore Beza supplemented Buchanan's first published text (T. I, 1566). By way of context, a near-complete listing of authors and titles of metrical Latin psalm translations for the period of 1500–1620 can be found in the study by Gaertner, arranged by date of first editions.[42]

My interest in this study primarily falls on psalm poetry written north of the Alps, particularly as they pertain to Dutch-English literary relations which, as noted above, were of particular importance to the genres of psalm poetry and love elegy. These connections among poets were cultivated during their study visits to Paris and have been described in the well-known studies of J.A. van Dorsten.[43] Van Dorsten emphasises the common humanist ideals that

---

38   Translations in Dutch and German were a common exercise for poets, shown by a col-lection of diverse meters in Dutch from 1540 and the French Psalter by Theodore Beza from 1565 translated into both Dutch and German. See Todd R., "'So well attired abroad': A Background to the Sidney-Pembroke Psalter and its Implications for the Seventeenth-century Religious Lyric", *Texas Studies in Language and Literature* 29.1 (1987) 74–93.

39   It would be very interesting and enlightening to conduct a study of poets who wrote in their native language as well as in Latin. A comparison of these Latin poets with others would be particularly exciting, as some stylistic differences come to light, such as the fact that Latin was written especially for the educated reader and thus sophisticated, ancient meters were to be used, while vernacular was to be easily understood. An investigation of this in this article would go beyond the scope, some examples are already comparatively examined by I. Bach and H. Galle, *Deutsche Psalmpoesie*, "Lateinische Psalterien des 16. Jahrhunderts in klassischen Versmaßen", 126–128.

40   See the eponymous chapter of R.P.H. Green in Houghton L.B.T. – Manuwald G. (eds.), *Neo-Latin Poetry in the British Isles* (London: 2012) 142–154.

41   Gaertner, "Latin Verse Translations of the Psalms" 275.

42   Ibid., 293–300. The author bases his data on the study of Vaganay H. *Les Traductions du Psautier en vers latins au XVIe siècle* (Fribourg: 1898).

43   Dorsten J.A. van, *Poets, Patrons and Professors. Sir Philip Sidney, Daniel Rogers and the Leiden humanists* (Leiden: 1962); Alter *The Radical Arts, First Decade of an Elisabethan Renaissance* (Leiden: 1970).

SHIFTING EMOTIONS IN NEO-LATIN PSALM POETRY AND EROTIC ELEGY 195

bound poets of both countries, as well as their shared interest in the political independence of the Northern Netherlands. He specifically mentions Daniel Rogers, Philip Sidney, Janus Dousa, Jan van Hout and many others. According to Van Dorsten, Daniel Rogers introduced Dousa as one of his best friends and an enthusiastic devotee of Buchanan when they were all staying together in Paris in 1576.[44] This is how Buchanan's works, especially his studies of the Psalms, became widely known. In addition to their basic humanistic and political ideals, the position of poets within their ecclesiastical-political circumstances must also be noted.[45] Whereas Flaminio was known as a Catholic reformer, Buchanan can certainly be classified as a Protestant or even Calvinist.[46] Both their collections have been interpreted as 'battle hymns' that can be decoded to favour a Catholic or Protestant reading. The poets themselves, however, were not interested in expressing their divergent theological views in the paraphrases, but rather, as Rivkah Zim writes, in competing to display their poetic skills and demonstrate 'that paraphrase was a highly skilled process, and one best reserved for a well-learned man. The duty of the humanist poet as a moral teacher, and the end to which he applied his art, was the exploitation of those works which he considered appropriate for the promotion of sound judgment. As biblical poetry, the Psalms had the capacity to promote spiritual values, wisdom and eloquence simultaneously. The art of the psalm imitator, like any imitator, lay in transposing the biblical models into decorous forms and language'.[47] Instead of focusing on exegesis and commentary, the poetic paraphrases aimed at personal and meditative engagement.[48] This might be

---

44   Van Dorsten, *Poets, Patrons and Professors* 42–3.

45   See Bostoen K., "Reformation, Counter-Reformation and literary propaganda in the Low Countries in the sixteenth-century: the case of Brother Cornelis", in Amos N.S. – Pettegree A. – Nierop H. van (eds.), *The Education of a Christian Society: Humanism and the Reformation in Britain and the Netherlands* (London: 1999) 164–189.

46   There is disagreement in the literature about Buchanan's religious views. Especially after his return to the now Protestant Scotland and his work as a tutor to Mary Stuart, Buchanan is attributed with "radical Calvinist" views. See Hadfield, A. "Spenser and Buchanan" in Erskine C., *George Buchanan: Political Thought in Early Modern Britain and Europe* (New York: 2012) 71–86, 72. Burgess sees "nothing discernably Calvinist" in the argument of the humanist intellectual Buchanan. Burgess G. "Political obedience" in Rublack U. (ed.), *The Oxford Handbook of the Protestant Reformations* (Oxford: 2017) 83–104, 93. McFarlane, however, illustrates a moderation of Buchanan's views through his travels and meetings: *Buchanan* 103–110.

47   Zim R., *English Metrical Psalms. Poetry as Praise and Prayer, 1535–1601* (Cambridge: 2011) 154. McFarlane, in *Buchanan* 281, is right, of course, to criticise the notion 'that Buchanan was essentially interested in a certain form of elegant classicism and that his concern with religion was at best indifferent'. Buchanan's writing of the Psalms already shows his interest in the religious ideas of his time, which is undeniable.

48   Green, *George Buchanan's Psalm Paraphrases* 27.

seen as the greatest difference from the medieval paraphrases of the twelfth and thirteenth centuries, in which the commentative character and interpretive amplification were fundamental. For medieval psalm poets, Peter Orth has shown in his study "Metrische Paraphrase als Kommentar", on the basis of two medieval Anonymi, linguistic transformation and Christian exegesis merge as a synthesis.[49] For these paraphrases, it was important to combine the exact biblical saying with paraphrase and exegesis. The later Renaissance paraphrases differ significantly not only in terms of content but also in form. A quote from the preface of Johannes Ganeius' psalm paraphrases reveals exactly what the psalm poets of the sixteenth century were aiming to achieve:

> metri genere psalmos perscripsissent, **elegiaco scilicet**, quod genus **lugu-bribus** primum & **miserabilibus querimoniis** iuxta vocabuli ἔτυμον accomodatum est; deinde uero ad **amatoria** transit. [...] **diversa** psalmorum **argumenta** commode tractari posse multoque; fore commodius, si variis odarum generibus describerentur: unius mihi opinionis auctores fuerunt Iosephus historicus ac Hieronymus, qui psalmos Hebraicos asserunt lyricis esse conscriptos. Ausus itaque sum, deo bene iuvante, in varia odarum genera psalmos transfundere, quod nemo, opinor, ante me tentaverat.[50]

Ganeius was not the first to publish his psalm paraphrases in elegiac meters in 1547; Flaminio preceded him in 1546 and achieved a much greater reputation. But he exemplifies exactly the trend that Orth describes for the psalm paraphrases of the sixteenth century as 'merely a variant of the transfer of classical Latinity to Christian subjects'.[51] The hexameter of the medieval paraphrases was no longer the mandatory meter; humanistic paraphrases were characterized on the one hand by a maximum variety of meters used in Greek

---

49   Orth, "Metrische Paraphrase als Kommentar" 203.
50   'They had probably written psalms in verse, namely in the elegiac, which was first – close to the etymological meaning – suitable for sad and miserable laments, indeed, it was only afterwards that the elegiac verse was used for love poetry. [They felt] that the diverse themes of the Psalms could be dealt with appropriately and would be much more suitable, if they were written down in the various metres of odes. The same opinion was handed down to me by the historian Josephus and Jerome, who argued that the Hebrew Psalms were composed in lyric verse. So, with God's help, I have dared to transcribe the Psalms into different meters of poetry, which I believe no one has ever attempted before me'. See the preface in Ganeius Joannes, *Psalmi Davidici Septuaginta quinque in lyricos versus* (Paris, Nicolaus Divitis: 1547) 2.
51   Orth, "Metrische Paraphrase als Kommentar" 200.

SHIFTING EMOTIONS IN NEO-LATIN PSALM POETRY AND EROTIC ELEGY 197

and Roman lyric poetry, and on the other hand by a preference for elegy.[52] This meter, which was used in antiquity first for the expression of mourning, and later also for grief in love, seemed most suitable for the expression of the psalms' contents.

One of the most famous Psalm poets who rendered the Psalms in a wide range of meters, but particularly in elegy, was the Scottish humanist George Buchanan (1506–1582). After spending some time in France, Buchanan came to the college in Coimbra as a professor in 1547 at the invitation of King João III of Portugal. The project of reviving the college by hiring famous, foreign-born professors failed; Buchanan was arrested by the Portuguese Inquisition and two years later sentenced to imprisonment in the Bento Monastery.[53] The literature on Buchanan has long asked whether this life crisis prompted Buchanan to write his well-known psalm paraphrases as penitential psalms. He himself wrote in his own *Vita* about this period: 'Hoc maxime tempore Psalmorum Davidicorum complures vario carminum genere in numeros redegit'. (It was in particular at this time that he set most of David's Psalms into several sorts of Latin metre.[54])

It does not seem to have been uncommon for sixteenth-century poets to be inspired by a trying situation such as imprisonment to write psalm paraphrases.[55] Although the subject of the psalm poetry is a fundamental confrontation with the Christian religion and faith, such poems also functioned as spiritual exercises for the poet himself, since the Psalms praise God in the first person and their translation leaves 'more scope for independent statement than other scriptural translation, because the ambiguous "I" of the Psalms leaves a space for the reader to insert a personal voice'.[56] Thus, for Buchanan,

---

52   It was a kind of artifice to include as many different meters as possible in a collection of psalm paraphrases. Ganeius used forty different meters for only seventy-five psalms in his version of 1547. See Gaertner, "Latin Verse Translations" 273.

53   On this episode see Aitken J.M., *The trial of Georg Buchanan before the Lisbon Inquisition* (Edinburgh: 1939). A useful reconstruction of Buchanan's life and career is offered by McFarlane I.D., *Buchanan* (London: 1981) 131–51 and Ford P.J., *George Buchanan: Prince of Poets* (Aberdeen: 1982) 1–11.

54   Green has vehemently rejected this as a misinterpretation of Buchanan's statement. Instead, he argues that Buchanan had shown great interest in the Psalms even before his incarceration, but that during this time he was able to work on them, 'more than any other time in his life'. Green, "George Buchanan, chieftain of neo-Latin poets" 146.

55   McEachern C., "Devotional Poetry", in Bates C. – Cheney P. (eds.), *The Oxford History of Poetry in English: Volume 4. Sixteenth-Century British Poetry* (Oxford: 2022) 351–370, 353.

56   Hannay M.P. – Kinnamon N.J. – Brennan M.G. (eds.), *The Collected Works of Mary Sidney Herbert Countess of Pembroke* Vol. 2 (Oxford: 1998) 8.

writing psalms involved a very personal meditative engagement with familiar texts – namely, those of the Davidian Psalms.[57]

In the following section, individual excerpts from Buchanan's psalm paraphrases are considered, and stylistic elements that are significant for his emotional expression are elaborated upon. The focus will be on the relation between his psalm poetry and love poetry. Is there a recognizable correspondence in poetic expression that ties the subjective poetry of the *Iuvenilia* to the first-person Davidic psalm poetry? How does the expression of emotion here compare to that in the love elegy?

5 Buchanan's Paraphrases: between Devotional and Elegiac Expression

Probably one of the most widespread literary echoes of the sixteenth century was *Psalm* 42. The psalm and its paraphrases are closely connected with the motif of the exile and the situation of imprisonment. The singer of the psalm, in distress, calls out for God, longing for his presence like a deer thirsting for water.

The psalmic 'thirst' is often associated with the thirst of the parched earth, the image of thirsting Israel, and the longing for God. *Psalm* 42 is about the feelings of longing and despair expressed in a contrasting image: the absence of water and yearning thirst versus the never-ending flow of tears of desperation, day and night:

> Quemadmodum desiderat cervus ad fontes aquarum, ita desiderat anima mea ad te, Deus. / Sitivit anima mea ad Deum fortem, vivum; quando veniam, et apparebo ante faciem Dei? / Fuerunt mihi lacrimae meae panes die ac nocte, dum dicitur mihi quotidie: Ubi est Deus tuus? (42,1–3)

> As the Hart brayeth for the rivers of water, so panted my soul after thee, O God. / My soul thirsteth for God, even for the living God: when shall I come and appear before the presence of God? / Mine tears have been my meat day and night, while they daily say unto me, Where is thy God?[58]

---

57   Green, "George Buchanan's Psalm Paraphrases in a European Context" 27.

58   All translations of the quoted Vulgate text into English are from the Geneva Bible published in 1560, one of the most famous Bible translations of the time, penned by a Calvinist. The translation claimed to be based on the original Hebrew text. It is not unlikely that Buchanan worked with this Bible translation and also glanced at the original, since he

SHIFTING EMOTIONS IN NEO-LATIN PSALM POETRY AND EROTIC ELEGY 199

In Buchanan's paraphrase of *Psalm* 42, we find a typical Ovidian lament written from the subject position of the *homo exul* – but not in elegiac verse:

> Non cervus fluvios sic avet algidos,
> cervus turba canum quem premit, ut tui
> cor desiderio carpitur anxio,
> rerum conditor optime.
> huc me raptat amor dulcis, et impotens
> ardor ferre moras. o niveum diem
> qui templo reducem me statuet tuo!
> o lucis iubar aureum!
> > [...]
> maeroris tenebras discutiet mihi
> lucis dulce iubar tuae.
> laudes interea non mihi nox tuas,
> non curae impedient: 'o columen meum',
> dicam 'et certa salus, ludibrium feris
> cur me deseris hostibus?'
>
> dirumpor, tacitis aestuat ignibus
> pectus, turba meis impia dum malis
> insultans rogat, 'heus, iste deus tuus
> cur nunc deserit exulem?'
>
> cur me sollicitis teque doloribus,
> mens aegra, exanimas? pone metum ac Deo
> te da; quo patriae vindice redditus,
> grates laetus adhuc agam.

The deer pursued by a pack of dogs is not so desperate for the ice-cool rivers as my heart is racked by worried longing for you, most excellent creator of all things. To you a sweet love impels me, a passion unable to bear delay. Day bright as snow, which will set me in your temple on my return! A day golden in its radiance! [...] the sweet radiance of your light will dispel the gloom of my sorrow. Meanwhile night will not hold me back from your praises, nor will anxieties: I shall say, 'O my sustainer and sure salvation, why do you leave me as a laughing-stock to the savage

---

knew Hebrew himself. On the influence of the Geneva Bible for reading the Psalms, especially in England, see Moul, *A Literary History of Latin & English Poetry* 100–108.

enemy'? I am torn apart, my heart is aflame with unseen fires, as the unholy crowd, gloating at my misfortunes, asks: 'Oh, why does that God of yours now leave you like an exile'? Why, my dejected soul, do you tire me and yourself with sickening worries? Put away fear and commit yourself to God, by whose protection I will return safe to my homeland and yet give thanks.[59]

Buchanan's paraphrase expands the original psalm in terms of emotional expression. He takes the oppositional emotions of longing and despair in the biblical original, bringing them together as the feeling of being torn apart. He portrays the lyrical persona of King David as one who suffers. The feeling of being torn asunder is closely comparable to that of the lovesick Dido in the fourth book of the Aeneid: 'At regina gravi iamdudum caeco *carpitur* igni' (But the queen has now for a long time burnt with hidden fire [IV,1]). In Buchanan, the lyrical self's heart is pursued by taunting enemies and tormented by loneliness and forlornness, while longing and unbridled love for the saving God eviscerates it. The opposing emotions (*desiderio – anxio*) Buchanan ascribes to the lamenting lyric I are also in tension: on the one hand, *desiderio* has love-elegiac and erotic connotations through the many ramifications in Catullus, Ovid, and Propertius. Moreover, the synaptic phrase *cor desiderio* is attested in Augustine: 'inquietum habes cor desiderio eius' (En 55,17). Indeed, the term *desiderium* is a key concept in the Augustinian anthropology.[60] Elwira Buszewicz remarks on Buchanan's psalm paraphrase that the substitution of *igni* for *desiderio* and *anxio* for *caeco* creates 'a chaste flame of divine love instead of erotic passion'.[61] I would add that the flame of love is also divided between divine and erotic love by the numerous allusions. From Catullus the expression *dulcis amor* is known, which is also ambiguous, since it is used both in reference to mourning for his dead brother and to erotic love for Lesbia.[62]

Commenting on a later passage, Roger Green says, 'Buch[anan] avoids the Biblical notion of grief [...]'.[63] This applies to the entire paraphrase of *Psalm* 42, but also to emotions other than grief: Buchanan avoids the biblical reference

---

59 Here and hereafter, Buchanan's Latin text and the English translation after Green in Buchanan G., *Poetic Paraphrase of the Psalms of David*, ed. – trans. – comm. R.P.H. Green (Geneva: 2011), here 224–225.

60 Rosenberger M., *Der Weg des Lebens. Zum Zusammenhang von Christologie und Spiritualität in der Verkündigung des hl. Augustinus* (Regensburg: 1996) 124–126.

61 Buszewicz E., "Homo exsul as the lyric persona of Buchanan's Psalms", in Ford P.J. – Green R.P.H. (eds.), *George Buchanan: Poet and Dramatist* (Swansea: 2009) 95–111, 104.

62 *Catullus* 68.

63 Buchanan, *Poetic Paraphrase of the Psalms of David* 553.

SHIFTING EMOTIONS IN NEO-LATIN PSALM POETRY AND EROTIC ELEGY   201

to the emotions and chooses instead the clearly secular one. Stylistically, the humanist Buchanan makes extensive use of ancient poetry, especially love-elegy. *Rapere* has fundamentally erotic connotations as, for example, in the Vergilian synaptic phrase *raptat amor dulcis* (*Verg.* G. III. 291–2), as noted by Green.[64] *Algidus* (1) is an unusual term that seems very Catullian, as in *O niveum diem*, actually a quote from Tibullus (3.3.25); the light metaphor *o lucis iubar aureum*, or later, *lucis dulce iubar tuae* (v. 35), has always been associated with erotic love (especially in Ovid's *Amores*), but also appears in biblical descriptions of Mary as well as in the neo-platonic conceptions of God. The divine figure of light generates a contrast with the figure of darkness in which the lyrical I is situated; feelings of hope and longing are juxtaposed to the fear and sorrow of the lonely and abandoned first-person speaker. Again, the inner conflict of the lyrical I is expressed through his clashing feelings, here lexically in *disrumpor* (torn). The passive diathesis of the verb clearly expresses that external events, not the subject himself, have caused this emotional state. His heart is inflamed by an invisible flame; as if in a mania, in love with his light-bringing God and full of hope, he is yet unable to prove his faith to his enemies.

The humanist reader is reminded of Dido's delusional, secretly ignited within her, which no one recognizes until it is too late. In this way, Buchanan plays with two ways of representing emotion: in-text, with respect to the linguistic-rhetorical design of the text, and out-of-text, by reference to culturally embedded models and schemas familiar to his readers. Thus far, I have looked at the multiple rhetorical devices that shape and intensify emotion, such as the lexical naming of emotive words, emotion-laden adjectives, speaker focalisation and the address to God in the *Du-Stil*.

On the level of meaning, nature becomes a semiotic representative of inner conflict and contradictory emotions: the dark, cold night is used to express grief, sorrow, worry, despair and fear (*maeroris tenebras*), as well as mockery by enemies, while the opposite, day, and also icy-cold snow in its alternative meaning (namely, brightness), express hope in a saving God. All the chosen expressions and rhetorical images are based on cultural knowledge about literary usage: Buchanan could assume that his educated readers, steeped in the humanist canon, knew how to decode the connotative references to Dido and interpret the images of nature as emotional formulas. The entire paraphrase of *Psalm* 42 vacillates between mixed feelings, longing and fear, but also between ancient-erotic and medieval-religious love, as if the poet were undecided about

---

64   Ibidem.

what sort of feelings of love he is trying to express. The discord culminates in the exilic isolation of the lyrical I in the midst of his enemies, in complete loneliness. Buchanan attributed the role of the *homo exul* to King David, suffering and surrounded by evil people, and, with witting references to Augustine, Boethius, and humanistic Neoplatonism,[65] he highlighted such themes as 'earthly imperfection, the body as a prison of the soul, life as pilgrimage'.[66]

A very different psalm, which has also received much attention, is *Psalm 45*, the so-called 'love song' and 'marriage song' (*carmen nuptiale*) for Solomon. The context of King Solomon's wedding is retained, but the usual Christian interpretation of the psalm, which is understood as the marriage of Christ and the Church, is avoided. Nevertheless, it is of no small consequence that the psalm itself repeatedly appears as an echo of the Song of Songs, thus mixing the tendencies of earthly eroticism and religious transcendence.

For our context, it is interesting to see to what extent the love-elegiac echoes mentioned earlier are present in this poem, whose basic tenor is linked to love (*Psalm 45*, 1–9):

> Cor micat, exsultant trepidis praecordia fibris,
> eructantque novum gravido de pectore carmen.
> certat lingua animum fando, manus aemula linguam
> scribendo exaequare, meo nova carmina regi
> dum cano, regi hominum cui nemo e semine cretus
> audeat eximiae contendere munere formae,
> quem decorat lepor, et roseis affusa labellis
> gratia, cui rerum caeli indulgentia spondet
> hunc fore perpetuum longaeva in saecla tenorem.[67]

> My heart is quivering, my breast dancing with excitement, and there issues from the fullness of my heart a new song. The speech of my tongue strives to match my mind, the writing of my hand to match my tongue, as I sing new songs to the king – the king with whose gift of exceptional beauty noone begotten of human seed would dare compete, who is adorned by comeliness and a charm that bathes his rose-red lips, to whom heaven's

---

65 See the chapter "Religious and Devotional Epigram and Lyric" in Moul V., *A Literary History of Latin & English Poetry* (Cambridge: 2022) 223–270 and 251; as well as Buszewicz, "Homo exsul as the lyric persona of Buchanan's Psalms" 96–97.

66 Buszewicz, "Homo exsul as the lyric persona of Buchanan's Psalms" 104.

67 Buchanan, *Poetic Paraphrase of the Psalms of David* 232.

SHIFTING EMOTIONS IN NEO-LATIN PSALM POETRY AND EROTIC ELEGY   203

benevolence promises that this state will continue unbroken for long ages to come.[68]

The hymnic character is omnipresent in the paraphrase and thus picks up on the biblical character of *Psalm* 45 (44, 2–3):

> Eructavit cor meum verbum bonum: dico ego opera mea regi. Lingua mea calamus scribae velociter scribentis. / Speciosus forma prae filiis hominum, diffusa est gratia in labiis tuis: propterea benedixit te Deus in aeternum.

> Mine heart will utter forth a good matter: I will entreat in my works of the king: my tongue is as the pen of a swift writer. / Thou art fairer than the children of men: grace is poured in thy lips, because God hath blessed thee forever.

Typical of a hymn is the undertone associated with the emotion of enthusiasm: as in the biblical psalm, Buchanan attributes to the singer of the hymn exuberant feelings from the depths of his heart, praising the perfection of the praised king. However, in comparing the paraphrase and the original psalm the shift in emphasis is striking: Buchanan uses the typically Ovidian phrase *cor micat*, also used by Tibullus: 1,10,2. Whereas in the original psalm with *verbum bonum* the hymnic content as respects the aforementioned king is foregrounded, in Buchanan it is the emotion of enthusiasm, exuberant joy, which leads to a not entirely positive restlessness of the lyrical I (*trepidis fibris*). This almost love-elegiac beginning of the paraphrase quickly changes its stylistic direction, demonstrating the more epic tone upon which Green has brilliantly elaborated in his study on this hexametric psalm paraphrase.[69] The Virgilian tone of Solomon's wedding is all about power, beauty and the luxury of the king. This is already echoed in the first section, even if some phrases are evocatively elegiac, such as the descriptions of the king's body, here the 'rose-red lips', later the hair, which is called '*flava*' in an Ovidian sense (see Ov. *Fast.* v,

---

68   Ibidem, 233.

69   Green R.P.H., "Classical voices in Buchanan's hexameter psalm paraphrases", in Davies C. – Law J.E. (eds.), *The Renaissance and the Celtic Countries* (Oxford: 2004) 55–89. In various passages, he evidences Virgilian echoes and the 'play[s] with the notion of a marriage between an Aeneas-figure and a Dido-figure', a repeated reference to the fourth book of the Aeneid. Ibidem, 67.

204   GIERE

609). Buchanan also refers to Ovid in later passages, using his tone to make statements about behaviour and emotion.[70]

As for Buchanan's sporadic recourse to the elegiac moment, let us return to the phrase *cor micat* at the beginning of the poem: in two other paraphrases, *Psalms* 55:13 and 88:36, he uses the synaptic phrase in a similar way. Here is a short excerpt from *Psalm* 55:

> **cor micat**, nervis **trepidant** solutis
> ossium nexus, animus labascit,
> semper et pallens oculis oberrat
>   mortis imago.[71]

> My heart trembles, my sinews go slack, the joints of my bones quiver, my mind collapses, and a pallid image of death hovers constantly before my eyes.[72]

This is the song of lamentation of a person deserted, similar to *Psalm* 42, a poem full of despair. Absolute hopelessness seems to have seized all the limbs of the lyrical self's body, creating a *'mortis imago'*. The passage *cor micat*, [...] *trepidis*, used in *Psalm* 45 to express the hymn's enthusiastic joy, here becomes an expression of the primary emotions of terror and fear. The movements of the body associated with the phrase are no longer expansive but instead become 'slack' and 'collapsing'. Green aptly describes the paraphrase as a 'versatile poem with vivid pictures of the Psalmist's feelings',[73] which Buchanan

---

70   One example is his paraphrase to Psalm 45 with allusion to Ovid's poetry of exile and references to Augustus-Caesar, referring to Ov. *Pont.* III,6,7 (*Quanta sit in media clementia Caesaris ira*) and Ov. *Pont.* 2,9,33 (*Caesar ut imperii moderetur frena precamur*). The metaphor *'frena currus'* is used intentionally, just as the phrase *clementia temperat iram* replaces the ruler's positive and mild behaviour, *veritatem, et mansuetudinem, et justitiam* in the biblical original, with *verum* und *aequum* in Buchanan's paraphrase. To this description of corrective justice, Buchanan adds an emotional component with the oppositional reactions of rage and clemency. In contrast to the Bible, Buchanan's portrayal of the king thus becomes human, for not only are positive reactions to be expected from this ruler, but also rage, an intensified form of the emotion of anger. Buchanan adopts the image of sharp arrows (*sagittae tuae acutae*) in the psalm as a metaphor for the conquest of peoples and enemies (in active diathesis for the ruler himself, rather than giving voice to the arrows: *coges*), but transforms the image lexically by again creating a love-elegiac undertone: The 'arrows affixed to the heart' is a characteristic love-elegiac metaphor, recurring especially in Neo-Latin literature (cf. Landino *Xand.* 1,3,33 or 1,2,35).

71   Buchanan, *Poetic Paraphrase of the Psalms of David* 261.

72   Ibidem, 263.

73   Ibidem, 563.

SHIFTING EMOTIONS IN NEO-LATIN PSALM POETRY AND EROTIC ELEGY   205

summarises as *mentis affectus* in verse 62. The connection of body and soul in relation to human emotions becomes particularly clear in this context. The same lexical expression can evoke a variety of emotions. This is also shown by the use of the phrase in the paraphrase to *Psalm* 88:

> sancte parens, animae auxilium cur subtrahis aegrae?
>   cur surda miseras respuis aure preces?
> me dolor et primis labor anxius urit ab annis;
>   me **trepidi** exanimant **corde micante** metus.
> me furor exagitat tuus, opprimit undique terror,
>   agmen ut hibernae, quod sata mergit, aquae .
> aeger, inops caris iaceo desertus amicis;
>   nec noti aerumnis ingemuere meis.[74]

But, o holy parent, I cry out to your divine majesty, as suppliant; and no time or place is untouched by my prayers. Holy parent, why do you withdraw your aid from my sick mind? Why do you reject my wretched prayers with a deaf ear? From my earliest years grief and anxious toil have tormented me, fretful fears have exhausted my trembling heart. Your fury harasses me, terror on every side overwhelms me, like the advance of a winter stream inundating sown fields. Sick and helpless, I lie deserted by my dear friends, and my acquaintances have not lamented my suffering.[75]

Despair is at its height in Buchanan's last example. The paraphrase of *Psalm* 88 is famously 'the bleakest of all the individual laments. The last word [referring to "*aerumnis meis*", v. 40 (my suffering)] expresses its mood'.[76] And *Psalm* 88 is one of the most autobiographical poems, almost certainly written during Buchanan's time in prison in Portugal, when he was ill and in exile.[77]

The heart, which in *Psalm* 45 bursts with happiness, in the same words now trembles with pain and fear (*dolor, labor anxius, metus, furor, terror*). No other psalm describes such a struggle in the face of complete hopelessness and fear of death. It is interesting to compare it with the Vulgate Psalm. Buchanan's version emotional extremes. In the Vulgate, *Psalm* 88(87),15–16 simply says:

---

74   Ibidem, 360.

75   Ibidem, 361.

76   Rodd C.S., "The Psalms", in Barton J. – Muddiman J. (eds.), *The Oxford Bible Commentary* (Oxford: 2007) 355–405, 391.

77   Wall J., "The Latin elegiacs of George Buchanan (1506–82)", in Aitken A.J. – McDiarmid M.P. – Thomson D.S. (eds.), *Bards and Makars: Scottish Language and Literature, Medieval and Renaissance* (Glasgow: 1977) 184–193.

Ut quid, Domine, repellis orationem meam; avertis faciem tuam a me? / Pauper sum ego, et in laboribus a juventute mea; exaltatus autem, humiliatus sum et conturbatus.

Lord, why dost thou reject my soul, and hidest thy face from me? / I am afflicted and at the point of death: from my youth I suffer thy terrors, doubting of my life.

Buchanan's dual focus on intensely felt single emotions as well as on compound and conflicting emotions appears clearly in an excerpt from his *Psalm* 39:

animum libido torquet, inflat gaudium,
 spes tollit, ac timor permit.
tumultur temere; [...][78]

Desire torments my mind, joy swells it, hope arouses and fear constricts it. We swing randomly between emotions.[79]

Summarising Buchanan's handling of mixed (conflicting) emotions in his Psalm paraphrases, some general statements can be made:

1. Emotions indicated in David's Psalms are adopted by Buchanan, but taken to extremes and contrasted with their opposites to build even greater tension between them.
2. The lyrical I is both a suffering *homo exul* and a joyful hymn-singer and thus his subjectivity is already caught in a contradictory tension. What the ego longs for is unattainable, whereby its earthly imperfection is always in contradiction with divine perfection. Its subjectivity is the central point of any emotional expression.
3. Every emotion is dependent on the basic motifs of grief and enthusiasm. Whether total despair and sadness or absolute enthusiasm and joy make up the basic mood, its extremes are shown by the existence of counter-feelings. The result is an inner conflict of the lyrical I that becomes 'palpable' for the reader.
4. The expression of emotions is made possible by various (semantic) rhetorical devices and their interpretation within the text, which is encoded in the humanistic style of expression that also characterises (and is therefore associated with) the love poetry of this period. Often the terms used

---

78 Buchanan, *Poetic Paraphrase of the Psalms of David* 216.
79 Ibidem, 217.

are situated between biblical expression and allusions to love poetry. The expression of ambiguity is taken to the extreme when the very same term (*cor micat*) is used to evoke completely different tones (elegiac and epic) and conflicting emotions.

The affinity with love elegy is an aspect that deserves to be particularly emphasised. Indeed, the influence of his own erotic poetry, in particular, *Neaera and Leonora*, which he wrote almost simultaneously while staying in Portugal,[80] resulted in the diverse overlaps of language, forms and styles. One of Buchanan's most important stylistic devices is certainly 'variety', which has always been seen as the 'highlight of his poetic paraphrases; perhaps indeed their guiding light'.[81] They are especially marked by metrical variety: he uses 30 different meters for 150 Psalms.[82] Unlike Eobanus Hessus, to cite one comparandum, who exclusively used the elegiac couplet for his paraphrases and thus seemed 'rather mournful or [...] associated in the reader's mind with Ovidian love poetry', Buchanan used 'diversity of metre' to correlate with 'variety of mood and theme' in the paraphrases.[83] Thus Buchanan's poems – regardless of metre – were associated with the processing of a wide variety of emotions, some of which had love-elegiac connotations.

In the last section of this essay, I look at ostensibly love-elegiac poetry collections of the sixteenth century, which are also characterised by a variety of metres and themes. To what extent are religious and transcendental elements discernible, perhaps inspired by the Psalms? How are the emotions processed?

6 Love Elegists between Religious Transcendence and Erotic Connotation

The love poetry of this period primarily offered a humanistic motivation for the demonstration of poetic skill. Buchanan had a great influence on the poets of the Pléiade in Paris (and later on poets in Portugal), and was himself inspired by Pléiade writers to compose erotic verse for the first time.[84] His religious and historical writings have received more attention than his erotic poetry. In the Low Countries, the *Basia* poems of Janus Secundus (1511–1536) were the

---

80   Brown P.H., *George Buchanan: Humanist and Reformer. A Biography* (Edinburgh: 1890) 135.

81   Green, *Poetic paraphrase* 33.

82   Moul, *A Literary History* 115.

83   McFarlane, *Buchanan* 280.

84   Ford P.J., "Leonora and Neaera. A consideration of George Buchanan's erotic Poetry", *Bibliothèque d'Humanisme et Renaissance* 40.3 (1978) 513–524, 524.

best known and imitated love poetry of the time (see *Basiorum Liber unus*, published posthumously by his brothers in the *Opera* of 1541). Even Buchanan, who was very much appreciated and revered by the Dutch poets, followed Secundus. His hendecasyllables about Neaera derive from Secundus, as also does the poem's style and the *puella*'s name, but the allure of the mouth and the kiss are replaced by the lover's gaze into the eyes of the beloved:

> Seu procacibus adnuas ocellis,
> Seu minacibus abnuas ocellis,
> Iuxta me miserum, Neaera, perdis;
> Spe torques modo credula timentem,
> Nunc formidine maceras dolentem.
> Spes, si lumine respicis benigno,
> Lentis ignibus ustulat medullas:
> Timor, lumine si aspicis maligno,
> Pigro frigore congelat medullas.[85]

> Either you nod at me with encouraging eyes or you refuse with threatening eyes, you ruin me in equal measure, Neaera. Sometimes you torment me, the fearful one, with credulous hope, at times you wear me down, the sufferer, with terror. Hope burns my innermost being with its gentle fires, when you return my gaze benevolently; fear freezes my innermost being with a numbing icy coldness, when you look at me with an evil eye.

Conflicting signals are sent from the eyes of the beloved herself: her gaze is full of eager desire and at the same time threatens rejection. The emotional reaction of the lyrical I is split into the antithesis of hope and fear, very similar to Petrarch's sentiments for Laura (e.g., in "Pace non trovo"). Thus, Buchanan already used mixed and contradictory emotions as expressive devices in his love poetry of the 1540s, later taking them up in his psalm poetry. In particular, the feeling of *spes* is, as we have seen above, characteristic of Buchanan's consideration of positive emotions in a distant future juxtaposed with negative feelings in the present. Less transcendent than personal in tone, Buchanan's composition presents characteristics of the neo-Catullan style.[86] The imitation of the lyrical soul-kiss tradition inspired by Secundus was more

---

85   *Poem* 2 of the "Hendecasyllabon liber" of George Buchanan, *Opera omnia historica, chronologica, iuridica, politica, satyrica et poetica*, Brittenburg 1725 (Brittenburg, Langerak: 1725).

86   Ford, "Leonora and Neaera" 523.

SHIFTING EMOTIONS IN NEO-LATIN PSALM POETRY AND EROTIC ELEGY   209

strictly orientated toward the Neoplatonic love concept of love and gradually merged into a broad Petrarchan tradition of love poetry in both Latin and the vernacular.[87] One of the first Dutch imitators of Secundus was certainly the Bruges poet Janus Lernutius (1545–1619), who wrote a collection of *Ocelli* poems (published with his *Carmina* in 1579) before his erotic *Basia*; they are reminiscent of Buchanan in their motifs and of Secundus' soul-kiss at the same time.

Lernutius and Buchanan may have met in Paris or later through Justus Lipsius and Janus Dousa in Leiden.[88] However, it can be assumed that Lernutius had knowledge of Buchanan's successful psalm poetry.[89] He himself did not write religious poetry, but was already a child of his turbulent, religious-political times. His father was initially close to the Reformation but later returned to the Catholic camp.[90] Like Buchanan, Lernutius is not known to have ever been a convinced Calvinist, although he was politically active in Bruges, which was Calvinist by the end of his life.[91] It seems likely that both sympathized at least in part with the ideas of the Reformation, or rather, that both adapted to the prevailing politico-religious circumstances without actually taking sides or choosing any religious orientation. They were interested to a certain extent in Christian doctrine, but did not focus on defending it.[92] What Buchanan and Lernutius had in common was the fate of having been imprisoned for a time.[93] Unlike Buchanan's psalm paraphrases, however, Lernutius' poetry was written before this drastic experience and should be treated accordingly.

A look at his *Ocelli* poetry reveals that Lernutius also takes up the neo-Catullan style in his use of the diminutive, parallelism, repetition and familiarity of tone.[94] He increasingly assimilates these stylistic features to Petrarchan antithesis, as here in *Carmen* 5:

---

87   Wong A., *The Poetry of Kissing in Early Modern Europe: From the Catullan Revival to Secundus, Shakespeare and the English Cavaliers* (Cambridge: 2017) 142.

88   McFarlane, *Buchanan* 242.

89   Some of their works were printed in the same place in Brittenburg; they will have known each other or at least met through mutual friends.

90   Crombruggen H. van, *Janus Lernutius, 1545–1619: een biografische studia* (Brussel: 1955) 60.

91   Ibidem, 64.

92   Van Crombruggen mentions the religious sect *Familia Charitatis*, which was close to Catholicism but adapted to the prevailing religious conditions and focused only on religious content, not on religious-political conditions. Platin, for example, was a member, Justus Lipsius also had connections to it. Ibidem.

93   Lernutius had been imprisoned in England between 1587 and 1592. His friend Justus Lipsius had pleaded for his release several times in vain.

94   Ford, "Leonora and Neaera" 523.

> Te Lux, te quoties video, subito aestuo totus,
>   Sulfur ut accensam cum rapuit faculam.
> Te Lux, te cum non video, subito algeo totus,
>   Ut cos Alpinis quae latet in nivibus. [...][95]

> You my brightness, as often as I see you, immediately I glow all over, while like sulfur she extinguishes the inflamed little torch. While I see you, brightness, you, suddenly I freeze completely, like an alpine stone lying in the snow.

As in Buchanan's poetry, Lernutius' psalm paraphrases and love poetry both associate emotional extremes with the antitheses of ice and fire, brightness and darkness, which are also typical nature-based signs signifying Petrarch's *dolendi voluptas* and inner conflict.

What is interesting about this poem is that Lernutius completely dispenses with lexical paraphrases of the lyrical I's feelings; metaphors from nature prove sufficient to express clearly, in the code of Petrarchist poetry, the contradictory feelings involved – love and passion imbued with painful suffering. This also becomes very clear in *Poem* 15:

> Ex oculis mea Hyella tuis modo gaudia mille;
>   At modo tristitiae semina mille traho.
> Cor micat, et trepidis exsultant pectora fibris:
>   Spem vultu quotiens candidiore facis.
> Mens cadit atque exspes iaceo in maerore, metuque
>   Spem vultu quotiens turbidiore negas.[96]

> In your eyes, my Hyella, is only a thousand-fold joy, but I carry a thousand germs of sadness. My heart sparkles, and my bowels' troubled, innermost parts leap, as often as you give hope with your glowing face. I get dizzy, and without any hope lie down in sorrow and fear, as often as you deny hope through your confusing face.

As in Buchanan's hendecasyllabic poem, the beloved's facial expression is contradictory from one moment to the next, confusing the emotions in the lyrical self; his hope, which had just been kindled into positive feelings, turns into

---

95   See Lernutius's *Carmen* 5 of his *Ocelli* in Janus Lernutius, *Initia, basia, ocelli* [*et*] *alia poemata*, Brittenburg 1614, (Brittenburg, Elzevir: 1614) 343.

96   Ibidem, 349.

SHIFTING EMOTIONS IN NEO-LATIN PSALM POETRY AND EROTIC ELEGY   211

complete hopelessness, into fear and sadness. The expression of these complementary or antithetical emotions is reflected by a perfect similarity of syntax
and semantics. The anaphora *Spem vultu quotiens* produces either a positive
or negative affect, according with Hyella's behaviour which has immediate
consequences on the lover's emotional state, with consequent shadings of one
emotion into another. With all the hope she gives or destroys, Hyella makes
her suitor feel either on top of the world or down in the slough of despair,
almost at the very same moment. The parallel position of *cor micat* and *mens
cadit* underlines the contradictory feelings of his heart and mind. On the other
hand, the expression of exuberant joy is intentionally modelled on Buchanan's
use of the phrase *cor micat* for ambiguous emotions. Lernutius borrows both
from *Psalm* 45 and Buchanan's paraphrase discussed above: 'Cor micat, exsult-
ant trepidis praecordia fibris'.

Lernutius' interplay of lexis, syntax and semantics leaves unanswered
whether the contradictory emotions merge and are thus mixed, or whether
they coexist at the very same moment. The juxtaposition of different feelings
in one and the same moment was a device already much used in the ancient
novel.[97] There conflicting emotions enumerated in a list express – according
to the Platonic philosophy – the partition of the soul into different emotions
in one and the same moment.[98] Lernutius constructs a syntactic combination
of opposing terms that engenders a contradiction, comparable to Petrarch's
oxymora expressing conflicting feelings and emotions. The linguist Michele
Prandi calls this 'coordination of two opposite predicates jointly applied to a
given subject' the most open of the three forms of a syntactic contradiction.[99]
In Lernutius, the syntactic typology, in conjunction with attributes such as
quotiens or *subito*, can indicate that a moment occupied by one emotion transitions into another that immediately follows and contradicts it. However, even
if the Platonic concept of soul-partition is not evident in Lernutius' poems,
basic Neo-platonic assumptions have been shown to occur in his *Ocelli* poems.
Eckart Schäfer has very plausibly analysed how the idea of Platonic reincarna-
tion is implicit in the epilogue of Lernutius' *Poem* 42 of the *Ocelli*-cycle, which
has also been identified as a parody of Horace's *Carm.* 2,20. Here the lyrical
I describes its deliverance from earthly bondage; enlightened by a heavenly

---

97   Fusillo M., "The Conflict of Emotions: A Topos in the Greek Erotic Novel" in Swain S. (ed.),
      Oxford readings in the Greek novel (Oxford: 1999) 60–82.

98   Repath I., "Emotional conflict and Platonic psychology in the Greek novel", in
      Morgan J.R. – Jones M. (eds.), *Philosophical Presences in the Greek novel. Ancient narrative.
      Supplementum 10* (Groningen: 2007) 53–84.

99   Prandi M., *Conceptual conflicts in metaphors and figurative language* (New York – London:
      2017) 91.

vision, it experiences an ecstatic ascent into the beyond, has a vision of the highest truth, becomes one with the divine – which takes the form of Venus as image of the *puella* Hyella – and finally unites with the divine itself.[100] The spirit tormented by earthly pangs of love is moved by old and new emotions as it makes its way toward heavenly liberation:

> Iam iam repulsa nocte animi, vigor
>> Conturbat intus atque hominem procul
>> Exturbat aegrum concitoque
>> Pectus obit agitatque motu.

> Iam mens inerti carcere libera
>> Supra maligni tramitis obices
>> Curru Cupidinis levata
>> Evehitur per inane magnum,
> […]
> Laetatur omni laetitia, et Deae
>> Agnoscit expressam effigiem suae
>> Ardetque miraturque et in se
>> Linquitur illecebra decoris.

The next moment, when the night of the soul had been pushed back, fresh vital force shook him within and expelled the suffering man into the distance, and with vehement movement the force hit the heart and moved it. Now the spirit, freed from the turbid imprisonment, is lifted beyond the obstacles of the malignant path from the chariot of Cupid and into the great void. […] The spirit, delighted with all the joy, recognises its goddess (= puella) in the imitated image and is inflamed (with love), admires her, and the lure of her adornment flows down upon him.

By using verb forms of *repulsare, conturbare, exturbare, concitare* and *agitare* in one of the stanzas, Lernutius characterises the act of liberation of the lyrical I as an inner chaos of feelings, a highly dynamic conflict of emotions as well as of *motus mixti*. In this powerful movement between the earthly and the divine, and the subsequent liberation (*carcere libera*) of *mens*, the soul can finally feel truly positive emotions toward the (now divine) beloved. Whereas Secundus only 'flirts' with the afterlife through his soul kiss, Lernutius makes the religious

---

100 See Lernutius's Alcaic ode 42 in Lernutius "*Initia, basia, ocelli*" 367f.

SHIFTING EMOTIONS IN NEO-LATIN PSALM POETRY AND EROTIC ELEGY   213

transcendence of the unattainable beloved more explicit.[101] Unlike Secundus, Lernutius only hints at the erotic overtones; the lyrical I and its mixed feelings, torn between joy and grief, between earthly desire and transcendent love fulfilment, are always the focus. Nevertheless, Lernutius demonstrates his talent for playing with his models, using ancient and contemporary Neo-Latin reminiscences alike, as well as erotic love elegy and Neo-Platonic philosophy. His explicit allusion to Psalm 45 and Buchanan's paraphrase demonstrates his literary skill and reveals his sense of his own poetry as the 'opposition of Eros and Mysticism',[102] of Eros and Agape. For Lernutius, love poems are not only humanistic *Iuvenilia* but also an expression of religious devotion. Thus, in his own collective edition of 1614, he included a personal statement on the later love poetic cycle *Basia*, distancing himself from Secundus: '[...] possunt / Basia Vestales haec capere atque dare' ([...] even nuns could read my poems). Schäfer situates Lernutius' 'erotic transcendence' in the contemporary historical context of Baroque and Counter-Reformation poetics and in ideas of de-individualisation and Christian reinterpretation of the Renaissance.[103] I propose adding an ironic Catullan component to this analysis. Among all Lernutius' religious-Christian allusions with erotic themes, the use of Psalm 45 is indeed significant. This psalm inclines toward both earthly eroticism and religious transcendence; Lernutius thus makes use of Buchanan's well-known poetic paraphrase of a psalm whose erotic status is as nebulous as that of Lernutius's own poetry.

More explicit is the religious tendency in the *Ocelli*-poetry of Adriaan van der Burch (1533–1557), a Dutch contemporary of Lernutius. Writing from a Catholic perspective, he called his love-elegiac collection of poems 'pious games' and added his *Oculli* poetry to them. Titled *Pii lusus, in quibus Oscula & Oculi, ac post illos Tristia et Funera*, his collection consists not only of elegiac *carmina* but also of psalm paraphrases focusing exclusively on psalm passages that refer to joyful or sad occasions, such as *oculi* or *funera*.[104] Thus, Van der Burch dwells on the contrast between joy and sorrow – *Seu Laetos, Tristes seu*,

---

101   Schäfer E., "Erotische Transzendierung bei Secundus und Lernutius", in Schäfer (ed.), *Johannes Secundus und die römsiche Liebeslyrik* (Tübingen: 2004) 262.

102   Ibidem, 261.

103   Ibidem, 262.

104   It is interesting that a completely different section of the aforementioned Psalm 45 is dealt with here – it is not about the heart and the innermost feelings, but about the eyes, which is why van der Burch takes up verse 11 of the psalm: "*Audi, filia, et vide, et inclina aurem tuam; et obliviscere populum tuum, et domum patris tui.*" Adriaan van der Burch, *Pii lusus: in quibus oscula & oculi, ac post illos tristia & funera*, Ultraiecti 1600 (Ultraiecti, Borculous: 1600) 20.

as stated in the preface of the 1600 edition. An introductory poem in the form of elegiac couplets summarises how Van der Burch's poetry issues from *motis procellis*, when he is moved by a multitude of emotions.[105]

There are numerous other examples of Dutch poets who similarly used the elegiac genre to demonstrate their love-lyrical humanistic style while also expressing religious-philosophical thoughts. One of them was certainly Janus Dousa, often considered a Secundus imitator who strayed 'appreciably nearer than his model to the realm of more serious Neo-Platonism, or of more chaste and earnest, if still metaphorical, Petrarchist love-poetry'.[106]

Regarding the handling of emotions, the following applies to all of these love-elegiac poets:

1. The Dutch love poets of the sixteenth century focus on the challenge posed by their variable feelings, for which both elegiac *Iuvenilia* and psalm poetry are proper genres.
2. The apparent opposition between erotic and devotional poetry is overcome by considering psalm paraphrases as a component of elegiac (love) poetry. As stylistic devices, passages from psalm paraphrases could be integrated into love poetry, or the paraphrases could appear in poetry cycles as stand-alone poems.
3. Different and contradictory emotions are negotiated in the poem cycles, which (can) integrate different styles and genre components, Neo-Catullian, Petrarchan and/or Neo-Platonic. By transcending style and genre, erotic love is elevated to a religious level, its potentially harmful effect neutralised.

7   Conclusion

For the humanists of the sixteenth century, the expression of emotions was elementary. Their readership was particularly interested in emotional-reflective and personal insights into the inner world of an autobiographical self. The lyrical medium, characterised by an inherent openness of form and content, seemed particularly appropriate for this kind of expression. Thus, the humanists composed psalm poetry to articulate feelings at a religious level, using love-elegiac

---

105   "*Sic Vanderburchi motis toto Orbo procellis, / Aegida dum Pallas concutit, atque fremit, / dum virtus afflicta iacet, probitasque fidesque / luditur, improbitas et scelus omne viget, / In coelum torques* OCULOS, *coelestia tractas, / solarisque animum* LUSIBUS *usque* PIIS." Ibidem, 5.

106   Wong A., *The Poetry of Kissing in Early Modern Europe* 180.

formats in collections of poems to illustrate earthly affections. My brief case study has revealed another phenomenon: both genres, the love elegy and the psalm paraphrase, were employed to express not only one-dimensional but also complex, contrary and antithetical emotions, often in one and the same poem. Poets, relying on absolute parallelism, concatenated one verse (or word) to another. The intention was to explore multi-perspectival emotions and to show how conflicting emotions could coincide or, better, collide head-on, but also shift, one into another. The reader was expected to empathise with the psychological-emotional process that had moved the humanist poet, also in a socially figurative sense: the sixteenth-century poet positioned himself in a dichotomous state between two dimensions, between earthly-human and transcendental-religious feelings, between poetic skills based on ancient models and a normative mode of expression drawn from the Bible.

What had formerly been evident in the demarcation between adolescent *Iuvenilia* and psalm poetry merged into a common process at the level of emotional strategies and modes of expression. In the poetic genres of love elegy and Psalm paraphrase, the same rhetorical strategies were used to emphasise ambivalent and contradictory emotions – namely, joy and grief, desire and frustration. These emotions were described in terms of their intensity and their fleeting movement, from one to the other, whereby the body and the environment could also be semiotic carriers of the emotional process.

By using the same communicative codes, both genres could describe emotions by means of similar rhetorical-stylistic techniques, related 'emotional terms' and semantic variants, as well as emotional expressions familiar to the humanistic style. As a result, psalm poetry sometimes utilises phrases with erotic connotations, while elegiac poetry sometimes includes psalm-poetic allusions or fragments of Psalms to secure religious-transcendental effects. Regardless of the poet's religious-political convictions, the content of the Psalms was as universal a shared literary source as the ambiguous Petrarchist and antic-erotic topoi of love elegy. It is the shared *elegiac motive* that enables the transition from one genre to another and promotes the complexity of emotional expression within both genres. This is because elegy, to which both lyric subgenres refer, is split into two opposing basic emotional states, grief and hymnic joy, expressing both lament and praise. The two genres of psalm poetry and love elegy, fundamentally different in their subject matter, adapt this dichotomy for their own purposes and – in accordance with their mutual historical connection to the lyric genre – make use of common strategies arising from their basic concern: the expression of emotions. The result is an emotional experience of inner conflict that evokes the vicissitudes and psychological torments of private individuals in an ambivalent state of ambiguity and self-division, between the uncertainty of unfulfilled longing and exuberant joy, between elation and mortal sadness. In portraying these emotions, the poet stirs similar emotions in the reader.

The manifestation of mixed emotions thus operates in three different registers – that of genre, of socio-psychological background and of individual skill of the humanistic poet. This holds true whether one discerns these emotions against the backdrop of the poet's *Iuvenilia* or in collections of poems that, though not exclusively love-elegiac, feature an antagonism between piety and verbal ingenuity.

Bibliography

Adriaan van der Burch, *Pii lusus: in quibus oscula & oculi, ac post illos tristia & funera*, Utrecht 1600 (Utrecht, Borculous: 1600).

Analecta hymnica medii aevi, ed. Blume C. – Dreves G.M., (Leipzig: 1886–1922).

Aitken J.M., *The trial of Georg Buchanan before the Lisbon Inquisition* (Edinburgh: 1939).

Beissner F., *Geschichte der deutschen Elegie* (Berlin: 1961).

Burgess G., "Political obedience" in Rublack U. (ed.), *The Oxford Handbook of the Protestant Reformations* (Oxford: 2017).

Bostoen K., "Reformation, Counter-Reformation and literary propaganda in the Low Countries in the sixteenth century: the case of Brother Cornelis", in Amos N.S. – Pettegree A. – Nierop H. van (eds.), *The Education of a Christian Society: Humanism and the Reformation in Britain and the Netherlands* (London: 1999) 164–189.

George Buchanan, *Opera omnia historica, chronologica, iuridica, politica, satyrica et poetica*, Brittenburg 1725 (Brittenburg, Langerak: 1725).

Brown P.H., *George Buchanan: Humanist and Reformer. A Biography* (Edinburgh: 1890).

Buchanan G., *Poetic Paraphrase of the Psalms of David*, ed. – trans. – comm. R.P.H. Green (Geneva: 2011).

Buszewicz E., "Homo exsul as the lyric persona of Buchanan's Psalms", in Ford P.J. – Green R.P.H. (eds.), *George Buchanan: Poet and Dramatist* (Swansea: 2009) 95–111.

Brown P.H., *George Buchanan: Humanist and Reformer, a Biography* (Michigan: 1890).

Chartier R., "Leisure and Sociability: Reading Aloud in Modem Europe", in Zimmerman S. – Weissman R.F.E. (eds.), *Urban Life in the Renaissance* (Newark: 1989).

Curtius E.R., *Europäische Literatur und lateinisches Mittelalter* (Tübingen – Basel 1993).

Colker M.L., "A Christianized Latin Psalter in Rhythmic Verse", *Sacris erudiri* 30 (1987–1988) 329–408.

Crombruggen H. van, *Janus Lernutius, 1545–1619: een biografische studia* (Brussel: 1955).

Dorsten J.A. van, *Poets, Patrons and Professors. Sir Philip Sidney, Daniel Rogers and the Leiden humanists* (Leiden: 1962).

SHIFTING EMOTIONS IN NEO-LATIN PSALM POETRY AND EROTIC ELEGY   217

Dorsten J.A. van, *The Radical Arts, First Decade of an Elisabethan Renaissance* (Leiden: 1970).

Dyck, J., *Athen und Jerusalem. Die Tradition der argumentativen Verknüpfung von Bibel und Poesie im 17. und 18. Jahrhundert* (München: 1977).

Eiswirth R., *Hieronymus' Stellung zu Literatur und Kunst* (Wiesbaden: 1955).

Ford P.J., *George Buchanan: Prince of Poets* (Aberdeen: 1982).

Ford P.J., "Leonora and Neaera. A consideration of George Buchanan's erotic Poetry", *Bibliothèque d'Humanisme et Renaissance* 40.3 (1978) 513–524.

Fries N., "Über die allmähliche Verfertigung emotionaler Bedeutung beim Äußern", in Kotin M.L. – Kotorova E.G. (eds.), *Die Sprache in Aktion: Pragmatik – Sprechakte – Diskurs* (Heidelberg: 2011) 15–32.

Galle H. – Bach I., *Deutsche Psalmendichtung vom 16. bis zum 20. Jahrhundert: Untersuchungen zur Geschichte einer lyrischen Gattung* (Berlin – Boston: 1989).

Gaertner J.A., "Latin Verse Translations of the Psalms, 1500–1620", *Harvard Theological Review* 49 (1956) 271–305.

Fusillo M., "The conflict of emotions: a topos in the Greek erotic novel", in Swain S. (ed.), *Oxford readings in the Greek novel* (Oxford: 1999) 60–82.

Gnüg H., *Entstehung und Krise lyrischer Subjektivität: Vom klassischen lyrischen ich zur modernen Erfahrungswirklichkeit* (Stuttgart: 1983).

Green R.P.H., "George Buchanan's Psalm Paraphrases in a European Context", in Hubbard T. – Jack R.D.S. (eds.), *Scotland in Europe* (Scottish Cultural Review of Language and Literature 7) 25–38.

Green R.P.H., "George Buchanan, chieftain of neo-Latin poets", in Houghton L.B.T. – Manuwald G. (eds.), *Neo-Latin Poetry in the British Isles* (London: 2012) 142–154.

Green R.P.H., "Classical voices in Buchanan's hexameter psalm paraphrases", in Davies C. – Law J.E. (eds.), *The Renaissance and the Celtic Countries* (Oxford: 2004) 55–89.

Hadfield A., "Spenser and Buchanan" in Erskine C. (ed.), *George Buchanan: Political Thought in Early Modern Britain and Europe* (New York: 2012) 71–86.

Hamlin H. *Psalm Culture and Early Modern English Literature* (Cambridge: 2006).

Julius Caesar Scaliger, *Iulii Caesaris epistolae et orations nunquam ante hac excusae* (Leyden, Franciscus Dousa: 1600).

Janus Lernutius, *Initia, basia, ocelli [et] alia poemata*, Brittenburg 1614 (Brittenburg, Elzevir: 1614).

Joannes Ganeius, *Psalmi Davidici Septuaginta quinque in lyricos versus* (Paris, Nicolaus Divitis: 1547).

Kugel J.L., *The Idea of Biblical Poetry: Parallelism and its History* (New Haven: 1981).

Kugel J.L., "Poets and Prophets: An Overview", in Kugel J.L. (ed.), *Poetry and Prophecy: The Beginnings of a Literary Tradition* (New York: 1990).

Lamping D., *Das lyrische Gedicht: Definitionen zu Theorie und Geschichte der Gattung* (Göttingen: 2000).

Lazarus R., *Emotion and adaption* (New York: 1991).

Lowth R., *Lectures on the Sacred Poetry of the Hebrews*, trans. G. Gregory, 2 vols. (London: 1787).

Marotti A.F., *Manuscript, Print and the English Renaissance Lyric* (Ithaca: 1995).

McEachern C., "Devotional Poetry", in Bates C. – Cheney P. (eds.), *The Oxford History of Poetry in English: Volume 4. Sixteenth-Century British Poetry* (Oxford: 2022) 351–370.

McFarlane I.D., *Buchanan* (London: 1981).

Meyer-Sickendiek B., *Affektpoetik: Eine Kulturgeschichte literarischer Emotionen* (Würzburg: 2005).

Moul V., *A Literary History of Latin & English Poetry* (Cambridge: 2022).

Moul V., "Lyric Poetry", in Knight S. – Tilg S. (eds.), *The Oxford Handbook of Neo-Latin* (Oxford: 2015).

Niefer J., *Inspiration and utmost art: the poetics of early modern English psalm translations* (Vienna – Zürich: 2018).

Ochs E. – Schieffelin B., "Language has a heart", *Text: Interdisciplinary Journal for the Study of Discourse* 9.1 (1989) 7–25.

Orth P., "Metrische Paraphrase als Kommentar: Zwei unedierte mittelalterliche Verifikationen der Psalmen im Vergleich", *The Journal of Medieval Latin* 17 (2007) 189–209.

Sidney P., *An apology of poetry or the defense of poesy*, ed. R.W. Maslen – G. Shepherd (Manchester – New York: 2002).

Repath I., "Emotional conflict and Platonic psychology in the Greek novel", in Morgan J.R. – Jones M. (eds.), *Philosophical Presences in the Greek Novel. Ancient narrative. Supplementum 10* (Grongingen: 2007) 53–84.

Rodd C.S., "The Psalms" in Barton J. – Muddiman J. (eds.), *The Oxford Bible Commentary* (Oxford: 2007) 355–405.

Rosenberger M., *Der Weg des Lebens. Zum Zusammenhang von Christologie und Spiritualität in der Verkündigung des hl. Augustinus* (Regensburg: 1996).

Prandi M., *Conceptual conflicts in metaphors and figurative language* (New York – London: 2017).

Schäfer E., "Erotische Transzendierung bei Secundus und Lernutius", in Schäfer (ed.), *Johannes Secundus und die römsiche Liebeslyrik* (Tübingen: 2004).

Shewder R.A., "'You're Not Sick, You're Just in Love': Emotion as an Interpretive System", in Ekman P. – Davidson R.J. (eds.), *The Nature of Emotion: Fundamental Questions* (New York – Oxford: 1994), 32–44.

Todd R., "'So well attired abroad': A Background to the Sidney-Pembroke Psalter and its Implications for the Seventeenth-century Religious Lyric", *Texas Studies in Language and Literature* 29.1 (1987) 74–93.

Tsur R., "Semantic Processes and Emotional Qualities in Poetry", in Rusch G. (ed.), *Empirical approaches to literature: Proceedings of the fourth biannual conference of the International Society for the Empirical Study of Literature, IGEL, Budapest, August 1994* (Siegen: 1995) 265–271.

Vaganay H., *Les Traductions du Psautier en vers latins au XVIᵉ siècle* (Fribourg: 1898).

Wall J., "The Latin elegiacs of George Buchanan (1506–82)", in Aitken A.J. – McDiarmid M.P. – Thomson D.S. (eds.), *Bards and Makars: Scottish Language and Literature: Medieval and Renaissance* (Glasgow: 1977) 184–93.

Wong A., *The Poetry of Kissing in Early Modern Europe: From the Catullan Revival to Secundus, Shakespeare and the English Cavaliers* (Cambridge: 2017).

Zim R., *English Metrical Psalms. Poetry as Praise and Prayer, 1535–1601* (Cambridge: 2011).

CHAPTER 6

On Red and White Cheeks: Jakob Balde's Poetic Ekphrases on a Triptych by Christoph Schwarz in the Light of the Scholastic Theory of the Passions

Aline Smeesters

Abstract

The Neo-Latin poetic corpus by the Jesuit Jakob Balde (Ensisheim 1604 – Neuburg-an-der-Donau 1668), the so-called "German Horace", contains several ekphrases of religious paintings from the 16th and 17th centuries. This contribution will focus on two of these poems, describing two panels of a religious triptych by the Munich painter Christoph Schwarz, representing respectively a St. Catherine of Alexandria and a Virgin and Child in a glory of clouds. It will try to show how Balde's insistance on a pictorial detail, the red-and-white colour of the characters' faces and cheeks, can refer to different levels of symbolic meaning, and in particular, how it can be read against the background of the scholastic theory of the passions and of their bodily impact.

Keywords

Neo-Latin poetry – Jesuit literature – ekphrasis – scholastic psychology – theory of passions – religious painting – Jakob Balde – Christoph Schwarz

1   Introduction

The Jesuit poet Jakob Balde (born in Alsace in 1604, died in Neuburg-an-der-Donau in 1668) was active mainly in Bavaria.[1] During his lifetime he enjoyed a

---

1   For a recent account of Jakob Balde's life and works, see Stroh W., "Balde, Jakob", in Arend S. et al. (eds.), *Frühe Neuzeit in Deutschland 1620–1720: Literaturwissenschaftliches Verfasserlexikon* (Berlin – Boston: 2019), vol. 1, 412–445. A directory of his works (with links to digitised early modern editions) and an up-to-date list of secondary literature under the care of Wilfried Stroh are available from: http://stroh.userweb.mwn.de/main7.html (accessed: 28.10.2022). See also Lebrecht Schmidt P., "Bemerkungen zu Biographie und Text im Werk

---

© ALINE SMEESTERS, 2025 | DOI:10.1163/9789004694613_007

European-wide reputation as a Neo-Latin poet (he is often called the German Horace).[2] His monumental, varied and virtuoso Latin work can be divided roughly into four periods, each one characterised by a predominance of certain meters and genres: Westermayer, the great nineteenth-century biographer of Balde wrote of an 'epic morning' (1626–37 – 'hexametric' would be more accurate than 'epic'), a 'lyric noon' (1637–1649), a 'satiric evening' (1649–1662) and an 'elegiac twilight' (1662–1668).[3]

Among Balde's many interests were the visual arts, and his poetic work notably contains several ekphrases of religious paintings from the 16th and 17th centuries, including paintings by Peter-Paul Rubens and by two artists active in Munich, Christoph Schwarz and Peter Candid.[4] In some of his texts, Balde wittily played with the colour suggestions evoked by these three surnames: red for Rubens, black for Schwarz, and white for Candid.[5] Colours also appear prominently in Balde's ekphrases of their paintings. The purpose of this essay will be to analyse the multi-layered symbolic value of these colour notations, and more precisely, of a detail present in Balde's two ekphrases of a triptych by Christoph Schwarz: namely, the red-and-white colour of the characters' faces and cheeks, a detail that I will argue can be read against the background of the scholastic theory of the passions.

---

des Jesuiten Jakob Balde", in Schnur R. (ed.), *Acta Conventus Neo-Latini Hafniensis* (Tempe, Arizona: 1997) 97–119.

2   The expression comes from his contemporary Sigmund von Birken (1626–1681) (Stroh, "Balde, Jakob" 423).

3   Westermayer G., *Jacobus Balde (1604–1668), sein Leben und seine Werke* (Munich: 1868; reprinted Amsterdam – Maarssen: 1998) 31. Lebrecht Schmidt, "Bemerkungen zu Biographie" 105–106, while acknowledging the general validity of this (admittedly somewhat caricatural) scheme, points out that the use of hexameter in Balde's youth (for parodic works, *epyllia*, exercises in style, etc.) cannot really be described as epic.

4   On Balde's ekphrastic poems, see: Kranz G., "Zu Jacob Baldes Bildgedichten", *Archiv für Kulturgeschichte* 60 (1978) 305–325; Hess G., "*Ut pictura poesis*. Jacob Baldes Beschreibung des Freisinger Hochaltarbildes von Peter Paul Rubens", in Weber A. (ed.), *Handbuch der Literatur in Bayern* (Regensburg: 1987) 207–220 (reedited in Hess G., *Der Tod des Seneca. Studien zur Kunst der Imagination in Texten und Bildern des 17. und 18. Jahrhunderts* (Regensburg: 2009) 166–180); Robert T., "Texttabernakel. Jacob Baldes sacrale Ekphrasen und die Krise des religiösen Bildes", in Burkard T. et al. (eds.), *Jacob Balde im kulturellen Kontext seiner Epoche* (Regensburg: 2006) 287–312; and Dekoninck R. – Smeesters A., "L'épode 15 de Jacob Balde, entre vision picturale et peinture visionnaire", in De Landtsheer J. – Della Schiava F. – Van Houdt T. (eds.), *Dulces ante omnia Musae. Essays on Neo-Latin Poetry in Honour of Dirk Sacré* (Turnhout: 2021) 475–494.

5   See, e.g., Balde Jakob, *Poema de Vanitate mundi* (Munich, Leysserius: 1638) 65, series 36, poem 5, lines 7–8: 'Quis placeat magis ? Anne Rubens, anne Albus, an Ater ?/ Hic pictor triplex, est simul ipse color' – 'Who do I like more, the Red, the White or the Black?/ These are three painters as well as three colours'.

2   Balde on Schwarz

Christoph Schwarz (Munich ca. 1548–Munich 1592) worked as a painter in Munich throughout his life.[6] He probably spent some time in Venice between 1570 and 1573, and his style combines elements of the German and Italian traditions. He carried out commissions for both the city's burghers (e.g., painting house façades) and for the court of the Wittelsbachs, particularly under William v (reigned from 1579 to 1597). His work at the request of the court was mainly in line with the Duke's confessional politics: Schwarz was notably in charge of commissions related to the new Jesuit foundations (the Munich college and St. Michael's church) favoured by the Duke. Schwarz also carried out commissions in Augsburg, e.g., for Octavianus Secundus Fugger and for the Jesuit St. Salvator church. During his lifetime, Schwarz enjoyed a great reputation, which earned him the title *primus pictor Germaniae*.[7] The Emperor Rudolf II even tried to bring Schwarz to his court, but his request was refused by William v. The precise status of the painter is unclear, since some clues tend to indicate that he was attached to the court, while others show that he did not enjoy the privileges usually accorded to court painters.[8] According to Balde, the painter died in poverty.[9] We know from other sources that he had problems with alcoholism ('plus vini quam olei in laboribus consumiert', 'he consumes more wine than oil while working', wrote Philipp Hainhofer in 1611), and that he had great difficulty, in his last years, in fulfilling his commissions.[10] Balde could not have met him, since Schwarz died twelve years before Balde was born, but he had first-hand experience of his paintings, and singled out for praise his consummate paintings of the Virgin and Child; in particular, he

---

6   On Christoph Schwarz, see: Volk-Knüttel B., "Candid nach Schwarz", *Münchner Jahrbuch der bildenden Kunst* 39 (1988) 113–132; Geissler H., "Schwarz, Christoph", in Turner J. (ed.), *The Dictionary of Art* (New York: 1996), vol. 28, 188–190; Diemer D. – Diemer P., "Schwarz, Christoph", in *Neue Deutsche Biographie* (Berlin: 2007), vol. 23, 804–805; Hess D. – Hirschfelder D., *Renaissance. Barock. Aufklärung. Kunst und Kultur vom 16. bis zum 18. Jahrhundert* (Nuremberg: 2010), esp. 131, 298–299; and, most importantly, Diefenthaler S.-K., "Ein städtischer Hofkünstler: Christoph Schwarz", in Eichberger D. – Lorentz P. – Tacke A., *The Artist between Court and City (1300–1600)* (Petersberg: 2017) 327–340.

7   Volk-Knüttel, *Peter Candid* 100.

8   On these questions, see the detailed analysis by Diefenthaler, "Ein städtischer Hofkünstler".

9   Balde Jakob, *Urania victrix* (Munich, Wagner: 1663) 68, elegy 1, 4, part 7.

10   Volk-Knüttel, "Candid nach Schwarz" 116. Volk-Knüttel quotes Hainhofer from: Doering O. (ed.), *Der Augsburger Patriciers Philipp Hainhofer Beziehungen zum Herzog Philipp II von Pommern-Stettin. Correspondenzen aus den Jahren 1610–1619* (Vienna: 1894–1896) 93 (letter dated 9/19.1.1611).

BALDE'S POETIC EKPHRASES ON A TRIPTYCH BY CHRISTOPH SCHWARZ   223

commends him for his ability to represent this subject with an illusion of presence and life, and to unite in Mary both virginal and maternal features.[11]

Three paintings by Christoph Schwarz held in Munich were the subject of poetic descriptions by Balde: two parts of a triptych dating from 1580–1581, painted by Schwarz for the *aula* of the Jesuit College in Munich;[12] and the *Fall of Lucifer* (1587–89), painted for the high altar of St. Michael's church linked to the Jesuit college in Munich.[13] The *Fall of Lucifer* is described in Balde's *Silva* VIII, 10 (lines 67–110); this long and complex poem, organized around the unifying theme of the Ignatian spiritual exercises, merits a separate study and will not be considered here.[14] This essay will rather concentrate on the two poems about the triptych [Fig. 6.1], whose left panel, featuring St. Catherine of Alexandria [Fig. 6.2] and centre panel, showing the Virgin and Child in a Glory of Clouds [Fig. 6.3], Balde describes respectively in a passage from the *Panegyricus de laudibus sanctae Catharinae* (lines 299–353),[15] and in *Ode* IV, 13.[16]

The triptych was painted at the request of Duke William V of Bavaria, who also contributed to the foundation of the Jesuit College in Munich. The outer wings (visible in the closed state) depict the Annunciation to Mary. The central panel shows the Virgin seated on a throne of clouds, her feet resting on a crescent moon. Standing on her lap, the Child Jesus reaches with his right hand for the flower held delicately by the Virgin. Above, two cherubs crown her with

---

11   Balde, *Urania victrix* 59–60, elegy I, 3, part 7.

12   Now in the Nuremberg Museum, Gm 900–902. On this painting, see Hess – Hirschfelder, *Renaissance. Barock. Aufklärung* 298–299, who mention that it became so well known that the Elector Palatine Johann Wilhelm later tried in vain to acquire it for his gallery in Düsseldorf.

13   The painting is still there today.

14   *Silva* VIII, 10, lines 67–110. The main early modern editions are: Balde Jakob, *Sylvae lyricae* (Cologne, Kalckhoven: 1646) 263; Balde Jakob, *De laudibus Beatae Mariae Virginis Odae Partheniae* (Munich, Wagner: 1648) 101 (ode 63); Balde Jakob, *Poemata*, 4 vols. (Cologne, Busaeus: 1660), vol. 1, 545 (*Silva* VIII, 9); and Balde Jakob, *Opera poetica omnia*, 8 vols. (Munich, Happach–Schlütter: 1729), vol. 2, 250. On this poem: Schäfer E., "Baldes Exerzitien-Tapisserien (*Silv.* 8, 10)", in Lefèvre E. (ed.), *Balde und Horaz* (Tübingen: 2002) 319–358, esp. 335–339.

15   Early modern edition: Balde, *Opera poetica omnia*, vol. 3, 295–305, 303–304. No detailed study of it has appeared, to our knowledge. Tilg S., *Die Hl. Katharina von Alexandria auf der Jesuitenbühne* (Tübingen: 2005) 9–10, provides a brief summary and the German translation of lines 353–361 and 366–372.

16   Main early modern editions: Balde Jakob, *Lyricorum libri IV. Epodon liber unus* (Munich, Leysserius: 1643) 220; Balde, *De laudibus Mariae*, 9 (ode 8); Balde, *Poemata*, vol. 1, 212; and Balde, *Opera poetica omnia*, vol. 1, 212. No in-depth study has been written on this ode, which is mentioned in passing by Robert in "Texttabernakel" 299–300.

FIGURE 6.1 Christoph Schwarz, *Marienaltar*, 1580–1581. Triptych with St. Catherine of Alexandria, the Virgin and Child in a Glory of Clouds, and St. Jerome, painted for the Jesuit College of Munich. Oil on wood, 183.1 × 64.4 cm – 197.6 × 152.8 cm – 181.8 × 64.2 cm. Nuremberg, Germanisches Nationalmuseum
IMAGE © GERMANISCHES NATIONALMUSEUM, NUREMBERG. LOAN FROM BAYERISCHEN STAATSGEMÄLDESAMMLUNGEN MÜNCHEN

the monogram IHS, accompanied by musician angels who sing and play various instruments. At the lower edge of the central panel, two miniature scenes depict the Flight into Egypt and the Massacre of the Innocents. The painting responds to Italian models (notably the musician angels who derive from Titian and Veronese) and German ones (Mary in glory, inspired by a painting by Albrecht Altdorfer).[17]

The two saints flanking the Virgin on the inner side wings were not chosen at random: St. Catherine, on the left wing, was the patron saint of the Jesuit College, while on the right wing, St. Jerome provided an example of learned sanctity.[18] St. Catherine stands with hand to heart, her other hand resting on the hilt of a sword, and the broken wheel of torture at her feet. As for the authorship of the Catherine's panel, although the painting is traditionnally attributed

17   Diefenthaler, "Ein städtischer Hofkünstler" 332–333.
18   Ibidem.

BALDE'S POETIC EKPHRASES ON A TRIPTYCH BY CHRISTOPH SCHWARZ 225

FIGURE 6.2
Christoph Schwarz, *St. Catherine of Alexandria*, 1580–1581. Part of Schwarz's *Marienaltar*, painted for the Jesuit College of Munich. Left panel. Oil on wood, 183,1 × 64,4 cm
IMAGE © GERMANISCHES NATIONALMUSEUM, NUREMBERG. LOAN FROM BAYERISCHEN STAATSGEMÄLDESAMMLUNGEN MÜNCHEN

FIGURE 6.3 Christoph Schwarz, *The Virgin and Child in the Glory of the Clouds*, 1580–1581. Part of Schwarz's *Marienaltar*, painted for the Jesuit College of Munich. Center panel. Oil on wood, 197,6 × 152,8 cm
IMAGE © GERMANISCHES NATIONALMUSEUM, NUREMBERG. LOAN FROM BAYERISCHEN STAATSGEMÄLDESAMMLUNGEN MÜNCHEN

BALDE'S POETIC EKPHRASES ON A TRIPTYCH BY CHRISTOPH SCHWARZ   227

to Schwarz, Balde's poem casts doubt on this attribution, since he ascribes the picture to 'the white Zeuxis or the black Apelles' ('Zeuxis *candidus* [...] vel *fuscus* Apelles', 300–301). The two adjectives, *candidus* and *fuscus*, certainly refer to Peter Candid and Christoph Schwarz. Is Balde hesitating between two attributions, or is he suggesting that both painters shared authorship of the painting? At least one case of a painting begun by Schwarz and completed by Candid is known and well documented.[19]

3   The Two Ekphrastic Poems

Before entering into a detailed analysis of the two poems (whose Latin text and English translation[20] are given in the appendix), it is worth briefly mentioning the context of their production, their generic characteristics and their construction.

Balde's *Panegyricus de laudibus Sanctae Catharinae, virginis et martyris, praesidis studiosorum* (*Panegyric on the glory of St. Catherine, virgin and martyr, patroness of students*), a long poem in 375 dactylic hexameters which remained unpublished until the *Opera poetica omnia* of 1729, probably dates from Balde's youth, and more precisely from his first period of teaching at the Jesuit college in Munich, between 1626 and 1628.[21] It belongs to a series of three poems in dactylic hexameters (together with the *Juditha Holophernis triumphatrix* and the *Pudicitia vindicata*) that seem to have been conceived as samples of the mythological-hagiographic epyllion genre, intended for Balde's Munich students.[22] One can assume that the editor of the *Opera poetica omnia* of 1729 (the Jesuit Franz Lang), who arrayed these three unpublished poems consecutively in volume 3 (pages 287 ff.), found them gathered in the same manuscript.[23] The *argumentum* that precedes the panegyric divides it

---

19   See the article by Volk-Knüttel, "Candid nach Schwarz".

20   Unless otherwise stated, all translations from the Latin in this essay are mine.

21   Proposed by Westermayer in *Jacobus Balde* 253, this dating still appears in recent literature (e.g., Tilg, *Die Hl. Katharina von Alexandria* 9); Wilfried Stroh, in his repertory of Balde's works, reproduces the date but follows it with a question mark (Stroh W., *Baldeana* (Munich: 2004) 319).

22   Lebrecht Schmidt P., "Bemerkungen zu Biographie" 105–106.

23   The monumental eight-volume edition of the *Opera poetica omnia* of 1729 is in fact based on a series of manuscripts and editions of Balde's work archived in Munich (as stated in the title and in the *Icon authoris et operis* which opens volume 1); it contains not only unpublished pieces such as the *Panegyric*, but also numerous authorial variants to pieces already published. On the relative value and sources of this 1729 edition, see the remarks of Lebrecht Schmidt, "Bemerkungen zu Biographie und Text" 102–111. The *Opera*

into three parts: the first concerns Catherine's birth and her early childhood, already marked by signs that she was destined to become the patron saint of students; the second part deals with her triumpant martyrdom; the third and final part consists of the *reliquae laudes* and offers a description of the painting of Catherine exhibited in the *aula* of the college of Munich. The ekphrasis of the painting begins at line 299. Balde's description of St. Catherine successively addresses the saint's face, eyes, hair, and mouth, then the position of her head, her neck, her garment, and finally her right hand resting on a sword. The poet then briefly mentions the wheel shown at her feet and the shadows in the background. Finally, he exhorts the youth of Bavaria to come and contemplate the painting (341 and following), as well as the altar on which it is placed (*ara*, 348).

Ode IV, 13 dates from the main period (1637–1650) of Balde's stay in Munich, where he worked as a teacher (at the Jesuit college) and as a court preacher and historiographer (at the court of the Dukes of Bavaria), and was also the president of a Marian congregation. He composed the poem, first published in the *Lyrica* of 1643, on the occasion of a vigil of the Assumption ('in pervigilio Assumptae Virginis'), according to the poem's title. The title further indicates that Balde wrote it while contemplating, in the company of a Michael Anguilla, the *Virgin and Child* by Schwarz that adorned the altar of the Virgin in the *aula* of the Jesuit college in Munich. The ode, composed of fourteen stanzas combining two minor asclepiads, a pherecratic, and a glyconic, is presented in the form of a dialogue between Balde and Anguilla, and more precisely, as an instance of 'Amoebaean singing', a dialogue in which each line builds on the previous one (by analogy, contrast or supersession).[24] The form is attested in Horace's *Odes* (III, 49), but is especially typical of Virgil's *Eclogues* (3 and 7) and, before him, of Theocritus' *Idylls*. Up to stanza 12, Balde's theme is the Virgin, while that of his interlocutor is the Child Jesus; the two speakers successively review the attitude, clothing, faces, looks, and gestures of the Virgin and Child. The poet doesn't pay any attention to the secondary characters or scenes – except for an allusion to the cherubic figures in the clouds who can probably be recognised as the *pennigeri Favonii* of line 10. The concluding stanzas 13 and 14 allude to the painter and redirect the reader's attention to his

---

  poetica omnia were republished in 1990 (Frankfurt am Main), with an introduction by W. Kühlmann and H. Wiegand.

24   As already pointed out by Benno Müller in the notes to his edition of Balde's *Carmina lyrica* (Munich: 1844) 100. Balde's *Silva* II, 3 (*De forma pueri Jesu et Mariae Virginis*) has a similar form and theme: two shepherds (Corydon and Menalcas) sing alternately about the beauty of Jesus and his mother.

prototypes, more beautiful than their portraits and surpassingly beautiful in their relation to each other.

4 The Illusionistic Powers of Painting

Balde's ekphrastic poetry as a whole frequently places pictorial representations in tension with, on the one hand, the real prototypes of the sacred figures represented (Christ, the Virgin, the saints), and, on the other hand, the other types of representations that can enable us to contemplate them, namely, poetic and mental ones. In various places in his work, Balde seems to put painting on the lowest rung: thus, in *Silvae* V, 1–3, painting is declared to be inferior to poetry, as it is unable to go beyond appearances and reproduce the realities of the mind;[25] and in the conclusion of *Silva* VIII, 10 – the poem which contains the ekphrasis of the *Fall of Lucifer* – Balde affirms the superiority of Ignatian 'tapestries', i.e., of mental images over the paintings of even the greatest painters, such as Zeuxis or Rubens: in pictorial images, the eye sees only the shadows and outlines of a vain beauty, whereas mental images allow the soul to see itself with greater clarity.[26]

In Balde's opinion, was painting really at the bottom of the scale of values, unable to go beyond the world of appearances and the stage of vain aesthetic satisfaction? This goes in tension with the importance of the theme of painting in Balde's poetic production, which indicates his keen interest in this visual art. The two ekphrases under consideration are cases in point of a more qualified view. In the ode on Schwarz's Virgin, Balde remarkably shows, through the dialogue between Anguilla and himself, how the contemplation of a painting can actually serve as a springboard to God: touched by the panel's beauty and impression of truth, the viewer becomes convinced of the divine nature of its subject (7–8: 'Even an ignorant man would say:/ He who is painted thus is a God'); aware of its status of representation, he conceives all the more admiration for the prototypes (50–52: 'What joys must flood the real faces/ If feigned faces spread such lucent joys / In an image!'). Similarly, in the ekphrasis of St. Catherine, the painting (produced by a talented hand) is compared to

---

25 First edition: Balde Jakob, *Sylvarum libri septem* (Munich, Leysserius: 1643) 106–113. In this sequence of three poems, the author receives from Apollo the gift that his compositions should materialise in images; in this way he realises that only poetry can picture a man's soul. On this poem, see Wiener C., "Menetekel an Münchner Wänden. Joachim Sandrart in Jacob Baldes Dichtungen", in Burkard T. et al. (eds.), *Jacob Balde im kulturellen Kontext seiner Epoche* (Regensburg: 2006) 313–337, esp. 313–330.

26 *Silva* VIII, 10, 383–390.

a moon that reflects the light of the sun, and is apt to provoke wonder and love (342–347).

Fascinated by the illusionist powers of painters, Balde, with genuine poetic virtuosity, regularly formulates his ekphrases in such a way as to suggest an indeterminacy between the image and the being it represents. Thus, in line 2 of *Ode* IV, 13, the Virgin is described as 'the living image of concentrated modesty' ('collectae species viva modestiae'). The expression *species viva*, 'the living image', can be applied to a being that seems to personify a virtue (as in Lucan VI, 254: 'vivam magnae speciem virtutis'); but in ekphrastic contexts, it also expresses the illusionary character of a work of art (e.g., Ausonius, *Epigr.*, 70, 4, on Myron's bronze cow as a 'living image' of a real cow). Balde thus blurs from the outset the boundary between the iconic representation and the represented being: the poem describes both the Virgin, who is modesty personified, and a work of art that represents her in an illusionistic way. Further in the poem, other poetic formulations reveal Balde's attention to the pictorial quality of the representation. E.g. in line 36, when he writes that the Virgin's pupil 'gleams with sweet oil', the expression seems to refer both to the brilliance of the woman's eyes, and to the medium used by the painter to admix his colours.

In the ekphrasis of St. Catherine, the physical surface of the painting appears to invite itself into the scene described. St. Catherine, the poet writes, searching for Christ with her eyes, fixes her gaze on the frame of the painting ('tabulae margo', 322) – which of course is not supposed to be part of her field of vision – as if it were this frame that prevented her from looking unimpededly at her beloved: the painting's frame thus bodies forth the invisible border that separates the earthly world from the kingdom of Heaven, humankind from the face-to-face encounter with the Lord God. If the painted figure of St. Catherine could really look beyond the frame, she would see the angel-filled heavens that occupy the upper zone of triptych's center – a space in which the forms, dissolving in fulgent light, prevent any clear view of the Creator. But the main subject of the central painting also offers viewers the opportunity to contemplate their God: the Virgin presents the infant Jesus – or, more precisely, a painted portrait of Mary proffers the infant Jesus, his image having been made available through the mystery of the Incarnation that rendered God representable to human eyes.

Both ekphrases also make use of the topical motif of the figure painted so illusionistically that it appears to move or to speak. In lines 41–45 of the ode, the characters are caught in mid-motion and mid-speech: the Virgin 'utters I know not what, and holds out a flower to her darling, that he may take it', while the child is either 'asking for I know not what, or nodding'. As for St. Catherine, Balde notes that her mouth is slightly open; in this almost imperceptible

BALDE'S POETIC EKPHRASES ON A TRIPTYCH BY CHRISTOPH SCHWARZ   231

movement, he reads complex emotions, both the suggestion of a smile and a moan. 'One would think she could speak', Balde continues, 'and if she moved her lips, that she would spread coloured words in our ears' (316–317). Colours being to painting what words are to poetry, the words of the saint could indeed only be *colorata verba*. Such words would in theory be unfit to touch the ears of the spectators; but the poet immediately adds that 'Far from being the cosmetic [*fucus*] of cunning, colour has learned to be eloquent' (318). The word *fucus*, whose primary meanings refer to a marine plant, and then to the purple dye derived from it, is used here to allude to sophistical and deceptive eloquence; but the colours of St. Catherine manage, according to Balde, to detach themselves from any association with 'dye' or 'make-up', and thereby attain a true eloquence.

5   The Eloquence of Colours

Colours are indeed much present in both poems. Throughout *Ode* IV, 13, indications are scattered that refer to shades of white, blue, and red, while in the *Panegyricus*, the main colours described are red and white. Balde uses a whole range of words that refer to images taken from the natural world: e.g., in the *Ode*, line 17, *viola*, the violet; 27, *pruina*, frost; 28, *ostrum*, purple; 30, *eburneus*, in ivory; 31, *mala* et *lilia*, apples and lilies; 32, *flammae* et *rosae*, flames and roses; 34, *ianthinus*, violet; 37, *lac*, milk; 38, *uva gemmea*, a gem-shaped grape; and in the *Panegyricus*, line 303, *ligustrum*, the privet flower; 304, *rosa* and *ignis*, the rose and the fire; 324–325, *pruina* and *gelu*, frost and ice. In the *Ode*, there are also terms expressing luminosity (lines 22 and 36, *lux*, light; 36, *nitere*, to shine; 38, *fulgor*, brilliance), and even the vibration of colours, first through ambiguous verbs like *micare* (14, to twinkle or scintillate) or *vibrare* (35, to vibrate or scintillate), and then through the magnificent expression in line 48, *apricus trepidat color*, literally 'a sunny colour trembles' (on the lip of the infant Jesus).[27]

We know that Schwarz was recognised by his contemporaries for his talent as a colourist. In his *Teutsche Academie der Bau-, Bild- und Mahlerey-Künste*,

---

27   *Apricus* means 'exposed to the sun', 'sunny'. In classical usage, the adjective does not directly describe a colour but is found in passages evoking the colour of sun-ripened fruits (Ovid, *Metamorphoses*, IV, 331: 'hic color aprica pendentibus arbore pomis' – 'This is the colour of apples hanging on a tree exposed to the sun'; Virgil, *Eclogues*, 9, 49: 'duceret apricis in collibus uva colorem' – 'the grapes take on colour on the sunny hillsides').

Joachim von Sandrart describes him as a 'herrlicher Colorirer'.[28] His palette is mainly characterised by its pastel shades, and by the light, sometimes ivory-coloured flesh tones of the figures.[29] It seems that Balde was indeed extremely attentive, not only to colours as such, but to colours as indicators of the painter's art. When the poet refers to the colour of the Virgin's cheeks, stating that 'her cheeks have drunk/ the German frosts,/ nicely diluted with purple' (26–28), the adjective *Teutonicus* (German) not only serves as a classical epithet that qualifies frost, but also refers to the painter's homeland; and the two verbs, *potare* (to drink) and *diluere* (to dilute), could be interpreted as allusions to the materiality of paint at the moment when the painter mixes the colours and applies them as a semi-liquid medium. In the *Panegyric*, the subtlety of the colour palette is emphasised twice. The face of St. Catherine, mingling the red of roses and fire with the white of the privet flower, is described as 'neither too red nor too pale,/ but more pale than red' (303–306), while the shade of Catherine's clothing is described as intermediate between the colour of a dyed garment (probably red, since the adjective *ruber* appears just above), and the natural colour of undyed fabric (that is, a shade of white) (328–329). This intermediate colour could correspond, according to Balde, to the qualifier *flavus*,[30] but it could also be an almost new colour ('colorem paene novum', 331–332) – that is, a colour invented by the painter.

Beyond the recognition of Schwarz's artistry, the emphasis on the colours red and white also has symbolic implications. In the Catherine ekphrasis, white is given a slight advantage over red (the face is 'more pale than red', and the cloth's red dye is associated with a poison, *venenum* (329)). The end of the ekphrasis provides a possible reading key, insofar as it closes with a kind of symbolic victory of white (chastity) over red (amorous passion): 'Admire the girl/ Who overcame the yoke of Venus and despised her torches,/ Untouched by the flame of her quiver. Embrace the Holy one/ Who extinguished the burning fires of Paphos in a white libation', Balde enjoins the youth of Bavaria. According to the legend, St. Catherine had aroused the passion of the emperor Maxentius who, mad with rage at her refusals, had her beheaded: from the neck of the young woman gushed not blood but milk.

---

28   Sandrart Joachim von, *Teutsche Academie der Bau-, Bild- und Mahlerey-Künste* (Nuremberg, J. von Sandrart – J.P. Miltenberger: 1675–1679), vol. 2, Book III, 485 (quoted in Diefenthaler, "Ein städtischer Hofkünstler" 337).

29   Diefenthaler, "Ein städtischer Hofkünstler" 329, 335.

30   Calepino's dictionary describes *flavus* as a mixture of green, red and white, and illustrates it with the examples of gold, honey and ripe ears of wheat (Calepinus Ambrosius, *Dictionarium* [Venice, in aedibus Manutianis: 1573] 280).

White and red, however, have still other symbolic meanings. When, in *Ode* IV, 13, Balde says that the Infant Child is 'two-coloured, white and red' ('bicolor, candidus et ruber', line 5), he evidently alludes to the bridegroom of the *Song of Songs*, who is *candidus et rubicundus* (5:10). Contemporary exegesis saw this dichromatism, amongst other interpretations, as a symbol of the union of divinity (white, the colour of purity and splendour) and humanity (red, the colour of blood).[31] Red is here given a more positive connotation in the Christian's symbolic palette. A few lines below, Balde emphasises another symbolic union of two abstract notions in Jesus's character: the harmonious blending of Majesty and Love ('conveniunt bene/ ac miscentur in uno/ Maiestas et Amor loco', 14–16).

6   Colourful Faces

Let us examine in more detail the particular colours of the main character's faces. On the face of the St. Catherine, as we have just seen, 'the natural colour of the rose/ balances the pallor of her cheeks, mingling fire with the privet flower, / and yet her face is neither too red nor too pale,/ but more pale than red' (303–306). On the Virgin and Child painting, 'the sun laughs on his [= the child's] ivory face;/ spring lilies bloom on his cheeks,/ and roses sharpen their flames' (30–32); as for his mother, 'her cheeks have drunk/ the German frosts,/ nicely diluted with purple' (26–28). Beyond the symbolic dimensions already outlined, what additional meaning is produced by the fact that this mixture of red and white is observed specifically on the characters' faces?

A first possible explanation is that these colours serve to affirm the beauty of the characters described. Just after having mentioned the red-white face of St. Catherine, Balde concludes: 'Whatever I say, will be an argument/ for her beauty' (306–307). The beauty of mother and child is also an important theme in *Ode* IV, 13, where it occupies the entire closing stanza. Both Catherine and the Virgin present throughout the two poems a harmonious blend of humility (Catherine: *modeste* 332; the Virgin: *modestia* 2, *pauper* 18) and majestic beauty (Catherine: *sublime* 303, *decor* 307, *regina* 342; the Virgin: *decet* 20, *augusta* 26).

---

31   Lapide Cornelius a, *Commentarii in Canticum Canticorum* (Lyon, Boissat: 1637) 320: 'Symbolice Christus est candidus ob purissimam et splendidissimam Deitatem, quam ab aeterno habet; rubicundus propter humanitatem cum sanguine rubro' (cited in Bauer B., "Apathie des stoischen Weisen oder Ekstase der christlichen Braut? Jesuitische Stoakritik und Jacob Baldes *Jephtias*", in Neumeister S. – Wiedemann C., *Res Publica Litteraria. Die Institutionen der Gelehrsamkeit in der frühen Neuzeit. Teil II* [Wiesbaden: 1987] 453–474, esp. 464, 472).

The description of a beautiful young person with a snowy white face, enhanced by touches of bright red (lips, blushing cheeks, etc.), is a very widespread topos in classical poetry.[32] The agreement of the two colours was unanimously thought to be a criterion of female beauty, and Balde's lines inevitably recall those passages in which the Latin poets, and in particular the elegiac poets of love, Tibullus, Propertius, and Ovid, described the faces of beautiful young women, with many supportive comparisons (whiteness of snow, milk, lilies, ivory; redness of fire, roses, etc.). This aesthetic dimension also derives from biblical exegesis of the *Song of Songs*: the Jesuit Cornelius a Lapide, for instance, commenting on 5:10, notes that 'the bride begins her praise of the bridegroom's beauty with the colour of his face, and shows that it is very beautiful, of mingled white with a sprinkling of red, i.e., of a pink comparable to that which the poets attribute to the magnificent Adonis'[33] (with references to Statius and Tibullus).[34]

But another possible explanation (compatible with the first), which I will now develop at more length, is that colours participate in the evocation of the characters' emotions. Indeed, some of the textual passages that evoke the colours of the characters' complexions are closely followed by references to emotions. In *Ode* IV, 13, just after having called the child Jesus 'bicolor' (5), Balde states that he 'breathes joy with all his limbs' (6); in the *Panegyricus*, the twenty lines (303–323) devoted to the description of Catherine's face, beginning with her white-and-red colour, further describe the emotions (ardent love, joy, sadness of separation) discernible in the movement of her lips and in her eyes. Her mouth, for instance, 'sketches the joy of a sacred smile / but without ceasing, however, to moan her tender loves' (314–315). Throughout both poems, particular attention is paid by the poet to the characters' emotions: the Virgin and Child radiate love and joy, while Catherine exudes a mixture of love, joy and sadness, three feelings intimately linked to her relationship with God. Presented as the bride (*sponsa*) of Christ, a word that directly evokes the *Song of Songs*, Catherine is also linked by implicit intertextual allusion to famous ancient characters of women in love, namely, Dido and Medea (see notes to lines 302, 321, 323).

---

32   For example, in Ovid, *Metamorphoses* III, 423, Narcissus admires himself: 'in niveo mixtum candore ruborem' – 'the redness mixed with a snowy whiteness'.

33   Lapide, *Commentarii* 320: 'Sponsa ergo pulchritudinis Sponsi elogia inchoat a colore faciei, docetque eum esse pulcherrimum, scilicet candidum rubore mixtum et vermiculatum, hoc est roseum, qualem Adonidi pulcherrimo dant poetae'.

34   Statius, *Achilleid*, I, 161–162; Tibullus, III, 4, 29–30.

7 Theory of Emotions

In terms of emotions, although Balde often showed a marked sympathy for neo-Stoicism, his first frame of reference must rather have been the scholastic theory of the passions (derived from Aristotelian ethics, but also and above all, from Thomas Aquinas's *Summa*),[35] which was part of the school and university training of every Jesuit.[36] This is evidenced by the fact that Balde himself briefly outlines this scholastic theory of the passions in the opening argument of his prosimetrum *Maximilianus Primus Austriacus* (1631), where he recalls the definitions of the eleven passions listed by scholastic philosophers.[37] My own following summary is based on a sample of texts that should not be understood as Balde's possible direct sources (some of them postdate one or two of the poems under discussion); rather, they bear witness to the widespread and very stable diffusion of this type of passion theory in Jesuit and non-Jesuit textbooks of scholastic philosophy,[38] as well as in a Jesuit treatise on poetics (that of the Italian Alessandro Donati).[39]

According to the scholastic *doxa*, the passions are basically eleven in number and are distributed in two series, depending on whether they fall under the concupiscible sensory appetite, which leads us to seek what seems pleasant and good to us and to reject what seems unpleasant and bad, or under the irascible sensory appetite, which operates particularly in those cases where

---

35   Thomas, *Summa*, Ia IIae, questions 22 to 48; but also *Summa*, Ia, q. 81; *De veritate*, q. 6 a. 3.

36   Recent research on Balde's relationship to Stoicism has emphasised that when he departs from it, he does so because Stoic apathy was in certain respects incompatible with the Christian conception of affects. See, for example, Bauer, "Apathie des stoischen Weisen". For a more nuanced view, see Arendt S., "*Nec Lapis esse volo* – 'Und kein Stein will ich sein'. Zum antistoischen Affekt in der Lyrik Jacob Baldes", in Burkard T. et al. (eds.), *Jacob Balde im kulturellen Kontext seiner Epoche* (Regensburg: 2006) 153–165.

37   First edition: Balde Jakob, *Maximilianus Primus Austriacus* (Ingolstadt, Hänlin: 1631). See Balde, *Opera poetica omnia*, vol. 8, 338–341. On this text, see Töchterle K., "Kraftvolle Keime. Zu Jacob Baldes Jugendwerk *Maximilianus Primus Austriacus*", in Burkard T. et al. (eds.), *Jacob Balde im kulturellen Kontext seiner Epoche* (Regensburg: 2006) 27–37.

38   [College of Coimbra], *In libros Ethicorum Aristotelis ad Nicomachum, aliquot Conimbricensis cursus disputationes, in quibus praecipua quaedam ethicae disciplinae capita continentur* (Lisbon, Simon Lopes: 1593) 47–59 ("Disputatio VII. De affectionibus animi quae passiones vocantur"); Saint-Paul Eustache de, *Summa philosophiae quadripartita de rebus dialecticis, moralibus, physicis et metaphysicis* (Paris, Chastellain: 1609), secunda pars, 99–134 ("Tractatus II. De passionibus animae"); Rhodes Georges de S.J., *Philosophia peripatetica ad veram Aristotelis mentem* (Lyon, Huguetan–Barbier: 1671) 559–573 ("Quaestio III. De passionibus prout sunt materia virtutis moralis").

39   Donati Alessandro S.J., *De arte poetica libri tres* (Rome, Guilielmus Facciotus: 1631) 215–251 (Book II, chapters 33–44 on the *affectus*).

the movement toward good or evil proves arduous. In all cases, the movement of the *appetitus* is directly linked to the perception of an object by the interior sense of imagination (or fantasy).[40] The table below summarises the main passions codified in this system:

Appetitus concupiscibilis	Ad bonum: AMOR
	Ad bonum absens: DESIDERIUM (= CONCUPISCENTIA)
	Ad bonum praesens: GAUDIUM (= DELECTATIO)
	Ad malum: ODIUM
	Ad malum absens: FUGA
	Ad malum praesens: TRISTITIA
Appetitus irascibilis	In bonum arduum
	absens et possibile: SPES, AUDACIA[41]
	absens et impossibile: DESPERATIO
	In malum arduum
	absens et imminens: TIMOR, AUDACIA
	praesens: IRA

Passions in general are considered to be the 'matter' of virtue, meaning that they can be put at the service of achieving or maintaining virtue. As such, they are deemed necessary even for the wise person[42] – in opposition, therefore, to

40 Saint-Paul, *Summa philosophiae* 101: 'Neque enim unquam appetitus ipse excitari potest, nisi prius imaginatio seu phantasia obiecti specie impulsa fuisset' – 'And the appetite itself can only be aroused if first the imagination or fantasy has been struck by the species of an object'.

41 *Audacia* is the only passion whose definition is subject to change according to the treatises: in Balde's *Maximilianus* (339) as well as in Rhodes' *Philosophia peripatetica* (561), *audacia* is the movement towards an absent good that is difficult but possible to obtain and that requires that a danger be overcome (the movement thus concentrates on the means toward the end); in the Coimbra commentary ([College of Coimbra], *In libros Ethicorum* 59) and in Saint-Paul, *Summa philosophiae* 110, *audacia* is the movement by which we prepare ourselves to face an absent evil. Similarly, in Donati, *De arte poetica* 217, *confidentia* concerns an evil that can be avoided.

42 Saint-Paul, *Summa philosophiae* 107: 'Denique cum virtus circa passionem tanquam propriam materiam versetur, sane is virtute careat necesse est qui passione caruerit: quare non sunt a sapiente viro penitus removendae' – 'Finally, insofar as virtue behaves towards passion as towards its own matter, the man who would be devoid of passion would necessarily be devoid of virtue; this is why the passions must not be totally removed from the wise'.

BALDE'S POETIC EKPHRASES ON A TRIPTYCH BY CHRISTOPH SCHWARZ   237

the Stoic viewpoint. Passions are also supposed to trigger a physiological reaction: the presence of a physical change (*mutatio corporis*) is even a defining feature of passion.[43] This physical impact is manifest above all in the dilation and contraction of the heart (considered as the seat of the passions), and in the heat and the movement of the blood. Under the *quaestiones* investigating the physical effect of the passions, one regularly finds mentions of paleness or, oppositely, of redness of the skin, caused by an influx or a reflux of blood. The effects of love are contradictory: on the one hand, love heats up the blood;[44] on the other hand, as the soul is entirely concentrated on the beloved object, it turns away from bodily functions, and especially from the digestion of food, which can cause a shortage of blood and thus leads to the characteristic pallor of lovers.[45] As for joy, all the texts agree that it causes a diffusion and effusion of blood throughout the superficial parts of the body, and thus colours the face red (*rubens vultus*);[46] anger and *furor* can also instigate redness.[47] On the other hand, a pale and discoloured face can be the effect of sadness (which prevents

---

43   The definition of passion given by the Coimbra commentary ([College of Coimbra], *In libros Ethicorum* 54) is: 'motus appetitus sensitivi ex apprehensione boni vel mali cum aliqua mutatione non naturali corporis' – 'a movement of the sensory appetite following the apprehension of a good or evil and accompanied by an unnatural bodily change'.

44   Ibidem 48: 'tam iis qui amant quam qui irascuntur, sanguis et calor effervescit' – 'in people who are in love and people who are angry, there is a heating and boiling of the blood'. See also Rhodes, *Philosophia peripatetica* 561.

45   Saint-Paul, *Summa philosophiae* 117: 'Sunt enim [...] quidam [...] physici [effectus], ut quod amantes pallidi, macilenti et squallidi sint. Dum enim tota vis animae ad rem amatam convertitur illucque intenta est, capiendo digerendoque alimento non sufficit; quo fit ut inopia cruditateque sanguinis membra extenuentur et pallescant'. – 'There are also some physical effects, such as the fact that lovers are pale, meagre and neglected. For while the soul turns all its strength to the beloved one and concentrates on it, it is no longer sufficient to take in and digest food, so that, through lack and crudeness of blood, the limbs become weak and pale'.

46   Ibidem 122: 'Primus [laetitiae effectus] est cordis et viscerum dilatatio [...] sequitur sanguinis ad externas partes diffusio' – 'The first [effect of joy] is the dilation of the heart and viscera [...] This leads to a diffusion of blood toward the external parts'. Cf. Donati, *De arte poetica* 225: 'Nec gaudium celari potest: rubentem in vultum, revocato ad extima sanguine, se fundit' – 'Joy cannot be hidden: it spreads over the flushed face, for the blood is called to the extremities'; see also Rhodes, *Philosophia peripatetica* 568.

47   Saint-Paul, *Summa philosophiae* 104–105: 'ut quod [...] sanguis [...] ira vero et furore ebulliat, et ad externas partes uberius diffundatur' – 'such as the fact that [...] blood [...] is boiled by anger and fury, and spreads abundantly to the outer parts'.

the natural dilation of the blood)[48] or of fear (which returns all the blood to the heart).[49]

Of course, it is risky to employ this interpretative key to give sense to the presence of white and red in poetic or pictorial portraits, on the one hand because each of the two colours can refer to a whole series of different emotions (white indicating love, sadness and fear, red indicating love again as well as joy, anger or fury), and on the other hand because they can both be charged with other (symbolic and aesthetic) values, as we have seen. But we can point out that some early modern commentators on classical poetry indeed used such emotional-physiological clues: for instance, commenting on the famous lines of Virgil describing Dido's face before her suicide, 'maculisque trementis/ interfusa genas, et pallida morte futura' – 'cheeks smeared with stains, pale with her future death',[50] Cristofore Landino notes that the stains on Dido's skin (near her bloodshot eyes) were due to the alternation of *furor* and *timor*, the *impetus furoris* causing the blood to push to the surface.[51]

If we try to read Balde's poems against the background of this theory, it appears that the subtle balance between red and white that characterises the descriptions of the faces of the three characters could well be interpreted as the outward sign of a balance between the various emotions (love and joy, plus sadness in the case of Catherine) that affect them internally. Their faces do not present the extreme pallor of frightened or desperate people, nor the extreme

---

48   Ibidem 125: '[tristitia] naturalem sanguinis et spirituum dilatationem praepedit' – 'Sadness prevents the natural expansion of blood and spirits'. See also Donati, *De arte poetica* 226, which mentions 'decolor vultus' – 'a pale face' among the signs of sadness.

49   Rhodes, *Philosophia peripatetica* 562: 'In timore sanguis et spiritus relictis exterioribus partibus confugit ad cor tanquam ad arcem ipsius vitae; unde sequitur in vultu pallor, tremor in externis partibus' – 'In fear, the blood and spirits, abandoning the external parts, flee to the heart as to the citadel of life; this leads to a paleness of the face and a trembling of the external parts'. See also Saint-Paul, *Summa philosophiae* 104.

50   Virgil, *Aeneid* IV, 643–644.

51   Landino Cristoforo, *Publii Virgilii Maronis Opera, cum Servii Mauri Honorati grammatici, Aelii Donati, Christophori Landini atque Domitii Calderini commentariis* (Nuremberg, Koberger: 1492), fol. 170r, ad *Sanguineam*: 'Nam furore accensae oculi ex furore veluti sanguinei rubebant. Nam ex vehementi furoris impetu sanguis ad exteriora pellitur, et spiritus veluti ardentes in oculis apparent ; et tamen genae, id est palpebrae et oculorum sinus, alternantibus furore simul et timore mortis maculis inficiuntur' – 'As she was inflamed with fury, her eyes, under the effect of this fury, became red and as if bloody. Indeed, under the vehement impulse of fury, the blood is driven to the extremities, and kinds of fiery spirits appear in the eyes; yet the cheeks, i.e. the eyelids and the contours of the eyes, are covered with spots because of the close alternation of fury and the fear of death'.

redness of people who are angry or overflowing with joy, nor the patches that mark Dido's tumultuous alternation of fury and fear; rather, a kind of noble serenity seems to transcend their emotions which are, so to speak, placed in the service of the Christian virtues (in contrast to the emotions of Dido or Medea, which drove them to suicide and crime). Behind the poet's admiration for the painter's art, we can therefore detect the affirmation of a balance, a harmony that is not only pictorial but also moral and emotional.[52]

8   Conclusion

As we have seen, poetic references to colour in Balde's ekphrases are loaded with multiple values. The poet is not only concerned with reporting on the workmanship of the paintings he observes: he also skilfully plays with the Christian's symbolic palette (white for chastity and red for amorous passion, white for divinity and red for humanity ...) and with the classical beauty standars (the topos of the beautiful young person whose snowy complexion is enhanced by red touches). Moreover, I hope I have demonstrated that Balde consistently combines colours to signify combinations of emotions, and that doing so, he is drawing upon, not Stoic philosophy as one might have thought, but rather the scholastic theory of the passions.

Balde's ekphrases thus have literary, religious as well as ethical implications. Balde himself would probably have considered this symbolic richness one of the proofs of the victory of poetry over painting: whereas the talented painter excels in creating subtle shades of colour, the talented poet succeeds in making sense of them on multiple levels, through his own art of combining not colours but words.

---

[52]   It should however be stressed that violent emotions are not always seen in a negative light by Balde, who also sang the praises of enthusiasms and ecstasies: see Smeesters A., "Enthousiasme, fureur poétique et puissance imaginative chez le jésuite Jacob Balde (1604–1668)", *Atlante. Revue d'études romanes* 9 (2018) 69–88, available from: https:// atlante.univ-lille.fr/04-enthousiasme-fureur-poetique-et-puissance-imaginative-chez-le -jesuite-jacob-balde-1604-1668.html (accessed: 28.10.2022).

Appendices

"Panegyricus de laudibus sanctae Catharinae, virginis et martyris, praesidis studiosorum"[53]
[Tertia pars circa reliquas laudes et descriptionem Catharinae in aula Monacensis Gymnasii depictae occupatur, atque ad eandem colendam auditores animat.][54]

[...]
Exere sidereos vultus, et suspice curas
Quas, ut adumbratos[55] viva daret icone Zeuxis   300
Candidus in terris habuit vel *fuscus* Apelles.
Stat subnixa solo.[56] Facies dignissima cerni
Nescio quid sublime gerit, mixtoque ligustris
Pallentes nativa genas rosa temperat igne.
Nec tamen aut nimium rubet, aut candore notatur,   305
Sed candore magis. Quidquid dicamus, id ipsum
Causa decoris erit. Gratae duo lumina frontis
Astra fuisse putes, fratres Phaetontis amoenos,
Sed pumilos cautosque magis, curruque paterno
Numquam non dignos. In nodum torta capilli   310
Regalem series ventorum sibila spernit.
Stemma tamen crinale refert formosius auro.
Os sacrum modice, quod vix advertere possis,
Panditur, et sancti delibat gaudia risus,
Sic tamen ut teneros etiam singultet amores.   315
Posse loqui credas et, si sua labra moveret,
Posse coloratis aures aspergere verbis;
Absque doli fuco didicit color esse disertus.
At caput erecta sensim cervice retrorsum
Abnatat in laevam, sursumque tuentibus absens   320

---

53   The Latin text comes from Balde, *Opera poetica omnia*, vol. 3, 303–304. The italics in line 301 appear in this edition. I have modernised the punctuation and the use of capital letters, removed the accents and transcribed the ampersands as 'et'.

54   Taken from the initial *argumentum* on p. 295.

55   I have correct *adumbratas* in consideration of its antecedent *vultus*. One could also read *adumbratam* with an implied *te* as antecedent.

56   Perhaps in deliberate contrast to Virgil's line where Dido is *subnixa*, not *solo* (on the ground), but *solio* (on a throne): Virgil, *Aeneid*, I, 506: 'saepta armis solioque alte subnixa resedit' – 'surrounded by people in arms, she sat atop a throne'. The expression *subnixa solio* was reused several times (Ausonius, *Cento nuptialis*, III, 45; Prudentius, *Against Symmachus*, I, 367; Claudian, *Epithalamium*, 10, 99–100).

BALDE'S POETIC EKPHRASES ON A TRIPTYCH BY CHRISTOPH SCHWARZ

"Panegyric on the glory of St. Catherine, virgin and martyr, patroness of students"[57]
[The third part deals with the remaining titles of glory and with the description of a painted Catherine in the great hall of the college of Munich; it exhorts the listeners to revere her.]

Bend[58] your starry face and admire the efforts
That the *white* Zeuxis, or the *black* Apelles,[59]
Have made on earth to sketch your living icon.
She is standing on the ground. Her face, very worthy of contemplation,
Has something sublime about it. The natural colour of the rose
Balances the pallor of her cheeks, mingling fire with the privet flower;[60]
And yet her face is neither too red nor too pale,   305
But more pale than red. Whatever I say, will be an argument
For her beauty. Under her pleasant forehead, her two eyes
Could be mistaken for stars, or charming brothers of Phaeton,
But in miniature, and more prudent than he, always proving worthy
Of the father's chariot.[61] Her hair, twisted   310
Into a royal bun, scorns the whistling winds,
And she wears a hair garland more beautiful than gold.
Her holy mouth is slightly open, almost imperceptibly,
And sketches the joy of a sacred smile –
But without ceasing however to moan her tender loves.   315
One would think she could speak, and if she moved her lips,
That she would spread coloured words in our ears:
Far from being the cosmetic of cunning, colour has learned to be eloquent.
Her head, thrown back, the neck slightly stretched,
Swims[62] to the left: turning her eyes upwards,   320

---

57   Translation is mine.
58   The poet is addressing St. Catherine in heaven.
59   Zeuxis and Apelles are two famous painters of Greek antiquity.
60   The privet flower or *ligustrum* is often used as a symbol of whiteness in classical Latin poetry (cf. Virgil, *Eclogues* 2, 18; Ovid, *Metamorphoses* XIII, 789; Martialis, I, 115, 3; or Claudian, *De raptu Proserpinae* II, 130).
61   Phaeton, son of the Sun, pleaded to drive his father's chariot but then proved unable to steer it.
62   This surprising image is apparently inspired by a passage from Statius, in which the marine goddess Thetis really swims: *Achilleides*, I, 382–383: 'Tunc excepta freto longe cervice reflexa / abnatat et blandis adfatur litora votis' – 'Then, received in the waves, she swims away, her head turned backwards, and making kind wishes to the shore'.

Nictibus absentem[63] sponsum sua sponsa requirit;
Quem tabulae quia margo negat, prolixius ardens
Haeret,[64] et aspectus in margine prodigit omnes.
Colla nitent cunctas Scythiae victura pruinas
Crystallique gelu. Nimium ne serica sindon   325
Pectus ad ornatum stringat, se nexa remittit
Carbasus, et rubro paulum laxatur amictu.
Talis inest habitus, qualem nec credere purum
Possis,[65] nec diri medicatum rore veneni,[66]
Sed magis in flavae vergentem stamina telae;   330
Inter utrumque tamen vestis repetita colorem
Paene novum mediumque facit. Demissa modeste
Palla fluit, fluxusque decet, confusaque rugis
Augustas lambit revoluto syrmate suras.
Dextra gerit gladium quem collum senserat olim,   335
Lactis adhuc memorem. Sed stridens verbere diro
Subter, humo propior, fumat rota, fractaque luget
Spicula virginei crudelis machina belli.
Caetera visurum vario pictura recessu
Ludit, et ambiguos reddunt mendacia sensus.   340
    Huc age, Boiugenum pubes Germana, tuamque
Reginam visura veni ! Quae dextera talem
Deliciosa sacrae radiavit imaginis umbram,
An solem potius radiaverit, anne Dianam
Fratre refulgentem, tecum disquire; sereni   345
Certe grande nimis pretium tibi fixit amoris:
Ingenio meritum debes. Circumspice pulchro
Signatam titulo generosi nominis aram,
Et vere regale decus. Mirare puellam,
Quae iuga contemptis vicit Cythereia taedis,   350

---

63   Virgil, *Aeneid*, IV, 83 (Dido in love with Aeneas): 'illum absens absentem auditque videtque' – 'Being absent herself, she sees and hears the absent man'.

64   Valerius Flaccus, *Argonautica* VI, 657–8 (Medea following Jason): 'At regina virum (neque enim deus amovet ignem) / persequitur lustrans oculisque ardentibus haeret' – 'But the queen follows the hero, contemplates him, devours him with her burning eyes (the god indeed never keeps the flame away from her)'.

65   For the construction, cf. Ps.-Calpurnius, *Laus Pisonis* 102–104: 'Talis inest habitus, qualem nec dicere maestum / nec fluidum, laeta sed tetricitate decorum / possumus' – 'His physiognomy is such that we cannot describe it as sad or languid, but as beautiful, with a cheerful severity'.

66   Silius Italicus, *Punica* VII, 453 (Venus's arrows): 'si mea tela dedi blando medicata veneno' – 'If I have given my arrows impregnated with a sweet poison'.

BALDE'S POETIC EKPHRASES ON A TRIPTYCH BY CHRISTOPH SCHWARZ   243

She is looking for her absent bridegroom as a lonely bride.
As the edge of the painting refuses him to her, she stares to it, ardent,
With more eagerness, and lavishes all her glances to this edge.
Her neck shines, brighter than all the frosts of Scythia,
Than the cold of the ice. So that the fine silk adorning her   325
Does not constrict her bosom too much, the knotted cloth
Loosens and relaxes a little, draping her in red.
Its composition is such that it cannot be thought of as pure,
Nor as impregnated with a poisonous dye,
But the colour of the fabric rather leans towards golden;   330
The garment, claiming a hue between these two colours,
Proposes an intermediate and almost new colour. Falling modestly,
The dress undulates, with a flutter full of decency, and licks
The august ankles, rolling up in a confusion of folds.
Her right hand carries the sword that her neck once felt,   335
And that still remembers the milk. Creaking under a terrible blow,
Below, closer to the ground, a wheel smokes; broken,
The cruel machine deplores the ravages of a virginal war.[67]
For the rest, the shaded background of the painting
Plays with the viewer, and its lies make the senses uncertain.   340
       O come to this place, you German youth of Bavaria,
To contemplate your queen! Ask yourself: did the marvellous hand
That produced such a brilliant reflection of the sacred image,
Rather make the sun shine, or the moon
Reflect her brother's light? In any case,   345
It has imprinted in you a serene love of great price,
And you must give its talent its due. Widen your gaze
At the altar bearing the beautiful inscription of a noble name,
And look at the truly royal pomp. Admire the girl
Who overcame the yoke of Venus and despised her torches,   350

---

67   According to the legend, at Catherine's prayer an angel of God descended and destroyed the machine of torture embedded with saws and nails.

Pura pharetratae flammae. Complectere Divam,
Quae niveo Paphios libamine diluit aestus,
Uberis in morem sparso. [...]

"Dialogus auctoris et Michaelis Anguillae de forma Virginis Matris et Pueri Iesu, cum in pervigilio Assumptae Virginis eiusdem aram celeberrimi artificis Schwartii manu depictam, in aula Monacensis gymnasii contemplarentur. Ode XIII"[68]

A – Quam sit tota, vides, mater amabilis: 1
Collectae species viva modestiae.
   Ex ipso licet ore
      Matrem discere virginem.
M – Infans ut bicolor, candidus et ruber,[69]   5
Membris laetitiam spirat ab omnibus!
   Ignorans quoque dicat:
      Qui sic pingitur, est Deus.
A – Virgo caeruleis nubibus insidet,
Inter pennigeros pulchra Favonios.   10
   Lunae fixa sinistro
      Livent sub pede cornua.
M – Erectus gremium molle premit puer,
Exultimque micat. Conveniunt bene,
   Ac miscentur in uno   15
      Maiestas et Amor loco.
A – Vesteis virgineas non ego divites,
Sed tinctas viola paupere dixerim,
   Ullis absque corymbis;
      Ut tanto deceant mage.   20
M – Investis nebula pusio non eget,
Tectus luce satis: sic quoque gratior.
   Pubescentibus altum
      Crinitur radiis caput.
A – Matris caesariem carbasus integit;   25

---

68   The Latin text comes from Balde, *Lyricorum liber* IV, 220–222. I have modernised the punctuation and the use of capital letters, removed the accents and transcribed the ampersands as 'et'. The text is basically identical in the editions of 1648 (*De laudibus Mariae* 9), 1660 (*Poemata*, vol. 1, 212) and 1729 (*Opera poetica omnia*, vol. 1, 212), except for the specification of the painter's first name (*Christoph.*) in the title in 1648.

69   Cant. 5, 10: 'Dilectus meus candidus et rubicundus' – 'My beloved is white and red'.

BALDE'S POETIC EKPHRASES ON A TRIPTYCH BY CHRISTOPH SCHWARZ   245

Untouched by the flame of her quiver. Embrace the Holy one
Who extinguished the burning fires of Paphos in a white libation,
Spread as from a breast. [...]

'A dialogue between the author and Michael Anguilla on the beauty of the
Virgin Mary and the Infant Jesus, while they were contemplating, during the
Assumption vigil, an altar of the Virgin painted by the hand of the most famous
artist Schwarz, in the great hall of the college in Munich. Ode 13'[70]

Author – You see how this mother is entirely lovable: 1
The living image of concentrated modesty.
    From her very face one can see
        That this mother is a Virgin.
Michael – How this two-coloured child, white and red,   5
Breathes joy with all his limbs!
    Even an ignorant man would say:
        He who is painted thus is a God.
A – The Virgin is seated on cerulean clouds,
Beautiful among the winged Zephyrs.   10
    The horns of the moon, fixed
        Under her left foot, are livid.
M – The upright child leans on her soft lap,
He hops and twinkles. What a beautiful meeting
    And mixture, in the same place,   15
        Of Majesty and Love!
A – The Virgin's garment, I would not call it
Lavish, but rather of the colour of a poor violet,
    Without any ornament:
        It suits her all the better.   20
M – Unclothed, the child does not need a cloud:
He is quite dressed by light – and also more charming this way.
    The top of his head is covered
        With a down of thin rays.
A – A veil adorns the mother's hair;   25

---

70   Translation is mine.

Frons augusta patet. Teutonicam genae
  Potavere pruinam,
    Ostrum quam bene diluit.
M – At crispata riget filioli coma,
Et sol in facie ridet eburnea.   30
  Malis lilia vernant
    Et flammas acuunt rosae.
A – Pondus non tetrici dulce supercili
Arcum supra oculos flectit ianthinum,
  Et quam pupula vibrat,   35
    Miti lux oleo nitet.
M – Huius luminibus lacte madentibus
Blandus fulgor inest, uvaque gemmea
  Quam permiscuit igni
    Electri teretis liquor.   40
A – Virgo nescio quid non tacet, et suis
Florem deliciis porrigit accipi.
  Commendare videtur
    Insertura volae manus.
M – Infans nescio quid vagit, an annuit?   45
Certe non dubiis gestit amoribus.
  Ex mulcente labello
    Apricus trepidat color.
A – Hanc pinxit tabulam Parrhasius niger.
Veris quanta fluent gaudia vultibus,   50
  Si tam limpida ficti
    Derivant in imaginem!
M – Formosi quia sunt et puer et parens,
An formosa parens, anne puer magis?
  Et formosa parens, et   55
    Formosus magis est puer.

BALDE'S POETIC EKPHRASES ON A TRIPTYCH BY CHRISTOPH SCHWARZ 247

Her majestic forehead is left free. Her cheeks
  Have drunk the German frosts,
    Nicely diluted with purple.
M – The son's hair is enhanced with curls,
And the sun laughs on his ivory face.   30
  Spring lilies bloom on his cheeks,
    And roses sharpen their flames.
A – The soft weight of an unsevere eyebrow
Draws a purple arc over her eyes:
  And the light vibrating through her pupil   35
    Gleams with sweet oil.
M – In the child's milk-wet eyes,
There is a gentle glow, and a gem-shaped grape
  That a melted and delicate electrum
    Has mixed with fire.   40
A – The Virgin utters I know not what, and holds out
A flower to her darling, that he may take it.
  She seems to be entrusting it to him,
    About to put it in the palm of his hand.
M – Is the child asking for I know not what, or nodding?   45
Surely, he is transported with an unmistakable love.
  On his charming little lip,
    A sunny colour trembles.
A – This picture was painted by the black Parrhasius.[71]
What joys must flood the real faces   50
  If feigned faces spread such lucent joys
    In an image!
M – Since both the child and his mother are beautiful:
Is the mother the more beautiful, or the child?
  Both the mother is more beautiful,   55
    And the child is more beautiful.

Bibliography

Primary Sources

Balde Jakob, *Maximilianus Primus Austriacus* (Ingolstadt, Hänlin: 1631).
Balde Jakob, *Poema de Vanitate mundi* (Munich, Leysserius: 1638).
Balde Jakob, *Lyricorum libri IV. Epodon liber unus* (Munich, Leysserius: 1643).

---

71   Parrhasius is another famous painter from Greek Antiquity.

Balde Jakob, *Sylvarum libri septem* (Munich, Leysserius: 1643).

Balde Jakob, *Sylvae lyricae* (Cologne, Kalckhoven: 1646).

Balde Jakob, *De laudibus Beatae Mariae Virginis Odae Partheniae* (Munich, Wagner: 1648).

Balde Jakob, *Poemata*, 4 vols. (Cologne, Busaeus: 1660).

Balde Jakob, *Urania victrix* (Munich, Wagner: 1663).

Balde Jakob, *Opera poetica omnia*, 8 vols. (Munich, Happach–Schlütter: 1729; republished Frankfurt am Main: 1990).

Balde Jakob, *Carmina lyrica*, ed. B. Müller (Munich: 1844).

Calepinus Ambrosius, *Dictionarium* (Venice, in aedibus Manutianis: 1573).

[College of Coimbra], *In libros Ethicorum Aristotelis ad Nicomachum, aliquot Conimbricensis cursus disputationes, in quibus praecipua quaedam ethicae disciplinae capita continentur* (Lisbon, Simon Lopes: 1593).

Donati Alessandro, *De arte poetica libri tres* (Rome, Guilielmus Facciotus: 1631).

Landino Cristoforo, *Publii Virgilii Maronis Opera, cum Servii Mauri Honorati, Christophori Landini, Aelii Donati et Domitii Calderini commentariis* (Venice, Bartholomaeus de Zanis de Portesio: 1491).

Lapide Cornelius a, *Commentarii in Canticum Canticorum* (Lyon, Boissat: 1637).

Rhodes Georges de, *Philosophia peripatetica ad veram Aristotelis mentem* (Lyon, Huguetan–Barbier: 1671).

Saint-Paul Eustache de, *Summa philosophiae quadripartita de rebus dialecticis, moralibus, physicis et metaphysicis* (Paris, Chastellain: 1609).

Scholarly Literature

Arendt S., "*Nec Lapis esse volo* – 'Und kein Stein will ich sein'. Zum antistoischen Affekt in der Lyrik Jacob Baldes", in Burkard T. et al. (eds.), *Jacob Balde im kulturellen Kontext seiner Epoche* (Regensburg: 2006) 153–165.

Bauer B., "Apathie des stoischen Weisen oder Ekstase der christlichen Braut? Jesuitische Stoakritik und Jacob Baldes *Jephtias*", in Neumeister S. – Wiedemann C., *Res Publica Litteraria. Die Institutionen der Gelehrsamkeit in der frühen Neuzeit. Teil II* (Wiesbaden: 1987) 453–474.

Dekoninck R. – Smeesters A., "L'épode 15 de Jacob Balde, entre vision picturale et peinture visionnaire", in De Landtsheer J. – Della Schiava F. – Van Houdt T. (eds.), *Dulces ante omnia Musae. Essays on Neo-Latin Poetry in Honour of Dirk Sacré* (Turnhout: 2021) 475–494.

Diefenthaler S.-K., "Ein städtischer Hofkünstler: Christoph Schwarz", in Eichberger D. – Lorentz P. – Tacke A., *The Artist between Court and City (1300–1600)* (Petersberg: 2017) 327–340.

Diemer D. and P., "Schwarz, Christoph", in *Neue Deutsche Biographie*, vol. 23 (Berlin: 2007) 804–805.

Doering O. (ed.), *Der Augsburger Patriciers Philipp Hainhofer Beziehungen zum Herzog Philipp II von Pommern-Stettin. Correspondenzen aus den Jahren 1610–1619* (Vienna: 1894–1896).

Geissler H., "Schwarz, Christoph", in Turner J. (ed.), *The Dictionary of Art*, vol. 28 (New York, NY: 1996) 188–190.

Hess D. – Hirschfelder D., *Renaissance. Barock. Aufklärung. Kunst und Kultur vom 16. bis zum 18. Jahrhundert* (Nuremberg: 2010).

Hess G., "*Ut pictura poesis.* Jacob Baldes Beschreibung des Freisinger Hochaltarbildes von Peter Paul Rubens", in Weber A. (ed.), *Handbuch der Literatur in Bayern* (Regensburg: 1987) 207–220 (reedited in Hess G., *Der Tod des Seneca. Studien zur Kunst der Imagination in Texten und Bildern des 17. und 18. Jahrhunderts* [Regensburg: 2009] 166–180).

Kranz G., "Zu Jacob Baldes Bildgedichten", *Archiv für Kulturgeschichte* 60 (1978) 305–325.

Lebrecht Schmidt P., "Bemerkungen zu Biographie und Text im Werk des Jesuiten Jakob Balde", in Schnur R. (ed.), *Acta Conventus Neo-Latini Hafniensis* (Tempe, AZ: 1997), 97–119.

Robert T., "Texttabernakel. Jacob Baldes sacrale Ekphrasen und die Krise des religiösen Bildes", in Burkard T. et al. (eds.), *Jacob Balde im kulturellen Kontext seiner Epoche* (Regensburg: 2006) 287–312.

Schäfer E., "Baldes Exerzitien-Tapisserien (*Silv.* 8, 10)", in Lefèvre E. (ed.), *Balde und Horaz* (Tübingen: 2002) 319–358.

Smeesters A., "Enthousiasme, fureur poétique et puissance imaginative chez le jésuite Jacob Balde (1604–1668)", *Atlante. Revue d'études romanes* 9 (2018) 69–88, available from: https://atlante.univ-lille.fr/04-enthousiasme-fureur-poetique-et-puissance -imaginative-chez-le-jesuite-jacob-balde-1604-1668.html (accessed: 28.10.2022).

Stroh W., *Baldeana* (Munich: 2004).

Stroh W., "Balde, Jakob", in Arend S. et al. (eds.), *Frühe Neuzeit in Deutschland 1620–1720: Literaturwissenschaftliches Verfasserlexikon (VL17)* (Berlin – Boston: 2019), vol. 1, 412–445.

Tilg S., *Die Hl. Katharina von Alexandria auf der Jesuitenbühne* (Tübingen: 2005).

Töchterle K., "Kraftvolle Keime. Zu Jacob Baldes Jugendwerk *Maximilianus Primus Austriacus*", in Burkard T. et al. (eds.), *Jacob Balde im kulturellen Kontext seiner Epoche* (Regensburg: 2006) 27–37.

Volk-Knüttel B., "Candid nach Schwarz", *Münchner Jahrbuch der bildenden Kunst* 39 (1988) 113–132.

Westermayer G., *Jacobus Balde (1604–1668), sein Leben und seine Werke* (Munich: 1868; reprinted Amsterdam – Maarssen: 1998).

Wiener C., "Menetekel an Münchner Wänden. Joachim Sandrart in Jacob Baldes Dichtungen", in Burkard T. et al. (eds.), *Jacob Balde im kulturellen Kontext seiner Epoche* (Regensburg: 2006), 313–337.

Websites

http://stroh.userweb.mwn.de/main7.html (accessed: 28.10.2022).

CHAPTER 7

Mixed Motives: the Art of Joachim Du Bellay, 1549–1558

Tom Conley

Abstract

Joachim Du Bellay (1522–1560), a founding member of the *Pléiade*, the 'brigade' of mid-century French poets steeped in classical mythology and verse, sought to reform and renew the vernacular idiom in appealing to the ode and the Petrarchan sonnet. In dialogue with Pierre de Ronsard, the acclaimed and determined leader of the group, he suffused an ample oeuvre with mixed motivation and contradiction, and their attendant affects. Focusing on the form and formatting of works issued during Du Bellay's lifetime, from *L'Olive* (1549) to *Les Antiquitez de Rome, Les Regrets* and *Les Jeux rustiques* (1558), this essay locates where pictorial and graphic design mobilise expressions of irony, self-deprecation, and a commanding sense of creative doubt.

Keywords

contradiction – solitude – self-negation – lyrical illusion – creative doubt – mixed motivation

Joachim Du Bellay (1522–January 1, 1560), pioneer member of the Pléiade, a coterie of French poets in the middle years of the sixteenth century dedicated to renewing and embellishing their vernacular tongue with classical aura, left in his verse a legacy of mixed intentions and designs. In his polemical *Deffence, et illustration de la langue francoyse* (Defense and Illustration of the French Language) of February 1549, a treatise that quickly led to controversy, he contended that French was no less suited for great poetry than the Greek and Latin of classical mentors. Borrowing much from *I dialogi* of Sperone Speroni, rejecting the idea of translating models of times past, he felt that poets would spur innovation and better the cause of French by 'imitating' them.[1] On the heels

---

1 Speroni Sperone, *I dialogi di messer Speron Sperone* (Venice, Aldus Manutius: 1542) was published in French translation by Claude Gruget two years after Du Bellay's *Deffence, et*

© TOM CONLEY, 2025 | DOI:10.1163/9789004694613_008

MIXED MOTIVES: THE ART OF JOACHIM DU BELLAY, 1549-1558   251

of the *Deffence*, in *L'Olive* (*The Olive*), a collection of fifty sonnets published several months later, Du Bellay mimed Petrarch and his adepts while refashioning contemporary material by neo-Petrarchan poets of French extraction, including Maurice Scève, avowed devotee of Petrarch and leader of the *École de Lyon*, and, without direct reference as such, Vasquin Philieul, who translated much of the *Rime sparse* in his *Laure d'Avignon* (Laura of Avignon) in the previous year.[2] Later in his brief career, changing his intentions and ways of writing, whether for creative ends, for the pleasure of thinking and living simultaneously in two traditions, two moments of time, and two idioms, as if contradicting himself, he excellently translated Virgil and other classical poets.

Whether in Latin or French, in the decade from 1549 to 1558, diverse, conflicted, and conflicting desires and ambitions – that can be taken as mixed motivations – inspired Du Bellay's writing. Not in the least, in the *Deffence*, staging an implicit 'dialogue of the ancients and the moderns' a century before Charles Perrault's *Parallèles entre les anciens et les modernes* (Parallels Between the Ancients and the Moderns) Du Bellay made a case for the force and beauty of the vernacular, but without disparaging Latin, which he mastered with Virgilian grace and ease.[3] In animated dialogue with his coequal and mentor, Pierre de Ronsard (1525–1584), proclaimed leader of the Pléiade and 'prince of poets' who wished to be eternised as such, Du Bellay strove for pedestrian immortality. Stating that his aims and ambitions were restricted to fostering an intimate (even narcissistic) relation with his verse, he internalised his classical forebears. Contrary to Ronsard, whose muses, readers often noted of the *Amours* of 1552 and 1553, spoke Greek and Latin, Du Bellay preferred *not* to emulate (while emulating and translating) classical poets. Advocating simple and unaffected French with often naggingly affected modesty, he sculpted his diction in a manner recalling the orders of classical architecture.[4]

---

illustration : *Les Dialogues de messire Speron Sperone italien, mis en vulgaire françoys* (Paris, Étienne Groulleau: 1551).

2   Philieul Vasquin, *Laure d'Avignon: Au nom et adveu de la Royne Catharine de Medici, Royne de France. Extraict du poete florentin, Françoys Petrarque, et mis en françoys par Vasquin Philieul de Carpentras* (Paris, Jacques Gazeau: 1548).

3   *Parallele des anciens el les modernes, en ce qui regarde les arts et les sciences* (Paris, Jean-Baptise Coignard: 1688).

4   In strong likelihood Du Bellay had in mind or at his side recent editions of Alberti, *L'Architecture et art de bien bastir*, trans. Jean Martin (Paris, Jacques Kerver: 1553); *Architecture ou art de bien bastir de Marc Vitruve Pollion, mis de latin en francoys par Jan Martin* (Paris, Jacques Gazeau: 1547); or Sebastian Serlio, *Premier livre d'archiecture* [...]. *Le second livre de perspective*, also translated by Jean Martin (Paris, Jean Barbé: 1545). The relation the sonnets hold with the three (or four) 'orders' can be felt in their disposition or *quadrature* on folios in the works Jacques Morel edited and published in 1558. On Du Bellay's 'sculpted' style see Glauser A., *Le Poème-symbole: de Scève à Valéry* (Paris, Nizet: 1967).

The rigor of form mediates expression of *feelings* Du Bellay otherwise conveys in a uniquely lyrical and emotive style. By virtue of their implicit stonework the sonnets (and, to a lesser degree, the odes) display a gamut of feelings that the mechanical aspect of print at once conveys and calls in question. The self or the "I" who speaks in writing often projects a condition of confusion or of mixed, doubly bound sentiments that strategically beg for their addressees' and reader's empathy and concern. Iterated in succession, conforming to strict measures of format (or *quadrature*), the aspect and disposition of the poems lay stress on their economy and affective urgency: hence between print and mixed motives and emotions an art of creative *contradiction*.[5] Ubiquitous in the verse, *ie* announces any of a number of staged or conflicts of the self, the poet who figures himself at odds with or in dialogue with his state of being. In his usage of the first-person singular, Du Bellay strikes affective notes of different tone and temper. The unrequited lover in *L'Olive* (1549) gives way to the obsequious subject in the synchronous *Recueil de poesie* who, at the end of the volume is countered comically by a fake alter ego, Narcissus in dialogue with Echo. He stands far from the grandiloquent observer of the Eternal City in times past and present in *Le Premier livre des Antiquitez de Rome* (1558). In the same year he is unlike the alternately abject, homesick, and satirical speaker of the *Regrets*. Readers cannot fail to see and hear in *Les Divers ieux rustiques* (also 1558) a diversity of selves, of I's who are other, in the graphic form of *ie-(e)ux* – whose motives and feelings, taken in aggregate, are profoundly confused.

In the paragraphs that follow, drawing on a severely restricted selection of texts, given the variously felt projections of the self, a primary aim is to assess the creative agency of contradiction, of self-questioning, and of mixed motivation that runs through the oeuvre in the decade of its composition and publication, from 1549 to the death of the author, at the age of 38, on January 1, 1560. The experimental and occasionally tentative character of the verse published in 1549, in *L'Olive* (The Olive) and the *Recueil de poesie* (Collection of Poetry), which Du Bellay meticulously revised and augmented in the early 1550s, stands

---

5 In the *Testament* François Villon uses contradiction to prod debate and dialogue; first and famously in "Les Contredits de Franc Gontier", a rewriting of a fourteenth-century poem by Philippe de Vitry in praise of rustic life; and second, the "Ballade de la Grosse Margot," in which the speaker implies that we lead our beleagured lives in contradiction [in *Œuvres complètes* ed. J. Cerquiglii-Toulet (Paris: 2014)] 130 and 136–39. Closer to Du Bellay, Charles Estienne praises open-endedness in *Paradoxe: Que le plaider est chose tresutile, et necessaire à la vie des hommes* (Paris, Charles Estienne: 1554). In the same vein, Claude Lévi-Strauss once remarked about the filiations and webbings of myth, *contredire*, to contradict, is tantamount to *conte redire*, to tell repeatedly, over and again in *Mythologiques IV: L'Homme nu* (Paris: 1971) 611.

in counterpoint to the poet's four major collections that appeared nine years later, upon the poet's return to France after spending three years in Rome on a diplomatic mission under the aegis of his cousin, Cardinal Jean Du Bellay. Granted its *privilège* on March 1, 1557, published in 1558, *Le Premier livre des Antiquitez de Rome, contenant une generele description de sa grandeur, et comme une deploration de sa ruine par Ioach. DuBellay. Plus un songe ou vision sur le mesme subiect, du mesme auheur* (The First Book of the Antiquities of Rome, containing a general description of its grandeur, and a deploration of its ruin by Ioach. Du Bellay, with a dream or vision by the same author on the same subject) aspired to grandiloquence and sublimity that soon after prompted Edmund Spenser to translate the fifteen sonnets of its appendix, *Le Songe* (The Visions) for an anglophone public.[6] The collection stands starkly adjacent to *Les Regrets*, published at the same moment, a collection of 191 sonnets of lyrical, satirical, and self-searching inspiration. In its gamut of tones that range from homesickness to bitter irony, and from irony to eulogy, the *Regrets*, a point of reference in the oeuvre, stands at the antipodes of *Les Divers Ieux* (or *Jeux*) *rustiques*, a final, lighter work of thirty-eight poems, some culled from the past, others written in face of the poet's imminent death, of different style, facture, and invention. Amateurs and specialists ask not only why and how these changes of mood are as they are, but also in what ways they seem compellingly modern.[7] In concert with the vision of this volume, despite the massive critical industry on Du Bellay of the last three decades, whether from the angle of what Meyer Schapiro called *style*, or fabled art historian Henri Focillon's *Vie des formes* titled, in English translation, 'the life of forms of art', or of biography and literary history, it remains pressingly pertinent to examine the mixed affective motives and motivations that ran through his writing from 1549 to 1558, the very years that witnessed the birth, growth, and decline of the Pléiade.[8]

---

6   Spenser Edmund, *Six Epigrams Translated from Petrarch, and Fifteen Sonnets from the 'Visions' of Joachim Du Bellay*, in Noot Jan van der, *Theatre for Worldlings* (London, Henry Bynneman: 1565). Readers today cannot fail to compare the *Songe* to Freud's vision, in *Civilization and its Discontents*, of the sedimented time and space of the Eternal City; see *The Standard Edition of the Complete Psychological Works of Sigmund Freud, Vol, 21*, ed. J. Strachey (London: 1968) 69–70.

7   Among others, poet-philosopher Michel Deguy, in *Tombeau de Du Bellay* (Paris: 1973), an extended essay that specialists in the critical industry tend not to address, calls Du Bellay a 'modern', no doubt for the minimalist character of the poems. See also Rigolot F., *Poésie et Renaissance* (Paris: 2002), esp. chapter 4.

8   Focillon H., *Vie des formes* and *Éloge de la main* (Paris: 1939); and Schapiro M., *Style* (Chicago: 1953).

Born of considerable nobility in the Angoumois, the 'author', who would be the self, the signatory "I" of one collection, is a vastly different persona or personae than those of each of the others. In keeping with the heritage of the name, the *auteur* on the title pages of the major works qualifies as an *acteur*, an actor, a mutable thespian in dialogue with the poems as he (such is Du Bellay's pronoun) writes them. Working through each of the collections, witnessing the self-consciousness of the verse, the reader is struck by a sense of the complexities of the *Je* or "I" who speaks and writes. From one collection to the next Du Bellay's *personæ* attest to what Michel de Montaigne, who praised Du Bellay and Ronsard for their lyrical innovations, would soon remark about the human character: "Certes, c'est un subject merveilleusement vain, divers et ondoyant, que l'homme" (Surely, the human being is a vain, diverse, and wavering subject).[9] The different inflections of Du Bellay in the first-person prompt recall of what psychoanalyst Joyce McDougall, in *Théâtres du je* (1982), notes about how patients who undertake treatment often play evasive games with their analyst. Fearing or deferring the effects of their joint labors, playing cat-and-mouse with their listener, they slip and skitter from one identity to another. Clinical experience with these patients, she adds, attests to the famous dictum from *As You Like It*, 'All's the world a stage [...]'.[10] Playactors on the divan, in their speech they evince a gamut of motives and emotions. In the same breath analysands often utter "I" to invent, display, and momentarily stabilise a subject-position, lending an air of authenticity (but also mendacity) to what they say about themselves. In appealing to the first-person singular, the 'self', or rather, the gamut of 'selves' becomes a plural entity, a welter of mixed expressions.[11] The different "*je*'s" who speak and write in the name of Du Bellay invite us to appreciate the poetry as a whole, but also to consider it in bits and pieces, in fragments, much like islands of an *isolario*, as an archipelago, possibly what fellow twentieth-century poet René Char brilliantly called

---

9   Montaigne M. de, "Par divers moyens on arrive à pareille fin", in *Essais*, I, I, ed. P. Villey (Paris: 1992); and Saulnier V.-L., *Les essais de Michel de Montaigne* (Paris: 1965; repr. ed., 1988) 6.

10   McDougall J., *Théâtres du je* (Paris: 1982); in English, eadem, *Theatres of the Mind: Illusion and Truth on the Psychoanalytical Stage* (New York: 1985).

11   In these situations the analyst might reconsider Arthur Rimbaud's dictum in his famous "Lettre du *voyant*" (dated April 13, 1871), delivered to Georges Izambard: begging his teacher and interlocutor to forgive him for a *jeu de mots*, in the spirit of challenge and defiance, Rimbaud fractured French grammar to yield a formula that would soon become foundational for the science of the mind: *je est un autre* (I is an other). In staging his own theater of the self, Du Bellay would be wont to say, *je sont des autres*, 'I are others', or, by implication, "I" is an assemblage of others. Rimbaud's correspondence is documented in *Œuvres complètes*, ed. A. Adam (Paris: 1972; repr. ed., 1988).

MIXED MOTIVES: THE ART OF JOACHIM DU BELLAY, 1549-1558 255

a 'parole en archipel'.[12] Such is the impression gained from the first instance of "Ie" in *L'Olive et quelques autres œuvres poeticques* (1549) (The Olive and Several Other Poetic Works), the first published collection, to the last, *Les Divers Ieux rustiques* (1558) (The Diverse Rustic Games), a collection synchronous with the publication of *Antiquitez* and *Les Regrets*.[13] In the latter, what seems to be *Du Bellay's* last work, thirty-one poems of different style and measure imply, as the author notes in several of the poems that look retrospectively upon the oeuvre, a plurality of selves (*divers "je"*) motivates and mobilises the verse. The task of this paper is to see how, why, and with what artistic consequences they mark a spectrum of affective styles and forms.

1 *L'Olive* in 1549 and 1550

The design and visual disposition of the fifty sonnets in the first edition of *l'Olive* play with and against its emotive content. As if, in allegiance to Du Bellay's praise of the anagram in the *Deffence*, the emblematic title suggests that the fruit of the fabled branch of peace can be seen as a veil (*voile*), and that the figure might be taken in different, even conflicting registers. Set under roman numerals, the poems are carefully allotted, displayed in their integrity, two per page, one atop the other. With the exception of the first and last sonnet, which occupy the full space of the folios on which they are printed, the volume seems formatted to stress what in the *Deffence*, in the context of caesura, Du Bellay calls *quadrature* – especially when the book is displayed in bifolio. Hence the remark in the preface that, promising a fuller work to come and admonishing printers for their errors, invites readers to behold the verse as might a painter standing before an unfinished painting: 'Ie croy (Lecteur) entendu ceste contrainte, que ie te iure par la troupe sacrée des neuf Sœurs estre veritable, que tu excusera benignement les faultes de cest Ouuraige precipité: semblable à ces Tableaux, auxquels le Peintre n'a encores donné la derniere Main'. (Given this constraint [dear Reader], I swear by the sacred troop of the nine Sisters

---

12 Char R., "Parole en archipel", (written circa 1962), in *Œuvres complètes* (Paris: 1982), can be read cartographically, to be sure, but also as a calling (an *appel*), 'arched', as it were, toward an originary (archi)absence.

13 Michel Magnien, Olivier Millet and Loris Petris, editors of the definitive critical edition of *Les Regrets* and *Les Divers jeux rustiques* (Paris: 2020) observe that because the works of 1558 lack colophons (*achevés d'imprimer*) indicating the month or day of their printing, it is impossible to discern their dates of publication. Their detailed comparison of the first and second printings of *Regrets*, in 1558 and 1559, has shown where printers' errors were corrected (p. 558).

to be true, that you will generously excuse the mistakes of this hastily printed work, like those Canvases a Painter has yet to finish.[14]) The sonnets' manner of display ensures that they are seen and glossed integrally, each in a rectangular frame measuring ten decasyllabic feet by fourteen lines. Placing two sonnets, one above the other, on facing folios, the arrangement invites the eye to contemplate the form of the collection and consider the architectural order that shapes its content, hence to follow the verse both sequentially (from line to line and from top to bottom) and diagonally (across the page, in fragments, notably where formulas are repeated or reshaped in adjacent sonnets, and reiterated to mark the wealth of potential in their beguiling simplicity) [Fig. 7.2].[15]

The brief preface of 1549 insists that the principle of *imitation* (and *not translation*) motivates the vernacular verse, whether the model be Petrarch or, closer to home, a 'S[aint] Gelays, un Heroët, un Ronsart, un Carles, un Sceve' (f. A.ii. v°). As he had already stated in the *Deffence*, after declaring his aim of enriching and ennobling his idiom, "ie" wishes to infuse familiar matter with elegantly unfamiliar twists and turns, even at the risk of obscurity. And, so, the stenographic I.D.B.A. on the title page (ostensibly Ioachim Du Bellay Angoumois), abbreviates (or skirts) the poet's proper name, at once attenuating and implicating the author's noble aura stemming from his Angevin parentage. Broadly, the formatting signals ambivalence about what it means to *name* or designate, to reify or to control the letters' referent. This ambivalence then becomes pervasive throughout the verse. Although the collections of 1558 spell out the author's name, it can be said (as Mallarmé would contend three centuries later) that the *nom*, if it does not quite negate, yet fails to 'caress' what it signifies, and instead infers its own negation (via *nom* with its homonymic *non*); the name functions like a mask or veil, much as the *olive* is a *voile* cast upon itself.[16]

---

14   Du Bellay Jacques, *L'Olive et quelques autres œuvres poeticques, par I. D. B. A.* (Paris, Arnoul L'Angelier: 1549), f. A.ii v°. (See BNF Gallica: https://gallica.bnf.fr/ark:/12148/btv1b 86095195.) *L'Olive augmentée depuis la premiere edition*, with *La Musagnoeomachie & aultres oeuvres poëtiques* (Paris, Gilles Corrozet – Arnoul L'angelier: 1550) contains 115 sonnets. Printed in italic, set under in roman numerals, the sonnets do not include roman majuscules. Despite appearing less than a year after the first edition, its self-contained and finished aspect distances it from the work of 1549.

15   Two of the most famous sonnets in the *Regrets*, the 9th and the 189th, vary a formula borrowed from the myths of Danaë and Narcissis and Echo. Respectively: 'Je rempliz de ton nom (i.e., "France" and/or the poem itself) les antres et les bois' has as a counterpart, 'Je rempliz d'un beau nom ce grand espace vide' (i.e., Rome and/or the poem itself).

16   Mallarmé expounds on allusion and obliquity throughout "Crayonné au théâtre", in *Œuvres complètes*, ed. H. Mondor (Paris: 1948).

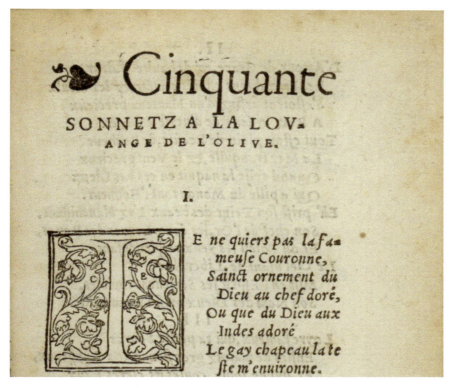

FIGURE 7.1   Sonnets 22 and 23 of *L'Olive* (Paris: Arnoul l'Angelier, 1549)

The first page of the inaugural collection is formatted to stress the ambivalence and mixed motivation that Du Bellay had just invoked in the preface [Fig. 7.1]. At its top, a horizontally placed fleuron points to the title, disposed in three lines of descending point-size, in roman majuscule, announcing that they are *in praise of* the fruit and its branch. The lineation of LOV-ANGE DE L'OLIVE breaks the name into two parts, as if to imply that the signifiers 'anticipate' what they designate, *lou-* giving way to the *ang*elic nature of the tree, branch, and fruit, that could be attributed to being rooted in the *Ang*oumois.[17]

---

17   Analyst Jacques Lacan contended that in the minuscule gap between the act of naming and cognition of what is named the listener's imagination floats freely, often in the context of thoughts that are dismissed to 'make sense', while at the same time what is felt (or anticipated) says much about the condition of the listener (or reader). Among others, poet Maurice Scève, whom Du Bellay admired and imitated in *L'Olive*, was a past master of the signifier. In *Délie* (Lyon, 1544), in the 76th *dizain*, addressing his 'obiet de plus haulte vertu' (object of the highest virtue), his beloved (and by inference, the poem he is writing), the author states,

The relation of the title to the numbering of the first sonnet and its historiated initial inaugurates the collection indicates that emotion and form are in play. Following the roman numeral 'I', an elegantly historiated initial encloses in an oblong frame two (quasi-symmetrical) garlands on either side of an immense historiated 'I' in majuscule [Fig. 7.1].

So also, the edition of 1550 splits the pronoun into two pieces to infer that the speaking and writing subject is divided [Fig. 7.2].

Famously, and for a third time, in 1558 Du Bellay's signature-incipit, "Ie ne", inaugurates the *Regrets*, cuts the self – as I/e – before the poem begins [Fig. 7.3].

The text of 1549 establishes the model. Displayed in an implicit perspective of vanishment, set between two quasi-symmetrical garlands in the square surround of a historiated initial, an immense "I" stands aside 'E' in lower-point majuscule.[18] Of divided motivation, using preterition to affirm and to deny, to avow and to disavow, "I/E" announces that it *will not* seek immortality nor, by inference, will it opine for the Laurel that Petrarch had worn (in the cognate of his beloved Laure). *Je ne* [...], reiterated in E*ncores moins veux-ie* (l. 4), gives way, finally, to the wish to undertake a project that will eternise the speaker. Far-fetched as it may seem, readers who gaze upon the page in the way a spectator studies a painting of Albertian design abruptly note how the lower-case "'in the center of 'ol-i-ve', marks a trajectory from 'ange de l'olive' (*ange* implying Du Bellay's native angoumois) to the initial above and back to the historiated "I" of the first line of the sonnet. In elegant contradiction, I/e manifests its desire at the end of the second quatrain to have force and drive (*hardiesse*, l. 14) enough to honor and immortalise the olive – branch or veil no matter – that stands for what is beyond nomination.

The sonnets that follow bear traces of experiment and of imitation and less, it seems, of identification with Petrarchan effects of unrealized or unrequited desire. Each poem resembles a miniature essay, and hardly an effect of emotive sincerity. Each, too, tends to evince a projective or mental geography of displacement and, for the sake of evading the Petrarchan style of Italian coequals,

---

> J'ouvris la bouche, & sur le point de dire
> *Mer*, un serain de son nayf soubrire
> M'entreclouit le poursuyvre du *ci*. (v. 4–6, stress added)
>
> (I opened my mouth, and on the point of saying / *Mer*, an evening song of her youthful smile / Held me from following with *ci*.). Scève and Du Bellay make the point with rapture that Lacan would take up from a psychoanalytical angle in "L'Instance de la lettre dans l'inconscient", in *Écrits* (Paris: 1966) 496–498.

18 For the sake of argument, it would not be unreasonable to remark how the writing anticipates R.D. Laing's reflections on the fractured nature of subjectivity in *The Divided Self* (New York: 1967).

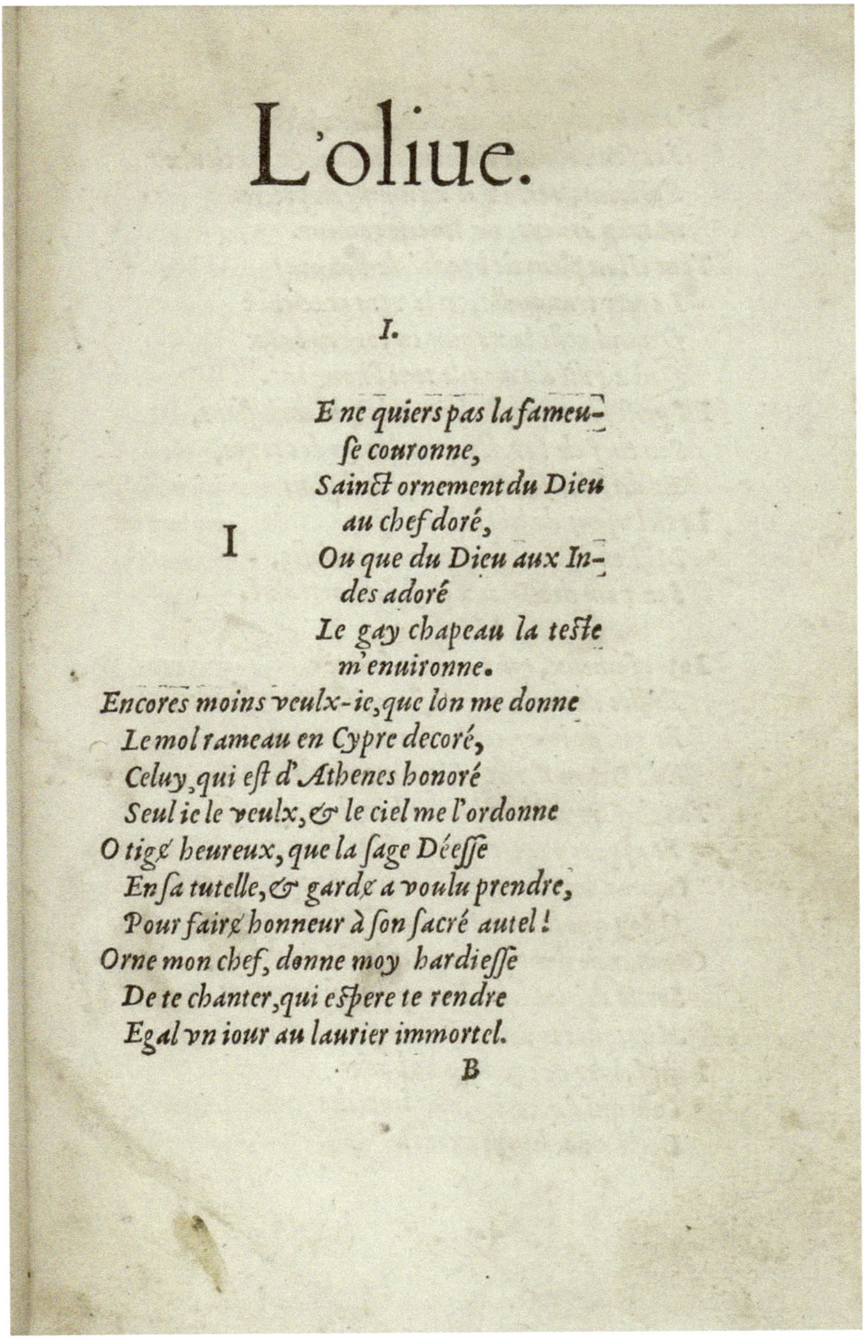

L'oliue.

I.

I

E ne quiers pas la fameu-
se couronne,
Sainct ornement du Dieu
au chef doré,
Ou que du Dieu aux In-
des adoré
Le gay chapeau la teste
m'enuironne.
Encores moins veulx-ie, que lon me donne
Le mol rameau en Cypre decoré,
Celuy, qui est d'Athenes honoré
Seul ie le veulx, & le ciel me l'ordonne
O tige heureux, que la sage Déesse
En sa tutelle, & garde a voulu prendre,
Pour faire honneur à son sacré autel!
Orne mon chef, donne moy hardiesse
De te chanter, qui espere te rendre
Egal vn iour au laurier immortel.

B

FIGURE 7.2 Incipit to *L'Olive* (Paris: Arnoul l'Angelier, 1550)

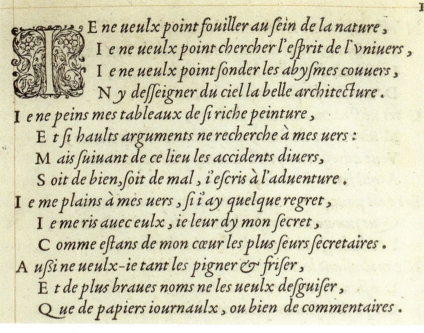

FIGURE 7.3 Title page, *Recueil de poesie* (Paris: Cavellat, 1558)

self-doubt in a mix with ambition. Hence the passage from the second to the third sonnet, from invocation of the 'world' and the heavens in the perspective of cosmography that mark the *Rime sparse*, to a fluvial topography of the French nation. '*Tout estoit plein de* Beauté' (II, l. 4), gives way to '*le M*onde', placed at the center, in the final line of the second quatrain, that implies to what degree each poem can be taken as a microcosm, an inclusive site mirroring a greater whole.[19]

> Tout estoit plein de Beauté, de Bonheur
>   La Mer tranquile, & le Vent gracieux
>   Quand celle la naquit en ces bas Lieux
>   Qui a pillé du Monde tout l'Honneur.

---

19   See Arnheim R., *The Power of the Center: A Study of Composition in the Visual Arts* (Berkeley: repr. ed. 2009); and Francastel P., *La Figure et le lieu: l'ordre visuel du Quattrocento* (Paris: repr. ed. 1980).

(All was full of Beauty, of Happiness / The Sea calm, and the Wind was gracious / When she gave birth to it in these lower Depths / Who stole from the world all its Honor.) The poem radiates an affective plenitude, a felicitous moment, when the "I" is one with ambient world. The form and content of the third sonnet, set immediately below on the same folio, strategically underscore the point: in praise of the *French* (and by inference via Petrarch, *not* Italian) locale, the third sonnet begins, like the Loire it describes, first at its native source and origin, and then in calm flow of its clear waters to the Mediterranean:

> *Loire fameux, qui ta petite Source*
> *Enfles de maintz gros fleuues & Ruysseaux,*
> *Et qui de loin coules des cleres Eaux*
> *En l'Occèan* [sic] *d'une assez lente Course.*
> *Ton chef royal bien hardiment bien hault pousse*
> *Et apparay entre les plus beaux*
> *Comme un Thaureau sur les menuz Troupeaux*
> *Quoy que le Pau envieux s'encourousse.* (f. A. iii. v°)

(Famous Loire, you, whose tiny source / Fills many great Rivers and Streams, / And, from afar, whose clear waters slowly flow to the Ocean. / The waters your royal leader mightily thrusts forward / And appears among the most handsome, / Like a Bull on the meager Herds / Even if the envious Po is angered and irritated.)

Despite its suave flow which mixes form with meaning, Du Bellay's description of his cherished Loire plots what might be taken to be the mental geography of a self at odds with its place in the world in the sonnets that follow, and perhaps by design, situated near the center of the assemblage, the twenty-third. Rife with formulas and turns in the synonymous *Recueil de poesie* and, later, in the great sonnets of *Les Regrets*, the poem might be a compass point of the volume [Fig. 7.4].[20]

---

20   Famously, in the twelfth line of the thirty-first sonnet, 'H *eureux qui, comme* Ulysse, *a fait un beau voyage*', perhaps the most renowned and most memorised in all of French literature, in its dazzling litany of anaphora:
P *lus me plaist le sejour qu'ont basty mes ayeux,*
Q *ue des palais* Romains *le front audacieux,*
P *lus que le marbre dur me plaist l'ardoise fine,*
P *lus mon petit Liré que le mont* Palatin
E *t plus que l'air marin la doulceur* Angevine.

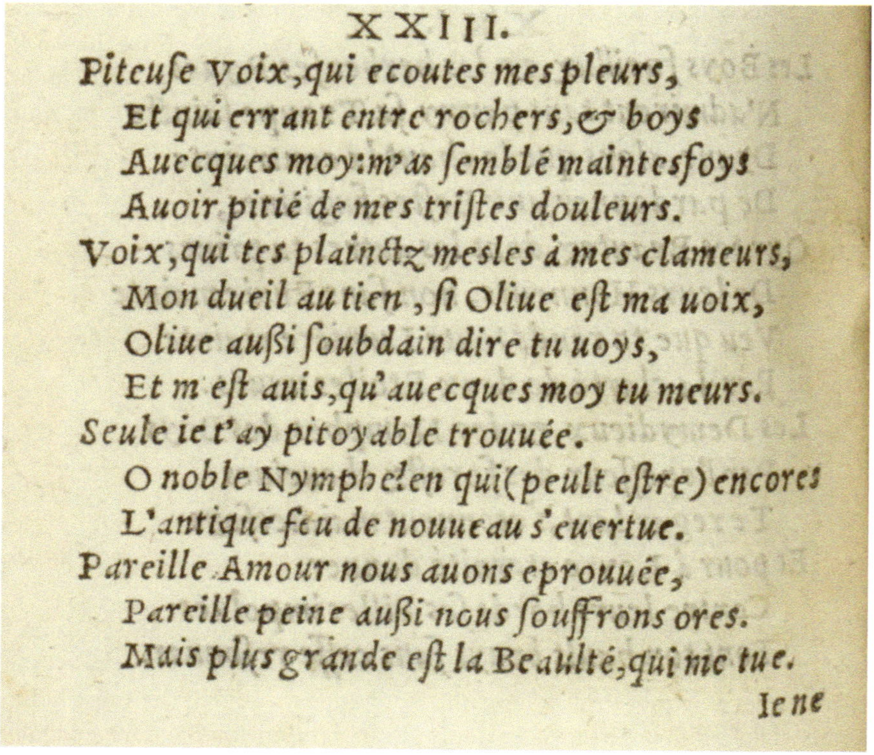

FIGURE 7.4 *L'Olive*, 1549, sonnet 23 and catchword (n.p.)

XXIII.

Piteuse Voix, qui escoutes mes pleurs,
  Et qui erroit entre les rochers, & boys
  Avecques moy: m'a semblé maintesfoys
  Avoir pitié de mes tristes douleurs.
Voix, qui tes plainctz mesles à mes clameurs,
  Mon deuil au tien, si Olive est ma voix,
  Olive aussi soubdain dire tu voys,
  Et m'est vis, qu'avecques moy tu meurs.
Seule ie t'ay pitoyable trouuée.
  O noble Nymphe! En qui (peult estre) encores
  L'antique feu de nouueau s'evertue.

MIXED MOTIVES: THE ART OF JOACHIM DU BELLAY, 1549-1558

Pareille Amour nous avons eprouuée,
Pareille peine aussi nous souffrons ores.
Mais plus grande est la Beaulté qui me tue.

Ie *ne*

(f. A. iv v °)

(Pitiful voice, you who listen to my woes, / and who wandered with me among the rocks and forests: / So often you seemed to take pity on my pains. / Voice, you whose cries are mixed with my clamors, / My grief with yours, if Olive is my voice, / Olive, when suddenly said, you see / and it appears to me, that with me you die./Alone, I found you pitifully. / O noble Nymph! In whom (perhaps), still / You strive to light the fire of antiquity. / A similar Love we have experienced, / A similar pain now afflicts us again. / But even greater is the Beauty that leaves me dead. [...] I not.)

An unnamed Narcissus pines for Echo's '*Piteuse voix*'. It could also be the voice of the 'Olive', a love lost, or a love of the poem concealed in the verse seeking to find and finish itself. Recalled 'wandering' with the poet among stony outcroppings and forests, then vanishing, the sorrowful voice leaves the speaker split between desiring not to desire – in other words, to die – and, as it had been for Petrarch, in a state of injurious pleasure, of unrequited grief, a confusion of pain and delight that is inferred to fuel the writing. In its graphic form the conventional formula that buckles the poem invites a reading of its paragrammar, of latent signs resonating in the spacing or syntactical order.[21] [L]*a* Beaulté *qui me tue* could be rendered as the 'Beauty that kills me', while *tue*, the past participle of *taire*, would also be evocative of a silence that comes when the poem reaches its end, and more so by 'corresponding' with silence through writing.[22] Further, if poems and their authors speak to each another across generations and different times, in its address to Echo, the conflicted voice of this poem recalls other iterations, not least François Villon, who would otherwise be at a light year's distance from the Petrarchan gist of *L'Olive*. In the most famous (and perhaps greatest) single poem in the French canon, the

---

21 For the paragrammar of verse, see Riffaterre M., *Semiotics of Poetry* (Indianapolis: 1984); and Meschonnic H., *Ethique et politique du traduire* (Paris: 2007).

22 The sonnet is remarkably close to "Correspondances", the fourth poem of *Les Fleurs du Mal* (1857), in which Baudelaire praises the faculty of free association and invention across different idioms, a faculty that, as happens, too, with Villon's poetry, reads across a mix of different linguistic registers.

"Ballade des femmes du temps jadis" (so named by Clément Marot in his critical edition of *Le Testament*, dated 1532), in addressing (and challenging) his prince, the speaker evokes the myth of Echo and Narcissus in the first six lines of the opening stanza:

> *Dictes moy ou nen quel pays*
> *Est Flora la belle romaine*
> *Archipiada ne Thais*
> *Qui fust sa cousine germaine*
> *Echo parlant quand bruyt on meine*
> *Sus riviere ou sus estang ...*

(Tell me where or in what country/ Is Flora the lovely Roman/Archipiada or Thaïs / Who was her germane cousin / Echo speaking when noise is led over river or pond.) Where Villon's Echo, speaking, makes the ballad flow in an audio-visual measure, Du Bellay's counterpart would qualify as an image, perhaps a Malrucian 'voice of silence'. Or would it? If to contradict, *contredire*, is to *conte redire*, to tell again, the deadened or muted voice (*mussée* in the idiolect of the Renaissance) speaks afresh in the single and sole *réclame* or catchword of the collection. And if *L'Olive* is to be seen as a *peinture parlant*e, a speaking picture, "Ie ne", reprinted in isolation and placed at a turning or vanishing point in the assembly of fifty sonnets, invites the reader to study the work as a painting.[23] Along a different line of inquiry, the *réclame* signals its usage and force of presence in the majority of other collections from the *Recueil de poesie* to the masterworks of 1558 (and their re-editions in 1559, shortly before Du Bellay's death) under (or in collaboration with) editor Fédérique Morel.

Closer to 1549, at the end of the first edition of the *Recueil de poesie*, published on the heels of Du Belllay's *Deffence*, "*Piteuse voix* [...]" acquires a deliciously facetious cast in the graphic character of "Dialogue entre Echo and un amoureux", an occasional or offhanded poem that caps the collection [Fig. 7.5]:

---

23   Du Bellay everywhere praises poetry that in its depictions qualifies as 'painting'; in *Les Regrets*, the poet's plume becomes a paintbrush (sonnet 148), and in *Les Divers Ieux rustiques*, in an ode (XIX) addressed to fellow poet Olivier de Magny on 'les perfections de sa dame', he writes, 'l'escriture / N'est qu'une parlante peinture' (ll. 215–16).

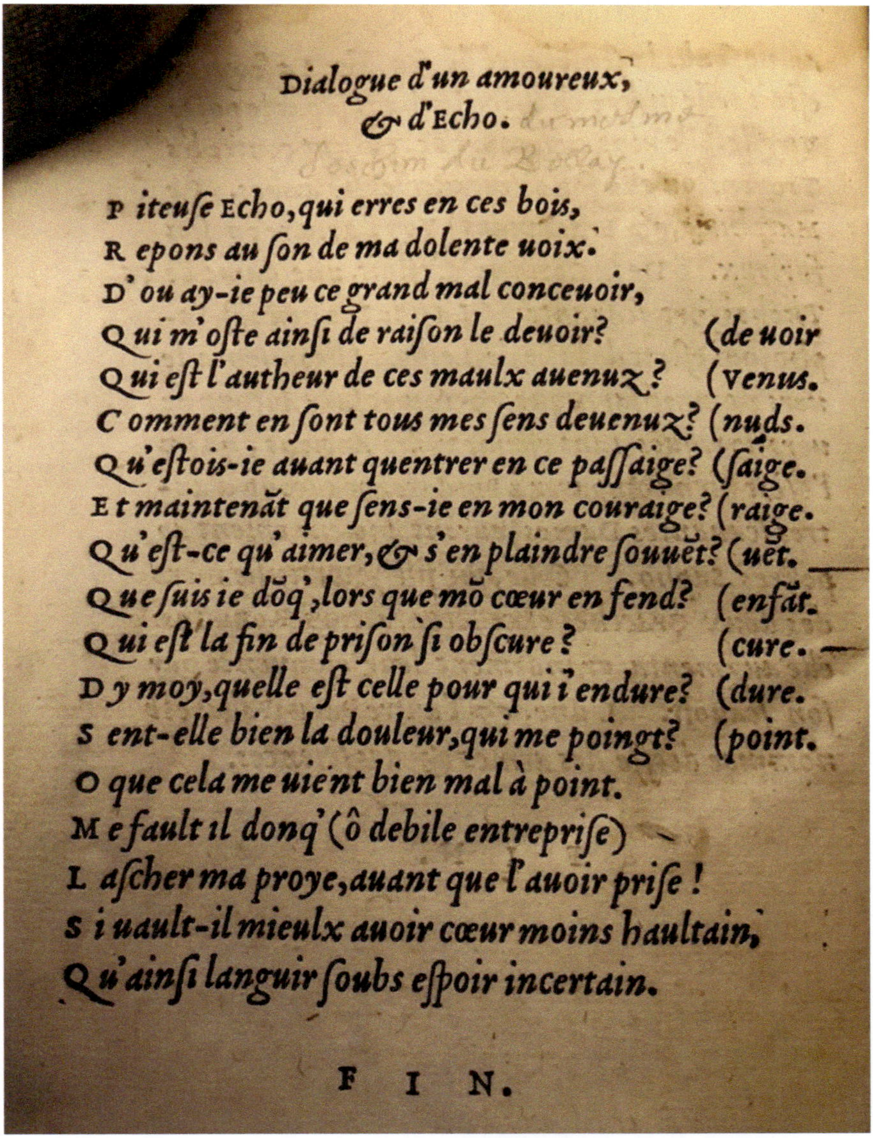

FIGURE 7.5 "Dialogue d'un amoureux et d'Echo," *Recueil de poesie* (1549), n.p.

Dialogue d'un amoureux & d'Echo.

P *iteuse* Echo, *qui erres en ces bois,*
R *epons au son de ma dolente voix.*
D'*où ai-ie peu ce grand mal concevoir,*
Q *ui m'oste ainsi de raison le devoir ?*　　　(*de voir*
Q *ui est l'autheur de ces maulx avenuz ?*　　(*Venus.*
C *omment en sont tous mes sens devenuz ?*　(*nuds.*
Q *u'estois-ie avant quentrer en ce passaige ?*　(*saige.*
E *t maintenant que sens-ie en mon couraige ?*　(*raige.*
Q *u'est-ce qu'aimer, s'en plaindre souvent ?*　(*vent.*
Q *ue suis ie donq, lors que mon cœur en fend ?*　(*enfant.*
Q *ui est la fin de prison si obscure ?*　　　(*cure.*
D *y moy, quelle est celle pour qui i'endure ?*　(*dure.*
S *ent-elle bien la douleur, qui me poingt ?*　(*point.*
O *que cela me vient bien mal à point.*
M *e fault il donq' (ô debile entreprise)*
L *ascher ma proye, avant que l'avoir prise !*
S *i vault-il mieulx voir cœur moins haultain,*
Q *u'ainsi languir soubs espoir incertain.*　　(96 v°)

(Pitiful Echo, you who wander in the woods, / Please respond to the sound of my sorrowful voice. / Whence could I have conceived this pain, / Which robs me of the duty of reason? (to see / Who is the author of these besetting ills? (Venus / What has become of all my senses? (nude / What was I before I entered into this phase? (sage / And now what do I feel in my heart? (rage / What is it to love, and often to complain of it? (wind / Who am I now that I am heartbroken? (an infant / What is at the end of this dark prison? (cure / Tell me, who is the one for whom I endure? (hardened / Does she really feel the pain assailing me? (not at all / Oh! How it all bereaves me. / Must I therefore (oh stupid enterprise) / Release my prey before capturing it! / Is it better to see my heart less haughty / Than thus to languish in uncertain hope.) Emotions are utterly entangled. On the one hand, alone in a sylvan setting, in tears, the poet searches for a lost love, while on the other, the printing of Echo's words flattens – but also both exacerbates and mocks – the feeling he has for an absent presence. *Echo*, however, speaks in the printed form of the appended syllables of the median lines (four to fourteen) of the poem. The open parentheses call in question the recitation of lament while playing on (or setting between inverted commas) self-pity, despond, or abjection.

MIXED MOTIVES: THE ART OF JOACHIM DU BELLAY, 1549-1558

At the core of the verse here and elsewhere in the oeuvre, the poet's self-questioning can be discerned as a force of creative doubt. The poet implies that a sense of inadequacy spurs the poetic drive, and that by way of equivocation and ambivalence, even if in echo or in silence, the poetry will listen to him. In the ninth sonnet of the *Regrets*, France, a maternal icon, is identified as Echo, an absence, but nonetheless the poet speaks to her. Even if she does not respond to his plaintive cries, although far and away from Rome, whence the poet writes, in the geography of the sonnet she is alive and present a poetic form.

> F *rance mere des arts, des armes, & des loix,*
> > T *u m'as nourry du lait de ta mamelle,*
> > O *res, comme un aigneau qui sa nourrice appelle,*
> > I *e rempliz de ton nom les antres & les bois.*
> S *i tu m'as pour enfant adoué quelque fois,*
> > Q *ue ne me respons-tu maintenant, ô cruelle ?*
> > F *rance, France respons à ma triste querelle :*
> > M *ais nul, sinon Echo, ne respond à ma voix.*
> E *ntre les loups cruels l'erre parmy la plaine,*
> > I *e sens venir l'yver, de qui la froide haleine*
> > D'*une tremblante horreur fait herisser ma peau.*
> L *as, tes autres aigneaux n'ont faute de pasture,*
> > I *ls ne craignent le loup, le vent, ny la froidure :*
> > S *i ne suis-ie pourtant le pire du troppeau.*

(France, mother of arts, of arms, and of laws, / You have nourished me with the milk of your breast, / And so, just as a lamb cries out for its mother, / I fill with your name the lairs and the woods. / If at times you have avowed me as your child, / Why, oh cruel mother, don't you respond? / France, France, respond to my sad dilemma: / But no one, only Echo, responds to my voice. / Among cruel wolves I wander about the plain, / I feel the coming of winter, whose cold breath / With trembling horror makes my hair stand on end. / Alas, your other lambs are not in want of pasture, / They fear neither wolves, wind, nor cold: / And yet I am not the worst of the flock.)

An emotive portrait of the self as a lost and wailing lamb, in a beguiling simplicity of form the sonnet plays with both geographical and affective proximity and distance. If it is a *peinture parlante*, which elsewhere, in *Les Ieux rustiques*, Du Bellay claims to be the aim of poetry, its vanishing point – *point de fuite* – would be marked by 'E*cho*' (l. 8), close to the center of the sonnet, the name of

268 CONLEY

the sylvan goddess of the "Dialogue" that capped the *Recueil de poesie*. 'France', whom the first line personifies as the matron of the arts (when in fact Italy held the distinction), becomes an absent presence in the multiple inflections of the fourth line.[24] Forlorn, isolated, in exile, the poet-lamb who had been suckled at the teats of its mother-sheep, separated from its nourishing source, is at a point of traumatic but vital entry *into* the world. In the second printing of the *Regrets* in 1559, at the onset of the second signature (or quire) of the collection, the initial vocative 'F *rance mere* [...]' is preceded by the aptly named *réclame*, 'France' (Fig. 7.4). Iterated twice in the seventh line, the proper name calls attention to the spacing and formatting of the sonnet. The motif of regret is inferred to be related to its economy – its condition of possibility – and, in sum, to the status the poet confers upon the poem as an aesthetic, political and economic object.

By striking contrast, in a rubricated copy of 1558, the final page of the gathering on which the seventh and eighth sonnets are printed lacks the *réclame*. Otherwise the 46 other catchwords are identical: Would Fédéric Morel, editor and designer who brought an elegantly minimal design to his books of poetry, have initially removed 'France' to attenuate the repetition and soon after, changing his mind in the second printing, added it to emphasise its resonance with sonnet on the next folio? Possibly in collaboration with Du Bellay, the editor deployed the *réclame* to lay stress not only on the tension of convention (fragments of words as simple particles signaling how the quires are ordered) versus motivation (in their spatial isolation, at appointed places, as intermediaries between the end of one sonnet and the beginning of another), but also on the 'entanglement' of the poet's emotive, economic and entrepreneurial aims?

The shape of the sonnet suggests an answer. Lost in the wintry landscape of the eighth sonnet's tercets, the bleating lamb wanders over a cold and windy plain:

> L *es costaux soleillez de pampre sont couverts,*
> M *ais des* Hyperborez *les eternelz hyvers*
> N *e portent que le froid, la neige, & la bruine.*

(The sunny vineyards are covered, / But the eternal winter of Hyperborean winters / Bear only chill, snow and drizzle.) In fear of 'cruel wolves' – by

---

24   In *Du Bellay et le sacré* (Paris: 1983), Gilbert Gadoffre astutely notes that in 1558 to call France the mother of the arts would be tantamount to a wish-fulfillment. See also Zerner H., *L'art de la Renaissance en France: L'invention du classicisme* (Paris: 1996), on the pre-classical inclinations of French artists and writers in the 1540s.

MIXED MOTIVES: THE ART OF JOACHIM DU BELLAY, 1549-1558

implication Italian brethren of the she-wolf (*la louve*), whom Romulus and Remus had suckled – and in a cold and unforgiving climate, the poet nonetheless finds himself in a site of creative possibility. Formatting the sonnet to contrast Roman and Italic typeface, Morel (assumably in collaboration with Du Bellay) assigns roman majuscules to the first letter of every sonnet.[25] Isolated by an em-space from the word to which they belong, the initials call attention to a condition of difference, a typeface recalling Rome of times past (depicted in *Les Antiquitez*, and whose capitals might count among its 'powdery relics') and Rome today (in the Italic forms, that in 1558 were of fairly recent usage in France).[26] Likewise, the initial letters of anthroponyms, toponyms, and concepts mentioned in the body of the poems are signaled in roman majuscule and followed by italic minuscule. Disruptive and disconcerting for many readers, as in "I *e ne*" that inaugurates both *L'Olive* and *Les Regret*s, the formatting draws attention to the proper names and place-names in the form of graphic signifiers. 'F *rance*', set atop the ninth sonnet (and reiterating the catchword in the reprinted edition of 1559), draws the eye to what is '-rance' or rancid for an instant before the name of the nation settles into place. For readers then and now, 'mere des arts' cannot be without recall or resonance of Rabelais's *Gargantua*, in whose thirteenth chapter on the 'propos torcheculatifs', the child-hero after whom the volume is named, in dialogue with Grandgousier, his earnest and benevolent father, exclaims, '*Mere de* [Dieu]' in the account of his experience – or experiment – with 68 different ways in wiping his rump.

The graphic character of contradiction and of confused motivation is further underscored when the poem is viewed and glossed in its 'quadrature', as a rectangular object, from left to right, from top to bottom (by dint of the isolated roman majuscules), and crosswise (when the book is opened to display its verso and recto folios). Surprising effects emerge from the ninth sonnet. In

---

25 In the preface to *Les Divers ieux rstiques*, in accord with convention, no doubt in unstated praise of Morel, Du Bellay takes to task printers who have a made a mess of his work: 'j'ayme mieux que tu le lises imprimé correctement, que depravé par une infinité d'exemplaires, ou, pis est, corrompu miserablement par un tas d'imprimeurs non moins ignorants que temeraires et impudens' (I prefer that you read it correctly printed than depraved by a pile of printers who are no less ignorant than reckless and impudent). See *Œuvres poétiques, vol. 2*, ed. D. Aris – J. Joukovsky (Paris: 1996) 144. In a letter addressed to Jean Du Bellay, he writes that after the pillage and mistreatment of his work he gave his poems to 'a printer, without otherwise seeing them', who is revealed to be Morel; see *Lettres de Joachim Du Bellay*, ed. P. de Nolhac (Paris: 1883) 45.

26 See Martin H.-J., *La Naissance du livre moderne: (XIVᵉ–XVIIᵉ siècles)* (Paris: 2000), chapter 4. Ronsard prints the sonnets of his *Amours* (1552 and 1553) exclusively in italic, and, like Morel's editions of Du Bellay prior to 1560, share a similar 'quadrature' without the numbering that appears in modern editions.

the cavalcade of incipit letters, for a passing instant, the lamb's mother is identified in acrostic, as *we*, the readers, who are addressed as *you*:

> F *rance mere des arts*
> T *u m'as nourry*
> O *res, comme un aigneau*
> I *e remplis*
> S *i tu m'as pour enfant ...*

As if in oblique allusion to the art for which François Villon was a past master (and whose *Testament* Clément Marot re-edited in 1532, replacing the *lettre bâtarde* with classical typeface), the first quatrain invites a vertical scansion whose initial signifiers spell the pronoun 'toi', the friendly reader, who would be *you*.[27]

Anaphora, for which Du Bellay's mastery goes without question, is manifest in the effect of repetition-as-contradiction in the median area of the poem – so intensely, and in such an uncommonly diagonal sense, that the quatrain seems isolated or vaguely related to the tercets that follow. Once again:

> S *i tu m'as pour enfant aduoué quelque fois,*
> Q *ue ne me **respons**-tu maintenant, ô cruelle ?*
> F *rance, France **respons** à ma triste querelle :*
> M *ais nul, sinon* Echo, *ne **respond** à ma voix.*

Where Echo's lament vanishes in a setting similar to that of the *Dialogue* of 1549, in "F *rance mere des arts* [...]" the voice inheres in the diagonal spacing or alignment of *respons* and *respond*. One iteration echoes another, and more so as the *réclame* on the preceding folio is doubled, effectively (or graphically) duplicating, indeed 'reclaiming' the lost ewe at the incipit of the sonnet on the following page. The critical or even psychic effect of anaphora invites return to the fourth line. Seeking its absent mother, the forlorn lamb bleats in distress,

> I *e remplis de ton nom les antres et les bois.*

Does he 'fill' the lairs and woods, as the partitive suggests, with pieces 'of' her, of 'your' name, or of *our* name? Given that the poem beckons the reader's

---

27 *Les Oevvres de Françoys Villon de Paris, reueues & remises en leur entier par Clement Marot valet de chambre du Roy* (Paris, Galiot du Pré: 1533), at https://gallica.bnf.fr/ark:/12148 /bpt6k71466p/f2.item.

MIXED MOTIVES: THE ART OF JOACHIM DU BELLAY, 1549-1558

attention to a Gallic matron of the arts, arms and letters, the distraught lamb may be endlessly 'filling' the forests and caverns in analogy with the rain of Zeus upon the (unnamed) goddess Danaë.[28] [N]*om* identifies what is not (*non*) visibly present. The lairs, *antres*, could be indeterminate areas between (*entre*) dark places and more abstractly, poetry *tout court*, and thus, at the beginning of the first tercet (l. 1), **E *ntre les loups*,** 'among' the wolves or between their jaws, would suggest that the poet is in a peril. The lamb would appear, too, to drink (*bois/t*) the liquid that showered the unnamed but allusively present deity.[29] The ambiguation of the verb and its homonymic noun, the forest in which the voice disappears, bears the virtue of complicating the emotional imagery. The lamb-poet is inferred to be a child who lacks symbolic means to cope with the absence or loss of a nurturing elder. The poems that follow can be seen and felt responding to the plaintive cries.

What it means to call out, and what may be the risky stakes of naming (such the ambiguation of France and Echo or Du Bellay and the bleating ewe) are queried elsewhere in the *Regrets*, seemingly at its compass-points. Near the center, in the 100th sonnet, the reifying effect of naming recalls the tenor of the third sonnet of the *Antiquitez de Rome*, in which the poet, addressing newcomers to the Eternal City who 'seek Rome in Rome', but who take little note of the milieu, reminds them (and his reader) to scrutinize '[c]es vieux palais, ces vieux arcs que tu vois, / E *t ces vieux murs, c'est ce que* R*ome on nomme*' (ll. 3–4) (these old palaces, these old arches that you see, / And these old walls, that's what Rome is named).[30] In the *Regrets*, a surfeit of names calls in doubt the act and instance of naming. 'Ursin', a bear of sorts, whom many critics believe is the humanist Fulvio Orsini, is named in the incipit:

> U *rsin, quand i'oy* **nommer** *de cs vieux* **noms** R*omains,*
>   D *e cs beaux* **noms** *cogneus de l'*I*nde iusqu'au* M*ore,*
>   **N** *on les grands seulement, mais les moindres encore,*
>   V *oire ceulx-la qui ont les ampoulles aux mains:*
> I *l me fasche d'ouir appeller ces uillains*
>   D *e ces* **noms** *tant fameux, que tout le monde honnore:*
>   E *t sans le* **nom** C*hrestien, le seul* **nom** *que i'adore,*
>   V *oudrois que de telz* **noms** *on appellast noz* S*aints.*

---

28   Because another motivating factor of the *Regrets* concerns its relation with Pierre de Ronsard, the line could be in dialogue with the twentieth sonnet of *Les Amours*.

29   If so, the sonnet would surely be in dialogue with Ronsard's *Amours* (1552 and 1553).

30   In the manner Gertrude Stein famously scattered the name of the rose in 'Rose is a rose is a rose is a rose', in "Sacred Emily", in *Geography and Plays* (Boston: 1922) 187. Du Bellay accumulates eleven instances of 'Rome' in twelve of the fourteen lines.

> L *e mien sur tous me fasche, & me fasche un Guillaume,*
> E *t mil autres sotz **noms** communs en ce royaume,*
> V *oiant tant de faquins indignement iouir*
> D *e ces beaux **noms** de* Rome, & *de ceulx de la Grece,*
> M *ais par sur tout* (Vrsin) *il me fasche d'ouir*
> N *ommer une* Thaïs *du nom d'une* Lucrece. (p, 25/ f. Hi v °, stress added)

(Ursin, when I hear the naming of these old Roman names, / Of these lovely names of renown from India to the Mores, / Not only the great, but the lesser still, / Indeed, those with callous and blister on their hands: / It angers me to hear these villains so named / With such famous names as these, which the world so honors: / And lacking the Christian name, the only name I adore, / I would wish that with such names our Saints be named. / My own especially angers me, and also a William, / And a thousand other foolish common names in this kingdom, / And seeing so many thugs indignantly make use / Of these lovely names of Rome, and those of Greece, / But especially (Ursin) it angers me to hear / A Thaïs named in the name of a Lucretia.) A sense of admiration for the person to whom the poem is addressed and named again near the end of the sonnet is mixed with frustration and anger over the titles given to those who are undeserving of nomination, while at the same time, in adoration of the classical and Christian legacy inhering many commonly used proper names the poet senses bitterly that their aura and presence are either forgotten or, simply go without saying. Couched in irony, the flaccid expressivity of 'ces beaux noms de Rome' suggests that the name and its referent are lacking in substance and that, in the same breath, they smack of glory. If it counts among the 'braves noms' (handsome names) that in the first sonnet of the collection Du Bellay wished to avoid in order not to veil (*desguiser* or disguise) his motives, a sense of negation – what is *non* in a *nom* – resounds in the 188th and 189th sonnets.

The former recalls (or echoes) the first, second, and fourth sonnets inaugurating the *Regrets*.[31] Addressing Pierre de Paschal, historiographer of Henri II, he declares, 'I *e ne veulz deguiser ma simple poësie /* S *ous le masque d'une fable*

---

31   In a vein similar to what is announced at the beginning of *L'Olive*, the *Regrets* are wrought in assertive negation; see, for instance, I, ll. 1–3 (emphasis added): 'I *ne veulx point fouiller au sein de la nature, /* I *ne veulx point chercher l'esprit de l'univers, /* I e *ne veulx point sonder les absymes couvers* [...]'. (I *no* longer wish to grope into the core of nature, I *no* longer wish to search for the soul of the universe, / I *no* longer wish to delve into the concealed abysses [...]). He addresses Paschal in the second sonnet, as he will again in sonnet 188: 'ie ne veulx pour un vers allonger, / M' accoursir le cerveau' (II, ll. 2–3) (to extend a line I wish not / To shorten my brain) (ll. 5–6); and famously, 'I *ne veulx fueilleter les exemplaires Grecs, /* I e

MIXED MOTIVES: THE ART OF JOACHIM DU BELLAY, 1549-1558   273

moisie, / N *y souiller d'un beau nom de monstres tant hideux*' (ll. 9–11, f. N v°) (I wish not to disguise my simple poetry / Under the mask of a musty fable, / Nor soil a handsome name with such hideous monsters). Like Paschal, he prefers to laud the monarch in an ordinary, unaffected, and factual (**'non fabuleux'**) line of poetry, but also, in the same breath, he wishes to bequeath praise upon 'ourselves, our children, and those who will be born of them' (ll. 13–14).

The antepenultimate sonnet (189) of the *Regrets* that follows begins uncannily *in medias res*, as if in the midst of an uninterrupted conversation. In feigned response to Jacques Peletier du Mans, poet, geometer, translator of Horace and author of an *art poétique* (1555) with which the *Deffence* was in dialogue, he writes,

> C *ependant* (P*elletier*) *que dessus ton* E*uclide*
> T *u montres ce qu'en vain ont tant cherché les vieux*

(However (Peletier), that over your Euclid / You show what elders had sought in vain) (ll. 1–2). He adds that despite the vice and envy of modern times, like another Hercules (*un second* A*lcide*) (l. 4) 'you hoist yourself' (*te guindes*) to the heavens. His friend's lofty point of view, he adds, leads him skyward from where, he implies, he can look down and remark, 'I *e rempliz d'un beau nom ce grand espace* vide' (I fill with a lovely name this great empty space) (l. 8, close to the center, possibly a vanishing point in the sonnet). Like Freud in his words on the space and history of Rome in *Civilization and its Discontents*, the line could be of mixed inflection, referring to the City, but also standing alone in abstraction, motivating the verse in an opposite sense. Praise of Jacques Peletier du Mans, longstanding friend and poet-geometer, either becomes vacuous or self-erasive. In the following tercets, contrary to his desire not to desire, he avows that while he *wanted* to abandon poetry to dedicate himself to higher causes, poetry is nonetheless the highest of all endeavors. In yet another emotive entanglement, in his desire to recount the honors of virtue, he wonders if with poetry he can fly heavenward as he would wish: 'A *vec la vertu ie veulx au ciel monter,* / P *ourrois-ie au ciel monter aveques plus haulte œlle*'? (With virtue I want to climb to the sky, / But can I climb to the sky on a higher wing?) Lacking a referent or an antecedent, what he calls 'this great empty space' could be Rome, but also and no less, in a sense close to Mallarmé, it could be the blank page on which poetry is written and forgotten.

---

ne veulx retracer les beaux traits d'un Horace' (IV, ll. 1–2) (I not at all wish to page through Greek copies, I not at all wish to redraw the handsome lines of a Horace).

In guise of a brutally abrupt conclusion, it could be wagered that *Les Divers Ieux rustiques*, entirely synchronous with the *Regrets* and the *Antiquitez*, can be taken as a space Du Bellay fills with vacuous words, be they in the shower of Zeus's golden rain in the myth of Danaë, or else also, those he pours into the delightfully leaky vessel of the *Divers Ieux*. Often received and appreciated as a tailpiece or addendum to the *Antiquitez* and the *Regrets*, a work of 'freedom of invention', *Les Ieux/Jeux* contains a variety of 'rustic games' assembled from earlier and current writing.[32] Composed of marginalia, described as a 'literary pastime', the assemblage includes translations of Virgil, Naugerius and others; poems of likely and unlikely form (some of seven lines, others of eight or ten, or even Alexandrines); airy verse that seems close to pure poetry, such as "D'un vanneur de blé, aux vents" (A Winnower of Wheat, in the Wind); satirical portraits and homages; tongue-in-cheek eulogies to his deceased cat and dog; rife with contradiction, a Petrarchan rejection of Petrarchan style ("Contre les Petrarchistes"), recalling his early works, and reminding readers and listeners that he has 'forgotten' his earlier manner and motivation; the confession of a courtesan who has lost her charm but little of her mordant wit; at the end, in a dialogue with Ronsard, who avowed that he became hard of hearing, a paradoxical encomium in praise of the poet's deafness. Editors have rightly alleged that in moving from one rubric to another, the passage or passing from one style of writing to another, the collection, a 'literary pastime', 'is underscored by imperceptible changes of tone' (1996: lxi).[33]

By virtue of *rustique*, the title designates at once a 'forest and a mixed work characterized by its variety'.[34] A reader of the first edition observes, as regards

---

32   I adhere to the orthography of the first printing, in which *Ieux*, possibly of richer connotation than *Jeux* (in modern editions), suggests that the "I" or "Ie" is a function of "them" or *eux*, hence proving that, as Émile Benveniste noted, pronouns are *shifters*, locative signs, not stable identities, whose essence is relational. "I" is a function of "you" that is mediated by a third term, an "it," a "he," a "she," a "they" or a "them", in *Problèmes de linguistique générale* (Paris: 1966). A poet – thus a Ronsard, Du Bellay, or another member of the Pléiade – would fantasise in "Ieux" a composite "I" and "them".

33   Noting the tone of the title, Daniel Aris and Françoise Joukowski remark that the poet gives himself freedom of expression in a context lesser constraint then that of the other works of the same year, in *Du Bellay: Œuvres poétiques*, vol. 2 (Paris: 1996) lxi.

34   Taking a cue from V.L. Saulnier's authoritative *Du Bellay* (Paris: 1951), Aris and Joukowski also remark that *Les Jeux rustiques* 'is a collection in which Du Bellay dares to be himself, in other words, a writer who knows how to limit himself so as to make more from less. He consents to minor genres that reduce the real to familiar and fleeting appearances', such as the breath of the winnower, a 'poem of the impalpable that verges on almost pure poetry'. Recently, Millet and fellow editors of the most recent critical edition of the *Œuvres complètes* (v. 4, Paris, 2020) have noted that the title 'announces a triple refusal (unity, seriousness, and elevation) that is based on a triple affirmation of programmatic value: variety,

MIXED MOTIVES: THE ART OF JOACHIM DU BELLAY, 1549-1558   275

Du Bellay's attention to formatting in the *Antiquitez* and the *Regrets*, that the poems make keen use of the plasticity and malleable nature of spoken and written language. The orthography plays a significant role. The format of the title page is indicative [Fig. 7.6]:

Ieux rustiques, et autres œvvres poetiques [...] (Paris, De l'Imprimerie de Federic Morel: 1558) implies that what follows is a motley, even macaronic assemblage of poems of different styles, origins and rationales, and that the *ieux* can surely be understood as a plurality of "I's", of selves of different facture and motivation; possibly, if analogy and association are part and parcel of early modern modes of thinking, *Ieux* could be understood in a visual sense, as games equivocating on the "I's" which in sound and print, are not far from *yeux*. Counting 76 pages in its first edition of 1558, the collection consists of thirty-eight poems. Contrary to those printed after the death of the author in 1560, it does not set the individual pieces below upper-case roman numerals. In the same format as Du Bellay's works that Morel published in the same year, slightly set apart by an em-space, upper-case roman majuscules inaugurate the lines in lower-case italic. In the body of the poetry, anthroponyms and toponyms are announced by roman capitals. The sense of a sequence or ordering of the poems is thus loose, given to casual reading, and the resultant effect is one absent of concatenation, sequence or overriding design.

If, nonetheless, every work of writing, although not forcibly in that order, contains a beginning, a middle, and an end, an axial piece might be the dedicatory poem to Duthier, councilor to the king and secretary of state, whose 'ordinary labors' (*ordinaire exercice*) appear to double those of the poet. In the fourth stanza "Ie" and "ieu" are contiguous:

> L *es vers qu'icy **ie** te chnte,*
> D *uthier, **ie** ne les presente*
> A *ces sourciz renfrognez,*
> A *uquelz tel **ieu** ne peut plaire,*
> E *t qui souvent à rien faire*
> S *ont les plus embesongnez.* (ll. 19–24)

(The lines here I sing for you, / Duthier, I do not offer / With a furrowed brow, / To which such playacting cannot be pleasing, / And that often are useless, / and moreover belaboured.)

---

playfulness [*ludisme*], and unaffectedness [*le naturel*]' (351). Without indicating the presence of the plural "I" in the title, the editors note that numerous and different iterations of "je" (which they put between inverted commas) run through the volume (351, 364, 365).

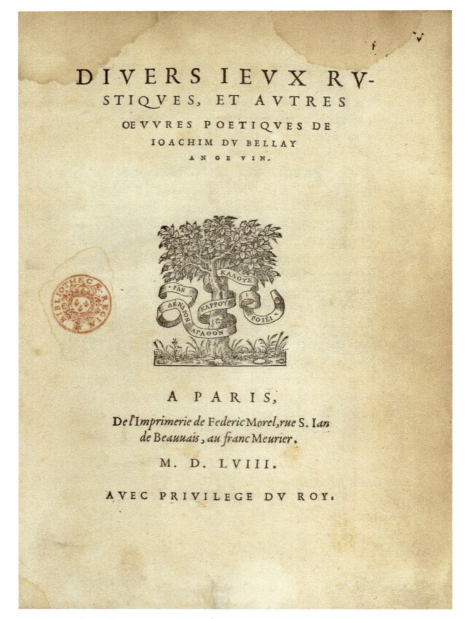

FIGURE 7.6 *Divers Ieux rustiques*, 1558, title page

MIXED MOTIVES: THE ART OF JOACHIM DU BELLAY, 1549-1558 277

The first poem, Du Bellay's free translation of Virgil in the "Moretum",
describes Marsault, a rustic hero who goes about his daily chores. Subsisting,
working meticulously with the objects of his household, including a broom
or a *ballay* (an echo of the author's name?), he cleans his millstone, 'using his
hands' to work his way through the duties of the day. Situated at the outset,
the poem and its hero awaken in the cold of winter when the sun ('l'estoile
journale') casts light upon what will be his *rustique séjour*. Toward the middle
of the collection, the ode on the perfections of fellow poet Olivier de Magny's
beloved lady (XIX) recounts the author's change of conviction, which he
describes famously in "Contre les petrarquistes" (XX). Du Bellay contradicts –
writes with and against – the lyric for which *L'Olive*, the *Recueil de poesie* and
other pieces of 1549–1550 were famous. 'Remotivating' his verse, he takes aim
at its feigned pathos and mendacious sincerity.

The ode to Olivier de Magny nonetheless shows him *revising* (seeing from a
different point of view while altering) the turns of phrase that were traits of the
signature in 1549 and 1550. Recalling the "Dialogue of the Lover and Echo, the
twenty-third sonnet of *L'Olive*, and recasting the ninth sonnet of the *Regrets*",
he opines:

> D *u temps que* l'*estois amoureux,*
> R *ien que les souspirs langoureux*
> N *e me plaisoit, et rien ma lyre*
> R *ien que l'Amour ne sçavoit dire.*
>
> P *ar tout ie trouvois argument*
> D *e me feindre un nouveau torment,*
> E *t ne trouvois roc ny fonteine*
> Q *ui ne representoit ma peine.*
>
> I *l me sembloit qu'****antres et bois***
> P ***iteux*** *respondoit à ma voix,*
> E *t me sembloit que mes prieres*
> A *rrestoient le cours des rivieres.* (ll. 53–64, stress added)

(In the time I was amorous / Nothing but languishing sighs / Could please me,
and my lyre / Could speak of nothing but Love. // Everywhere I found a reason
/ To feign a new torment, / And whatever rock or fountain I found could only
represent my pain. // It seemed to me that lairs and woods / Pitifully responded
to my voice, / And it seemed to me that my prayers stopped the course of the
rivers.) Mocking himself and his past at the same time he includes poems of

earlier inspiration in the verse, Du Bellay encourages his reader to appreciate and to savor the mixed motivations that in this volume become its overriding topic. If, in its critical reception *Les Ieux* and its many "I's" can be imagined belonging to a late and self-liberating enterprise, it can be added that the gamut of sentiment, moods, and projections of the self might also attest to an unparalleled art of mixing a variety of motives and motivations.

Bibliography

Arnheim R., *The Power of the Center: A Study of Composition in the Visual Arts* (Berkeley: 2009).

Benveniste É., *Problèmes de linguistique générale* (Paris: 1966).

Char René, *Œuvres complètes*. Paris: Éditions Gallimard/Pléiade, 1982.

Deguy, M., *Tombeau de Du Bellay*. Paris: 1973.

Du Bellay Joachim, *L'Olive et quelques autres œuvres poeticques, par I. D. B. A.* (Paris, Arnoul L'Angelier: 1549).

Du Bellay Joachim, *Œuvres poétiques*, 2 v. Ed. D. Aris & F. Joukovski (Paris, Éditions Garnier: 1996).

Du Bellay Joachim, *Les Divers Ieux rustiques* (Paris, Federic Morel: 1558).

Du Bellay Joachim, *L'Olive augmentée depuis la premiere edition, & La Musagnoeomachie & aultres oeuvres poëtiques* (Paris, Gilles Corrozet et Arnoul L'angelier: 1550).

Du Bellay Joachim, *Les Dialogues de messire Speron Sperone italien, mis en vulgaire françoys* par Clude Gruget (Paris, Étienne Groulleau: 1551).

Du Bellay Joachim, *Œuvres complètes*, v. 4.1, ed. Michel Magnien, Olivier Millet and Loris Petris. (Paris, Classiques Garnier: 2020).

Focillon H., *Vie des formes suivi par Éloge de la main*. Paris: 1939.

Francastel P., *La Figure et le lieu: l'ordre visuel du Quattrocento* (Paris: 1980).

Freud, Sigmund, *The Standard Edition of the Complete Psychological Works of Sigmund Freud*, ed. J. Strachey. 24 v. (London, Hogarth Press: 1968).

Gadoffre G., *Du Bellay et le sacré* (Paris: 1983).

Laing R.D., *The Divided Self* (New York: 1967).

Lévi-Strauss C., *Mythologiques IV: L'homme nu* (Paris: 1971).

Mallarmé Stéphane, *Œuvres complètes*, ed. H. Mondor (Paris: 1948).

Martin, H.-J., *La Naissance du livre moderne: (XIVᵉ–XVIIᵉ siècles)* (Paris: 2000).

McDougall J., *Théâtres du je* (Paris: 1982).

McDougall J., *Theatres of the Mind: Illusion and Truth on the Psychoanalytical Stage* (New York: 1985).

Meschonnic H., *Ethique et politique du traduire* (Paris: 2007).

Montaigne Michel de, *Les Essais*. 3 v. Ed. Pierre Villey (Paris: PUF. 1965; repr. ed., 1988).

Philieul Vasquin, *Laure d'Avignon. ... Extraict du poete florentin, Françoys Petrarque, et mis en françoys par Vasquin Philieul de Carpentras* (Paris, Gazeau: 1548).

Riffaterre M., *Semiotics of Poetry* (Indianapolis: 1984).

Rimbaud, Arthur, *Œuvres complètes*, ed. A. Adam (Paris: 1972; repr. ed., 1988).

Saulnier V.-L., *Du Bellay* (Paris: 1951).

Scève Maurice, *Délie: Obiet de plus haulte vertu* (Lyon: Constantin, 1544).

Schapiro M., *Style* (Chicago: 1953).

Spenser Edmund, *Six Epigrams Translated from Petrarch, and Fifteen Sonnets from the 'Visions' of Joachim Du Bellay*, in Noot Jan van der, *Theatre for Worldlings* (London, Henry Bynneman: 1565).

Speroni, Sperone, *I dialogi di messer Speron Sperone* (Venice, Aldus Manutius: 1542).

Stein Gertrude, *Geography and Plays* (Boston: 1922).

Villon Franços, *Les Oevvres de Françoys Villon de Paris, reueues & remises en leur entier par Clement Marot valet de chambre du Roy* (Paris, Galiot du Pré: 1533).

Zerner H., *L'art de la Renaissance en France: L'invention du classicisme* (Paris: 1996).

SECTION C

Mixed Emotions in Prose Literature

∵

CHAPTER 8

Tears of Love and Sorrow: the Affective Regime of the European Pastoral Tradition

Anita Traninger

Abstract

Textual Arcadia differs from Arcadia as represented in the visual arts in that it is centred around a specific constellation of motus mixti: textual Arcadia is the location of endless tears, tears of love and sorrow. Taking Jorge de Montemayor's seminal Siete libros de la Diana (1559) as its starting point, the chapter discusses this language of tears in the context of early modern theories of weeping, from religious penance to anthropology, and shows that Arcadian tears are of a fundamentally different character, as they are meant to flow incessantly. The reason for this is literary, not anthropological: The God Amor feeds on tears, as Vergil's tenth eclogue notes, which is why lovers have to produce an endless supply. While Arcadia affords female and male characters different liberties, it subjects them to the same affective regime. What is more, the bucolic landscape in which all of this plays out comes alive in consonance with the affective afflictions of its inhabitants. The chapter shows how the shepherds' affective disposition and the landscape are symbiotically related to one another. It demonstrates how the resonant landscape materialises a certain idea of motus mixti, the entwinement of love and sorrow, in the media of tears and nature. Arcadian love, the chapter argues, is the ultimate mixed emotion, and the locus amoenus is not just its compassionate abode, but the space in which a motus mixtus is shared by human and non-human actors.

Keywords

Arcadia – love – sorrow – nymph – tears – gender – nature

Arcadia is a foreign land. Of course, as virtually every handbook on the Classical tradition tells us, it was originally a region on the Peloponnese peninsula. The early moderns, however, could not care less. They frequently imagined Arcadia to be located right outside their city gates, incredibly close

© ANITA TRANINGER, 2025 | DOI:10.1163/9789004694613_009

and yet quite different (a different planet, as some would say today).[1] Despite the early moderns frequently imagining Arcadia as bordering on urban dwellings, they conceived of it as informed by a fundamentally different affective regime. Dedicated to the leisurely lives of shepherds and shepherdesses whose only concern in the world was not – as one would assume – their flocks, but love, Arcadia afforded a leisurely existence, one, however, that was endlessly complicated by compound emotions. Love was inextricably linked to sorrow in Arcadia, and tears were constantly shed for both love and sorrow.

In what follows, I will focus on the Spanish tradition, which, however, ties into a European discourse of astonishing stability and continuity. To begin with, a brief glance at gender relations will help to grasp the specific constellation of *motus mixti* that informs Arcadia. The foundation for Arcadia's particular affective regime is laid by certain liberties enjoyed by female and male protagonists respectively – liberties that differed significantly from the early-modern real-world social order.

1   Arcadian Freedom: a Gendered Experience

Arcadian shepherdesses were free from the social constraints that severely curtailed early modern women's range of motion. Women were relegated to clearly delimited spaces, allowing them to leave their home only for a a highly selective number of occasions.[2] Of course, the didactic literature of the day

---

1   In the wake of Garcilaso de la Vega's *Third Eclogue*, in which the river Tajo is referenced repeatedly, the mention of local toponyms became a common feature of the Spanish pastoral, see Garcilaso de la Vega, *Poesías castellanas completas*, ed. E.L. Rivers (Madrid: 1996) 209–226. See on the *idea* of Arcadia, independent of a particular geographical location, Snell B., "Arkadien. Die Entdeckung einer geistigen Landschaft (1945/1955)", in Garber K. (ed.), *Europäische Bukolik und Georgik* (Darmstadt: 1976) 14–43.

2   Much of the recent literature on early modern women is centred around the insistence that women did indeed transgress and subvert the spaces granted to them. Scholars have e.g. sought to overcome spatial models such as gendered spaces, cf. the collection Helly D.O. – Reverby S.M. (eds.) *Gendered Domains: Rethinking Public and Private in Women's History* (Ithaca, NY: 2018). The anecdotal evidence of individuals who sought to carve out spaces of agency beyond what they were officially granted by the authorities does not thwart, however, the fact that women were essentially policed out of public life. Edited collections such as Helly – Reverby, *Gendered Domains* offer excellent contributions on cloisters and harems, but are light on reflections on every-day life of married and unmarried women. For heuristic purposes, it is useful to recognise today's tendency towards 'retrospective identification' (Joan W. Scott), i.e., the desire to find in early modern women precursors of modern emancipatory movements. Cf. Scott J.W., "Fantasy Echo: History and the Construction of Identity", *Critical Inquiry* 27/2 (2001) 284–304. Recent studies of gendered spaces in

THE AFFECTIVE REGIME OF THE EUROPEAN PASTORAL TRADITION   285

put forward norms that were not universally complied with; still, the sentiments these authors uttered are not to be easily dismissed: women should be careful, as Fray Luis de León put it, not to become 'callejeras', or streetwalkers. They should be seen neither '[por] las calles, ni las plazas, ni las huertas, ni las casas ajenas' ('in the streets nor in the squares nor in the gardens nor in other houses').[3] Women were relegated to particular sections in church as well as in the theatre, and even within their homes, the sitting rooms were compartmentalised according to gender: while men were seated on chairs, women lounged about, hidden by a curtain, on cushions and low benches on an elevated platform called *estrado*.[4] This secluded space did in fact happen to afford women a certain liberty, as Mme de Aulnoy reported back to Paris from Madrid in her *Voyage d'Espagne* in 1692:

> Il n'entre jamais d'hommes où elles [i.e. les femmes] sont; un mari jaloux auroit beau venir chercher sa femme, l'on s'en moqueroit et l'on ne se donneroit pas même la peine de lui répondre, elle y est ou elle n'y est pas. Elles sont fines, les bonnes Dames, et cette liberté ne leur sert pas mal; car vous observerez qu'il n'y a pas une maison qui n'ait sa porte de derrière par où elles peuvent sortir sans être vûes.[5]

> No man ever enters where they [i.e., the women] are; a jealous husband could come looking for his wife, but no one would care, and no one would even bother to answer: either she is there or she is not. They have the freedom, the good ladies, and this freedom does them no harm; for you will

---

early modern Europe have rightly challenged the anachronistic projection of the modern public/private dichotomy on early modern phenomena. Still, their rejection of the notion of public space as a male-gendered space e.g. in Kuehn T. – Schutte A.J., "Introduction", in Schutte A.J. – Kuehn T. – Seidel Menchi S. (eds.), *Time, Space, and Women's Lives in Early Modern Europe* (University Park: 2002) ix–xix, here xvii, is not particularly helpful when it comes to grasping the spatial constraints women were subjected to in early modern Europe.

3   León Luis de, "La perfecta casada", in León Luis de, *Obras completas castellanas*, ed. F. García (Madrid: ³1959) 233–342, ch. 16, 323–325: 'No han de ser las buenas mujeres callejeras, visitadoras y vagabundas, sino que han de amar mucho el retiro, y se han de acostumbrar a estarse en casa' ('Good women should not be streetwalkers, visitors and vagabonds, but should love reclusiveness and should be accustomed to stay at home'). All translations are my own if not indicated otherwise.

4   See Del Río Barredo M.J., "Espacios de mujeres en el Madrid del siglo XVII: el estrado, entre la casa y la calle", in Amelang J.S. et al. (eds.) *Palacios, plazas, patíbulos: La sociedad española moderna entre el cambio y las resistencias* (Valencia: 2018) 789–800.

5   Aulnoy, Marie-Catherine d', *Relation du voyage d'Espagne*, vol. 3 (The Hague, Henry van Bulderen: ²1692) 132.

observe that there is not a house that does not have a back door through which they can leave without being seen.

Of course travel reports need to be taken with a grain of salt, and Mme d'Aulnoy's *Relation* in particular has been likened to the *contes de fées* she is above all known for.[6] Still, the literature, from humanist treatises to seventeenth-century travelogues, is in agreement on the fact that women were neither to be seen nor heard in public and that they were reduced to exploiting what little leeway they had by circumventing conventions and secretly pursuing their interests.[7] Whatever contact with men women cared to have beyond the closest family needed to be organised clandestinely and pursued furtively.

Arcadia's mixed cast of characters, to the contrary, including shepherds and shepherdesses, but also nymphs, wild men, and wise women, interacts with each other in an unconstrained manner, in a way completely unthinkable in reality, in particular for women. What is more, Arcadia also permitted women to wander the forests on their own, stay out overnight in the company of both men and women, and in general to roam freely wherever they pleased. Cervantes' story of Marcela, which is today commonly read as a tale of female emancipation, cannot be overestimated in the shocking toppling of established order her antics meant at the time. As the protagonist in an episode of the first part of *Don Quijote*, Marcela rejects all the candidates who are presented to her for marriage, claiming to be too young to commit to matrimony. Her family gives in and decides to grant her the time she needs – until one morning when she emerges dressed as a shepherdess, she joins a group of shepherd girls and leaves town with their flock. The city's young men continue to court her, however, following her around in the woods and meadows. There is even a small grove with two dozen tall beeches with the name "Marcela" carved into the bark of each. When a young shepherd, Grisostomo, dies of his unhappy love for Marcela, she makes a surprise appearance at his funeral. Accused of relentless cruelty, she defends her right to reject an unwelcome admirer in a powerful speech:

> 'tengo libre condición y no gusto de sujetarme; ni quiero ni aborrezco a nadie. No engaño a éste, ni solicito aquél; ni burlo con uno, ni me

---

6 See most recently Balguerie V., "Voyage en terre colonisatrice: Relation du Voyage d'Espagne de Marie-Catherine d'Aulnoy", *Early Modern French Studies* (2023) 1–15.

7 See on the humanist debate Martínez-Góngora M., *Discursos sobre la mujer en el humanismo renacentista español: los casos de Antonio de Guevara, Alfonso y Juan de Valdés y Luis de León* (York, SC: 1999).

THE AFFECTIVE REGIME OF THE EUROPEAN PASTORAL TRADITION

entretengo con el otro.' [...] Y en diciendo esto, sin querer oír respuesta alguna, volvió las espaldas y se entró por lo más cerrado de un monte que allí cerca estaba, dejando admirados, tanto de su discreción como de su hermosura, a todos los que allí estaban.[8]

'I am free, and I have no desire to submit myself; I neither love nor hate anyone. I neither deceive this one, nor court that one; I neither joke with this one, nor amuse myself with the other.' [...] And having said this, without waiting for an answer, she turned her back and went into the innermost part of nearby mountains, leaving all those who had gathered stunned by her discretion and her beauty.

In the narrated world of Don Quijote, Marcela's behaviour is scandalous. Yet just like Quijote himself, she has adopted a literary mode of existence – in her case, that of Arcadia.[9] What Marcela chose is only superficially the life of a herder; rather, she cast herself as an Arcadian shepherdess, turning into a mode of existence what generations of aristocratic ladies had subscribed to for courtly festivals and entertainments. Much like the courtiers who staged tournaments in the mould of the major battles and duels in the *Amadís de Gaula*, Arcadia was the preferred pattern for courtly pastimes, from Renaissance *intermedi* to baroque festivals.[10] Jorge de Montemayor's *Los siete libros de la Diana* (first printed in 1559), the first and most influential example of the Spanish *novela pastoril* or pastoral romance, in turn insists that the world evoked in the text is the same as that of courtly entertainment: all characters are nobles in disguise, done up as 'unos rústicos pastores', for whom it is precisely the highly artificial construct of Arcadia that allows them to conduct themselves 'desnudos de artificio y de vestidos', ('without artifice and [elaborate] dress') as Lope de Vega put it in his pastoral romance of the very name, *Arcadia*.[11] The

---

8   Cervantes Miguel de, *El ingenioso hidalgo Don Quijote de la Mancha*, ed. L.A. Murillo, 2 vols. (Madrid: 1978) vol. 1, 187–188.

9   Marcela's stance has been discussed as an unjustified claim to freedom, cf. the classical study by Köhler E., "Wandlungen Arkadiens: die Marcela-Episode des 'Don Quijote' (1, 11–14)", in Köhler E., *Esprit und arkadische Freiheit. Aufsätze aus der Welt der Romania* (Frankfurt/Main – Bonn: 1966) 302–327. But it is indeed not a generalised philosophical principle that is at stake with Marcela's refusal of having to accept and return a man's love, but a literary convention. Cf. also Iventosch H., "Cervantes and Courtly Love: The Grisóstomo-Marcela Episode of *Don Quixote*", PMLA 89/1 (1974) 64–76.

10   See Brusa P. – Traninger A., *Lesekontext und Affektregime: Probleme der Gattungsmischung in der Erzählprosa des Siglo de Oro*, Working Papers der FOR 2350 "Diskursivierungen von Neuem" 11 (Berlin: 2018).

11   Lope de Vega, *Arcadia, prosa y versos*, ed. A. Sánchez Jiménez (Madrid: 2012) 181.

textual world of the pastoral becomes a space in which real-life desires can be turned into fictional experience – to a certain degree, as I will demonstrate below. Montemayor promises true stories under the guise of the pastoral, in which the names have been changed ('muy diversas historias, de casos que verdaderamente han sucedido, aunque van disfrazados debajo de nombres y estilo pastoril').[12]

For men, Arcadia was above all defined by a liberation from duties. Alonso Núñez de Reinoso, a Portuguese converso writing in Venice, had one protagonist of his *Historia de los amores de Clareo y Florisea y de los trabajos de Isea* (1552) end a long odyssey from the Eastern Mediterranean towards the Iberian Pensinsula on one *ínsula Pastoril*, the pastoral island. The shepherds who live on this island distinguish themselves by rejecting the usual manly occupations of the time:

> Había por aquellos valles muchos pastores que tañendo sus flautas rodeaban sus ganados, sin de otra cosa ninguna tener cuidado más que de levantarse cuando el sol salía, y guardar sus ovejas, y pasar el día en honestos ejercicios; [...] no les daba cuidado el conquistar reinos, adquirir ciudades, vencer batallas, desear señoríos, querer mandar, buscar las Indias, servir al mundo, perder la vida, destruir el alma.[13]

> There were many shepherds in those valleys, who, playing their flutes, circled their flocks, with no other care but to rise when the sun rose, and keep their sheep, and spend the day in honest pursuits; [...] they did not care at all for conquering kingdoms, acquiring cities, winning battles, desiring lordships, wanting to command, seeking the Indies, serving the world, losing their lives, destroying their souls.

Liberated from all traditional expectations for male upper-class activity, men who adopt the life of a shepherd are at the same time subjected to a fictional power dynamics that is dictated by female prerogatives. That real-world male prerogatives are decidedly curtailed in this fictional world is the precondition for women's enlarged radius of action.

---

12 Montemayor, *La Diana*, 108, "Argumento de este libro". On the supposed historical identity of Diana, see García Abad A., "Sobre la patria de la *Diana*", *Revista de literatura* 27/53–54 (1965) 67–77.

13 Núñez de Reinoso Alonso, *Los amores de clareo y Florisea y los trabajos de la sin ventura Isea*, ed. M.A. Teijeiro Fuentes (Cáceres: 1991) 191–192.

THE AFFECTIVE REGIME OF THE EUROPEAN PASTORAL TRADITION

2   The Language of Tears

The Arcadian population is above all concerned with one emotion – love – but the prevailing sentiment is pain. Textual Arcadia differs from Arcadia as represented in the visual arts in that it is centred around a specific constellation of *motus mixti*: textual Arcadia is the location of endless tears, tears of love and sorrow.

On occasion, these tears are shed in mourning. Death is indeed present in Arcadia, and the lamentation of the dead does have a firm place in the bucolic environment. When a group of shepherds gathers at the Meliso's grave in the 'valle de los Cipreses' in Cervantes' *Galatea*, the shepherd Telesio calls for a collective rite of mourning, including of course the shedding of tears in commemoration of the deceased shepherd:

> Veis allí, gallardos pastores, discretas y hermosas pastoras; veis allí, digo, la triste sepultura donde reposan los honrados huesos del nombrado Meliso, honor y gloria de nuestras riberas. Comenzad, pues, a levantar al cielo los humildes corazones, y con puros afectos, abundantes lágrimas y profundos sospiros, entonad los sanctos himnos y devotas oraciones.[14]

> You see there, gallant shepherds, discreet and beautiful shepherdesses; you see there, I say, the sad tomb where the venerated bones of the reputable Meliso, honour and glory of our shores, have been laid to rest. Begin, then, to lift up your humble hearts to heaven, and with pure affections, abundant tears and deep sighs, chant the holy hymns and devout prayers.

The 'holy valley', 'el sagrado valle', in which the graves are located, is described as remote – it can only be reached through a narrow passage –, and it is characterised by a particular kind of vegetation: it is not in the shade of the customary alder (*aliso*) that the congregation sings and weeps, but under the tree of the dead, the cypress; and it is not the white backs of grazing sheep that dot the green pastures, but white marble stones that mark the burial places of those shepherds who have earned the privilege of being buried on this extraordinary

---

14   Cervantes Miguel de, *La Galatea*, ed. F. López Estrada – M.L. Gracía Berdoy (Madrid: 2011) 545.

site.[15] Telesio performs a ceremony that is reminiscent of the Catholic rite:[16] he delivers a funeral sermon (only summarily reproduced in the narrative), the shepherds kneel, incense is burned, prayers are said and concluded with a collective 'Amen'.

Beyond solemn occasions such as funerals which may equally allow for and even demand tears in the real world, pastoral narratives, and Montemayor's *Diana* in particular, abound in random scenes where weeping is the first and foremost everyday occupation of the characters. Before I take a closer look at some essential passages, let me briefly outline the *Diana*'s plot. At the centre of the narrative is the beautiful shepherdess Diana, with whom the shepherds Sireno and Sylvano both have fallen in love. Diana initially returns Sireno's feelings, but rejects Sylvano. Yet while Sireno is away on a long journey, Diana marries the rich Delio at her parents' request. Sireno's grief over this marriage and the loss of Diana lets him bond both with Sylvano as well as other shepherds and shepherdesses on his return. They lament each others' lovesickness, share their stories and sing about love. Finally, three nymphs lead the shepherdesses and shepherds to the wise Felicia who knows how to remedy 'pasiones enamoradas', enamoured passions.[17] Through a mysterious potion (simply called 'agua'), which Felicia administers to the lovers, they are relieved of their suffering. Sireno is now able to master his passion and attains a certain indifference towards Diana: he finds his happiness not in freedom *to* love, but in freedom *from* love.[18] Diana, in turn, after returning to the group of shepherds, regrets her behaviour towards Sireno, who has now definitely turned his back on her.

---

15 Cf. Damiani B.M., "El valle de los cipreses en *La Galatea* de Cervantes", *Anales de Literatura Española* 5 (1986) 39–50. Damiani points out the intertextual reference to the story of Cyparissus in Ovid's *Metamorphoses* (x, 106–142) who is transformed into a cypress at his own request in order to be able to mourn eternally. On death in Arcadia, see of course Panofsky E., "Et in Arcadia Ego: On the Conception of Transience in Poussin and Watteau", in Klibansky R. – Paton H.J. (eds.), *Philosophy and History: Essays Presented to Ernst Cassirer* (Oxford: 1936) 223–254, and specifically on the pastoral novel Damiani B.M. – Mujica B., *Et in Arcadia Ego. Essays on Death in the Pastoral Novel* (Lanham – New York – London: 1990).

16 These echoes of Catholic rites are in tension with Shepard/Shepard's argument that this is supposed to be a pagan, pre-Christian world in which Christian institutions play no role, cf. Shepard S. – Shepard M., "Death in Arcadia. The Psychological Atmosphere of Cervantes' *Galatea*", in Labrador Herraiz J.J. – Fernández Jiménez J. (eds.), *Cervantes and the Pastoral* (Cleveland, OH: 1986) 157–168, here 168.

17 Montemayor Jorge de, *Los siete libros de La Diana*, ed. A. Rallo (Madrid: 2008) 192. Unless otherwise stated, I quote from this edition.

18 There is a broad scholarly tradition that situates 'freedom to love' at the core of pastoral discourse, taking its cue in particular from Sannazaro's *Arcadia*, see Petriconi H., "Die verlorenen Paradiese", *Romanistisches Jahrbuch* 10 (1959) 167–199, esp. 180. But scholars of the

THE AFFECTIVE REGIME OF THE EUROPEAN PASTORAL TRADITION 291

In the *Diana*, everybody weeps all the time. The word 'lágrimas' is found in more than one hundred instances, and this is not counting related words, such as *llanto*.[19] Stories are without exception told 'con muchas lágrimas', songs are performed under tears and interrupted by sighs. What is more, weeping is a collaborative effort. When listening to songs and stories, the shepherd community does not remain idle, but matches the word accents in each performer's delivery with sighs and accompanies each others' songs with tears in the style of a *basso continuo*: 'No estaba ocioso Sireno al tiempo que Sylvano estos versos cantaba, que con sospiros respondía a los últimos acentos de sus palabras, y con lágrimas solemnizaba lo que dellas entendía'.[20] ('Sireno was not idle while Sylvano was singing these verses, and answered the last accents of his words with sighs, and solemnised with tears what he understood of them'.)

Tears are so ubiquitous in the *Diana* that the shepherdess Selvagia, for example, can report on her colleague (if this is the appropriate term) Ysmenia's reaction to a letter without having been present at the scene: 'No pudo Ysmenia acabar de leer esta carta, porque al medio della fueron tantos los sospiros y lágrimas que por sus ojos derramaba, que pensó perder la vida llorando'.[21] ('Ysmenia could not finish reading this letter, because halfway she sighed so much and had so many tears in her eyes that she thought she would lose her life weeping'.) When someone is overwhelmed by tears, the community is ever prepared to join them: 'Acabado de decir esto la hermosa Selvagia comenzó a derramar muchas lágrimas, y los pastores le ayudaron a ello por ser un oficio de que tenían gran experiencia'.[22] ('When she had finished saying this, the beautiful Selvagia began to shed many tears, and the shepherds helped her to

---

Spanish tradition have insisted that Spanish pastoral is rather characterised by a privileging of the 'freedom from love', see Matzat W., "Subjektivität im spanischen Schäferroman", in Friedlein R. – Poppenberg G. – Volmer A. (eds.), *Arkadien in den romanischen Literaturen. Zu Ehren von Sebastian Neumeister zum 70. Geburtstag* (Heidelberg: 2008) 21–39, here 33.

19   Moreno Báez E., "Prólogo", in Jorge de Montemayor, *Los siete libros de La Diana*, ed. E. Moreno Báez (Madrid: 1955) XXVII–XCII, here XLVI, counts 102 occurrences. Castillo Martínez C., "De las lágrimas a la risa: análisis de la decadencia de los libros de pastores", in Lobato M.L. – Domínguez-Matito F. (eds.), *Memoria de la palabra. Actas del VI Congreso de la Asociación Internacional Siglo de Oro. Burgos-La Rioja, 15–19 de julio 2002*, 2 vols. (Frankfurt/Main: 2004) vol. 1, 497–510, here 499, points out that related metaphors ('los ojos hechos fuentes', 'eyes turned into springs', etc.) would still have to be added.

20   Montemayor, *La Diana* 119.

21   Montemayor, *La Diana* 147. Cf. Juan Montero's remark on this reaction as an infringement of narrative point of view, Montemayor Jorge de, *La Diana*, ed. J. Montero (Madrid: 1996) 51, note 238.

22   Montemayor, *La Diana* 156.

do so, as it was a activity in which they had great experience'.) This inevitably sounds like irony to us, but *oficio* is to be taken seriously as a key word here. *Officium pastorum* is the traditional concept that is evoked here, not without, however, subjecting it to a significant semantic shift: while *oficio* was the conventional term for the shepherds' adoration of the Christ child in Medieval spiritual plays,[23] it now refers to the shepherds' lovesick weeping that figures as their habitual occupation, possibly even duty or profession.

There is indeed, as Roland Barthes suggested with a view to the modern discourse of love, a differentiated language of tears at play in Arcadia.[24] Tears are not so much an authentic expression of affect in an 'unalienated world of shepherds',[25] but rather a highly coded sign system. The pastoral world is not one of liberation from or discharge of affects.[26] Rather than affording an "authentic" life, Arcadia demands extreme restraint, in particular with regard to expressions of desire, and coded behaviour that crucially includes the practice of weeping. What is more, this practice of weeping is informed by literary and religious intertexts.

Even though the pastoral landscape is characterised as a place of relief from the duties and constraints of everyday life that allows for an exclusive focus on love, the protagonists do not hesitate to think of themselves as wandering the biblical vale of tears. Selvagia laments '[que] Amor [...] me puso 'n este valle de lágrimas [...]'.[27] ('that love put me in this vale of tears'). The phrase references Ps 83:7, in which the human life is described as a pilgrimage 'in valle lacrimarum' ('in a vale of tears'), a phrase that would reappear in the Middle Ages in a hymn to the Virgin Mary, the *Salve Regina*: 'Ad te suspiramus, gementes et flentes in hac lacrimarum valle' ('To thee we sigh, mourning and crying in this vale of tears').[28] With this blending of religious and pastoral discourse the Arcadian love cult is elevated to the rank of a civil religion.

In the early modern period, it was only in the field of religious experience that tears were unreservedly conceived as a desirable 'gift' for both genders, insofar

---

23   Avalle Arce J.B., *La novela pastoril española* (Madrid: 1974) 15–16.

24   Barthes R., *Fragments d'un discours amoureux* (Paris: 1977) 214.

25   Gumbrecht H.U., *Eine Geschichte der spanischen Literatur*, 2 vols. (Frankfurt/Main: 1990) vol. 1, 322.

26   For this line of argumentation, see. e.g. Johnson C.B., "Montemayor's Diana: A Novel Pastoral", *Bulletin of Hispanic Studies* 48/1 (1971) 20–35.

27   Montemayor, *La Diana* 163.

28   See Büttner F., "Zur Geschichte der Marienantiphon 'Salve Regina'", *Archiv für Musikwissenschaft* 46/4 (1989) 257–270.

THE AFFECTIVE REGIME OF THE EUROPEAN PASTORAL TRADITION 293

as they were ascribed an evidential power of genuine religious feeling.[29] As a sign of repentance, of compassion for the crucified and altogether as a complement of spirituality, tears were so highly valued that weeping and provoking tears was widely practised.[30] Religious discourse does not discern between the genders with regard to weeping[31] – and neither does Arcadia.

Early modern anthropology, on the contrary, did reflect on the genderedness of the physiology of tears. Juan Luis Vives described weeping not even as an expression of an emotion, but as the discharge of excess moisture through the eyes: drunk people, children, women, and the sick are among the most susceptible to crying.[32] The grouping of women in this category of the weak or debilitated is not least due to the doctrine of humoral pathology, which classified the female body as cold and moist and thus as deficient in comparison to the warm and dry male body.[33] This decided hierarchisation of the possible combinations of bodily fluids provided the explanation of and justification for female tears: for the weaker sex it is not only physiologically necessary to let moisture escape, their pathological condition also explains their weakness in the face of adversity. Male tears, on the other hand, although permissible, require more elaborate legitimation; the situations in which men are permitted to cry are severely limited, or, as the debating shepherds in Lope de Vega's *Arcadia* put it, 'el hombre robusto, y finalmente hombre, ¿cómo podrá llorar

---

29   See Benke C., *Die Gabe der Tränen. Zur Tradition und Theologie eines vergessenen Kapitels der Glaubensgeschichte* (Würzburg: 2002); Nagy, *Le Don des larmes*; Tausiet M., "Agua en los ojos: El 'don de lágrimas' en la España moderna", in Tausiet M. – Amelang J.S. (eds.), *Accidentes del alma. Las emociones en la Edad Moderna* (Madrid: 2009) 167–202. On religious weeping in a transcultural context, see the contributions in Patton K.C. – Hawley J.S. (eds.), *Weeping in the Religious Imagination* (Princeton – NJ – Oxford: 2005).

30   Christian, Jr. W.A., "Provoked Religious Weeping in Early Modern Spain", in Davis J. (ed.), *Religious Organization and Religious Experience* (London – New York: 1982) 97–114.

31   Benke, *Die Gabe der Tränen* 412.

32   Vives Juan Luis, "De anima et vita", in Juan Luis Vives, *Opera omnia*, ed. G. Mayans y Siscar, vol. 3 (Valencia, Benito Monfort: 1782) 300–520, III, ch. 20, "De lacrimis", 500–501, here 500. Spanish translation: Vives Juan Luis, *El alma y la vida*, trans. and ed. I. Roca (Valencia: 1992) 355: 'las lagrimas fluyen cuando el cerebro está humedecido, cual sucede en los ebrios, o cuando es muelle y tierno, como en los niños, en las muchachas y en los enfermos'.

33   See on the theory of gender in the combinatorial four-part scheme of humoral theory Schöner E., *Das Viererschema in der antiken Humoralpathologie* (Wiesbaden: 1964) 31 (Corpus Hippocraticum) and 92 (Galen). For a general orientation see Klibansky R. – Panofsky E. – Saxl F., *Saturn and Melancholy: Studies in the History of Natural Philosophy, Religion, and Art* (Montreal: 2019) 3–66; Redondo A., *Otra manera de leer* El Quijote (Madrid: 1997) 121–146.

sin verdadero dolor?' ('the sturdy man, and finally man, how can he weep without real pain?').[34]

Tears, as Thomas Aquinas stated in his discussion of human emotions in the *Summa theologiae*, are actually intended to alleviate pain, and in this sense, their purpose is their own superfluousness: weeping alleviates pain and thus in turn eliminates the reason for tears.[35] In Arcadia, however, tears flow incessantly, and this is due to literary tradition. It is not an *imitatio naturae*, but an *imitatio auctorum* that justifies the shepherds' and shepherdesses' uninterrupted flow of tears. It is Virgil's tenth eclogue that supplies the actual reason for the endless crying. The god of the shepherds, Pan, instructs lovesick Gallus that cruel Amor would never tire of tears:

> 'ecquis erit modus?' inquit. 'Amor non talia curat:
> nec lacrimis crudelis Amor nec gramina rivis
> nec cytiso saturantur apes nec fronde capellae.'

> 'Will there be no end?' he cried. 'Love recks naught of this: neither is cruel Love sated with tears, nor the grass with the rills, nor bees with the clover, nor goats with leaves.'[36]

It is not amor, love, which *causes* tears, but capital-letter Amor, the god of love, who *feeds* on tears; his demand, therefore, knows no limit. Weeping is the shepherds' permanent sacrifice to their greedy deity. This sacrifice is to be offered by men and women alike – in this sense, Arcadian tears are gender-neutral. While Arcadia affords female and male characters different liberties, as I have shown above, it subjects them to the same affective regime. This is a gender norm that depends on a genre norm, and it is not indicative of a historical change in gender relations or social order tout court.[37]

---

34 Cf. also Weinand H.G., *Tränen. Untersuchungen über das Weinen in der deutschen Sprache und Literatur des Mittelalters* (Bonn: 1958) 66–81. For a review of more recent research on the history of emotions, however with scarce references to tears, see Schnell R., "Historische Emotionsforschung", *Mittelalterliche Studien* 38 (2005) 173–276.

35 Thomas Aquinas, *Summa theologiae. Latin text and English translation, introductions, notes, appendices, and glossaries*. Vol. 20. *Pleasure (1a2ae. 31–39)* (London: 1975) 1a 2ae q38 a2. This is not a specifically Christian position, cf. Plutarch, "On the Control of Anger (De cohibenda ira)" in Plutarch, *Moralia*. Vol. 6, trans. W.C. Helmbold (Cambridge, MA: 1939) 455 B.

36 Virgil, *Eclogues. Georgics. Aeneid: Books 1–6*, trans. H. Rushton Fairclough, rev. G.P. Goold (Cambridge, MA: 1999) Eclogue x, 28–30.

37 See Hempfer K.W., "Ariosts *Orlando Furioso*. Die (De-)Konstruktion von Helden im generisch pluralen Diskurs", in Aurnhammer A. – Pfister M. (eds.), *Heroen und Heroisierungen*

THE AFFECTIVE REGIME OF THE EUROPEAN PASTORAL TRADITION 295

Women as well as men in Arcadia shed tears for the sake of love and sorrow, both individually and in groups. By contrast, crying was clearly gendered in the early modern (as of course in the contemporary) world, even if there is no consensus among scholars regarding the precise distribution of the licence to weep – above all with a view to the cultural history of tears: some argue that crying became an exclusively female practice only from the eighteenth century onwards,[38] while others see the pastoral novel in particular as indicative of an emerging conception of masculinity that was linked to a new tolerance towards the open display of emotions.[39]

Early modern writers did indeed comment on gender-specific differences regarding weeping. In Cervantes' last novel, *Los trabajos de Persiles y Sigismunda* (1617), the 'prudent man' is granted the licence to cry on no more than three occasions: 'Por tres cosas es lícito que llore el varón prudente: la una, por haber pecado; la segunda, por alcanzar perdón dél; la tercera, por estar celoso. Las demás lágrimas no dicen bien en un rostro grave'.[40] ('A prudent man may weep for three reasons: first, for having sinned; second, to obtain forgiveness for it; third, for jealousy. Other tears are not suitable for a serious face'). The licences are predominantly – and hardly surprisingly – linked to the religious sphere,

---

in der Renaissance (Wiesbaden: 2013) 45–69, here 47. The constitution of gender relations in line with generic conventions suggests that it is not useful to speak of an early modern tradition of weeping that 'found expression' in literature, as proposed by Ulbrich C., "Tränenspektakel. Die Lebensgeschichte der Luise Charlotte von Schwerin (1731) zwischen Frömmigkeitspraxis und Selbstinszenierung", *L'Homme* 23/1 (2012) 27–42, here 27. At best, Arcadia can be described as an 'anthropological experimental setting', see Wehle W., "Menschwerdung in Arkadien: Die Wiedergeburt der Anthropologie aus dem Geist der Kunst", in Wehle W. (ed.), *Über die Schwierigkeiten, (s)ich zu sagen: Horizonte literarischer Subjektkonstitution* (Frankfurt/Main: 2001) 83–106, here 98.

38 Nagy P., *Le Don des larmes au Moyen Âge. Un instrument spirituel en quête d'institution, V^e–XIIIe siècle* (Paris: 2000) 26.

39 Vaught J.C., "Men who Weep and Wail: Masculinity and Emotion in Sidney's *New Arcadia*", *History Compass* 2/1 (2005) 1–16, here 1. Rhodes, "Skirting the Men" 139, argues in the same vein, but links this fact to the loss of prestige of the Spanish nobility. Other voices see a tolerance for male tears caused by the rise of sentimentalism in the eighteenth century, cf. Carter P., "Tears and the Man", in Knott S. (ed.), *Women, Gender, and Enlightenment* (Basingstoke: 2005) 156–173; Vincent-Buffault A., *Histoire des larmes, XVIIIe–XIXe siècles* (Marseille: 1986); analogously for the *drame larmoyant* and its Spanish variant, the *comedia lacrimosa*, see García Garrosa M.J., *La retórica de las lágrimas. La comedia sentimental española, 1751–1802* (Valladolid: 1990).

40 Cervantes Miguel de, *Los trabajos de Persiles y Sigismunda*, ed. C. Romero Muñoz (Madrid: 2004) 303. See (Madrid: 2009) 167–202. See Teijeiro Fuentes, M.Á., "La novela bizantina: de la antigüedad pagana al contrarreformismo cristiano", in Teijeiro Fuentes, M.Á. – Guijarro Ceballos J. (eds.), *De los caballeros andantes a los peregrinos enamorados. La novela española en el Siglo de Oro* (Cáceres – Madrid: 2007) 111–175, esp. 117.

except for jealousy which is the only legitimate cause for tears beyond sin and contrition.[41] Lope de Vega, in his *Arcadia*, stages an extended discussion among shepherds about male tears which references both established contemporary theories of weeping and Arcadian doctrines. While Rústico, who assumes the comical role of *gracioso*, contemplates faking tears to conquer his beloved and thus negotiates a strategic position between real-life masculinity and Arcadian conventions, love-sick Celio emulates his god Amor and feeds on tears, while abundantly producing them himself: 'De ellas – dijo Celio – vivo, bebo y me sustento. No me acuerdo haber tenido fiesta sin lágrimas. Todo soy llanto: mi pecho es un océano, mis ojos, un Nilo y un Éufrates. La primera cosa que hice en naciendo fue llorar' ('"They are", said Celio, "what I live on, drink on, and feed on. I do not remember to have had a feast without tears. I am all tears: my breast is an ocean, my eyes, a Nile and a Euphrates. The first thing I did when I was born was to weep"').[42]

Other shepherds were depicted as deliberately provoking their own tears. Diana's scorned lover Sireno seems to be leaning into his pain by repeatedly touching and handling his beloved's belongings – and shedding copious amounts of tears when doing so. He keeps a lock of Diana's hair and some of the green silk strings that held it together in his knapsack. Surrendering to sad memories, he spreads these tokens of a lost love out on the grass in front of him, only to accuse memory, in an emotional apostrophe, of being the 'destruidora de mi descanso', the destroyer of his peace of mind.[43] Sireno's tears in the face of the material traces of lost love read as an authentic emotional response. His tearful reaction appears to be in line with modern notions of tears as uncontrolled and uncontrollable physical expressions of the inner self.[44] This would correspond with interpretations of the pastoral landscape as a place of authenticity, '[...] characterised by a simplicity and purity that allows for an authenticity of feeling, both happy and sorrowful, which urban artificiality negates.'[45] Yet nothing in Arcadia is natural. Rather, as indicated

---

41 See Capp B., "'Jesus Wept' but did the Englishman? Masculinity and Emotion in Early Modern England", *Past and Present* 224 (2014), 75–108.

42 Lope de Vega, *Arcadia*, 235–247, esp. 238, 241. The discussion goes back and forth for some time time and can by no means be reduced to an overall rejection of "effeminating" tears, as proposed by Cull J.T., "Androgyny in the Spanish Pastoral Novels", *Hispanic Review* 57 (1989) 317–334.

43 Montemayor, *La Diana* 112.

44 Söntgen B. – Spiekermann G., "Tränen. Ausdruck – Darstellung – Kommunikation. Eine Einführung", in Söntgen B. – Spiekermann G. (eds.), *Tränen* (Munich: 2008) 9–16, here 9.

45 Hernández-Pecoraro R., *Bucolic Metaphors. History, Subjectivity, and Gender in the Early Modern Spanish Pastoral* (Chapel Hill: 2006) 84; see also Wallace J.C., "El llanto como

by how the green of the silk blends in with the green of the meadow, and the curl of Diana's 'dorados cabellos' becomes one of the 'doradas flores',[46] nature herself partakes in the continued manifestation of Sireno's unfulfilled desire.[47]

3 Nature Talks Back

At first glance, Arcadia projects a perfect state of blissful contentment. A land of *plaisir*, Arcadia boasted a landscape to match. Although the action used to be precisely located through the mention of European toponyms and city names,[48] the elements that make up the landscape were deliberately generic. Across a long and extensive textual tradition, it consisted of the very same standardised building blocks which Ernst Robert Curtius packaged as the *topos* of the *locus amoenus*.[49] Curtius claimed it consisted of just six 'charms', as he called them: a little river or a clear fountain, luscious meadows strewn with fragrant flowers and populated by trees that offer refreshing shade, a cool breeze, and birdsong.[50]

Despite various attempts at constructing a "realism" of the pastoral, with scholars claiming, e.g., that Spanish pastoral in particular celebrated the importance of shepherding for the early modern Iberian peninsula,[51] the landscape is no more natural than the literary *pastores* are shepherds. The landscape is not just of a prefabricated and generic beauty, it also comes alive in consonance with the affective afflictions of its inhabitants. It is in particular their tears and

---

elemento dramático en *La Galatea*", in Labrado Herraiz J.J. – Fernández Jiménez J. (eds.), *Cervantes and the Pastoral* (Cleveland, OH: 1986) 185–196, here 188.

46 Montemayor, *La Diana* 114, 110.

47 Cf. on the corresponding colours of clothing and nature in Lope's *Arcadia* Mujica B., "Lope de Vega's *Arcadia*: A Step Toward the Modern Novel", *Hispanic Journal* 2 (1981) 27–49, here 29.

48 See above note 1.

49 Garcilaso already combined the localisation of the pastoral landscape with a description of nature that emphasised its artificiality, see Rivers E.L., "The Pastoral Paradox of Natural Art", in Rivers E.L., *Talking and Text: Essays on the Literature of Golden Age Spain* (Delaware: 2009) 83–101, esp. 89.

50 Curtius E.R., *Europäische Literatur und lateinisches Mittelalter* (Tübingen: [11]1993) 202–206, esp. 203.

51 See Krauss W., "Localización y desplazamientos en la novela pastoril española", in Sánchez Romeralo J. – Poulussen N. (eds.), *Actas del Segundo Congreso Internacional de Hispanistas* (Nijmegen: 1967) 363–369; Damiani B.M., "Realismo histórico y social de *La Diana* de Jorge de Montemayor", in Kossoff A.D. et al. (eds.), *Actas del VIII congreso de la Asociación Internacional de Hispanistas 22–27 agosto 1983*, 2 vols. (Madrid: 1983) vol. 1, 422–431.

sighs that reverberate through this simulacrum of nature, whose boundaries are 'where nature begins'[52] and which responds to and even partakes in the protagonists' afflictions. The shepherdess Belisa articulates this very idea in a passionate speech in *La Diana*:

> ¿Quién pensáis que hace crecer la verde yerba desta isla y acrecentar las aguas que la cercan sino mis lágrimas? ¿Quién pensáis que menea los árboles deste hermoso valle sino la vos de mis sospiros tristes que inflamando el aire, hacen aquello que él por sí no haría? ¿Por qué pensáis que cantan los dulces pájaros por entre las matas cuando el dorado Phebo está en toda su fuerza, sino para ayudar a llorar mis desventuras? ¿A qué pensáis que las temerosas fieras salen al verde prado, sino a oír mis continuas quejas?[53]

> Who do you think makes the green grass of this island grow, and the waters near it swell, but my tears? Who do you think moves the trees of this fair vale, but the voice of my sad sighs, which, inflaming the air, do that which it would not do itself? Why do you think the sweet birds sing among the bushes when the golden Phebus is in his full strength, but to help to mourn my misfortunes? Why do you think that the fearful wild beasts come out into the green meadow, but to hear my continual complaints?

The shepherds' affective disposition and the landscape are symbiotically related to one another. The relationship between weeping shepherds and pastoral nature is one of empathetic communion: the rivers leave their beds, not due to rain (which does not exist in Arcadia), but because of the tears shed by shepherds and shepherdesses. And protagonists themselves turn into nature, 'los ojos hechos fuentes',[54] their eyes turned into springs. Juan Luis Vives, in his commentary on Virgil's tenth eclogue, stressed the close connection between the Arcadian landscape and Amor's need for tears: just as the meadows must

---

52   Strosetzki C., "Arkadiens Grenzen: Natur und Naturzustand", in Friedlein R. – Poppenberg G. – Volmer A. (eds.), *Arkadien in den romanischen Literaturen. Zu Ehren von Sebastian Neumeister zum 70. Geburtstag* (Heidelberg: 2008) 161–174, here 173.

53   Montemayor, *La Diana*, 229–230. Montemayor was certainly not the first to employ this device, cf. Petrarca Francesco, *Canzoniere*, ed. M. Santagata (Milan: 1996) 301, esp. v. 1–2; cf. Warning R., "Petrarcas Tal der Tränen. Poetische Konterdiskursivität im Canzoniere", in Hempfer K.W. – Regn G. (eds.), *Petrarca-Lektüren. Gedenkschrift für Alfred Noyer-Weidner* (Stuttgart: 2003) 225–246.

54   Montemayor, *La Diana* 111.

THE AFFECTIVE REGIME OF THE EUROPEAN PASTORAL TRADITION

always be moistened by the streams, so Amor must constantly be offered tears.[55] Modern critics have accused early modern writers of a misguided pathetic fallacy,[56] but in fact the resonant landscape materialises a certain idea of *motus mixti*, the entwinement of love and sorrow in the media of tears and nature, that is not a representation of an anthropological fact, but a concept forged and explored in fiction. Arcadian love is the ultimate mixed emotion, and the *locus amoenus* is not just its compassionate abode, but the space in which a *motus mixtus* is shared by human and non-human actors.

4   Negotiating Mixed Emotions

These concepts are typically spelled out and subjected to negotiation when the action deviates from the iterative paths, from the endless songs and conversations about love that give the genre its distinct, yet utterly expectable profile.

A case in point is the episode in Montemayor's *Diana* in which three nymphs are being ambushed by three wild men (*salvajes*). When en route from the meadow of the laurels ('prado de los laureles, por donde pasa el arroyo que corre de esta clara fuente')[57] to another meadow, which surely looked just like the one they just left behind ('se iban por el verde prado adelante'),[58] the three nymphs are attacked by three savages who break out from some shrubbery. For contemporary readers there was no doubt that the sheer designation of the attackers as *salvajes* implied sexual transgression.[59] What is more, their typical feral appearance with their hairy bodies just partly covered in animal hides is used to signal that these are men in their animal state, untouched by civilisation and not controlled by reason.[60] Accordingly, critics have described their appearance in *La Diana* as an intrusion of the ugly and uncivilised into the idealised space of Arcadia.[61]

---

55   Vives Juan Luis, "Bucolicorum Vergilii interpretatio potissimum Allegorica", in Juan Luis Vives, *Opera omnia*, ed. G. Mayans y Siscar, vol. 2 (Valencia, Benito Monfort: 1782) 5–71, here 69.

56   Montemayor, *La Diana*, ed. Montero, 138, note 19.

57   Montemayor, *La Diana* 168.

58   Montemayor, *La Diana* 185.

59   See Avalle-Arce, *La novela pastoril* 87.

60   Egido A., *El gran teatro de Calderón. Personajes, temas, escenografía* (Kassel: 1995) 37–61, ch. "El vestido de salvaje", esp. 39.

61   See Wardropper B.W., "The *Diana* of Montemayor: Revaluation and Interpretation", *Studies in Philology* 48 (1951) 126–144, here 130; Schönherr G., *Jorge de Montemayor. Sein Leben und sein Schäferroman, die 'Siete libros de la Diana'* (Halle/Saale: 1886) 38.

But the episode is rather more complex. The *salvajes* do indeed appear as wild men being partly covered by their own body hair, partly by pelts. But they are also dramatically decked out with tiger-hide skullcaps, armbands made from snake heads, shields made from fish shells, and lion heads for helmets.[62] They are not of a kind with the satyrs who populated one of the architexts of early modern pastoral narrative, Jacopo Sannazaro's *Arcadia*, and who engaged with the nymphs in a perpetual sequence of chase and flight.[63] Rather, Montemayor's *salvajes* resemble actors representing barbarians on a courtly stage, performing and at the same time exaggerating an exotic ferocity.

They are also perfectly capable of engaging in polite discourse with their victims. Rushing out from their hiding place, the *salvajes* do not immediately lay hands on the nymphs, but rather address them to explain the motivation for the assault. They are rather confident of victory and convinced that the outcome of the episode is a foregone conclusion:

> A tiempo estáis, oh ingratas y desamoradas ninfas, que os obligara la fuerza a lo que el amor no os ha podido obligar, que no era justo que la fortuna hiciese tan grande agravio a nuestros cativos corazones, como era dilatalles tanto su remedio.[64]

> You are in time, o ungrateful and unloving nymphs. Now force will compel you to do what love could not compel you to do. It was not right that fortune should do so great a wrong to our captive hearts, and it was not right to delay their remedy for so long.

The nymphs, who do not seem to have been aware of the salvajes' love, are in shock and respond with tears ('no supieron responder a la soberbias palabras que oían, sino con lágrimas'). Then one of them, Dorida, finds the strength to speak up: she does not beg for mercy nor does she surrender; rather, she accuses her assailants of cowardly behaviour: how could they take up arms against women while claiming to act out of love? Her speech is to no avail, the *salvajes* tie the nymphs' hands with the strings from their bows. Some shepherds and

---

62   Montemayor, *La Diana* 186.
63   Gazzetti M., "Das selten glückliche Zusammentreffen von weiblicher Maßlosigkeit und männlicher Attacke", in Gazzetti M. (ed.), *Der Liebesangriff – "Il dolce assalto". Von Nymphen, Satyrn und Wäldern. Von einer Möglichkeit, über die Liebe zu sprechen = Rowohlt Literaturmagazin Sonderheft* 32 (1993) 21–42, here 21; on the figure of the Satyr, see the comprehensive study Lavocat F., *La Syrinx au bûcher. Pan et les satyres à la Renaissance et à l'âge baroque* (Geneva: 2005).
64   Montemayor, *La Diana* 186.

THE AFFECTIVE REGIME OF THE EUROPEAN PASTORAL TRADITION   301

shepherdesses who witness the scene from afar try to drive away the attackers by shooting them with their slingshots, but they do not achieve much. Rather, the *salvajes* start to charge at them. In the nick of time, an inevitably exceptionally beautiful shepherdess, Felismena, emerges from the thicket of the forest, armed with a bow and a staff of wild oak with a tip of steel. Not missing a beat, she pierces two of the wild men's breasts with her arrows, and when she is not quick enough to incapacitate the third in the same manner, she instead brings him to his knees with a blow of her staff, only to then push the staff's tip through the socket of his eye, piercing his brains through to the other side of the skull until he gives a frightful cry and falls dead on the ground.

What began as an almost polite conversation in accordance with pastoral convention, which demands the *sermo humilis* be used in combination with refined forms of address, now ends in extreme violence, but certainly not in the way expected, neither by the assailants – nor by the reader. Before the scene escalated into bloodshed, the *salvajes* had made it clear what they erroneously believed to be able to gain from the attack:

> En fin tenemos en la mano el galardón de los sospiros, con que a causa vuestra importunábamos las aves y animales de la escura y encantada selva do habitamos; y de las ardientes lágrimas con que hacíamos crecer el impetuoso y turbio río que sus temerosos campos va regando.[65]

> At last we have in our hand the reward for our sighs, with which we disturbed the birds and animals of the wild and enchanted forest where we live – all because of you; as well as the reward for the burning tears with which we made the impetuous and turbulent river swell, which waters these fearful fields.

Far from being outsiders to the pastoral world, the *salvajes*, too, participate in a culture of weeping prompted by spurned love, and the landscape willingly reverberates with their affects. But they fundamentally misunderstand the meaning of tears: capturing the nymphs is, for them, a kind of compensation for all the sighs and feverish tears they shed out of their burning longing for the nymphs. They do not understand (or accept) that in Arcadia the discourse of love *ends* in and with tears: a beloved rejects the lover; the rejected responds with tears. As an act of communication, tears do not afford further negotiation. It is the savages' error, the *soberbia* they are accused of, that they

---

65   Montemayor, *La Diana*, 186–187.

are convinced that they do not have to content themselves with shedding tears over their rejection, but that they are rather entitled to compensation for their trouble – which consists in them forcing the nymphs into submission and violating them – because of the pain they had to endure.

Since the *salvaje*'s attack, in its initial stages, consists of an explanatory statement that details both the motivation for and the expected outcome of the attack, it offers the opportunity for a reflection on what is possible in Arcadia; the episode is in effect an exposition of the rules that govern pastoral life. The *salvajes* are presented as already rejected men, who are thus already subject to the shepherds' *officium* of weeping. They deviate from it, however, because they do not accept that weeping marks the end point – and not the beginning – of the practice of pastoral love. Tears in Arcadia may be in limitless supply, but they nevertheless mark the end of the love protocol.

5   Conclusion: the Tears/Water Continuum and Arcadian Affect Management

Arcadia is, above all, a universe dedicated to, and what is more, created through discourse. As Bruce Wardropper remarked, it enables lovers to speak of love, not to live it.[66] While the practice of love at the *locus amoenus* is predominantly verbal, it is a prolonged conversation about love that regularly involves singing – and just as often weeping. If Arcadia is the landscape of love, then it is the landscape – in particular in the Spanish case – of an artificially cut down practice of love, tamed and reduced to discourse, purged of all manifestations of libidinal desire.

Male desire in particular is reduced to being expressed in speech, in verbal expressions of longing. Even those lovers who are, for a brief moment, enjoying their love (while separation inevitably looms) show their dedication to each other by way of the most restrained gestures of affection. In Montemayor's *Diana*, Sireno and Diana hold hands just once and hug just once – this being all the physical contact the two lovers are shown to have.[67]

Arcadian landscape, typically suggested only by means of a few highly coded building blocks, is closely connected with an equally highly coded rhetoric of emotion. The tears that are cried in Arcadia do not cause dripping noses and

---

66   Wardropper, "The *Diana* of Montemayor" 128.

67   See Rhodes E., "Skirting the Men: Gender Roles in Sixteenth-Century Pastoral Books", *Journal of Hispanic Philology* 11/2 (1987) 131–149, here 134. Rhodes challenges the customary view that pastoral discourse was above all informed by 'eroticism'.

THE AFFECTIVE REGIME OF THE EUROPEAN PASTORAL TRADITION 303

red eyes. Rather, '[t]hey are rhetorical tears, parts of a rhetorical game played according to rhetorical rules'.[68] Just as the standardised *locus amoenus* is a simulacrum of nature, the tears shed there are not a direct expression of authentic emotion but rather an integral part of a fictional tradition.

The inhabitants of Arcadia are not exactly torn between love and sorrow. Rather, they exist in a state of compound emotions: the default mode is that of unhappy love, with modulations happening within that register. While there is a differentiated language of tears that variably applies to emotional states from shock to regret and to sorrow, there is also a community-building practice of compassion and shared emotions that is expressed by liberally and effortlessly joining in with others' weeping. It is the Arcadian shepherds' habitual practice (*oficio*) to use tears as a comment, a response, or simply as a token of sympathy.

Arcadia's affective regime is extended to nature, which customarily resonates with the desperate lovers' sighs and tears. Yet it is specifically the mysterious interdependence between shepherds' tears and the rivers' waters that is the primary medium of Arcadia's mixed emotions; presenting as a continuum, it is by means of tears and water that the community of lovers and their communion with nature is initiated, consolidated, and eventually also terminated. As the second main storyline of Montemayor's *Diana* demonstrates, it is water that is used both in a rite of initiation into the unhappy love cult and as its cure. To make this point, a one last detour to bring to mind Felismena's back story may be in order.

Felismena, the courageous archer who defeated the *salvajes* (and who is the secret heroine of the novel), is given special treatment at Felicia's palace. While the other shepherds, including in particular Sireno, are given a drink of the magical *agua* and are cured from their mixed emotions, Felismena's cure is delayed. She is tasked with mastering further (unspecified) travails. This appears fitting since her backstory, to which almost all of Book two is dedicated, is a breathtaking adventure: After having been persistently wooed by don Felis, she falls in love with him. But his father opposes the marriage and sends Felis away to the court of the princess Augusta Cesarina. Lovesick Felismena dresses as a man in order to be able to trail his steps. Upon her arrival at court she is promptly recruited as a page for the very same don Felis, who has, however, shifted his romantic intentions to the noble Celia in the meantime. Broken-hearted Felismena puts on a shepherdess' dress and flees the town to eventually join the Arcadian community of unhappy lovers.

---

68   Lange M.E., *Telling Tears in the English Renaissance* (Leiden: 1996) 63.

In the *Diana*'s Book seven, following the sojourn at Felicia's palace, Felismena is again on the road as a *pastora* when she overhears fighting noises, only to spot a single knight who has to ward off three aggressors. He is only able to fend off one of them before getting in dire straits. As she did against the *salvajes* in Book one, Felismena again intervenes with her bow and defeats the remaining aggressors. The relieved *caballero* removes his helmet – it is none other than don Felis. Felismena allows herself to be recognised as his spurned lover and is prepared to accept this state as her permanent fate:

> En traje de dama te he querido como nunca nadie quiso; en hábito de paje te serví, en la cosa más contraria a mi descanso que se puede imaginar, y aun ahora en traje de pastora vine a hacerte este pequeño servicio. Ya no me queda más que hacer si no es sacrificar la vida a tu desamor si te parece que debo hacello, y que tú no te has de acordar de lo mucho que te he querido y quiero [...].[69]

> In the dress of a lady I have loved thee as no one ever loved thee; in the habit of a page I served thee, in the most contrary thing to my rest that can be imagined; and even now in the dress of a shepherdess I have come to do thee this little service. There is nothing left for me to do but to sacrifice my life to your unlove, if it seems to you that I must do so, and that you must not remember how much I have loved and loved you.

Yet Felis asks for forgiveness, and Felismena is prepared to grant it because 'si pensara no perdonalle, no se hubiera por su causa puesto a tantos trabajos' ('if she had thought of not forgiving him, she would not have put herself to so much trouble for his sake').[70] Now the nymphs can declare the end of Felismena's *trabajos* and announce that her contentment is imminent ('el fin de tus trabajos es llegado y el principio de tu contentamiento').[71] Unlike Sireno, who was freed from his passion by having been made to forget about Diana through Felicia's potion, Felismena is headed towards a mutual and contented relationship with Felis, which is equally outside the Arcadian affective regime. Yet the administering of Felicia's potion is still necessary for them to achieve this state. The ritual, however, is different this time. Now the nymphs present two cups, one in silver, one in gold. Before they make Felis drink from the golden cup in order for him to achieve amorous contentment, they splash his face with water from

---

69   Montemayor, *La Diana* 373.
70   Montemayor, *La Diana* 375.
71   Montemayor, *La Diana* 374.

the silver cup. Obviously simulating tears streaming down his face, the sprayed water clearly signifies Felis' initiation to the community of suffering lovers. It is only then that he can be administered the aquatic cure that signifies both the beginning of his reciprocal, contented relationship with Felismena and the relinquishment of the Arcadian affective regime.

Just like tears, water assumes several and even diametrically opposed qualities in Arcadian affect management. By way of Felicia's magic, it is specifically water, which is otherwise shown as continuous with pastoral tears, that is used to set an end point to the endless streaming of tears. At the same time, the swelling of rivers from copious amounts of tears that are being shed for lost love is a dynamic image in an otherwise constant and equilibrious nature. Curiously, the rivers are only ever described as swelling, never as calming down or even drying out. More than anything else, this speaks to the interest in the dynamics inherent in compound emotions, and in general to the effort of grasping the transient experience of *motus mixti*.

Bibliography

Sources

Aulnoy Marie-Catherine d', *Relation du voyage d'Espagne*, vol. 3 (The Hague, Henry van Bulderen: [2]1692).

Cervantes Miguel de, *La Galatea*, ed. F. López Estrada – M.L. Gracía Berdoy (Madrid: 2011).

Cervantes Miguel de, *El ingenioso hidalgo Don Quijote de la Mancha*, ed. L.A. Murillo, 2 vols. (Madrid: 1978).

Cervantes Miguel de, *Los trabajos de Persiles y Sigismunda*, ed. C. Romero Muñoz (Madrid: 2004).

Montemayor Jorge de, *La Diana*, ed. J. Montero (Madrid: 1996).

Montemayor Jorge de, *Los siete libros de La Diana*, ed. A. Rallo (Madrid: 2008).

Garcilaso de la Vega, *Poesías castellanas completas*, ed. E.L. Rivers (Madrid: 1996).

León Luis de, "La perfecta casada", in León Luis de, *Obras completas castellanas*, ed. F. García (Madrid: [3]1959) 233–342.

Lope de Vega, *Arcadia, prosa y versos*, ed. A. Sánchez Jiménez (Madrid: 2012).

Núñez de Reinoso Alonso, *Los amores de clareo y Florisea y los trabajos de la sin ventura Isea*, ed. M.A. Teijeiro Fuentes (Cáceres: 1991).

Petrarca Francesco, *Canzoniere*, ed. M. Santagata (Milan: 1996).

Plutarch, "On the Control of Anger (De cohibenda ira)", in Plutarch, *Moralia*. Vol. 6, trans. W.C. Helmbold (Cambridge, MA: 1939) 89–159.

Sannazaro Jacopo, *Opere volgari*, ed. A. Mauro (Bari: 1961).

Thomas Aquinas, *Summa theologiae. Latin text and English translation, introductions, notes, appendices, and glossaries*. Vol. 20. *Pleasure (1a2ae. 31–39)* (London: 1975).

Virgil, *Eclogues. Georgics. Aeneid: Books 1–6*, trans. H. Rushton Fairclough, rev. G.P. Goold (Cambridge, MA: 1999).

Vives Juan Luis, "De anima et vita", in Juan Luis Vives, *Opera omnia*, ed. G. Mayans y Siscar, vol. 3 (Valencia, Benito Monfort: 1782) 300–520.

Vives Juan Luis, "Bucolicorum Vergilii interpretatio potissimum Allegorica", in Juan Luis Vives, *Opera omnia*, ed. G. Mayans y Siscar, vol. 2 (Valencia, Benito Monfort: 1782) 5–71.

Vives Juan Luis, *El alma y la vida*, trans. and ed. I. Roca (Valencia: 1992).

Secondary Literature

Avalle Arce J.B., *La novela pastoril española* (Madrid: 1974).

Balguerie V., "Voyage en terre colonisatrice: Relation du Voyage d'Espagne de Marie-Catherine d'Aulnoy", *Early Modern French Studies* (2023) 1–15.

Barthes R., *Fragments d'un discours amoureux* (Paris: 1977).

Benke C., *Die Gabe der Tränen. Zur Tradition und Theologie eines vergessenen Kapitels der Glaubensgeschichte* (Würzburg: 2002).

Brusa P. – Traninger A., *Lesekontext und Affektregime: Probleme der Gattungsmischung in der Erzählprosa des Siglo de Oro*, Working Papers der FOR 2350 "Diskursivierungen von Neuem" 11 (Berlin: 2018) http://dx.doi.org/10.17169/refubium-508.

Büttner F., "Zur Geschichte der Marienantiphon 'Salve Regina'", *Archiv für Musikwissenschaft* 46/4 (1989) 257–270.

Capp B., "'Jesus Wept' but did the Englishman? Masculinity and Emotion in Early Modern England", *Past and Present* 224 (2014), 75–108.

Carter P., "Tears and the Man", in Knott S. (ed.), *Women, Gender, and Enlightenment* (Basingstoke: 2005) 156–173.

Castillo Martínez C., "De las lágrimas a la risa: análisis de la decadencia de los libros de pastores", in Lobato M.L. – Domínguez-Matito F. (eds.), *Memoria de la palabra. Actas del VI Congreso de la Asociación Internacional Siglo de Oro. Burgos-La Rioja, 15–19 de julio 2002*, 2 vols. (Frankfurt/Main: 2004) vol. 1, 497–510.

Christian Jr. W.A., "Provoked Religious Weeping in Early Modern Spain", in Davis J. (ed.), *Religious Organization and Religious Experience* (London – New York: 1982) 97–114.

Cull J.T., "Androgyny in the Spanish Pastoral Novels", *Hispanic Review* 57 (1989) 317–334.

Curtius E.R., *Europäische Literatur und lateinisches Mittelalter* (Tübingen: 11 1993).

Damiani B.M., "Realismo histórico y social de *La Diana* de Jorge de Montemayor", in Kossoff A.D. et al. (eds.), *Actas del VIII congreso de la Asociación Internacional de Hispanistas 22–27 agosto 1983*, 2 vols. (Madrid: 1983) vol. 1, 422–431.

Damiani B.M. – Mujica B., *Et in Arcadia Ego. Essays on Death in the Pastoral Novel* (Lanham – New York – London: 1990).

Del Río Barredo M.J., "Espacios de mujeres en el Madrid del siglo XVII: el estrado, entre la casa y la calle", in Amelang J.S. et al. (eds.) *Palacios, plazas, patíbulos: La sociedad española moderna entre el cambio y las resistencias* (Valencia: 2018) 789–800.

Egido A., *El gran teatro de Calderón. Personajes, temas, escenografía* (Kassel: 1995).

García Abad A., "Sobre la patria de la *Diana*", *Revista de literatura* 27/53–54 (1965) 67–77.

García Garrosa M.J., *La retórica de las lágrimas. La comedia sentimental española, 1751–1802* (Valladolid: 1990).

Gazzetti M., "Das selten glückliche Zusammentreffen von weiblicher Maßlosigkeit und männlicher Attacke", in Gazzetti M. (ed.), *Der Liebesangriff – "Il dolce assalto". Von Nymphen, Satyrn und Wäldern. Von einer Möglichkeit, über die Liebe zu sprechen = Rowohlt Literaturmagazin Sonderheft* 32 (1993) 21–42.

Gumbrecht H.U., *Eine Geschichte der spanischen Literatur*, 2 vols. (Frankfurt/Main: 1990).

Helly D.O. – Reverby S.M. (eds.) *Gendered Domains: Rethinking Public and Private in Women's History* (Ithaca, NY: 2018).

Hempfer K.W., "Ariosts *Orlando Furioso*. Die (De-)Konstruktion von Helden im generisch pluralen Diskurs", in Aurnhammer A. – Pfister M. (eds.), *Heroen und Heroisierungen in der Renaissance* (Wiesbaden: 2013) 45–69.

Hernández-Pecoraro R., *Bucolic Metaphors. History, Subjectivity, and Gender in the Early Modern Spanish Pastoral* (Chapel Hill: 2006).

Iventosch H., "Cervantes and Courtly Love: The Grisóstomo-Marcela Episode of *Don Quixote*", *PMLA* 89/1 (1974) 64–76.

Johnson C.B., "Montemayor's Diana: A Novel Pastoral", *Bulletin of Hispanic Studies* 48/1 (1971) 20–35.

Klibansky R. – Panofsky E. – Saxl F., *Saturn and Melancholy: Studies in the History of Natural Philosophy, Religion, and Art* (Montreal: 2019).

Köhler E., "Wandlungen Arkadiens: die Marcela-Episode des 'Don Quijote' (I, 11–14)", in Köhler E., *Esprit und arkadische Freiheit. Aufsätze aus der Welt der Romania* (Frankfurt/Main – Bonn: 1966) 302–327.

Krauss W., "Localización y desplazamientos en la novela pastoril española", in Sánchez Romeralo J. – Poulussen N. (eds.), *Actas del Segundo Congreso Internacional de Hispanistas* (Nijmegen: 1967) 363–369.

Kuehn T. – Schutte A.J., "Introduction", in Schutte A.J. – Kuehn T. – Seidel Menchi S. (eds.), *Time, Space, and Women's Lives in Early Modern Europe* (University Park: 2002) ix–xix.

Lange M.E., *Telling Tears in the English Renaissance* (Leiden: 1996).

Lavocat F., *La Syrinx au bûcher. Pan et les satyres à la Renaissance et à l'âge baroque* (Geneva: 2005).

Martínez-Góngora M., *Discursos sobre la mujer en el humanismo renacentista español: los casos de Antonio de Guevara, Alfonso y Juan de Valdés y Luis de León* (York, SC: 1999).

Matzat W., "Subjektivität im spanischen Schäferroman", in Friedlein R. – Poppenberg G. – Volmer A. (eds.), *Arkadien in den romanischen Literaturen. Zu Ehren von Sebastian Neumeister zum 70. Geburtstag* (Heidelberg: 2008) 21–39.

Moreno Báez E., "Prólogo", in Jorge de Montemayor, *Los siete libros de La Diana*, ed. E. Moreno Báez (Madrid: 1955) XXVII–XCII.

Mujica B., "Lope de Vega's *Arcadia*: A Step Toward the Modern Novel", *Hispanic Journal* 2 (1981) 27–49.

Nagy P., *Le Don des larmes au Moyen Âge. Un instrument spirituel en quête d'institution, V^e–XIIIe siècle* (Paris: 2000).

Panofsky E., "Et in Arcadia Ego: On the Conception of Transience in Poussin and Watteau", in Klibansky R. – Paton H.J. (eds.), *Philosophy and History: Essays Presented to Ernst Cassirer* (Oxford: 1936) 223–254.

Patton K.C. – Hawley J.S. (eds.), *Weeping in the Religious Imagination* (Princeton, NJ – Oxford: 2005).

Petriconi H., "Die verlorenen Paradiese", *Romanistisches Jahrbuch* 10 (1959) 167–199.

Redondo A., *Otra manera de leer* El Quijote (Madrid: 1997).

Rhodes E., "Skirting the Men: Gender Roles in Sixteenth-Century Pastoral Books", *Journal of Hispanic Philology* 11/2 (1987) 131–149.

Rivers E.L., "The Pastoral Paradox of Natural Art", in Rivers E.L., *Talking and Text: Essays on the Literature of Golden Age Spain* (Delaware: 2009) 83–101.

Schnell R., "Historische Emotionsforschung", *Mittelalterliche Studien* 38 (2005) 173–276.

Schöner E., *Das Viererschema in der antiken Humoralpathologie* (Wiesbaden: 1964).

Schönherr G., *Jorge de Montemayor. Sein Leben und sein Schäferroman, die 'Siete libros de la Diana'* (Halle/Saale: 1886).

Scott J.W., "Fantasy Echo: History and the Construction of Identity", *Critical Inquiry* 27/2 (2001) 284–304.

Shepard S. – Shepard M., "Death in Arcadia. The Psychological Atmosphere of Cervantes' *Galatea*", in Labrador Herraiz J.J. – Fernández Jiménez J. (eds.), *Cervantes and the Pastoral* (Cleveland, OH: 1986) 157–168.

Snell B., "Arkadien. Die Entdeckung einer geistigen Landschaft (1945/1955)", in Garber K. (ed.), *Europäische Bukolik und Georgik* (Darmstadt: 1976) 14–43.

Söntgen B. – Spiekermann G., "Tränen. Ausdruck – Darstellung – Kommunikation. Eine Einführung", in Söntgen B. – Spiekermann G. (eds.), *Tränen* (Munich: 2008) 9–16.

Strosetzki C., "Arkadiens Grenzen: Natur und Naturzustand", in Friedlein R. – Poppenberg G. – Volmer A. (eds.), *Arkadien in den romanischen Literaturen. Zu Ehren von Sebastian Neumeister zum 70. Geburtstag* (Heidelberg: 2008) 161–174.

Tausiet M., "Agua en los ojos: El 'don de lágrimas' en la España moderna", in Tausiet M. – Amelang J.S. (eds.), *Accidentes del alma. Las emociones en la Edad Moderna* (Madrid: 2009) 167–202.

Teijeiro Fuentes M.Á., "La novela bizantina: de la antigüedad pagana al contrarreformismo cristiano", in Teijeiro Fuentes, M.Á. – Guijarro Ceballos J. (eds.), *De los caballeros andantes a los peregrinos enamorados. La novela española en el Siglo de Oro* (Cáceres – Madrid: 2007) 111–175.

Ulbrich C., "Tränenspektakel. Die Lebensgeschichte der Luise Charlotte von Schwerin (1731) zwischen Frömmigkeitspraxis und Selbstinszenierung", *L'Homme* 23/1 (2012) 27–42.

Vaught J.C., "Men who Weep and Wail: Masculinity and Emotion in Sidney's *New Arcadia*", *History Compass* 2/1 (2005) 1–16.

Vincent-Buffault A., *Histoire des larmes, XVIIIᵉ–XIXᵉ siècles* (Marseille: 1986).

Wallace J.C., "El llanto como elemento dramático en *La Galatea*", in Labrado Herraiz J.J. – Fernández Jiménez J. (eds.), *Cervantes and the Pastoral* (Cleveland, OH: 1986) 185–196.

Wardropper B.W., "The *Diana* of Montemayor: Revaluation and Interpretation", *Studies in Philology* 48 (1951) 126–144.

Warning R., "Petrarcas Tal der Tränen. Poetische Konterdiskursivität im Canzoniere", in Hempfer K.W. – Regn G. (eds.), *Petrarca-Lektüren. Gedenkschrift für Alfred Noyer-Weidner* (Stuttgart: 2003) 225–246.

Wehle W., "Menschwerdung in Arkadien: Die Wiedergeburt der Anthropologie aus dem Geist der Kunst", in Wehle W. (ed.), *Über die Schwierigkeiten, (s)ich zu sagen: Horizonte literarischer Subjektkonstitution* (Frankfurt/Main: 2001) 83–106.

Weinand H.G., *Tränen. Untersuchungen über das Weinen in der deutschen Sprache und Literatur des Mittelalters* (Bonn: 1958).

CHAPTER 9

'How We Weep and Laugh at the Same Thing': Conflicting Emotions in Rabelais and Montaigne

Paul J. Smith

Abstract

The oppositional theme of joy and sadness plays an essential role in the work of Rabelais and Montaigne. In thematising these emotions, both Rabelais and Montaigne set themselves against traditional discourses on them, each in their own way. Rabelais uses the theme as a source for laughter and literary parody, but also, in his paratexts, as a source for metadiscursive reflection on his own authorship. For Montaigne, in the first instance, that is, in the 1580 edition of the *Essais*, scholarly but conversational reflection on these emotions has the function of self-advertising that focuses on the French king Henri III as implied reader. In the second instance, in the 1588 and 1595 editions of the *Essais*, when self-advertising is no longer necessary, the thematisation of joy and sadness takes on a more and more personal character.

Keywords

Gargantua and *Pantagruel* – Montaigne's *Essays* – Palace Academy of Henry III – joy – sadness – *perplexitas*

1 Introduction

This chapter addresses the topic 'conflicting and shifting emotions' in the work of the two most important prose writers of 16th-century France: François Rabelais and Michel de Montaigne. I will limit my argument to two opposing emotions: joy and sadness. The opposition between these two emotions forms the very basis of the writing of Rabelais, the author of the comic narratives about the giants Gargantua and Pantagruel. One of the most quoted passages from Rabelais – 'Mieux est de ris que de larmes escrire, / Pource que rire est le propre de l'homme' – can be found in the threshold poem "Aux lecteurs"

© PAUL J. SMITH, 2025 | DOI:10.1163/9789004694613_010

CONFLICTING EMOTIONS IN RABELAIS AND MONTAIGNE

from his book *Gargantua* (1535).[1] As the subject of his writing, Rabelais opts for laughter, and rejects sadness:

> Vray est qu'icy peu de perfection
> Vous apprendrez, si non en cas de rire :
> Autre argument ne peut mon coeur elire,
> Voyant le deuil qui vous mine et consomme,
> Mieux est de ris que de larmes escrire,
> Pource que rire est le propre de l'homme.[2]

> Little perfection here may hide
> Save laughter: little else you'll find
> No other theme comes to my mind
> Seeing such gloom your joy doth ban.
> My pen's to laughs not tears assigned.
> Laughter's the property of Man.[3]

The last line is a translation of the tag 'Risus proprium hominis', a cliché, which can be traced back to Aristotle, and which was much quoted and discussed by scholastics in the Middle Ages and by humanists in the 16th century.[4] There is no unanimity among the Rabelais scholars as to whether (and if so, to what extent) Rabelais, in his critique of scholastics, would have parodied this cliché.[5]

Be that as it may, this tag is a trait d'union between Rabelais and Montaigne. It forms the conclusion of Montaigne's chapter "On Democritus and Heraclitus",[6]

---

1   All quotations from Rabelais refer to Rabelais François, *Œuvres complètes*, ed. M. Huchon (Paris: 1994). English translations of Rabelais are taken from Rabelais François, *Gargantua and Pantagruel*, transl. M.A. Screech (London: 2006).

2   Rabelais, *Œuvres* 3.

3   Rabelais, *Gargantua and Pantagruel* 203.

4   For an overview, see Bowen B.C., *Enter Rabelais, Laughing* (Nashville – London: 1998) 19–28.

5   Thus, for Romain Menini the final verse of the dizain is a parody in imitation of Lucian, who mocks such futile sophistic distinctions as: 'man is capable of laughter, and a donkey is not' (Lucian, *Bion Prasis* [The Auction of Lives]); see Menini R., *Rabelais altérateur* (Geneva: 2014) 544–547. Other critics are more cautious: La Charité C., "Les *Angeli Politiani Opera* (Lyon, S. Gryphe, 1533) et ce que d'iceulx Rabelais a desrobé pour son *Gargantua*", *L'Année rabelaisienne* 3 (2019) 57–69 (here 62–63), and Cappellen R., "Sur quelques vers en quête d'auteur(s). Les emprunts poétiques dans l'œuvre de Rabelais", in Huchon M. – Le Cadet N. – Menini R. – Thomine M.-C. (eds.), *Inextinguible Rabelais* (Paris: 2021) 223–246 (here 240–246).

6   As is customary in contemporary Montaigne criticism, I use the term 'chapter' here, following Montaigne's own usage, and not 'essay', as is the customary practice in less specialised works.

but in an interesting variant: '[a]Notre propre condition est autant ridicule que risible' (Our own specific property is to be equally laughable and able to laugh).[7] This conclusion stems from the choice Montaigne makes: he prefers the laughing Democritus to the weeping Heraclitus. Montaigne comes to this choice by the following argumentation:

> I prefer [Democritus's] temperament, not because it is more agreeable to laugh than to weep but because it is more disdainful and condemns us men more than the other – and it seems to me that [...] we cannot be despised enough. Lamentation and compassion are mingled with some respect for the things we are lamenting: the things which we mock are judged to be worthless. I do not think that there is so much wretchedness in us as vanity; we are not so much wicked as daft; we are not so much pitiful as despicable.[8]

The subject of joy and sadness is also addressed by Montaigne from a very different perspective in his chapter "How we weep and laugh at the same thing" – we will focus on this chapter in particular. We will see how, in dealing with this topic, both authors, Rabelais and Montaigne, respond to discussions of their time.

2 'Ho' and 'Ha' – Rabelais on Joy and Sadness in the Context of *perplexitas*

Let us start with a chapter from the beginning of Rabelais' first published book, entitled *Pantagruel* (1532), named after its protagonist, the comic giant Pantagruel. According to the literary and rhetorical conventions, after the hero's genealogy (*genus*), the miraculous birth of the hero is told (*genesis*).[9] The mother Badebec gives birth to a son so large that she dies in childbirth. The father, Gargantua, doesn't know whether he should be sad at the death of

---

7 All quotations from Montaigne refer to Montaigne Michel de, *Œuvres complètes*, ed. A. Thibaudet – M. Rat (Paris: 1962). English translations of Montaige are taken from Montaigne Michel de, *The Complete Essays*, transl. M.A. Screech (Harmondsworth: 1991). With a few exceptions, for the sake of the readability of this contribution, I will only quote Montaigne in translation. The indications (a), (b) and (c) refer to the textual layers of the three principal editions of the *Essais*, 1580, 1588, and 1594 respectively.

8 Montaigne, *The Complete Essays* 339.

9 See Smith P.J., *Dispositio: Problematic Ordering in French Renaissance Literature* (Leiden – Boston: 2007) 29–31.

CONFLICTING EMOTIONS IN RABELAIS AND MONTAIGNE 313

his wife or happy at the birth of his son Pantagruel. He is 'ebahy et perplex': the word 'perplex' must be understood as a technical term: Gargantua is in a state of *perplexitas*, perplexity.[10]

This episode needs a close reading. The episode is particularly dense and complex, as it is subject to a continual shifting, not only from one emotion to another, but also from reason to passion, and the other way round. There is also shifting from satire (of scholastic argumentation) to literary parody (of the *deploratio* – the funeral mourning), and, within the treatment of each emotion, the shift of register: from high to low. This is how the initial stage of Gargantua's internal conflict is explained:

> Le doubte que troubloit son entendement estoit assavoir s'il devoit plorer pour le deuil de sa femme, ou rire pour la joye de son filz. D'un costé et d'aultre il avoit argumens sophisticques qui le suffocquoyent, car il les faisoit très bien *in modo et figura*, mais il ne les povoit souldre, et, par ce moyen demouroit empestré comme la souriz empeigée ou un milan prins au lasset.[11]

> The doubt which troubled his mind was namely this: ought he to weep out of grief for his wife or laugh out of joy for his son? He had good dialectical arguments for both sides. They choked him, for he could marshall them very well in syllogistic modes and figures but he could come to no conclusion. So he remained caught like a mouse in pitch, or a kite in the nets of a fowler.[12]

The comparison with a mouse stuck in pitch may have been inspired by Erasmus's adagium *Mus in pice*,[13] and is also used elsewhere by Rabelais to indicate perplexity.[14]

---

10 On *perplexitas* in Rabelais and other 16th-century authors, see Geonget S., *La notion de perplexité à la Renaissance* (Geneva: 2006).

11 Rabelais, *Œuvres* 225.

12 Rabelais, *Gargantua and Pantagruel* 25.

13 This adagium is also used by Montaigne, *The Complete Essays* 1211 (III, 13, "On experience"). Most critics see this as borrowing from Erasmus, "Mus picem gustans", in *Adages*, II, iii, 68. However, Michel Magnien points to an old legal adage closer to Montaigne and Rabelais than to Erasmus's "Mus picem gustans"; see Magnien M., "Montaigne et Érasme: bilan et perspectives", in Smith P.J. – Enenkel K.A.E. (eds.), *Montaigne and the Low Countries (1580–1700)* (Leiden – Boston: 2007) 17–45 (here 28 n. 27).

14 Rabelais, *Œuvres* 467; idem, *Gargantua and Pantagruel* 551.

This initial situation marks the start of an intertextual play with literary conventions and genres. After this initial passage we first get a parody of the funeral *deploratio*:

> O mon dieu, que te avoys je faict pour ainsi me punir? Que ne envoyas tu la mort à moy premier que à elle? car vivre sans elle ne m'est que languir.[15]

> O God of mine! What have I done that you should punish me so? Why didn't you send death to me rather than her? To live without her is for me but to languish.[16]

The combination 'mourir', 'vivre' and 'languir' is commonplace in French elegiac and love poetry since the Middle Ages. Thus, in the poetry of the poet-prince Charles d'Orleans, we find the verse 'Car mieulx me vault tout à ung cop morir / Que longuement en desaise languir' (For I would rather die suddenly than slowly languish in grief)[17] and elsewhere: 'Car j'ayme mieulx prouchainement / Mourir, que languir en tourment' (For I would rather die soon, than languish in torment).[18]

After this initial sentence there is an abrupt comical shift from high, serious poetry to a low, scabrous and saucy non-poetical register:

> Ha Badebec, ma mignonne, mamye, mon petit con (toutesfois elle en avait bien troys arpens et deux sexterées) ma tendrette, ma braguette, ma savate, ma pantofle jamais je ne te verray.[19]

> Alas, Badebec, my sweeting, my beloved, my quim so little and lovely – hers covered three acres and two square poles though – my tenderling, my codpiece, my slippers, my slip-on: never again shall I see you![20]

Then Gargantua returns to the high register of the elegy:

> Ha faulce mort tant tu me es malivole, tant tu me es oultrageuse de me tollir celle à laquelle immortalité appartenoit de droict.[21]

---

15   Rabelais, *Œuvres* 225.
16   Rabelais, *Gargantua and Pantagruel* 25.
17   Charles d'Orléans, *Poésies*, ed. P. Champion (Paris: 1966) 9.
18   Charles d'Orléans, *Poésies* 81.
19   Rabelais, *Œuvres* 225.
20   Rabelais, *Gargantua and Pantagruel* 25.
21   Rabelais, *Œuvres* 225.

CONFLICTING EMOTIONS IN RABELAIS AND MONTAIGNE   315

> Ha, false Death, how malevolent, how cruel you are, to take from me her
> who, as of right, deserves immortality.[22]

The vocabulary deployed is appropriate for high-pitched elegiac poetry: 'faulce
mort' is a frequently used apostrophe in elegiac poetry; 'malivole' is a recent
latinism, that belongs to the elevated style;[23] 'oultrageuse' is an epithet, frequently used in conjunction with 'mort' in the 16th century;[24] and 'tollir' is a
word regularly used by Rabelais, but already archaic in the 16th century (and to
which Rabelais wants to give its original Latin form).[25]

Then follows a transition sentence:

> Et ce disant pleuroit comme une vache, mais tout soubdain rioit comme
> un veau, quand Pantagruel luy venoit en memoire.[26]

> And so saying he bellowed like a cow. Then all of a sudden he remem-
> bered Pantagruel, and began to laugh like a calf.[27]

This is a variation on the early modern popular expression 'pleurer comme une
vache', to which Rabelais adds the phrase 'rire comme un veau', laugh like a calf
('calf' in the sense of "fool").[28]

The sadness is characterised by the plaintive exclamation 'Ha'; the merri-
ment is displayed with the exclamation 'Ho'. The passage from 'Ha' to 'Ho' parallels the passage from high to low register, as can be seen in the use of the
words 'coillon' and 'peton':

> Ho mon petit filz (disoit il) mon coillon, mon peton, que tu es joly, et tant
> je suis tenu à dieu de ce qu'il m'a donné un si beau filz tant joyeux, tant
> riant, tant joly! Ho, ho, ho, ho, que suis ayse, beuvons ho, laissons toute
> melancholie.[29]

---

22 Rabelais, *Gargantua and Pantagruel* 25.
23 Sainéan L., *La Langue de Rabelais. II. Langue et vocabulaire* (Paris: 1923) 76.
24 See for instance La Porte Maurice de, *Les épithètes* (Paris, Gabriel Buon: 1582) fol. 272r.,
    s.v. 'mort'.
25 Godefroy F., *Dictionnaire de l'ancienne langue française*. Tome septième (Paris: 1892) 737,
    s.v. 'tolir'.
26 Rabelais, *Œuvres* 225.
27 Rabelais, *Gargantua and Pantagruel* 25.
28 See Rey A., *Dictionnaire historique de la langue française* (Paris: 2022), s.v. 'veau'.
29 Rabelais, *Œuvres* 225–226.

'O my little son,' he said. 'My little bullock, my imp, how pretty you are; how beholden I am to God for having given me so fine a son, one so happy, so laughing, so pretty. Ho, ho! Ho, ho! How joyful am I! Let us drink, ho! And banish all melancholy'.[30]

Then follows a third stage, again in the high register:

> Ce disant ouyt la letanie et les mementos des prebstres qui portoyent sa femme en terre, dont laissa son bon propos et tout soubdain fut ravy ailleurs, disant, 'Seigneur dieu, fault il que je me contriste encores?'[31]

> As he was saying that, he heard the litany and the dirges of the priests as they bore his wife to her grave. At which he gave over his happy talk and was caught away in ecstasy, saying: 'Jesus! Must I go on being sad?'[32]

A kind of divine intervention takes place, which transports Gargantua into ecstasy, and extricates him from perplexity: there is no need to be sad, because Badebec is in heaven, and is happier than we are.

According to Stéphan Geonget, in his study *La notion de perplexité*, we are dealing here with the second of the three types of perplexity distinguished by the scholastics. 'La première consiste en une hésitation sur le sens d'un passage de la Bible, la deuxième sur un comportement et la troisième sur le moyen de sortir d'une situation de péché nécessaire' (The first consists of a hesitation on the meaning of a passage of the Bible, the second on a behavior and the third on the way out of a situation of necessary sin).[33] Gargantua's perplexity corresponds to the second type of perplexity, which, according to the scholastic William of Auxerre, in his *Summa aurea*, referring to Augustinus, 'can only be solved one way, namely by the Spirit'.[34]

The theme of perplexity in Rabelais is a comic theme, which is at the basis of entire episodes, and even books: This is, for example, the case with the character Panurge, who does not know whether to marry or not – another well-known topic of scholastic debate. Just like Gargantua, Panurge is also compared to a mouse stuck in pitch.[35] His doubts provide the rationale for a

---

30   Rabelais, *Gargantua and Pantagruel* 25.
31   Rabelais, *Œuvres* 226.
32   Rabelais, *Gargantua and Pantagruel* 26.
33   Geonget, *La notion de perplexité* 295.
34   Ibidem.
35   Rabelais, *Œuvres* 467, and idem, *Gargantua and Pantagruel* 551.

CONFLICTING EMOTIONS IN RABELAIS AND MONTAIGNE 317

long series of consultations on the pros and cons of marriage in the *Third Book* of Rabelais, and, as a result of those unsuccessful consultations, a quest for the oracle of the Dive Bouteille (which can be seen as a parody of the Holy Grail), which occupies the entire *Fourth* and *Fifth Books*.

A good example of perplexity, but which cannot be placed exactly in the above mentioned scholastic scheme, is the episode of the sophist Janotus de Bragmodo, who, half drunk, coughing and spluttering, delivers a speech in a hybrid macaronic mixture of French and kitchen Latin. The audience bursts out laughing, and Janotus then laughs along unwillingly – which ends in a fit of laughter that seizes everyone. Let's take a closer look at the scene:

> Ensemble eulx, commença rire maistre Janotus, à qui mieulx, mieulx, tant que les larmes leurs venoient es yeulx : par la vehemente concution de la substance du cerveau: à laquelle furent exprimées ces humiditez lachrymales, et transcoullées jouxte les nerfz optiques. En quoy par eulx estoyt Democrite Heraclitizant, et Heraclyte Democritizant representé.[36]

> Magister Janotus began to laugh with them, each outdoing the other until tears came to their eyes from the mind-shaking concussion of the matter of their brains by which the lachrimatory fluids were expressed and sent flowing around the optic nerves. By which, in them, Democritus was shown heraclitizing and Heraclitus democritizing.[37]

This combination of laughing and weeping is important for our argument, in which the opposing figures Heraclitus and Democritus coincide. In the end, it is laughter that wins. Notable in this passage is the medical terminology ('concution', 'substance', 'humiditez lachrymales', 'nerfz optiques') used to describe the phenomenon of laughter.

This medical perspective is also important for describing the relationship between writer and reader. In his many Prologues Rabelais, who was a medical doctor himself, regularly returns to the therapeutic effect of literature. The reader is seen as a patient suffering from an excess of black bile. The reader's condition is described in the same terms as Gargantua's perplexity at the birth of his son and the death of his wife. Reading the comic books about Gargantua and Pantagruel quickly moves the reader from gloom to joy.

This healing power of literature is a literary commonplace in the 16th century. What is not commonplace is the comic exaggeration of this topic: Rabelais

---

36   Rabelais, *Œuvres* 53.
37   Rabelais, *Gargantua and Pantagruel* 265.

not only makes us laugh by using this commonplace, but he also makes us laugh *at* this commonplace. He already does so in the Prologue of his first book *Pantagruel*. The commonplace of the healing book is drawn into the absurd: The book heals against the sadness of a failed hunt, but also against a toothache, if you put the book on the sore spot of the cheek, and finally the book is a tried and tested remedy for syphilis.[38]

To summarise: in Rabelais we find laughter that is accompanied by a reflection on laughter, or that wants to provoke in the reader a reflection about laughter. It is striking that Rabelais is aware of the many theories about passions and emotions, especially joy and sadness, but that he refuses to go into them in a methodical way. If he already refers to existing theories, he does so in a comical way, whereby it is usually unclear whether he really accepts (or rejects) the theories.

3   Montaigne on Joy and Sadness

Recent studies, such as Anita Traninger's on Montaigne's chapter on anger,[39] have shown that Montaigne, in his discussion of emotions, responds to intellectual discussions of his time. This is particularly true of the discourses held between 1576 and 1579 in the so-called Académie du Palais,[40] the Palace Academy, which were held at the request of King Henri III on important intellectual topics, such as the passions, and among those discourses, the six on joy and sadness.[41] What is special is that among the Academy intellectuals were several poets, not the least of them: Pibrac, Ronsard, Jamyn, Baïf and the young Desportes, who would later become Ronsard's competitor and successor. Some of these oral discourses are written out fully, others consist only of a title or a short summary. First of all, it is remarkable how much the opinions differ. But it is also remarkable how strongly the argumentation of these discourses

---

38   Smith P.J., "Le Prologue du *Pantagruel*: une lecture", *Neophilologus* 68 (1984) 161–169.

39   Traninger A., "Anger Management and the Rhetoric of Authenticity in Montaigne's *De la colère* (II, 31)", in Enenkel K.A.E. – Traninger A. (eds.), *Discourses of Anger in the Early Modern Period* (Leiden – Boston: 2015) 97–125.

40   Traninger A., "Essai und discours. Montaigne, die Praxis der Lektüre und die Académie du Palais", in Mahler A. (ed.), *Der Essay als 'neue' Form* (Wiesbaden: 2020) 99–118. On the Académie du Palais, see Frémy E., *L'Académie des derniers Valois* (Paris: 1887; Geneva: 1969), and Sealy R.J., *The Palace Academy of Henry III* (Geneva: 1981).

41   That is, Jamyn ("Des Passions humaines: de la Joye et de la Tristesse et quelle est la plus véhémente"); Ronsard ("Quelle est plus forte, aigre et poignante, la joye ou la tristesse"); and four anonymous debaters (of which two medical doctors; no titles given).

CONFLICTING EMOTIONS IN RABELAIS AND MONTAIGNE

follows a formal scholastic line of reasoning, with precisely formulated definitions, which rely strongly on Aristotelianism and on the prevailing Ramism. This applies not only to the philosophers and the medical doctors present, but also to the poets. This abstract-theoretical approach was not to the liking of the king, who decreed that examples should be given – something with which Ronsard, among others, complied.

It is against this context of formal argumentation that Montaigne's chapters on emotions should be read. According to the latest insights, formulated by Montaigne specialist Philippe Desan, Montaigne wrote his essays mainly for Henri III to present himself as a candidate for the ambassadorship in Rome.[42] This is the reason why Montaigne travelled from Bordeaux to Paris in 1580, immediately after the publication of his book, in order to personally present his book to the king. This also explains the form and content of Montaigne's first chapters. Many of the topics have a military context, dealing with special decisions of wartime leaders, combined with a great deal of attention to passion and emotion, and their unexpected and often contradictory changes: for example, whole chapters are devoted to anger, laziness, indecision, bravery, cowardice, cruelty, etc.

As in the six discourses of the Palace Academy, sadness and joy get Montaigne's attention. However, the way these emotions are handled by Montaigne is very different from the Academy's discourses on the subject – besides, as far as I know, his *Essais* do not contain any borrowing from these discourses, which he probably did not read himself. In Montaigne's working method there is no room for formally presented theoretical abstractions: instead he relies on free argument, without a rhetorical structure imposed from outside, also without an unambiguous conclusion, and in a conversational tone throughout. And contrary to the Palace Academy's discourses, Montaigne does not provide definitions – that would go against his relativistic view of life. Neither does he start from abstract Aristotelian or Ramistic definitions; he commences from historical examples, just as Henri III wished. These examples are taken from the distant and more recent past, and he explains them in an unexpected and unconventional way.

However, due to all kinds of political events, the *Essais* did not have the final desired result: the coveted Roman ambassadorship did not go to Montaigne, but the king appointed him mayor of Bordeaux. This explains why the later editions of the *Essais* become much more personal, including Montaigne's chapter "How we weep and laugh at the same thing" – as we shall see.

---

42   Desan P., *Montaigne. Une biographie politique* (Paris: 2014) 277.

4   'The Pliancy and Mutability of Our Soul' in the 1580 Edition of the *Essais*

Let's now subject this chapter to a close reading, as I did with Rabelais, and as I have done with Montaigne in some other publications.[43] I start with the text of the first edition of 1580, in text-critical editions usually indicated as textual layer (a). The chapter opens with a long syntactically complex sentence, which does not give short, concise definitions, but three historical examples,[44] as I have indicated in the diagram on the next page.

The long sentence opens with a short dependent adverbial clause, '[a]When we read in our history books', clearly indicating that historical examples are the starting point (just as Henri III wished). Then there are three dependent declarative content clauses, each containing an example, which by the way are not that well known at all. I have indicated between brackets respectively the historical events discussed (272 BC, 1477, and 1364) and the textual sources, which are very different from each other: Plutarch, Fulgosus (1508), and Froissart (end 15th century) respectively. Then follows the very brief main clause: '[a]we should not at once exclaim', followed by a quotation in Italian from the first quatrain of sonnet 81 by Petrarch – in translation: 'Thus does the mind cloak every passion with its opposite, our faces showing now joy, now sadness'. In this quotation Montaigne plays an extremely complex intertextual game. That is, Petrarch refers, in the verses not quoted by Montaigne, to Julius Caesar's remarkable mourning over the death of his opponent Pompey. It is clear that Montaigne would not agree with Petrarch's interpretation (namely, that Caesar's mourning was feigned).

Skipping three other arguments and quoted authorities – Plutarch (*Life of Caesar*), Lucan (*Pharsalia*), Publilius Syrus apud Aulus Gellius (*Noctes Atticae*)[45] – the reader comes to Montaigne's partial conclusion; to wit: You cannot just say automatically in all cases that tears are feigned, if you would logically expect joy:

> [a]For while it is true that most of our actions are but mask and cosmetic, and that it is sometimes true that

---

43   See for instance Smith, *Dispositio* 171–224.

44   Montaigne favoured argumentation in three parts, both at the macro level of the *dispositio* of the various chapters and at the micro level of sentences and phrases. See Smith P.J., "'Ma façon simple, naturelle et ordinaire': triades et trinômes chez Montaigne", in Desan P. – Knop D. – Perona B. (eds.), *Montaigne: une rhétorique naturalisée?* (Paris: 2019) 161–176.

45   I quote the references given by M.A. Screech in Montaigne, *The Complete Essays* 262–263.

CONFLICTING EMOTIONS IN RABELAIS AND MONTAIGNE

Dependent adverbial clause: When we read in our history books
Three dependent declarative content clauses:

- (1) that Antigonus was severely displeased with his son for having brought him the head of his enemy King Pyrrhus who had just been killed fighting against him and that he burst into copious tears when he saw it, [historical event: 272 BC; source: Plutarch, *Life of Pyrrhus*, circa 100 AD; translation by Jacques Amyot, 1559][a]

- (2) and that Duke René of Lorraine also lamented the death of Duke Charles of Burgundy whom he had just defeated, and wore mourning at his funeral, [historical event: 1477; source: Fulgosus, *De dictis factisque memorabilibus*, 1509][b]

- (3) and that at the battle of Auroy which the Count de Monfort won against Charles de Blois, his rival for the Duchy of Brittany, the victor showed great grief when he happened upon his enemy's corpse, [historical event: 1364; source: Froissart, *Chroniques*, II, XCCI; end 15th century][c]

Independent (or main) clause:

- we should not at once exclaim,

Quoted speech:

- 'Et cosi aven che l'animo ciascuna / Sua passion sotto et contrario manto / Ricopre, con la vista hor' chiara hor bruna' (Thus does the mind cloak every passion with its opposite, our faces showing now joy, now sadness [source: Petrarch, sonnet 81])[d]

---

a Plutarch, *Les Vies des hommes illustres*, trad. J. Amyot, ed. G. Walter. Volume I (Paris: 1951) 915. This reference and the following ones are given by the editors of Montaigne M. de, *Les Essais*, eds. J. Balsamo – M. Magnien – C. Magnien-Simonin (Paris: 2007) 1440.

b Fulgosus Baptista, *De dictis factisque memorabilibus collectanea a Camillo Gilino Latina facta* (Milano, Jacobus Ferrarius: 1509) IV, v.

c The editors of Montaigne, *Les Essais* refer more specifically to Gilles Nicole, *Annales et croniques de France* (Paris, Guillaume Le Noir: 1562) I, fol. 117v and II, fol. 130r.

d The editors of Montaigne, *Les Essais* refer to Petrarch, *Canzoniere* (Lyon, G. Rouillé: 1550) 162.

'Haeridis fletus sub persona risus est';
(Behind the mask, the tears of an heir are laughter)

nevertheless we ought to consider when judging such events how our souls are often shaken by conflicting emotions.[46]

To substantiate this, Montaigne uses first a medical comparison, and then he comes up with examples taken from everyday life. The medical perspective is given in a long sentence in which Montaigne, with his typical circumspection ('there is said to be'),[47] draws a parallel with medical humoral theory, without thereby explaining the change of emotions, because emotions, Montaigne seems to believe, are movements of the soul, not of the (medical) body. This caution and refusal to give a definition, are in stark contrast to the Palace Academy's trenchant way of arguing and defining. However, in spite of his indecisive way of arguing, Montaigne does show to his ideal reader (Henri III) that he is au courant of current scientific insights. One also notices how Montaigne weaves military imagery into his argument, which would also have been to the taste of the king:

[a]Even as there is said to be a variety of humours assembled in our bodies, the dominant one being that which normally prevails according to our complexion, so too in our souls: although diverse emotions may shake them, there is one which must remain in possession of the field; nevertheless its victory is not so complete but that the weaker ones do not sometimes regain lost ground because of the pliancy and mutability of our soul and make a brief sally in their turn.[48]

After this hypothetical medical analogy, Montaigne uses examples that are recognisable to everyone, examples from everyday life: for instance, you can be sad when you say goodbye to your friends and family, at the start of a journey that you enjoy taking; and – another example – girls who are happy to get married weep when they say goodbye to their mothers.

These are all examples of genuine, sincere emotions that are conflicting precisely because they are perceived as simultaneous. Montaigne then goes on to argue that in reality these emotions are not simultaneous. To do so, Montaigne

---

46   Montaigne, *The Complete Essays* 263. The quoted passage is Aulus Gellius, *Noctes Atticae* XVII, 14.

47   Montaigne, *The Complete Essays* 263.

48   Ibidem.

comes up with an interesting explanation for our perception of simultaneous conflicting emotions. This is indeed a question of perception, as Montaigne explains by referring to the physical phenomenon of light. Emotions follow each other so quickly that they seem to be simultaneous and therefore inexplicably contradictory:

> [a]The sun, they say, does not shed its light in one continuous flow but ceaselessly darts fresh rays so thickly at us, one after another, that we cannot perceive any gap between them.

> [b]Largus enim liquidi fons luminis, aetherius sol
> Inrigat assidue coelum candore recenti,
> Suppeditatque novo confestim lumine lumen.

> (That generous source of liquid light, the aethereal sun, assiduously floods the heavens with new rays and ceaselessly sheds light upon new light)

> [a]So, too, our soul darts its arrows separately but imperceptibly.[49]

So, everything is a matter of perception: if we observe an inexplicable emotion in someone, then that emotion may be feigned – because the emotion that is played masks the real emotion. But Montaigne shows that the emotional effect is mostly comprised by a succession of emotions, which proceed so quickly that it seems as if these emotions occur simultaneously. And if there is succession (so Montaigne argues), then the emotion in question does not have to be a feigned emotion. For man is a changeable being, and ceaselessly falls from one state of mind to another, without there being any doubt as to the sincerity of that state of mind. And therefore, you should not judge a person on the basis of a single state of mind.

If we now compare Montaigne's explanation of the mourning of historical persons with the explanation given by his source texts and the authors quoted, we see Montaigne's critical distance. In some authors (such as Fulgosus and Froissart) he finds no explanation, and he provides one himself; in others (such as Plutarch and Petrarch) he finds an explanation with which he does not (fully) agree, and which he nuances or corrects. The chapter is thus a

---

49 Montaigne, *The Complete Essays* 264. The Latin quotation in the (b) layer (translated by M.A. Screech) is from Lucretius's *De natura*, v, 282–285.

324 SMITH

wonderful example of scholarship, presented in an unlearned, conversational way – a form of indirect self-advertising, with as ideal reader, King Henri III.

5 Montaigne's 1588 and 1595 Additions

All this applies to the first edition of 1580 (textual layer [a]). If we now look at the later editions, of 1588 (textual layer [b]) and of 1595 (textual layer [c]), we see that the need for self-advertising aimed at the French king is no longer necessary. The emphasis is increasingly placed on Montaigne's own individuality – this movement towards himself we see in all his chapters. Thus, in the 1588 edition Montaigne gives the following addition:

> 1588 edition: [b]When I rail at my manservant I do so sincerely with all my mind: my curses are real not feigned. But once I cease to fume, if he needs help from me I am glad to help him: I turn over the page.[50]

And in the 1595 edition, he elaborates upon this personal example:

> 1595 edition: [c]When I call him a dolt or a calf I have no intention of stitching such labels on him for ever: nor do I believe I am contradicting myself when I later call him an honest fellow. No characteristic clasps us purely and universally in its embrace.[51]

And in 1588 he speaks of his changing attitudes towards his wife: '[b]If anyone should think when he sees me sometimes look bleakly at my wife and sometimes lovingly that either emotion is put on, then he is daft'.[52] The example of his attitude to his wife is, rather unexpectedly, immediately followed by the example of Nero's mourning for his mother, whom he had had murdered: '[b]When Nero took leave of his mother whom he was sending to be drowned, he nevertheless felt some emotion at his mother's departure and felt horror and pity'.[53] These unexpected, associative turns in his argument keep the reader on his toes. They are typical of Montaigne, who, in his chapter "On vanity", labelled ideal writing (of others, and implicitly his own) as a '[b] gait

---

50 Montaigne, *The Complete Essays* 263–264. The indication of the (b)-layer is lacking in Screech's translation.

51 Montaigne, *The Complete Essays* 264.

52 Ibidem.

53 Ibidem.

of poetry, all jumps and tumblings', and on the same page: 'I change subject violently and chaotically'.[54]

6   By Way of Conclusion

Rabelais and Montaigne give their own twist to the topic of laughter and weeping. But they both oppose the contemporary, formal way of discussing this topic. And in doing so, they show their scholarly awareness of the contemporary discussions on the topic, which allows them to formulate their own basis of their writing, each in their own inconclusive way. For Rabelais, these discussions are a source of satire and entertainment (learned or otherwise), but they also prompt a paratextual metadiscursive reflection on his work. For Montaigne, this topic serves initially (in the 1580 edition of his *Essais*) as self-advertising to present himself as an unconventional thinker, with King Henri III as an ideal intended reader, and secondly (in the 1588 and 1595 editions) as an increasingly personal case study of the instability of human action, including his own.

Bibliography

Bowen B.C., *Enter Rabelais, Laughing* (Nashville – London: 1998).

Cappellen R., "Sur quelques vers en quête d'auteur(s). Les emprunts poétiques dans l'œuvre de Rabelais", in Huchon M. – Le Cadet N. – Menini R. – Thomine M.-C. (eds.), *Inextinguible Rabelais* (Paris: 2021) 223–246.

Desan P., *Montaigne. Une biographie politique* (Paris: 2014).

Frémy E., *L'Académie des derniers Valois* (Paris: 1887; Geneva: 1969).

Fulgosus Baptista, *De dictis factisque memorabilibus collectanea a Camillo Gilino Latina facta* (Milano, Jacobus Ferrarius: 1509).

Geonget S., *La notion de perplexité à la Renaissance* (Geneva: 2006).

Gilles Nicole, *Annales et croniques de France* (Paris, Guillaume Le Noir: 1562).

Godefroy F., *Dictionnaire de l'ancienne langue française*. Tome septième (Paris: 1892).

La Charité C., "Les *Angeli Politiani Opera* (Lyon, S. Gryphe, 1533) et ce que d'iceulx Rabelais a desrobé pour son *Gargantua*", *L'Année rabelaisienne* 3 (2019) 57–69.

La Porte Maurice de, *Les épithètes* (Paris, Gabriel Buon: 1582).

---

54   Montaigne, *The Complete Essays* 1125.

Magnien M., "Montaigne et Érasme: bilan et perspectives", in Smith P.J. – Enenkel K.A.E. (eds.), *Montaigne and the Low Countries (1580–1700)* (Leiden – Boston: 2007) 17–45.

Menini R., *Rabelais altérateur* (Geneva: 2014).

Montaigne Michel de, *Œuvres complètes*, eds. A. Thibaudet – M. Rat (Paris: 1962).

Montaigne Michel de, *The Complete Essays*, transl. M.A. Screech (Harmondsworth: 1991).

Montaigne Michel de, *Les Essais*, eds. J. Balsamo – M. Magnien – C. Magnien-Simonin (Paris: 2007).

Petrarch, *Canzoniere* (Lyon, G. Rouillé: 1550).

Plutarch, *Les Vies des hommes illustres*, trad. J. Amyot, ed. G. Walter. Volume I (Paris: 1951).

Rabelais François, *Gargantua and Pantagruel*, transl. M.A. Screech (London: 2006).

Rabelais François, *Œuvres complètes*, ed. M. Huchon (Paris: 1994).

Rey A., *Dictionnaire historique de la langue française* (Paris: 2022).

Sainéan L., *La Langue de Rabelais. II. Langue et vocabulaire* (Paris: 1923).

Sealy R.J., *The Palace Academy of Henry III* (Geneva: 1981).

Smith P.J., "Le Prologue du *Pantagruel*: une lecture", *Neophilologus* 68 (1984) 161–169.

Smith P.J., *Dispositio: Problematic Ordering in French Renaissance Literature* (Leiden – Boston: 2007).

Smith P.J., "'Ma façon simple, naturelle et ordinaire': triades et trinômes chez Montaigne", in Desan P. – Knop D. – Perona B. (eds.), *Montaigne: une rhétorique naturalisée?* (Paris: 2019) 161–176.

Traninger A., "Anger Management and the Rhetoric of Authenticity in Montaigne's *De la colère* (II, 31)", in Enenkel K.A.E. – Traninger A. (eds.), *Discourses of Anger in the Early Modern Period* (Leiden – Boston: 2015) 97–125.

Traninger A., "Essai und discours. Montaigne, die Praxis der Lektüre und die Académie du Palais", in Mahler A. (ed.), *Der Essay als 'neue' Form* (Wiesbaden: 2020) 99–118.

CHAPTER 10

The Troubles of Christian Perfection: Berinzaga, Gagliardi, Borromeo

Wietse de Boer

Abstract

Conflicting emotions are a recurrent feature of early-modern meditative practices. Their role, and the appropriate strategies for handling them, were central issues in the genesis of a classic of meditative literature, the *Breve compendio intorno alla perfettione christiana*. This brief guidebook was grounded in the experiences of the Milanese mystic Isabella Berinzaga (*c.* 1551–1624), distilled from several accounts of these, and redacted by Berinzaga's Jesuit spiritual director, Achille Gagliardi (1537–1607). The present chapter shows how the mystic's meditative ventures, originally cast in the mold of spiritual exercises, were transformed into a method of denial of the will. Paradoxically, this method both generated and was meant to transcend conflicting emotions. Berinzaga's experiences, her relationship with her spiritual director, and the resulting program all became contested and led to official prohibitions. To explain the cultural context, including the operative language of emotion, the chapter contrasts the *Compendio* with a contemporary work of moral psychology, Lelio Pellegrini's *De affectionibus animi noscendis et emendandis*. This book offered an alternative regimen of emotional self-control, and pointed for inspiration at the example of an archbishop with whom Berinzaga and Gagliardi were well acquainted, Carlo Borromeo of Milan.

Keywords

pathology – history of emotions – mysticism – self-annihilation – quietism – Isabella Berinzaga – Achille Gagliardi

The case is well-known. In 1584 the Milanese mystic Isabella Berinzaga developed a close partnership with her spiritual director, the Jesuit Achille Gagliardi.[1]

---

1 For biographies of the protagonists, see Cozzi G., "Berinzaga, Isabella Cristina", in *Dizionario biografico degli Italiani* 9 (1967); Brunelli G., "Gagliardi, Achille", in *Dizionario biografico degli Italiani* 51 (1998); Pavone S., "Gagliardi A.", in *Dizionario storico dell'Inquisizione*, ed.

© WIETSE DE BOER, 2025 | DOI:10.1163/9789004694613_011

Their bond became controversial, however, was forcibly dissolved, and ended in a papal condemnation in 1601. Yet it also produced a small meditation manual, the *Breve compendio intorno alla perfettione christiana*, which, despite formal disapprovals, was printed in multiple languages and, from the early seventeenth century, rapidly became a classic of spiritual literature [Fig. 10.1]. Official prohibition by the Congregation of the Index in 1702, lifted only in 1899, caused the *Breve compendio* to fade into oblivion. Its scholarly rediscovery in the early 1930s, thanks to Marcel Viller, Henri Bremond, Jean Dagens, and Giuseppe De Luca, produced an outpouring of research, in which historians reconstructed the affair in great detail and debated questions of authorship and influence. The *Breve compendio* came thus to be seen as a fountainhead of seventeenth-century spirituality, in France, Italy, and elsewhere.[2] During the last few decades, the book and the relationship in which it was rooted have received renewed attention as scholars discovered their relevance for the history of female mysticism, sanctity, and authority, and, more recently, for the contested direction of the Jesuit order under General Claudio Acquaviva.[3]

The *Breve compendio* is known especially for its focus on the will – more precisely, on the 'annihilation' of the self and surrender of the will in pursuit of divine union. That was the book's distinctive feature, as has long been recognised, explaining both its enormous resonance and the suspicions and prohibitions it provoked. This method, and the personal experiences from which it was forged, also make the work a prime candidate for a case study in the history of emotion. Despite unfortunate losses, the surviving documentation

---

Prosperi A. – Lavenia V. – Tedeschi J., 4 vols. (Pisa: 2010) 2: 633–634. Brief introductions on their relationship and the background of the *Breve compendio* can be found in Pozzi G. – Leonardi C. (eds.), *Scrittrici mistiche italiane* (1988; Genoa: 1996) 392–398; Malena A., *L'eresia dei perfetti. Inquisizione romana ed esperienze mistiche nel Seicento Italiano* (Rome: 2003), 293–299; Friedrich M., *The Jesuits: A History*, trans. J.N. Dillon (2016; Princeton, NJ: 2022) 89–90, 221–222.

2   For an overview of this early historiography, see Petrocchi M., *Storia della spiritualità italiana* (Turin: 1996) 123–132; of special importance is Bremond H., *Histoire littéraire du sentiment religieux en France*, 12 vols. (1916–1933; Paris: 1933) 11:3–56.

3   Signorotto G., "Gesuiti, carismatici e beate nella Milano del primo Seicento", in Zarri G. (ed.), *Finzione e santità tra medioevo ed età moderna* (Turin: 1991) 177–201, at 183–184; Sluhovsky M., *Believe Not Every Spirit: Possession, Mysticism, and Discernment in Early Modern Catholicism* (Chicago: 2007) 97–136, esp. 114–115; Pelosi O., "'Spoliata di sé e d'ogni cosa': la scrittura negata di Isabella Berinzaga (1551–1624)", *Annali d'Italianistica*, vol. 25: *Literature, Religion, and the Sacred* (2007) 311–323; Mostaccio S., "Per via di donna. Il laboratorio della mistica al servizio degli Esercizi Spirituali. Il caso Gagliardi/Berinzaga", in Zarri G. (ed.), *Storia della direzione spirituale*, vol. 3: *L'età moderna* (Brescia: 2008) 311–329; ead., *Early Modern Jesuits between Obedience and Conscience during the Generalate of Claudio Acquaviva (1581–1615)*, trans. by C. Copeland (London-New York: 2016) 113–130; Catto M., *La Compagnia divisa. Il dissenso nell'ordine gesuitico tra '500 e '600*, 2nd ed. (Brescia: 2022) 63–100.

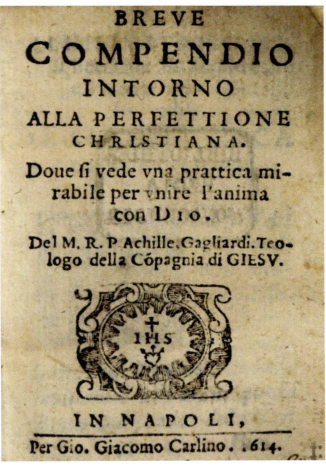

FIGURE 10.1   Gagliardi Achille, *Breve compendio intorno alla perfettione Christiana, dove si vede una prattica mirabile per unire l'anima con Dio* (Naples, per Gio. Giacomo Carlino: 1614), frontispiece
© BAYERISCHE STAATSBIBLIOTHEK, MUNICH, ASC. 1988, URN:NBN:DE:BVB:12-BSB10262716-1

offers rich materials for an examination of what a founder of that field has called 'the navigation of feeling'.[4] In early-modern moral thought, in contrast to modern psychology, this refers especially to the forms of control exercised by reason over involuntary determinants of behaviour, physical, sensory, and

---

4 Reddy W., *The Navigation of Feeling: A Framework for the History of Emotions* (Cambridge-New York: 2008).

affective.[5] To some degree, my approach is also indebted to the investigation of 'emotional scripts' – performative instructions aimed at eliciting desired affective states – that has animated recent studies of medieval and early-modern meditative literature.[6] But the following pages examine the *Breve compendio* especially as a guide for managing the conflicting emotions that could arise during contemplation. The genesis of this method may be clarified by a confrontation with the documentary record of Isabella Berinzaga's troubled life and mystical experiences.[7] Such a comparative approach has been pursued to some extent as a matter of philological study, but has otherwise remained

---

5 Alfieri F., "Tracking Jesuit Psychologies. From Ubiquitous Discourse on the Soul to Institutionalized Discipline", in Županov I.G. (ed.), *The Oxford Handbook of the Jesuits* (Oxford: 2019) 783–810, esp. 787.

6 The term, originating in the psychology of emotion, has penetrated historical studies as well, developing and supplementing concepts denoting the culturally-specific features of emotion, such as 'emotional communities' (B. Rosenwein) and 'emotional ecology'. See McNamer S., *Affective Meditation and the Invention of Medieval Compassion* (Philadelphia: 2010); Karant-Nunn S.C., *The Reformation of Feeling: Shaping the Religious Emotions in Early Modern Germany* (Oxford: 2010); Hillman J., "Internal Theater and Emotional Scripts in French Jesuit Meditative Literature", in Marculescu A. – Morand Métivier C.-L. (eds.), *Affective and Emotional Economies in Medieval and Early Modern Europe* (Cham: 2018) 143–163. On directed emotional engagement in meditative practice, see further Graham H. – Kilroy-Ewbank L. (eds.), *Emotions, Art, and Christianity in the Transatlantic World, 1450–1800* (Leiden-Boston: 2021), especially the introduction and chapters 1 (Fleming A.C., "The Emotions of Ignatius of Loyola and the Mental Pictures of the *Spiritual Exercises*", 33–70) and 2 (Melion W.S., "Allegory and Affective Experience in Thomas Sailly, S.J.'s *Thesaurus precum et exercitiorum spiritualium* of 1609", 71–125).

7 The present essay is a report on research in progress. Other, complementary approaches largely remain outside its scope, especially the study of the *Breve compendio*'s place within the mystical tradition. This includes its possible connections with the medieval Free Spirit movement and Rheinland mysticism (on which see Marín J.M., "A Beguine's Spectre: Marguerite Porete († 1310), Achille Gagliardi († 1607), and Their Collaboration across Time", *The Way* 15, 3 [2012] 93–110 and Faesen R., "Achille Gagliardi and the Northern Mystics", in Maryks R. (ed.), *Companion to Jesuit Mysticism* [Leiden – Boston: 2017] 82–111) and with sixteenth-century Lombard spirituality; on the latter see Bonora E., *I conflitti della Controriforma. Santità e obbedienza nell'esperienza religiosa dei primi barnabiti* (Florence: 1998) esp. 103–146; Caravale G., *L'orazione proibita. Censura ecclesiastica e letteratura devozionale nella prima età moderna* (Florence: 2003) 211–212; Mazzonis Q., *Riforme di vita cristiana nel Cinquecento italiano* (Soveria Mannelli: 2020), Engl. trans. *Reforms of Christian Life in Sixteenth-Century Italy* (London – New York: 2022). Nor can we here examine in any detail the censorship and publication history of the *Breve compendio*, its connection with the Ignatian *Spiritual Exercises* and the debates that produced the *Directoria*. On this aspect, see (besides the literature cited in n. 3) Stroppa S., "Achille Gagliardi e Giuseppe Blondo a Milano. La riflessione sugli *Esercizi Spirituali* e la mistica", *Studia Borromaica* (2007) 307–327. On the history of censorship more generally, see Caravale G., *Libri proibiti. Censura e cultura italiana in età moderna* (Bari – Rome: 2022).

THE TROUBLES OF CHRISTIAN PERFECTION

largely unexplored. The goal, then, is to trace the 'passage of the discourse from experience to systematic reflection'.[8] Any such analysis needs of course to be mindful of the coeval language of emotion, which was part of what may be called the moral psychology of the day.[9] Consideration of this issue will also serve as an introduction into the cultural milieu in which the Berinzaga affair unfolded. This is where we start.

1   Pellegrini on Affections

Pathology, declared the influential encyclopaedist Johann Heinrich Alsted in 1630, is 'the doctrine concerning the knowledge and improvement of the affects'.[10] If, in modern terminology, this suggests a notion of 'mental health', in the early seventeenth century the discipline pertained, in part or entirely, to physiology, oratory, ethics, and theology. A range of publications developed one or more of these strands, whose origins can be partially traced back to ancient medicine, natural philosophy, rhetoric, and ethics.[11] Alsted observed that he had drawn especially on the recent work of the Roman philosopher Lelio Pellegrini (1551–1602). In fact, his discussion of the affects relied heavily on a book by Pellegrini whose very title had inspired Alsted's definition of pathology,

---

8   Stroppa S., "L'annichilazione e la censura: Isabella Berinzaga e Achille Gagliardi", *Rivista di storia e letteratura religiosa* 32, 3 (1996) 617–625, at 622.

9   For appropriate words of caution against assumptions of equivalency between modern 'emotions' and early modern 'affects', see the useful conceptual analysis in Champion M. – Garrod R. – Haskell Y. – Feros Ruys J., "But Were They Talking about Emotions? *Affectus, affectio*, and the History of Emotions", *Rivista storica italiana* (2016) 521–543.

10   Alsted Johann Heinrich, *Encyclopaedia septem tomis distincta* (Herbornae Nassoviorum, s.e.: 1630), *Tomus septima* 2360: 'Pathologia est doctrina de affectibus noscendis et emendandis'. Recent work on Alsted includes Hotson H., *Johann Heinrich Alsted 1588–1638: Between Renaissance, Reformation and Universal Reform* (Oxford: 2000); Störkel R., *Bildungsgut für Europa – Die Encyclopaedia des Johann Heinrich Alsted von 1630* (Berlin: 2019).

11   See, e.g., Gutberleth Henricus, *Pathologia, hoc est doctrina de humanis affectibus, physice et ethice tractata* (Herbornae Nassoviorum, s.e.: 1615); Magirus Johannes, *Pathologia, sive morborum et affectuum omnium praeter naturam, qui corpus humanum invadere solent, enumeratio* (Francofurti, ex officina Paltheniana: 1615); Weiganmeir Johann Baptist, *ΠΑΘΟΛΟΓΙΑ sive disputatio de affectibus* (Tubingae, Theodoricus Werlin: 1623); Macdowell William, *Pathologia sive discursus ethico-politicus de affectibus* (Groningae, typis Ioannis Sassi: 1623); Dannhawer Johann Conrad, *Pathologia rhetorica sive disputatio de affectibus generatim ad publicam proposita* (Argentorati, Johann Repp: 1632); Alardus Lambert, *Pathologia sacra novi testamenti, continens significantiora eiusdem et cum emphasi singulari usurpata loca* (Lipsiae, sumptibus Henningi et A.M. Gross: 1635); Moles Vicente, *De morbis in sacris literis pathologia* (Matriti, ex officina Joannis Sancii: 1642).

De affectionibus animi noscendis et emendandis (1598).[12] This treatise offered a moral-psychological analysis of the affects grounded in a Thomist-Aristotelian philosophy of the soul – Pellegrini's list of affects was practically identical to that of Aquinas – and supplemented with insights from Stoicism and other classical sources.[13] If the soul consisted of vegetative, sensitive, and rational parts, the focus here was on the sensitive. That was the area in which affects came into motion when an object, perceived by the external senses and processed by the internal ones (particularly, the imagination), stirred up one or more appetites. The latter, in turn, were distinguished according to two categories, the concupiscible and the irascible. Their object might be good or bad, and they could result in either pleasure or pain. Particular affects might relate differently to the same object: love connoted an 'inclination towards a body'; desire constituted a 'motion' in its direction; pleasure resulted from reaching this goal. Among further variables, affects could be moderate or immoderate, orderly or disordered, instantaneous or lasting, simple or mixed. Pellegrini offered a chart of the latter – previewing the structure of his subsequent chapters – in which simple affects (such as love, hate, hope, and fear) were distinguished from minor or mixed ones. He explained mixed affects with a few examples: shame (*verecundia*) combined sadness with the fear of unseemliness; competitiveness (*aemulatio*) was an 'effort born from sadness and hope'; and so forth. But as his detailed treatment later in the book showed, even the 'simple' affects often consisted of complex, even contradictory impulses.

Taken together, Pellegrini concluded, the affects could cause 'disturbances of the soul' that had 'such force that they often pull a person down into depression [...] but if they are tamed, they arise gently and more evenly, without force or tumult'.[14] Hence the 'utility of this disputation': to show how these disturbances could be contained by reason – defined by the scholastics as the rational part of the soul operating through the intellective and appetitive powers, that is, the intellect and the will. Thus Pellegrini's project was disciplinary in nature: its goal was not merely to know, but to restrain (*frenare*) the affects.[15] Yet his higher aim was moral. Pellegrini devoted a chapter to the question as to whether 'the affections of the soul, however moderated, can be conjoined with virtue'. The answer was certainly affirmative, but the philosopher took

---

12 Pellegrini Lelio, *De affectionibus animi noscendis et emendandis commentarius* (Romae, apud Vincentium Pelagallum: 1598).

13 See for his introductory discussion, Pellegrini, *De affectionibus* 1–29. For Aquinas, see Rosenwein B.H., *Generations of Feeling: A History of Emotions, 600–1600* (Cambridge: 2016) 144–168.

14 Pellegrini, *De affectionibus* 30.

15 Pellegrini, *De affectionibus*, fol. † 2 r.

THE TROUBLES OF CHRISTIAN PERFECTION

care to criticise the Stoics' approach as too blunt and ineffective. Citing Zeno's definition of affection as 'a commotion of the soul contrary to nature, averse to right reason', he described their aspiration to achieve *apathia* (impassibility) as futile. Instead, Pellegrini agreed with the Aristotelian tradition – along with 'all of humankind' – on the need to correct affections when 'immoderate' but 'to retain them as useful where they can serve reason'.[16] For '[e]xperience teaches that the functions of mortals are much helped and promoted by the affects: when an appetite (*appetitus*) is aroused, we will carry out our plans more easily and with greater effort'.[17]

The basic principles of Pellegrini's system were no doubt commonly shared. The philosopher taught moral philosophy at the Sapienza in Rome between 1586 and his death in 1602, and it is in that city that *De affectionibus* appeared in 1598.[18] As has been observed, the book has a 'parallel' in commentaries on Aristotle's *Ethics* produced around that time at the Collegio Romano and elsewhere.[19] In the same years, the Jesuit theologian Juan Azor (1535–1603) was at work on his massive *Institutiones morales*, published in three volumes between 1600 and 1611. Azor was a prominent insider: he taught at Alcalà and Rome, and in 1584 he was named to the commission charged by Claudio Acquaviva to establish the *Ratio studiorum*. In the first volume of his *Institutiones morales*, Azor offered a long treatment of the affects, which was more theoretical than Pellegrini's, but built on similar premises.[20] Achille Gagliardi, himself an expert in these fields – he had taught ethics (1562–1563) and scholastic theology (1566–1567, 1576–?) at the Collegio Romano – was surely familiar with the Aristotelian-Thomist assumptions underpinning the work on the affects of both Pellegrini and Azor.[21]

But Pellegrini's *De affectionibus* also deserves our attention for other reasons. While Azor's work was purely academic, Pellegrini's book was not directly tied

---

16 Pellegrini, *De affectionibus* 15; Pellegrini derived Zeno's definition from Cicero, *Tusc. Disp.* 4:11 (where the definition is of *perturbatio*, not *affectio*).

17 Pellegrini, *De affectionibus* 16.

18 On Pellegrini, see Lines D.A., *Aristotle's Ethics in the Italian Renaissance. The Universities and the Problems of Moral Education* (Leiden – Boston: 2002) 340–345, 452, 514–515, and passim; Carella C., *L'insegnamento della filosofia alla "Sapienza" di Roma nel Seicento. Le cattedre e i maestri* (Florence: 2007) 48.

19 Lines, *Aristotle's Ethics* 342, with further discussion of moral philosophy at the Collegio Romano at 348–383; on this see also Knebel S.K., *Wille, Würfel und Wahrscheinlichkeit. Das System der moralischen Notwendigkeit in der Jesuitenscholastik 1550–1700* (Hamburg: 2000).

20 On Jesuit moral philosophy, and Azor's in particular, see Alfieri F., "Tracking Jesuit Psychologies".

21 Lines, *Aristotle's Ethics* 454–455.

to his teaching, unlike his commentary on Aristotle's *Ethics*, which appeared in 1600.[22] But in *De affectionibus* the Roman philosopher offered precious clues about how he wished to see its principles enacted. One such application was in the political sphere. The Roman philosopher dedicated his book to Ferdinando de' Medici, a former cardinal but now Grand Duke of Tuscany, and took the opportunity to promote its importance as a lesson in princely moderation. The discipline of reason over passion, he noted, was especially important for the ruler: who would restrain a prince who is 'unbridled and measures the greatness of his fortune by his license to sin?' But Pellegrini's true compass was the Milanese archbishop Carlo Borromeo, who had died in 1584 but whose posthumous fame was alive and growing in Counter-Reformation Italy. To his memory Pellegrini dedicated his book, not only on account of the archbishop's 'strength of mind, tolerance of labour, and contempt for pleasure', but because 'he controlled his own affects and the full turbulence of his soul with such exertion' as to be peerless in his own day and find his equal only in ancient heroes. This is why Pellegrino chose Borromeo's portrait – resembling the famous coeval painting, now in the Pinacoteca Ambrosiana, attributed to Ambrogio Giovanni Figini – to grace his book's frontispiece [Fig. 10.2]. The image was to aid the very project of emotional control that was Pellegini's goal:

> We have placed Carlo's portrait at the beginning of this work, both because the sole memory of such a man fills the soul with holiness, and his image when observed brings order to one's inner motions; and in order that the readers may understand that, to illustrate certain points, we use examples from ancient and recent history in such a way that what Carlo did and said, we must always follow.

Throughout the book, then, the figure of Borromeo reappeared to illustrate important points. The first chapter, on love, detailed the power of this affect by celebrating it – with an abundance of classical references – as the principal source of good. But it ended with a cautionary warning against familial love: 'Cardinal Carlo was always suspicious of the power of consanguineous love. When his relatives requested something, he preferred to hear them through intermediaries, to avoid that an impulse of the blood would drive him imprudently to consent to harmful things'.[23] The opening chapter of the second section, on joy and pleasure, concluded with an endorsement of Borromeo's spirituality. Here Pellegrini promoted the highest form of pleasure, 'which

---

22   Lines, *Aristotle's Ethics* 342.

23   Pellegrini, *De affectionibus* 39.

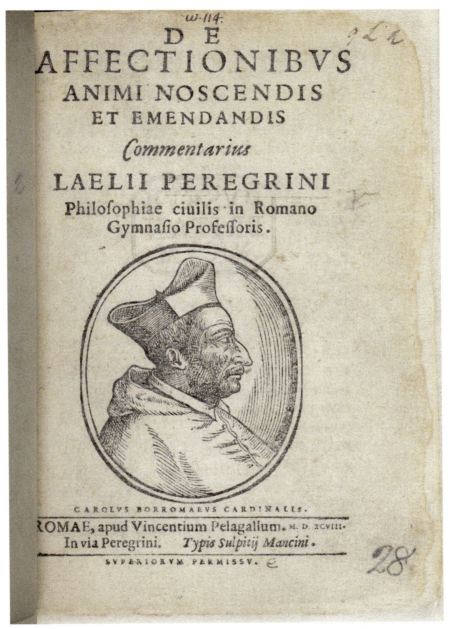

FIGURE 10.2   Pellegrini Lelio, *De affectionibus animi noscendis et emendandis commentarius* (Rome, apud Vincentium Pelagallum: 1598), frontispiece
© THE BRITISH LIBRARY BOARD, 0 COLL DRT DIG STORE 716.A.2. BY PERMISSION OF THE BRITISH LIBRARY

emanates from the knowledge of God and the love of the highest good', leaving his readers with the image of Carlo Borromeo as he 'stayed in church at night to spend long periods absorbed in the contemplation of divine things, focused on singing his creator's praises'. Thus, for all the bodily and mental stresses of his pastoral work, he found quiet and joy in 'the bosom of riches and the garden of delights'.[24] And so it went on: in a discussion of desire, Borromeo was mentioned for his rejection of his worldly possessions as he settled in Milan. Immunity from aversion was illustrated by his scorn for the loss of patrimony and physical comforts. Tolerance for physical pain was exemplified by the archbishop's stoic demeanour as he suffered an agonising foot injury during a procession of the Holy Nail. And to illustrate resistance to fear, Pellegrini told the famous story of the attempt on Borromeo's life in 1569: absorbed in prayer near his private chapel, he was undisturbed when bullets grazed him, just when his terrified assistants sang the gospel words, *Non turbetur cor vestrum, neque formidet* (John 14:27, 'Let not your heart be troubled, neither let it be afraid').[25]

In sum, Borromeo embodied Pellegrini's notion of *disciplina*, 'by which to order the motions of the soul and to drive away any vexation (*molestia*) that holds back contemplation'.[26] A diligent student of Epictetus, he 'vanquished all affects and his self', without, however, embracing the 'entirely useless' Stoic ideal of *apathia*.[27] In this way the archbishop's example revealed how the affects were involved in moral edification, spiritual uplift, and even hagiographic purpose. In fact, in a reflection of Borromeo's growing fame of sanctity in the years leading up to his canonisation process, Pellegrini referenced the preacher Francesco Panigarola, who in a much-publicised funeral oration had praised this prelate born to wealth for aspiring to the 'condition of dogs' (*canum condicionem*).[28] Likewise, the Roman philosopher had lifted the anec-

---

24   Pellegrini, *De affectionibus* 89–90.
25   See, respectively, Pellegrini, *De affectionibus* 83–84, 111, 123, 164–165.
26   Ibidem 32 (where, to be sure, the term *contemplatio* refers to the pursuit of 'those who examine the secrets of nature and investigate the causes of things'; but the same psychological point applies).
27   Ibidem 19.
28   Pellegrini, *De affectionibus* 22. The reference appears to be to Panigarola's remark that Borromeo 'per la sua persona altro non godeva, che poco pane et acqua che mangiava, et un poco di paglia ove dormiva': Panigarola Francesco, *Oratione fatta dal R.do Padre Panicarola nel Duomo di Milano nelle essequie dell'Illustriss.mo et Rever.mo Cardinale di S. Prassede Archivescovo di Milano* (Roma, per gl'Heredi d'Antonio Blado: 1584), fol. B 2 v. A later hagiography used the same comparison with dogs to characterise Panigarola's remark: Giussano Giovanni Pietro, *Vita di S. Carlo Borromeo Prete Cardinale di Santa Prassede Arcivescovo di Milano* (Roma, Stamperia della Camera Apostolica: 1610) 636 ('come disse il sopra nominato Panigarola in quella oratione funebre nella morte d'esso

THE TROUBLES OF CHRISTIAN PERFECTION

dotes about Borromeo's foot injury and assault almost verbatim from Carlo Bascapè's biography, published in Ingolstadt in 1592.[29] Pellegrini's remark about Epictetus's influence no doubt also relied on Borromeo's early biographers: it had been discussed by both Agostino Valier, author of a *vita* published in 1586, and Bascapè. The latter noted that the archbishop studied the *Enchiridion* 'to restrain his emotions (*perturbationes*)' and 'achieve a perfect moderation of his soul (*animi perfectam moderationem*)'.[30] Neither author, however, had raised Pellegrini's reservations about *apathia* – an issue whose significance will become clear later. In this context the Roman philosopher also cited the occasion where Borromeo had encountered the Stoic tradition, the so-called *Noctes Vaticanae* – a series of learned disquisitions on classical and religious virtues written by a group of humanists and ecclesiastics (including Agostino Valier) whom the young cardinal-nephew had assembled in the Vatican in the early 1560s.[31] The remark underscores not only the deep connection in Pellegrini's mind between affect theory and ethics, but also how both were recycled in edifying and hagiographic discourse. These points will prove to be relevant as we analyse the relationship between Berinzaga and Gagliardi.

There is one more reason why Borromeo's image in *De affectionibus* matters: it brings us closer to the intellectual and religious orbit within which the Berinzaga-Gagliardi affair unfolded. In fact, the Milanese experiences of both were intertwined with Carlo Borromeo's reform efforts in the Lombard archdiocese. Isabella Cristina Berinzaga, born into the middle-class Lomazzo family of Milan in or around 1551, developed an intense spiritual life while still a child. Entrusted to the care of maternal relatives following her mother's death, she

---

Santo, non usava più delle sue facoltà di quello si faccia un povero cane nella casa del suo padrone, che è pane, acqua, e paglia'). The point about the *conditio canum* has evident biblical overtones: see Matt. 15:26–27. On Borromeo's canonisation process, see Turchini A., *La fabbrica di un santo. Il processo di canonizzazione di Carlo Borromeo e la Controriforma* (Casale Monferrato: 1984).

29 Bascapé Carlo, *De vita et rebus gestis Caroli S.R.E. Cardinalis tituli S. Praxedis Archiepicopi Mediolani* (Ingolstadii, ex officina typographica Davidis Sartoris: 1592) 280–281 and 73, respectively; in a modern edition, Bascapè C., *Vita e opere di Carlo Archivescovo di Milano Cardinale di S. Prassede* (Milan: 1983) 662 and 178.

30 Zardin D., "Il 'Manuale' di Epitteto e la tradizione dello stoicismo cristiano" (2006), in idem, *Carlo Borromeo. Cultura, santità, governo* (Milan: 2010) 29–54, at 31. The passage cited by Zardin is in Bascapè, *De vita et rebus gestis* 11 (*Vita e opere* 30–31). Valier's discussion of Borromeo's encounter with Epictetus and Stoicism can be found in Valier Agostino, *Vita Caroli Borromei Cardinalis Sancti Praxedis Archiepiscopi Mediolani* (Verona, apud Hieronymum Discipulum: 1586) 7–8.

31 Pellegrini, *De affectionibus* 18. See Sassi Giovanni Antonio (ed.), *Noctes Vaticanae seu sermones habiti in academia a S. Carolo Borromeo Romae in Palatio Vaticano instituta* (Mediolani, Typographia Bibliothecae Ambrosianae: 1748).

assumed the family name Berinzaga Rabia; an uncle, Girolamo Rabia, a fervent priest and future collaborator of Borromeo, was a vital supporter. From 1567 Berinzaga frequented the church of San Fedele, which the archbishop had turned into the base of a new community of Jesuits he had invited to Milan. But Isabella developed a strained relationship with her confessor, who was evidently discouraging her spiritual path; and rumours of her assiduous frequenting of the Jesuits reached the ears of General Everard Mercurian, who ordered an envoy, Father Sebastiano Morales (or Morais), to look into the situation. Morales's findings, however, were so positive that Berinzaga was accepted as a 'daughter of the Society'. But the true turning point in Berinzaga's career came in 1584, when the Paduan Jesuit Achille Gagliardi was named provost of San Fedele. Gagliardi had moved to Milan in the early 1580s at the behest of Archbishop Borromeo, who esteemed him greatly and sought him out as his collaborator and confessor. But it was in his capacity as provost that Gagliardi met Berinzaga and took on responsibility for her spiritual direction. Upon her insistence he agreed to guide her through a series of spiritual exercises, which took place from the beginning of May until mid-September 1584. These became the basis for a set of manuscripts out of which the *Breve compendio* grew. Unlike *De affectionibus*, the work did not articulate its method explicitly in terms of a theory of the affects. Yet a comparison between the two works is nevertheless helpful: it may help determine to what extent the *Breve compendio*, and the draft texts that contributed to it, shared common ground with contemporary assumptions about the affects, and where it went its own way.

Befitting its genre, the *Breve compendio* set out to be both systematic and normative: it led the practitioner on a prescribed contemplative path. This obviously implies severe limitations in the insights the text may provide about our theme. Yet, as noted, the background of the book is unusually well documented. This documentation consists, on the one hand, of the *Breve compendio*, supplemented by several manuscript additions (some of which made it into seventeenth-century editions under the title *Secondo compendio*), along with records of the Jesuit censorship process. On the other, we have a detailed account of Isabella Berinzaga's spiritual exercises, which Gagliardi assembled from his notes on Berinzaga's oral accounts and some of her own writings, none of which is extant. This text, which includes multiple biographical passages, sheds light on Berinzaga's emotional life and clarifies how Gagliardi translated her spiritual practices and experiences into the streamlined itinerary proposed in the *Breve compendio*. This process has not been adequately studied, even though the key sources have been published. Following remarkable archival discoveries made in the mid-twentieth century, notably by the Jesuit P. Pirri,

THE TROUBLES OF CHRISTIAN PERFECTION   339

another member of the same order, Mario Gioia, published editions of both
sets of documents in 1994 and 1996.[32]

2   Berinzaga's *Vita*

We turn first to the documents Gioia published under the title *Per via di
annichilazione*, based on a set of manuscripts commonly referred to as the
Vita. These form the record of Berinzaga's meditations and life events. In 1931
the Jesuit Marcel Viller proposed that the *Breve compendio* was Gagliardi's
attempt at systematising the meditative experiences he had recorded in the
Vita.[33] This assumption has been tacitly accepted by much of the later historiography, but only minimally demonstrated. Viller cited as an example the culminating experience of the surrender of the will, whose source he identified in
a passage of Berinzaga's *Vita*: between 1576 and 1580 'the Lord always gave her
a great desire to renounce her free will entirely to him' until 'in 1580, suddenly,
without any thought on her part, he took every liberty away from her, that is,
by telling her that in the future he did not want her to be free to want or desire
anything, except for what he would inform her was his divine wish'.[34] This
raises the question: if the destination of the contemplative journey consisted
in the vacation of the will, was the path to get to this point, as sketched out in
the *Breve compendio*, similarly grounded in Berinzaga's lived experiences?

A brief word on the structure and content of the relevant source materials
is in order. The main text edited in *Per via di annichilazione* consists of three
parts, written and assembled certainly in the period 1584–1601, but much of it
probably completed by 1588: 1) a brief narrative explanation of how Berinzaga
got to make her spiritual exercises with Gagliardi; 2) the list of 'spiritual points'
Gagliardi gave her as the basis of these exercises; and 3) the bulk of the text,
containing the account of Berinzaga's meditative trajectory. The document
survives in three largely identical manuscripts, one of which is entitled *Vita*

---

32   Gioia M. (ed.), *Per via di annichilazione. Un testo di Isabella Cristina Berinzaga redatto da
       Achille Gagliardi S.I. Edizione critica, introduzione e note* (Rome-Brescia: 1994); idem (ed.),
       *Breve compendio di perfezione cristiana. Un testo di Achille Gagliardi S.I. Saggio introdut-
       tivo ed edizione critica* (Rome-Brescia: 1996). These works offer dependable transcriptions
       and annotations without being critical editions, as has been pointed out by Stroppa,
       "L'annichilazione e la censura".

33   Viller M., "L'abrégé de la perfection de la Dame milanaise", *Revue d'ascétique et de mystique*
       12 (1931) 76; see also Gioia's discussion in *Breve compendio* 98–100.

34   For this passage, compare Gioia, *Per via di annichilazione* 173–174 and Gioia, *Breve compen-
       dio* 236–237.

Isabellae et Cristinae Bellinzagae seu Lomazzae. The third part is presented as a methodical treatment of Berinzaga's pursuit of perfection, divided up into the stages of purgation, illumination, and union. Sections within this structure are typically introduced by general lessons on specific points and fleshed out by examples from Berinzaga's life or contemplative experiences. Some sections, including meditations on the life of Christ, forms of adoration of God, and instances of mystical union may at first have been separately drafted.[35] A fourth, significantly different manuscript of the *Vita*, held at the Biblioteca Nazionale Centrale in Rome (henceforth BNR), no doubt represents an earlier stage of composition and hence sheds further light on the text's elaboration.[36] BNR largely coincides with the three other manuscripts in the first two parts and the beginning of the third. However, two meditative points early in the Way of Purgation – one on physical pains and ailments, and the next one on 'exterior persecutions' – are here developed into extensive narratives. The manuscript thus traces Berinzaga's life back to her childhood, based on recollections (Gagliardi notes) which she had written down herself at the request of the Jesuits. Presumably, this happened at the occasion of the 1579 investigation, an account of which appears at the end of this manuscript.[37] At that point, then, the text was effectively evolving into a *vita*, assuming hagiographical overtones. Gagliardi must have realised this, as it is precisely here that the manuscript ends and he must have resumed the more succinct narrative of Berinzaga's meditations based on the structure and the points he had proposed. To these the aforementioned manuscripts adhere throughout; the biographical narratives of BNR return under their respective points, but much abbreviated. The entire document, Gagliardi explained during Bellarmino's 1601 investigation, was based on information Berinzaga had reported to him 'in writing and by mouth'. He had assembled it in 'many notebooks (*cartuccie*)' which he had burned once he had finished the composition of his own text.[38] The latter thus represented his ordering and framing of the original source

---

35   See Gioia's introduction in *Per via di annichilazione* 42–50. These excursus appear to be the texts identified during the censorship investigations: in 1601 Roberto Bellarmino referred to them as 'one containing a *Vita* of Madonna Isabella', 'another, a *Vita* of Christ', 'the third about the unions (*unioni*)', 'the fourth on the divinity (*divinità*)' (ibidem 26 n. 54).

36   Ibidem 43, 46–47. My examination of the manuscript (Biblioteca Nazionale Centrale, Rome, ms. 3440, Fondo Gesuitico 1311) confirmed these observations.

37   Gioia, *Per via di annichilazione* 291–292.

38   Pirri P., "Il P. Achille Gagliardi, la Dama milanese, la riforma dello spirito e il movimento degli zelatori", *Archivum Historicum Societatis Iesu* 14 (1945) 70.

THE TROUBLES OF CHRISTIAN PERFECTION   341

texts. Hence, as has been noted, 'an almost inextricable superimposition of the language of the theologian over that of the woman'.[39]

In BNR Gagliardi explained the rationale of the meditation points he had given his spiritual daughter. Her high degree of virtue had prompted him to bypass the 'ordinary and common' exercises – a reference, no doubt, to the Ignatian exercises. Instead, he had, on the one hand, followed the classic Pseudo-Dionysian scheme of the stages of meditation (purgation – illumination – union) and, on the other, made adjustments to her 'state'. Her blameless conscience had rendered unnecessary the meditation on sins in the Way of Purgation. Gagliardi had replaced this with 'universal points on the purgation of all created things' and 'the parts of man, both external and corporeal and internal and regarding the soul'. In the Way of Illumination, he had proposed meditations on the virtues (subdivided into those concerning oneself, one's neighbour, and God), on the life of Christ, acts of internal worship of God and invocation of the saints, and an explanation of the process of contemplation. The Way of Union was focused on 'love, unions and ecstacies (*rapti*), and the affects of the Song of Songs'.[40]

Within the scope of this chapter, we will examine especially the stage of purgation. The reason is that this section encompasses practically the entire process of annihilation up to mystical union – the foundation, as we shall see, of the entire meditative system of the *Breve compendio*. In accordance with the structure explained in BNR, the Way of Purgation contained meditations on general principles, physical experiences and persecutions, exterior sensations and actions, the passions, will and judgment, temptations, and finally annihilation and the resulting illumination. The Way of Illumination being differently oriented (inspired, in part, by the Ignatian exercises), the Way of Union took up where the Way of Purgation had ended. This unevenness resulted no doubt from Gagliardi's strained efforts to fit a complex set of experiences into the conceptual matrix he had initially proposed. The surviving manuscripts thus offer a mere snapshot of the process by which he sought to turn Berinzaga's meditations into a coherent system of contemplation.

We focus here on three critical themes of the Way of Purgation. The first concerns Berinzaga's intense physical ailments and external life challenges, such as the hostility of family members and a confessor. In the main text of the *Vita*, Gagliardi presented these dual challenges as tokens of God's paternal

---

39   Stroppa, "L'annichilazione e la censura" 619.
40   Gioia, *Per via di annichilazione* 99 n. 40. It should be noted that the final chapter, on the 'affects of the Song of Songs' is lacking in all manuscripts. See ibidem 239 n. 707 for further commentary.

love, which was 'pure and sincere', 'unlike that of earthly fathers, which is mixed with interests' – a hint of the earthly conflicts that hindered Berinzaga's spiritual progress.[41] These obstacles were the means by which God allowed his spiritual daughter to repent her sins, purge her soul, and rejoice in the ensuing 'feast in paradise'.[42] The following pages illustrate such afflictions in the biographical mode. The account includes elements of the much more detailed narrative of BNR, which was organised along similar lines. In one long chapter the latter manuscript catalogued a vast spectrum of pains Berinzaga suffered during her childhood – piercing pains in her head, teeth, nose, stomach, abdomen, and especially her heart – along with fainting spells, fevers, nervous spasms, colds, and infections. It also described a parade of ineffective doctors and their cures, as well as religious remedies such as exorcisms. Amidst this avalanche of medical facts, the central religious message almost receded into the background – the lesson that Berinzaga accept her bodily afflictions as gifts and graces of God, that is, as opportunities to confess his goodness, accept her pains as 'great illuminations (*lumi*) in the knowledge of God and her own lowliness', and aids in facing her 'illnesses, tribulations, and [in] her inner conformation with the divine Majesty'.[43] How she responded emotionally to these challenges remains unclear.

That is different in the next chapter, which highlights 'external travails and persecutions' caused by three groups of people: 'lowly people', the educated elite, and the mystic's inner circle. Among them were several women who resisted her desire to join a monastery, marriage contenders prodding her to accept their offers, her father and brothers, whose disorderly conduct upset her peace of mind, and the aunt and uncle in whose house she grew up. But it was especially a confessor who for eight years opposed her independent spiritual path. It is a critical passage, worth quoting in extenso:

> The reason was that, whereas the Lord guided her inwardly in her own way – especially in certain unions and ecstasies (*unioni et rapti*), to which we shall return in the proper place in the Unitive Way – the father [confessor] wanted her to follow the common and secure path by which he guided his other women penitents, and which our Society ordinarily uses, being strongly opposed to spiritual novelties, especially where there is any danger of illusions, and in women, who are more prone to being deceived. The Lord, however, did not allow this, but steadily continued

41 Gioia, *Per via di annichilazione* 109.
42 Ibidem.
43 Ibidem 254.

THE TROUBLES OF CHRISTIAN PERFECTION   343

in this high mode (*in queste alte maniere*) and at the same time, to refine
her virtues, permitted the confessor strenuously to try to divert her from
all that he wrought in her, suspecting that she was being deceived, but
neither understanding nor penetrating what she told him about her
inner life.[44]

In this dense passage, Gagliardi uncovered the seeds of Berinzaga's conflict
with the Jesuits in her past, came to her defence, and suggested how her biography informed the method he was elaborating. But here we should note especially the emotional fallout produced by Berinzaga's conflict of loyalties:

> This created great suffering in her, because she wanted to obey but could
> not, and then she saw that [her confessor] got worked up because of this
> situation and confronted her in great anger; and this provoked intolera-
> ble distress in her, as it seemed to her that in this way the Lord wanted to
> abandon her, having in God's place her confessor, who prescribed what
> she had to do, and who forbade her to go beyond the time, the matter, and
> the mode [of meditation] he gave her; and she, forcing herself to obey,
> felt her feelings break down under the great violence.[45]

In short, Berinzaga's 'persecutions' consisted in large part of the obstacles others put in the way of her aspirations, resulting in agonising conflicts of interest and loyalty. Yet if the confessor's behaviour allowed the devil to lead her
into desperation, the 'superior part' of her soul remained 'contented', because
'the Lord comforted her with the good will she felt in not offending him'. What
is more, he made her 'feel that he allowed everything for his greater glory'.[46]
Contentment overruled distress.

Emerging here, in other words, is a form of regulation of contending emotions as the basis of meditative progress: Berinzaga invoked the 'superior
part' of her soul to override the negative affects that pulled her back from her
upward path. This turned into a more emphatic lesson that framed the shorter
biographical notes, common to the three other manuscripts, which Gagliardi
inserted in his account of Berinzaga's spiritual exercises. Thus, he explained, a
Jesuit father taught Berinzaga 'happily to suffer' her physical tribulations 'as a
means to acquire the glory of paradise'; and she herself told Gagliardi that the
Lord 'purged her soul by giving her a great desire' for persecutions, 'more than

---

44   Ibidem 275–276.
45   Ibidem 275–276.
46   Ibidem 277.

the greedy desire riches'.[47] In this context, Gagliardi reduced the biographical narrative of BNR to a more succinct but still impressive catalogue of adversities. It continued to lay blame on Berinzaga's relatives and longtime confessor; and it retained a summary of the inner turmoil caused by the latter: 'What, in all this, gave her the greatest pain and grief was that she felt herself to be guided by God, and almost forced (*violentata*) along an extraordinary path, and on the other side pulled back by the confessor, to whom, nonetheless, she wished to obey as to God: from this derived great perplexity and distress in her soul'.[48] Yet, immediately afterwards, the passage ends in an upbeat confirmation of the mystic's exemplary embrace of God's lesson: 'In all these persecutions and trials, and many more which are left out for brevity's sake, she never confessed any resentment, nor ever felt herself to be moved by inner blows'.[49]

The second theme worth highlighting concerns the contemplation on the affects. Here Gagliardi's meditation points follow scholastic faculty psychology, not unlike Pellegrino's *De affectionibus*. After a section on the external senses, Gagliardi turned to the affects, dividing them into the irascible and concupiscent. In the first category, he offered a lesson in self-discipline: those prone to anger should be embarrassed before God, avoid occasions that would trigger the urge, or repress it 'after the first motions'. However, when employing it to a good end, e.g., to correct others, they should be sure 'to move themselves to anger for the glory of God, not allowing it to go beyond the boundaries of reason [...].'[50] The following examples from Berinzaga's life show this self-discipline in action. From early childhood, she 'felt a great horror when seeing anger in others'. 'When feeling the start of a first motion of anger, she immediately felt an inner restraint (*freno*) which did not let her go further'. If such a 'motion' was intended to chide others, she 'waited until her soul was calm'. As soon as God allowed her to react, her anger was tempered by reason and untainted by 'any disordered resentment'. She went three years 'without any motion of anger' and 'felt great quiet of mind'. This was a wonder to behold, Gagliardi concluded, given the many illnesses and persecutions she endured.[51]

Dealing with concupiscence similarly required self-discipline but entailed a more differentiated and progressive process of purification in which even positive affects were submitted to divine approval. Gagliardi's introductory lesson distinguished bestial, natural, and spiritual desires. The first, the uncontrolled

---

47   Gioia, *Per via di annichilazione* 110 and 121.
48   Ibidem 124–125.
49   Ibidem 125.
50   Ibidem 128–129.
51   Ibidem 129–130.

THE TROUBLES OF CHRISTIAN PERFECTION

'sensual appetites' common to all animals, were always evil and in need of being restrained. The second, the natural human desire for food, leisure, and the like, was good or bad depending on its purpose. Purging it meant abstaining from it for the love of God. The third, the spiritual pursuit of virtue or suffering in Christ's name, was good by itself, unless it was spoiled by an evil goal or excess, in which case it was to be purged by conforming this desire to God's will. On this point Gagliardi's biographical account is brief. Berinzaga had always lacked the first desire – or rather, God 'in his goodness had preserved her from it'. She had often faced the second as a child, as God allowed her to 'feel difficulty in repressing it', but 'over time she had always acquired greater perfection, and for several years now, as she submitted herself to God, she was entirely free of it'. As for the third, from the age of three she had felt 'a great spiritual desire to be better than all other creatures for the glory of God'. Furthermore, she greatly desired the pursuit of virtues, 'such as doing all kinds of jobs' but 'at times felt some difficulty'. But now her 'desire to love God [wa]s so great as to melt her heart' and 'the Lord has given her complete moderation also of that desire'. This gift, in turn, consisted in seeking 'divine approval' for every spiritual desire, including the pursuit of virtue.[52]

This was the pivot point towards the third theme, the purgation of the will. Here the double-edged sword of self-negation and subordination to God was to be wielded to resolve a state of conflicting emotions. Gagliardi distinguished the inferior from the superior will. The inferior, directed towards human concerns, was purged by marshalling embarrassment and humility in the face of an offence against God; by relying on God when a wish to pursue an indifferent goal had failed; by drawing on obedience to God to conquer resistance on a human level (*nell'humanità*); by self-humiliation when the contemplative relied on her own power rather than God's; and by offering her will to God and her superiors. Also the superior will, aimed at divine matters, was to be purged: the contemplative not only had to 'dispossess' herself of the very gifts and graces received from him, but even ought to feel contentment about this dispossession.

Purgation of the will, Gagliardi noted in his biographical comment, had deep roots in Berinzaga's past. She had sought to surrender her inferior will 'from the time she sucked milk': by refusing, resisting, or feeling discontent about anything she had to undertake of her own volition and without an express order of her superiors; and by mortifying her will and seeking delight in opposing and conquering it. The most concrete detail here is that 'for more

---

52   Ibidem 130–131.

than sixteen years' – a clear reference to her association with the Jesuits of San Fedele – she was determined 'to die and do the will of her superiors rather than living without it'. Often, Gagliardi noted, she had thus done things she knew would remain unsuccessful or cause harm, adding 'and she knew it by divine revelation'. God had also let her know that he had granted her, in matters concerning the superior will, the necessary resignation to suffer 'physical illnesses', 'tribulations of the soul', 'falling prey to shortcomings', the loss of 'all light and sensation', lacking support from superiors and others, 'going to hell' (including even her sense of unworthiness 'that divine justice would be executed in her'), and 'being separated from God if that were to please him'. In all this, Gagliardi observed, Berinzaga might 'at times feel some disgust, but was nevertheless most resolute, feeling a deep quiet and contentment of spirit'.[53] Along similar lines, Gagliardi recorded lessons and meditations on self-judgment and temptations.

The pinnacle of this trajectory was annihilation, which Gagliardo described as 'the end and perfection of the purgative path'. From the beginning this component appears to have had a unique place in Berinzaga's 1584 cycle of spiritual exercises. Here, and only here, the list of basic meditation points Gagliardi had ostensibly proposed – but evidently recorded only later in the surviving manuscripts – offers a glimpse of his spiritual daughter's input and takes on a retrospective quality: it mentioned the 'progress she wants to make' in this regard; and it spoke of the 'light which God let her receive from this annihilation'.[54] This distinctiveness is confirmed in Gagliardi's subsequent account. The exercise consisted of three steps. 1) A sense of one's lowliness should be cultivated in prayer and spiritual practice generally: everywhere the soul should seek out opportunities to be 'despised and vilified' rather than resenting them. 2) By extension, it should 'feel an effective desire to be known and held by all to be vile and nothing (*da niente*)', which would produce 'greater fervour in divine service'. 3) Finally, the soul should feel 'great joy' about its nothingness, because it redounded to God's greater glory. This degree of annihilation would produce such a great 'light of cognition of God' as to unite the soul with God, who would then 'engage the soul with a greater excess of affection than in any other way and by any other means'. At this point no 'medium' (*mezzo*) stood between God and the soul, whose will would coincide with God's.

Gagliardi then detailed the 'means' of achieving annihilation, ranging from self-deprecation to disaffection to self-hate. Berinzaga, he said, 'often used to

---

53   Ibidem 132–133.
54   Ibidem 100.

THE TROUBLES OF CHRISTIAN PERFECTION

347

tell me, and the Lord now showed her more clearly in this meditation, that an annihilation in which the soul remains dejected and confused is not a perfect one'. To achieve that goal required an 'illumination (*lume*) which raises the soul up to God'. Hence the description of seven kinds of illumination tied to the abovementioned stages of annihilation, only briefly punctuated with examples from Berinzaga's experience.[55] The chapter thus became a brief treatise on the final steps towards mystical union and the full renunciation of free will. Its concluding page, however, again turned biographical:

> Finally, the Lord showed her why it pleased him to draw her to himself by this way of annihilation, namely: 1) because this is the most perfect step by which God draws a soul to himself; 2) because he had *ab aeterno* elected her to this [end], to bestow her with gifts and graces among and above all other creatures who now are marked (*segnalate*); 3) to produce an idea and a portrait of all virtues, in support of others. Moreover, he showed her that he had done this out of pure love, making her feel in part the love with which he had destined her for such a great good. And in this elevation, a melody formed between her and God, and it was of love.[56]

This was the remarkable outcome of Berinzaga's path of purgation. Whereas the points her director had proposed contained numerous conventional exercises – cleansing of the senses and affects, meditations on the life of Christ, on the virtues, and so forth – the way in which it was realised assumed a singular focus, that is, to win a contest of conflicting emotions. In Gagliardi's telling, it came to be Berinzaga's overarching goal to override negative affects with positive ones by an appeal to God's will, and in the process to void her own. And her success in this effort not only resulted in mystical union – a 'melody [...] of love' – but it also yielded the extraordinary understanding that all was divinely ordained. Berinzaga came to believe (and Gagliardi with her) that she had a direct conduit to God, was his elect, and was destined to serve as an exemplary 'idea and portrait of all virtues'. It was a claim to sanctity.

3 Gagliardi's *Compendio*

How, then, was the complex, layered document known as the *Vita* translated into the method proposed in the *Breve compendio*? It is obvious that Berinzaga's

---

55   Ibidem 140–141.
56   Ibidem 142.

conflicted religious loyalties and the adversities meted out to her by hostile relatives did not make their way into that treatise, which removed all identifiable vestiges of her life story. This was not merely a process of elimination. As will become clear, it entailed significant revisions of the method itself. Further, in a continued effort to systematise the method, Gagliardi reduced even the structural elements of the *Vita*'s section on purgation to focus exclusively on the will – on its engagement in the suppression of the self and its eventual surrender to God's will. In contrast, as we shall see, the Jesuit also introduced warnings against the elevation of the intellect. What implications did this choice between the two faculties of reason have for the sensitive functions of the soul, particularly the affects?

The *Breve compendio* presented itself, not unlike Pellegrini's *De affectionibus*, as a program of self-discipline, offering a path across the hurdles of the contemplative process. The first prerequisite for the practitioner was in fact a strong commitment to spiritual perfection. That was aimed at 'the mortification of the senses and the passions' and hence 'full control' (*pieno dominio*) of these forces by conquering their resistance (their *ripugnanze*). This required, above all, the mortification of one's own will and judgment. In their place came the obedience to – and even the alignment 'of one's entire inner life' with – the superior's directives.[57] Here Gagliardi clearly assumed a context of Jesuit spiritual direction and reaffirmed the principle of ecclesiastical mediation. In so doing he erased a conflict that had deeply shaped Berinzaga's experiences: she had reluctantly submitted to her confessor's instructions, which she construed and accepted as a divinely ordained impediment to her spiritual progress, while remaining firm in her conviction of being guided directly by God. Even without this wrinkle, however, Gagliardi's point about obedience served to introduce his method's paradoxical objective – the application of the will in pursuit of its own annulment.

Gagliardi described this itinerary as gradual and systematic. It was articulated in three stages (*stati*), each of which contained six steps (*gradi*), 'which, one after the other, form a kind of ladder, going from one stage to the next and on to the last'.[58] Each level combined two distinct approaches. The first pursued the inner rejection of all created things, especially the self, based on their 'lowliness' (*bassezza*); the successive means to this end were annihilation, expropriation, and indifference. The second approach, 'the highest esteem for God', consisted in the submission of the will leading to 'a complete conformity with the divine will' in all 'daily plans, affects, and actions'. This dual effort produced

---

57 Gioia, *Breve compendio* 179–180.
58 Ibidem 186.

THE TROUBLES OF CHRISTIAN PERFECTION   349

a 'union and transformation into God called deification'.[59] Essentially, then, the method proposed here reduced Berinzaga's program of meditation to the one element the *Vita* had explained in the concluding pages of the Way of Purgation, with brief elaborations in parts of the Ways of Illumination and Union. But the promised outcome of 'deification' stayed true to the extraordinary claim, in the *Vita*, of Berinzaga's divine election and mystical union. Both the term and the claim were to raise the eyebrows of later critics.

Gagliardi clearly had an awareness of entering treacherous territory here. Hence his repeated words of caution against forms of mystical illumination associated with the intellect, along with their physical and affective expressions. Thus, in describing deification, he noted that spiritual union and transformation ought not to be 'mystical, by way of the raptures, mental elevation, and vehement affects (*affetti*) that derive from it. For that [form of deification] is subject to many illusions and much effort, with the risk of physical illness and mental ruin; and this effort for the most part remains unsuccessful, because few achieve it'.[60] The same warning returned towards the end of the book. Here the Jesuit underscored, in describing deification, that the renunciation of the will was superior to the mystical elevation of the intellect: 'intellective ecstasies are dangerous, [suitable only] for the few, and full of occasions of curiosity and self-interest (*proprietà*)'.[61] These passages echoed contemporary concerns over the appropriateness of the Ignatian *Spiritual Exercises*, especially in their more advanced phases, for the inexperienced, the young, and the female. More generally, they reflect the suspicions surrounding the behaviours of many aspiring saints.[62] Instead, Gagliardi emphasised, the intended deification pursued by the transformation of the will was 'solid (*soda*), real (*reale*) and

---

59   Ibidem 183, and cf. n. 67. It should be noted that an elaboration of this text, the *Secondo compendio*, developed this dual process into a triad: inserted between 'conformity' and 'deiformity' was now 'uniformity', defined as 'conformation with God's will in oneself, thanks to his immediate regard and love, which removes the resistance': ibidem 250, with another variant noted in n. 24.

60   Ibidem 183–184; and cf. ibidem 182, where the author cautions that the 'esteem of God' should not be channeled 'by the penetration of theological concepts and similar aspects of divinity, for this pertains to the few and is unnecessary'.

61   Ibidem 234.

62   De Boer W., "Invisible Contemplation: A Paradox in the *Spiritual Exercises*", in Enenkel K. – Melion W.S. (eds.), *Meditatio – Refashioning the Self. Theory and Practice in Late Medieval and Early Modern Intellectual Culture* (Leiden – Boston: 2011) 235–256, at 250–252. The literature on the pretence of sanctity is extensive. On Italy, see especially Zarri, *Finzione e santità*; Schutte A.J., *Aspiring Saints: Pretense of Holiness, Inquisition, and Gender in the Republic of Venice, 1618–1750* (Baltimore: 2001); Malena, *L'eresia dei perfetti*; Modica M., *Infetta dottrina. Inquisizione e misticismo nella Roma del '600* (Rome: 2009).

common'. Of this, he said, 'all are capable, and they can achieve it with ease and clarity, albeit not without suffering'.[63]

Here a comparison with the *Vita* suggests a noteworthy revision. As we have seen, that text was premised on the belief that Berinzaga's spiritual experiences were authentic and unmediated. As spiritual director, Gagliardi insisted, he had provided nothing except the 'spiritual points' of the exercises he had proposed to her; all the rest consisted not of his teachings but God's unfiltered revelations to Berinzaga, often rendered in her own words. In his account of them, Gagliardi repeatedly referred to these as the knowledge or 'illuminations' God had imparted to her. He seemed unconcerned about the 'intellective' forms of mysticism he warned about in the *Compendio*; and his descriptions of the ecstasies – the *'unioni e rapti'* – Berinzaga experienced in the Unitive Way are devoid of any concerns about the affective excess that seemed to worry the author of the *Breve compendio*. The beginning of Berinzaga's first union, as described in the *Vita*, unfolded as follows:

> As she got ready for prayer in a state of great rebellion, she subjected herself to the greatest effort and violence; and having arrived at her place of prayer, the Lord made her aware that he had promised her repeatedly to unite her with himself, and that now was the time. And right away, he suddenly gave her a stupendous light (*lume*) by which she instantly knew all the sins she had committed, which gave her a grief so intense (she told me) as to make her die, if God had not given her strength.[64]

And shortly thereafter:

> By means of this annihilation and self-knowledge, further enflamed by the love of God [...] she was drawn to the divine presence, that is, to that presence with which God resides in heaven and above all created things; and there she saw with the intellect a light in the form of a ray descending from God into her soul, which caused another, greater light in her to return to God in reflection of the first, in the way in which a ray of sunlight reflected in a mirror doubles its light. And these lights not only brought about God's presence, but also the soul's absorption in God himself.[65]

---

63   Gioia, *Breve compendio* 183–184, and n. 67.
64   Gioia, *Per via di annichilazione* 230.
65   Ibidem 231.

THE TROUBLES OF CHRISTIAN PERFECTION 351

The *Breve compendio*, in contrast, here described only briefly the divine union achieved by the surrender of the will, foregoing any reference to emotional turmoil or intellective illumination. The reason is easy to guess: Gagliardi realised that these elements might raise suspicions about the method.

Yet as the element of affective struggle was removed from the stage of union, it became an intrinsic element of the *Breve compendio*'s preceding meditative stages. There Gagliardi translated the narrative of Berinzaga's personal troubles into the abstract terms of a spiritual contest of emotions. What is more, he presented this as unfolding in a crescendo of inner conflict. The first step of self-annihilation was taken by affect and action. By action, those aiming for spiritual perfection were to reduce their lifestyle to the barebones requirements of their religious institution and the directions of the superior – another reference to the institutional setting the author of the *Breve compendio* had in mind. By affect, they were 'entirely to renounce every wish and desire' for created things considered indifferent, including life, death, health, illness, status, and office. Thus, contemplatives had to 'detach themselves from every design, affection, and intention vis-à-vis those things and deprive themselves completely of every comfort and taste (*gusto*) associated with these, as if they were dead'.[66] The second step took this effort to a higher and more deceptive level: the intended detachment was here applied, not to indifferent things, but to those that were 'holy and spiritual', that is, the very 'means to unite the spirit with God'. In these, 'self-love and self-interest can and tend to become mixed in (*meschiare*) and hide under the appearance of holiness'. Among these inappropriate emotions, Gagliardi listed 'spiritual consolations and tastes'. The reference was to 'the sensitive affects of the heart' stirred up 'by tenderness, fervour, tears, sweetness in every action, great facility in conquering oneself, an abundant taste [for this], etc.' Such 'softness and tenderness', attuned to one's own satisfaction and delight, not only deviated from the 'solid' path of perfection, but amounted to the 'abuse of holy things for our self-interest'.[67]

Even after purging these mixed emotions, however, the contemplative often ran into further impediments, of human or divine origin, either because of the distractions of human life or because God did not allow smooth progress. As a result, the soul would feel 'pained, anxious, and worried by such impediments, and aggrieved by them'. Again, Gagliardi suspected the interference of self-interest, 'albeit very much hidden and disguised'. The resulting anxiety and worry might be without sin but were nevertheless 'a created thing' (*cosa creata*). Indirectly, they revealed a wish to dictate the law to God; certainly, the

---

66   Gioia, *Breve compendio* 191.
67   Ibidem 195–196.

soul's unrest did not come from God. For successful progress led to a state of 'conformity, quiet, and cheerfulness'.[68] But things would get worse again:

> [despite the] great dominion of the superior part over the inferior, by the great habit and facility [the soul] has acquired in controlling the flesh and the passions, the Lord is used to allow, at this point or whenever he pleases, that [the soul] again feels grave temptations, similar to and worse than those suffered at the beginning of the conversion – of the flesh, impatience, fear, difficulty, et cetera – so that [the soul] begins to feel a great rebellion of the inferior part against the superior, and the devil tempts it severely.[69]

Renewed battle was necessary, until the 'superior part wins by a wide margin'. Even so, the return of the devil and 'the movements of sensuality' at this advanced stage had the potential of giving the soul the impression of turning backwards, and hence inducing desperation. New remedies were in order, based on the realisation that the soul was actually at an advanced level.[70]

When, finally, the soul had reached 'the superior part where the virtues and the spirit reside', it would abandon 'the light of the intellect and, in the affective sphere, the intentions, desires and inclination geared to what is good, [as well as] strength and patience'. Now the process of perfection ceased to be a struggle: 'Where previously [the soul] fought with great vigour, now it feels without strength, unable to resist'. But it was precisely here that new dangers lurked, for in this state, 'every twig seems like a beam'. Thus the soul experienced such 'obscurity, blindness and darkness, anxiety, weariness, difficulty, rebellion, and great timidity, confusion, and depression' as to be unable 'to return to its former good intentions'. It was a moment of 'great peril'. Gagliardi listed six forms of emotional backlash: grief provoked by the sense of disaster, misguided guilt over one's perceived defects, a great but pointless effort to address these, renewed frustration at the lack of success, resulting impatience, and finally fear, timidity, and the risk of desperation.[71] And he spent the remainder of his discussion of the first stage of perfection outlining the remedies that would return the soul to its intended detachment from the self and its conformation and submission to God.

---

68   Ibidem 203.
69   Ibidem 211.
70   Ibidem 211–215.
71   Ibidem 217–218.

THE TROUBLES OF CHRISTIAN PERFECTION

The second stage largely followed the same playbook; in this regard the *Breve compendio* differs from the *Vita*, where purgation gave way to something substantially different, illumination. However, deepening advances were again jeopardised by new setbacks, even more heightened. But what further detachment was needed when the soul, upon the successful conclusion of the first stage, had fully geared itself to the enactment of virtue? The answer was that this activity, however blameless, was still the result of our 'election and will operating with its own active virtue and imposing acts of virtue on other forces'. In other words, a residue of one's own will and interest remained, and hence something to strip off: the very potential of acting on one's will.[72] Here an opening for renewed turmoil appeared:

> Experience, however, proves that the soul finds itself so oppressed by weariness and afflictions, and assailed by so many distractions and miseries that, even as it tries to force itself, no act results, neither of thanking God, nor [any act of] strength, or patience, or anything else, except for desiring what pleases God and remaining thus [in a state of] suffering and transfixed to the core by a thousand temptations.[73]

To be sure, this impasse did not remove the progress the soul had made. Its new condition resembled that of martyrs exposed to the blows of their attackers: lacking in 'active force', they were reduced to 'suffer[ing] everything for the love of God and be[ing] contented with that'. The contemplative likewise was reduced to 'passive quiet' and to giving in to God's will. This stage, like the first one, required the annihilation crucial to the entire process of perfection. But now it was joined by the 'withdrawal (*sottrazione*) of all that is active in the soul'.[74] In a new, critical paradox, the will thus had to elect its own surrender. But here, again, trouble awaited:

> Very often there ensue woes and afflictions far greater than before, because [at this point the soul] has lost the shelter of the acts of virtue. Moreover, in the kindling of its inner depths, new, vehement and disordered emotions (*movimenti*) are stirred up, different from anything ever experienced in life, so that [the soul] feels as if in a hell.[75]

---

72   Ibidem 226–227.

73   Ibidem 227–228.

74   Ibidem 228–229.

75   Ibidem 231.

The response to this further challenge was again expressed in paradoxical terms: 'Here one ought to arm oneself (*armarsi*) with nothing except submission and passive quiet to suffer everything to satisfy God who wants it'. This attitude provided 'the greatest power' – power, however, that was not active, but consisted in self-exposure and self-surrender. The suffering soul was weak and patient as a lamb: it embraced a passive conformity with God's will that was the premise of deification. It was not an act of self-sacrifice, but 'almost a giving oneself in prey to God'.[76] This effort was twofold. On the one hand, the soul, being thus reduced to quiet, exposed itself and was prepared most willingly (*volenterissime*) to suffer 'all woes, afflictions, and miseries'. On the other, in this inward state (or *apex animae*), it opened itself to God so that he might operate through it with its consent, which was both free and passive. The soul then offered thanks – consisting of love, union with God, and election of every virtue – without experiencing these sentiments expressly (*expresse*), for this would involve active engagement, but 'accepting them and cooperating with them with all one's heart and in freedom'. Hence a double state of ecstasy. Withdrawn from the senses, the intellect was devoid of its natural powers, but 'receive[d] divine lights and insights'. This was, Gagliardi said – in one remaining acknowledgement of a mystical experience he had previously warned against –, 'what the mystics call *pati divina*'. But he hastened to add that God operated to greater effect through the will, 'raising it up in a practical and most virtuous ecstasy': this was 'an even higher form of *pati divina*'.[77]

What was left was the third stage. It required far less discussion, barely a page of text. The reason was simple: here the will was entirely denuded and impotent. Its 'power of freedom' reached its apex where it 'entirely renounc[ed] its own will ('tutto il suo proprio volere') and liberty'. Gagliardi adopted legal language here. 'In making this renunciation, the will disowns itself ('la volontà si fa non propria volontà'), because it entirely cedes and surrenders itself by its own right ('juri suo') into the hands of another will'.[78] In this way, Gagliardi added in a telling (apocryphal) simile, Paulinus of Nola had offered his own freedom to liberate a young man enslaved by Vandal raiders. If the soul's surrender was thus a form of self-enslavement, it promised freedom from emotional struggle.

---

76   Ibidem.

77   Ibidem 232–234.

78   Ibidem 237–238. It should be noted that Gagliardi's original text referred to 'tutto il suo volere' ('its entire will') and 'non volontà' ('non-will'). The word *proprio/propria* was added in the process of censorship, no doubt to avoid the more radical implication that the will was entirely erased.

THE TROUBLES OF CHRISTIAN PERFECTION

4 Borromeo's Spiritual Exercises

Let us return once more to the comparison that served as our point of departure – the ascetic discipline ascribed to Carlo Borromeo. Lelio Pellegrini suggested that this regimen extended to his spirituality, but did not go into detail. On this subject Borromeo's canonisation process and the hagiographical tradition provide rich, if carefully tailored, information. Particularly relevant are descriptions of the Jesuit *Spiritual Exercises* of which the Milanese archbishop was a known devotee. The last occasion on which he made them was to become the edifying capstone of his life and a key episode in later hagiographies.[79] The retreat, directed by the Jesuit Francesco Adorno, took place on the Sacred Mount of Varallo over two weeks in October 1584, within days of his death on November 3. The routine was focused on penitential exercises and the contemplation of the scenes of Christ's passion: the site, of course, offered an ideal setting for the Ignatian practice of *compositio loci* in full engagement of the senses.[80] The account of Giussano, echoing that by Bascapè, offers further details. At Varallo Borromeo, through physical deprivation and hours-long mental prayer, pursued a penitential practice that left him in tears. He reportedly spent a long time in the chapels of the Garden of Gethsemane and, especially, the Sepulchre. His contemplation of Christ's dead body was intensified by the premonition of his own approaching end,

---

79   Bascapè, *De vita et rebus gestis* 258–260 (quote at 260; *Vita e opere* 610–616, at 614); Giussano, *Vita* 482–483. See also Giussano's account of the spiritual exercises which Borromeo made, again under Adorno's direction, at Varallo in 1578, ibidem 344–345.

80   This aspect is (along with Borromeo's involvement with renovations of the sanctuary) a key focus of recent art-historical studies. See Göttler C., "The Temptation of the Senses at the Sacro Monte di Varallo", in De Boer W. – Göttler C. (eds.), *Religion and the Senses in Early Modern Europe* (Leiden-Boston: 2013) 393–451; Harpster G.T., *Carlo Borromeo's Itineraries: The Sacred Image in Post-Tridentine Italy* (PhD dissertation, University of California-Berkeley: 2018) 76–106; Benzan C., "Alone at the Summit: Solitude and the Ascetic Imagination at the Sacro Monte of Varallo", in Enenkel K. – Göttler C. (eds.), *Solitudo: Spaces, Places and Times of Solitudo in Late Medieval and Early Modern Cultures* (Leiden – Boston: 2018) 336–363; eadem, "Coming to Life at the Sacro Monte di Varallo: the Sacred Image *al vivo* in Post-Tridentine Italy", in Balfe T. – Woodall J. – Zittel C., *Ad vivum? Visual Materials and the Vocabulary of Life-Likeness in Europe before 1800* (Leiden – Boston: 2019) 224–246; Fleming, "The Emotions of Ignatius of Loyola" 51–52; Casper A.R., *An Artful Relic. The Shroud of Turin in Baroque Italy* (University Park, PA: 2021) 33–36. Longo P.G., "Il Sacro Monte di Varallo nella seconda metà del XVI secolo", in *I sacri monti di Varallo e Arona dal Borromeo al Bascapè* (Novara: 1995) 41–140 remains a critical earlier study.

as if 'he wished to be dissolved and to be with Christ' (Phil. 1:23).[81] Penitence thus turned into *ars moriendi*: he stepped up his devotions 'as if there were little time left to gain merit'. If this suggested an active will – rather than its renunciation – otherwise he was found (by Adorno and others) to be 'entirely alienated from the things of this world'. Giussano was clearly aware of the inability to see into Borromeo's soul: in a token of his humility (the biographer noted), the archbishop was wont to keep 'concealed the inner celestial favours' he received. But now these favours 'abounded to the point that, no longer able to resist, he showed the most manifest signs of them, so that it appeared that his blessed soul was entirely united with God and already enjoyed the heavenly delights'. When celebrating mass, in particular, 'it was evident that he was all transported (*rapito*) in spirit and, because of the interior commotion of his soul, he shed tears in such abundance' as sometimes to have to interrupt the mass. Bascapè had already used similar language: Adorno and others had found Borromeo 'divinely moved (*divinitus commotum*) in a most unusual and singular way'. Giussano cited the testimony of Bishop Bernardino Morra of Aversa, who on this occasion had seen his face 'luminous and resplendent' and 'conjectur[ed] that this was caused by the celestial light that irradiated his soul, spread to his exterior, and communicated to the body part of that brightness with which he will be endowed in the heavenly fatherland'.[82]

For all its limitations, this account essentially aligns with Pellegrini's understanding of the Borromean ethos of self-control, aided by Ignatius's contemplative techniques. The reference to the 'interior commotion of his soul' is the only indication of the contemplative's emotional state. We can find this assessment confirmed, unexpectedly, by the same Jesuit who had guided Isabella Berinzaga's spiritual exercises in the months before Borromeo undertook his last. On December 13, 1603 – hence barely more than two years after the papal condemnation of Berinzaga's 'life and revelations' – Achille Gagliardi wrote Archbishop Federico Borromeo a long letter to testify to Borromeo's sanctity. The document was certified and introduced as evidence in the canonisation process and quoted extensively in Giussano's biography.[83] The letter is important for two reasons. On the one hand, because of its terminology: Gagliardi called Borromeo an exceptional model of 'Christian perfection' in both the

---

81   This scene took poignant iconographic form in Giovanni Battista Crespi's *Carlo Borromeo Adoring the Dead Christ at Varallo* (c. 1610): see Casper, *An Artful Relic* 34–36.

82   Giussano, *Vita* 482.

83   Marcora C., "Il processo diocesano informativo sulla vita di S. Carlo per la sua canonizzazione", *Memorie storiche della diocesi di Milano* 9 (1962) 635–652. Cf. the long quotation in Giussano, *Vita* 513–514.

THE TROUBLES OF CHRISTIAN PERFECTION

active and contemplative spheres; and he observed in Borromeo's demeanour a 'quiet' resulting from quotidian prayer. As we have seen, both terms were central to the *Breve compendio*; and the latter may have contributed to suspicions about its method of mystical annihilation. On the other hand, Gagliardi agreed with the biographers in emphasising the strenuous energy – even the violence – with which Borromeo sought the virtuous life in defiance of his own bodily impulses. Thus, in his pursuit of vigilance – literally, his battle against sleep – 'he had an enormous taste for pure violence, however long it would last'. Unlike other fights, he could not prevail in this one; he was able to 'grab the prey from his enemy's hands without taking his power'. If Borromeo could 'win but not defeat' this adversary, he nevertheless demonstrated his unrelenting activation of the will to obtain virtue. As for prayer and contemplation, Gagliardi discerned 'many manifest signs' that the archbishop was 'full of God'. His soul displayed a 'quiet, peace, tranquility, evenness, stability and immobility' unperturbed by 'the slightest annoyance, slackening, or relaxation'. Yet, like other eyewitnesses, even Borromeo's former confessor could not plumb his depths: 'he never opened up with me to reveal the slightest feeling, but always talked about what he read in [the works of] others or asked for clarifications and instructions, like one who wants to learn'.[84] Thus, if Gagliardi's description of Borromeo's spirituality adopted some language he had also used in the *Breve compendio*, and if the references to the 'violence' of the archbishop's austerities seem to echo those concerning Berinzaga, this is not sufficient to assume deeper similarities. There is no hint of a surrender of the will, nor of deepening emotional crises on the way to divine union.

5   Conclusion

If the nascent early-modern discipline of pathology was motivated by the interest in knowing, interpreting, steering, and/or suppressing the affects, the

---

84   Marcora, "Il processo diocesano informativo" 640–641. The point about Borromeo's 'violenza a se stesso' in pursuit of 'virtù' returns in Giussano, *Vita* 610. Borromeo's efforts to collect and record rules for meditation and prayer are known. Thus we know of a set of 'ricordi e regole d'essercitii spirituali', including 'punti di passione', on which Borromeo was working and which he had asked Gagliardi 'to review and bring to perfection' (letter of Borromeo to Gabriele Paleotti, October 20, 1584, cited in Longo, "Il Sacro Monte di Varallo" 98); cf. Göttler, "Temptations of the Senses" 437, and Buzzi F., "'Ante orationem praepara animam tuam': il *De oratione* di Carlo Borromeo e la spiritualità del suo tempo", *Studia borromaica: saggi e documenti di storia religiosa e civile della prima età moderna* 20 (2006) 43–90.

pursuit of impassibility occupies a distinctive place in it. In the religious realm the contested ventures of Isabella Berinzaga and Achille Gagliardi offer a noteworthy example. While their place in the longer tradition of European mysticism deserves further study, the influence they exercised through the *Breve compendio* is undisputed.[85] This chapter has sought some insights into the genesis of its method, particularly as far as the engagement with the affects is concerned. Three points are worth noting by way of conclusion.

First, the different versions of the *Vita*, the *Breve compendio*, and several related manuscripts suggest that the process by which Achille Gagliardi sought to turn Isabella Berinzaga's religious experiences into a spiritual method was dynamic and unfinished. Further analysis, especially of the *Secondo compendio*, along with Gagliardi's other writings, may shed additional light on this process. But this much is clear. The Jesuit penned a biographical narrative – hagiographic in style if not intent – as well as a record of Berinzaga's spiritual exercises in which some biographical elements served as illustrative material. The document thus assumed hybrid features: it was part hagiography, part meditative journal, part spiritual guide. Subsequently, Gagliardi turned a single, distinctive element of one of the three stages – self-annihilation – into the basis of a drastically revised meditative system, in which elements from his earlier account, both physical and affective, returned in abstract form as challenges to be overcome in the conquest of the self and the surrender to God. In the process, the Jesuit removed aspects which he knew to be controversial, including any references to the mystical pretences and emotional experiences of religious women. His emphasis in the *Vita* on the authenticity of Berinzaga's spirituality, and on his own limited role in its expression, gave way to reminders of clerical supervision and warnings against potential pitfalls.[86]

Second, as he sought to distill a method out of Berinzaga's lived experiences, disentangled from the categories with which he (and she) had started, Gagliardi developed a sustained reflection, if not a theory, on the functioning

---

85 But see the literature cited above in n. 7. An important source in this longer history is constituted by the detailed *censure*, commissioned by the Congregation of the Index, which led to the placement of the *Breve compendio* on the Index of Forbidden Books in 1702. At that point, the book was read in light of the seventeenth-century controversies over Quietism and the resulting condemnations of Miguel de Molinos, François Fénelon, and others. See Archivio del Dicastero per la Dottrina della Fede, Rome, C.L.C.L. 1701–1702, fasc. 45, fols. 481–510.

86 Gagliardi's insistence, in later years, that his role was limited to defining the points of meditation was a double-edged sword: it supported his claims about the authenticity of Berinzaga's experiences, but it also allowed Gagliardi to distance himself from her 'pericolose imaginationi o illusioni': see Signorotto, "Gesuiti, carismatici e beate" 184.

THE TROUBLES OF CHRISTIAN PERFECTION 359

of the will. On the one hand, he considered how negative emotions could be deliberately overridden by positive ones. On the other, he examined the consequences of transforming the application of the will to control the affects into an experiment in relinquishing it. Paradoxically, he found that the exercitant's very spiritual progress – marked by a deliberate yielding of the will – was accompanied by ever greater affective turmoil up to the point of divine union. The issue was sufficiently worrisome to Gagliardi that he devoted a brief separate treatise to it. It explained how the *apathia* pursued by the practitioner created the potential for serious temptations and 'troubles of the soul': hence the need for a determined response inspired by the passion of Christ and the ancient martyrs.[87] Over time – but the precise chronology and context remain unclear – he developed a further awareness of the pitfalls of *apathia*. Of several contemplative treatises Gagliardi penned in his later years – unpublished and largely unexamined by scholars – the *Praxis cultus interni* (1590) suggests as much. This guidebook for Jesuit novices, meant to lay the foundations of contemplative practice, ended with a reference to 'annihilation and conformity with God' as a culminating experience, 'which has its own compendium' dedicated to it – an obvious reference to the *Breve compendio*.[88] Yet the *Praxis* also issued a stern warning against '*apathia*, which means impassibility', more precisely against 'the vain and laborious pretext of acquiring and affecting this impassibility, almost in the way of the Stoics, and recovering Adam's innocence – and this by one's own efforts and diligence, and not without the hidden danger of some form of Pelagianism'. Hence the need to 'establish principles and foundations containing the true path to perfection'.[89] Gagliardi's reference to Pelagianism suggests that what was ostensibly a critique of *apathia* may actually be an implicit defence of the method he had laid out in the *Breve compendio*. The point certainly touched on the core of that method – the surrender of the will – and suggests the following, final comparison with Pellegrini's book.

Third, then, Berinzaga's spiritual exercises, as Gagliardi had defined them, shared some common ground with the program of moral improvement Lelio Pellegrini articulated in *De affectionibus noscendis et emendandis*. Yet as the mystic practiced these exercises, and more definitively when her spiritual director turned them into a method, the goal of annihilation and the resulting

---

87 Gioia, *Breve compendio* 266–275.

88 Gagliardi Achille, *Praxis cultus interni*, Biblioteca Nazionale Centrale, Rome, Fondo Gesuitico 1115, fol. 66r: 'Postquam [corr. from *postquem*] sequitur annihilationis ac conformitatis cum Deo status omnium altissimus, de quo in proprio compendio'.

89 Ibidem, fols. 57 v–58 r.

apathia set them apart from Pellegrini's prescriptions. In another respect, too, the two books and their models diverged, reflecting larger fissures in Counter-Reformation religion. Central to this split, undoubtedly, were gendered notions of acceptable emotional expression and engagement with the divine. Pellegrini was not shy to draw on the stoic, masculine aura of a soon-to-be saint like Carlo Borromeo to illustrate his treatise on enhancing the affective life. Gagliardi's project, in contrast, moved in the opposite direction. While some spiritual directors of the time were able to write the *vitae* of their spiritual daughters to promote their sanctity, this proved impossible for Gagliardi.[90] As clouds of suspicion formed over the turbulent spirituality of this post-Tridentine *divina madre*, and over his relationship with her, his writings moved from hagiography to abstract treatise.[91] Whereas Borromeo's profile loomed large in Pellegrini's book – and the emerging iconography of the Counter-Reformation – Berinzaga was not to be the 'idea and [...] portrait of all virtues' Gagliardi wished to promote. And as far as we know, no image of her has been preserved. Ironically, however, this erasure prevented neither the censorship of the *Breve compendio intorno alla perfettione christiana* nor its wide diffusion and profound influence.

Selective Bibliography

Alardus Lambert, *Pathologia sacra novi testamenti, continens significantiora eiusdem et cum emphasi singulari usurpata loca* (Lipsiae, sumptibus Henningi et A.M. Gross: 1635).

Alfieri F., "Tracking Jesuit Psychologies. From Ubiquitous Discourse on the Soul to Institutionalized Discipline", in Županov I.G. (ed.), *The Oxford Handbook of the Jesuits* (Oxford: 2019) 783–810.

Alsted Johann Heinrich, *Encyclopaedia septem tomis distincta* (Herbornae Nassoviorum, s.e.: 1630).

---

90 Bilinkoff J., *Related Lives: Confessors and Their Female Penitents (1450–1750)* (Ithaca, NY: 2005). For the medieval roots of the phenomenon, see Mooney C.M. (ed.), *Gendered Voices. Medieval Saints and Their Interpreters* (Philadelphia: 1999); Coakley J.W., *Women, Men, and Spiritual Power. Female Saints and Their Male Collaborators* (New York: 2006).

91 Cf. Prosperi A., "Dalle 'divine madri' ai padri spirituali" (1986), in Id., *Eresie e devozioni. La religione italiana in età moderna*, vol. III, *Devozioni e conversioni* (Rome: 2010) 65–88; note, at 88, the reference to Borromeo's disciple Giovanni Fontana, bishop of Ferrara (1590–1611), who remarked in his *Avertimenti per la sanità dell'anime* (1610) that 'non si legge che Dio sia apparso in forma di donna ma solamente d'huomo maschio'.

THE TROUBLES OF CHRISTIAN PERFECTION 361

Bascapé Carlo, *De vita et rebus gestis Caroli S.R.E. Cardinalis tituli S. Praxedis Archiepicopi Mediolani* (Ingolstadii, ex officina typographica Davidis Sartoris: 1592).

Bascapé Carlo, *Vita e opere di Carlo Archivescovo di Milano Cardinale di S. Prassede* (Milan: 1983).

Benzan C., "Alone at the Summit: Solitude and the Ascetic Imagination at the Sacro Monte of Varallo", in Enenkel K. – Göttler C. (eds.), *Solitudo: Spaces, Places and Times of Solitudo in Late Medieval and Early Modern Cultures* (Leiden – Boston: 2018) 336–363.

Benzan C., "Coming to Life at the Sacro Monte di Varallo: the Sacred Image *al vivo* in Post-Tridentine Italy", in Balfe T. – Woodall J. – Zittel C. (eds.), *Ad vivum? Visual Materials and the Vocabulary of Life-Likeness in Europe before 1800* (Leiden – Boston: 2019) 224–246.

Bilinkoff J., *Related Lives: Confessors and their Female Penitents (1450–1750)* (Ithaca, NY: 2005).

Bonora E., *I conflitti della Controriforma. Santità e obbedienza nell'esperienza religiosa dei primi barnabiti* (Florence: 1998).

Bremond H., *Histoire littéraire du sentiment religieux en France*, 12 vols. (Paris: 1916–1933).

Brunelli G., "Gagliardi, Achille", in *Dizionario biografico degli Italiani* 51 (1998).

Buzzi F., "'Ante orationem praepara animam tuam': il *De oratione* di Carlo Borromeo e la spiritualità del suo tempo", *Studia borromaica: saggi e documenti di storia religiosa e civile della prima età moderna* 20 (2006) 43–90.

Caravale G., *L'orazione proibita. Censura ecclesiastica e letteratura devozionale nella prima età moderna* (Florence: 2003).

Caravale G., *Libri proibiti. Censura e cultura italiana in età moderna* (Bari – Rome: 2022).

Carella C., *L'insegnamento della filosofia alla "Sapienza" di Roma nel Seicento. Le cattedre e i maestri* (Florence: 2007).

Casper A.R., *An Artful Relic. The Shroud of Turin in Baroque Italy* (University Park, PA: 2021).

Catto M., *La Compagnia divisa. Il dissenso nell'ordine gesuitico tra '500 e '600*, 2nd ed. (Brescia: 2022).

Champion M. – Garrod R. – Haskell Y. – Feros Ruys J., "But Were They Talking about Emotions? *Affectus, affectio*, and the History of Emotions", *Rivista storica italiana* (2016) 521–543.

Coakley J.W., *Women, Men, and Spiritual Power. Female Saints and Their Male Collaborators* (New York: 2006).

Cozzi G., "Berinzaga, Isabella Cristina", in *Dizionario biografico degli Italiani* 9 (1967).

Dannhawer Johann Conrad, *Pathologia rhetorica sive disputatio de affectibus generatim ad publicam proposita* (Argentorati, Johann Repp: 1632).

De Boer W., "Invisible Contemplation: A Paradox in the *Spiritual Exercises*", in Enenkel K. – Melion W.S. (eds.), *Meditatio – Refashioning the Self. Theory and Practice in Late Medieval and Early Modern Intellectual Culture* (Leiden – Boston: 2011) 235–256.

Faesen R., "Achille Gagliardi and the Northern Mystics", in Maryks R. (ed.), *Companion to Jesuit Mysticism* (Leiden – Boston: 2017) 82–111.

Fleming A.C., "The Emotions of Ignatius of Loyola and the Mental Pictures of the *Spiritual Exercises*", in Graham H. – Kilroy-Ewbank L. (eds.), *Emotions, Art, and Christianity in the Transatlantic World, 1450–1800* (Leiden – Boston: 2021) 33–70.

Friedrich M., *The Jesuits: A History*, trans. J.N. Dillon (2016; Princeton, NJ: 2022).

Gioia M. (ed.), *Per via di annichilazione. Un testo di Isabella Cristina Berinzaga redatto da Achille Gagliardi S.I. Edizione critica, introduzione e note* (Rome – Brescia: 1994).

Gioia M. (ed.), *Breve compendio di perfezione cristiana. Un testo di Achille Gagliardi S.I. Saggio introduttivo ed edizione critica* (Rome – Brescia: 1996).

Giussano Giovanni Pietro, *Vita di S. Carlo Borromeo Prete Cardinale di Santa Prassede Arcivescovo di Milano* (Roma, Stamperia della Camera Apostolica: 1610).

Göttler C., "The Temptation of the Senses at the Sacro Monte di Varallo", in De Boer W. – Göttler C. (eds.), *Religion and the Senses in Early Modern Europe* (Leiden – Boston: 2013) 393–451.

Graham H. – Kilroy-Ewbank L. (eds.), *Emotions, Art, and Christianity in the Transatlantic World, 1450–1800* (Leiden – Boston: 2021).

Gutberleth Henricus, *Pathologia, hoc est doctrina de humanis affectibus, physice et ethice tractata* (Herbornae Nassoviorum, s.e.: 1615).

Harpster G.T., *Carlo Borromeo's Itineraries: The Sacred Image in Post-Tridentine Italy* (PhD dissertation, University of California-Berkeley: 2018).

Hillman J., "Internal Theater and Emotional Scripts in French Jesuit Meditative Literature", in Marculescu A. – Morand Métivier C.-L. (eds.), *Affective and Emotional Economies in Medieval and Early Modern Europe* (Cham: 2018) 143–163.

Hotson H., *Johann Heinrich Alsted 1588–1638: Between Renaissance, Reformation and Universal Reform* (Oxford: 2000).

Karant-Nunn S.C., *The Reformation of Feeling: Shaping the Religious Emotions in Early Modern Germany* (Oxford: 2010).

Knebel S.K., *Wille, Würfel und Wahrscheinlichkeit. Das System der moralischen Notwendigkeit in der Jesuitenscholastik 1550–1700* (Hamburg: 2000).

Lines D.A., *Aristotle's Ethics in the Italian Renaissance. The Universities and the Problems of Moral Education* (Leiden – Boston: 2002).

Longo P.G., "Il Sacro Monte di Varallo nella seconda metà del XVI secolo", in *I sacri monti di Varallo e Arona dal Borromeo al Bascapè* (Novara: 1995).

Macdowell William, *Pathologia sive discursus ethico-politicus de affectibus* (Groningae, typis Ioannis Sassi: 1623).

Magirus Johannes, *Pathologia, sive morborum et affectuum omnium praeter naturam, qui corpus humanum invadere solent, enumeratio* (Francofurti, ex officina Paltheniana: 1615).

Malena A., *L'eresia dei perfetti. Inquisizione romana ed esperienze mistiche nel Seicento Italiano* (Rome: 2003), 293–299.

Marcora C., "Il processo diocesano informativo sulla vita di S. Carlo per la sua canonizzazione", *Memorie storiche della diocesi di Milano* 9 (1962) 635–652.

Marín J.M., "A Beguine's Spectre: Marguerite Porete († 1310), Achille Gagliardi († 1607), and Their Collaboration across Time", *The Way* 15, 3 (2012) 93–110.

Mazzonis Q., *Riforme di vita cristiana nel Cinquecento italiano* (Soveria Mannelli: 2020), Engl. trans. *Reforms of Christian Life in Sixteenth-Century Italy* (London-New York: 2022).

McNamer S., *Affective Meditation and the Invention of Medieval Compassion* (Philadelphia: 2010).

Melion W.S., "Allegory and Affective Experience in Thomas Sailly, S.J.'s *Thesaurus precum et exercitiorum spiritualium* of 1609", in Graham H. – Kilroy-Ewbank L. (eds.), *Emotions, Art, and Christianity in the Transatlantic World, 1450–1800* (Leiden – Boston: 2021) 71–125.

Modica M., *Infetta dottrina. Inquisizione e misticismo nella Roma del '600* (Rome: 2009).

Moles Vicente, *De morbis in sacris literis pathologia* (Matriti, ex officina Joannis Sancii: 1642).

Mooney C.M. (ed.), *Gendered Voices. Medieval Saints and Their Interpreters* (Philadelphia: 1999).

Mostaccio S., "Per via di donna. Il laboratorio della mistica al servizio degli Esercizi Spirituali. Il caso Gagliardi/Berinzaga", in Zarri G. (ed.), *Storia della direzione spirituale*, vol. 3: *L'età moderna* (Brescia: 2008) 311–329.

Mostaccio S., *Early Modern Jesuits between Obedience and Conscience during the Generalate of Claudio Acquaviva (1581–1615)*, trans. C. Copeland (London – New York: 2016).

Panigarola Francesco, *Oratione fatta dal R.do Padre Panicarola nel Duomo di Milano nelle essequie dell'Illustriss.mo et Rever.mo Cardinale di S. Prassede Archivescovo di Milano* (Roma, per gl'Heredi d'Antonio Blado: 1584).

Pavone S., "Gagliardi A.", in *Dizionario storico dell'Inquisizione*, ed. Prosperi A. – Lavenia V. – Tedeschi J., 4 vols. (Pisa: 2010) 2: 633–634.

Pellegrini Lelio, *De affectionibus animi noscendis et emendandis commentarius* (Romae, apud Vincentium Pelagallum: 1598).

Pelosi O., "'Spoliata di sé e d'ogni cosa': la scrittura negata di Isabella Berinzaga (1551–1624)", *Annali d'Italianistica*, vol. 25: *Literature, Religion, and the Sacred* (2007) 311–323.

Petrocchi M., *Storia della spiritualità italiana* (Turin: 1996).

Pirri P., "Il P. Achille Gagliardi, la Dama milanese, la riforma dello spirito e il movimento degli zelatori", *Archivum Historicum Societatis Iesu* 14 (1945) 1–72.

Pozzi G. – Leonardi C. (eds.), *Scrittrici mistiche italiane* (1988; Genoa: 1996).

Prosperi A., "Dalle 'divine madri' ai padri spirituali" (1986), in Id., *Eresie e devozioni. La religione italiana in età moderna*, vol. III, *Devozioni e conversioni* (Rome: 2010) 65–88.

Reddy W., *The Navigation of Feeling: A Framework for the History of Emotions* (Cambridge – New York: 2008).

Rosenwein B.H., *Generations of Feeling: A History of Emotions, 600–1600* (Cambridge: 2016).

Sassi Giovanni Antonio (ed.), *Noctes Vaticanae seu sermones habiti in academia a S. Carolo Borromeo Romae in Palatio Vaticano instituta* (Mediolani, Typographia Bibliothecae Ambrosianae: 1748).

Schutte A.J., *Aspiring Saints: Pretense of Holiness, Inquisition, and Gender in the Republic of Venice, 1618–1750* (Baltimore: 2001).

Signorotto G., "Gesuiti, carismatici e beate nella Milano del primo Seicento", in Zarri G. (ed.), *Finzione e santità tra medioevo ed età moderna* (Turin: 1991) 177–201.

Sluhovsky M., *Believe Not Every Spirit: Possession, Mysticism, and Discernment in Early Modern Catholicism* (Chicago: 2007).

Störkel R., *Bildungsgut für Europa – Die Encyclopaedia des Johann Heinrich Alsted von 1630* (Berlin: 2019).

Stroppa S., "L'annichilazione e la censura: Isabella Berinzaga e Achille Gagliardi", *Rivista di storia e letteratura religiosa* 32, 3 (1996) 617–625.

Stroppa S., "Achille Gagliardi e Giuseppe Blondo a Milano. La riflessione sugli *Esercizi Spirituali* e la mistica", *Studia Borromaica* (2007) 307–327.

Turchini A., *La fabbrica di un santo. Il processo di canonizzazione di Carlo Borromeo e la Controriforma* (Casale Monferrato: 1984).

Valier Agostino, *Vita Caroli Borromei Cardinalis Sancti Praxedis Archiepiscopi Mediolani* (Verona, apud Hieronymum Discipulum: 1586).

Viller M., "L'abrégé de la perfection de la Dame milanaise", *Revue d'ascétique et de mystique* 12 (1931) 44–89.

Weiganmeir Johann Baptist, ΠΑΘΟΛΟΓΙΑ *sive disputatio de affectibus* (Tubingae, Theodoricus Werlin: 1623).

Zardin D., "Il 'Manuale' di Epitteto e la tradizione dello stoicismo cristiano" (2006), in idem, *Carlo Borromeo. Cultura, santità, governo* (Milan: 2010) 29–54.

Zarri G. (ed.), *Finzione e santità tra medioevo ed età moderna* (Turin: 1991).

Zarri G. (ed.), *Storia della direzione spirituale*, vol. 3: *L'età moderna* (Brescia: 2008).

PART 2

Portraying Mixed Emotions in the Visual Arts

∵

SECTION A

Mixed Emotions in Image-based Spiritual Exercises

∵

CHAPTER 11

O vos omnes: Recognition, Tragic Emotion, and the Passerby Topos in Northern European Art around 1500

Mitchell Merback

Abstract

This paper examines a dynamic tendency discernible in late medieval devotional images, especially the portrayal of the Man of Sorrows by Netherlandish and south German artists around 1500, and its grounding in the prophetic address of Lamentations 1:12 ('O all ye that pass by the way, attend, and see if there be any sorrow like to my sorrow'), which interpellates the anonymous 'passerby' as a potential agent of compassionate identification, ethical attention, and reciprocal care. Tracing the varied uses of the stich *O vos omnes* as a meditative commonplace and a caption for Passion imagery reveals it to be a powerful structuring principle within the moral-spiritual economy of late medieval devotions. Three dimensions of this structuring are treated: its *deictic structure*, which imposed certain inescapable ethical demands on the beholder; the *sequence of emotions* the address could instigate; and its capacity as an experiential trope. Approached in these terms, Lamentations 1:12 can be seen to implant a specific challenge at the heart of premodern Christian subjectivity – the challenge to undergo a *conversion*, not only as a redirection of one's narrative of self, but as an assent to a cluster of emotions associated with the ideal of 'penitential sorrow' (*penthos*) and 'compunction of the heart' (*compunctio cordis*). A key to their unfolding in the devotional encounter is the experience of *recognition*, a term that technically derives from Aristotelian poetics but operates in the context of devotional performance as a catalyst and driver of this inner 'turning' of the sinner toward God.

Keywords

Lamentations (biblical text) – passersby – recognition – pity – fear – conversion – *penthos* ("penitential sorrow") – compunction

© MITCHELL MERBACK, 2025 | DOI:10.1163/9789004694613_012

In the late medieval image-type known as "Christus im Elend" (Christ in Misery), "Christus in der Rast" (Christ in Repose), and "Herrgottsruhbild" (Our Lord at Rest),[1] Jesus is portrayed at an imagined station of the Cross immediately prior to his crucifixion. Seated in contemplation, alienated and derelict, he reflects on the Passion from a space outside its action and seems to hold the totality of its significance in his mind. Drawing the image away from any specific narrative moment, sculptors such as the Upper Rhenish master who carved the figure now in Cologne learned to depict Christ hunched in misery upon the "cold stone" of Golgotha – a prisoner often bound with ropes, silently awaiting execution [Fig. 11.1].[2] Of course the synoptic gospel writers recount no such moment of rest after the soldiers had 'led him away to crucify him' (Matt. 27:31; cf. Mark 15:20). Only the brief encounter with Simon of Cyrene and Jesus's consoling address to the "daughters of Jerusalem" (Luke 23:28–31) are interposed between the mocking by Pilate's goons and the arrival at 'the place that is called Golgotha' (Matt 27:33). The scene of dejected repose, like 'the many other things Jesus did' which Gospel writers passed over in silence (John 21:25), had to be reconstituted exegetically, a process of creative embroidery F.P. Pickering famously described as a 'translation of ancient prophecies, metaphors, similes and symbols [...] into "history".'[3] Such a progressive elaboration of Passion narrative took place in both Italian and German art from around 1300. By the end of that century, the multiplication of scenic units we see, for example, in the Passion altarpiece now in Hannover, known as the *Goldene Tafel* [Fig. 11.2], was already being complemented by new "devotional close-up" portraits based on this iconography.[4] In both of these developments altar painters initially led the way.

---

1   Fundamental are Von der Osten G., "Job and Christ: The Development of a Devotional Image", *Journal of the Warburg and Courtauld Institutes* 16.1–2 (1953) 153–58; idem, "Christus im Elend (Christus in der Rast) und Herrgottsruhbild", in *Reallexikon zur deutschen Kunstgeschichte*, vol. 3 (Stuttgart: 1953) 644–58; and Dobrzeniecki T., "Debilitatio Christi: A Contribution to the Iconography of Christ in Distress," *Bulletin du Musée National de Varsovie* 8 (1967) 93–111.

2   See the informative study by Surmann U., *Christus in der Rast* (Frankfurt am Main: 1991). In the Low Countries the theme was called "Christus op de koude steen"; see for example the work of *circa* 1480–90 by a north Netherlandish follower of Derick Baegert in Esztergom, in Smeyers M. (ed.), *Dirk Bouts (ca. 1410–1475), een Vlaams primitief te Leuven*, exh. cat. (Leuven: 1998) no. 53.

3   Pickering F.P., *Literature and Art in the Middle Ages* (Coral Gables: 1970) 234.

4   See Köllermann A.-F., "Die Goldene Tafel. Gestalt und Programm", in Köllermann A.-F. – Unsinn C. (eds.), *Zeitenwende 1400. Die Goldene Tafel als europäisches Meisterwerk* (Petersberg: 2019) 25–49; and on the multiplication of narrative units, see Merback M.B., "Passion of Christ", in *The Grove Encyclopedia of Medieval Art and Architecture* (Oxford: 2012); also *Grove*

FIGURE 11.1   Upper Rhine, Christ in Misery, c.1480. Limewood with traces of polychromy, 81.6 cm in height. Cologne, Kolumba
IMAGE: © LOTHAR SCHNEPF; KOLUMBA, COLOGNE

Heirs to that period of innovation, the generation of German painters working in the decades before the Reformation devoted themselves to refining the scenographic conception of Christ in repose, while also developing new devotional versions of the theme. Both types can be found in the oeuvre of Hans Holbein the Elder (c.1460–1524). For the so-called *Gray Passion*, a set of twelve panels from a now-dismembered altarpiece of unknown provenance, Holbein arranged the players in what were by then more or less traditional

---

Art Online. Oxford Art Online (available at http://www.oxfordartonline.com/subscriber/article/grove/art/T2217023).

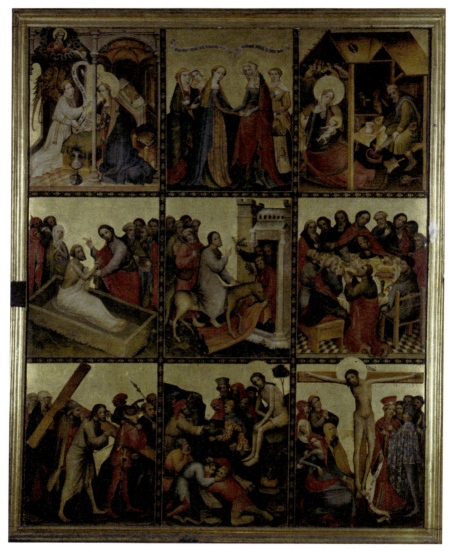

FIGURE 11.2   North German, Passion Scenes, inner face of the left wing of a Passion Altarpiece known as the *Goldene Tafel*, c.1410–18. Mixed technique on oak panel, 231 × 184 cm (wing dimensions). Hannover, Landesmuseum
IMAGE: LANDESMUSEUM HANNOVER – ARTOTHEK

O VOS OMNES: NORTHERN EUROPEAN ART AROUND 1500

terms [Fig. 11.3].[5] About ten years later, the artist evacuated Golgotha of all its actors save two, placing Christ, collapsed in exhaustion upon the Cross with his wrists crossed and bound, opposite the weeping Virgin in a desolate landscape stewn with bones [Fig. 11.4].[6] Inspiration for this rare pairing of the Sorrowing Virgin with a Christus in Elend figure may have come from a Passion tract such as the one composed by Heinrich of Sankt Gallen (late 14th century), which includes a scene where Christ is momentarily forgotten by the soldiers and Jews on their way to Golgotha. Seated on a stone, he espies his mother among the mourning women and seeks to console her – though his address is rudely cut short as the soldiers whisk him away again.[7] Such a slender narrative backbone, if that is indeed what Holbein had in mind, freed the artist to organize the composition purely along the intersubjective axes connecting his protagonists to the beholder and to one another. Modeling perfect fortitude, the statuesque Virgin gazes upon her son while he trains his gaze upon us with a plaintive expression both consoling and accusing. This organization of the image into complementary axes of address may look fairly conventional to students of "late Gothic" (*spätgotische*) art and piety, but its incorporation into a total poetic treatment of the scene –the tokens of desolation scattered about the landscape, the road that snakes into the distance, the strategically placed songbirds[8] – makes our interpellation as spectators especially gripping. This

---

5   See Krause K., *Hans Holbein der Ältere* (Munich – Berlin: 2002) 119–39. Holbein did, however, introduce a rare motif: amidst the barrage of insults and blows, Jesus presses his little finger against his lips, expressing his will to keep silent to the end, "like a lamb before its shearer" (*quasi agnus coram tondente obmutescet*), in the words of Isaiah 53:7. The gesture has a further source in the Book of Psalms; see Dobrzeniecki, "Debilitatio Christi" 109.

6   See Von der Osten, "Christus im Elend" 655; *Hans Holbein der Ältere und die Kunst der Spätgotik*, exh. cat. (Augsburg: 1965) no. 43; Surmann, *Christus in der Rast* 26; and Lüdke D. et al., *Grünewald und seine Zeit. Große Landesaustellung Baden-Württemberg*, exh. cat. (Karlsruhe: 2007) 379 (no. 140). The panel's reverse bears coat of arms of one Jörg Vetter, who hailed from Donauwörth and served as *Bürgermeister* of Augsburg in 1514. The nimbuses crowning the two figures were at some point overpainted.

7   Discussed in Dobrzeniecki, "Debilitatio Christi" 99–100, who illustrates pendant panels by an unidentified Polish painter, one depicting the disconsolate Christ seated upon the Cross, the other Mary standing with her arms crossed (figs. 4–5); see also Fehlemann S., "Christus im Elend: Vom Andachtsbild zum realistischen Bilddokument", in Brock B. – Preiß A. (eds.), *Ikonographia: Anleitung zum Lesen von Bildern* (*Festschrift Donat de Chapeaurouge*) (Munich: 1990) 79–96, at 86. Heinrich's Passion tract was translated into every German dialect and widely disseminated in manuscript and incunables; see Ruh K., *Das Passionstraktat des Heinrich von St. Gallen* (Thayngen: 1940) 29–60.

8   Though species are hard to discern, Holbein may have intended to contrast the goldfinch, perched in the tree above Christ's head, with a magpie snooping around the bones at the picture's left margin; see Roth-Bojadzhiev G., *Studien zur Bedeutung der Vögel in der*

FIGURE 11.3   Hans Holbein the Elder, Christ in Repose before the Crucifixion, panel from the *Gray Passion*, c.1495–1500. Oil on panel, 88.5 × 88 cm. Stuttgart, Staatsgalerie
IMAGE © STAATSGALERIE STUTTGART

combination of formal and iconographic elements strongly suggests that we are dealing with an image built up, as it were, around a specific topos.

That topos I believe can be found in the timeless words of Lamentations 1:12: 'O vos omnes qui transitis per viam, attendite, et videte si est dolor sicut dolor meus! quoniam vindemiavit me, ut locutus est Dominus, in die irae furoris sui' (O all ye that pass by the way, attend, and see if there be any sorrow like to my sorrow: for he hath made a vintage of me, as the Lord spoke in the day of

mittelalterlichen Tafelmalerei (Vienna: 1985) 67, who notes only the rarity of such landscapes in Holbein's oeuvre.

FIGURE 11.4   Hans Holbein the Elder, Mary and Christ at Rest on Golgotha, c.1503–04. Oil on limewood panel, 41.5 × 32.8 cm. Hannover, Landesmuseum
IMAGE: LANDESMUSEUM HANNOVER – ARTOTHEK

his fierce anger).[9] Long associated with the Passion portrait tradition, and frequently used as a devotional caption attached to the Man of Sorrows, the Pietà, as well as certain kinds of Crucifixion images (discussed below), the lament was most effective rhetorically when it was imaginatively placed the mouth of the suffering Christ. So performed, Jeremiah's call to Israel to awake from its collective servitude to sin becomes an accusation leveled at the individual, calling the soul to repentance.

---

9   Unless otherwise noted, biblical passages in English are from the Douay-Rheims Bible, accessed online at http://www.drbo.org/index.htm.

In what follows I demonstrate the importance of the stich *O vos omnes* as a structuring principle within the moral-spiritual economy of late medieval devotions by attending to three aspects of its use as an address to the Christian subject. First is its *deictic structure*, which imposed certain demands on beholders of late medieval devotional images such as Holbein's; second is the sequence of *emotions* it could instigate and inform; and third – a consequence of the first two aspects – is its capacity as an *experiential* trope. Framed thus, in experiential terms, Lamentations can be seen to impose a specific challenge to premodern Christian subjectivity: a notional *role* to which the devout beholder assents, so that, in the course of his or her prayerful meditation on Christ's innocent suffering, he or she must undergo a kind of conversion, a conversion that is not only a redirection in one's narrative of self, but an assent to certain complex emotions. I call this interpellation of the beholder *the passerby principle*, and do so for several reasons. As a performed topos, *O vos omnes* calls for a renunciation of the role of the bystander, a second notional role which I take to be the negative mirror-image of the passerby.[10] Instead of coming to the aid of the other, the bystander is the one who retreats into isolation, condemning him- or herself to a state of spiritual inattention and waywardness. Passingby can of course be its own form of spiritual neglect, an abrogation of piety: late medieval reformers complained about the widespread practice of entering church only 'to see God in passing' (*pour veoir Dieu en passant*) before again departing.[11] But, as we will see, there are ample grounds for positing the beholder-as-passerby in positive terms, as a figure for the Christian who heeds the call of suffering and, with heart "softened" by contrition, recognizes his or her vocation within the spectacle of life, recognizing, that is, the need to *attend*. The clearest expression of this subject-position in Christian tradition is Augustine's definition of *misericordia* in book nine of *The City of God*. After endorsing Cicero's view of pity as the noblest of emotions, Augustine asks, 'But what is pity [*misericordia*] except a kind of fellow-feeling in our own hearts for the sufferings of others that in fact impels us to come to their aid as far as our ability allows?'[12] Late medieval artists loved to portray this sympathy dawning

---

10   Art historical work on the bystander as a special category of beholder has only recently gotten started; see the essays in Fricke B. – Krass U. (eds.), *The Public in the Picture: Involving the Beholder in Antique, Islamic, Byzantine, Western Medieval and Renaissance Art* (Chicago: 2015).

11   Among the many signs of late medieval piety's degeneration remarked by reformers and memorably diagnosed by Huizinga J., *The Autumn of the Middle Ages*, trans. R.J. Payton and U. Mammitzsch (Chicago: 1996) 178.

12   "Quid est autem misericordia nisi alienae miseriae quaedam in nostro corde compassio qua utique si possumus subvenire compellimur?" (*City of God*, 9,5); in Augustine,

FIGURE 11.5   Housebook Master, Crowd beneath the Cross, detail from Calvary scene, central panel of a Passion Altarpiece, 1480–85. Tempera and oil on pine panels, 131 × 173 cm (central panel). Freiburg im Breisgau, Augustinermuseum
PHOTO © AUGUSTINERMUSEUM, MICHAEL JENSCH, CC BY 4.0

on the faces of those who bear witness to the Passion at close range. Observe, for instance, the subtly differentiated forms of attentiveness produced by that talented late medieval physiognomist, the Housebook Master, for his Golgotha tableau now in Freiburg [Fig. 11.5].[13]

To encounter suffering along the "way" in the *pèlerinage de la vie humaine* – which was, as the Cistercian Guillaume de Deguileville's inspired allegory makes clear, always a *pèlerinage de l'âme*[14] – to pause in sympathy, to feel impelled to attend – these are *emotional* events to which pious beholders were enjoined by certain kinds of devotional images. To heed the call of "heartfelt sympathy" means figuratively stepping off the way and abstracting onself

City of God Against the Pagans, 7 vols., trans. G.E. McCracken (Cambridge, Mass: 2014) 3:168–69; see also the discussion in Keaty A., "The Christian Virtue of Mercy: Aquinas' Transformation of Aristotelian Pity", *Heythrop Journal* 46 (2005) 181–98, at 186, who construes the passage as a discussion of *mercy*.

13   For catalogue basics, see Zinke D. (ed.), *Augustinermuseum. Gemälde bis 1800* (Freiburg: 1990) 38–42, with older literature.

14   See Hagen S.K., *Allegorical Remembrance: A Study of* The Pilgrimage of the Life of Man *as a Medieval Treatise on Seeing & Remembering* (Athens – London: 1990).

FIGURE 11.6 Workshop of Cornelis Engebrechtsz, Christ in Repose with Nun and Saint Augustine, *c*.1500. Oil on panel, 52 × 41 cm. Antwerp, KMSKA
PHOTO: COLLECTION KMSKA – FLEMISH COMMUNITY, PUBLIC DOMAIN MARK 1.0

from time's ceaseless flow.[15] This is what the Augustinian nun portrayed in the panel by Cornelis Engebrechtsz, now in Antwerp, must have imagined herself doing. In the open air of Golgotha she kneels; as the executioners prepare the cross she attends Christ in his misery and joins him in meditation [Fig. 11.6].[16]

15 See Davis I., "'Ye that pasen by þe Weiye': Time, Topology and the Medieval Use of Lamentations 1.12", *Textual Practice* 25.3 (2011) 437–72.
16 Discussed in Falque I., *Devotional Portraiture and Spiritual Experience in Early Netherlandish Painting* (Leiden: 2019) 64–65 (cat. 351).

O VOS OMNES: NORTHERN EUROPEAN ART AROUND 1500

Modeling decorum in the face of unspeakable suffering and unsurpassable love, the nun's outward appearance is completely impassive. By convention, however, this outward control of emotions betokens an active, inner cognition in which all the vital energy associated with *affectus* is cycled back into meditative attention and kept below the surface of appearances, producing an ethical model for others to follow.[17] So long as affect is controlled at the appetitive level and rendered invisible, meditation can open itself to a veritable cascade of emotions; and that cascade, as I will argue, is initiated by the experience and practice of *recognition*. Among the lyrical elements of Holbein's picture that prompt such an experience, and which we see thematized in the Engebrechtsz panel, is Christ's imploring look. That look solicits our attention in a way that outstrips all the stops and starts of Passion narrative and condenses it at the point where our gaze crosses his, that is, where a *mutual recognition* takes place. For everything else they strove to be, pictures structured around this principle realized their devotional and therapeutic potential as virtual spaces for cognitive work and spiritual performance, making them theaters of encounter where reciprocities of the kind I am describing could be enacted. As it unfolds within these overlapping processes, emotion itself, we will see, likewise takes on the character of a *praxis*.[18]

1   *O vos omnes*, **Liturgical Seeing, and the Man of Sorrows**

Lamentations 1:12 has a long and complex reception history to which we can hardly do justice in a short space. Its earliest literary adaptation occurs in the antiphons and responses for Good Friday, also known as the *Improperia* (ninth to tenth century). In performed couplets, which drew tragic content from Hebrew prophecy to stoke an affective response to the Passion, Christ reproaches "his people" for the insults and injuries inflicted by their many ingratitudes, and demands accountability: 'My people, My people what have I done to you, how have I offended you, answer me!' (*Popule meus, quid feci tibi? aut in quo constristavi te? responde mihi!*). Within this preeminent ritual

---

17   On the psychological "conjunction of opposites" that determines the decorous meditative attitude in donor portraits, see Merback M.B., "Pain and Memory in the Formation of Early Modern *Habitus*", *Representations* 146, Special Issue, Ablow R. (ed.) (2019): 59–90, esp. 61–67, with further references.

18   A valuable reconceptualization of emotion as a mode of practice, stemming largely from the work of Pierre Bourdieu, is Scheer M., "Are Emotions a Kind of Practice (And is that what makes them have a history?): A Bourdieuian Approach to Understanding Emotion", *History and Theory* 51.2 (2012) 193–220.

context the address to "my people," traditionally interpreted as "the Jews," extends to every sinning Christian – all who harbor a "judaizing" impulse within. A strong structural continuity unites the many diverse liturgical uses of *O vos omnes* from its earlier Frankish-Gregorian paraphrasing to more expansive later adaptations such as the Venetian *depositio hostiae* ceremony (the ritual entombment of the *corpus Christi* on Good Friday) and the Venetian *planctus Marie*, both studied by Nils Petersen.[19] That the stich in such contexts principally invited the congregation to 'identify with the divine sufferings of Christ and Mary' is beyond doubt, but there is more to its operation. In the *depositio* rite, for example, poetic laments incorporating *O vos omnes* are used to punctuate the moments of frozen suspension in what Petersen calls the 'linear unfolding of a liturgico-memorial happening.' Collective contemplation of the host at these "stational halts" is structurally fused to the individual's sense that he or she is directly implicated in the epiphany of Christ's suffering body.[20] Alternating moments of physical movement and its suspension, processional passage and its cessation, intensify those moments of *pro me* confrontation when Christ (or Mary) addresses "my people," imploring the individual in transit to stop, look, feel, and attend.

Embedded within the changing aspects of *O vos omnes*'s liturgical use over its history is the very trope of response with which this paper is concerned, *recognition*, a trope often worked out in specifically ocular terms. In the connections drawn by Hans Belting in his important study of the Passion portrait, the Good Friday antiphons stage 'a climax of the intensifying pathos of suffering of the one whose "eyes became blind from weeping," and the *Videte* is taken up in the echo: "Now they saw whom they had pierced" (*Viderunt in quem transfixerunt*) and recognized in him the Son of God.'[21] The Gospel source of this imagery is John 19:36–37,[22] where the collective recognition of those assembled around the crucified Jesus is explicitly framed as the fulfillment of

---

19   Petersen N.H., "Liturgical Representation and Late Medieval Piety", in Lillie E.L. – Petersen N.H. (eds.), *Liturgy and the Arts in the Middle Ages: Studies in Honour of C. Clifford Flanigan* (Copenhagen: 1996) 181–204, who considers the ceremony, compiled by the Dominican Alberto Castellani (1480–1522) and published in 1523, a compound based on the *Improperia* and the traditional *adoratio crucis* ceremony for Good Friday.

20   Petersen, "Liturgical Representation" 187; for the *depositio* rites, see also Young K., *The Drama of the Medieval Church*, 2 vols. (Oxford: 1933) 1:112–48, esp. 128 for the antiphons and responses using *O vos omnes* and its paraphrases, 130 for the uses of the *Improperia*.

21   Belting H., *The Image and its Public in the Middle Ages: Form and Function of Early Paintings of the Passion*, trans. M. Bartusis – R. Meyer (New Rochelle: 1990) 199, with reference to *S. Gregorii Magni Liber Responsalis* (PL 78, 767).

22   "For these things were done, that the scripture might be fulfilled: You shall not break a bone of him (*Facta sunt enim haec ut Scriptura impleretur: Os non comminuetis ex eo*). And

O VOS OMNES: NORTHERN EUROPEAN ART AROUND 1500

Scripture (the reference is to Zacharias 12:10). A parallel linkage of epiphany and recognition punctuates the phases of the liturgical *depositio*, when the same antiphons were sung during the procession to the sepulcher and then at the display of the Host, as we have seen. Attending clergy perform the lament Christ addresses to the Daughters of Zion, imploring them to "see my sorrow" (*Videte dolorum meum*). Further verses from Jeremiah are placed in the mouth of the Sorrowing Virgin at the moment of the entombment: 'I am entirely desolate, because there is no one to console me' (*Desolata sum nimis, non est qui consolatur me*).[23]

It was with good reason, then, that Belting called *O vos omnes* 'a locus classicus in the rhetoric of the Middle Ages.'[24] Likewise, its uses in medieval sermon literature were so widespread that Siegfried Wenzel could call it a 'meditative commonplace.'[25] Within a devotional context, the call to stop, listen, and look (*aspice*), constitutes the Christian individual as a guilty sinner – the *causa* of Christ's pain – but also a potential agent of consolation. This implies an obligation at once existential and ethical, the fullest realization of the devotional goal of psychologically identifying with Christ or Mary. To a degree not fully grasped by scholars, the devotional culture of the later Middle Ages encouraged devotees to make themselves both the subject and the object of *pietas*, an untranslatable word that merges the meanings of "pity" and "piety" but also, if we look at its classical origins, obligation and "dutifulness." The image-type that stages this consolatory dimension of religious emotion most powerfully is widely known as the *imago pietatis*, a name that became attached to the micro-mosaic icon promoted since the late fourteenth century by the Carthusians of Santa Croce in Rome [Fig. 11.7].[26] Less important than the name, of course,

---

again another scripture saith: They shall look on him whom they pierced (*Et iterum alia Scriptura dicit: Videbunt in quem transfixerunt*)."

23   Belting, *Image and Its Public* 199.

24   Belting, *Image and Its Public* 197–201 (Appendix B), quote at 201.

25   Wenzel S., *Verses in Sermons: 'Fasciculus Morum' and its Middle English Poems* (Cambridge MA: 1978) 122, also 115.

26   As John Lansdowne explains, *pietas* meant obligation or duty long before it connoted pity or compassion; the represention of Christ *in formam pietatis*, the earlier name given in the sources, shows him as "the manifestation of *pietas* [...] the agent of *pietas*, not its passive recipient"; Lansdowne J., *The Micromosaic of the Man of Sorrows at Santa Croce in Gerusalemme in Rome*, 2 vols. (Ph.D. dissertation, Princeton University: 2019) 113; see also Belting, *Image and its Public* 32–33, commenting on the 14th-century Bohemian diptych in Karlsruhe (Kunsthalle): "The Bohemian artist [...] annuls this definitive passivity by allowing the dead man to make a gesture betraying that he is not dead and can therefore not only receive piety, but can grant it as well. Jesus begins a subtle dialogue with the viewer who is attuned to this nuance." Thankfully, a great deal of the older bibliography

FIGURE 11.7
Late Byzantine (Constantinople), Micromosaic Icon of the King of Glory, early 14th century. Colored stones, 13 × 19 cm. Rome, Basilica di Santa Croce in Gerusalemme
PHOTO: SOPRINTENDENZA SPECIALE PER IL PATRIMONIO STORICO, ARTISTICO ED ETNOANTROPOLOGICO, ROME

is the capacity of the visual formula to hold opposites in suspension, a structure which captures the polyvalence of *pietas*. Pictorially condensed in the formula of the dead-but-alive Christ, that polyvalence establishes the Passion portrait as a prime locus of therapeutic reciprocities between Christ and the beholder.[27]

Those same reciprocities testify to the deep emotional power of Lamentations as a *deictic* text.[28] Linguistically it can be said to operate across three deictic fields, wherein the two more familiar kinds of deixis, a person-based deixis ("you" and "I") and a space-based deixis ("passing by the way") are projected onto a notional third deictic domain. This third kind of deixis is at once temporal and, if I may use the word, *existential*. As we will shortly see, it is the axis along which affective response meets appraisal and judgment and will; where the subject experiences the challenge of Christian discipleship in a dawning *self*-recognition, the *peripeteia* of a life-story, the soul's transit back to God.

has now been superceded by Lansdowne, but still indispensible is Bertelli C., "The *Image of Pity* in Santa Croce in Gerusalemme", in Fraser D. – Hibbard H. – Lewine M.J. (eds.), *Essays in the History of Art Presented to Rudolph Wittkower* (London: 1967) 40–55.

27 See Merback M.B., "The Man of Sorrows in Northern Europe: Ritual Metaphor and Therapeutic Exchange," in Puglisi C.R. – Barcham W.L. (eds.), *New Perspectives on the Man of Sorrows* (Kalamazoo: 2013) 77–116.

28 Pandit L., "Emotion, Perception and Anagnorisis in the Comedy of Errors: A Cognitive Perspective", *College Literature* 33.1 (2006) 94–126, at 99.

FIGURE 11.8
Israhel van Meckenem, Man of Sorrows Standing in the Tomb, later 15th century. Engraving, 10 × 7.6 cm. Vienna, Albertina
PHOTO: ALBERTINA, PUBLIC DOMAIN MARK 1.0

By 1500 European painters, sculptors, and printmakers had fully transformed the Byzantine type of the dead Christ into an animated presence who, kneeling or standing under his own power, with eyes open, wields the instruments of the Passion, offers himself to the beholder, or spouts blood into the chalice. Along with these well-known developments we find Lamentations 1:12 and its variants increasingly used as a rhetorical-devotional caption, for example, in one of several reproductions of the Santa Croce icon made by the Rhenish engraver Israhel van Meckenem after 1450 [Fig. 11.8]. This reveals both the inherent capaciousness of the Passion portrait and its specific capacity as an image cut to the measure of the passerby principle. More sophisticated in its application of the verse is the indulgenced broadsheet by an artist in the circle of Albrecht Dürer (most likely Wolf Traut). Published in Nuremberg by Hieronymus Höltzel, first in Latin and then a year later in German, the sheet combines a sixty-eight line poem by Sebastian Brant, an eight-line prayer by Benedict Chelidonius, an indulgence, and the large woodcut by Traut [Fig. 11.9].[29] Today in Washington, the version shown here is a rare exemplar of that first edition,

---

29   On the broadsheet, see Schilling E., "An Indulgence Printed at Nuremberg in 1512," in Goetz O. (ed.), *Essays in Honor of Georg Swarzenski* (Chicago: 1951) 125–28; Bühler A., "Die Heilige Lanze. Ein ikonographischer Beitrag zur Geschichte der deutschen Reichskleinodien", *Das Münster* 16.3/4 (1963) cat. 23; and Smith J.C., *Nuremberg. A Renaissance City, 1500–1618*, exh. cat. (Austin: 1983) no. 59. For the German version of 1512 (exemplar in the Albertina, inv. DG 1934/494), see Lüdke et al., *Grünewald und seine Zeit* no. 141.

FIGURE 11.9 Wolf Traut, Man of Sorrows and Mother of Sorrows, indulgenced broadsheet published by Hieronymus Höltzel in Nuremberg, 1512, with typographical text. Woodcut highlighted with red ink, 42.5 × 26 cm. Washington, D.C., National Gallery of Art, Rosenwald Collection

PHOTO © NATIONAL GALLERY OF ART

FIGURE 11.10
Jacob Binck, Man of Sorrows – Ecce Homo, 1520–30. Hand-colored engraving on a manuscript leaf, 133 × 96 mm, from a disassembled Flemish prayerbook. London, British Museum
PHOTO © TRUSTEES OF THE BRITISH MUSEUM

highlighted with red ink, possibly by the sheet's first owner. Performing his part of Brant's dialogical lament, and looking consolingly at his mother, Christ rests his left hand on the edge of the woodblock's lower frame, inscribed ASPICE QVI TRANSIS QVIA TV MIHI CAVSA DOLORIS (Look, you who pass by, you who are the cause of my sorrow). This same variant of *O vos omnes* reappears about a decade later in the banderolle which the peripetetic painter-engraver Jakob Binck (1485–1568/9) placed above a Man of Sorrows who cradles the Cross and the Column while displaying his wounds [Fig. 11.10]. This seems to paraphrase an older formula in which angels mediate the exhortation to the beholder, as seen in the small ivory relief carved somewhere in south Germany around 1500, and now in New York [Fig. 11.11].[30] Despite the loss of polychromy and gilding on the banderole that twists and darts between the winged messengers hovering above the three-figure *Pietà* (derived, evidently, from a widely copied engraving by Martin Schongauer), the incipit is unmistakeable: *O vos om[nes] qui transi[tis] per [viam, atten]dite et vid[ete si est dolor sicut dolor meus]*. With such innovations and repetitions, the silent dead Christ in the Passion portrait has become an active, virtual partner in meditative dialogue.

30 The ivory has been little studied; in the short piece written to mark its 1999 accession, Barnet, while admirably placing the work in the context of late Gothic ivory production, declared the inscription illegible; Barnet P., "An Ivory Relief of the *Man of Sorrows* in New York", *The Sculpture Journal* 4 (2000) 1–5.

FIGURE 11.11
South German, Man of Sorrows between Mary and Saint John, c.1500. Elephant ivory with paint and gilding, 8.6 × 6.5 × 1.0 cm. New York, Metropolitan Museum of Art
PHOTO COURTESY OF THE METROPOLITAN MUSEUM OF ART, WWW.METMUSEUM.ORG

Not surprisingly, as part of the long evolution of the affective image in the Latin church, the prophetic-penitential appeal of "Aspice qui transis" was coordinated directly with other kinds of Passion imagery as well. The earliest instance I am aware of is the *imago Crucifixi*, a mosaic installed above the entrance to the monastery complex constructed by Latin crusaders during the renovations of the Church of the Holy Sepulchre in Jerusalem. From the twelfth-century *Libellus de locis sanctis* (Little Book of the Holy Places), a Latin guidebook and travelogue composed by a certain German monk known only as Theodoricus, we know that the image was reknowned for its affective power, for it was 'painted in such a way that it imbued every beholder with deep remorse' (*ita depicta ut cunctis intuentibus magnam inferat compunctionem*).[31] Whatever its actual appearance, to ensure the image would produce this emotional effect, Theodoricus continues, its authors arrayed the verses from Lamentations around it: *Aspice qui transis quia tu mihi causa doloris. / Pro te*

---

31   Theodoricus, *Libellus de Locis Sanctis* (1164–74), eds. Bulst M.L. – Bulst W. (Heidelberg: 1976) 18; quoted in Belting, *Image and Its Public* 6; see also Bulst-Thiele M.L., "Die Mosaiken der 'Auferstehungskirche' in Jerusalem und die Bauten der 'Franken' im 12. Jahrhundert", *Frühmittelalterlichen Studien* 13 (1979) 442–71, and esp. 461–62. For the *Libellus* in translation, see Theoderich, *Guide to the Holy Land*, trans. Stewart A., 2nd edn, ed. Musto R.G. (New York: 2006) 16. Also discussed in Lillie E.L., "O vos omnes qui transitis per viam [...]: The Quotation from Lamentations 1, 12 in Danish Medieval Art", in Lillie – Petersen (eds.), *Liturgy and the Arts* 205–220, at 215n23.

O VOS OMNES: NORTHERN EUROPEAN ART AROUND 1500 387

passus ita, pro me noxia vita.[32] At the far end of this development, long after the western devotional image had learned to make visible the beholder's penitential communion with the Savior, the same verbal address was still being used in conjunction with the Crucifixion and other Passion themes. We find it, for example, set beneath the visionary grisaille of Christ on the Cross – flanked by Saint Jerome in penitence – by the Lübeck painter Hermen Rode (*c.*1468–*c.*1504), a work commissioned by the brothers Heinrich and Adolf Greverade for their family chapel in the city's Marienkirche, destroyed by fire in 1942.[33] Arrayed clockwise around its wooden frame, in crisp Roman letters, the full verse of Lamentations 1:12 hails the beholder of Quentin Massys's boldly theatrical *Ecce Homo* of *c.*1518–20, today in the Prado – offering a counter-deixis, one might say, to the conspiratorial whisper of the Jewish tormentor in the panel's lower right corner.[34]

In rarer instances the Mother of Sorrows could be assigned the lines from Lamentations. In the famous passionale commissioned by Abbess Kunigunde from the convent of St. George in Prague (*c.*1312–20), the second of the book's five major segments, devoted to the *Planctus* and the *collaetatio Mariae*, revisits the events of Good Friday through the plaintive meditations of the Virgin. Turning from her portrait on folio 11 recto, where she is pictured in mute desolation at the foot of the Cross – though she's alone on the page – the reader is implored to stop, look, and join in the universal recognition of the Mother's pain: *Attendite igitur, universi populi, et videte dolorum meum, si unquam visus, dolor similis, sicut dolor meus* (Pay attention, all my people, and see my sorrows, whether there is to be seen any sorrow like unto mine).[35]

---

32   Belting, *Image and Its Public* 228 n13.

33   Hermen Rode, Crucifixion in Grisaille, exterior face of the *Greverade Diptych* (Crucifixion and the Dormition of the Virgin), dated 1494 by an inscription, formerly in the Marienkirche Lübeck; see Hasse M., *Die Marienkirche zu Lübeck* (Munich: 1983) 114, fig. 62.1; and Rasche A., "Hermen Rode: The Painter of Medieval Lübeck and His Art Production", in Jahnke C. (ed.), *A Companion to Medieval Lübeck* (Leiden: 2019) 306–51 at 340–43, and figs. 11.17–18, 11.34 (Crucifixion), and 11.35–36, with further references.

34   Research has not yet shown whether the frame is exactly contemporary with the panel or – more likely – of a slightly later date; for the most recent discussion, see Schütt F. *Quentin Massys: Bildstrategien der Affekterzeugung* (Petersberg: 2021) 70–74.

35   *Pasionál abatyše Kunhuty* (Prague, National Library of the Czech Republic, Sign. XIV A 17), fol. 11v; for the manuscript's contents, see Toussaint G., *Das Passional der Kunigunde von Böhmen: Bildrhetorik und Spiritualität* (Paderborn: 2003) esp. 14–21, 158–61; cf. Belting, *Image and Its Public* 198. For the digitized manuscript, see http://www.manuscripto rium.com/apps/index.php?direct=record&pid=AIPDIG-NKCR__XIV_A_17____2GWPZB8 -cs#search.

FIGURE 11.12 Claus Sluter, Jeremiah, from the *Well of Moses*, c.1400–06. Dijon, Chartreuse de Champmol.
Artwork in the public domain
PHOTOGRAPH BY THE AUTHOR

Naturally the spoken lines from Lamentions could also be given to their putative author, Jeremiah, as in the powerful figure Claus Sluter and his workshop conceived for the monumental Fountain of Mercy (*fons pietatis*) installation, popularly known as the "Well of Moses," at the Carthusian monastery at Champmol, outside Dijon, around 1400 [Fig. 11.12]. It is not enough, however, to draw the parallel with liturgical mystery plays and other performed spectacles, where Old Testament prophets appealed directly to spectators, summoning them to co-experience the Passion in the most intimate, arresting terms.[36]

---

36 The parallel threads through the modern literature on Sluter, beginning with Huizinga's account in *The Autumn of the Middle Ages* 308–11, but it also appears early in the

O VOS OMNES: NORTHERN EUROPEAN ART AROUND 1500

Because Sluter's figure addresses a beholder who is both physically mobile and notionally "in transit" between the old self and a new one, the injunction to "look" and "recognize" Christ's suffering unfolds across all three deictic axes at once – the person-based deixis, the space-based deixis, and the time-based deixis.[37] This is the axis along which the subject experiences *self-recognition* as well, the reorientation of the soul back toward God. Without an adequate theory of the emotional *process* behind this performance – without, that is, some sense of how sensation and thought, modulated as experience, move along and across these axes – the "affective power" of images, a concept routinely invoked in discussions of response, remains little more than hermeneutical slogan. It is to that problem we can now turn.

2   **Recognition and Compound Emotions: Definitions and Problems**

Earlier I claimed that the complex affective event we call *recognition* is central to the passerby topos and its realization in devotional performance. Its history and psychological contours merit attention. Audiences of the Greek tragedians will recall the passionate intensity of the encounter between brother and sister in Sophocles's *Electra*, a twinned climax of *coming-to-know* as true identities unfold one after the other. Overhearing Electra's lament over the ashes of her brother and contemplating her sufferings, Orestes suddenly realizes it is *his* sister standing before him; then comes Electra's realization that the one before her is indeed the one for whom she mourns. 'The only one, indeed,' Orestes pronounces, 'who has ever come knowing your sorrows as his own.'[38] That moment of revelation in the play provides a classic instance of what Aristotle, in Chapter 11 of *The Poetics*, calls *anagnôrisis* – an unusual word typically translated as "recognition," but sometimes as "discovery" or even "disclosure." In the closest thing he gives to a formal definition, Aristotle calls it 'a change from ignorance to knowledge.'[39] In Sophocles's scene, which

---

modern literature on religious drama; for commentary and additional sources, see Lindquist S.C.M., *Agency, Visuality and Society at the Chartreuse de Champmol* (Aldershot: 2008) 172 and 186–87 n175.

37   On these deictic modes in the reading process, see Stockwell P., *Cognitive Poetics: An Introduction*, 2nd edn. (Independence: 2019) 49–69, esp. 51–53.

38   See esp. Boitani P., "Recognition: The Pain and Joy of Compassion," in *Recognition: The Poetics of Narrative*, ed. P.F. Kennedy – M. Lawrence (New York: 2009) 213–26, at 213.

39   *Poetics* 2.11 (1452a, 30–33); translation from Aristotle, *Poetics*, trans. A. Kenny (New York: 2013) 30.

exemplifies what Aristotle calls 'mutual recognition between a pair,'[40] those wrenching trials of proof which bring a release of passionate joy when knowledge become certain qualify as the *anagnôrisis*, while the attendant realization that Orestes will take his revenge against Clytemnestra after all counts as the *peripeteia*, or reversal. Within his scheme for the tragic arts, recognition was therefore one of two key ingredients poets and playwrites should deploy in crafting the kind of plot (*mythos*) that the philosopher thought best. By means of these two narrative devices the poet discharges his essential duty: to arouse the emotions of the spectator in preparation for their "purification," or *katharsis*.[41]

Modern commentators on the *Poetics* have, by a common effort reaching across several disciplines, revealed how vast in scope the inheritance of these aesthetic principles has been in the western tradition of imaginative literature and drama. Not only Homer and the tragedians cited by Aristotle availed themselves of this dynamic paradigm of narrative. So too did the authors of medieval epics and romances (both Christian and Islamic); Shakespeare the tragedian, Shakespeare the comedian, and other Elizabethans; and a host of modern novelists, playwrights, and filmmakers too numerous to mention.[42] Each in their own way has elevated recognition and reversal to positions of structural importance on a par with *mimesis* itself, the fundamental concept in the *Poetics*. In registering its ubiquity and variety, recent literary studies have highlighted the ways recognition doubles as a device for structuring action within narrative *and* as a trope for the reader's comprehension of truth's disclosure outside the narrative (this, as I explain below, is the dimension that promises the most for our purposes). To a large degree, this dynamic is already implicit in Aristotle's theory of tragedy, since the key emotions aroused by tragic incident – pity most of all – demand of the spectator a relational attitude toward characters, one marked especially by compassion. Literary historians and critics who have pursued the theme now speak of a broadbased "poetics of revelation" that enfolds aesthetic concepts old and new – concepts

---

40 "Since detection is something that takes place between people, it may be either the detection of one person by another (whose own identity is clear) or mutual recognition between a pair"; *Poetics* 2.11 (1425b, 4–7); Kenny (trans.), *Poetics* 30.

41 "Tragedy is a representation of an action of a superior kind – grand, and complete in itself – presented in embellished language, in distinct forms in different parts, performed by actors rather than told by a narrator, effecting, through pity and fear, the purification of such emotions"; *Poetics* 2.6 (1449b, 24–28); Kenny (trans.), *Poetics* 23.

42 See esp. the editors' introduction in Kennedy – Lawrence (eds.), *Recognition* 1–12.

O VOS OMNES: NORTHERN EUROPEAN ART AROUND 1500

such as "epiphany," "insight," "luminous perception," even the "experience of coherence."[43] And some art historians have followed suit.[44]

Any account of the emotional coordinates of recognition is hemmed in by several difficulties. Not least is Aristotle's notorious omission of any sustained account of the tragic emotions from the *Poetics*, where – apart from the importance he accorded pity and fear – the discussion of emotion is focused on *katharsis*, the primary function of tragedy.[45] For his systematic treatment of emotion commentators turn instead to the *Rhetorics*, where we find, among others, the following definition of pity:

> Let pity then be a kind of pain about an apparent [*phainomenos*] evil, deadly or painful, that befalls one who does not deserve it; an evil that one might expect also to come upon himself or one of his friends, and when it seems near.[46]

Within Aristotle's scheme for the arousal of emotions through the arts of persuasion, this definition covers the three foundational things every speaker must take into account: the *type of person* toward whom pity is to be directed; the *characteristic circumstances* that makes the victim seem pitiable; and the *disposition of mind* of the person in whom feelings of pity are to be aroused (i.e., the kind of person inclined to feel pity). The importance of all three features for tracking recognition's affective movements in the way I have in mind will soon become evident. Immediately noteworthy is the singular importance of sense perception, indexed by Aristotle's use of the word *phainomenos*. However it may present itself to knowledge, whether directly or by some other evidence, that evil which has caused or is likely to cause harm must be *manifest* to the onlooker.

Within the confines of the *Poetics* tragic incident is never defined as a function of an agent's moral qualities, virtues or vices. Although Aristotle does allow

---

43   Discussed in Adams B.B. *Coming-to-Know: Recognition and the Complex Plot in Shakespeare* (New York: 2000) 15.

44   See Merback M.B. "Recognitions: Theme and Metatheme in Hans Burgkmair the Elder's *Santa Croce in Gerusalemme* of 1504", *Art Bulletin* 96.3 (2014) 288–318, with further references.

45   See Rorty A.O., "The Psychology of Aristotelian Tragedy," in *Essays on Aristotle's* Poetics, ed. A.O. Rorty (Princeton: 1992) 1–22, reminding us that the *Poetics* is, at the end of the day, "a book of technical advice, as well as a functionally oriented anatomy" (3).

46   Aristotle, *Rhetoric*, 1385b; trans. from Aristotle, *Art of Rhetoric*, trans. J.H. Freese, ed. G. Striker (Cambridge: 2020) 221; see discussions in Konstan D., *Pity Transformed* (London: 2001) 128; and Keaty, "The Christian Virtue of Mercy" 182.

that a person's character (*ēthos*) can determine choices and actions, he insists that tragedy is a mimesis not of emotions but actions (*praxeis*), in particular the electrifying errors or "mistakes" (*harmatiai*) that arise from "not-knowing" (*agnoia*). Unintentional deeds are the source of suffering (*pathos*), and it is they that inspire fear, pity, and compassion in their audiences. At the same time, in his definitions Aristotle is very careful to insist on the thoughts that always accompany emotion; as Richard Sorabji and others have pointed out, the philosopher's accounts of emotions are 'shot through with cognitive terms,' for 'both the orator and the poet need to know exactly what thoughts go into various emotions if they are to act on those emotions.'[47] The two primary emotions worked on by the tragedian, fear (*phobos*) and pity (*eleos*), are prime examples. Fear is not only our distress or disturbance from the appearance (*phantasia*) of an evil that is unavoidably dangerous or destructive; it is always-already accompanied by an expectation (*prosdokia*) that we will suffer as a result. A specific judgment, the *thought* of suffering, then, informs the reflexive feeling of fear.[48] Likewise, when Aristotle defines pity as a form of distress arising from the appearance that a destructive evil has or will afflict someone undeserving of it, he assumes that feeling is accompanied by the expectant thought that we, or someone close to us, will also suffer, since that same evil is seen (*phainesthai*) as near.[49] To make these emotions functional, the dramatist has to mobilize a type of fear that incorporates an expectant fear for oneself, and/or those close to us. Similarly, the pity provoked by plot is best when it amounts to a fear that misfortune will afflict someone like ourselves (*homoious*). 'Aristotle's only restriction,' Sorabji concludes, 'is that if fear for oneself is excessive, it will drive out the pity which it is the function of tragedy to produce.'[50] Tragedy does all this, to repeat, not by imitating emotions – or the attendant mental and moral states of characters – but by imitating fearful and pity-inspiring *events*.

Grasping recognition in this complex sense – as both tragic event and tragic process, cognitive as much as affective in both its temporal and spatial dimensions – is all the more difficult when the "event" is the Christian

---

47   Sorabji R., *Emotion and Peace of Mind: From Stoic Agitation to Christian Temptation: The Gifford Lectures* (Oxford: 2000) 22 and 23 respectively.

48   Sorabji, *Emotion and Peace of Mind* 23.

49   Sorabji, *Emotion and Peace of Mind* 23. Why Aristotle is so careful in calibrating our "distance" from destructive suffering in his definition of pity is worth more than passing attention. As affective responses, pity and fear operate in a delicate equilibrium. If the evil associated with misfortune is so near that we perceive it as personally destructive, pity quickly shades into fear. But if the pain-causing misfortune is too distant from us, we will feel neither fear nor pity.

50   Sorabji, *Emotion and Peace of Mind* 24.

O VOS OMNES: NORTHERN EUROPEAN ART AROUND 1500

beholder's recognition of Christ in his identity as the suffering Savior. There is one main reason for this, which can be indicated only briefly in the present discussion: the form of "coming-to-know" demanded by the Christian image begets an equally powerful, countervailing movement, a *reflexive* passage out of ignorance and into knowledge, identifiable as self-recognition. I have written elsewhere about the structural symbiosis between christological recognition and those reflexive disclosures of "the self" facilitated by visual imagery, and suggested that the mutual enfolding of these two forms of recognition formed the twin requirements, alongside participation in the sacraments, for the restoration of God's image (*imago Dei*) in the soul.[51] Salvific recognition and self-recognition were always intertwined in a kind of ethical-spiritual double-helix as it were, and they involved an intricate play of compound emotions which we must now try to describe.

To that end it will be useful to show, as an integrated hypothesis, how I am connecting recognition to a distinct set of emotions associated with the devotional scenario in which a notional "passerby" becomes a self-recognizing witness to the suffering Christ. The following scheme charts those emotions (in an unavoidably artificial way) across three stages of affective response:

1. Imaginatively "passing by the way" and encountering the spectacle of pain and sorrow, the subject interpellated by Lamentations 1:12 is called upon to enact a recognition of Christ in his identity as the suffering Savior (cf. Isaiah 53) and the Son of God. By virtue of this recognition, the subject stands within an unstable set of situational coordinates (i.e., mobility, alienation from God, waywardness, "ignorance"). This phase is marked by the occurrence of a compound emotion closely akin to the tragic emotion of pity.

2. Christological recognition and the intensification of reciprocal attention demand, in turn, the subject's self-recognition as both disciple (one whose vocation it is to attend to suffering) and sinner (one who is the "cause" of Christ's suffering). This phase is also marked by the occurrence of a compound emotion; this one, however, is closely akin to the tragic emotion of fear.

3. Once enfolded, the two recognitions move the subject toward a new set of situational coordinates (i.e., fixity, attentiveness, "knowledge") and culminate in a conversion. The entire process resolves itself in the inversion of the first compound emotion into its mirror-image (more on this below).

---

51 Merback, "Recognitions."

A full justification or testing of this scheme would be impractical here, but some review of the psychosomatic models of emotion – ancient and medieval – that can lend it proper substance and historicity are in order. But before proceeding to flesh out the hypothetical model in these terms, two brief clarifications are in order.

Firstly and obviously, with the present scheme I am moving *anagnôrisis* beyond the purely technical meaning assigned to it in Aristotelian poetics, where it denotes an element of plot. Considering it instead as a structural principle of response, I am trading in that limited definition for a range of higher powers – psychological, aesthetic, epistemological. Along with its partner, *peripeteia*, it may be understood now as constituting a psychic event in the experience of the individual and – just as important – an event which bears an "existential" relationship to the self's narrative of its relation to God. So whereas Aristotle treats recognition as a functional part of the poetic structure which, when handled properly by the dramatist, produces a certain emotional effect in his audience, I am interested in recognition *as an effect unto itself*. To some extent this move is anticipated in Aristotle's account, which already grants recognition a degree of existential reflexivity. As Amelie Rorty points out, recognition moments in the plots Aristotle favors 'typically fulfull the ancient command to know oneself (*gnōthi seauton*).' In Oedipus's discovery that he is the son of Jocasta, for example, recognition enfolds the knowledge of both who he is *and* the transgressions he has committed. 'As his [prior] ignorance was not merely an intellectual error, but a waywardness that pervaded his actions,' Rorty explains, 'so too his acknowledgement of his waywardness is not merely a cognitive recognition. It consists in his living out his life, a blind man wandering, "a horror, a pollution to be avoided".'[52]

Second, in order to cope with two big problems – the problem of specifying the nature of pity in a Christian devotional context and the problem of determining the flow of emotional experience occurring in pity's wake – I am appealing to the profound transformation Aristotelian emotion underwent in the Middle Ages, notably in the writings of Thomas Aquinas. In his account of Christian mercy, part of his treatise on the theological virtues in the second-second part of *Summa Theologica* (qq1–46), Thomas conserves all three conditions which Aristotle deemed necessary for evoking pity: the undeserving character of the sufferer, the chance circumstances of the evil afflicting him, and the sense of our own vulnerability when witnessing another person's suffering. When it came to organizing his four articles on the topic and

---

52   Rorty, "The Psychology of Aristotelian Tragedy" 12 (both quotes).

O VOS OMNES: NORTHERN EUROPEAN ART AROUND 1500

explaining their Christian meaning, however, Thomas appealed to Augustine of Hippo's definition of pity in *De civitate Dei*. There, as we noted earlier, Augustine defines it as 'a kind of fellow-feeling in our own hearts for the sufferings of others that in fact impels us to come to their aid as far as our ability allows.'[53] Anthony Keaty has highlighted the two immediately relevant features of this definition: on the one hand, what brings about the sympathy for the suffering person characteristic of mercy is "another's distress" (the various instances of which Thomas goes on to analyze); and on the other, what impels the merciful person to aid the sufferer is a certain "subjective disposition" (an inner inclination associated with virtuous action, which is likewise the subject of further analysis by Thomas).[54] This account of mercy reframes pity, then, as an active human charity that manifests the 'friendship love that is God's own.'[55] It combines a clearsighted projection of our own vulnerability onto the situation of suffering, and a necessary transformation of affective response into therapeutic action. With these clarifications and caveats we are better prepared to see why the two types of recognition, along with their accompanying reversals, should be classed as *mixed emotions*.

3   Mixed Emotion and Ambivalence

While considering that both Christ-recognition and self-recognition are grounded in the complex nature of the tragic emotions, we have nevertheless seen that neither one can be simply correlated with the "singular" emotions of pity or fear. On the surface this should be obvious, given that definitions of emotion going back to Aristotle already presuppose a composite nature, wherein bodily sensations and fluctuations occur in a continuous interchange with thoughts and judgments about things. In some quarters such an inclusive conception is called "cognitive emotion." Since mixed emotions are by definition composite responses, we might begin to get a handle on things by simply identifying their component parts. We have already located the delicate equilibrium between pity and fear at the heart of tragic emotion, and seen how Aquinas's transformation of Aristotelian pity into Christian mercy, by presupposing a virtue that inclined the beholder to therapeutic action on behalf of the victim, introduced the emotion of love into the equation. But now we are aiming for something more: a schema that accounts for the entire process

---

53   Augustine, *City of God* 9,5 (as cited above).
54   See Keaty, "The Christian Virtue of Mercy" 186ff.
55   Keaty, "The Christian Virtue of Mercy" 194.

whereby the tandem dawning of Christ-recognition and self-recognition bring about a change in the total "complexion" of emotions experienced in the devotional encounter. To arrive there requires sorting through the other emotions that come into play.

One framework for doing this derives from the classic division of the motive faculty into "concupiscible" and "irascible" parts – i.e., those reactions that count as acts of desiring things held to be pleasurable, set against those driven by the desire to overcome adverse things.[56] Neatly organized along this divide is the classification of emotions put forth by the Cistercian Isaac of Stella (*c*.1100–*c*.1170s) in the mid-twelfth century. Isaac constructed his list as a supplement to the fourfold scheme – a scheme with Stoic origins – adopted by a number of his contemporaries.[57] In thinking about the unfolding of knowledge out of ignorance that defines recognition as an emotional event, we might initially single out from Isaac's list of concupiscible emotions *dilectio* (affection) and *spes* (hope) (although *surprise* is not on Isaac's list, it, too, would seem to play a part whenever identities are disclosed). But the moment recognition in the Passion portrait moves beyond the simple phenomenal "facts" of christological identity to reveal the abject *condition* of the sufferer, as a prerequisite for pity the perception of "some destructive evil" must also enter the picture. On the irascible side of the ledger, and thinking about the recognition of Christ's abject state in the Passion, we might next imagine that pity is mixed with the arousal of *indignatio* (indignation), perhaps also the *odium* (hate) felt toward those who "caused" Christ's wounds – a group that medieval Christians knew included the Pharisees who delivered him, the executioners who pierced him, the blasphemers who reviled him, and above all the Jews who rejected him.

But already we've run into another problem. By the logic of late medieval penitentialism, the ranks of those historical agents seen as worthy of hate and scorn for inflicting harm on the innocent Jesus must include the passerby him- or herself. After all, it is *our* sins, the sins of an ungrateful humanity, that continue to wound the Savior in a perpetual present – an existential culpability enshrined and performed in the *Improperia* from at least the eleventh century

---

56   See Knuuttila S., *Emotions in Ancient and Medieval Philosophy* (Oxford: 2004) 222, who refers to Avicenna's *De anima* I.5 and IV.4. In this famous commentary on Aristotle's *De anima*, the author added a third to the two opposed powers of the soul, one not present in animals: the internal sense of "estimation," or *wahm* in Arabic; see Hasse D.N., *Avicenna's De Anima in the Latin West: The Formation of a Peripatetic Philosophy of the Soul 1160–1300* (London: 2000) 127–53.

57   Knuuttila, *Emotions* 232. On the Stoics' fourfold scheme of generic emotions, which distinguished distress (*lupē, aegritudo*), pleasure (*hēdonē, laetitia*), fear (*phobos, metus*), and appetite (*epithumia, libido, appetitus, cupiditas*), see Sorabji, *Emotion and Peace of Mind* 29–32.

FIGURE 11.13
Jan van Eyck and workshop assistant, Christ as Judge, detail from *Last Judgment*, ca. 1430. Oil on canvas, transferred from wood, 56.5 × 19.7 cm (one panel of a diptych). New York: Metropolitan Museum of Art
PHOTO COURTESY OF THE METROPOLITAN MUSEUM OF ART, WWW.METMUSEUM.ORG

onward, as noted earlier in this essay. Since the origins of the image-type, the epiphany of the Man of Sorrows in the Passion portrait was an experience charged with just this kind of ambivalence. Echoing the serene self-display of the stigmata by the Apocalyptic Judge, seen for example in Jan van Eyck's diptych in New York [Fig. 11.13],[58] the wounded Man of Sorrows at once promised mercy to the blessed and leveled a terrifying accusation against sinners.[59] This ambivalence suggests that the recognition prompted by the Passion portrait, and likewise some powerfully deictic versions of the Mass of Saint Gregory, such as the Middle Rhenish panel in St. Petersburg [Fig. 11.14],[60] always produces a "mixed" emotion: the joy and affectionate desire for a loving God, combined with fear over God's judgment and a painful anticipation of his wrath. Recognition of Christ in his salvific identity paves the way for both emotions,

58   For basics and bibliography, see Ainsworth M.W. – Christiansen K. (eds.), *From Van Eyck to Bruegel: Early Netherlandish Painting in the Metropolitan Museum of Art* (New York: 1998) 86–89 (cat. 1).

59   Panofsky E., "'Imago Pietatis.' Ein Beitrag zur Typengeschichte des 'Schmerzensmanns' und der 'Maria Mediatrix'", in *Festschrift für Max J. Friedländer zum 60. Geburtstage* (Leipzig: 1927) 261–308, at 284–88; and for further discussion, see Merback M.B., *Pilgrimage and Pogrom: Violence, Memory, and Visual Culture at the Host-Miracle Shrines of Germany and Austria* (Chicago: 2013) 286–88.

60   That the inscription is a 16th-century overpainting strongly suggests that an epitaph was repurposed to become an indulgenced panel; see Nemilov A.N., "Gedanken zur geschichtswissenschaftlichen Befragung von Bildern am Beispiel der sog. Gregormesse in der Ermitage," in Tolkemitt B. – Wohlteil R. (eds.), *Historische Bildkunde. Probleme – Wege – Beispiele* (Berlin: 1991) 123–33, with the older literature.

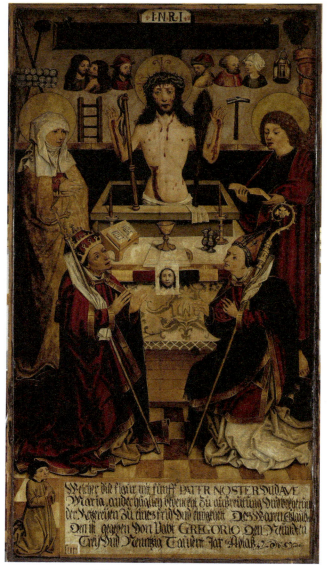

FIGURE 11.14 Middle Rhenish, Mass of Saint Gregory, second half of 15th century, with 16th-century indulgence text. Oil on panel, 141.5 × 71.5 cm. St. Petersburg, The State Hermitage Museum
PHOTO © THE STATE HERMITAGE MUSEUM

O VOS OMNES: NORTHERN EUROPEAN ART AROUND 1500

as does the reciprocal recognition of the passerby as a sinner in need of rescue. The first manifests as a virtuous response of the "intellective appetite" – the reasoned expectation of future happiness in the radiance of God's love – the second as a base passion, a reflex of the "sensitive appetite" to pains that have, in a flash, drawn terrifyingly close.

Admittedly this account remains abstract – as if recognition was only a motif in need of interpretation rather than a transformative event in the life of the devout beholder. This latter, existential dimension needs to be fleshed out further. As I suggested earlier, the twinned disclosures of God and self inherent in all recognition events set in motion a profound reorientation of the self toward God, in a word, a *conversion*. From late antique and medieval witnesses such as Augustine, as well as modern writers including Karl Morrison and Pierre Hadot, we know that conversion is always much always more than a "change of mind," let alone the outward embrace of a new group identity. Conversion is nothing less than the disclosure of a *new self* springing up in place of the old, and its recognition by oneself (and, subsequently, others).[61] When regarded in this light, self-recognition reveals its emotional core and its direction. And it encourages us to return to our sources in search of specific historical models we might map onto its structure. In my final section I wish to test one such model.

4   Gregory the Great and the Two Compunctions

When, in the third century, Origen wrote of the complementarity that existed between an intensified awareness of one's sinfulness and the fervent hope for God's mercy, he relied on the idea of "penitential sorrow," known in Greek as *penthos* (πένθος; lit. "mourning") and in Latin – through the intermediary *katanuxis* (κατάνυξις) – as *compunctio*.[62] Origen no doubt knew all 120 instances of the verb *penthos* appearing in the Septuagint (as helpfully counted by Joseph Pegon). With them he sought for a more compelling exegesis of Matthew 5:4: 'Blessed are those who mourn, for they shall be comforted.'

---

61   Hadot P., "Conversion," in *The Selected Writings of Pierre Hadot: Philosophy as Practice*, trans. M. Sharpe – F. Testa (London: 2020), 93–103; Morrison K.F., *Conversion and Text: The Cases of Augustine of Hippo, Herman-Judah, and Constantine Tsatsos* (Charlottsville – London: 1992); and idem, *Understanding Conversion* (Charlottesville – London: 1992).

62   Pegon J., "Componction", *Dictionnaire de la Spiritualité*, vol. 2, part 2 (1953) 1312–21; cited and discussed in Hunt H., *Joy-Bearing Grief: Tears of Contrition in the Writings of the Early Syrian and Byzantine Fathers* (Leiden: 2004) 24. See also esp. Hausherr I., *Penthos. The Doctrine of Compunction in the Christian East*, trans. A. Haufstader (Kalamazoo: 1982).

The etymologies of these two, closely related words are revealing of the emotional dynamism patristic writers attributed to them. *Penthos* is one of the principal nouns based on *pascho* (πάσχω), typically translated "to suffer" but more accurately rendered as 'to receive an impression or sensation, experience a feeling (good or bad), to endure, be chastised.'[63] Penitential weeping is therefore something that *happens* to bodies and minds, something that befalls them, something they "suffer" once set in motion by the active powers of the soul. It is, then, quite the opposite of both an active power of the soul and a passion erupting as it were from within. As a paradigmatic "mixed" emotion that brings with it its own *katharsis*,[64] the therapeutic value of *penthos* has been widely interpreted as closely akin to the extirpation of the emotions associated with Stoic ascetic exercises. This equation ignores the fact that, prior to the patristic period, the Stoic model for struggle against the passions coexisted with a more "optimistic" attitude, one that promoted the value of a redirection or "transposition" (μετάθεσις, *metáthesis*) of the passions' vital energies to make them "helpers" of the intellect, as Philo of Alexandria put it.[65] Accordingly, we find *penthos* at the boundary between passive experience and active practice; it seems to be as much, if not more, about purposefully sustaining the painful emotions associated with the awareness of sin than working them off. F.E. Peters explains that *páthē* in its early philosophical meaning likewise sat at the crossroads of a materialist account of sensation wherein 'a *pathos* of the senses [...] is capable of triggering a *pathe* of the soul.'[66] On the basis of its close connection with *pathos*, *penthos* is perhaps best understood, then, as a "passive activation" of the soul's own "active powers" (*dynameis*) through a deeply experience-based, embodied knowledge of sin.[67] Expressive of the soul's mournful exile from God, it becomes the most characteristic practical and productive state of mind for the cenobite – a continuous movement of the soul back to God.

Compunctio, meanwhile, rather than being 'practically synonymous with *penthos*,' as Irénée Hausherr and Tomaš Špidlík have framed it, refers to a singular revelatory event, a sudden awakening to the consciousness of sin.[68]

---

63   Hunt, *Joy-Bearing Grief* 4.

64   Knuuttila, *Emotions* 125.

65   Ware K.T., "The Meaning of 'Pathos' in Abba Isaisas and Theodoret of Cyrus", *Studia Patristica* 20 (1989) 315–22, at 317 (for Philo).

66   Peters F.E., *Greek Philosophical Terms: A Historical Lexicon* (New York: 1967) 152–53.

67   This is my formulation based on Peters's discussion of *pathos*; Peters, *Greek Philosophical Terms* 152–55; cf. Hunt, *Joy-Bearing Grief* 5.

68   Hunt, *Joy-Bearing Grief* 16. For the earlier views, see Hausherr, *Penthos* 3–10; and Špidlík T., *Prayer: The Spirituality of the Christian East, Volume 2*, trans. A.P. Gythiel (Kalamazoo: 2005) 259–61 and 285.

O VOS OMNES: NORTHERN EUROPEAN ART AROUND 1500   401

Its locus classicus is found in the experience of listeners to Peter's prophetic sermon after the Holy Spirit's descent (Acts 2:37): 'Now when they had heard these things, they had compunction in their heart.' What the Vulgate renders as *compunctio* was originally the feminine noun *katanuxis* (κατάνυξις), which covers the sense of a "pricking or wounding" of the heart or the soul. Thus it captures the "severe sorrow" that settles upon the conscious soul characteristic of *penthos*, but also the kind of "stupefaction" or "bewilderment" that results from being violently struck. This is why, elsewhere in the New Testament, notably in Romans 11:8, *katanuxis* can be nearly synonymous with "sleep," or a "falling into a mental stupor," thus an absence of consciousness.[69] *Compunctio* shocks the wayward soul out of its complacency, awakens it from ignorance into a knowledge of sin, and plunges the penitent into a temporary state of disorientation or "bewilderment" while also sparking the process of return. 'κατάνυξις is thus a sudden shock,' writes Hausherr, 'an emotion which plants deep in the soul a feeling, an attitude, or a resolution.'[70] Noteworthy is the close structural affinity *compunctio* shares with Aristotle's *anagnôrisis*. It may even be correct to say that, in the passerby's encounter with the suffering Christ, recognition and compunction overlap so closely as to become indistinguishable.

It was Gregory the Great (*c*.540–604) who reframed the problem of how the triad of emotions associated with recognition and *compunctio* – fear, pity, and love – undergoes its own therapeutic clarification in the experience of penitential weeping. In his *Dialogues* Gregory relies on a dichotomized conception of *compunctio* in which one form of spiritual sorrow gets displaced by another; the description even recalls Aristotle's balance of proximity and distance in the rhetorical production of pity and fear. Unstable emotions blend, catalyze, and finally resolve into a new equilibrium:

> Who first cried that he should not be led to the punishment, afterward begins to cry more bitterly since he is delayed from the kingdom. For the mind contemplates what the choirs of angels, the very society of saints, and the majesty of inward vision of God might be like and it laments more being removed from these everlasting blessings than it cried earlier when it feared eternal punishment. So it happens that when the compunction of fear is perfect it draws the soul to the compunction of love.[71]

---

69   In Paul's letter God is said to have imposed a "spirit of insensibility" (*spiritum compunctionis*) upon a stiffnecked Israel; for the etymology, see *Bible Hub*, no. 2659: *katanuxis* (accessed at https://biblehub.com/greek/2659.htm).

70   Hausherr, *Penthos* 8.

71   Gregory the Great, *Dialogues* 3.34.2; translation from Straw C., *Gregory the Great: Perfection in Imperfection* (Berkeley: 1988) 223; also discussed in Knuuttila, *Emotions* 174–75.

Two kinds of recognition have occurred. As awareness of one's distance from God is aroused, the corresponding awareness of sin intensifies. The soul in this emotional alchemy becomes "supersaturated" with the bitter, painful form of compunction, producing a kind of stupefaction. Resolution demands that an inversion of perspective takes place. Hope that God's plan for humankind will close the wayward soul's distance from Him now allows fear of punishment to crystallize into its opposite, producing a new admixture, a yearning for the Kingdom, and a foretaste of that inner vision which is both bitter *and* sweet: the compunction of love. One form of compunction has transmuted into another. 'Simultaneously the compunction of fear becomes less ardent,' Simo Knuuttila explains, 'a new self begins to emerge, and the Christian deems his or her future life to be an offering of loving obedience.'[72] But this only becomes possible when that compound form of awakening-to-knowledge (where compunction is inseparable from recognition) is matched by a second compound form (where compunction is inseparable from self-recognition). Both compounds contain their own admixtures of fear, pity, and love, but it takes the forceful recognition of the self – as always-already implicated in suffering – to invert the relation of irascible and concupiscible elements. Fear is displaced by the "compunction of love" yet the irascible element remains. On the surface that element looks to be hatred of sin, aversion to that distance from God sin imposes. But equally so, it is the soul's zealous "desire" to see the destructive power of guilt forever banished.

A similar therapeutic logic appears in the work of late medieval authors who adapted the Gregorian doctrine of compunction for their readers. In his *De Spiritualibus Ascensionibus*, a key text for the Devotio Moderna, Gerard Zerbolt van Zutphen (1367–1398) charted the penitent's journey from a sorrowful *compunctio ex timore* to a joyous *compunctio ex amore*.[73] Both were accompanied by the "gift of tears" (*gratia lacrimarum*), a sign of divine favor intuitively grasped as *both* the body's passive activation through an awakening to sin, and an active, even strategic cultivation of emotional experience for the sake of hastening the soul's passage into a new set of situational coordinates. *Compunctio* here stands revealed as a practical technique for forging a new relationship to God – prompted by the call to attend, sparked by the experience of recognition, and borne upon the shifting flow of emotion.

---

72   Knuuttila, *Emotions* 174–75.

73   Discussed with further references in Roodenburg H., "Imagination Over Matter? Tears, Touch and 'Ornamenta Sacra' Among Women of the *Devotio Moderna*", in Dekoninck R. – Claes M.-C. – Baert B. (eds.), *'Ornamenta Sacra': Late Medieval and Early Modern Liturgical Objects in a European Context* (Leuven: 2022) 165–85.

5   Conclusions

With this analysis we have arrived at the fundamental Christian experience of sorrow and repentence for sin, that fear of God which is "the beginning of wisdom" (Prov. 9:10; cf. Job 28:28), and the expectation that the prodigal soul will, upon its return, receive God's mercy – what may seem a rather conventional conclusion. If the model presented here has any exceptional heuristic value, it may lie in the indication that emotional "mixtures" are always capable of both equilibrium and entropy. And further: if we still wish to speak of a *katharsis* of emotions in the devotional encounter, we should perhaps understand it not via the medical analogy, where purgation means the the removal of elements thought to impede proper functioning, nor according to the "educative" theory of catharsis (although this is closer to my suggestion). Catharsis in my account looks more like a *clarification* of emotions.[74] Not only are emotions elevated above the level of the sensory appetite. Catharsis-as-clarification *sanctifies* those emotions and makes them touchstones for every impending form of reciprocity: prayer, meditation, liturgy, sacrament, and the devotional encounter with the visual image as well.

In a deeply sensitive analysis Isabel Davis has characterized the text of Lamentations 1:12 as medieval piety's privileged vehicle for 'topological deformations of time.' She calls attention to several poetic and dramatic adaptations in which 'the language both of passing and attending spoke directly to medieval understandings of time in motion.'[75] This, together with the examples adduced here from late medieval visual culture, gives us a rather different picture of the "mobile observer" than the one described in recent studies of the kinetics of medieval art.[76] Now the defining aspiration of the observer in transit is the *cessation* of movement, the *stilling* of action at the moment of the subject's interpellation. Halting the soul's journey across the terrain of existence, the mobile observer heeds the call to attend and comes to rest in the adoption of a new vantage point. The emotion-rich encounter with suffering, the ethical turn toward attentiveness, and the performance of a reciprocity all "take place"

---

74   See the important essay by Golden L., "The Clarification Theory of *Katharsis*", *Hermes* 104.4 (1976) 437–452.

75   Davis, "'Ye that pasen by þe Weiye'" 453.

76   For example, the essays collected in Ganz D. – Neuner S. (eds.), *Mobile Eyes: Peripatetisches Sehen in den Bildkulturen der Vormoderne* (Munich: 2013). Richly transformative of many older assumptions in this field of interpretation is Jung J.E., *Eloquent Bodies: Movement, Expression, and the Human Figure in Gothic Sculpture* (New Haven: 2020).

404   MERBACK

at this sanctified station of rest, a place not unlike the one occupied by Christ on Golgotha, where he broods over humanity's ingratitude.[77]

This principle is operative across a much broader field of contexts than the one pinpointed in this paper. Over the *longue durée* of western mortuary practices and the cult of memory, for instance, the obligation to pause along the thoroughfares of the living and "attend" to the dead turned the anonymous passerby into an especially valued figure. To enact *memoria* before the tomb meant recognizing one's place in a world of mutual obligation. Medieval funerary inscriptions preserved a tradition traceable back to Roman cemetaries, in which those in transit on earth were called upon to pray for the souls of those who have transitioned from this world to the next. Those marvelously morbid double-decker memorials known as "transi" tombs often addressed the passerby with words borrowed from Lamentations, in fact, as did admonitions to pray for the extended community of the purgatorial dead. Upon a plaque displayed on the outer wall of a cemetery in fifteenth-century Beauvais, an anonymous, worm-eaten corpse once solicited prayers from all those who pass (*passez*) for the benefit of all those who have departed (*trespassez*):

> *Vous qui per cy devant passez*
> *Priez dieu pour les trespassez*
> *C'est cimitière.*

> (You who pass by here
> Pray to God for the departed.
> This is a cemetary).[78]

Under the spell of the *transi* tomb's macabre address, where the beholder is likewise urged to imagine him- or herself in transit towards death, the passerby's act of recognition intertwines closely with self-recognition; devotion and the rites of mutual obligation becomes inescapable adjuncts to existence. The desire to stimulate – and perhaps even *simulate* – such an affective "turning" before the spectacle of suffering may have also been the inspiration behind a novel conception of the Crucifixion appearing in German and Netherlandish art around 1500, and developed in the succeeding decades – the so-called "oblique Crucifixion." Lucas Cranach the Elder, Albrecht Altdorfer, Wolf Huber, Sebald Beham, and Jan Mostaert all experimented with this rotated

---

77 For the metaphorical, mythical, and ritual dimensions of the time's emplacement, see Smith J.Z., *To Take Place: Toward Theory in Ritual* (Chicago: 1987).

78 See Cohen K., *Metamophosis of a Death Symbol: The Transi Tomb in the Late Middle Ages and the Renaissance* (Berkeley: 1983) 74, and fig. 23, but with no additional references.

FIGURE 11.15 Jan Mostaert, Calvary, c.1530. Oil on panel, 114.6 × 74.6 cm. Philadelphia, Philadelphia Museum of Art
PHOTO: THE JOHN G. JOHNSON COLLECTION, PHILADELPHIA MUSEUM OF ART (CAT. 411), PUBLIC DOMAIN

perspective. For his Crucifixion in Philadelphia Mostaert added (in the lower right corner) a mysterious hooded traveler who, in arriving before the spectacle of suffering, falls to his kneels and mediates our gaze as it follows the diagonal over his shoulder and toward the body of Christ [Fig. 11.15].[79] Such images belong in that extended family of images structured by the passerby principle.

79 On the oblique Crucifixion and its dynamisms, see Merback M.B., *The Thief, the Cross and the Wheel: Pain and the Spectacle of Punishment in Medieval and Renaissance Europe* (London – Chicago: 1999), 257–63; Schlie H., "Exzentrische Kreuzigungen um 1500. Zur Erfindung eines bildlichen Affektraums", in *Golgotha in den Konfessionen und Medien der Frühen Neuzeit*, ed. J.A. Steiger – U. Heinen (Berlin: 2010), 63–92; and Bohde D., "Schräge Blicke – exzentrische Kompositionen: 'Kreuzigungen' und 'Beweinungen' in der altdeutschen Malerei und Graphik", *Zeitschrift für Kunstgeschichte* 75.2 (2012) 193–222.

In its total framing the passerby principle urges an encounter with salvific suffering that bears an existential relationship to one's own life story. It is structured by the subject's inner narrative of conversion to Christ, and its stages are marked by a sanctification of emotion, felt as such when the crisis comprising these twinned moments of discovery, Christ-recognition and self-recognition, is resolved. To re-orient one's life around the vocation of the disciple, the friend of God and follower of Christ, co-bearer of his Cross – this entails a reenactment of that fundamental recognition of Christ, a "seeing-through" the twin veils of the Incarnation and the Death on the Cross. The subject passing "by way and street" steps out of time, turns with attention toward that fixed point, and in doing effects a recognition, a change that also brings about a *peripeteia*, a reversal in one's life story.

Bibliography

Adams B.B. *Coming-to-Know: Recognition and the Complex Plot in Shakespeare* (New York: 2000).

Ainsworth M.W. – Christiansen K. (eds.), *From Van Eyck to Bruegel: Early Netherlandish Painting in the Metropolitan Museum of Art* (New York: 1998).

Barnet P., "An Ivory Relief of the *Man of Sorrows* in New York", *The Sculpture Journal* 4 (2000) 1–5.

Belting H., *The Image and its Public in the Middle Ages: Form and Function of Early Paintings of the Passion*, trans. M. Bartusis – R. Meyer (New Rochelle: 1990).

Bertelli C., "The *Image of Pity* in Santa Croce in Gerusalemme", in Fraser D. – Hibbard H. – Lewine M.J. (eds.), *Essays in the History of Art Presented to Rudolph Wittkower* (London: 1967) 40–55.

Bohde D., "Schräge Blicke – exzentrische Kompositionen: 'Kreuzigungen' und 'Beweinungen' in der altdeutschen Malerei und Graphik", *Zeitschrift für Kunstgeschichte* 75.2 (2012) 193–222.

Boitani P., "Recognition: The Pain and Joy of Compassion," in *Recognition: The Poetics of Narrative*, ed. P.F. Kennedy – M. Lawrence (New York: 2009) 213–26.

Bühler A., "Die Heilige Lanze. Ein ikonographischer Beitrag zur Geschichte der deutschen Reichskleinodien", *Das Münster* 16.3/4 (1963).

Bulst-Thiele M.L., "Die Mosaiken der 'Auferstehungskirche' in Jerusalem und die Bauten der 'Franken' im 12. Jahrhundert", *Frühmittelalterlichen Studien* 13 (1979) 442–71.

Cohen K., *Metamophosis of a Death Symbol: The Transi Tomb in the Late Middle Ages and the Renaissance* (Berkeley: 1983).

Davis I., "'Ye that pasen by pe Weiye': Time, Topology and the Medieval Use of Lamentations 1.12", *Textual Practice* 25.3 (2011) 437–72.

O VOS OMNES: NORTHERN EUROPEAN ART AROUND 1500

Dobrzeniecki T., "Debilitatio Christi: A Contribution to the Iconography of Christ in Distress," *Bulletin du Musée National de Varsovie* 8 (1967) 93–111.

Falque I., *Devotional Portraiture and Spiritual Experience in Early Netherlandish Painting* (Leiden: 2019).

Fehlemann S., "Christus im Elend: Vom Andachtsbild zum realistischen Bilddokument", in Brock B. – Preiß A. (eds.), *Ikonographia: Anleitung zum Lesen von Bildern (Festschrift Donat de Chapeaurouge)* (Munich: 1990) 79–96.

Fricke B. – Krass U. (eds.), *The Public in the Picture: Involving the Beholder in Antique, Islamic, Byzantine, Western Medieval and Renaissance Art* (Chicago: 2015).

Ganz D. – Neuner S. (eds.), *Mobile Eyes: Peripatetisches Sehen in den Bildkulturen der Vormoderne* (Munich: 2013).

Golden L., "The Clarification Theory of *Katharsis*", *Hermes* 104.4 (1976) 437–452.

Hadot P., "Conversion," in *The Selected Writings of Pierre Hadot: Philosophy as Practice*, trans. M. Sharpe – F. Testa (London: 2020), 93–103.

Hans Holbein der Ältere und die Kunst der Spätgotik, exh. cat. (Augsburg: 1965).

Hagen S.K., *Allegorical Remembrance: A Study of* The Pilgrimage of the Life of Man *as a Medieval Treatise on Seeing & Remembering* (Athens – London: 1990).

Hasse D.N., *Avicenna's De Anima in the Latin West: The Formation of a Peripatetic Philosophy of the Soul 1160–1300* (London: 2000).

Hasse M., *Die Marienkirche zu Lübeck* (Munich: 1983).

Hausherr I., *Penthos. The Doctrine of Compunction in the Christian East*, trans. A. Haufstader (Kalamazoo: 1982).

Huizinga J., *The Autumn of the Middle Ages*, trans. R.J. Payton and U. Mammitzsch (Chicago: 1996).

Hunt H., *Joy-Bearing Grief: Tears of Contrition in the Writings of the Early Syrian and Byzantine Fathers* (Leiden: 2004).

Jung J.E., *Eloquent Bodies: Movement, Expression, and the Human Figure in Gothic Sculpture* (New Haven: 2020).

Keaty A., "The Christian Virtue of Mercy: Aquinas' Transformation of Aristotelian Pity", *Heythrop Journal* 46 (2005) 181–98.

Kennedy P.F. – Lawrence M., "Introduction," in *Recognition: The Poetics of Narrative*, ed. P.F. Kennedy – M. Lawrence (New York: 2009) 1–12.

Köllermann A.-F., "Die Goldene Tafel. Gestalt und Programm", in Köllermann A.-F. – Unsinn C. (eds.), *Zeitenwende 1400. Die Goldene Tafel als europäisches Meisterwerk* (Petersberg: 2019) 25–49.

Knuuttila S., *Emotions in Ancient and Medieval Philosophy* (Oxford: 2004).

Konstan D., *Pity Transformed* (London: 2001).

Krause K., *Hans Holbein der Ältere* (Munich – Berlin: 2002).

Lansdowne J., *The Micromosaic of the Man of Sorrows at Santa Croce in Gerusalemme in Rome*, 2 vols. (Ph.D. dissertation, Princeton University: 2019).

Lillie E.L., "O vos omnes qui transitis per viam [...]: The Quotation from Lamentations 1, 12 in Danish Medieval Art", in Lillie E.L. – Petersen N.H. (eds.), *Liturgy and the Arts in the Middle Ages: Studies in Honour of C. Clifford Flanigan* (Copenhagen: 1996) 205–220.

Lindquist S.C.M., *Agency, Visuality and Society at the Chartreuse de Champmol* (Aldershot: 2008).

Lüdke D. et al., *Grünewald und seine Zeit. Große Landesaustellung Baden-Württemberg*, exh. cat. (Karlsruhe: 2007).

Merback M.B., *The Thief, the Cross and the Wheel: Pain and the Spectacle of Punishment in Medieval and Renaissance Europe* (London – Chicago: 1999).

Merback M.B., "Passion of Christ", in *The Grove Encyclopedia of Medieval Art and Architecture* (Oxford: 2012).

Merback M.B., *Pilgrimage and Pogrom: Violence, Memory, and Visual Culture at the Host-Miracle Shrines of Germany and Austria* (Chicago: 2013).

Merback M.B., "The Man of Sorrows in Northern Europe: Ritual Metaphor and Therapeutic Exchange," in Puglisi C.R. – Barcham W.L. (eds.), *New Perspectives on the Man of Sorrows* (Kalamazoo: 2013) 77–116.

Merback M.B. "Recognitions: Theme and Metatheme in Hans Burgkmair the Elder's *Santa Croce in Gerusalemme* of 1504", *Art Bulletin* 96.3 (2014) 288–318.

Merback M.B., "Pain and Memory in the Formation of Early Modern *Habitus*", *Representations* 146, Special Issue, Ablow R. (ed.) (2019): 59–90.

Morrison K.F., *Conversion and Text: The Cases of Augustine of Hippo, Herman-Judah, and Constantine Tsatsos* (Charlottsville – London: 1992).

Morrison K.F., *Understanding Conversion* (Charlottesville – London: 1992).

Nemilov A.N., "Gedanken zur geschichtswissenschaftlichen Befragung von Bildern am Beispiel der sog. Gregormesse in der Ermitage," in Tolkemitt B. – Wohlteil R. (eds.), *Historische Bildkunde. Probleme – Wege – Beispiele* (Berlin: 1991) 123–33.

Pandit L., "Emotion, Perception and Anagnorisis in the Comedy of Errors: A Cognitive Perspective", *College Literature* 33.1 (2006) 94–126.

Panofsky E., "'Imago Pietatis.' Ein Beitrag zur Typengeschichte des 'Schmerzensmanns' und der 'Maria Mediatrix'", in *Festschrift für Max J. Friedländer zum 60. Geburtstage* (Leipzig: 1927) 261–308.

Pegon J., "Componction", *Dictionnaire de la Spiritualité*, vol. 2, part 2 (1953) 1312–21.

Peters F.E., *Greek Philosophical Terms: A Historical Lexicon* (New York: 1967).

Petersen N.H., "Liturgical Representation and Late Medieval Piety", in Lillie E.L. – Petersen N.H. (eds.), *Liturgy and the Arts in the Middle Ages: Studies in Honour of C. Clifford Flanigan* (Copenhagen: 1996) 181–204.

Pickering F.P., *Literature and Art in the Middle Ages* (Coral Gables: 1970).

Rasche A., "Hermen Rode: The Painter of Medieval Lübeck and His Art Production", in Jahnke C. (ed.), *A Companion to Medieval Lübeck* (Leiden: 2019) 306–51.

Roodenburg H., "Imagination Over Matter? Tears, Touch and 'Ornamenta Sacra' Among Women of the *Devotio Moderna*", in Dekoninck R. – Claes M.-C. – Baert B. (eds.), *'Ornamenta Sacra': Late Medieval and Early Modern Liturgical Objects in a European Context* (Leuven: 2022) 165–85.

Rorty A.O., "The Psychology of Aristotelian Tragedy," in *Essays on Aristotle's* Poetics, ed. A.O. Rorty (Princeton: 1992) 1–22.

Roth-Bojadzhiev G., *Studien zur Bedeutung der Vögel in der mittelalterlichen Tafelmalerei* (Vienna: 1985).

Ruh K., *Das Passionstraktat des Heinrich von St. Gallen* (Thayngen: 1940).

Scheer M., "Are Emotions a Kind of Practice (And is that what makes them have a history?): A Bourdieuian Approach to Understanding Emotion", *History and Theory* 51.2 (2012) 193–220.

Schilling E., "An Indulgence Printed at Nuremberg in 1512," in Goetz O. (ed.), *Essays in Honor of Georg Swarzenski* (Chicago: 1951) 125–28.

Schlie H., "Exzentrische Kreuzigungen um 1500. Zur Erfindung eines bildlichen Affektraums", in *Golgotha in den Konfessionen und Medien der Frühen Neuzeit*, ed. J.A. Steiger – U. Heinen (Berlin: 2010), 63–92.

Smeyers M. (ed.), *Dirk Bouts (ca. 1410–1475), een Vlaams primitief te Leuven*, exh. cat. (Leuven: 1998).

Smith J.C., *Nuremberg. A Renaissance City, 1500–1618*, exh. cat. (Austin: 1983).

Smith J.Z., *To Take Place: Toward Theory in Ritual* (Chicago: 1987).

Sorabji R., *Emotion and Peace of Mind: From Stoic Agitation to Christian Temptation: The Gifford Lectures* (Oxford: 2000).

Špidlík T., *Prayer: The Spirituality of the Christian East, Volume 2*, trans. A.P. Gythiel (Kalamazoo: 2005).

Stockwell P., *Cognitive Poetics: An Introduction*, 2nd edn. (Independence: 2019).

Straw C., *Gregory the Great: Perfection in Imperfection* (Berkeley: 1988).

Surmann U., *Christus in der Rast* (Frankfurt am Main: 1991).

Toussaint G., *Das Passional der Kunigunde von Böhmen: Bildrhetorik und Spiritualität* (Paderborn: 2003).

Von der Osten G., "Job and Christ: The Development of a Devotional Image", *Journal of the Warburg and Courtauld Institutes* 16.1–2 (1953) 153–58.

Von der Osten G., "Christus im Elend (Christus in der Rast) und Herrgottsruhbild", in *Reallexikon zur deutschen Kunstgeschichte*, vol. 3 (Stuttgart: 1953) 644–58.

Ware K.T., "The Meaning of 'Pathos' in Abba Isaisas and Theodoret of Cyrus", *Studia Patristica* 20 (1989) 315–22.

Wenzel S., *Verses in Sermons: 'Fasciculus Morum' and its Middle English Poems* (Cambridge MA: 1978).

Young K., *The Drama of the Medieval Church*, 2 vols. (Oxford: 1933).

Zinke D. (ed.), *Augustinermuseum. Gemälde bis 1800* (Freiburg: 1990).

CHAPTER 12

Mixed Emotion and Spiritual Perfection in Abraham Bloemaert's *Sylva anachoretica* of 1619

Walter S. Melion

Abstract

The affective conjunction of fear and joy, and the complex layering of other discrepant emotions, are characteristic of the eremitical life of the desert Fathers, as portrayed by Abraham Bloemaert in the series of fifty desert Fathers and Mothers that illustrate Joannes Risius (Ryser), s.j.'s *Sylva anachoretica* (Anachoretic Woodland) of 1619. Ultimately based on Heribert Rosweyde, s.j.'s *'t Vaders boeck* (Book of the Fathers) of 1617, Bloemaert's pregnant images, like Risius's textual digests, distil the complex emotional life of the Fathers, their constant struggle to control multifarious, often contrary feelings, and their heroic efforts to subdue these emotions as they strive to achieve a state of contemplative repose. Engendered by the many trials and tribulations they encounter in the desert – a hell on earth that their hard-won sanctity converts into a foretaste of paradise – their bodily expression of mixed emotion signals the precise moment when fear of the Lord turns into joy and, in the words of *Psalm* 125, what is sown in tears is harvested in felicity. In bodying forth the admixture cum transposition of sorrow into joy, Bloemaert adapted the criteria for portraying sorrow codified by Karel van Mander in his *Grondt der edel, vry Schilder-const* (Foundation of the Noble, Free Art of Painting): Van Mander presents sorrow as a compound of pity, fear, and heaviness of heart shading into desolation of the spirit like unto sickness or death. And yet, Bloemaert also follows another of Van Mander's figural canons, assimilating every anchorite to that graceful form of serpentine contrapposto which the *Grondt* canonised as the most perfect of bodily attitudes. The affective complexity of the *Sylva anachoretica*, in that it exemplifies the struggle to attain spiritual perfection, jointly exemplifies the perfection of Bloemaert's art.

Keywords

anchorite – consolation – desert father – hermit – illumination – solitude – tribulation

© WALTER S. MELION, 2025 | DOI:10.1163/9789004694613_013

MIXED EMOTION & PERFECTION IN BLOEMAERT'S *SYLVA ANACHORETICA*   411

Engraved by Boëtius à Bolswert after designs by Abraham Bloemaert, the *Sylva anachoretica Aegyti et Palestinae, figuris aeneis et brevibus vitarum elogiis expressa* (Anachoretic Woodland of Egypt and Palestine, Portrayed in Copperplate Figures with Brief Epitaphs of the Lives) (Antwerp, Ex Typographia Henrici Aertssij: 1619) consists of fifty full-length images of hermit saints – twenty-five anchorites and twenty-five anchoresses – who furnish an array of spiritual models worthy of the reader-viewer's contemplative imitation [Figs. 12.1–12.30].[1] Each opening comprises a text written by Joannes Risius (Ryser), S.J., whose condensed *vitae* largely derive from Heribert Rosweyde, S.J.'s *Vitae Patrum* (Lives of the Fathers) (Antwerp, Ex officina Plantiniana, apud Viduam et filios Jo. Moreti: 1615), and, on the facing folio recto, an engraved portrait of the respective hermit saint in penitential prayer, usually accompanied by distinguishing attributes, such as the enshrouding body-length hair of Saint Onuphrius, whose daily portion of bread (or alternatively, whose Sunday Eucharist) a diaphanous angel is shown bringing

---

1   Risius Joannes, S.J., *Sylva anachoretica Aegypti et Palaestinae. Figuris aeneis et brevibus vitarum elogiis expressa. Abrahamo Blommaert inventore. Boetio a Boswert sculptore* (Antwerp: Ex typographia Henrici Aertsii, sumptibus auctoris, 1619). Underlying the *Sylva*, which portrays the Fathers and Mothers in word and image, is the extended analogy between painting (and sculpting) and hagiographical writing propagated by Heribert Rosweyde, S.J., in *Fasti sanctorum, quorum vitae in belgicis bibliothecis manuscriptae* (Antwerp, Ex officina Plantiniana: 1607) [2]: 'Quemadmodum pictores, cum imaginem ex imagine pingunt, exemplar identidem respectantes, lineamenta eius transferre conantur magno studio ad suum opificium'. For Rosweyde, hagiographical portraits compounded of texts and images are said to provide affective and incontrovertible evidence of the saints' exemplary lives; he goes so far as to compare them to holy relics – *trophaea* such as the martyr's blood or vestments. As if painted by the brush or sculpted by the chisel, they affect the attentive reader-viewer both materially and spiritually; see ibid. 3: 'Qui apud posteros nomen amant, duo potissimum in votis habent, eruditum calamum, et penicillum, caelumve ductile. Illo hominis pars potior, animi virtus; hoc corporis rerumque gestarum decus propagator. Gemina haec felicitas SS. Martyribus, animosis Christi Athletis, ab omni aevo obtigit; qui dum generose in hoc vitae Circo decertant, cadendo vincunt, superati hostem sternunt, trophaeum de corporis sui exuviis statuunt, non tenuit spectator manum. Hic namque verba ceratis tabulis excipit, ille stylo certaminum rudimenta adumbrat; hic Martyris vestem rapit, fidele spolium; ille sanguinem colligit, fidei obsidem. Ita sibi superstes vivit Martyr; et post gladium, post cineres, certamini suo testimonium dicit'. On Rosweyde's application of the criteria of pictorial mimesis in the *Fasti sanctorum*, see Machielsen J., "Heretical Saints and Textual Discernment: The Polemical Origins of the *Acta Sanctorum* (1643–1940)", in Copeland C. – Machielsen (eds.), *Angels of Light? Sanctity and the Discernment of Spirits in the Early Modern Period* (Leiden – Boston: 2012) 103–141, esp. 135–138; and Melion W.S., "'Niet te verladen': The Manner and Meaning of Abraham Bloemaert and Boëtius à Bolswert's *Sylva anachoretica* of 1619," in Marquaille L. (ed.), *New Perspectives on Abraham Bloemaert and his Workshop* (Turnhout: 2022) 89–142, esp. 110–125.

[Fig. 12.10].[2] The publisher, Hendrik Aertssens, ascribes publication of the *Sylva* to Risius, who assumed the project's costs ('Sumptibus Auctoris'). The book's prolonged genesis, exhaustively traced by Marcel Roethlisberger in his monograph on Bloemaert, unfolded in several stages.[3] Aertssens finally published the *Sacra eremus ascetarum* in 1619, with Risius's texts printed on the versos of the images; the monastic canon, as codified therein, encompasses cenobitic monks from the Roman West, such as Benedict and Dominic, as well as the reclusive desert Fathers and Mothers. Between the typographical title-page, *Sylva anachoretica* [...], and the textual preliminaries, Bolswert interpolated an allegorical landscape of the eremitical life that depicts the *eremus* (waste, desert, wilderness) not as an arid wasteland but as a verdant forest, wherein the hermit's flourishing soul is analogised to a greenwood [Fig. 12.3].[4] The introductory matter includes an epigraph from Basil's *Liber de laude vitae solitariae* (Book in Praise of the Solitary Life), a long excerpt from Jerome's *Epistola 1. ad Heliodorum* on the paradisiacal joys of desert solitude, and Risius's dedicatory preface to the Benedictine Abbot Antonius de Winghe, a strong supporter

---

2 On Bloemaert's *Saint Onuphrius*, see Roethlisberger M., *Abraham Bloemaert and his Sons: Paintings and Prints*, 2 vols. (Doornspijk: Davaco, 1993) 1:177. On Risius, a scion of the 'oude burgerij' of Amsterdam and a major figure in the Holland Mission, see ibid., 172; Allard H.J., *Pater Adrianus Poirters, s.j.: een historisch-letterkundige schets* (Amsterdam: 1871) 17–19; and *Societatis Jesu in Neerlandia historiae compendium, ab anno 1592, quo primum missio nostra Hollandica sanctissim. Domino nostro Clemente VIII instituta est, usque ad haec nostra tempora* ('s-Hertogenbosch: 1860) 40–41. Preparatory drawings survive for *Saints Anthony, Hilarion, Malchus, Macarius Aegyptius, Abraham Hermit, Ephraem, John in Lyco, Elias Aegyptius, Theonas, Helenus Ammon Nitriota, Bonosus, Euphraxia, Mary Neptis of Abraham, Thais, Melania the Elder*, and *Melania the Younger*. On the complex publication history of Rosweyde's *Vitae Patrum*, see, in addition to the sources cited in note 3 *supra*, Judson J.R. – Van de Velde C., *Corpus Rubenianum XXI: Book Illustrations and Title-Pages*, 2 vols. (London and Philadelphia: Harvey Miller/Heyden and Son, 1978) 1:246–249; Begheyn P., s.j., "Jesuit Book Production in The Netherlands, 1601–1650", in Lucas T.M. (ed.), *Spirit, Style, Story: Essays Honoring John W. Padberg, s.j.* (Chicago: 2002) 303–326; and idem, "Heribert Rosweyde, s.j., *Leven vande heylighe Maghet ende Moeder Godts Maria* (1629)", in Begheyn et al. (eds.), *Jesuit Books in the Low Countries, 1540–1773: A Selection from the Maurits Sabbe Library* (Leuven: 2009) 70–71, esp. 70.

3 Roethlisberger, *Bloemaert and his Sons* 171–183.

4 Roethlisberger attributes the design of this print, signed 'Bolswert fecit', to Bolswert himself, who in this instance closely emulated the manner of Bloemaert; see ibid. 175. Based on *Psalm* 101:7 – 'I am become like to a pelican of the wilderness' – this allegory serves to assure the reader-viewer that the eremitical penitents s/he is about to peruse had confidence in the power of God to save and console them.

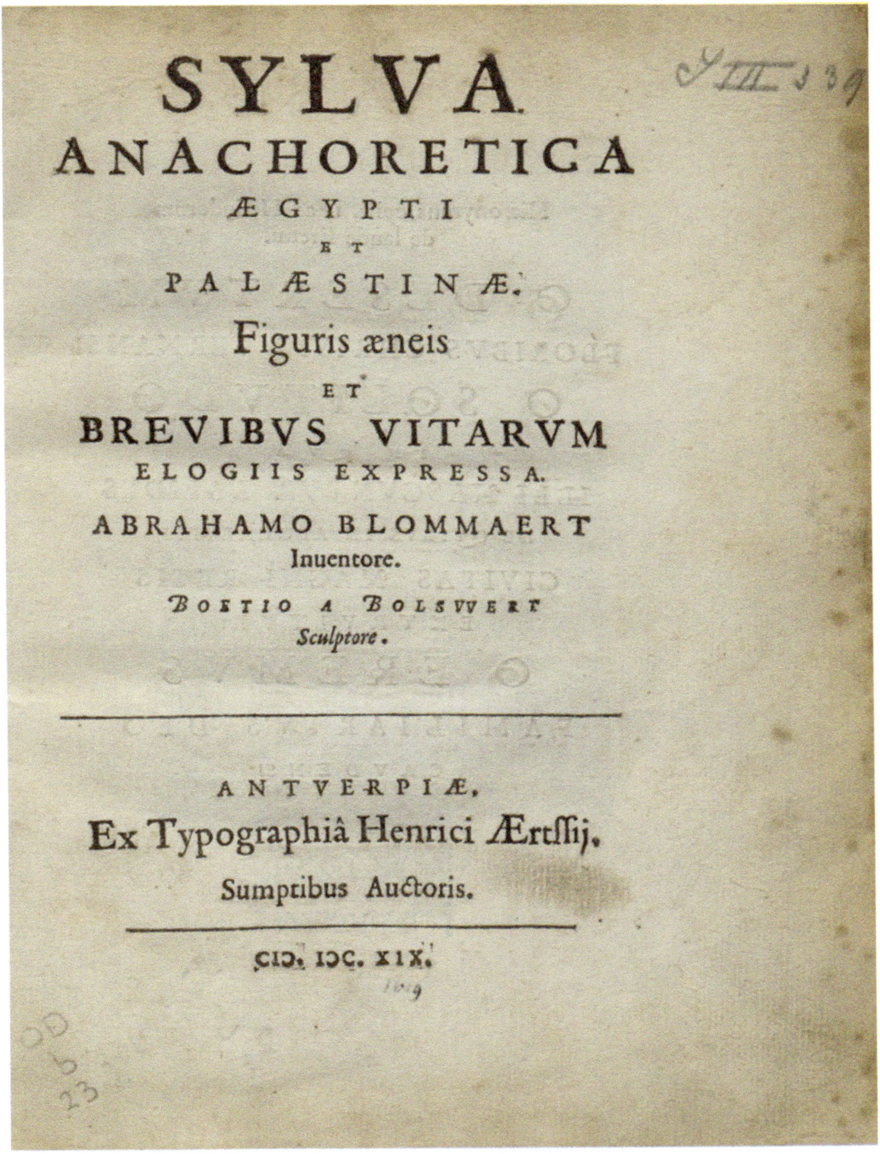

SYLVA
ANACHORETICA
ÆGYPTI
ET
PALÆSTINÆ.
Figuris æneis
ET
BREVIBVS VITARVM
ELOGIIS EXPRESSA.
ABRAHAMO BLOMMAERT
Inuentore.
BOETIO A BOLSVVERT
Sculptore.

ANTVERPIÆ,
Ex Typographiâ Henrici Ærtssij,
Sumptibus Auctoris.

CIↃ. IↃC. XIX.

FIGURE 12.1 Abraham Bloemaert, *Title-Page: Sacra eremus ascetarum* (Antwerp, Hendrik Aertssens: 1619), quarto. Rijksmuseum, Amsterdam

FIGURE 12.2 Boëtius à Bolswert after Abraham Bloemaert, *Frontispiece: Ad sacrum speculum*, ca. 1612/reissued 1619. Engraving, ca. 125/30 × 85/88 mm. Rijksmuseum, Amsterdam

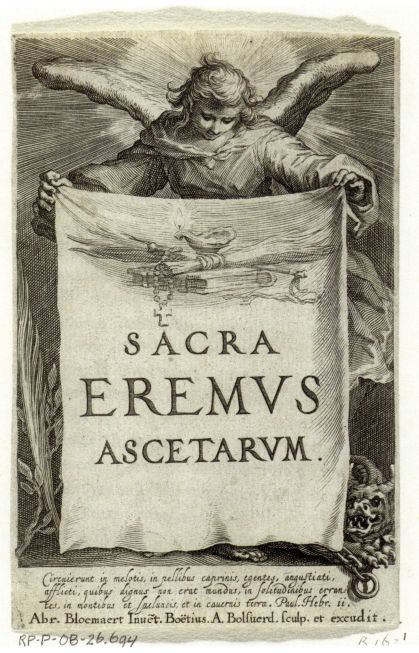

FIGURE 12.3   Boëtius à Bolswert, *Similis factus sum pellicano solitudinis: Wooded Landscape with Hermits*, ca. 1612/reissued 1619. Engraving, ca. 145 × 90 mm. Rijksmuseum, Amsterdam

FIGURE 12.4   Boëtius à Bolswert after Abraham Bloemaert, *Jesus is led into the desert: Temptation of Christ*, ca. 1612/reissued 1619. Engraving, ca. 125/30 × 85/88 mm. Rijksmuseum, Amsterdam

MIXED EMOTION & PERFECTION IN BLOEMAERT'S *SYLVA ANACHORETICA* 417

FIGURE 12.5   Boëtius à Bolswert after Abraham Bloemaert, *Saint John the Baptist*, ca. 1612/ reissued 1619. Engraving, ca. 125/30 × 85/88 mm. Rijksmuseum, Amsterdam

FIGURE 12.6 Boëtius à Bolswert after Abraham Bloemaert, *Saint Paul Hermit*, ca. 1612/reissued 1619. Engraving, ca. 125/30 × 85/88 mm. Rijksmuseum, Amsterdam

MIXED EMOTION & PERFECTION IN BLOEMAERT'S *SYLVA ANACHORETICA* 419

FIGURE 12.7   Boëtius à Bolswert after Abraham Bloemaert, *Saint Anthony Hermit*, ca. 1612/
reissued 1619. Engraving, ca. 125/30 × 85/88 mm. Rijksmuseum, Amsterdam

FIGURE 12.8   Boëtius à Bolswert after Abraham Bloemaert, *Saint Hilarion*, ca. 1612/ reissued 1619. Engraving, ca. 125/30 × 85/88 mm. Rijksmuseum, Amsterdam

FIGURE 12.9 Boëtius à Bolswert after Abraham Bloemaert, *Saint Malchus*, ca. 1612/reissued 1619. Engraving, ca. 125/30 × 85/88 mm. Rijksmuseum, Amsterdam

FIGURE 12.10 Boëtius à Bolswert after Abraham Bloemaert, *Saint Onuphrius*, ca. 1612/ reissued 1619. Engraving, ca. 125/30 × 85/88 mm. Rijksmuseum, Amsterdam

FIGURE 12.11   Boëtius à Bolswert after Abraham Bloemaert, *Saint Pachomius*, ca. 1612/ reissued 1619. Engraving, ca. 125/30 × 85/88 mm. Rijksmuseum, Amsterdam

FIGURE 12.12 Boëtius à Bolswert after Abraham Bloemaert, *Saint Macarius Aegyptius*, ca. 1612/reissued 1619. Engraving, ca. 125/30 × 85/88 mm. Rijksmuseum, Amsterdam

FIGURE 12.13   Boëtius à Bolswert after Abraham Bloemaert, *Saint Macarius Alexandrinus*, ca. 1612/reissued 1619. Engraving, ca. 125/30 × 85/88 mm. Rijksmuseum, Amsterdam

FIGURE 12.14   Boëtius à Bolswert after Abraham Bloemaert, *Saint Abraham Hermit*, ca. 1612/ reissued 1619. Engraving, ca. 125/30 × 85/88 mm. Rijksmuseum, Amsterdam

FIGURE 12.15   Boëtius à Bolswert after Abraham Bloemaert, *Saint Basil the Great*, ca. 1612/reissued 1619. Engraving, ca. 125/30 × 85/88 mm. Rijksmuseum, Amsterdam

FIGURE 12.16   Boëtius à Bolswert after Abraham Bloemaert, *Saint Ephraem*, ca. 1612/reissued 1619. Engraving, ca. 125/30 × 85/88 mm. Rijksmuseum, Amsterdam

FIGURE 12.17   Boëtius à Bolswert after Abraham Bloemaert, *Saint Simeon Stylita*, ca. 1612/ reissued 1619. Engraving, ca. 125/30 × 85/88 mm. Rijksmuseum, Amsterdam

FIGURE 12.18 Boëtius à Bolswert after Abraham Bloemaert, *Saint Frontonius*, ca. 1612/reissued 1619. Engraving, ca. 125/30 × 85/88 mm. Rijksmuseum, Amsterdam

FIGURE 12.19   Boëtius à Bolswert after Abraham Bloemaert, *Saint John in Lyco*, ca. 1612/reissued 1619. Engraving, ca. 125/30 × 85/88 mm. Rijksmuseum, Amsterdam

FIGURE 12.20   Boëtius à Bolswert after Abraham Bloemaert, *Saint Elias Aegyptius*, ca. 1612/ reissued 1619. Engraving, ca. 125/30 × 85/88 mm. Rijksmuseum, Amsterdam

FIGURE 12.21 Boëtius à Bolswert after Abraham Bloemaert, *Saint Theonas*, ca. 1612/reissued 1619. Engraving, ca. 125/30 × 85/88 mm. Rijksmuseum, Amsterdam

FIGURE 12.22 Boëtius à Bolswert after Abraham Bloemaert, *Saint Helenus*, ca. 1612/ reissued 1619. Engraving, ca. 125/30 × 85/88 mm. Rijksmuseum, Amsterdam

FIGURE 12.23　Boëtius à Bolswert after Abraham Bloemaert, *Saint Ammon Nitriota*, ca. 1612/reissued 1619. Engraving, ca. 125/30 × 85/88 mm. Rijksmuseum, Amsterdam

FIGURE 12.24   Boëtius à Bolswert after Abraham Bloemaert, *Saint Paul Simplex*, ca. 1612/ reissued 1619. Engraving, ca. 125/30 × 85/88 mm. Rijksmuseum, Amsterdam

FIGURE 12.25   Boëtius à Bolswert after Abraham Bloemaert, *Saint Arsenius*, ca. 1612/
reissued 1619. Engraving, ca. 125/30 × 85/88 mm. Rijksmuseum, Amsterdam

FIGURE 12.26 Boëtius à Bolswert after Abraham Bloemaert, *Saint Bonosus*, ca. 1612/ reissued 1619. Engraving, ca. 125/30 × 85/88 mm. Rijksmuseum, Amsterdam

FIGURE 12.27   Boëtius à Bolswert after Abraham Bloemaert, *Saint Jerome*, ca. 1612/reissued 1619. Engraving, ca. 125/30 × 85/88 mm. British Museum, London

FIGURE 12.28   Boëtius à Bolswert after Abraham Bloemaert, *Title-Page: Sacra eremus ascetriarum*, ca. 1612/reissued 1619. Engraving, ca. 125/30 × 85/88 mm. Rijksmuseum, Amsterdam

MIXED EMOTION & PERFECTION IN BLOEMAERT'S *SYLVA ANACHORETICA* 441

FIGURE 12.29   Boëtius à Bolswert after Abraham Bloemaert, *Virgin Mary, Mother of God*, ca. 1612/reissued 1619. Engraving, ca. 125/30 × 85/88 mm. Rijksmuseum, Amsterdam

FIGURE 12.30   Boëtius à Bolswert after Abraham Bloemaert, *Saint Mary Magdalene*, ca. 1612/ reissued 1619. Engraving, ca. 125/30 × 85/88 mm. Rijksmuseum, Amsterdam

FIGURE 12.31 Willem de Passe after Abraham Bloemaert, *Angel Gabriel*, ca. 1610. Engraving, 273 × 186 mm. Rijksmuseum, Amsterdam

FIGURE 12.32　Crispijn van de Passe after Abraham Bloemaert, *Virgin Annunciate*, ca. 1610. Engraving, 275 × 187 mm. Rijksmuseum, Amsterdam

MIXED EMOTION & PERFECTION IN BLOEMAERT'S *SYLVA ANACHORETICA* 445

FIGURE 12.33   Willem van Swanenburg after Abraham Bloemaert, *Peter Mourning his Betrayal of Christ*, from *Biblical Penitents*, 1609–1611. Engraving, 268 × 171. Rijksmuseum, Amsterdam

FIGURE 12.34　Willem van Swanenburg after Abraham Bloemaert, *Paul's Contrition over his Former Persecution of Christ*, from *Biblical Penitents*, 1609–1611. Engraving, 267 × 170 mm. Rijksmuseum, Amsterdam

FIGURE 12.35   Willem van Swanenburg after Abraham Bloemaert, *Zachaeus Grieving over his Riches*, from *Biblical Penitents*, 1609–1611. Engraving, 272 × 173 mm. Rijksmuseum, Amsterdam

FIGURE 12.36   Willem van Swanenburg after Abraham Bloemaert, *Repentant Mary Magdalene in the Wilderness*, from *Biblical Penitents*, 1609–1611. Engraving, 271 × 174 mm. Rijksmuseum, Amsterdam

MIXED EMOTION & PERFECTION IN BLOEMAERT'S *SYLVA ANACHORETICA* 449

FIGURE 12.37　Jan Saenredam after Abraham Bloemaert, *Ahijah Divides his Cloak before Jeroboam*, from *Prophecies of Ahijah*, 1604. Engraving, 270 × 199 mm. Rijksmuseum, Amsterdam

FIGURE 12.38   Jan Saenredam after Abraham Bloemaert, *Ahijah Predicts the Fall of Jeroboam*, from *Prophecies of Ahijah*, 1604. Engraving, 270 × 194 mm. Rijksmuseum, Amsterdam

MIXED EMOTION & PERFECTION IN BLOEMAERT'S *SYLVA ANACHORETICA* 451

FIGURE 12.39 Jan Saenredam after Abraham Bloemaert, *Expulsion*, from *History of Adam and Eve*, 1604. Engraving, 278 × 200 mm. Rijksmuseum, Amsterdam

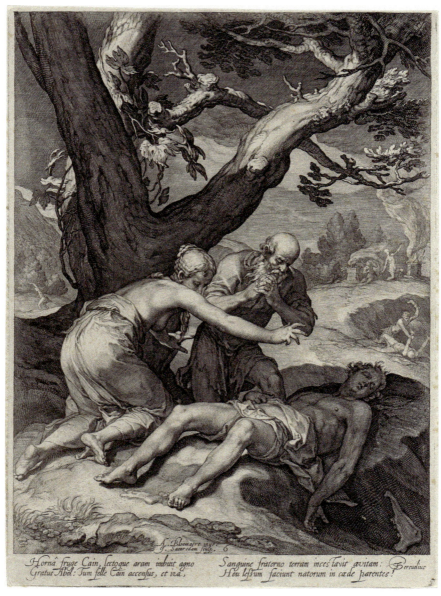

FIGURE 12.40 Jan Saenredam after Abraham Bloemaert, *Lamentation of Adam and Eve, from History of Adam and Eve*, 1604. Engraving, 279 × 200 mm. Rijksmuseum, Amsterdam

of Rosweyde's project of composing a new *vitae patrum* based on the principles of humanist philology and historiography.[5]

1   Bloemaert and the Visual Markers of Mixed Emotion

How does Bloemaert portray emotion, in particular mixed emotion, in the *Sylva*, and how do the Fathers compare to other paragons of emotional expression designed by him? First and foremost, the Fathers are epitomes of sorrow, varying only in the degree of melancholy they register, which encompasses, at one end of the scale, the gentle sorrow of John the Baptist, whose grave features, tempered by a slight smile, simultaneously allude to the sad sacrifice of Christ the lamb and to the happy, redemptive effects this sacrifice will procure (Roethlisberger 165), and at the other end, the extreme sorrow of Bonosus, whose twisted face and body reveal how intense is his horror of sin, and how agonising (Roethlisberger 187) [Figs. 12.5 & 12.26]. John and Bonosus, indeed all the Fathers, display amalgams of the traits codified by Karel van Mander in Book I of the *Schilder-Boeck*, the *Grondt der Edel, vry Schilder-const* (Foundation of the Noble, Free Art of Painting), for the depiction of sorrow tinged by pain and fear. In stanzas 44–45 of chapter 6, "Portrayal of the Affects, Passions, Desires, and Sorrows of Persons", Van Mander describes these gestural and physiognomic features as follows:

> To fashion a mournful expression, full of pity
> And inner feeling, without a flow
> Of tears, as sometimes occurs,
> One shall turn the eyebrows sideways, to the left,
> Somewhat raising them and the half-shuttered eye,
> And let the little fold running from nose to cheek
> Be pulled in the same direction, and abridged:
> Thus shall one portray a fearful person.
>
> The head shall also hang tilted to one side,
> The cheek, raised toward the aforesaid eye,
> Shall pull the mouth open, sidewise.

---

5 De Winghe, Abbot of the Benedictine monastery of Lessines (Liessies) in the Archdiocese of Cambrai, later edited the complete works of the French Benedictine mystic François-Louis de Blois; see Bosius Fredericus-Ludovicus, *Opera omnia*, ed. Antonius de Winghe (Antwerp: Ex officina Plantiniana Balthasaris Moreti, 1632).

One hand shall strike the bosom at the heart,
The other attach to its proper shoulder,
With its innermost surface turned outward,
Positioned as if to seize or avert something:
Thereby one shall plumb a heavy heart.

With hands on heart, laid crosswise,
[And] the head pressing down on one shoulder, yea all
The body's fellow citizens behaving as one,
[The eyes] like red clouds raining temperately
Onto the pale fields of the cheeks, moistening them,
The hands joined, with the fingers plaited;
Contrariwise, like West and East,
The face shall look dispiritedly in the opposite direction.[6]

---

6 Mander Karel van, *Den Grondt der Edel vry Schilder-const: Waer in haer ghestalt, aerdt ende wesen, de leer-lustighe Jeught in verscheyden Deelen in Rijm-dicht wort voor ghedraghen*, in idem, *Het Schilder-Boeck* (Haarlem, Paschier van Wesbusch: 1604), fol. 26v:

   'Om nu een droef ghelaet, vol medelijden,
En inwendighe passy, sonder storten
Der tranen, te maken, alst beurt somtijden,
Salmen de wijnbrauwen ter slincker sijden
Met d'ooghe half toe wat om hoogh' opschorten,
En laten derwaert trecken en vercorten
T'vouken, dat van de neuse loopt in wanghe/
Soo salmen uytbeelden een wesen banghe.
   'T'hooft sal oock hanghen eensijdich ghestopen,
De wanghe nae t'voornoemt ooghe verheven
Sal op die sijde den mondt trecken open,
D'een handt op t'herte den boesem sal nopen,
En d'ander haer eyghen schouder aencleven,
Soo met t'binnenste uytwaert ghewent, even
Ghestelt, als om yet te vatten oft schutten,
Om een gheperst ghemoedt wel uyt te putten.
   'De handen op't herte, cruyswijs gheleghen,
T'hooft druckend' een schouder, jae vry soo mochten
Oock al s'Lichaems borghers wel mede pleghen,
Als die roode wolcken met laeuwen reghen
De bleycke wange-velden nat bevochten,
De handen t'samen met vinghers doorvlochten,
Contrary van een, als Westich en Oostich,
Sal t'aenschijn elderswaert op sien mistroostich'.

On Van Mander's detailed treatment of the passions and other states of feeling in chapter 6 of the *Grondt*, "Wtbeeldinghe der Affecten, passien, begeerlijckheden, en lijdens der Menschen", see Melion W.S., *Karel van Mander and his* Foundation of the Noble, Free Art

Bonosus, like the similarly contorted Hilarion (Roethlisberger 168), tilts the brows sidewise, one cheek raised, eyes heavy-lidded, mouth pulled askew (though open in Bonosus's case, closed in Hilarion's), while canting the head to one side [Figs. 12.8 & 12.26]. Bonosus clasps his hands, plaiting his fingers, which swivel away from his arcing head and dispirited face. Malchus and Alexandrinus follow suit, though in near *profil perdu* (Roethlisberger 169 and 173) [Figs. 12.9 & 12.13]. Every Father is a variation on "Jesus led into the desert", the series' opening plate, in which Christ models the lineaments of sorrow variously displayed by his eremitical followers (Roethlisberger 164) [Fig. 12.4]. His left-hand gesture eschewing the devil's invitation to turn stone into bread precisely matches the aversive gesture described by Van Mander in stanza 45. One of the Fathers, Arsenius, weeps despondently, in the fashion endorsed by Van Mander in stanza 47, propping up his sorrow-laden head, a kerchief clutched in his left hand, his elbow anchored by the rock against which he leans, his other arm and lower body cascading downward listlessly [Fig. 12.25]:

> To press or wipe the tearful eye,
> The hand or a kerchief shall sometimes come forward,
> And the head, heavy-laden with mournful damp,
> Shall stand steadfast, helpful to the hand,
> With the elbow propped up;
> Indeed all the limbs ought, virtually without exception,
> To lie slack or hang down
> As if dead or wholly overcome by sickness.[7]

To the extent that Bloemaert based his Fathers on the *Grondt*'s criteria for portraying sorrow, he was indicating, like Van Mander, that sorrow is a compound state, admixed with pity, fear, and heaviness of heart shading into desolation of the spirit like unto sickness or death. And yet, Bloemaert consistently follows

---

of Painting: *First English Translation, with Introduction and Commentary* (Leiden – Boston: 2023) 431–446.

7   Van Mander, *Grondt*, fol. 26:
> 'Om de tranend' ooghe drucken oft dwaden,
> Sal somtijts handt oft doeck daer comen vooren,
> En t'hooft, met droeve vochticheyt beladen,
> Sal de handt behulpelijck slaen in staden,
> En dat met den elleboogh onderschooren,
> Jae alle leden souden schier behooren
> Daer slappelijck te ligghen oft te hanghen,
> Als doot, oft gheheel met sieckten bevanghen'.

another of Van Mander's figural canons, assimilating every Father to the form of serpentine contrapposto endorsed in chapter 4 of the *Grondt*, "On the Attitude, Decorum, and Decorous Motion of a Human Figure", stanzas 10–11 and 13 of which state:

> One sees a Human Figure display
> This sort of swaying motion in running or walking,
> Both while working and standing still:
> Closely to observe this
> With respect to all persons – Children, Men, and Women –
> Will crown our works with success.
> We ought never to extend the arm and leg of a Figure
> Forward on the same side.
>
> We should be mindful to alternate them,
> Letting the right arm come forward,
> And the right leg sink backward,
> The left leg project, and, conversely, the left
> Arm back away by degrees,
> Always crosswise; whether the Figures sit
> Or stand, their faces should turn
> Toward the arm that extends outward.
>
> In Figures standing naturally, one observes
> How the head usually turns
> In the direction of the foot, and one also sees
> How the Body tends to move itself
> As does the head, giving it support:
> But in posing [Figures] according to the rules of Attitude,
> It is considered especially praiseworthy
> To move the Head away from where the Torso turns.[8]

---

8 Ibid., fol. 12v:
>   'Sulcke roerend' acty, loopend' oft gaende,
> Sietmen den Mensche natuerlijck vertoonen,
> Soo wel werckend' als in postuere staende,
> In onsen dinghen dit wel gade slaende,
> Soo in Kinders, Mannen, als Vrouw persoonen,
> Sal onsen arbeydt welstandich becroonen,
> Op een sijd' eens Beeldts wy niet en behooren
> Arem en been uyt te doen steken vooren.

MIXED EMOTION & PERFECTION IN BLOEMAERT'S *SYLVA ANACHORETICA*   457

Throughout the *Schilder-Boeck*, the contrappostal turning figure is praised as the acme of graceful motion, and this must be one of the reasons why Bloemaert, whose signature *handelinge* (manner, handling) Van Mander himself considered uncommonly graceful, insisted on thus rotating his figures so conspicuously, in spite of the admonition, inserted as an addendum to stanza 14, that 'no such turning is to be tolerated / In sacred Figures, which one must do one's best / To make devout and modest'.[9] For Bloemaert, it would seem, maintaining the canon of grace trumped the canon of decorum: surely this was due to the longstanding association between *gratie* (in Latin, *gratia*, in Italian *grazia*) as a term of art virtually synonymous with beauty and as a theological category signifying an afflatus of the Holy Spirit. The Fathers' torsion implicitly ascribes their penitential devotion or, better, their grace of vocation to the inspiriting action of God who, bodied forth in Christ, is the true source of the eremitical life. That torsion sometimes pushes close to contortion discloses the strength of their commitment to the rigors of the solitary life, which remains spiritually beautiful even in *extremis*.

The emotional reach of the *Sylva*'s Fathers becomes all the more apparent when they are compared with the nuancedly emotive figures featured in other prints after Bloemaert. For example, the *Virgin Annunciate* of ca. 1610,

---

> 'Maer dat wy een wisselinghe ghedincken,
> Den rechten arem voor uyt comen laten,
> En t'rechter been achter doen henen sincken,
> T'slincke been voor uyt, daer teghen den slincken
> Arem achter wech laten gaen by maten,
> Altijt cruyswijs, t'zy of de Beelden saten,
> Oft stonden, soo sal haer de troenge weynden
> Naer den arem, die men voor uyt sal seynden'.
> [...]
> 'Natuerlijck sietmen in staende postueren,
> T'hooft ghemeynelijcken ghekeert te wesen
> Soo den voet gherecht is, noch salmen spueren,
> Dat t'Lijf hem altijt wil schicken en rueren
> Nae t'wendyn des hoofts, als steunsel van desen:
> Maer dit wordt in de stellinghe ghepresen
> Werckelijcker, nae *Actitudens* orden,
> T'Hooft elders als t'Lichaem gheweynt te worden'.

On Van Mander's criteria of well-tempered bodily disposition in chapter 4 of the *Grondt*, "Van der *Actitude*, welstandt, ende weldoen eens Beeldts", see Melion, *Karel van Mander and his Foundation* 402–408.

9   Van Mander, *Grondt*, fol. 12v:

> 'Doch gheen omdraeyen is wel te ghedooghen
> Aen gheestlijcke Beelden, die men op't beste
> Soeckt te maken devotich en modeste'.

On this passage, see Miedema H., *Karel van Mander, Den grondt der edel vry schilder-const*, 2 vols. (Utrecht: 1973), 2:453.

engraved and published by Crispijn van de Passe as a pendant to Willem de Passe's *Angel Gabriel*, depicts Mary neither quite joyful nor sorrowful, overshadowed by the Holy Spirit at the moment she assents to become the mother of Christ [Figs. 12.31–12.32].[10] Half-closed, heavily shaded, her eyes resemble the somber eyes of Christ in "Jesus led into the desert", John the Baptist, Onuphrius (though in near silhouette), Abraham Hermit, Frontonius, Helenus, and Ammon Nitriota (Roethlisberger 170, 174, 179, 183, and 184) [Figs. 12.4, 12.5, 12.10, 12.14, 12.18, 12.22, & 12.23]. This is ostensibly a moment of supreme joy, as the quatrain below, excerpted from the *Magnificat*, emphasises: 'My soul doth magnify the Lord, and my spirit hath rejoiced in God my Saviour. Because he hath regarded the humility of his handmaid: for behold from henceforth all generations shall call me blessed'.[11] And yet, that grave joy is overlaid with many of the vestiges of great sorrow enumerated by Van Mander in the *Grondt*, not least the gestures he associates with mournful compassion and fear, one hand striking the bosom at the heart, the other turned palm outward as if 'to seize or avert something' [Fig. 12.32]. The Virgin's attitude, gestures, and facial expression communicate a congeries of entangled affects: her fear of the Lord, trepidation at the sudden appearance of the angel ('Fear not, Mary'), wonder at his God-sent salutation ('How shall this be done'?), grateful recognition of divine mercy (*Magnificat*: 'And his mercy is from generation unto generations, to them that fear him'), and anticipatory sorrow, in proleptic expectation of the Passion whereby the 'Son of the Most High' obtains salvation 'from generation unto generations', to them that fear the Lord. Bloemaert weaves these affects together or, rather, laminates them: experienced sequentially in *Luke* 1:28–55, they are made to attach indissolubly to the multivalent event enacted in the *Annunciation*, which amalgamates Mary's manifold responses to its various phases – Gabriel's arrival and message, her illumination by God and overshadowing by the Holy Spirit, and her prescient knowledge of the joyful and sorrowful circumstances that the mystery of the Incarnation portends.

The Virgin Annunciate's multiple registers of reactive emotion ultimately derive from Ludolphus of Saxony's *Vita Christi*, in Book I, chapter 5 of which, "On the Saviour's Conception", she is described as *mare amarum*, the 'bitter sea for the conversion of sinners [...], changing the water of earthly pleasures into the wine of compunction', ever bitter in this life 'because of her desire to

---

10   On these pendants, see Roethlisberger, *Abraham Bloemaert* 1:215–216.

11   'Magnificat anima mea Dominum et exultavit Spiritus meus in Deo salutari me[o] / Quia respexit Humilitatem ancille sue ecce enim / Ex hoc beatam me dicit omnes generationes etc. Luc, 1'. Cf. the inscription on the *Angel Gabriel*: 'Ave gratia plena Dominus tecum: / Benedicta tu in Mulieribus. Luc. 2'.

MIXED EMOTION & PERFECTION IN BLOEMAERT'S *SYLVA ANACHORETICA*   459

see her son in his kingdom'.[12] Even as Gabriel strives to induce her 'to accept [Jesus] joyfully as her son', praising her as 'full of grace', she remains *turbata* (troubled), first, 'by the splendour of this novel apparition', second, 'because of the modesty of her virginal purity', third, 'because of the novel form of [the angel's] salutation', fourth, because 'such is the view of the humble that the more highly they are praised, the more uncomfortable they become'.[13] The expressive features shared by Mary and the Fathers bear witness to the complex affective states that she and they enshrine bodily.

Bloemaert assayed the figural trope he would later use for the Fathers, in four of plates from a series of six *Biblical Penitents*, engraved and published by Willem van Swanenburg between 1609 and 1611: *Peter Mourning his Betrayal of Christ, Paul's Contrition over his Former Persecution of Christ, Zachaeus Grieving over his Riches*, and *Repentant Mary Magdalene in the Wilderness* [Figs. 12.33–12.36].[14] Each of these prints turns on the Aristotelian device of *peripeteia*, defined in the *Poetics* as a sudden, unexpected change of circumstances that often carries with it a cathartic shift of emotion.[15] A small background scene depicts an earlier or later episode from the protagonist's life, the nature and affective character of which are reversed in the foreground scene of penitence. In *Zachaeus*, the distant encounter between Christ and the tax collector can be seen through the doorway at right; as *Luke* 1:4 recounts, Zachaeus, who was chief of the publicans, had climbed a tree to get a better view of Jesus on his way into Jericho [Fig. 12.35]. Saviour and sinner are shown turning toward each other, the one blessing, the other rejoicing to receive the Lord and be so blessed (*Luke* 19:6: 'And he made haste and came down and received him with joy'). By contrast, the anterior Zachaeus appears in the guise of a penitent, per the assertion he makes in *Luke* 19:8: 'Behold, Lord, the half of my goods I give

---

12   See *Ludolph of Saxony, The Life of Jesus Christ, Part One, Volume 1, Chapters 1–40*, trans. – introd. M.T. Walsh (Colegeville: 2018) 83. Cf. *Vita Christi Domini Salvatoris nostri a A.R.P. Ludolpho Saxone Cartusiano*, ed. Johannes Dadraeus (Venice, Apud Guerraeos Fratres et Franciscum Zilettum, 1581) 22.

13   *Ludolph of Saxony*, trans. – introd. Walsh, 88–89. Cf. *Vita Christi Domini Salvatoris nostri*, ed. Dadraeus, 23.

14   On the series and these four prints in particular, see Roethlisberger, *Abraham Bloemaert* 1: 162–165.

15   Aristotle introduces *peripeteia* in part 6 of the *Poetics*, and discusses it in parts 10–11; see *Aristotle's Poetics*, trans. – comm. G. Whalley (Montreal – Buffalo: 1997) §36, 36A, 37, and pp. 86–87, 89–91, 96, 102, 114, 128. On Daniel Heinsius's Latin edition of the *Poetics* as a possible source for Bloemaert's interest in *peripeteia*, see note 96 *infra*. It is important to note, however, that Aristotle does not elaborate on labile or mixed emotion as a necessary consequence of *peripeteia*. In dwelling on these complex emotional effects, Bloemaert, perhaps responding to the conventions of rhetorical theatre, draws a causal analogy between peripetal change and emotional expression.

to the poor; and if I have wronged any man of any thing, I restore him fourfold'. Head, cheek, and eyes tilted sideward, right hand pressed against his heart, his face and other hand inclined contrariwise, he musters the attributes of mournful fear/fearful sorrow systematised by Van Mander. Enhancing the affective antithesis between near and far, foreground and background, is the distinction between the serpentine figure of Christ pointing up and the rigidly aligned figure of Zachaeus pointing down, the former diffusely lit, the latter in strong chiaroscuro.[16] The paired tercets, composed *ex tempore* by Petrus Scriverius, give voice to the penitent's remorse laced with hope for forgiveness, and put a second antithesis, between faith and incredulity, into words:

> I confess, Lord, that I have sinned against an exhausted people,
> Alas, having filled my coffers with heaped up riches.
> Being clement, bestow mercy and purify me of my grave faults.
>
> And may you wish for Zachaeus amongst your own.
> Whatever coinage I procured, formerly without faith,
> All that I now confer on your poor.[17]

Conversely, the rearward scene confirms that Zachaeus, ever fearful of God, sorrowful yet impelled by penitent hope, has, as Jesus asseverates in *Luke* 19:9, been saved: 'This day is salvation come to this house, because he also is a son of Abraham'.

The *Repentant Magdalene*, who again derives from Van Mander's canon of sorrow, though more sweetly, reverses the terms of the antithesis laid out in *Zachaeus* [Figs. 12.35 & 12.36]: there, kneeling in the foreground, Zachaeus rigidly aligns his thighs, torso, and head, while gracefully twisting in the background, where his pose echoes that of Christ. Inverting this relation, the foreground Magdalene, like the tree trunks around her, emphatically rotates her body, in one sense turning away from the world, in another toward thoughts of imminent death and the cross of Christ, but also toward God on high, source of illuminative grace. In the background, by contrast, she stands erect, no longer turning, while angels nourish her bodily and spiritually, raising her heavenward. As in the *Zachaeus*, the contrast between the Magdalene's two

---

16   That Zachaeus's pose, unlike that of Peter, Paul, and Mary Magdalene, is not serpentine perhaps has to do with the fact that he remained a publican, putting his profits to good use rather than fully eschewing, i.e., *turning* entirely away, from his former life.

17   'Peccavi, fateor Domine, exhaustoque popello / (Heu!) mea congestas arca flagella topes. / Da veniam Clemens, gravibus meque balue culpis, // Zachaeumque tuos inter habere velis. / Quidquid nummorum corrasi incredulus olim, / Id nunc pauperibus largior omne tuis'.

MIXED EMOTION & PERFECTION IN BLOEMAERT'S *SYLVA ANACHORETICA*   461

personae distinguishes sinner from saved, the former's remorseful penitence from the latter's assurance of salvation. The tercets, composed by Cornelis Plempius, underscore the peripetal shift between the worldly and the penitent Magdalene, which both presages and heightens the print's contrast between the repentant Magdalene and her heavenly counterpart:

> A seeming Venus to the young (ah, sensory pleasure, fit to be deplored!),
> Beyond measure was I, the dark/dismal Magdalene, pleasing to myself.
> I saw myself, as in a mirror, most foul,
>
> When Christ turned his face to mine.
> Let the Venuses come to observe; themselves let them see;
> Deprived of her haughty looks, a proud [Venus] perishes instantly.[18]

The inscriptions by Scriverius and Plempius invite us to consider how *peripeteia* itself is the subject that fills the penitents' thoughts: just as Zachaeus admits to being painfully aware of his former incredulity, now supplanted by Christian charity, so the Magdalene recalls how she once delighted in her voluptuous, Venus-like charms, now noisome to behold. Coterminous with this peripetal disparity between past and present, is the distinction Bloemaert draws, with implied reference to Van Mander's affective precepts, between the complex, discordant emotions felt by the penitent – Zachaeus's sorrow, fear, and hope, shared, too, by the Magdalene, but overtopped by self-loathing – and the concordant experience of the soul made one with its Saviour. Viewed from the vantage point of the penitent's conflicting emotions, her/his torsion, more than a reference to grace, can also be seen, contradictorily, as an allusion to the push and pull of emotional impulses that cause her/him to sway, now this way, now that, as s/he strives to find common cause with Christ. *Zachaeus* and the *Repentant Magdalene*, seen in this way, provide useful yardsticks for reading the emotional significance of the penitential poses, gestures, and facial expressions in the *Sylva* [Figs. 12.35 & 12.36].

An earlier pair of prints illustrating the two key prophecies of Ahijah, respectively addressed to Jeroboam in 3 *Kings* 11:29–39 and to Jeroboam's wife in 3 *Kings* 14:5–16, performatively stages how penitence may best be enacted and expressed through the motions of the face and body [Figs. 12.37 & 12.38].[19]

---

18   'Visa iuventuti Venus (ah, deflenda voluptas!) / Plus nimio placui Magdalis atra mihi. / Ipsa ego me velut in speculo teterrima vidi, // Os mea cum Christus vertit in ora suum. / Spectatum Veneres veniant; spectentur et ipsae; / Pompa superciljs protinus orba cadet'.

19   On these two prints, the second states of which were paired with another two, *Elijah Fed by Ravens* and *Elisha and Elijah's Chariot of Fire* (Roethlisberger 81 and 82), see Roethlisberger, *Abraham Bloemaert* 1:127–128.

Engraved and published by Jan Saenredam, both prints carry inscriptions by Theodoor Schrevelius that paraphrase and, to some extent, diverge from Scripture in ways that highlight how the true subject of the two-part series is Jeroboam's fall from grace. In plate 1, *Ahijah Divides his Cloak before Jeroboam*, the prophet conveys to Jeroboam that he has been elected by God to succeed errant Solomon: ten of the twelve tribes of Israel will henceforth be his to govern [Fig. 12.37]. Whereas 1 *Kings* 11:30–31 clearly states that Ahijah divided his new garment into twelve parts, giving ten to Jeroboam in order to elucidate his prophecy, Schrevelius instead imputes the garment to Jeroboam, associating it with the sin of pride which will lead inevitably to the new king's downfall:

New in vesture, swelling with arrogance, proud in public honor,
Jeroboam, you meet the holy scion of Shiloh;

Who cuts the garment into twelve parts, and
Having rendered ten, unfolds the mysteries of the rent mantle.[20]

Bloemaert positions Ahijah beside the seated Jeroboam, to whom he hands strips of the cut-up mantle. In plate 2, *Ahijah Predicts the Fall of Jeroboam*, Bloemaert embeds the prophet within his vision of Jeroboam's fallen house, the king's dead progeny eaten by dogs in the city, by birds in the country [Fig. 12.38]. The crown beside the dead youth at left identifies him as the king's son Abia whose fate his mother the queen had asked Ahijah to reveal:

Now deviant error had turned Jeroboam from the true path,
When Ahijah threatened disaster and ruin:

In the market places filthy dogs, in the crossroads savage birds of ill-omen
Will consume the scattered bodies.[21]

Again consonant with Van Mander's canon of pitiable sorrow and disconsolate fear, Ahijah now sits at right, his standing pose in plate 1 transformed into a forebodingly penitent version of Jeroboam's seated pose there [Figs. 12.37 & 12.38]. Whereas the future king's relaxed attitude and ready grasp upon the

---

20 'Veste novus, fastuque tumens, et honore superbus / Jeroboa occurris sancto Schilonis alumno; // Qui duodena secat vestem in fragmenta, decemque / Reddidit, et scissae pandit mysteria pallae'.

21 'Devius a recto iam tramite flexerat error / Jeroboam, cum cladem Achia exitiumque minat: // Per fora depascent fusos, per compita truncus / Obscoenique canes importunaeque volucres'.

MIXED EMOTION & PERFECTION IN BLOEMAERT'S *SYLVA ANACHORETICA*   463

proffered strips of cloth signaled Schrevelius's sense of him as swollen with pride, Ahijah's inflection of this pose, dynamically turning, head titled, brows lifted, eyes shaded, left hand extended as if to avert, communicates the tragic horror and miserable sorrow of the king's present condition. The prophet not only prophesies but also reacts to the dread oracles he delivers, giving us to see, jointly and ironically, the penitent fear and remorse that might have saved Jeroboam had he been less proud, but which can save him no longer. The affective transposition of Ahijah into a vatic substitute for the chastised Jeroboam was surely a response to 3 *Kings* 14:6, which has the prophet empathetically declare to the king's wife that his oracle will be well-nigh unbearable to hear: 'But I am sent to thee with heavy tidings'. In plate 2, Ahijah shows how these tidings must be received, performing the king's part.

Designed ca. 1604, Ahijah's body, gesture, and face in *Ahijah Predicts the Fall of Jeroboam* constitute Bloemaert's earliest full-fledged exploration of the penitential affects he would later exemplify variously in the *Sylva*, most notably in the case of those anchorites who appear almost to personate their forebear: not only *John the Baptist, Malchus, Macarius Alexandrinus, Abraham Hermit, Frontonius, Ammon Nitriota*, and *Bonosus*, but also *Christ Led into the Desert* (Roethlisberger 164, 165, 169, 173, 174, 179, 184, and 187) [Figs. 12.5, 12.9, 12.13, 12.14, 12.18, 12.23, 12.26, & 12.38]. The emotional tenor of these Fathers' faces and gestures derives, too, from another series of 1604, the six-part *History of Adam and Eve*, engraved and published by Jan Saenredam, especially the features of Eve in the *Expulsion*, horrified and grief-stricken at the consequences of her sin [Fig. 12.39]. Pleading with her eyes, mouth agape, hands tightly clasped in a prayer of supplication, she gazes up at the angel driving her and Adam from paradise; she is an exemplar of horror, bewilderment, and shame, as the inscription by Theodoor Schrevelius asserts:

> The eye's light having been restored, shame and horror rush in upon the
> > thunderstruck [Adam and Eve]:
> While the serpent, tracing [its] tortuous convolutions
>
> Scrapes the ground: The winged attendant hurtles down from the high
> > citadel,
> He who defends the chaste grove with punishing flame.[22]

---

22   'Reddita lux oculus; pudor, et gravis ingruit horror / Attonitis: Cum torta legens sinuamina serpens // Verrit humum: Supera ruit aliger arce satelles, / Qui flamma intactas defendat vindice silvas'.

Schrevelius's couplets imply that Eve's newfound consciousness of sin, now visible to her eyes of the spirit, has filled her with a complex of emotions as involuted as the serpent's windings. In transferring her diagnostic traits to the Fathers, Bloemaert conferred upon them a consciousness of sin like hers, and with it, a compound of horrified and confused shame entirely appropriate to the ascetic's vocation of weighing daily the wages of original sin. Similarly, he transferred the countenance of Adam, woebegone at the death of Abel in *Lamentation of Adam and Eve*, to *Anthony Hermit, Hilarion, Macarius Aegyptius, Basilius Magnus, Ephraem, Simeon Stylita, John in Lyco, Theonas, Paulus Simplex*, and *Arsenius* (Roethlisberger 167, 168, 172, 175, 176, 177, 180, 182, 185, and 186) [Figs. 12.7, 12.8, 12.12, 12.15, 12.16, 12.17, 12.19, 12.21, 12.24, 12.25, & 12.40]. By layering the markers of painful anguish onto the monks' evident contrition, he declares that the Fathers' penitential remorse was no less intense than the grief felt by a parent over a murdered son. Schrevelius's couplets again punctuate Bloemaert's display of emotion, contrasting the bitter, murderous rage of Cain with the doleful wailing of his stricken parents:

> Cain with the year's produce, grateful Abel with the chosen lamb stained the altar:
> And thence [was] Cain inflamed with bitter rage.
>
> He defiled the ancestral earth with fraternal blood:
> Alas, the sons' parents bewail the slaughter.[23]

It bears repeating that Bloemaert, in depicting the Fathers, allows for a measure of indeterminacy, less as regards emotional kind than degree. It is just this quality of openness to complementary affective readings that enhances the mixed emotional effects so characteristic of the series.

2 Mixed Emotion in Heribert Rosweyde, s.j.'s *'t Vaders boeck*

The ultimate source for Bloemaert's conception of the desert Fathers as exemplars of mixed emotion was Heribert Rosweyde's *'t Vaders boeck, 't Leven ende spreucken der Vaderen* [...], *in thien boecken by een vergadert* (Book of the Fathers: Lives and Sayings of the Fathers [...] Assembled in Ten Books)

---

23 'Horna fruge Cain, lectoque aram imbuit agno / Gratus Abel: Tum felle Cain accensus, et ira, // Sanguine fraterno terram incestavit avitam: / Heu lessum faciunt natorum in caede parentes'!

(Antwerp, Hieronymus Verdussen: 1617), a compendious chronicle in ten parts of their deeds and sayings, translated from his 1615 edition of the *Vitae patrum* and published by Hieronymus Verdussen in 1617.[24] His early Christian sources, ranging from Jerome and Athanasius to Theodoretus of Cyrus and Johannes Moschus, are enumerated in the first eight chapters of the General Preface. The complex emotional life of the Fathers, their constant struggle to control multifarious, often contrary feelings, and their heroic efforts to subdue these emotions and achieve a state of contemplative repose, are central concerns of *'t Vaders boeck* that thread their way through the whole of it. Engendered by the many trials and tribulations they encounter in the desert, episodes of mixed emotion recur throughout their lives, but in particular, they regularly accompany the moment of conversion. This pattern is set early on, in the General Preface, chapter 10 of which, citing Book 8, chapter 6 of Augustine's

---

24   Based on the *Vitae patrum* of Evagrius (wrongly ascribed to Jerome by Rosweyde's teacher Martin Delrio, s.j.), *'t Vaders boeck* consists of ten parts: first, 16 *Vitae virorum* and twelve *Vitae mulierum*, including lives of Sts. Paul Hermit, Anthony Hermit, and Jerome; second, the *Historia monachorum* of Rufinus; third, the *Verba seniorum*, ascribed to Rufinus; fourth, texts on the monastic life by Sulpicius Severus and Cassian; fifth, the *Verba seniorum* of Pelagius; sixth, the *Verba seniorum* of John the Subdeacon; seventh, the *Verba seniorum* of Poschasius; eighth, the *Paradise* of Heraclides, translated by Gentianus Hervet and rightly identified by Rosweyde as the *Lausiac History* of Palladius; ninth, the *Philotheus* (*Theophiles*) of Theodoretus; tenth, the *Spiritual Meadow* of Moschus, translated by Ambrogio Traversari. In all these cases, as noted in Machielsen, in "Heretical Saints and Spiritual Discernment" 122–133, Rosweyde made every effort to retain and restore the original sources' simple style of writing, which he viewed as a mark of authenticity and the essential attribute of early Christian hagiography. Rosweyde censured his predecessor, the Carthusian hagiographer Laurentius Surius, whose *Vitae sanctorum patrum ordinis praedicatorum* (Leuven, Apud H. Wellaeum: 1575), based on the earlier collection by Luigi Lipomani, had been edited to conform to normative criteria of Latin diction, style, and decorum. Philological discernment, in Rosweyde's view, precluded tampering of this sort. On Rosweyde's *Vitae patrum*, a revised edition of which was published by the Plantin press in 1628, see Delehaye H., s.j., *L'oeuvre des Bollandistes à travers trois siècles, 1615–1915* (Brussels: 1959) 17–21; Peeters P., *L'oeuvre des Bollandistes* (Brussels: 1961) 11; Coens M., "Héribert Rosweyde et la recherche des document", *Analecta bollandiana* 83 (1965) 50–52; Fatouros G., "Rosweyde, Heribert, s.j.", in *Biographisch-Bibliographisches Kirchenlexikon*, ed. F.W. Bautz et al., 44 vols. (Hamm: 1970–1979) 15: cols. 1213–1214; and Godding R., "L'oeuvre hagiographique d'Héribert Rosweyde", in Godding – Joassart B. – Lequeux X. – De Vriendt F. (eds.), *De Rosweyde aux Acta Sanctorum: La recherche hagiographique des Bollandistes à travers quatre siècles* (Brussels: 2009) 35–62, esp. 48–49. The *Vitae patrum* is the closest Rosweyde came to realising the grand project of a comprehensive *Acta sanctorum*, presaged in the *Fasti sanctorum*, and ultimately inaugurated by Johannes Bollandus and his followers, on which see ibid. 38–49; and Machielsen, "Heretical Saints and Textual Discernment" 109–115, 122–139.

Confessions, rehearses the circumstances of his conversion to Christ.[25] Crucial to his change of heart, explains Rosweyde, was the inspiring story told him by a visitor, his countryman Potitianus: one day, chancing upon a manuscript life of the Egyptian monk Anthony, two courtiers were astonished to read about his spiritual accomplishments. Filled with wonder at his life and works, they were jointly seized, like him, by love for the Lord, but also by a sense of shame mingled with self-anger at the years they had misspent chasing after imperial honors. The leader of the two, moved by his surging emotions ('beroeringe sijns gemoets'), constantly sighing ('versuchte hy altemets'), finally avowed that peace of mind could be found only by embracing the anchoretic life, in imitation of Anthony ('ende met dat hy hem gerustich vandt [nu u, Heere, verkosen hebbende]').[26] The mixed effect this tale exercises on Augustine is profound: his loving admiration of the two courtiers merges with self-loathing at his soul's sorry state:

> While Potitianus recounted this, you caused me, Lord, to come to myself, taking me away from behind my back where, unwilling to pay myself heed, I had set myself, and placing me before my face, so that I might see how ugly, misshapen, foul, heartsore I was. This I saw, and it frighted me, and I found not where to turn to hide myself from myself. So, I tried to avert my eyes, and yet [Potitianus] went on telling his tale: and you, Lord, set me again before myself, placing me before my conscience, so that I might find and hate my wickedness. My wickedness was well known to me, but I feigned not to know it: I covered it over and forgot it. The more fierily I loved these two courtiers [...], the more I hated myself for being loathsome in comparison with them.[27]

---

25 Cf. *The Confessions of St. Augustine*, trans. J.G. Pilkington (Garden City: 1900) 148–151.
26 Rosweyde, s.j., *'t Vaders boeck*, fol. ****2r.
27 Ibid.: 'Terwijle Potitianus dit verhaelde, dede ghy, Heere, my tot my selven komen; my wech nemende van mijnen rugge, daer ick my ghestelt hadde, doen ick op my selven niet letten en wilde; ende my stellende voor mijn aensicht, op dat ic sien soude, hoe leelijc, hoe mismaect, hoe vuyl, hoe zeerich ic was. Dit sach ick, ende verschrikte my; ende werwaerts ick my wenden soude, om my selven voor my selven te verbergen, en vont ick niet. So ic poochde mijne oogen van my af te keeren, ginck hy niettemin voort met my te vertellen dat hy vertelde: ende ghy, Heere, stelde my wederomme voor my selven, stelde my voor't aensicht mijnder conscientie, op dat ick mijne boosheyt vinden ende haten soude. Mijne boosheyt was my wel bekent; maer ick veysde my, al oft ickse niet en kende: ick hielse bedect ende vergatse. Hoe ick vierichlijcker beminde dese twee hovelinghen [...] hoe ick my selven by hen vergeleken verfoeyelijcker haette'?

MIXED EMOTION & PERFECTION IN BLOEMAERT'S *SYLVA ANACHORETICA* 467

Burning with love, consumed by hate, his emotions wavering or intermingled, Augustine's heart sorely longs for the solitary life, which he believes to be the sole and surest path to God.

Rosweyde's account of this anecdote, though twice removed from its origins in the *Confessions* (he tells the story of a story's effect on the future saint), exemplifies the response he hoped to elicit by adverting to desert Fathers such as Onuphrius or Pachomius. They, too, are presented as paragons of mixed emotion, which has the power to shake the sinner's false complacency, impelling him to strive after virtue. Take Onuphrius, who attests, in "Life of the Hermit Saint Onuphrius, Described by Abbot Paphnutius", that he was moved to become a solitary hermit at a young age: what does it mean for him to have been thus moved? First, this movement entails baring one's soul to the onset of troublesome emotions, the most trying of which Onuphrius's spiritual advisors compare to devilish incursions:

> But the monks who dwell in the wilderness neither receive nor enjoy any consolation from the world but alone from God. For when on occasion anxiety and tribulation assault them, or the devil, our most sworn enemy, attacks, who is there to stand by them?[28]

Second, it requires the monk steadfastly to cultivate fear of the Lord, while battling against the devil's snares and entrapments ('ende strijden voor al, in Godts vreese vastelijck te staen').[29] Third, it transports the heart from stillness to fiery ardor, causing it to burn with divine love, to scorn worldly pleasure, and to place all its hope in God:

> Finally, I, poor Onuphrius [...] began in the stillness of my heart to consider the glorious deliverance perforce enjoyed by them who suffer to battle mightily here on earth for love of the Father: my heart burned with his love, my spirit blazed with desire to attain to the kingdom of heaven with my utmost strength, and wholly to disdain the pleasures of the world, just as David teaches [in *Psalm* 72:28], saying: 'But it is good for me to cleave to my God, to put my hope in the Lord God'.[30]

---

28 Ibid. 60: 'Maer de monicken die de wildernisse bewoonen, en ontfanghen noch ghenieten gheenen troost ter werelt dan alleen van Godt. Want is dat hun somwijlen angst ende tribulatie is bestormende, oft indien haer den duyvel, onser aller ghesworen vyandt bestrijdt, wie is die haer bystaet'?

29 Ibid. 61.

30 Ibid.: 'Ick dan eyndelijcken armen Onuphrius [...] heb begonst stillekens in mijn hert te dencken, wat glorieuse salicheydt sy in den hemel moeten ghenieten, die sware strijden

These motions of the soul – toward love, disdain, and hope – experienced simultaneously or in tandem, fortify Onuphrius in his decision to forsake the company of men, even his fellow monks, and to dwell deep in the desert, where, as he admits, God will continuously test his resolve, allowing devilish assaults to buffet him as instruments of probation. Onuphrius, speaking to his would-be disciple Paphnutius, recalls what the holy hermit who initiated him into the rigors of the solitary life once said:

> Stand up, son, and go with me; you must journey into the depths of the desert and dwell alone in another cave: where (if you struggle manfully) you shall withstand every kind of devilish temptation. For God desires you to be tried in this desert, [to see] if you resolutely desire to keep his commandments.[31]

During the seventy years that God relentlessly tested him, confesses Onuphrius, there were times he came near to death or despaired of life, feeling himself barely capable of breath.[32] By his own account, hope oscillates with near despair as he struggles to maintain his love God and contempt for the world, contends with anxiety and tribulation, and holds fast to fear of the Lord.

Mixed emotions never cease to jostle and torment Onuphrius, ever proving him as he exerts himself night and day, almost without end, in rigorous spiritual exercises. His biographer Paphnutius presents them as affective trials that he willingly undertakes, made more difficult by the many demons that daily attempt to distract him. Onuphrius's ability to weather his raveling emotions functions as the gauge of his virtues and the crucible of his sanctity.

Other Fathers – Pachomius, for instance – eventually achieve a hard-won, God-given equanimity, which grants them a foretaste of heavenly bliss, but such a state is reached only by way of tangled emotions, some complementary,

---

hier op der aerden om de liefde des Heeren geleden hebben: mijn herte wierdt van zijne liefde brandende, mijnen gheest yverich begeerde de ghenoechelijckheden der wereldt gansschelijck te versmaden, ende naer het hemels rijck met alle uyterse kracht te trachten, ghelijcker-wijs David leert, segghende: "My is goedt Gode aen te hangen, ende mijne hope in Godt den Heere te stellen".

31   Ibid. 62: 'Staet op sone, ende gaet met my, ghy moet gaen treden naer't binnenste der woestijne, ende in eenen andere speloncke alleen woonen: al waer (indien ghy manlijcken strijdt) ghy sult alderhande bekoringhen der duyvelen verwinnen. Want u Godt begheert in dese woestijne te proeven, oft ghy Godts gheboden ghetrouwelijck begheert t'onderhouden'.

32   Ibid. 62: 'Ick hebbe in dese woestijne soo veel gheleden, dat ick dickwijls meynde dat my de doodt verwan; hebbe menich-werven soo hopeloos van leven gheweest, dat ic naus en ghevoelde dat daer noch eenighen aessem in mijn lichaem resteerde'.

MIXED EMOTION & PERFECTION IN BLOEMAERT'S *SYLVA ANACHORETICA*   469

others contradictory, that inevitably buffet every true anchorite. As Rosweyde, or rather, his source Dionysius, Abbot of Rome, puts it in "Life of Pachomius, Abbot of Tabenna", this erstwhile desert Father and eventual founder of cenobitic monasticism took as his exemplars the monks Anthony, Ammon, and Theodorus, for whom happiness and joy arose from sorrow and sighs, felicity and repose from disquiet and misery ('voor droefheydt ende suchten, blijdschap ende vreucht: ende voor sorch-vuldicheyt ende ellende, gheluck ende gherustheydt ghekomen is').[33] One of the key episodes in the "Life" narrates the affective tug-of-war Pachomius bravely endured while enlarging the monastic house at Tabenna; falsely accused of prideful ambition by a fellow monk, Pachomius, deeply aggrieved at the reproach, having taken it to heart ('swaerlijck opghenomen'), finds himself grappling with other powerful emotions, against all of which he wrestles simultaneously. He prays to be relieved of impatience ('onverduldicheyt'), to be troubled no more by despondency ('droefheyt'), to be jostled no longer by rage ('rasernije'), to be freed from the provocations of indignation ('gramschappe'). These affects torment him ('ghequelt worde'), propel him hither and thither ('herwaerts ende derwaerts loope'), angrily goad him ('geterght worde'), forcing him to admit that he remains hostage to the 'passions of the flesh that strive against his soul, as yet unmastered by him' ('noch niet de passien mijns vleeschs, die teghen mijn siele strijden, verwonnen en hebbe').[34] His sole recourse is to anchor himself to 'fear of the Lord' ('vreese des Heeren'), the key therapeutic that underlies these other knotty emotions and, in spite of all, ultimately enables him to hold fast to God amidst waves of turbulent sensation that he likens to demonic onslaughts.[35] Only through fear of the Lord does he manage to keep his sights on the joy that God alone can bestow: 'For when I was small and fruitless, and altogether without knowledge of my life, you generously gifted me with the feeling and understanding of your fear: that seeing the outermost darkness and torments unending, [and yet] knowing you as the true light and eternal felicity, I might come perpetually to enjoy you'.[36]

Throughout *'t Vaders boeck*, Rosweyde treats the Fathers like living martyrs, proclaiming them no less worthy of veneration; their fervent embrace of solitude, if it finally leads to spiritual repose and felicity, first requires them at

---

33   Ibid. 67.
34   Ibid. 72–73.
35   Ibid. 73.
36   Ibid. 75: 'Want doen ick kleyn ende verworpen was, ende gantsch gene kennisse mijns levens en hadde, hebt ghy my met het ghevoelen ende verstant uwer vreese mildelijcken begaeft: op dat ick d'uyterlijcke duysternisse ende d'eeuwighe tormenten schouwende, u het waerachtich licht ende oneyndelijcke blijdschappe kennende eeuwelijck soude ghenieten'.

length to be surfeited by distress and affliction. In the "Life of Pachomius", quoting *Hebrews* 11:37–38, he insists on the link between their emotional travails and the suffering of martyrs, praising both as equivalent sources of angelic merits:

> 'They wandered about in sheepskins, in goat skins, being in want, distressed, afflicted; of whom the world was not worthy; wandering in deserts, in mountains, and in dens, and in caves of the earth'. Finally, having a great desire for the peace of solitude, they obtained for themselves the joy of sanctity and faith, and at once gave to their fellows an example of a more worthy and holy life. For scorning all earthly things, cutting themselves off from worldly affairs, they strove to attain to the holiness of angels, even while still in this fragile body, [and] thereby climbing to the summit of virtue, they were raised beyond every wonderment of men; thus, making their merits equal to those [of the martyrs] who devoutly strove to shed their blood in the name of Jesus Christ our Lord, smashing the snares of invisible foes, they became alike to the ancient Fathers in every virtue.[37]

When he later celebrates Pachomius's accomplishments as an abbot, stating that God graced him with the gift of equanimity, so that 'he remained always the same, alike to himself in everything, carefully conserving his spirit in the Lord's discipline', he construes composure as the terminus of the saint's yearslong efforts, first as an anchorite, then as a cenobite, to contain his mixed, often vexatious affects.[38] (Alternatively, he may be implying that Pachomius appeared imperturbable to his brothers in Christ, even though internally he

---

37 Ibid. 66: "'Sy hebben omghegaen in schaeps-vellen, in gheyten vellen, ghebreck lijdende, benauwt, ghepynicht; der welcken de wereld niet weerdich en was; in woeste plaetsen dolende, op berghen, als oock in speloncken ende holen der aerden". Eyndelijcken groote begheerte hebbende tot de ruste der eenicheyt, hebben de blijdschap haerder salicheydt ende gheloove, door de Goddelijcke gave verkreghen, ende hebben terstont den anderen tot een exempel van een weerdigher ende heyligher leven ghegheven. Want sy alle aerdtsche saken versmaedt hebbende, ende hun van alle wereldtlijcke dinghen afgesneden, noch in dit broos lichaem zijnde, hebben de heylicheydt der Enghelen seer soecken naer te volghen, door welcke tot het hoochste der deuchden op-klimmende, hebben sy boven alle verwonderinge der menschen verheven gheweest; soo dat sy de oude Vaders in alle deuchden ghelijck waren, makende haer-lieder verdiensten gelijck met de ghene die voor den naem Jesu Christi onsen Heere tot uytstortinghe huns bloedts vromelijck ghestreden hebben, de laghen der onsienlijcker vyanden vernielende'.
38 Ibid. 85: 'Maer hy hadde dese Goddelijcke gave, dat hy altijdt den selven, ende in alles hem selven ghelijck was, ende sijnen gheest in de discipline des Heeren sorchvuldich bewaerde'.

MIXED EMOTION & PERFECTION IN BLOEMAERT'S *SYLVA ANACHORETICA*   471

continued to be roiled by emotions.) In the *Sylva*, Bloemaert portrays the key moment when the anchorite Pachomius received the monastic rule of Tabenna, conveyed to him by a heavenly voice; disguised as a monk, the devil sitting beside him signifies that the holy man, even now, at the threshold of his founding of the cenobitic life, is shadowed by evil, plagued by Satan's insidious *lagen* (snares, ambushes), the chief symptoms of which are runaway emotions [Fig. 12.11]. By comparison, Onuphrius is shown with the angel who daily fed and comforted him, giving him the strength to withstand the many menaces, bodily and spiritual, that imperilled his love of God, not least the fear of death and onset of despair [Fig. 12.10]. Gazing at the angel's face, a suppliant Onuphrius enjoys an interval of respite, even while mortifying his body, holding one knee bent to the hard ground, to discipline his unruly spirit.

The Fifth Book of *'t Vaders Boeck*, based on Pelagius the Cardinal Deacon's Latin translation from a Greek collection of anchoritic and cenobitic exempla, consists of a treatise in eighteen chapters on monastic affects, positive or negative. Each chapter focuses on a specific motion of the heart (or set of correspondent motions), as well as on the patterns of behavior that either stir or curb these emotions. Although Book 5 opens and closes respectively with chapters on peace of mind and contemplative repose, it mainly comprises clusters of exempla on affective virtues such as patience and steadfast fortitude, or on affective vices such as vainglory and lustful desire. Mixed emotions are discussed most fully in chapter 3, "On Motion and Sorrow of the Heart" ("Vande bewseginghe ende berou des herten"), chapter 5, "On Unchastity" ("Vande onkuyscheydt"), chapter 7, "On Patience and Strength of Spirit" ("Vande verduldicheydt oft sterckmoedicheydt"), chapter 13, "One Must Be Hospitable and Charitable, with a Joyful Countenance" ("Datmen moet gastsaem zijn, ende bermhertigh met een vrolijck ghelaet"), chapter 16, "On Patience" ("Van verduldigheydt"), and chapter 17, "On Love" ("Vande Liefde"). I want briefly to examine what each chapter has to say about mixed emotion, since Book 5, in my view, underlies Bloemaert's clear interest in evincing such emotions, therewith showing them to be characteristic of the desert Fathers' solitary lives.

He broaches this theme in chapter 3, citing one of the sayings of Evagrius, who instructs the monk to remain firm in his chief vocation, which is to cultivate sorrow ('aenveert droefheyt', i.e., 'undertake to be sorrowful').[39] If he is to hold to this intention, he must diligently exercise his imaginative faculty, visualising the affects to be felt on the day of Judgement, not only by the damned but also by the saved. Thoughts of both things, damnation and salvation, and

---

39   Ibid. 475.

472 MELION

of their attendant emotions, must be experienced in tandem, in order to purge foul, dark thoughts from the mind and heart. The ekphrastic passage, since it specifically encourages training in mixed emotion as crucial to expelling monastic vice and impelling monastic virtue, deserves to be quoted in full:

> Abbot Evagrius said: when you sit in your cell, gather unto you your senses, and be mindful of the day of death; and you shall then observe the dying of your body. Consider its decay, and undertake to be sorrowful. Have revulsion for the vanity of this world. Be still and attentive, in order always to preserve your firm intention; and you shall not be diverted. Consider, too, those who are in hell. Consider to yourself how the souls exist there, with what bitter loss of speech, with what most oppressive sighs, with what fear and strife, with what distress and pain, and without illumination, in endless lamentation and melancholy. Consider, too, the day of resurrection, and conceive to sense that godly, ghastly, and fearsome judgement. Bring to view the shame that sinners shall suffer in the sight of Christ, in the presence of Angels, Archangels, Powers, and all men. Think, too, of all the punishments, of the eternal fire, of the undying worm, of the obscurity of hell, and above all, of the gnashing of teeth, of the fear and torments. Place, too, before your eyes the goodness made ready for the righteous, [their] fidelity before God the Father and his son Christ, before the Angels, Archangels, Powers and all peoples, the kingdom of heaven, and [God's] gifts, joy and repose. To yourself have thought of both these things, and sigh over the judgements upon sinners; weep, take on a sorrowful attitude, also fearing to fall into the same [judgements]: but rejoice, exult, be jubilant over the goodness prepared for the righteous. And hasten to possess these goods and escape these punishments. See to it that you never forget this, be it sitting in your cell, or elsewhere outside it; and cast not from your heart the thoughts of these things, to ensure that at the least you eschew foul and dark thoughts.[40]

---

40 Ibid.: 'Den Abt Evagrius heeft geseyt: Als ghy sit in uwe celle, vergadert by u uwe sinnen, ende zijt ghedachtich den dach des doots; ende dan suldy bemercken de verstervinghe van u lichaem. Peyst op de neder-laghe, ende aenveert droefheyt. Hebt een schroomen vande ydelheydt deser werelt. Zijt stil ende sorchvuldich, op dat ghy altoos meught blijven in u gherust voornemen; ende ghy en sult niet beswijcken. Peyst oock op de ghene, die inder hellen zijn. Peyst by u selven, hoe de sielen daer zijn, in wat bitter stil-swijgen, in wat alderswaertste suchten, in wat vreese ende strijdt, in wat vertoeven ende pijne, ende sonder verlichtinge in oneyndelijc schreyen ende droefheyt. Peyst oock op den dagh der verrijsenisse, ende begrijpt in uwen sin dat goddelijck, afgrijselijck, ende vreeselijck oordeel. Brenght ten voorschijn de beschaemtheyt, die de sondaren sullen lijden

MIXED EMOTION & PERFECTION IN BLOEMAERT'S *SYLVA ANACHORETICA*   473

Sorrow provides the foundation for this multi-storied complex of emotions, as another pregnant saying, voiced by the holy Abbot Pastor, asserts; adducing an inconsolable woman to his fellow monks, he draws an affective moral: 'Were all the pleasures of the world to come her way, her heart would not turn away from sorrow. So, too, must a monk always have sorrow in himself'.[41] Other sayings of the Father support this view. One adjures his brothers always to live as if the soul were about to die from fear and anxious dread in the presence of God to whom an accounting of our every passion must finally be given ('als die van alle onse beroerten in't besonder aen Godt sullen rekeninghe gheven').[42] Another enjoins his brothers to live in constant regret at the shadow cast by our bodies upon our souls ('soo moeten wy het weenen ende leetwesen altoos by ons hebben waer dat wy zijn'); yet another insists that a monk must never cease to shed tears of remorse ('wy moeten altoos weenen').[43] And chapter 3 concludes by affirming that 'God desires that the soul be thus tormented, that [like the Israelites in the desert] it ever desire to enter into that [promised] land'.[44] The torment to which this monk refers is the tension between the anchorite's desire bitterly to weep and the regrettable weakness of spirit that sometimes leaves him incapable of weeping as he should. This torment, too,

---

in't aenschouwen van Christus, in de teghenwoordicheyt der Engelen, Artschengelen, Machten, ende allen menschen. Denckt ooc op alle de straffingen, op het eeuwigh vier, op dien onsterffelijcken worm, op de duysternisse der hellen, ende boven al op de knersselinghe der tanden, op de vreesen ende tormenten. Stelt u oock voor ooghen 'tgoet, dat den rechtveerdigen bereyt is, het betrouwen voor Godt den Vader ende sijnen sone Christum, voor d'Enghelen, Artsch-engelen, Machten ende allen volcke, 'trijck der hemelen, ende sijne gaven de blijdschap ende ruste. Hebt de ghedachtenisse van beyden dese dingen by u, ende versucht over de oordeelen der sondaren; weent, neemt aen een droevich wesen, vreesende oock inde selve te vallen: maer verblijdt u, verheught u, ende zijt vrolijck over 'tgoet, dat den rechtveerdighen bereyt is. Ende haest u om de goederen te besitten, ende om de straffen te ontgaen. Siet voor u, dat ghy dit noyt en vergeet, 'tzy als ghy in uwe celle sit, 'tzy als ghy elders buyten zijt; ende dat u herte de ghedenckenisse van dese dinghen niet en verworpe; op dat ghy hier door ten minsten moocht schouwen vuyle ende schadelijcke ghedachten'.

41 Ibid. 476: 'Al quamender alle de ghenuchten des werelts, soo en sullense haer herte niet afkeeren van droefheyt. Alsoo moet oock eenen monick altoos droefheyt in sy-selven hebben'.

42 Ibid. 477.

43 Ibid.

44 Ibid. 478: 'Want Godt begheert, dat de siele alsoo ghequelt wort, datse altijdt begheerte heeft om te gaen in dat landt'. The notion that God tests his followers, proving them like a goldsmith purifies gold, derives from *Wisdom* 3:5–6: 'Afflicted in few things, in many they shall be well rewarded: because God hath tried them, and found them worthy of himself. As gold in the furnace he hath proved them, and as a victim of a holocaust he hath received them, and in time there shall be respect had to them'.

is sent by God to intensify the monk's many causes of purgative sorrow. These many endorsements of sorrow, constitutive of a kind of doctrine of sorrow, and the edifice of mixed emotion built upon it, more than likely informed Bloemaert's decision to depict every Father as grave, by turns gently or severely sorrowful, their attitudes, gestures, and faces further redolent of other affects that admix with foundational *droefheyt*.

Chapter 5 concerns unchastity (*onkuyscheydt*), which is repeatedly described as the most prevalent and intractable of negative emotions. Lustful thoughts are the devil's favoured deadfall, whereby he toils to ensnare the monk, diverting him from his chosen way of life; they can be resisted only if the monk recognises that temptations of this kind, though not insuperable, are yet inescapable, challenges he must meet head-on and labour ceaselessly to overcome. With reference to Anthony's tripartite theory of bodily motion, chapter 5 begins by defining sexual response as threefold: first, as an autonomic function of the body that operates irrespective of any accompanying or precipitating emotion; second, as an effect of the fiery motion of blood overheated by an excess of food and drink; third, as an errant stimulus induced by demonic agency for the express purpose of weakening the virtuous resolve of truly devout persons.[45] Monks above all, who struggle to lead a very pious life, are constantly subjected to such stimuli which, since they propagate by means of pleasurable mental images, are especially difficult to overcome. The following anecdote about consent of the will makes this point with the utmost clarity:

> An elderly Father asked a brother: 'Have you the habit of speaking with women'? The brother answered: 'No, not I. But', said he, 'I have inside me new and old painters who are my musings and thoughts, which portray the women to my heart, and thereby scatter my senses'. Then the old Father said to him: 'Fear not death; but instead contemplate what lives, that is, the consent to sin and the workings thereof; and prolong your prayers'.[46]

---

45   Ibid. 483–484.

46   Ibid. 485: 'Eenen out-vader heeft eenen broeder ghevraecht, segghende: Hebt ghy gene ghewoonte van met eene vrouwe te spreken? Den broeder heeft gheantwoort: Neen ick. Maer (seyde hy) ick hebbe by my nieuwe ende oude schilders, de welcke mijne ghedachten ende gepeysen zijn, die my de vrouwen in mijn herte voorbeelden, ende also mijne sinnen verstroyen. Doen heeft den out-vader tot hem geseyt: En vreest de doode niet; maer schouwt de levende, dat is, het consent ende de wercken der sonden; ende maeckt u ghebedt langher'.

MIXED EMOTION & PERFECTION IN BLOEMAERT'S *SYLVA ANACHORETICA*   475

Far from evading such vividly forceful, picture-like thoughts, the monk must allow the existence of such 'ghedachten en gepeysen', because acknowledging them, fearing them more than death, is the crucial first step toward thwarting them. Otherwise, as Abbot Syrus of Alexandria surprisingly puts it, bodily sin will always have its way, for sin can be opposed only if it first comes to consciousness:

> Abbot Syrus of Alexandria, asked about unchaste thoughts, likewise answered: were you without thoughts, then you would have only deeds. Which is to say that he whose thoughts neither battle against sin nor gainsay it, is the one who commits bodily sin: but he who sins bodily is the one who has no difficulty of thought.[47]

In support of this adjuration, the Abbess Sara is cited, for even after struggling mightily for thirteen years against lustful thoughts, she never once expressed a wish to escape this ongoing tribulation: rather, she asked only that God be pleased to fortify her.[48] So, too, an unnamed abbot who patiently heard the repeated confessions of a fellow monk whose thoughts doggedly inclined to lust, consoled him by admitting that he, too, often fell prey to such thoughts, the intensity of which the younger monk, were he to know and feel them, could neither be fathomed nor borne.[49]

The point of these anecdotes is summarised in a valedictory proverb: the monk must be like the man who smells meat roasting in a roadside winehouse and walks on by, rejecting to eat what his nose savours: 'For we are no extirpators of bad thoughts but only wrestlers against the same'.[50] Sexual longing, precisely because it calls forth and even intensifies fear of the Lord, requires to be experienced along with it, no less surely than fear occasions hope in God ('maer is alleenlijck hopende').[51] As a matter of fact, the monk who most

---

47   Ibid.: 'Den Abt Syrus van Alexandrien, ghevraeght zijnde van onkuysche gepeysen, heeft also gheantwoort: Hebt ghy gheene gepeysen, soo en hebt ghy gheene hope: want en hebt ghy gheene gepeysen, soo hebt ghy de wercken. Dat is te seggen, want die met het ghepeys tegen de sonde niet en vecht noch en weder-seyt, die sondight lichamelijck: maer die lichamelijck sondight, die en heeft gheene moeyelijckheyt van ghepeysen'.

48   Ibid.

49   Ibid. 485–486.

50   Ibid. 486: 'Want wy gheen uyt-roeyers en zijn van quade gepeysen, maer alleenlijck worstelaers teghen de selve'.

51   Ibid. The monk who gives in to lust, then struggles to regain his chastity, is compared to a householder who rebuilds a collapsed house upon its former foundations, striving to make it structurally sound, more hopeful that this time it will stand than fearful that it will crumble again. So, too, a sinner's fear of the Lord should beget and fortify hope.

suffers from such impediments to virtue, will finally be the one to approach soonest and closest to the Lord, falling into temptation again and again, and each time rising ever higher above it by mustering the *materialen* (materials) at his disposal: namely, 'consideration of the commandments, prayers of praise, labour of the hands, and spiritual exercises'.[52] Moreover, the co-mingling of emotions such as lust, fear, and hope increases the yearning for eternal rest, envisaged as a transcendent escape from the multiplex impulses prevalent in this life, according to *Psalm* 124:1: 'They that trust in the Lord shall be as Mount Sion: he shall not be moved for ever that dwelleth in Jerusalem'. This passage implicitly summons up several passages in *Proverbs* 14, cited earlier in a marginal gloss to chapter 5, that acknowledge the penitential necessity of mixed emotion: for example, 'The heart that knoweth the bitterness of his own soul, in his joy the stranger shall not intermeddle' (14:10); or 'Laughter shall be mingled with sorrow: and mourning taketh hold of the end of joy' (14:13).[53]

Of course, this does not mean that Rosweyde countenances pleasure taken in lustful thoughts. A follow-up anecdote argues to the contrary: an older monk who was adviser to a younger once asked God why his charge never progressed in virtue. He was then given to see the young man in a vision, playing cards with the Spirit of Unchastity, all the while ignoring and angering his guardian angel. The monk, surmised the Father, not only felt lust but continued, unbeknownst to himself, to draw pleasure from his desires. His struggle against temptation was at best halfhearted.[54] Far better were it for him to have realised, in the words of another disciple monk, quoted shortly thereafter: 'I see that even though I am tormented, I yet pluck fruits from the difficulty of this labour'.[55] Thoughts of sexual pleasure, and the feelings they arouse, are to be controverted by calling bitter things to mind, principally death and the hellish torments attendant upon a sinful death ('de ghedachtenisse des doots ende der tormenten').[56]

Rosweyde's source Pelagius explicitly returns to the topic of mixed emotion three more times before the close of chapter 5. First, he tells the curious tale of two monks, both members of the same monastic house, who gave way to sexual

---

52 Ibid.: 'Alsoo is oock eenen monick: indien hy inde bekoringhe ghevallen is, ende hem bekeert tot den Heere, die heeft veel gereetschaps; te weten, overpeysinghe der wet Godts, lof-sanghen, 'twerck der handen, ghebeden, ende andere gheestelijcke oeffeninghen; de welcke hem als materialen zijn dienende'.

53 Cf. ibid. 484 and 486.

54 Ibid. 486–487.

55 Ibid. 487: 'Abt, ick sien al is't dat ick gequelt worde, dat ick nochtans vruchten verkrijghe door de moeyelijckheyt van desen arbeyt'.

56 Ibid. 489.

MIXED EMOTION & PERFECTION IN BLOEMAERT'S *SYLVA ANACHORETICA*   477

desire; having abandoned their order, they took wives. But soon overcome with remorse, they returned and asked to be imprisoned in their respective cells for a year and punished with near starvation. When they finally emerged, one appeared healthy and robust, the other wan and drawn. Amazed, their fellow brothers questioned the two men about their year spent in penitence: one answered, that he always rejoiced, trusting in the redemptory mercy of the Lord, the other that he had spent the entire time in abject fear of final judgement. The moral that the monks rightly draw is that both joy *and* fear of the Lord ought to be cultivated by the penitent since both emotions are equally meritorious ('de penitentie van beyde is by Godt van gelijcke verdiensten').[57]

Second, there is the story of an elderly, intensely pious anchorite who was visited by a courtesan acting as Satan's agent. The woman knocked at the monk's door, claiming that she had lost her way and was overcome by fear. Moved by pity, he admitted her into his anteroom and then locked himself in his cell. Again she knocked, alleging that the wild beasts of that desert place terrified her, and again the old monk, feeling compassion, opened his door; but this time pity and fear were intermingled, for by letting a woman draw near, he worried that he had broken his monastic vows and offended God. The devil now seized his opportunity, launching countless arrows of desire, until pierced through and through, the monk lay with the woman. His fear and remorse now redoubled, but still he blazed with lust, and so, desperate for a remedy, he resolved to punish himself, burning away his fingers, one by one, in the flame of a nearby lamp. Regardless, fear, remorse, and bodily pain remained ineffective against desire: 'And he stuck his finger in the lamp, and when it burned he felt no pain due to the greater fire of his desire; and he continued to do this until morning dawned, so that all his fingers were burnt away'.[58] It was not until every finger had been lost, and God had struck the woman dead, that the monk finally recovered; remarkably, continuing to feel compassion for the woman, by the power of God he not only raised her from the dead but also converted her, layering pity onto fear and remorse as previously he had layered fear and remorse onto pity.

A third and final tale concerns a righteous monk who, insidiously tempted by the devil, secretly lay with a woman; after giving way to carnal desire, he found himself caught between hope and despair, his consciousness of having rejoiced the devil matched by his consciousness of having provoked God. Acute

---

57   Ibid. 490.

58   Ibid. 491: 'En hy stack sijnen vinger inde lampe, ende als dien brande, soo en ghevoelde hy de pijne niet door den seer grooten brant sijnder begeerlijckheyt; ende dit dede hy tot 'smorgens toe, tot dat hy alle sijne vingeren af ghebrant hadde'.

478 MELION

fear of final damnation contended with forlorn hope in the Lord's boundless mercy; the antipodes between which the monk wavered were his joint advertencies of God the Father and Satan, and dual images of his hell-bound soul strewn like dust and his risen body redeemed by Christ on the Judgement day.

> be merciful to me, [Lord,] who embittered you, and made the devil glad; and see, I am dead, having given ear to him. [...] For nothing is impossible to you, though my soul be like dust strewn in hell. Show your creature mercy, for you are kind and loving, who on the day of resurrection shall raise the bodies of them that are no more. [...] and he fell again upon his face, beseeching God thus: 'Lord, I know that the battle (*strijt*) is waged that I might be crowned'.[59]

Through this strife of warring emotions, the monk was finally given to experience hope shading into joy, admixed with astonishment at divine forebearance, all this built upon an ever present foundation of fearful remorse. The sign that certified forgiveness was a lamp long extinguished, now miraculously lit by God.

> Then spare me, Lord: for once again I confess my impurity before your goodness, before your Angels and all who are justified; and did I not fear to cause more offense, I would confess it to all men. [...] And rising, he found the lamp burning brightly. And glad with hope, he was fortified in joy of heart, wondering at the grace of God who had forgiven his sins and heard his heart's desire; and he said: 'I thank you, Lord; for you have shown mercy to one who was unworthy to live, giving an assurance with this great and wondrous sign; for being merciful, you spare the souls of them you have created'.[60]

---

59 Ibid. 493–494: '[...] zijt mijns bermhertich, die u seer verbittert hebbe, die den vyant seer verblijdt hebbe; ende siet, ick ben doot, hem ghehoor gevende. [...] Want by u en is niet onmogelijc, hoe wel mijne siele by de hellen ghelijck stoffe verstroyt is. Thoont bermherticheyt aen u schepsel, want ghy goedertieren ende bermhertich zijt; die oock de lichamen, die nu niet en zijn, sult inden dagh der verrijsenisse verwecken. [...] Ende hy is weder op sijn aensicht ghevallen, den Heere aldus biddende: Heere, ick weet dat den strijt gheschiet is, om dat ick gecroont soude worden'.

60 Ibid. 494: 'Spaert my dan, Heere: want ick belijde mijne vuylicheyt weder aen uwe goetheyt voor uwe Enghelen ende alle rechtveerdigen; ende 't en ware dat ick vreesde voor meerdere verargheringhe, ick soude het voor alle menschen belijden. [...] Ende opstaende heeft hy de lampe klaer brandende ghevonden. Ende hem door hope verheugende, is versterckt met blijdschap des herten; hem verwonderende van Godts gratie, die hem sijn sonden also hadde vergheven, ende hem verhoort na de begheerte sijns herten; ende hy seyde: Ick dancke u, Heere; want ghy hebt bermherticheyt gethoont aen den genen, die

MIXED EMOTION & PERFECTION IN BLOEMAERT'S *SYLVA ANACHORETICA*   479

This exemplum, like the two that precede it, testifies to the generative properties of mixed emotion, the cultivation of which is treated by Rosweyde like a monastic exercise. The complex process of harnessing libidinal energies to penitential feelings produces purgative and illuminative effects, that make sin apparent and incline the sinner to atonement, thus assisting the monk who has turned away from God to return to him. Both motions, along with the emotions that precipitate and are precipitated by them, are regularly evoked by Rosweyde's frequent use of the verbs *afkeeren* (turn away), *bekeeren* (turn toward, i.e., convert), and *weder-keeren* (return, turn back or around), not only in chapter 5 but throughout 't Vaders boeck.[61] In chapter 1 of the opening "Life of Anthony", for example, the temptations and tribulations heaped upon him by Satan are said to have as their chief purpose the estrangement of his soul from God; Anthony is urged to eschew his monkish vocation by turning away from the Lord:

> finally, he made him consider the oppressive weight that lies in the virtues, as also the difficult labour of approaching to them, and likewise the sickness and fragility of the body, and the long span of time: he excited in him a very great obscurity of thought, wishing him to turn away (*afkeeren*) from his good purpose.[62]

Here and elsewhere in the *Book of the Fathers*, negative emotions such as these, along with the counter-emotions they engender, and the controvertible strife that ensues, set the stage for the monk's turning round or back toward God: '[...] if he has fallen into temptation, and turns toward the Lord (*bekeert*), he has many tools [at his disposal]'.[63] These tools are the materials (*materialen*) mentioned in the proverb, cited above, about the monk who chooses to wrestle against bad thoughts (and feelings) rather than merely extirpating them.[64] Or alternatively, as in the case of the two apostate monks who married women

---

    niet weerdich en was om te leven; gevende een betrouwen met dit groot ende selsaem teecken: want ghy bermhertich zijnde, spaert de sielen, die ghy gheschapen hebt'.

61   See, for example, the uses *af-keeren* at fol. ****2r and pp. 8, 562, 601, 813; of *bekeeren* at 154, 162, 225, 276, 282, 289, 404, 521; of *weder-keeren* (or *wederom keeren*) at fol. ****2r and pp. 9, 11, 27, 29, 42, 50, 75, 107, 109, 158, 162, 183, 334, 367, 383, 395, 428, 452, 488, 668, 821.

62   Ibid. 8: '[...] ten laetsten dede hem ghedencken de swaricheyt die in der deuchden ghelegen is, als moeyelijcken arbeydt om tot die te gheraken, oock insghelijcks des lichaems kranckheyt ende broosheyt, met de langhduericheyt des tijts: hy toestoockte hem een over groote duysternisse der ghepeysen, willende hem van sijn goedt voornemen afkeeren'.

63   Ibid. 486: '[...] indien hy inde bekoringhe ghevallen is, ende hem bekeert tot den Heere, die heeft veel gereetschaps'.

64   See notes 52 and 53 *supra*.

480 MELION

then realised to their chagrin that the angelic life of a monk is preferable by far, mixed feelings of penitential joy and sorrow facilitate a re-turn: 'Then let us return to the wilderness ('na de wildernisse *weder-keeren*), and let us do penance for that which we perpetrated in an ungodly manner'.[65] The figure of emotional contestation (*strijt*), bodied forth in the imagery of turning away and toward, calls to mind the serpentine contrapposto that is perhaps the most telling feature of Bloemaert's desert Fathers.[66] Boëtius à Bolswert's signature line (assimilated from the prints of Hendrick Goltzius), which swells and tapers in graduated concentric arcs, enhances the effect of turning that portrays the ongoing struggle (*strijt*) of the Fathers (and Mothers), subject as they are to the push and pull of their emotions, to sensations of aversion and attraction, toward or away from virtue, toward or away from vice [Figs. 12.4–12.30].

Mixed emotion is endemic to the monastic vocation, as two closely related chapters – 7, "On Patience and Strength of Spirit", and 16, "On Patience" – demonstrate by means of exempla taken from the sayings of such luminaries as Abbots Theodorus of Pherme and Pastor, and the anchoress Syncletica. Two closely related anecdotes make the case: first, a brother went to Abbot Theodorus to complain of the many emotions that constantly disquieted him; whatever his circumstances, whether he lived alone or amongst other monks, they never abated. Theodorus answered by posing a question about the monastic life:

> 'If you find repose neither alone nor amongst others, [ask yourself] why you wished to become a monk. Was it not to endure torments and adversity? But tell me, how many years have you worn this habit'? Whereupon he answered: 'Eight'. The old man replied: 'Believe me, I have lived in this habit seventy years and found not a single day's rest, and do you wish to find rest after eight years' time'?[67]

---

65 Ibid. 490: 'Laet ons dan na de wildernisse weder-keeren, ende laet ons penitentie doen van 'tghene wy ongoddelijck bedreven hebben'.

66 On *strijt*, see notes 59 and 60 *supra* and note 68 *infra*. As Rosweyde states in the dedicatory preface, fol. **2r, struggle against the devil's wiles is what unites the Fathers and Mothers in their shared penitential vocation. Further on *strijt*, see ibid. 46, 54, 137, 196, 227, 256, 264, 268, 273, 293, 303, 309, 316, 317, 323, 344, 408, 473, 474, 476, 493, 497, 500, 531, 570, 594, 618, 648, 649, 681, 710, 728, 738, 742, 751, 766, 770.

67 Ibid. 497: 'Indien ghy een-samich zijnde niet en rust, noch oock by andere, waerom hebdy willen monick worden? Is't niet om dat ghy quellinghen ende tegenspoet sout verdraghen? Maer segt my, hoe veel jaren hebt ghy dit habijt ghedraghen? Waer op hy gheantwoort heeft: Acht. Den ouden man seyde weder tot hem: ghelooft my, ick hebbe seventich Jaren in dit habijt geleeft; ende ick en heb niet eenen dach ruste ghevonden, ende wilt ghy in den tijdt van acht jaren ruste hebben'?

MIXED EMOTION & PERFECTION IN BLOEMAERT'S *SYLVA ANACHORETICA*   481

Second, the monk Johannes Nanus once said to Abbot Pastor that he lived a life free of care, at peace with himself, exempted from toilsome struggle ('die geenen strijt en heeft'). Pastor at once protested that though contemplative rest is a monk's distant goal, his present circumstances require him continually to endure inquietude, since 'the soul makes progress through struggle' ('want de siele inden strijdt voortganck neemt').[68] One of the sayings of Syncletica identifies the affray of emotions that course through the soul without cease: delight in praise and glory ('lof ende glorie'), feelings of satiety and bodily lust ('versaetheydt des lichaems [...] ende met de wellusten'), and faint-heartedness ('kleyn-moedich makende').[69] They roil just beneath the surface of the love of God that every monk or nun persistently strives to maintain. Quoting *Psalm* 4:1, Syncletica declares that such emotions, and the distress they cause, magnify the heart even while entangling it; they are spiritual exercises that test the soul, training it to repel the Tempter's stratagems and incursions: 'For you shall be perfected through distress of this kind. For he [i.e., the Lord] says: "When I was in distress, thou hast enlarged me". Then let us best prove our souls in these exercises; for we have our enemy in sight'.[70] Tacking into not sailing away from these emotional headwinds, the soul must lift the cross like a sail, setting it against the gusts of a contrary spirit.[71]

Patience is defined as the ability to collect one's jointly felt thoughts and consider them in concert, not allowing them aimlessly to disperse the soul's energies from pillar to post. It is as if Rosweyde, speaking through Pelagius, were advising the monk or nun to gather his/her emotions, condensing them in the heart, from where their coincident effects can be assayed:

> A brother said to an elderly Father: 'My thoughts are scattered hither and yon, and I am anxious'. And he [i.e., the Father] said: 'Sit in your cell, and those thoughts shall return to you; for like a tethered she-ass whose foal wanders hither and thither, yet always comes home to its mother, whithersoever it roamed, so, too, thoughts return to them who shall have sat

---

68   Ibid.

69   Ibid. 499.

70   Ibid.: 'Want ghy sult volmaeckt zijn door dusdanighe benautheyt. Want hy seyt: "In benautheydt hebdy mijn herte verbreyt". Laet ons dan in dese oeffeningen aldermeest onse sielen beproeven; want wy hebben onsen vyant voor oogen'.

71   See ibid.: 'Alsoo als wy ontmoeten eenen contrarien gheest, laet ons oock het cruys in plaetse van een seyl oprechten; ende wy sullen sonder perijckel door de zee van deser werelt Voort-varen, ende inde havens komen'.

patiently in their cell, [conforming] to the will of God; for even if they stray for a short time hither and yon, yet do they always return to him'.[72]

Coincident emotion is likewise the subject of chapter 13, "One Must Be Hospitable and Charitable", and its complement, chapter 17, "On Love". Loving hospitality rendered to a fellow monk visiting from a desert cell or monastic house requires the monk[s] visited to prioritise joy over sorrow; the visitor is given a felicitous welcome, expressions of delight are exchanged, the perennial fast is broken, and so, during the visit, happiness takes the prior position, while the monk's native condition of penitential remorse becomes auxiliary. This affective state of affairs is contingent, of course, and momentary; upon the visitor's departure, sorrow regains the upper hand. An anecdote told about Abbot Joseph of Panepho underscores this point: one day a delegation of monks visited him to inquire whether they should mitigate their customary practice of abstinence and instead offer good cheer to some visiting brothers. In response, Joseph retired to his cell and reemerged, dressed in rags; he then retired again and returned wearing his former habit. Asking the monks whether he was still the same person, irrespective of what he wore, and receiving the answer yes, he explained that so, too, the monk who shows kind welcome to a visitor has not fundamentally changed. He is the same person: his sorrow is subordinated to joy but not effaced, just as joy will soon once again be submerged in sorrow. Altering one's mood as circumstances licitly require involves mixing two affective kinds – sorrow and joy – varying them by degree, keeping one *in potentia* while the other comes to the fore:

> Just as I am the same in both attires, and not altered by the first costume, nor impaired by the second, so must we behave in the reception of brothers, as the holy Gospel reads: [*Matthew* 22:21, *Mark* 12:17, *Luke* 20:25] "Render therefore to Caesar the things that are Caesar's, and to God the things that are God's". Thus, when the brothers are present, we

---

72   Ibid. 502: 'Eenen broeder heeft tot eenen out-vader gheseydt: "Mijne ghepeysen zijn verstroyt ende herwaerts ende derwaerts loopende, ende ick ben benaut". Ende hy heeft gheseyt: "Sit in uwe celle, ende die ghepeysen sullen wederom tot u keeren: want ghelijck als eene eselinne ghebonden is, al is't dat haer jonck loopt herwaerts ende derwaerts, het komt nochtans altijts weder by sijne moeder, waer dat het oock gheloopen heeft: soo oock sullen de ghepeysen weder-keeren tot den genen, die om Godts wille verduldelijc in sijne celle sal gheseten hebben; want al zijn sy eenen korten tijt herwaerts ende derwaerts verstroyt; nochtans keeren sy altijts weder tot hem"'.

MIXED EMOTION & PERFECTION IN BLOEMAERT'S *SYLVA ANACHORETICA*   483

should receive them with joy: but when we are solitary, then must we be sorrowful.[73]

That Rosweyde/Pelagius is talking about joy in sorrow, sorrow in joy becomes all the more apparent from another anecdote that cleverly characterises joyful hospitality as self-abnegation in another guise:

> Once upon a time, two brothers came to an elderly Father whose custom it was to refrain from eating all day. When he saw the brothers, he happily received them and said: 'Fasting has its reward'. And then he added: 'They who eat on account of love fulfill two commandments: for they suppress their own will [i.e., their inclination to fast], and fulfill the [other] commandment by refreshing [their] brothers'.[74]

The one commandment is the perennial rule of penitence, the other is the rule of loving hospitality, but the moral of the story is that in showing good-natured kindness to visitors, the monk yet partakes of a kind of penitential sorrow, for he goes against himself. Conversely, hospitable joy never ceases to exist as an option to be exercised, even by the most melancholy of anchorites.

Throughout the two chapters on *liefde*, as also in the chapters on *verduldigheydt*, the exemplary sayings of the Fathers put stress on the relation between the affects and the will. The latter faculty must ever tend toward the love of God, and the monk's or nun's task is to ensure that his/her emotions, howsoever complex and varied, lend support to this overarching purpose. Love of one's fellow monks, especially visitors, is seen as analogous to the love of God, to express it in small, just as patience steadfastly mustered in the face of shifting or divergent emotions is appreciated as a manifestation of that anchoring love. A neat anecdote distills these ready truths: an elderly monk was interrogated by a group of philosophers as to what distinguished him from

---

73   Ibid. 532: "'Ghelijck ick in beyde die selve ben, ende met d'eerste cleedt niet verandert en ben, noch door het tweede niet beschadicht; also moeten wy doen in de onthalinge der broederen, gelijck in 'theylich Evangelie wort ghelesen: 'Gheeft den Keyser dat den Keyser toe-behoort: ende gheeft Godt dat Godt toe-behoort'. Als dan de broeders teghenwoordich zijn, soo moeten wy die met blijdschap ontfanen: maer als wy alleen zijn, dan moeten wy droevich zijn'".

74   Ibid. 533: 'Op eenen tijt zijn twee broeders ghekomen tot eenen out-vader, die gheene ghewoonte en hadde van alle daghe te eten. Als hy de broeders ghesien hadde, heeft hy die blijdelijck ontfanghen, ende gheseyt: "'tVasten heeft sijnen loon". Ende noch seyde hy: "Die om der liefden wille eet, volbrenght twee gheboden; want hy verlaet sijnen eyghen wille, ende heeft 'tghebodt voldaen, vermakende de broeders'".

them. After all, they, too, fasted, chastised their bodies, sat alone with their thoughts in the wilderness. How then was he different for them. The Father answered: 'We hope in the grace of God and preserve our heart'.[75] A saying of Abbot Marcus, in defence of the solitary life, is cited to preface and augment this insight: '[...] but I cannot be with God and [also] with men: for many thousands of the highest powers have but a single will, but men have many wills. And so, I cannot leave God to come and be with men'.[76] The will to love God takes absolute priority, subsuming the monk's other faculties and the full range of his affects – sorrow, fear, remorse, hope, pity, desire, et alia. If the bedrock of these emotions is penitential sorrow, their summit is love, not only of one's neighbor monks but of God above all.

Inflections of these affects are legible in the attitudes, gestures, and especially the faces, but also the attributes, of Bloemaert's *vaderen*. Take John: the gentle tilt of his head, the softness of his upturned eyes, the slight smile on his mouth, and his proximity to that supreme symbol of divine love – the lamb of God – communicate the love that animates the prophet's penitential devotion, his turnings away and toward as he struggles to maintain his purpose of lovingly serving Christ his Saviour [Fig. 12.5]. The conch alludes to his efforts to trumpet the coming of Jesus, while the root vegetables, single fruit, and stalk of bitter herb signify the rigors of the solitary life. Onuphrius gently gazes in loving thanks at the angel, but his body strenuously twists even as it holds a punishing pose suggestive of his daily efforts to chastise himself and prolonged struggles to contain his troublesome emotions [Fig. 12.10]. Theonas, cowled like a Capuchin, expresses his intense affection for Christ by gazing lovingly at a crucifix, but he, too, twists though less forcefully than Fathers such as Hilarion, Paul Simplex, or Bonosus [Figs. 12.8, 12.21, 12.24, 12.26]. Other Fathers, even while turning and striving, are closer to a state of composure – Anthony, for instance, even though two demons attack him from behind – whereas others are more expressive of deep remorse, e.g., the tearful Arsenius or Ammon Nitriota, or penitential distress, e.g., Macarius Alexandrinus, Abraham Hermit, or Helenus, or suppliant hope, e.g., Malchus or Frontonius [Figs. 12.7, 12.9, 12.13, 12.14, 12.18, 12.22, 12.23, 12.25]. As discussed in section 3 of this essay, below, comparison of Bloemaert's Fathers with key figures in his biblical prints of peripetal scenes reveals further affective inflections discernible in the *Sylva*: horror, bewilderment, shame, bitter regret, pitiable sorrow, disconsolate fear.

---

75   Ibid. 552: "'Wy hopen inde gratie Godts, ende bewaren onse herte'".
76   Ibid. 553: "'[...] maer ick en can niet zijn met Godt ende met de menschen: want veel duysenden vande bovenste crachten hebben eenen wille, maer de menschen hebben veel willen. Ick en can dan Godt niet verlaten, ende comen, ende zijn met de menschen'".

MIXED EMOTION & PERFECTION IN BLOEMAERT'S *SYLVA ANACHORETICA*   485

Indeed, the series as a whole, since it consists of Fathers markedly similar in pose, might be read as intonations of one and the same figure, which is to say, as variations on a single theme. Together they enunciate the complex affective life of the desert Fathers. Their setting – in Latin, *eremus* (waste, desert, wilderness) – amplifies the expression of mixed emotion and, on top of this, by way of Bolswert's striking frontispiece which depicts the desert wilderness as an arboreal paradise, as if transformed by the monks' contemplative devotions, serves to highlight Bloemaert's ability to describe or, better, produce such a transformative effect. (Probably conceived by Bolswert, the print was designed and engraved in the manner of Bloemaert, to fit integrally into the series upon which it comments.[77]) Risius's dedicatory preface as well, in calling attention to the series' artifice, whereby saints and *eremus* are converted into representational images and transported from distant desert wastes to the Southern Netherlands, further invites appreciation of the *Sylva* as an epitome of Bloemaert's art. In the *Schilder-Boeck*, Van Mander had identified efflorescent grace as one of the master's most distinctive qualities, praising him in terms that can be seen to apply equally to the subjects and pictorial manner of the *Sylva*.

3   **Landscape and Mixed Emotion as Epitomes of Bloemaert's Art in the *Sylva***

The close correspondence between Bloemaert's designs and Rosweyde's and Risius's texts on the desert Fathers and Mothers indicates that he devised his canon of illustrious hermit saints with their conception of the anachoretic life in mind.[78] As Roethlisberger plausibly supposes, Bloemaert, who was Roman Catholic and Latinate, very likely compared notes with Risius and Jan van Gorcum, s.j., author of a condensed Dutch edition of Rosweyde's

---

77   Roethlisberger attributes the design of this print, signed 'Bolswert fecit', to Bolswert himself, who in this instance closely imitated the manner of Bloemaert, paying homage to him. See Roethlisberger, *Bloemaert and his Sons* 175. Based on Psalm 101:7 – 'I am become like to a pelican of the wilderness' – this allegory assures the reader-viewer that the eremitical penitents s/he is about to peruse had confidence in the power of God to save and console them. It was meant to function, and was surely received by most reader-viewers, as a plate by Bloemaert himself.

78   In what follows, I focus on Bloemaert's portraits of the Fathers; the Mothers, gathered under the heading "Sacra eremus ascetriarum", are portrayed similarly to the Fathers, although Bloemaert habitually enhances their sweetness of facial expression [Figs. 12.28–12.30].

Vitae Patrum;[79] he may also have corresponded with Rosweyde. As we shall see, his distinctive *handelinge* (pictorial handling) – punningly described by Van Mander as his 'artful/natural/subtle method of drawing with the pen' ('aerdighe wijse van teyckenen, en handelinge metter Pen') and his 'painterly floral manner/quality' ('schilderachtigen bloem-aerdt') – was perfectly suited to epitomising the special virtues of the hermits and hermitesses; conversely, their peculiar way of life or, better, grace of vocation, can be seen to have served as a platform for showcasing the master draftsman's 'still and salutary character, heartily loving and ever inclined to search after the utmost power and beauty of the art of Picturing' ('stil en bequamen wesen, hertlijck verlieft en gheneghen meer en meer nae te soecken d'uyterste cracht en schoonheyt der Const *Pictura*').[80]

Featured in part two of Book iv of the *Schilder-Boeck*, the "Life of Abraham Bloemaert, Excellent Painter of Gorcum" praises the *aerdt* (subtlety/naturalness) of the master's landscapes, which then stand proxy for his art as a whole in the peroration that closes the "Life". Bloemaert's works are epitomes of relative restraint: like nature, they are 'niet te verladen', overburdened neither by incidentals, such as anecdotal scenes, nor by an excess of plants, foliage, or landscape particulars.[81] In this sense, too, they are decidedly natural, the opposite of artificial and overwrought, and as such, the apt expressions of a man inclined to stillness and solitude, a man of salutary character ('van stil en bequamen wesen'). It is as if Van Mander were describing Bloemaert himself as one of the desert Fathers, inviting the reader-viewer to see him and them as mutually referential or connotative. On this reading, the draughtsman's ability to portray multilayered meditative affects is construed as complementary to the very affects he himself bodies forth, both subtly and naturally, through his devoted practice of *schilderconst*.

The frontispiece to the *Sylva* takes Rosweyde's imagery of the martyrs as *arbores*, branching and fruiting in Lord's service, and applies it to the desert saints, who daily punished their bodies, martyring them in their efforts to achieve spiritual perfection [Fig. 12.2]. Interspersed throughout the woodland landscape, coenobites and anchorites are seen wandering and praying, each positioned beside and beneath trees that function as their eremitical

---

79 See Gorcum Jan van, s.j., *Het leven der HH. Eremyten ende Eremytinnen, beschreven door verscheyden Autheuren* [...] (Antwerp, Hieronymus Verdussen: 1619).

80 Mander Karel van, "Het leven van Abraham Bloemaert, uytnemende Schilder van Gorricum", in *Het Schilder-Boeck* (Haarlem, Paschier van Wesbusch: 1604), Book iv, fol. 298r.

81 Ibid.: 'Dees dinghen, hoewel niet te seer verladen met werck, staen besonder en uytnemende wel, en (na mijn duncken) niet te verbeteren'.

analogues. Poised at threshold of the forest, the image of the pelican in its piety feeding three young chicks alongside a cross signifies the saving presence of Christ who pervades and sustains the monastic *eremus*. The bifurcate tree stumps at right, the jagged one the remnant of a fallen tree, the smooth one the remnant of a hewn one, allude to various biblical passages that attest the power of God to punish sin and reward virtue: for example, *Psalm* 29:5 – 'The voice of the Lord breaketh the cedars; yea, the Lord shall break in pieces the cedars of Lebanon'; or *Jeremiah* 6:6 – 'For thus saith the Lord of hosts: Hew down her trees, cast up a trench about Jerusalem. This is the city to be visited: all oppression in in the midst of her'. They also call to mind *Matthew* 3:10 – 'For the axe is laid to the root of the trees. Every tree therefore that doth not yield good fruit shall be cut down and cast into the fire' – and related passages such as *Matthew* 7:19 and *Luke* 3:9, 13:7, and 13:9. But these scriptural admonitions to cast sin out, condensed into the symbolic stumps, open onto a verdant landscape whose woodland vales and meandering stream look more like the paradisiacal vale of Tempe than a desert wilderness. Of course, the term *eremus* can mean 'desert waste' or, more generically, a 'wilderness', such as a virgin woodland, but this landscape really does appear pastoral rather than inhospitable. It differs in this respect from the rough, rocky, barren, and cavernous settings, sometimes marked by the gnarled trunk or branches of a solitary tree, where the Fathers and Mothers sit or kneel in prayer [Figs. 12.5–12.6, 12.8–12.10, 12.12–12.14, 12.1–12.18, 12.20, 12.22, 12.25–12.27, 12.30]. The frontispiece image portrays these settings in a new light, revealing how the sanctity of their inhabitants' lives has made what was forbidding appear strangely welcoming. Traces of the wasteland and wilderness, inhospitable places that inspire terror, are absorbed into a verdant vista wherein the abject fear of the sinner and the fearsomeness of the *eremus* elide into the contemplative joy of the anchorite and the lush, inviting umbrage of his solitary dwelling place. The affective conjunction of fear and joy, and the complex layering of other disparate emotions, are characteristic, as we have seen, of the eremitical life of the desert Fathers and Mothers epitomised by Rosweyde in *'t Vaders boeck*, published just two years prior. The strenuous spiritual exercises whereby they strive to secure eternal salvation require them to bring their competing impulses to consciousness and choose amongst them, even while feeling their push and pull concurrently. This is to say that just as the Fathers are peerless models of mixed emotion, paragons of the struggle to achieve spiritual mastery by resolving contrary emotions into contemplative repose, so the relation between the landscapes in the frontispiece and the series proper – the former being, after all, notionally the same as the latter – operates analogously. The *eremus* as *paradisus* issues from and remains rooted in the *eremus* as wasteland.

488   MELION

The mixed metaphor of *eremus/paradisus* is thus one of the visual means harnessed by Bloemaert to the task of portraying the internal tug-of-war of the eremitical life, externalising it as crucial to the Fathers' solitary lives and quintessential to their grace of vocation. The layering of *eremus* and *paradisus* has another function as well. In combination with Risius's treatment of place in his dedicatory preface, and seen against the backdrop of Van Mander's "Life of Bloemaert", it also alludes to the master's artistic *bona fides*, his manifest virtues as a consummate *teyckenaer/schilder* (draughtsman/painter), above all his dynamic yet graceful *handelinge*. Here the notion of virtue expands, shifting from the register of moral and spiritual virtues, to encompass artisanal virtue, too.

How does the merger of desert and paradise, or better, the affective conversion of one into the other, serve to exemplify these virtues? The answer can partly be found in the *Sylva's* three epigraphs and the opening *vita*, "Iesus ductus est in desertum" (Jesus led into the desert).[82] Excerpted from Jerome's "First Letter to Heliodorus, in Praise of the Desert", the first epigraph identifies the *eremus* as a florid, flourishing place populated by the eremitical followers of Christ, each of whom is like a jewel-like blossom: 'O Desert verdant with the flowers of Christ! O Solitude in which those stones spring forth wherewith in the Apocalypse the city of the great king is raised! O Woodland / Wilderness, rejoicing familiarly with God'![83] The layering of the lapidary and floral metaphors characterises the desert saints as the foundation stones upon which God constructs his spiritual city. They are flowers as precious and luminous as the gems enumerated in *Apocalypse* 21:17–21 – jasper, sapphire, chalcedony, emerald, sardonyx, etc. – burgeoning in verdancy. The poetic, artisanal imagery of gardening and building combines with the second epigraph, from Basil's *Liber de laude vitae solitariae* (Book in Praise of the Solitary Life), which equates the solitary life with a school of theory and practice, where celestial doctrine and divine *artes* (principles, foundations, but also, skills, handicrafts) are taught: 'The solitary life is the school of celestial doctrine, the discipline of divine arts, where God is the whole of what is learned'.[84] The first two epigraphs are then complementary to the third, which consists of a longer excerpt from Jerome's "First Epistle to Heliodorus" praising the desert as the paradisiacal threshold

---

82   On this plate, see Roethlisberger, *Bloemaert and his Sons* 175–176.

83   Risius, *Sylva anachoretica*, n.p.: 'O Desertum floribus Christi vernans! O Solitudo in qua illi nascuntur lapides de quibus in Apocalypsi civitas magni Regis extruitur! O Eremus familiarius Deo gaudens'. For the text of Jerome's letter, now generally numbered 14, see https://www.newadvent.org/fathers/3001014.htm (accessed 20 April 2020).

84   For the text of *De laude vitae solitariae*, see Jacques Paul Migne, *Patrologia graeca*, t. CXLV, 246–252 (http://patristica.net/graeca/#t145).

MIXED EMOTION & PERFECTION IN BLOEMAERT'S *SYLVA ANACHORETICA* 489

between the burdensome terrestrial life and the lightsome heavenly life soon to be revealed:

> Believe me, I have more light than you. Sweet it is to lay aside the weights of the body and to soar into the pure bright ether. [...] Does the boundless solitude of the desert terrify you? In the spirit you may walk always in paradise. Do but turn your thoughts thither, and you will be no more in the desert. [...] 'The sufferings of this present time are not worthy to be compared with the glory' which shall come after them, 'which shall be revealed in us' [*Romans* 8:18].[85]

The three epigraphs lead into the opening *vita*, "Iesus ductus est in desertum", which paraphrases *Romans* 5:12–21, 1 *Corinthians* 15:22, and *Colossians* 3:9–10, to argue that Christ, the image of God incarnate, whose divine personhood transcends the Lord's judgement upon the sin of Adam, is alone capable restoring the paradise lost by the first man. He guides humankind out of the desert of sin, by himself going into the desert where, having conquered Satan, he converts it into the paradise once lost and now regained:

> But he who leaderless in paradise lost the accepted path, how could he resume the way he had lost, leading out of the desert, without a guide, the temptations being so many, the striving after virtue so difficult, the stumbling into error so easy? Therefore was Jesus, full of the spirit, led into the desert: that by counsel he might challenge the devil, for had he not fought, he would not have conquered on my behalf: that by example he might show us who strive after better things, how all the more to guard against the devil, lest infirmity of mind/heart forfeit the grace of the mystery.[86]

---

85   Risius, *Sylva anachoretica*, n.p.: 'Crede mihi, nescio quid plus lucis adspicio. Libet sarcina corporis abiecta ad purum aetheris evolare fulgorem. [...] Infinita eremi vastitas te terret? sed tu paradisum mente deambula. Quotiescumque illuc cogitatione conscenderis, toties in eremo non eris. Scabra sine balneis attrahitur cutis? sed qui in Christo semel lotus est, non illi necesse est iterum lavare. Et ut breviter ad cuncta, audias Apostolum respondentem: "Non sunt", inquit, "condignae passiones huius saeculi ad superventuram gloriam, quae revelabitur in nobis"'.

86   Ibid. 1: 'Sed qui in paradiso sine duce iter amisit acceptum, quemadmodum de deserto sine duce iter repetere posset amissum, ubi tentationes plurimae, nisus ad virtutem difficilis, lapsus facilis ad errorem. Plenus igitur Iesus spiritu agitur in desertum: consilio, ut diabolum provocaret; nam nisi ille certasset, non mihi iste vicisset: mysterio, ut Adam illum de exilio liberaret: exemplo, ut ostenderet nobis diabolum ad meliora tendentibus invidere, et tunc magis esse cavendum, ne mysterij gratiam deserat mentis infirmitas'.

All three epigraphs in one way or another claim that the desert, thanks to the efforts of Christ and his eremitical satellites, has becomes a lush, leafy paradise where suffering is transmuted into a foretaste of heavenly glory. The woodland retreat in Bolswert's frontispiece alludes to this mysterious process of penitential, contemplative transmutation. It stands for the terrifying *eremus* become a welcoming *sylva*, for the attendant emotions of fear and horror become felicity and peace of mind.

The reference to the desert as a place where *artes* are cultivated, and to the hermit saints as jewel-like flowers, who by constantly battling against the death of sin preserve the living grace of the mystery of salvation ('mysterij gratiam'), sets the stage for the reflexive character of the *Sylva* – its ability to reflect back upon the nature of Bloemaert's art, and to foreground his command of *teyckenconst*. The *Sylva*, on this account, is the *locus* where his *const* is seen to be cultivated. The notion that the *Sylva* consists of floral specimens speaks to his reputation as a *bloem-aerdige schilder* and *teyckenaer* (efflorescent painter and draughtsman), who richly adorns *Pictura* with his 'bloeyende bloem-aerdige vercieringe mildlijck' (blooming, bloom-like, salutary finery).[87] The series' function of celebrating the *flores Christi* who devoted themselves to cultivating the *mysterij gratiam Christi* redounds to Bloemaert's reputation for graceful invention and execution, manifest in his mastery of figural (and arboreal) devices such as the *figura serpentinata*. His *ars* is presented, implicitly, as the *machina* that discovers beauty in the *eremus*, layering joy onto this place of desolation and sorrow, not only as a matter of the spirit but also as a matter of art. Risius's dedication of the *Sylva* to Antonius de Winghe, Abbot of the Benedictine Abbey of Lessines, underscores the series' reflexivity, its heightened allusion to *ars/const*, by developing the clever conceit that the *Sylva*'s plates, rather than simply depicting a selection of hermit saints, instead represent how they portray themselves for the benefit of votaries such as De Winghe. These are images about image-making. The conceit originates in the image-based spiritual exercises of the Jesuits, whose approach to prayer,

---

87 The pun on Bloemaert's name ('Bloemaert' = 'bloem-aerdige') opens and closes Karel van Mander's "Het leven van Abraham Bloemaert", in Book IV of *Schilder-Boeck*, fols. 297r and 298r. It appears first as cited here, a second time in the peroration on Bloemaert's lifelong search for whatever is most forceful and beautiful about the art of Picturing; see note 80 *supra*: 'Hy is een Man [...] gheneghen meer en meer nae te soecken d'uyterste cracht en schoonheyt der Const *Pictura*: welcke, ghelijck sy Bloemaert, om zijnen schilderachtigen bloem-aert (van hem bloemigh verciet wesende) gheheel vriendlijck toeghedaen en gunstigh is, doet sy uyt rechte danckbaerheyt van Wtrecht zijnen naem recht uyt de Weerelt over loflijck voeren en dragen [...]'.

MIXED EMOTION & PERFECTION IN BLOEMAERT'S *SYLVA ANACHORETICA*

both meditative and contemplative, was intensely visual, centering on the mental production of images. Risius affirms:

> Now these selfsame [hermits] come and represent themselves by their image ('sua se specie repraesentant'); and indeed, they bear with them their broken household utensils, their cup, rush mat, and goats' hair coverlet. In truth, they sit fast in their fearful caves, but thence speedily gain access to the forecourts of heaven: semi-nude they endure the injuries of the open air, but are sheltered sufficiently, lying hid under the shadow of Christ: frightful in appearance, as if buried underground, they send their suppliant tears heavenward. Thus they come to you, ambassadors of the human race. [...] Whether in the country or the city, they carry all things with them.
>
> Given by a friendly hand, you hold the effigies, to which, that they be made more graceful, it has pleased [another] friend to attach brief maxims from the *Lives of the Fathers*. Maxims given virtually in their authors' words, lest they be cosmeticised.[88]

Risius tacitly construes the hermits as comely, and made more graceful still through the addition of their holy words; yet at the same time, imagining a face-to-face encounter, he calls them frightful, and finds their cavernous hermitages terrifying. It is their images, in other words, which are a joy to behold; discrepancy in reaction is a way of emphasising that the Fathers become present to Van Winghe only by way of their images, which they send him in lieu of appearing in person. Despatched from the *eremi* of Egypt and Palestine, their portraits have now reached Lessines and Antwerp, having been sanctioned by the very men and women they portray. These graceful images and texts, then, are insistently representational, and accordingly, their artful character, which is to say, Bloemaert's *const*, is brought to the fore. The elision/conversion of horror into pleasure, fear into joy, discussed above apropos the hermits' appearance

---

88   Ibid., n.p.: 'Veniunt nunc ipsi, et sua se specie repraesentant; quin et curtam supellectilem suam secum deferunt, caucum, psiathium, cilicium. Formidolosis quidem antris haerent, sed inde celerius caeli atria penetrant: seminudi aëris iniurias excipiunt, sed sat tecti sunt, qui sub Christi umbra latitant: terrae velut insepulti horrent, deprecatorias tamen ad caelum lacrymas mittunt. Veniunt igitur ad Te, humani generis legati. Non quaerenda illis loca lautia; suis ipsi antris, suis tuguriis, suis lautumiis sunt contenti. Ne labora de ferculis; inemptis dapibus famem sedant, dactylis, oleribus, lapsanis. Seu ruri seu in urbe sunt, Omnia secum portant.
       'Effigies habes ab amica manu; quae ut gratiores essent, placuit amico brevia e Vitis Patrum concinnare elogia. Quae Auctorum fere verbis dedit, ne fucum faceret'.

and setting, proves finally to be a mixed consequence not only of eremitical artifice but also of inspired and transcendent *teyckenconst/schilderconst*.

Unsurprisingly, many of the texts place special emphasis on the theme of image-making. Saint Anthony Hermit, for instance, is said to have attended closely to any praiseworthy examples of virtue he saw, and to have recast himself in their image ('ut quemcumque videret aliqua virtutis laude excellentem, illium imitari studeret') (Roethlisberger 167) [Fig. 12.7].[89] Saint Pachomius is described like an artist: when he reads Scripture, 'he examines it with skill/dexterity/resourcefulness/fertility of contrivance, and works upon/strokes/passes his hand over it with a pious mind/heart, applying himself daily to perfect through labor/workmanship whatsoever his memory retains' ('sed solerter examinans ac pia mente pertractans, studebat indies opere perficere, quae memoria retinebat') (Roethlisberger 171) [Fig. 12.11].[90] The term *memoria* implies that Pachomius has fixed an image in his mind and/or heart. The "Life of Saint Bonosus", excerpted from Jerome's "Letter 41 to Ruffinus", portrays him as a living image of various Old Testament types as well as a parabolic exemplum [Fig. 12.26].[91] Virtuous beyond measure, he climbs the ladder of Jacob (*Genesis* 28:12) while carrying the cross of Christ upon his back (*Matthew* 16:24), looking ever forward, never backward (*Luke* 9:62). He sows in tears, yet harvests in joy (*Psalm* 125:5), and as Moses in the desert set up the brazen serpent, so he sets himself up as a sacramental image (*Numbers* 21:8–9). The scriptural lens through which Jerome views Bonosus forms part and parcel of his tendency to see every aspect of the saint's life pictorially. His description of the hermit's desert cell, a vivid exercise in word-painting, models for Ruffinus how the saint's life should be visualised: 'Place all this before your eyes, dearest friend, and with all the faculties of your mind and spirit picture to yourself the scene. When you realise the effort of the fighter then you will be able to praise his victory'.[92] The pictured scene answers to the rhetorical question posed by

---

89   Ibid. 4. On this plate, see Roethlisberger, *Bloemaert and his Sons* 176.

90   Risius, *Sylva anachoretica* 8. On this plate, see Roethlisberger, *Bloemaert and his Sons* 177.

91   Risius, *Sylva anachoretica* 24. On this plate, see Roethlisberger, *Bloemaert and his Sons* 179. For Jerome's letter, now generally numbered 3, see https://www.newadvent.org/fathers /3001003.htm (accessed 20 April 2020).

92   *D. Hieronymi Stridoniensis epistolae selectae, et in libros tres distributae*, ed. P. Canisius, S.J. (Lyons, Antonius Beaujolius: 1677) 204: 'Propone tibi ante oculos, amice dulcissime, et in praesentiam rei totus animo ac mente convertere. Tunc poteris laudare victoriam cum laborem praeliantis agnoveris'. 'Picture to yourself the scene' is an idiomatic translation; a more literal one would be 'apply yourself to making the thing itself present in mind and spirit'. Whether translated idiomatically or literally, Jerome's text urges his interlocutor to fashion a mental image.

MIXED EMOTION & PERFECTION IN BLOEMAERT'S *SYLVA ANACHORETICA*   493

Christ in *Matthew* 11:7–8: 'What went you out into the desert to see? A reed shaken with the wind? But what went you out to see'? In response, as proof of the saint's mettle, Jerome, whose words Risius distills, describes the *eremus* of Bonosus with exceptional clarity and intensity. The dreadful place, violent and forlorn, is as if pacified, civilised by the saint's indomitable virtue:

> like a new inhabitant of paradise, he sat on a shipwrecked island encompassed by the roaring sea, by razor-sharp escarpments, naked rocks, and appalling solitude. [...] alone (nay rather, with Christ as his sole companion) he there sees the glory of God, which even the apostles discerned only in the wilderness. Nor does he catch sight of turreted cities, for instead he inscribes his name in the rolls of the new city [of God]. [...] All around him the sea madly rages, and resounding, dashes against winding cliffs. Not a blade of green grass grows, nor pressed close by shady places is any field flourishing: stony precipices hem in like a prison. Secure, intrepid, armed by the apostle [Paul], now he hears God [...] and perchance, sees while he dwells on that island, something like unto the example of John [the Evangelist].[93]

This ekphrasis pictures the *eremus* as a protean place, by turns hostile and generative, where a different kind of encounter with images transpires: the typological and parabolic images invoked earlier in the "Life" metamorphose into the Augustine image of the City of God and the Johannine vision of the Apocalypse. The many kinds and degrees of image engendered by and around Bonosus ultimately resolve into an extended account of the cunning images conjured by the devil to tempt Christ in the desert (*Matthew* 4:1–16); the triad of seductive images – of food, riches, and glory – calls up a triple sequence of scriptural rejoinders excerpted from *Deuteronomy* 8:3, 1 *Timothy* 6:9, and 2 *Corinthians* 12:10.[94]

---

93   Risius, *Sylva anachoretica*, 24: '[...] insulam pelago circumsonante naufragam, cui asperae cautes, et nuda saxa, et solitudo terrori est, quasi quidam novus paradisi colonus insedit. [...] solus ibi (immo iam Christo comitante non solus) videt gloriam Dei, quam etiam Apostoli nisi in deserto non viderant. Non quidem conspicit turritas urbes, sed in novae civitatis censu dedit nomen suum. [...] Totam circa insulam fremit insanum mare, et sinuosis montium illisum scopulis aequor reclamat. Nullo terra gramine viret, nullis vernans campus densatur umbraculis: abruptae rupes quasi quendam horrore carcerem claudunt. Ille securus, intrepidus, et totus de Apostolo armatus, nunc Deum audit [...] et fortasse, ad exemplum Ioannis, aliquid videt, dum in insula commoratur'.

94   Ibid.: 'Forsitan antiquae fraudis memor, famem suadere tentabit; sed iam illi responsum est: "Non in solo pane vivit homo". Opes forsitan gloriamque proponet; sed dicetur illi. "Qui cupiunt divites fieri, incidunt in muscipulam et tentationes". Fessa membra ieiuniis,

Amongst the *Sylva*'s hermits, Bonosus is one of the most contorted, his hands the most tightly clenched, his face the most pleading if not tormented, and these features comport with the text's characterisation of him as planting in sorrow, defiant even under the perturbations of the devil, and bearing witness to the apocalyptic glory of God (Roethlisberger 187) [Fig. 12.26]. The plate is not only the perfect expression of the text's personation of the saint; it is also a placeholder for the many other images whereby Bonosus is meant to be seen and understood. Beside him, the open book of Scripture refers to the source of the proliferating affective images, by turns or at once desolatory and consolatory, he sets in motion.

This brief excursus on selected hermits from the *Sylva*'s litany of desert saints drives home the point that the book's images reflexively convert image-production into one of its central themes. This is the context within which Bloemaert's images could themselves be adduced for the appreciative eye of the book's *amatores artis picturae* and *liefhebbers van const*, though, of course, the line between votary and *amator/liefhebber* would have been quite porous, allowing the reader-viewer to see through Bloemaert to the anchorites, through the anchorites to Bloemaert.[95] But the *Sylva*'s plates, more than mere models of *teyckenconst/schilderconst* are also heartfelt epitomes of affective complexity, of consolation snatched from desolation, of fear and sorrow transposed into joy.

4   Conclusion: Bloemaert and Ignatian Prayer

Given Bloemaert's strong connections with the Society of Jesus, an important source for his considerable investment in portraying mixed emotions would surely have been Ignatius's embrace of tearful expression as an indispensable

---

morbo gravante concutiet; sed Apostoli repercutietur eloquio: "Quando infirmor, tunc fortior sum". (Perhaps mindful of an olden trick, [the devil] will urge hunger [upon him]; but already he is answered: 'Man does not live by bread alone' [*Deuteronomy* 8:3]. Perhaps he will lay glory and riches before him; but he is answered: 'For they that will become rich fall into temptation and into the snare of the devil' [1 *Timothy* 6:9]. He will strike limbs wearied by fasting and oppressed by illness; but by their eloquence, the apostles will drive him back: 'For when I am weak, then am I powerful' [2 *Corinthians* 12:10]).

95   On the term *kunstliefhebber*, which begins to appear in documents of the Antwerp Guild of St. Luke ca. 1600, and on the allied Latin term *artis pictoriae amator*, see Held J.S., "*Artis pictoriae amator*: An Antwerp Art Patron and his Collection", in idem, *Rubens and his Circle: Studies by Julius S. Held*, ed. A.W. Lowenthal – D. Rosand – J. Walsh, Jr. (Princeton: 1982) 35–64, esp. 59 n. 3. On codification of the term *liefhebbers der schilderyen* to refer to elite 'collectors and enthusiasts' of painting in Antwerp, see Filipczak Z.Z., *Picturing Art in Antwerp, 1550–1700* (Princeton: 1987) 47–72, esp. 51.

component of intensely spiritual, divinely inspired prayer.[96] His ready tears, howsoever saintly, were characteristic not just of him but also of fellow religious such as Filippo Neri, François de Sales, Teresa of Ávila, and, famously, the

---

96 Another possible source for Bloemaert's interest in the representation of mixed emotions may have been Daniel Heinsius's Latin edition of Aristotle's *Poetics* (*Aristotelis De poetica liber* [Leiden, Ioannis Balduinus: 1610]), along with his theoretical elaboration upon Aristotle, *De tragoediae constitutione liber* (Leiden, Ioannis Balduinus: 1611), in which the mixed emotions of fear and pity are put forward as the cathartic affects that the dramatic poet must aspire to produce above all. Catharsis is secured through the staged enactment of *peripeteia* (sudden reversal of fortune or circumstances) and *anagnorisis* (recognition by a principal character of her/his true identity or situation) as the necessary climax of a *fabula implex* (morally complicated story). If *peripeteia* and *anagnorisis* appear convincingly to emerge from a coherent structure of storytelling, they will necessarily compel the playwright's audience to feel fearful compassion/compassionate fear, as Heinsius declares apropos of Sophocles's *Oedipus rex*; see Heinsius D., *Aristoteles De poetica liber* [...] *Accedit Daniel Heinsius "De tragoedia[e] constitutione"*, ed. W.A. Koch (Hildesheim: 1976) 92:

> 'Quippe quis [...] non horret, non commiseratione commovetur, cum momento uno de felicitate sua eo deturbatur Oedipus; ut se parricidam, virum matris, liberorum avum esse intelligat? Idque ex ipsa argumenti dispositione, si quis domi legat. Licet in theatro nihil videat'.
>
> [Who is it who [...] does not fear, is not moved to pity, when in a single moment Oedipus is cast down from his felicity, to such an extent that he recognises himself as a patricide, a husband to his mother, a grandfather to his sons? And this from the selfsame arrangement of the play, even if one were [merely] to read it at home rather than seeing it at the theatre.]

For Heinsius, as for his foremost follower, the poet-playwright Joost van den Vondel, catharsis results as a literary or performative effect when an abrupt turn of events causes the protagonist to realise how that headlong turn pertains to her-/himself, thereby eliciting fear and pity (*schrick* and *meedogen*) in the audience (or reader-viewer). The trope of turning, thus viewed, has both a peripetal and an agnaroristic function. Conversely, Bloemaert's frequent reliance on turning figures to signal the experience of conversion, as in the *Biblical Penitents*, especially *Zachaeus* and *Mary Magdalene*, and his use of the same twisting figural type throughout the *Sylva* to convey the eremitical monk's constant, hypervigilant struggle to turn away from sin and toward salvation, can be identified as allusions to the experience of *peripeteia* and *anagnorisis*. Viewed through the lens of Heinsius's Aristotelian poetics, Bloemaert's serpentine penitents and desert Fathers might best be thought of as conveyors of that cathartic fear and pity which figures gripped by spiritual changes have the power to arouse in the beholder. On fear and pity in Aristotle's *Poetics* as interpreted by Heinsius in *De tragoediae constitutione*, see Konst J.W.H., "'Medoogen en schrick uit te wercken': Der emotionale Effect von Vondels *Jeptha* (1659)", in Steiger J.A. (eds.), *Passion, Affekt und Leidenschaft in der frühen Neuzeit*, 2 vols. (Wiesbaden: 2005) 2:803–815. On Heinsius's *De tragoediae constitutione* and his translation of the *Poetics*, see Bremer J.M. – Schouten D.C.A., "Hoe Aristoteles' *Poetica* een weg vond naar Nederland", *Spektator* 16 (1986–1987) 270–286; and Meter J.H., *The Literary Theories of Daniel Heinsius: A Study of the Development and Background of his Views on Literary Theory and Criticism during the Period from 1602–1612* (Assen: 1984), passim.

496 MELION

Capuchin Lorenzo da Brindisi.[97] As Joseph Imorde has argued in an important article, tears were appreciated as the sine qua non of meditative and contemplative sincerity.[98] With respect to the topic at hand, it is important to note that flowing tears were equally associated with the overwhelming experience of divine love, sweet beyond endurance, and the equally overwhelming experience of heartsore contrition, abject beyond description. In describing the tearful joy of living saints, their followers tended to elide the distinction between joy and sorrow, construing tears as attributes of powerfully mixed emotions. Typical is a later account of Father Lorenzo that paraphrases from eyewitness reports gathered to make the case for beatification; as he speaks, he weeps, and so, he brings his listeners, too, to tears:

> for whether from the pulpit before crowds of people who oft gathered [to hear him], or in cloisters before his spiritual sons and brothers, or before secular authorities, discoursing privately on the bitter Passion and death [of Christ], his words were so gripping, so affecting that the hearts of whoever were present, even those obdurate and stubborn, were perforce made soft thereby, since the burning love for the suffering Jesus that was in Lorenzo gave such force to his words as to draw compassionate tears of contrition and sorrow even from hard stones.[99]

Another report describes how the tears of sorrow he shed from the pulpit were at one and the same time tears of consolation triggered by the sight of

---

97   On the theological justification of tears as discernible signs of grace, see Benke C., *Die Gabe der Tränen: Zur Tradition und Theologie eines vergessenen Kapitels der Glaubensgeschichte* (Würzburg: 2002).

98   Imorde J., "'Gustus Mysticus': Zur Geschichte und Metaphorik geistlicher Empfindsamkeit", in Steiger et al. (eds.), *Passion, Affekt und Leidenschaft* 2:1105–1133.

99   See Rossi Angelo Maria de, *Leben, Wandel und Todt des Grossen Wunderthätigen Diener Gottes Laurentii von Brundusio, Weiland gewesten Ministri Generalis des Gesammten Capuc. Ordens* [...] (Augsburg – Innsbruck, Joseph Wolff: 1751) 109; as cited in Imorde, "Geschichte und Metaphorik geistlicher Empfindsamkeit", 115: '[...] da er eintweders auf der Cantzel vor häuffig-versammleter Volcks-Menge, oder in den Clösteren vor seinen geistlichen Söhnen und Mit-Brüderen oder aber vor weltlichen Stands-Personen in einem Privat-Discurs von dem bitteren Leyden und Sterben eine Anred hielte, seine Wort dermaßen eingreiffend und beweglich waren, daß die Hertzen der Anwesenden, ob sie schon verstockt und hartneckig, sich gleichwohl müßten andurch erweichen lassen, weil nehmlich die in Laurentio brinnende Liebe zu dem leidenden Jesu seinen Worten ein solche Krafft gabe, welche sogar aus harten Felsen mitleidige Buß- und Trauer-Zäher kunten hervor locken'.

MIXED EMOTION & PERFECTION IN BLOEMAERT'S *SYLVA ANACHORETICA*   497

his audience weeping contritely in response to his words.[100] For Lorenzo, as for Ignatius, Teresa, et al., tears compounded of joy and sorrow testify to the saints' power to convert, i.e., to [re]turn the faithful to God. The central place of tears within spiritual exercises, not least in the Ignatian *Spiritual Exercises*, where they are enshrined in the fourth point of the fifth exercise of the first week, the "Meditation on Hell", accords with the emphasis on the mixed experience of love, hope, and disdain for sin in Rosweyde, where in life after life, purgative sorrow and penitential distress grapple with divine love, and grave joy and great sorrow coalesce.[101] In turn, many of Bloemaert's Fathers, as noted above, appear simultaneously to register love and sorrow. To circle back to a point made above, the gathering of Fathers thus bears witness to the affective richness of Bloemaert's art.

In sum, I have approached the *Sylva* from three vantage points. Section 1 of this essay argued that Bloemaert aligned the gestural and physiognomic traits of the desert Fathers and Mothers with the lineaments of mixed emotion codified in Van Mander's *Grondt*, especially the figural canons detailed in chapter 4, "On the Attitude, Decorum, and Decorous Motion of a Human Figure". The turning poses of the figures, who pivot robustly yet gracefully across multiple axes of orientation, indicate that they are shifting from one emotional state to another or, rather, given how elegantly they turn, merging emotion into emotion. The peripetal shifts and emotional range on view in earlier prints by Bloemaert demonstrate the degree of his commitment to exploring complex, compound, multilayered emotions in biblical scenes and portrayals of saints such as Peter, Paul, and Mary Magdalene. In section 2, I drew parallels between Rosweyde's *'t Vaders boeck*, Bloemaert's and Risius's chief source, and the *Sylva*, showing how concerned both Rosweyde and Bloemaert were to plumb the Fathers' and Mothers' contrary feelings and record their ceaseless efforts to endure if not fully master these labile emotions. The moment of conversion from the secular to the sacred life, from the life of a coenobite to that of an anchorite, was particularly fraught, and it is this change in spiritual condition that the serpentine contrapposto of Bloemaert's figures displays so evocatively. In section 3, by way of an excursus on the *Sylva*'s settings and their relation to the book's paradisiacal frontispiece, I called attention to the way in which

---

100   Ibid. 17: '[...] indeme er selbst auf der Cantzel zu mehrmahlen häuffige Zäher-Perlen liesse herunter fallen, den Verlust der so kostbaren Seelen andurch gebührend zu beweinen, sahe er mit grossen Hertzens-Trost, daß auch hingegen seine Zuhörer in Erwegung der begangenen Sünden sich ergüßten in haüffige Buß-Thränen'.

101   See Ignatius of Loyola, s.j., *Exercitia spiritualia* (Rome, Societas Iesu: 1548), n.p.: "Quintum exercitium est contemplatio de inferno, continetque ultra orationem praeparatoriam, et duo praeludia, puncta quinque, et unum colloquium".

mixed emotion – bodied forth by the figures and heightened by the merger of *eremus* and *paradisus* – also functions as an index of Bloemaert's artistic virtue: his ability as a draughtsman and painter, or to be more accurate, his 'artful/natural/subtle method of drawing with the pen' and his 'painterly floral manner/quality'. These pictorial virtues were surely seen to complement the moral and spiritual virtues epitomised by the *Sylva*'s saintly protagonists, which is to say that Bloemaert himself acts the part of a protagonist. The implication is that his art, adapted to the task of illustrating the desert saints' deeds, fully involved him in the spiritual exercise of parsing their inner lives and embracing the range, complexity, and, in time after much struggle, the virtuous outcome of their emotional striving after perfection. As they were examples to Bloemaert, so they are presented as examples to us of the emotional exercises whereby the willing votary comes closer to Christ.

Bibliography

Allard H.J., *Pater Adrianus Poirters, s.j.: een historisch-letterkundige schets* (Amsterdam: 1871).

Aristotle's Poetics, trans. – comm. G. Whalley (Montreal – Buffalo: 1997).

Begheyn P., s.j., "Jesuit Book Production in The Netherlands, 1601–1650", in Lucas T.M. (ed.), *Spirit, Style, Story: Essays Honoring John W. Padberg, s.j.* (Chicago: 2002) 303–326.

Benke C., *Die Gabe der Tränen: Zur Tradition und Theologie eines vergessenen Kapitels der Glaubensgeschichte* (Würzburg: 2002).

Bleyerveld Y. – Elen A.J. – Niessen J., *Bosch to Bloemaert: Early Netherlandish Drawings in Museum Boijmans Van Beuningen*, exh. cat., Museum Boijmans Van Beuningen, Rotterdam; Fondation Custodia, Paris (Paris: 2014).

Bloemaert Abraham – Bloemaert Frederick, *Artis Apellae liber hic, studiosa juventus aptata ingenio fert rudimenta tuo* (Utrecht, Frederick Bloemaert: ca. 1650).

Bloemaert Abraham – Bloemaert Frederick. *Artis Apellae liber hic, studiosa juventus aptata ingenio fert rudimenta tuo* (Amsterdam, Nicolaus Visscher: 1682).

Bloemaert Abraham – Bloemaert Frederick, *Oorspronkelyk en vermaard konstryk tekenboek van Abraham Bloemaart, geestryk getekent, en meesterlyk gegraveert by zyn zoon Frederik Bloemaart. Hooglyk dienstig en nut voor Schilders, Beeldhouwers, Plaatsnyders, Tekenaars en Konstbegeerige Leerlingen van de beyde Sexen* (Amsterdam, Reinier and Josua Ottens: 1740).

Bolten J., *Method and Practice: Dutch and Flemish Drawing Books, 1600–1750* (Landau Pfalz: 1985).

Bolten J., *Abraham Bloemaert, c. 1565–1651: The Drawings* (Amsterdam: 2007).

Bolten J., *The Drawings of Abraham Bloemaert: A Supplement* (New York: 2017).

Bosius Fredericus-Ludovicus, *Opera omnia*, ed. Antonius de Winghe (Antwerp, Ex officina Plantiniana Balthasaris Moreti: 1632).

Bremer J.M. – Schouten D.C.A., "Hoe Aristoteles' *Poetica* een weg vond naar Nederland", *Spektator* 16 (1986–1987) 270–286.

Coens M., "Héribert Rosweyde et la recherche des document", *Analecta bollandiana* 83 (1965) 50–52.

Delehaye H., s.j., *L'oeuvre des Bollandistes à travers trois siècles, 1615–1915* (Brussels: 1959).

Delehaye H., s.j., "Heribert Rosweyde, s.j., *Leven vande heylighe Maghet ende Moeder Godts Maria* (1629)", in Begheyn et al. (eds.), *Jesuit Books in the Low Countries, 1540–1773: A Selection from the Maurits Sabbe Library* (Leuven: 2009) 70–71.

Fowler C.O., *Drawing and the Senses: An Early Modern History*, Harvey Miller Studies in Baroque Art (Turnhout: 2016).

Fowler C.O., "Abraham Bloemaert and Caritas: A Lesson in Perception", in Melion W.S. – Ramakers B. (eds.), *Personification: Embodying Meaning and Emotion*, Intersections 41 (Leiden – Boston: 2016) 545–571.

Fatouros G., "Rosweyde, Heribert, s.j.", in *Biographisch-Bibliographisches Kirchenlexikon*, ed. F.W. Bautz et al., 44 vols. (Hamm: 1970–1979) 15: cols. 1213–1214.

Filipczak Z.Z., *Picturing Art in Antwerp, 1550–1700* (Princeton: 1987) 47–72.

Godding R., "L'oeuvre hagiographique d'Héribert Rosweyde", in Godding – Joassart B. – Lequeux X. – De Vriendt F. (eds.), *De Rosweyde aux Acta Sanctorum: La recherche hagiographique des Bollandistes à travers quatre siècles* (Brussels: 2009) 35–62.

Gorcum Jan van s.j., *Het leven der HH. Eremyten ende Eremytinnen, beschreven door verscheyden Autheuren* [...] (Antwerp, Hieronymus Verdussen: 1619).

Heinsius D., *Aristoteles De poetica liber* [...] *Accedit Daniel Heinsius "De tragoedia[e] constitutione"*, ed. W.A. Koch (Hildesheim: 1976).

Held J.S., "*Artis pictoriae amator*: An Antwerp Art Patron and his Collection", in idem, *Rubens and his Circle: Studies by Julius S. Held*, ed. A.W. Lowenthal – D. Rosand – J. Walsh, Jr. (Princeton: 1982) 35–64.

Helmus L.M., *The Bloemaert Effect: Colour and Composition in the Golden Age*, exh. cat., Centraal Museum, Utrecht; Staatliches Museum, Schwerin (Petersberg: 2011).

Imorde J., "'Gustus Mysticus': Zur Geschichte und Metaphorik geistlicher Empfindsamkeit", in Steiger J.A. (eds.), *Passion, Affekt und Leidenschaft in der frühen Neuzeit*, 2 vols. (Wiesbaden: 2005) 2:1105–1133.

Jong T.T. de., *Bote en Schelte, Boëtius en Schelte van Bolswert naar Antwerpen: Gouden eeuwgravures naar Blemaert, Rubens en Van Dyck*, exh. cat., Museum Titus Brandsma, Bolsward (Bolsward: 2013).

Judson J.R. – Van de Velde C., *Corpus Rubenianum XXI: Book Illustrations and Title-Pages*, 2 vols. (London – Philadelphia: 1978).

Konst J.W.H., "'Medoogen en schrick uit te wercken': Der emotionale Effect von Vondels *Jeptha* (1659)", in Steiger J.A. (eds.), *Passion, Affekt und Leidenschaft in der frühen Neuzeit*, 2 vols. (Wiesbaden: 2005) 2:803–815.

Vita Christi Domini Salvatoris nostri a A.R.P. Ludolpho Saxone Cartusiano, ed. Johannes Dadraeus (Venice, Apud Guerraeos Fratres et Franciscum Zilettum, 1581).

Ludolph of Saxony, The Life of Jesus Christ, Part One, Volume 1, Chapters 1–40, trans. – introd. M.T. Walsh (Colegeville: 2018).

Machielsen J., "Heretical Saints and Textual Discernment: The Polemical Origins of the *Acta Sanctorum* (1643–1940)", in Copeland C. – Machielsen (eds.), *Angels of Light? Sanctity and the Discernment of Spirits in the Early Modern Period* (Leiden – Boston: 2012) 103–141.

Mander Karel van, *Den Grondt der Edel vry Schilder-const: Waer in haer ghestalt, aerdt ende wesen, de leer-lustighe Jeught in verscheyden Deelen in Rijm-dicht wort voor ghedraghen*, in idem, *Het Schilder-Boeck* (Haarlem, Paschier van Wesbusch: 1604).

Mander Karel van, *Het Schilder-Boeck* (Haarlem, Paschier van Wesbusch: 1604).

Mander Karel van – Schuere Jacques van der et al., *Den nederduytschen Helicon, eygentlijck wesende der maet-dicht beminders lust-tooneel (1610)* (Alkmaar – Haarlem, Paschier van Wesbusch: 1610).

Marquaille L., *La peinture hollandaise et la foi catholique au XVIIe siècle* (Rennes: 2019).

Marquaille L. (ed.), *New Perspectives on Abraham Bloemaert and his Workshop* (Turnhout: 2022).

Melion W.S., "Pictorial Artifice and Catholic Devotion in Abraham Bloemaert's *Virgin of Sorrows with the Holy Face* of c. 1615," in Kessler H. – Wolf G. (eds.), *The Holy Face and the Paradox of Representation* (Bologna: 1998) 319–340.

Melion W.S., *The Meditative Art: Studies in the Northern Devotional Print, 1550–1625*, Early Modern Catholicism and the Visual Arts 1 (Philadelphia: 2010).

Melion W.S., "'Niet te verladen': The Manner and Meaning of Abraham Bloemaert and Boëtius à Bolswert's *Sylva anachoretica* of 1619", in Marquaille L. (ed.), *New Perspectives on Abraham Bloemaert and his Workshop* (Turnhout: 2022) 89–142.

Melion W.S., *Karel van Mander and his* Foundation of the Noble, Free Art of Painting: *First English Translation, with Introduction and Commentary* (Leiden – Boston: 2023).

Meter J.H., *The Literary Theories of Daniel Heinsius: A Study of the Development and Background of his Views on Literary Theory and Criticism during the Period from 1602–1612* (Assen: 1984).

Miedema H., *Karel van Mander, Den grondt der edel vry schilder-const, uitgegeven en van vertaling en commentaar voorzien*, 2 vols. (Utrecht: 1973).

Miedema H. (ed.), *Karel van Mander, The Lives of the Illustrious Netherlandish and German Painters*, trans. D. Cook-Radmore, 6 vols. (Doornspijk: Davaco, 1999).

Peeters P., *L'oeuvre des Bollandistes* (Brussels: 1961).

Risius, Joannes, S.J., *Sylva anachoretica Aegypti et Palaestinae. Figuris aeneis et brevibus vitarum elogiis expressa. Abahamo Blommaert inventor. Boetio a Bolswert sculptore* (Antwerp, Ex typographia Henrici Aertssij, sumptibus auctoris: 1619).

Roethlisberger M., *Abraham Bloemaert and his Sons: Paintings and Prints*, 2 vols. (Doornspijk: Davaco, 1993).

Roethlisberger M. – Metzler S., *Abraham Bloemaert and his Time*, exh. cat., Museum of Fine Arts, St. Petersburg, FL (St. Peterburg: 2001).

Rossi Angelo Maria de, *Leben, Wandel und Todt des Grossen Wunderthätigen Diener Gottes Laurentii von Brundusio, Weiland gewesten Ministri Generalis des Gesammten Capuc. Ordens* [...] (Augsburg – Innsbruck, Joseph Wolff: 1751).

Rosweyde Heribert, S.J., *Fasti sanctorum quorum vitae in belgicis bibliothecis manuscriptae. Item Acta praesidalia SS. martyrum Tharaci, Probi, et Andronici* (Antwerp, Ex officina Plantiniana, apud Ioannem Moretum: 1607).

Rosweyde Heribert, S.J., *Vitae Patrum. De vita et verbis Seniorum libri X. historiam eremiticam complectentes* (Antwerp, Ex officina Plantiniana, apud viduam et filios Ioannis Moreti: 1615).

Rosweyde Heribert, S.J., *Vitae Patrum. De vita et verbis Seniorum libri X. historiam eremiticam complectentes* (Antwerp, Ex officina Plantiniana: 1615).

Rosweyde Heribert, S.J., *'t Vaders boeck. 't Leven ende spreucken der Vaderen* (Antwerp, Hieronymus Verdussen: 1617).

Seelig G., *Abraham Bloemaert (1566–1651): Studien zur Utrechter Malerei um 1620* (Berlin: Gebr. Mann, 1997).

Societatis Jesu in Neerlandia historiae compendium, ab anno 1592, quo primum missio nostra Hollandica sanctissim. Domino nostro Clemente VIII instituta est, usque ad haec nostra tempora ('s-Hertogenbosch: 1860).

Surius Laurentius, *Vitae sanctorum patrum ordinis praedicatorum* (Leuven, Apud H. Wellaeum: 1575).

Wisse J., *Ethos and Pathos from Aristotle to Cicero* (Amsterdam: 1989).

CHAPTER 13

Spiritual Joy in the Face of Death: Compound Emotions in Texts and Images of the Martyrs of the Japan Mission

Raphaèle Preisinger

Abstract

The 'eager martyrdom' of the victims of the early modern persecution of Christians in Japan became a recurring topos of reports recounting their last moments. As news of their martyrdom spread, the 26 Christians crucified in Nagasaki in 1597 during the first great Christian martyrdom in Japan became widely known. Pictorial renderings of these martyrs, who were beatified in 1627, direct attention to their emotional states by adopting visual strategies predicated on the perception of the mystical experiences of Francis, Ignatius and Francis Xavier, the respective founders and first saints of the Franciscan order and the Society of Jesus.

Keywords

illuminatio – alumbrado – converso – exemplarity – illuminative contemplation – Nagasaki – red martyrdom – white martyrdom

In his book on Christian martyrdom in the Roman Empire, Glen Warren Bowersock describes how martyrs would erupt into displays of radiant joy, smiling and even laughing as they awaited imminent death. This eagerness for martyrdom, which is reported in countless narratives of Roman persecution of the early Church, was so widespread that Church leaders such as Cyprian of Carthage were prompted publicly and repeatedly to condemn voluntary martyrdom. Yet Tertullian argued that a Christian should strive for suffering and that peace comes through struggling and dying for an honourable cause: in defeat lies victory.[1]

---

1 Bowersock G.W., *Martyrdom and Rome* (Cambridge – New York – Melbourne: 1995) 59–64.

© RAPHAÈLE PREISINGER, 2025 | DOI:10.1163/9789004694613_014
This is an open access chapter distributed under the terms of the CC BY 4.0 license.

EMOTIONS IN TEXTS & IMAGES OF THE MARTYRS OF THE JAPAN MISSION 503

The motif of Christian martyrs' spiritual joy in the face of death would travel through time and space to reemerge more than one millennium later in written reports and printed publications recounting the violent deaths of the victims of the early modern persecution of Christians in Japan. Christian efforts to spread the faith on the archipelago of Japan started when the Jesuit Francis Xavier reached the shores of Kagoshima on August 15, 1549. The missionary enterprise in Japan would henceforth produce thousands of martyrs, and the 'eager martyrdom' of Christians who fell victim to persecution by the Japanese authorities became a recurring topos of reports recounting their last moments.[2]

In his *Historia de las islas del archipiélago filipino y reinos de la Gran China, Tartaria, Cochinchina, Malaca, Siam, Cambodge y Japón*, printed in Barcelona in 1601, the Franciscan Marcelo de Ribadeneira narrates the events leading up to the crucifixion of 26 Christians who fell victim to the first great execution of Christians in Japan. Even though these individuals weren't the first Christians killed for their faith there, the 26 put to death in 1597 would be beatified in 1627 and remain the only blesseds among the victims of the Japanese persecution of Christians until the 19th century.[3] The Japanese ruler Toyotomi Hideyoshi had sentenced a group of Christians to death by crucifixion at Nagasaki for the crimes of violating the law of the realm and disturbing the public peace. On February 5, 1597, these 26, among whom were six Franciscan missionaries and 17 of their Japanese acolytes, as well as three Japanese Jesuit lay brothers, were crucified in Japanese fashion at Nagasaki.

Ribadeneira's description of the ostentation of the martyrs on chariots for public humiliation in Miaco (Kyoto) stresses the spiritual joy discernible in the physiognomy of their leading figure, Fr. Pedro Bautista, and his display of triumphant gratification in view of death. The Franciscan *comisario*, who was positioned in the first of the train of chariots, is said to have faced backwards toward his disciples to comfort them by making a show of his rapturous attitude.[4] After the long forced journey from Miaco to Nagasaki to reach the site of execution, the condemned were notified of their approaching death. This news is said to have in no way troubled them, as their wish to die for Christ

---

2 For a listing of the known victims classified by martyrdom, see Ruiz-de-Medina J., *El martirologio del Japón, 1558–1873* (Rome: 1999).

3 According to Ruiz-de-Medina, *El martirologio del Japón* 275–785, the first martyrdom of Christians in Japan occurred in 1558. Many more took place before the 1597 crucifixion in Nagasaki, but these events never included as large a group of victims as in 1597.

4 Ribadeneira Marcelo de, *Historia de las islas del archipiélago filipino y reinos de la Gran China, Tartaria, Cochinchina, Malaca, Siam, Cambodge y Japón*, ed. J.R. de Legísima (Madrid: 1947), chapter VI 448–449.

was greater than the natural aversion to death: 'no recibieron turbación alguna, porque el deseo que traían de morir por Cristo sobrepujaba al aborrecimiento natural que el hombre tiene a la muerte' (they did not at all feel confounded, because their desire to die for Christ surpassed the natural revulsion of man towards death).[5] Needless to say, this last formulation, though expressive of faith triumphant over fear, still speaks of an emotional state of rather mixed emotions.

In this essay I analyse the iconography of these 26 martyrs which developed in Europe in relation to the rendering of 'mixed emotions' by contextualising the pictorial formulations developed by both the Franciscan and the Jesuit order within the textual and visual traditions to which they adhere and which enframe them. Taken as a whole, the iconography of the martyrs developed by both orders evolved separately. Careful examination of the pictorial schemes devised by the Franciscans and Jesuits reveals that, with respect to the rendering of the martyrs' emotional states, compositions were strongly influenced by the perception of their founders' mystical experiences. While neither St. Francis, St. Ignatius of Loyola nor St. Francis Xavier experienced physical martyrdom, St. Francis's reception of the stigmata on mount La Verna came to be perceived as an experience of spiritual martyrdom, and St. Francis Xavier, who became known for his heart ignited by divine love, came to be perceived as the prototype of the Jesuits who died on mission abroad.

1   St. Francis as a Model of 'Mixed Emotions'

The earliest datable extant depiction of the martyrdom of 1597 is to be found in the German translation of the earliest printed report on the subject, authored by the governor of Luzon Francisco Tello de Guzmán. Originally published in Seville and Granada in 1598, the brochure was widely diffused by the Franciscans and immediately translated from Spanish into many European languages. The German translation of Guzmán's report was published in Munich in 1599 in two different versions, one containing woodcuts and the other engravings identical in their iconography, to which an image of St. Francis receiving the stigmata was added.[6] On the title page, this publication refers explicitly to the

---

5   Ribadeneira, *Historia de las islas*, chapter XVIII 475. Translations are mine unless otherwise indicated.

6   Guzmán Francisco Tello de, *Relation, Auß befelch Herrn Francisci Teglij Gubernators, vnd general Obristens der Philippinischen Inseln* [...] (Munich, Adam Berg: 1599). On this brochure, see Omata Rappo H., *Des Indes lointaines aux scènes des collèges. Les reflets des martyrs de*

'six spiritual brothers from the Spanish Empire belonging to the Observant branch of the Franciscan Order', while mentioning the other victims only in passing: 'together with 20 Japanese recently converted by them'.[7] Throughout the brochure, there is no explicit mention of the three victims affiliated with the Society of Jesus among the 'Japanese', whom the Jesuits would slowly, but not without hesitation, come to accept as martyrs from their own ranks.[8]

Two narrative scenes refer to the events surrounding the martyrs' death in each of the brochure's German versions. The first shows the six Franciscan brothers being hauled to their execution by horses on a flat chariot, with their hands tied. In this version of the account, they lie close to the ground, while the Japanese soldiers triumphantly hold up a panel with the martyrs' death sentence [Fig. 13.1].[9] The second is intriguing because of the effort expended visually to approximate the martyrs' crucifixion to that of Christ [Fig. 13.2]. The analogy to images of Christ crucified amidst two thieves is evident at first glance. Visual convergence is primarily achieved by showing only three bodies lifted high on the cross instead of six or even more. Moreover, the way in which the bodies are shown turning toward or away from each other and the way the blood pours from the side wound of the central martyr follow European pictorial conventions for representing the Crucifixion of Christ. Surprisingly, only two of the three bodies tied to three crosses are tonsured and can thus be identified as Franciscans. Indeed, as the lower part of the scene includes the four other brothers mentioned in the text, who are being freed of their bonds upon arrival at the site, the martyr on the right must be one of the Japanese converted by them. Just like the Franciscan missionaries beneath the cross, the crowd of captives seen standing next to them – the rest of the condemned – is about to share the fate of those already crucified. The question of why the artist chose to leave the cross at right to one of the Franciscans' followers is quickly answered. In an image so clearly modelled

---

la mission japonaise en Europe (*XVIᵉ–XVIIIᵉ siècle*) (Münster: 2020) 259, 263–268. The two versions differ only with respect to their images; the more complete version can be found in the Bayerische Staatbibliothek in Munich under the call number Res/4 H.eccl. 870,49, while the other has the call number Res/4 H.eccl. 873,30 in the same library. Because of the close resemblance of the prints in both versions, they will be referred to jointly, and differences only pointed out where relevant.

7 Guzmán, *Relation*, title page: 'sechs geistliche Brüder auß Hispania / deß Ordens S. Francisci von der Obervanß / sambt andern 20. newlich von inen bekehrten Japonesern'.

8 On the Jesuits' initial reticence to recognise 'their' three martyrs among the twenty-six, see Omata Rappo, *Des Indes lointaines aux scènes des collèges* 117–122.

9 Omata Rappo, *Des Indes lointaines aux scènes des collèges* 330–332, convincingly argues that the motif of the flat chariot to which the Franciscan missionaries are attached cites depictions of the Catholics martyred in England at that time.

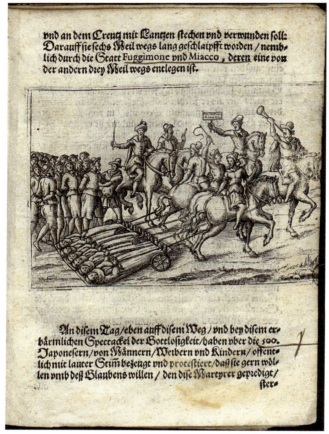

FIGURE 13.1 The 26 Japan Martyrs of 1597 on the Way to their Crucifixion, 1599, engraving. From: Guzmán Francisco Tello de, *Relation, Auß befelch Herrn Francisci Teglij Gubernators, vnd general Obristens der Philippinischen Inseln* [...] (Munich, Adam Berg: 1599), fol. A iv r. Munich, Bayerische Staatsbibliothek Res/4 H.eccl. 870,49, 10. CC BY-NC-SA 4.0, https://creativecommons.org/licenses/by-nc-sa/4.0/

on Christ's Crucifixion, whoever was depicted on the right-hand cross – the one reserved for the so-called bad thief – would carry at least slightly negative connotations, thus making it necessary to avoid showing any Franciscan in this position.[10]

10   The figure depicted at a smaller scale to the right of the central cross is somewhat puzzling. It is included in both versions of Guzmán's *Relation*, but looks quite different in each. The figure in Res/4 H.eccl. 873,30 may perhaps be identified as a Jesuit observing the

FIGURE 13.2   The Crucifixion of 1597 in Nagasaki, 1599, engraving.
From: Guzmán Francisco Tello de, *Relation, Auß befelch Herrn Francisci Teglij Gubernators, vnd general Obristens der Philippinischen Inseln* [...] (Munich, Adam Berg: 1599), fol. B ii r. Munich, Bayerische Staatsbibliothek Res/4 H.eccl. 870,49, 14.
CC BY-NC-SA 4.0, https://creativecommons.org/licenses/by-nc-sa/4.0/

What is interesting is the information not provided by the artist who designed the image. Even though the shape of the Japanese crosses on which the twenty-six martyrs died, which included a lateral plank at foot level, is found in several contemporaneous publications, no reference is made to it here [Fig. 13.3]. Depictions of these crosses contained in the letters and reports

scene without intervening on the martyrs' behalf, an accusation leveled by the Franciscans against the Jesuits.

FIGURE 13.3   Title page of Fróis Luís, *Drey Japonische Schreiben* [...] (Mainz, Johan Albin: 1599). Munich, Bayerische Staatsbibliothek 4 Jes. 268
PHOTO COURTESY OF BAYERISCHE STAATSBIBLIOTHEK MÜNCHEN

of the missionaries who were present at this event show four planks assembled in the shape of a cross, of which a short central one holds up the dying body.[11] In his 1597 report on the crucifixions, an abridged version of which was published in several languages two years later, the Jesuit Luís Fróis describes the method of attaching the bodies to the crosses with ropes and metal clasps: The hands, feet, and the neck of the condemned were thereby fastened to the cross.

---

11   On the Japanese crosses, see Omata Rappo, *Des Indes lointaines aux scènes des collèges* 251–260.

EMOTIONS IN TEXTS & IMAGES OF THE MARTYRS OF THE JAPAN MISSION   509

Fróis also describes the method of piercing the hanging bodies with lances to bring about death: two lances intersecting through the ribcage in an x-shape were thrust into the condemned person's chest.[12] Betraying an almost scientific interest in this method of execution, the multiple sketches of the cross that accompanied the early reports show a large lateral plank placed under the martyrs' feet. Indeed, the tied-up bodies of the martyrs were attached to the cross with legs apart – a detail not seen here. Only women would have been tied to the cross with their legs joined.[13]

The image in the German translation of Tello's report clearly conforms more closely to traditional European representations of the Crucifixion of Christ than to Fróis' description of the Japanese cross. The only clear deviations from representations of Christ's Crucifixion reside in the ropes used to tie the bodies to the crosses, and in the depiction of two lances piercing the bodies on the crosses at the left and right of the picture's centre instead of one piercing only the central figure. Even though a multitude of pictorial formulations was sought, the Crucifixion of Christ would remain the paradigmatic visual matrix for representations of the crucifixion of the 26 martyrs of 1597.

The physiognomical details of the three crucified persons looking down at those gathered around them are difficult to discern. Still, their bodily stances and overall facial expressions connote a serene attitude; they certainly do not bear the pain-stricken expressions one would expect, given their wounded torsos. In the woodcut, the crucified missionaries are even seen clearly smiling. Tello's text indeed speaks of the Franciscan commissary Pedro Bautista's fearlessness and joyous eagerness to be crucified, which strengthened his companions' hearts; according to Tello, Bautista and his fellow missionaries prayed and preached the Gospel, even after they were wounded. His report also mentions how the martyrs inspired an intense wish to die for the Christian faith among the five hundred Japanese who witnessed the spectacle of their denigrating journey to the place of crucifixion.[14]

In the version of the German translation with engraved illustrations, the contextual framework for the story of the martyrs is pinpointed by the insertion of an additional printed scene on the verso of the title page, preceding the textual narrative. It shows St. Francis lovingly embracing a crucifix after

---

12   See, for instance, the German version of Fróis' report: Fróis Luís, *Drey Japponische Schreiben* [...] (Mainz, Johan Albin: 1599) 54.

13   On the Japanese method of crucifixion, see Omata Rappo, *Des Indes lointaines aux scènes des collèges* 260–263. See also the description of the 1597 crucifixion provided by Ribadeneira, in *Historia de las islas*, chapter xx 480.

14   Guzmán, *Relation*, fol. B ii v and text following the depiction of the flat chariot carrying the Franciscans on A iv r–A iv v.

FIGURE 13.4 St. Francis Lovingly Embracing a Crucifix, engraving. From: Guzmán Francisco Tello de, *Relation, Auß befelch Herrn Francisci Teglij Gubernators, vnd general Obristens der Philippinischen Inseln* […] (Munich, Adam Berg: 1599), fol. A i v. Munich, Bayerische Staatsbibliothek Res/4 H.eccl. 870,49, 5. CC BY-NC-SA 4.0, https://creativecommons.org/licenses/by-nc-sa/4.0/

having received the stigmata [Fig. 13.4]. Interestingly, it is not the event of St. Francis receiving the marks of Christ's passion that is shown here, in spite of its importance to the Franciscans, who believed that their founder had thus been singled out from among other founders and saints. Instead, the focus is on St. Francis' intense, tearful gaze at Christ crucified and thus quite explicitly on his inner emotional state. The carnal excrescences protruding from the

EMOTIONS IN TEXTS & IMAGES OF THE MARTYRS OF THE JAPAN MISSION   511

back of St. Francis' hands and the side wound from which blood still pours point to the emotions triggered by the visionary encounter with Christ 'sub specie seraph' on Mount La Verna.

In the *Legenda maior*, the official biography of St. Francis written by St. Bonaventure in the 13th century, which came to shape the perception of the saint for centuries to come, the state of simultaneous joy and distress felt by Francis upon perceiving the seraph is described as follows: 'Hoc videns, vehementer obstupuit, mixtumque moerore gaudium cor eius incurrit. Laetabatur quidem in gratioso aspectu, quo a Christo sub specie Seraph cernebat se conspici, sed crucis affixio compassivi doloris gladio ipsius animam pertransibat' (At this sight Francis was bewildered; joy and sorrow simultaneously filled his heart. The tender apparition which had Christ's gaze rest upon him, filled him with joy; the sight of his painful crucifixion, however, pierced his soul with the sword of dolorous compassion).[15] Throughout his lifetime, St. Francis had striven for martyrdom. Even though he died naked on the ground, having endured many illnesses and afflictions, he never did suffer actual, 'red' martyrdom. Instead, his fate was that of so-called 'white martyrdom'.[16] Indeed, according to St. Bonaventure, upon seeing the seraphic apparition, St. Francis understood through divine revelation that: 'se non per martyrium carnis, sed per incendium mentis totum in Christi crucifixi similitudinem transformandum' (not corporeal martyrdom, but the blaze of his spirit must transform him, the friend of Christ, into the image of Christ crucified).[17]

St. Francis' eagerness for martyrdom thus led to an intense spiritual experience, not to corporeal martyrdom. As they suffered real, 'red' martyrdom, the Japan martyrs could potentially have been perceived as surpassing St. Francis in this regard. It is to counter any such view that the image of St. Francis contemplating the cross was inserted in the brochure: the readers were reminded that it is 'inner' transformation that leads to salvation. The 1599 Italian edition of Tello's report makes a similar point by inserting a depiction of Francis'

---

15   Bonaventure (Di Fidanza Giovanni), *Legenda maior sancti Francisci*, in *Fontes franciscani*, ed. E. Menestò – S. Brufani (Assisi: 1995) 775–961, chapter XIII 891.

16   The juxtaposition of the terms 'red martyrdom' and 'white martyrdom' originates in the works of early Christian writers such as Jerome, Cyprian, and Augustine. Hoel succinctly describes these terms as follows: 'Red martyrdom in the medieval thought world was physical death on behalf of God, while white martyrdom was asceticism. As a result, the emphasis in describing white martyrdom, as opposed to red, is placed not so much on the individual martyr, but on the process of martyrdom'. See Hoel N.O., "Hues of Martyrdom: Monastic and Lay Asceticism in Two Homilies of Gregory the Great on the Gospels", *The Downside Review* 138.1 (2020) 3–18, 11.

17   Bonaventure, *Legenda maior sancti Francisci*, chapter XIII 892.

stigmatisation at the end of the text.[18] By alluding to the martyrs' outbursts of joy in the face of death, written reports of their execution underlined precisely this: the condemned had reached the state of detachment from the world considered necessary to conform with Christ. The many manuals of contemplation that assisted readers to assimilate themselves to Christ, from St. Bonaventure's *Lignum vitae* to St. Ignatius's *Spiritual Exercises*, all emphasised that true conformity was to be achieved first and foremost through compassion, or, to quote the Epistle to the Galatians, by spiritually 'dying with Christ on the cross' (Gal. 2:19). The engraving showing the three crucified martyrs of Japan in Tello's report showcases the detachment from the world the three martyrs have achieved by depicting them with serene facial expressions.

The idea of approximating the martyrs of 1597 to representations of the Crucifixion of Christ between the two thieves would continue to inform visual schemes as the iconography of the Nagasaki martyrdom evolved. A tripartite structure governs the composition of the etching by Jacques Callot, most probably executed shortly after the Japan martyrs were beatified [Fig. 13.5].[19] In this print, only the six Franciscan missionaries, hardly discernible among the martyrs, and their seventeen Asian acolytes are shown.[20] No special status is awarded to the six missionaries among the victims, for all are shown haloed. Some of the martyrs look up to Christ who descends from heaven, their hands turned upward in anticipation of salvation, while others are shown with their heads hanging down, either dead or in a state of transition between life and death.

However, the threefold structure of the Callot print is exceptional among explicitly Franciscan images. There were 23 followers of St. Francis among those crucified in 1597, which made adherence to compositions showing the Crucifixion of Christ difficult. The Jesuits, in turn, who contributed only three martyrs, could fully exploit the rhetorical power residing in the number of victims from their ranks. Indeed, owing to the strong tensions between the Franciscans and the Jesuits regarding the Japan mission, the iconography of the 26 martyrs would for the most part evolve separately for each order:

---

18   Guzmán Francisco Tello de, *Relazione mandata da don Francesco Teglio gouernatore e Capitano Generale dell'Isole Filippine* [...] (Florence, Giacomo Carlino & António Pace: 1599).

19   See Rijksmuseum, Amsterdam, object number RP-P-1925-15 at http://hdl.handle.net/10934 /RM0001.COLLECT.400108 (accessed 30.10.2023); Koshi K., "Die 26 Märtyrer von Japan in der Kunst: ein Werkkatalog", *Bulletin annuel du musée national d'art occidental* 8 (1974) 16–72, 34–35 (Nr. 3).

20   The missionaries, identifiable thanks to their habits, occupy the first three rows at left, the central position, and the first two rows at right.

FIGURE 13.5　　Jacques Callot, The Crucifixion of the 23 Franciscan Martyrs of 1597 in Japan, 1627 or later, etching, 11,4 × 16,8 cm, Amsterdam, Rijksmuseum, object number RP-P-1925-15. CC0 1.0, https://creativecommons.org/publicdomain/zero/1.0/deed.en

pictures of the martyrs crucified at Nagasaki in 1597 tended to portray either the Franciscan *or* the Jesuit victims, rather than showing them together.[21]

The tendency to separate the Franciscan and the Jesuit martyrs seems at least partially linked to their beatification in 1627, as the cardinals in Rome decided to separate the rights of veneration accorded to the two groups of martyrs. Henceforth, each order should venerate only its own martyrs. The beatification of the martyrs was correspondingly declared in two distinct briefs on two consecutive days.[22] Before the 1627 beatification, Franciscans favoured two pictorial approaches. In one, they showed the twenty-six as a group, while omitting to mark the presence of Jesuits among them, a strategy observable in the text and images of the German translation of Tello's report, which, in a general way, corresponds with the Franciscan reports on the Nagasaki martyrdom written immediately after the events. In the other approach, they depicted only the 23 Franciscan martyrs, extracting them from the larger group of twenty-six.[23] In some cases, certain groups of martyrs, such as the missionaries among them, were singled out pictorially.[24] The Jesuits, in turn, only started truly capitalising on their martyrs after their beatification in 1627.

An almost entirely unknown painting located in the church of Santa Maria della Croce in Francavilla Fontana in Puglia is fascinating for combining the iconography of the twenty-three Franciscan martyrs with the utterances of Christ on the cross [Fig. 13.6].[25] It shows the six Franciscan missionaries prominently displayed in the foremost picture plane, and the seventeen Japanese martyrs associated with the same order depicted at a very small scale in the

---

21   On the history of Christian mission in Japan, see the fundamental studies Boxer C.R., *The Christian Century in Japan 1549–1650* (Berkeley: 1951); Fujita N.S., *Japan's encounter with Christianity. The Catholic Mission in pre-modern Japan* (New York: 1991); Hesselink R.H., *The Dream of Christian Nagasaki. World Trade and the Clash of Cultures, 1560–1640* (Jefferson: 2016); and Vu Thanh H., *Devenir japonais. La mission jésuite au Japon (1549–1614)* (Paris: 2016).

22   On the beatification of the martyrs, see Omata Rappo, *Des Indes lointaines aux scènes des collèges* 160–161.

23   On the Franciscans' overall silence in their early reports as regards the presence of Jesuit martyrs among their own, see ibidem 118–119. A picture showing only the 23 Franciscan martyrs is known to have been displayed in the Roman church of Santa Maria in Aracoeli after the positive decision taken by the Rota regarding these martyrs in 1625. See ibidem, 157, 353–354.

24   For instance, Ribadeneira reports that the Franciscan Minister General Francisco de Sosa had a print made showing an emblem invented by him of the six Franciscan missionaries among the victims of the 1597 crucifixion. See Ribadeneira, *Historia de las islas* 11–12.

25   On this painting, see Galante L., "Aspetti dell'iconografia sacra dopo il concilio di Trento nell'area Pugliese", in Pellegrino B. – Gaudioso F. (eds.), *Ordini religiosi e società nel mezzogiorno moderno*, Volume II (Lecce: 1987) 515–534, 525–526.

FIGURE 13.6   The Crucifixion of the 23 Franciscan Martyrs of 1597 in Japan, 1627, oil on canvas, ca. 220 × 350 cm, Francavilla Fontana, Santa Maria della Croce, Fototeca SABAP-BA n. inv. 205091 cat.D. Su autorizzazione della Soprintendenza Archeologia, Belle Arti e Paesaggio per la città metropolitana di Bari – MiC

background. The inscription at the bottom of the painting reports two dates, that of the actual martyrdom and the date their martyrdom was declared. This occurred on July 10, 1627, preceding the beatification of these martyrs by about two months.[26] Such an indication makes it possible to date the image very precisely, as it must have been created in the interval between their declaration as martyrs and their beatification, which is not mentioned.

The names of the Franciscan missionaries are inscribed on their haloes, making it possible to identify them. The Franciscan commissary Pedro Bautista is depicted centrally in the uppermost part of the painting, gazing to heaven as he commends his spirit to God, uttering Christ's words: 'IN MANUS TUAS DOMINE'. This is an unequivocal allusion to the last words spoken by Christ just before dying (Luke 23:46): 'Pater in manus tuas commendo spiritum meum'.[27] The martyr depicted next to him on the right is seen repeating the same words ('IN MANUS TUAS'), his eyes already shut, while the Franciscan missionary on the upper left of the painting utters the words 'IESUS IESUS IESUS' with an air of great despair. Overall, the martyrs in the lower part of the composition appear more vital than those depicted above; they look up to heaven in great agony. The first from the left repeats Christ's words asking his father to forgive his malefactors (Luke 23:34), as known from the Church fathers, such as St. Augustine: 'DOMINE IGNOSCE ILLIS QUIA NESC[...]'.[28] The lower centrally depicted martyr pronounces the words: 'GLORIA PATRI E FILIO', which mark the beginning of a Trinitarian avowal,[29] while an executioner sticks a finger in his side wound, underlining the parallels to the Crucifixion of Christ. To the right, the last of the six Franciscan missionaries utters the words 'MEMENTO MEI DOMINE' (taken from Neh 6:14: 'memento Domine mei pro Tobia et Sanaballat [...]', but altering them to refer to the speaker himself). This is a rather unique example of how the *Christiformitas* of the Franciscan martyrs could be quite blatantly stated, but it appears not to have met with much approval, as there are no other depictions of this kind known.

After the 23 crucified martyrs affiliated with the Franciscan order had been beatified, Franciscan pictorial schemes generally opted to show only these twenty-three, distributed evenly across the surface of an image. The Franciscan

---

26   See Omata Rappo, *Des Indes lointaines* 161.

27   Unless indicated otherwise, the Latin Bible citations are taken from the Vulgate.

28   See Augustine, Sermo XLIV, De verbis Isaiae, chapter LIII v. 2–9 at www.monumenta
      .ch/latein/text.php?tabelle=Augustinus&rumpfid=Augustinus, Sermones, 10,%20%20 44
      &level=4&domain=&lang=0&links=&inframe=1&hide_apparatus=1 (accessed 15.08.2023):
      'Pater, ignosce illis, quia nesciunt quid faciunt'.

29   Eham M., "*Gloria patri*", in Kasper W. (ed.), *Lexikon für Theologie und Kirche, 3rd edition,
      volume 4* (Freiburg im Breisgau: 1995) 752–753.

EMOTIONS IN TEXTS & IMAGES OF THE MARTYRS OF THE JAPAN MISSION 517

FIGURE 13.7   Raphaël Sadeler II, *The Crucifixion of the 23 Franciscan Martyrs of 1597 in Japan*, 1627–1632, engraving, 39 × 48,9 cm, Amsterdam, Rijksmuseum, object number RP-P-1926-631. CC0 1.0, https://creativecommons.org/publicdomain/zero/1.0/deed.en

martyrs' sheer number made visual conflation with the Crucifixion of Christ between the two thieves difficult if not impossible. Instead, the Franciscans resorted to exploiting fully the rhetorical power that resided in showing the multitude of victims from their ranks, as seen in horizontal compositions such as the 1627–1632 engraving by Raphaël Sadeler (II) in the Rijksmuseum [Fig. 13.7].[30] As in Callot's etching, a range of emotions is expressed. The martyrs oscillate between steadfast calmness, or even joy, as seen in the smiling face of the Franciscan commissary Pedro Bautista, shown with downcast eyes, his right hand blessing his followers – and agony, as some are depicted writhing in pain, about to die.

---

30   See Rijksmuseum, Amsterdam, object number RP-P-1926-631 at http://hdl.handle.net/10934/RM0001.COLLECT.169168 (accessed 04.01.2023).

Although reports on the event narrate that the martyrs were forced to strip off their habits when they were crucified,[31] in the iconographical schemes, affiliation with the martyrs' respective order was generally expressed by the means of the figures' habits. Their garb made the victims recognisable and distinguishable from victims of persecution that came from other religious orders. But apart from the habits, the shape of the crosses and other visual particularities of the execution were altered to exemplify the idea of *Christiformitas*, in spite of what was known about the specific circumstances of the mass crucifixion.

2 Conforming to the Society's Founders and First Saints

The Jesuit iconography of the martyrs evolved quite differently from the Franciscan schemes. Whereas the Franciscans supported the cause of the 1597 martyrs from the very beginning, the Jesuits at first expressed doubts about the affiliation of the three further victims with the Society of Jesus and even about the status of their deaths as martyrdoms. Overall, it took the Jesuits some time to recognise them as martyr candidates for beatification from their own ranks and to support their cause in Rome.[32]

Initially, the Jesuits incorporated images of their three martyrs into larger compositions showcasing an array of martyrs. The earliest depictions of the Jesuit Japan martyrs appeared in 1608. An engraving in Bartolomeo Ricci's *Triumphus Jesu Christi crucifixi*, a compilation volume published in Antwerp as part of the campaign for the beatification of Ignatius of Loyola, shows the three Jesuit martyrs as part of the larger group of 26 martyrs, composed of Jesuits and Franciscans alike [Fig. 13.8].[33] This depiction of the 26 martyrs of 1597 is embedded in the larger context of a pictorial enumeration of 70 crucified martyrs. The figure of a Jesuit priest speaking to those Jesuits about to be affixed to their crosses corresponds to written reports on the martyrs' death. Here, this motif has the function of showcasing the Society's involvement in a positive light and of testifying to the veracity of the events depicted. The martyrs on the ground seem grateful, almost cheerful, to be allowed to die after having talked to a priest. Even the child among them rushes to his cross, while the ones already on their crosses patiently await their execution.

---

31   Ribadeneira, *Historia de las islas*, chapter XX 480.

32   Omata Rappo, *Des Indes lointaines aux scènes des collèges* 117–131.

33   Ricci Bartolomeo, *Triumphus Jesu Christi crucifixi* (Antwerp, Joannes Moretus: 1608) 4r. On this image of the 26 Japan martyrs, see Omata Rappo, *Des Indes lointaines aux scènes des collèges* 272–275.

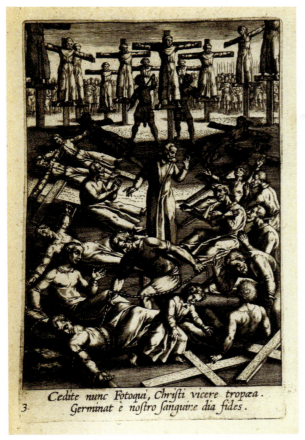

FIGURE 13.8   The Martyrs of 1597 Preparing for Crucifixion, 1608, engraving. From: Ricci Bartolomeo, *Triumphus Jesu Christi crucifixi* (Antwerp, Joannes Moretus: 1608), fol. B iv r, Vienna, Österreichische Nationalbibliothek. Public domain: http://rightsstatements.org/vocab/NoC-NC/1.0/

Another depiction of the three Jesuit victims of the Nagasaki crucifixion can be found in an engraving published by Matthäus Greuter and Paul Maupin in Rome in 1608. According to the title, *Effigies et nomina quorundam è societate Jesu qui pro fide vel pietate sunt interfecti ab 1549 ad 1607*, it portrays members of the Jesuit order martyred during these years. The three victims of Japanese persecution can be seen in the lowest row of the central plate [Fig. 13.9]. Martyrological portrait series such as this print started to appear shortly after the publication of Giovanni Camerota's *Centuria prima*, the first, German,

FIGURE 13.9 Matthäus Greuter and Paul Maupin, *Effigies et nomina quorundam è societate Jesu qui pro fide vel pietate sunt interfecti* [...], 1608, engraving, 182,5 × 50 cm, middle section of the print, Paris, Bibliothèque nationale de France, BnF ms. Français 15782, fol. 423r

edition of which was published in Munich in 1605. This history of the first hundred martyrs of the Society of Jesus also inspired several now lost martyrological cycles that very likely included the Society's three Japan martyrs, such as the 102 Jesuit martyr portraits commissioned by Pedro de Ribadeneyra for the Jesuit College of Madrid.[34] The now-lost series, perhaps dating to 1606, displayed in the novitiate complex of Sant'Andrea al Quirinale in Rome and described in Louis Richeome's treatise *La peinture spirituelle* of 1611, is known to have included the Jesuit martyrs of 1597.[35]

These martyrological portrait series have been interpreted as the Society's attempt to capitalise on their martyrs before their first saints were officially canonised. They associate the martyrs with notions of Christian exemplarity and apostolic succession.[36] The three Japan martyrs in the Greuter/Maupin print are shown at the moment of execution. This makes them stand out among the martyrs, as most of the others, though also shown with their instruments of death, adhere much more closely to the conventions of portraiture. The latter are depicted in an upright position, as if engaged in dialogue with the beholder, to whom they explain the circumstances of their deaths. The decision to proceed differently with the Japan martyrs by focusing on their last moments betrays an interest in the precise way they were executed. Additionally, it attests to the Jesuits' realisation of the argumentative power residing in the existence of crucified martyrs among the members of the Society.

Showing the martyrdom as it took place required a different depiction of emotional states than representing persons actively explaining how their martyrdom occurred. The Greuter/Maupin engraving shows a range of emotions in the depiction of the three Nagasaki martyrs, as Iacobus Kisai (also known as Diogo Kisai) is portrayed in a state of thoughtful, though steadfast, resistance; Paul Miki is seen holding the martyr's palm brought to him by an angel, in hopeful anticipation of the glories to come; and João Goto is depicted as already dead.[37] Although in this early Jesuit depiction there is not much

---

34 See Harpster G., "Illustrious Jesuits: The Martyrological Portrait Series circa 1600", *Journal of Jesuit Studies* 9 (2022) 379–397, 381–382.

35 Richeome Louis, *La peinture spirituelle ou l'art d'admirer, aimer et louer Dieu en toutes ses oeuvres, et tirer de toutes profit salutere* (Lyon, Pierre Rigaud: 1611), livre III, tableau VII, section III 135 (should be 235).

36 Harpster, Illustrious Jesuits, *passim*.

37 The conspicuous 'erasure' of any allusion to the Japanese parentage of the martyrs crucified in Nagasaki in 1597 in this print, as also in most of the other European depictions that soon followed, may have something to do with the fact that no one originating from newly Christianised territories had yet been officially recognized as a saint by the post-Tridentine Church. Indeed, among the 26 Japan martyrs beatified in 1627 would be the first individuals from territories encountered by European polities in the early

difference with the Franciscan visual strategy of showing a range of emotions, the upward gaze of the centremost martyr triumphantly holding a martyr's palm branch, Paul Miki, can be seen as announcing the direction in which Jesuit iconography would develop.

The very number of the Jesuit Japan martyrs of 1597 – three – lent itself to pictorial analogy with the Crucifixion of Christ, on the one hand. However, explicitly stressing that analogy could attract reprovals of all kinds, as it elicited questions as to the nature of the relationship between the prototypes and their followers. An elegant way of avoiding suspicion was to cast the Japan martyrs as followers of the Society's founding fathers. Once St. Ignatius and St. Francis Xavier were canonised in 1622, their paradigmatic sanctity was declared in no uncertain terms. Neither had died as martyrs, but the perception of St. Francis Xavier as the model martyr in the context of the Society's mission in Asia certainly facilitated the presentation of many portraits of Jesuit martyrs along the nave of the Church of the Gesù in Rome during the celebrations in honour of Francis Xavier and Ignatius's joint canonisation, and also in other Jesuit churches, on this festive occasion.[38]

The recognition of asceticism as a form of 'martyrdom' paved the way for the fashioning of visual analogies between the 'red' Japan martyrs and their 'white' mystical counterparts.[39] Such pictorial solutions, if they were to be successful, however, would have to recognisably refer to visual schemes already applied to St. Ignatius and St. Francis Xavier, for instance by including the glorifying connotations in their iconography of the strong downward lighting from heaven that was perceived, by its very nature, as characterising 'illuminative' contemplation.[40] The three crucified Jesuit Japan martyrs were progressively cast not only as followers of Christ, but also of the Society's founding fathers. Besides eulogising the Society's founders, this pictorial strategy also held off the danger of showing too emphatic a link between these crucified followers of Christ and Christ himself.

---

modern period to be ranked in the Roman hierarchy of the saints. Obscuring the martyrs' origins may have been thought to increase the chances for official recognition of a saintly status at some point in the future.

38   On St. Francis Xavier as the prototype of Jesuit martyrs in Asia, see Cañeque A., "In the Shadow of Francis Xavier: Martyrdom and Colonialism in the Jesuit Asian Missions", *Journal of Jesuit Studies* 9 (2022) 438–458. On the display of Jesuit martyr portraits during the canonisation celebrations for St. Ignatius of Loyola and St. Francis Xavier, see Harpster, *Illustrious Jesuits* 383.

39   See note 16 above.

40   Traditionally, the mystical path, in Christianity, is understood according to a three-step model. The first step is purgation, the second illumination and in the third, mystical union with the Divine is reached.

Other dangers, however, loomed. Despite the emergence of the Society itself from St. Ignatius' experience of interior illumination – the famous vision at *La Storta* from which the new congregation would receive its name – certain theologians criticised Ignatius' proposal of spiritual purification and discernment for its illuminist elements.[41] As charges of illuminism and quietism directed at Jesuit spirituality would need to be warded off continuously – Ignatius' spirituality had proven attractive to the *converso/alumbrado* circles of Alcalá, where he had studied in 1526–27 – the Society was constantly cautious to monitor the mystical impulses of its members.[42] To avert suspicion, the interpretation of martyrdom as illuminative contemplation would entail adhering to well-established pictorial schemes and cautiously exploring what was permissible in altering them.

A print made shortly after the martyrs' beatification introduces visual parallels with the founding fathers' mystical experiences rather subtly. The engraving by Wolfgang Kilian, *Three Beatified Martyrs of the Society of Jesus, who testified to the name of Jesus with 23 others* […], published in Augsburg in 1628, prominently places the three Jesuit martyrs at centre stage in the foremost picture plane, while the Franciscan martyrs, only summarily mentioned in the caption, are shifted to the background [Fig. 13.10].[43] The centremost martyr is distinguished by the intensity of his emotions; he writhes in agony, his gaze turned to heaven, the words 'Iesu, Maria' issuing from his mouth. These words are mentioned, in the text of the broadsheet and in several written accounts of the martyrdom, as having been uttered by the condemned before dying.[44] St. Francis Xavier allegedly cried out these same words on his deathbed, as represented, for instance, in the cycle painted by André Reinoso in the sacristy of São Roque in Lisbon in 1619 – a coincidence underlining the saint's prototypical role for martyrdom in Asia. The broadsheet's textual explanation of the scene attributes them to Paul Miki and situates his outcry in the moments immediately before the martyrs were transpierced with lances, just as shown in the engraving. Paul Miki's facial expression and bodily stance thus reveal his emotional, rather than physical

---

41 On St. Ignatius' vision at La Storta as foundational for the Society of Jesus, see Fleming A.C., "St. Ignatius of Loyola's 'Vision at La Storta' and the Foundation of the Society of Jesus", in Schraven M. – Delbeke M. (eds.), *Foundation, Dedication and Consecration in Early Modern Europe*, Intersections 22 (Leiden – Boston: 2012) 225–249.

42 On the accusations directed at Jesuit spirituality, see Maryks R.A., "Introduction", in Maryks R.A. (ed.), *A Companion to Jesuit Mysticism* (Leiden – Boston: 2017) 1–5.

43 See Bayerische Staatsbibliothek, Munich, object number Einbl. VII,24 l at https://www .digitale-sammlungen.de/de/view/bsb00064463?page=,1 (accessed 15.06.2023).

44 See, for example, Fróis Luís, *Relación del Martirio de los 26 cristianos crucificados en Nangasaqui el 5 Febrero de 1597*, ed. R. Galdos (Rome: 1935), chapter XVI 99–105 and Ribadeneira, *Historia de las islas*, chapter XX 481.

FIGURE 13.10 Wolfgang Kilian, *Drey Seelige Martyrer der Societet Jesu* [...], 1628, engraving, 14,5 × 27 cm, Munich, Bayerische Staatsbibliothek Einbl. VII,24 l
PHOTO COURTESY OF BAYERISCHE STAATSBIBLIOTHEK MÜNCHEN

state, as the lances have just barely reached his chest. His right hand and upward gaze show him engaged in a conversation with God, recalling Christ's utterance, 'My God, my God, why hast thou forsaken me?' (Matt. 27: 46), before dying. Thus, what is presented to us in the figure of Paul Miki here is not the stoicism that would characterise later depictions of these martyrs, but a rather human, yet steadfast, experience of suffering.

Kilian avoided the somewhat negative connotations ascribed to the martyr at right seen in Tello's German translation by choosing to present the bodies and crosses of the two 'outer' martyrs in a more nuanced way; however, the harsh light falling on the scene from a source located at the top right corner does cast a strong shadow on this figure, leaving this martyr in a somewhat ambiguous position. His fingers turned upwards suggest he is still alive and participates in the agony of the martyr at centre, encouraging the viewer to do the same. The other martyrs are shown either dead or in fearful awe of the lances coming to transpierce their bodies, thus underlining the cruelty of the Japanese executioners and of the population that came to observe the spectacle.

In fact, the stress laid on the martyrs' emotions in this engraving is explained by the characterisation of the audience. Typically, scenes depicting the 1597 crucifixion in Nagasaki include individuals from the local Christian population gathering under the crosses to collect relics. Here, in contrast, the crowd of mostly sitting spectators shows no signs of compassion, but seems either merely entertained (as seen in the row of people seen from behind gazing at the three Jesuit martyrs); completely disinterested (as seen in the figures engaged in conversation in the background on the right); approving of the events (as seen in the people represented sitting or standing in the back); or even displaying a sense of cruel pleasure at the spectacle of the dying martyrs (as can be observed in the smiling figure standing on the far left side). In Kilian's print, the death sentence, which usually occupies a prominent place in depictions of this martyrdom, as it explains the reason for the martyrs' execution, was altered to fit the stress laid on the audience. Instead of paraphrasing, as in Sadeler's print, the historical sentence, which revolved around the prohibition of Christianity and the martyrs' act of preaching the Christian 'law' despite it, here, reference is made to 1 Cor 1:23:

QUOD PRAEDICABANT
CHRISTUM CRUCIFIXUM
IUDAEIS, SCANDALUM
GENTIS, STULTITIAM.

Stress is thus laid on the foolishness of the 'heathens', consisting of, in turn, perceiving the Christians as fools. The emotional suffering of the Christian martyrs was emphasised in this engraving so as to invite the viewer to identify with them, marking a sharp contrast with the Japanese depicted watching the scene.

The motif of the heavenward gaze, combined with written words, as seen in the centremost martyr, is well known from images showing the 'true effigy' of St. Francis Xavier [Fig. 13.11]. This portrait type was of particular relevance in the context of post-Tridentine canonisations.[45] The words 'Satis est Domine, satis est', uttered by St. Francis Xavier in images of the true portrait-type, are mentioned in his bull of canonisation, and refer to his mystical experiences in Goa between September 1551 and mid-April 1552.[46] By adding a *titulus* to the upward gaze of the centrally depicted Jesuit Japan martyr, the Augsburg print of 1628 establishes a visual analogy with St. Francis Xavier's 'true portrait'.

Visual parallels with St. Ignatius and St. Francis Xavier would increasingly permeate images of the three Jesuit Japan martyrs. Iconographical schemes showing either or both St. Ignatius and St. Francis Xavier engaged in illuminative contemplation became particularly influential for images of the Jesuit martyrs. An engraving by Schelte Adamsz. Bolswert codified the motif of dazzling heavenly light shining down on Ignatius and Francis Xavier, both of whom gaze into it [Fig. 13.12].[47] In this print, both saints' heads are surrounded by rays of light to express their exalted state. The position of Francis Xavier's hands crossed over his chest and his heavenward gaze allude to images of the *vera effigies*-type referring to his moments of *extasis* [Fig. 13.11]. Even though Ignatius' and Francis Xavier's facial expressions are serene, teardrops are shown falling from the former's eyes, pointing to how he is overwhelmed with emotions. A vision of the Trinity at Manresa, recorded in St. Ignatius' so-called autobiography, is said to have provoked a reaction of uncontrollable tears and sobbing due to the action of divine grace. This gift of tears, which he experienced recurringly, was most often interpreted as an expression of spiritual

---

45   On 'true effigies' of saints in the post-Tridentine era, see Niedermeier N., *Die ersten Bildnisse von Heiligen der frühen Neuzeit. Porträtähnlichkeit in nachtridentinischer Zeit* (Regensburg: 2020); in particular, on the true effigy of St. Francis Xavier, see Andueza Unanua P., "La *Vera Effigies* de San Francisco Xavier: la creación de una imagen postridentina", in Fernández Gracia F. (ed.), *San Francisco Javier en las artes. El poder de la imagen*, exh. cat., Castillo de Javier (Pamplona: 2006) 96–119.

46   Osswald M.C., "La imagen del santo en Goa y en Oriente", in *Los mundos de Javier* (Pamplona: 2008) 239–262, 245.

47   See Metropolitan Museum of Art, New York, accession no. 51.501.7129 at https://www.met museum.org/art/collection/search/770374?sortBy=Relevance&ft=Schelte+Adams +%c3%a0+Bolswert&offset=0&rpp=40&pos=11 (accessed 15.06.2023). An example showing St. Ignatius only, gazing at a heavenly source of light, his head surrounded by a halo of rays, can be seen in the engraving published by Joannes Galle in Antwerp ca. 1626–1676, kept in the Rijksmuseum, Amsterdam, object number RP-P-1904-460 at http://hdl.handle.net/10934/RM0001.COLLECT.226356 (accessed 30.09.2023).

FIGURE 13.11 Hieronymus Wierix, The 'True Effigy' of St. Francis Xavier, before 1619, engraving, 7,3 × 11 cm, Paris, Musée du Louvre
PHOTO © MUSÉE DU LOUVRE, DIST. RMN-GRAND PALAIS / MARTINE BECK-COPPOLA

consolation and joy rather than sorrow. As Darcy Donahue points out, tears 'became the most common external characteristic of Ignatian spirituality'.[48]

---

48 Donahue D., "The Mysticism of Saint Ignatius of Loyola", in Maryks R.A. (ed.), *A Companion to Jesuit Mysticism* (Leiden – Boston: 2017) 6–35, 17. St. Ignatius' spiritual diary is published as Tylenda J.N. (trans. and ed.), *A Pilgrim's Journey: The Autobiography of Ignatius of Loyola* (Wilmington: 1985).

FIGURE 13.12   Schelte Adamsz. Bolswert after Peter Paul Rubens, Saint Francis Xavier and Saint Ignatius of Loyola, ca. 1633–1659, engraving, 24,1 × 34,2 cm, New York, The Metropolitan Museum of Art, Accession Number: 51.501.7129. CC0 1.0, https://creativecommons.org/publicdomain/zero/1.0/deed.en

EMOTIONS IN TEXTS & IMAGES OF THE MARTYRS OF THE JAPAN MISSION   529

This same light, this same halo of rays, and these same tears began to appear in images of the three crucified martyrs. Bolswert's engraving *Primitiae Martyrum Societatis Iesu in Ecclesia Iaponica* after Abraham van Diepenbeeck, which shows how the three martyrs are being tied to crosses, one of which has already been raised – an accurate record of the Japanese method of raising the condemned onto crosses – features just the kind of heavenly illumination experienced by the founding fathers in the other Bolswert engraving [Fig. 13.13].[49] Rays of light shine directly onto their faces, highlighting how calmly, and indeed joyfully, they accept their fate. Here, martyrdom is depicted as *illuminatio*, resulting in the martyrs' serene heroic stance. Quite unlike their depiction in Kilian's engraving, here, Diogo Kisai, Paul Miki and João Goto willingly accept to die on the cross. Their illuminated state also makes them immune to the temptations that their idolatrous executioners confront them with – as represented in the motif of the veiled statue raised toward the martyr at right by the figure kneeling at the foot of his cross. This element, which resonates with the figure wearing a turban in the background at center, ties the martyrs of the Japan mission to the narrative and pictorial conventions of early Christian martyrs such as St. Lawrence or St. Batholomew, who are typically confronted with the choice between the adoration of a heathen idol or death by a tyrant in early modern depictions of their martyrdom.[50]

The composition seen in Bolswert's engraving of the three Jesuit Japan martyrs was soon copied and its rendering of Diogo Kisai's, Paul Miki's and João Goto's martyrdom as *illuminatio* transferred to other compositions representing this pictorial subject. Even though this wouldn't be the only Jesuit iconography of the Japan martyrs that would persist, it certainly became a rather dominant strand. It is unknown how the painting by Johann Heinrich Schönfeld in the Museo Civico di Castel Nuovo in Naples fits into this chronology, but it is interesting for its close resemblance to the Bolswert engraving.[51] Another engraving, also after Abraham van Diepenbeeck, created in 1667, is

---

49   See Rijksmuseum, Amsterdam, object number RP-P-BI-2563 at http://hdl.handle.net/10934/RM0001.COLLECT.84531 (accessed 30.10.2023); Koshi, *Die 26 Märtyrer von Japan in der Kunst* 47 (Nr. 27). The original composition by Abraham van Diepenbeeck is kept in the Hermitage Museum, St. Petersburg, Inventory number OP-2782 at https://www.hermitagemuseum.org/wps/portal/hermitage/digital-collection/02.+drawings/221612 (accessed 30.09.2023).

50   As an example, see the etching by Jan de Bisschop after a painting by Bartholomeus Breenbergh showing the martyrdom of St. Lawrence in the Rijksmuseum, Amsterdam, object number RP-P-OB-67.482 at http://hdl.handle.net/10934/RM0001.COLLECT.335850 (accessed 31.10.2023).

51   On this painting, see Prieto M. – Muñoz A., *Primeros mártires en Japón, Nagasaki. Historia e Iconografía, second edition* (Madrid: 2021) 215–216. A rather crude copy of the Bolswert print, which mirrors it symmetrically, can be found on the title page of the book

FIGURE 13.13　Schelte Adamsz. Bolswert after Abraham van Diepenbeeck, The Crucifixion of the Three Jesuit Martyrs of 1597, 1628–1659, engraving, 27,1 × 43 cm, Amsterdam, Rijksmuseum, object number RP-P-BI-2563. CC0 1.0, https://creativecommons.org/publicdomain/zero/1.0/deed.en

FIGURE 13.14
After Abraham van Diepenbeeck, The Crucifixion of Jesuit and Franciscan Martyrs in Japan in 1597, 1667, engraving, Wellcome Collection, Reference: 11014i. Public Domain Mark, https://creativecommons.org/public domain/mark/1.0/
SOURCE: WELLCOME COLLECTION

noteworthy for its focus on the Jesuit and Franciscan martyrs alike, as it lets the Franciscans partake in the heroic stoicism characterising the compositions following Bolswert's engraving [Fig. 13.14].[52] The heads of all the martyrs are shown surrounded by the typical rays connoting illuminative contemplation, while heavenly light shines down on them.

A painting of unknown date most likely created in Spanish Flanders, now located in the Kyushu National Museum, refers, in the inscription on its frame,

---

Tag-Zeiten/oder Siebenstündige Gemüts-Erhebungen [...], printed in Munich in 1674. On this print, see Koshi, *Die 26 Märtyrer von Japan in der Kunst* 48 (Nr. 28).

52 On this engraving, see https://wellcomecollection.org/works/bmgzujzs (accessed 31.10.2023). It was copied and adapted to a horizontal format in an engraving illustrating a book authored by Cornelius Hazart, S.J., titled *Kirchen-Geschichte/Das ist:/Catholisches Christenthum/durch die ganze Welt außgebveitet* [...], published in Vienna in 1678. On this print, see Koshi, *Die 26 Märtyrer von Japan in der Kunst* 59 (Nr. 54).

to 'Three crucified Japanese': 'Drij ghekruijste Japonoisen, Wt de Soci^t. Jesu, den 5. Febr. 1597. S. Paulus Michi. oudt 33. S. Jacobus Khisai. oudt 64. S. Joannes Goto. oudt 19' [Fig. 13.15].[53] It hyperbolises the Jesuit martyrs' stoic anticipation of heaven by conspicuously interpreting the heavenly light shining down upon them as a phenomenon that counteracts natural weather. The martyrs' heads are seen extending into a dark cloud bank, which is only disrupted by the rays of divine light shining down from above to illuminate them, while blood is seen flowing in streams out of the martyrs' bodies pierced by two lances each.

The motif of heavenly light shining down from above also appears in an oil painting of 1635 by Guido Cagnacci in the church of San Francesco Saverio in Rimini, which amounts to a painted epitome of *illuminatio*. It offers a dramatic close-up of the crucifixion of the martyrs; in this close view, iconographical elements that deviate from the Crucifixion of Christ, such as the metal cuffs used to strap the crucified to their crosses, are described in detail and prominently featured [Fig. 13.16].[54] The evident parallels with the Crucifixion of Christ that are naturally present in a picture focusing so strongly on three crucified men made it necessary for the artist to emphasise difference, thus allowing for a clearly positive presentation of the martyr at right. While the two 'outer' martyrs are positioned at the same angle with respect to the martyr at centre, the martyr on the left, João Goto, is shown already dead. This is not surprising given the two swords or lances that are seen piercing the bodies of all three diagonally.

In this painting, Paul Miki and Diogo Kisai are depicted gazing at the heavenly source of light above them. The typical rays surrounding the martyrs' heads and connoting illumination were not considered necessary to convey the concept of martyrdom as *illuminatio* here, as this notion was instead conveyed through the martyrs' serene expressions and tearful gazes. Indeed, in both Paul Miki and Diogo Kisai, illuminative experience is seen to evoke the tears typical of Ignatian spirituality, a response to divine grace and an index of spiritual consolation.

3 Conclusion

This essay aimed at shedding some light on the beginnings of European iconographies of the martyrs of the early modern missionary enterprise in Japan,

---

53   Basic information on this painting is provided in ibidem 45 (Nr. 23); and Omata Rappo, *Des Indes lointaines aux scènes des collèges* 366.

54   On this painting, see https://www.beweb.chiesacattolica.it/benistorici/bene/5231822 /Cagna ...1%2ovon (accessed 15.06.2023); Koshi, *Die 26 Märtyrer von Japan in der Kunst* 46 (Nr. 24). There exists a close copy of this painting in the Pinacoteca Comunale of Rimini, see Koshi, *Die 26 Märtyrer von Japan in der Kunst* 46 (Nr. 25).

EMOTIONS IN TEXTS & IMAGES OF THE MARTYRS OF THE JAPAN MISSION 533

FIGURE 13.15 *Drij ghekruijste Japonoisen*, oil on canvas, 117,5 × 89 cm, Kyushu National Museum
SOURCE: COLBASE (HTTPS://COLBASE.NICH.GO.JP/COLLECTION_ITEMS/KYUHAKU/A27?LOCALE=JA)

FIGURE 13.16 Guido Cagnacci, *Tre martiri del Giappone*, 1635, oil on canvas, 250 × 140 cm, Rimini, San Francesco Saverio
REPRODUCED WITH THE PERMISSION OF COMMISSIONE DIOCESANA PER L'ARTE SACRA E I BENI CULTURALI, DIOCESI DI RIMINI

and on the visual schemes and notions that would impact Franciscan and Jesuit renderings of the martyrs' emotions. Overall, the pictorial formulations developed by these two orders evolved quite differently, not least with respect to how the martyrs' emotional states were described.

Early on, the Franciscans situated their missionaries' martyrdoms abroad within the context of the mystical experience of their founder St. Francis, described as an experience of spiritual martyrdom triggering a set of mixed emotions. This was later abandoned, but it seems to have continued influencing the compositions showing the Franciscan martyrs with respect to the characterisation of their emotions. Indeed the Franciscans, who had a large number of martyrs to depict, typically expressed a range of emotions, reaching from expressions of joy to the silent acceptance of (a painful) death. If there is one figure among the Franciscan martyrs whose emotional state is recurringly, though not always, characterised in a distinct way, it is that of their commissary Pedro Bautista, who assumes his leadership role by showing a joyous attitude to his followers. Overall, however, Franciscan textual descriptions put more weight than their visual counterparts on the eager martyrdom of the members of their order.

By contrast, the Jesuits, who were initially reticent to promote their Japan martyrs' veneration in the first place, at first set these martyrs within broader contexts and adopted a variety of solutions with regard to the martyrs' emotional states. As soon as they turned to more openly embracing their martyrs, the iconography changed. The Society's founding fathers' 'white martyrdoms' would increasingly provide the visual matrix to be followed and the standard iconographical strand would depict the martyrs' crucifixion in Nagasaki as an experience of illuminative contemplation. With the campaigns to promote the cults of Ignatius and Francis Xavier, both saints' mystical experiences came to be perceived in an emotion-laden, heroic light, which was transferred to renderings of the Japan martyrs. At times showing pain-stricken martyrs, at others, a heroic stance, images of the victims of Christian persecution abroad would continue to fascinate European audiences for centuries to come.

Acknowledgements

This publication is part of a project that has received funding from the European Research Council (ERC) under the European Union's Horizon 2020 research and innovation programme (grant agreement No. 949836). Views and opinions expressed are, however, those of the author only and do not necessarily reflect those of the European Union or the European Research Council Executive Agency. Neither the European Union nor the granting authority can be held responsible for them. This project was also funded by a Swiss National Science Foundation PRIMA grant.

Bibliography

Andueza Unanua P., "La *Vera Effigies* de San Francisco Xavier: la creación de una imagen postridentina", in Fernández Gracia F. (ed.), *San Francisco Javier en las artes. El poder de la imagen*, exh. cat., Castillo de Javier (Pamplona: 2006) 96–119.

Augustine, Sermo XLIV, De verbis Isaiae, chapter LIII at www.monumenta.ch/latein/text.php?tabelle=Augustinus&rumpfid=Augustinus,Sermones,10,%20%2044&level=4&domain=&lang=0&links=&inframe=1&hide_apparatus=1 (accessed 15.08.2023).

Bonaventure (Di Fidanza Giovanni), *Legenda maior sancti Francisci*, in *Fontes franciscani*, ed. E. Menestò – S. Brufani (Assisi: 1995) 775–961.

Bowersock G.W., *Martyrdom and Rome* (Cambridge – New York – Melbourne: 1995).

Boxer C.R., *The Christian Century in Japan 1549–1650* (Berkeley: 1951).

Cañeque A., "In the Shadow of Francis Xavier: Martyrdom and Colonialism in the Jesuit Asian Missions", *Journal of Jesuit Studies* 9 (2022) 438–458.

Donahue D., "The Mysticism of Saint Ignatius of Loyola", in Maryks R.A. (ed.), *A Companion to Jesuit Mysticism* (Leiden – Boston: 2017) 6–35.

Eham M., "Gloria patri", in Kasper W. (ed.), *Lexikon für Theologie und Kirche, 3rd edition*, volume 4 (Freiburg im Breisgau: 1995) 752–753.

Fleming A.C., "St. Ignatius of Loyola's 'Vision at La Storta' and the Foundation of the Society of Jesus", in Schraven M. – Delbeke M. (eds.), *Foundation, Dedication and Consecration in Early Modern Europe*, Intersections 22 (Leiden – Boston: 2012) 225–249.

Fróis Luís, *Drey Japponische Schreiben [...]* (Mainz, Johan Albin: 1599).

Fróis Luís, *Relación del Martirio de los 26 cristianos crucificados en Nangasaqui el 5 Febrero de 1597*, ed. R. Galdos (Rome: 1935).

Fujita N.S., *Japan's encounter with Christianity. The Catholic Mission in pre-modern Japan* (New York: 1991).

Galante L., "Aspetti dell'iconografia sacra dopo il concilio di Trento nell'area Pugliese", in Pellegrino B. – Gaudioso F. (eds.), *Ordini religiosi e società nel mezzogiorno moderno*, Volume II (Lecce: 1987) 515–534.

Guzmán Francisco Tello de, *Relation, Auß befelch Herrn Francisci Teglij Gubernators, vnd general Obristens der Philippinischen Inseln* [...] (Munich, Adam Berg: 1599).

Guzmán Francisco Tello de, *Relazione mandata da don Francesco Teglio gouernatore e Capitano Generale dell'Isole Filippine* [...] (Florence, Giacomo Carlino & António Pace: 1599).

Harpster G., "Illustrious Jesuits: The Martyrological Portrait Series circa 1600", *Journal of Jesuit Studies* 9 (2022) 379–397.

Hesselink R.H., *The Dream of Christian Nagasaki. World Trade and the Clash of Cultures, 1560–1640* (Jefferson: 2016).

Hoel N.O., "Hues of Martyrdom: Monastic and Lay Asceticism in Two Homilies of Gregory the Great on the Gospels", *The Downside Review* 138.1 (2020) 3–18.

Koshi K., "Die 26 Märtyrer von Japan in der Kunst: ein Werkkatalog", *Bulletin annuel du musée national d'art occidental* 8 (1974) 16–72.

Maryks R.A., "Introduction", in Maryks R.A. (ed.), *A Companion to Jesuit Mysticism* (Leiden – Boston: 2017) 1–5.

Niedermeier N., *Die ersten Bildnisse von Heiligen der frühen Neuzeit. Porträtähnlichkeit in nachtridentinischer Zeit* (Regensburg: 2020).

Omata Rappo H., *Des Indes lointaines aux scènes des collèges. Les reflets des martyrs de la mission japonaise en Europe (XVIe–XVIIIe siècle)* (Münster: 2020).

Osswald M.C., "La imagen del santo en Goa y en Oriente", in *Los mundos de Javier* (Pamplona: 2008) 239–262.

Prieto M. – Muñoz A., *Primeros mártires en Japón, Nagasaki. Historia e Iconografía, second edition* (Madrid: 2021).

Ribadeneira Marcelo de, *Historia de las islas del archipiélago filipino y reinos de la Gran China, Tartaria, Cochinchina, Malaca, Siam, Cambodge y Japón*, ed. J.R. de Legísima (Madrid: 1947).

Ricci Bartolomeo, *Triumphus Jesu Christi crucifixi* (Antwerp, Joannes Moretus: 1608).

Richeome Louis, *La peinture spirituelle ou l'art d'admirer, aimer et louer Dieu en toutes ses oeuvres, et tirer de toutes profit salutere* (Lyon, Pierre Rigaud: 1611).

Ruiz-de-Medina J., *El martirologio del Japón, 1558–1873* (Rome: 1999).

Tylenda J.N. (trans. and ed.), *A Pilgrim's Journey: The Autobiography of Ignatius of Loyola* (Wilmington: 1985).

Vu Thanh H., *Devenir japonais. La mission jésuite au Japon (1549–1614)* (Paris: 2016).

CHAPTER 14

Materialities of Mixed Emotions and Spiritual Martyrdom between the Grand Duchy of Lithuania and Grand Duchy of Tuscany

Ruth Sargent Noyes

Abstract

This essay takes up the Italo-Baltic translation of the relic of Polish-Lithuanian prince, St. Kazimierz Jagiellończyk, from Vilnius to Florence as a case study in the cross-cultural portrayal of entangled emotions during the Counter-Reformation. Focusing on Florentine religious culture under Grand Duke Cosimo III, I consider the transcultural reception and recontextualisation of Jagiellończyk's cult, corporeal remains, and the reliquary made to transport, safeguard, and encapsulate his relic. The essay draws on distinct genres of source material to frame the significance of St. Kazimierz as a spiritual martyr and also calls attention to the symbolic materiality of the reliquary made to cultivate shifting emotions as instruments of devotion.

Keywords

relics – reliquaries – Tuscany – Lithuania – Medici – Pacowie – amber – ivory

Quivi con ogni toleranza non curava il christiano giovane d'esporre il nobile, e delicato corpo a' crudeli colpi dell'orrido inverno, et alle malagevoli intemperie della fuocosa estate. Onde postotsi così prostrato con la faccia in terra, lungamente orava, e divotamente salmeggiava, godendo la dolce compagnia de gl'Angioli, e del suo caro Signore. Quivi tal'ora contemplando la di lui dolorosa Passione tutto si distruggeva di pietà, e lacrimando considerava le pene di Christo, e le nostre perversità, che'l condussero da Cielo in terra à morir per salvarci. Quivi sentiva un gaudio incomparabile, rivolgendosi per la memoria i dolci frutti, che n'ha tratto la Chiesa Santa. Quivi anche muovevasi tal'ora la sua lingua à cantar con dolci laudi la carità di Christo Crocifisso, e ciò facendo prendeva gusto, e diletto grandissimo il suo inservatore spirito, e solo Dio era di questa

© RUTH SARGENT NOYES, 2025 | DOI:10.1163/9789004694613_015

sua opera testimonio. Ma continuando egli lungamente in questo santo essercitio ogni notte ... quivi vedevasi l'anima del santo giovane contemplante nel profondo silentio della mezza notte i divini misterii tutta sollevata, e rapita in Dio. ... entrava di lui spirito acceso in questi celesti chiostri, e godeva della divina essenza tutti i beni. E dopo sì lunghe contemplationi, si sentiva dentro l'anima tutto sparso d'un celeste lume, e contento indicibile.

With the utmost tolerance the young Christian did not hesitate to expose his noble and delicate body to the cruel blows of the horrible winter, nor to the evil intemperance of searing summer. Thus positioned prostrate with his face to the earth, for a long time he prayed and devoutly chanted, taking pleasure in the sweet company of the Angels and his dear Saviour. There sometimes while contemplating the Saviour's painful Passion, all was destroyed with pity, and crying he considered the sufferings of Christ, and our own perversions, which brought him from Heaven to earth, to die for our salvation. This brought him an incomparable joy, turning his memory to the sweet fruits of this for the Holy Church. He also sometimes moved his tongue to sing with sweet lauds of the charity of Christ Crucified, and in so doing his humble spirit found the greatest enjoyment and delight [...] Continuing at great length these sacred exercises every night [...] contemplating in the profound silence of the night the divine mysteries, the saintly youth's soul was elevated in rapture with God [...] his enraptured spirit ascended to the celestial choirs, and enjoyed all the benefits of the divine essence. And after such long contemplations, he felt his soul within pierced by a celestial light and unspeakable contentment.[1]

The above passage from a 1629 hagiography published in Naples describes the self-induced midnight ecstasies of Polish-Lithuanian Prince Kazimierz

---

1 Research for this article has received funding from the European Union's Horizon 2020 research and innovation program under the Marie Sklodowska-Curie grant agreement No 842830 (TRANSLATIO), hosted by the National Museum of Denmark. Additional support for field research has been provided by the following: Böckler-Mare-Balticum-Stiftung Travel Grant, Latvian State Fellowship for Research, Fritz Thyssen Stiftung Travel Grant, Bourse Robert Klein (Kunsthistorisches Institut Florenz – INHA Paris – Villa Finaly Chancellerie des Universités de Paris-Sorbonne), and Archimedes Estonian National Scholarship. Unless otherwise indicated, translations are the author's.

MIXED EMOTIONS BETWEEN THE GRAND DUCHIES 539

Jagiellończyk (1458–1484).[2] Called *Casimiro* in the Italian text, Jagiellończyk descended from the venerable Jagiellons of medieval Lithuania.[3] Rather than taking up the crown after his father, Prince Kazimierz instead rejected kingship to pursue a life of holiness marked by extreme self-abnegation and spiritual exercises, his rapturous episodes hastening his early death as a young spiritual or white martyr.[4] Another Italian seventeenth-century hagiography affirmed that 'si portia questo castissimo Prencipe ragionevolmente chiamare Martire di Castità, perche ne fù così studioso osservatore, che elesse più tosto morire, che pigliar moglie, come dai Parenti, et dai Medici n'era instantissimamente pregato, essendo egli in una infermità per la quale restava solo, et unico tal remedio' (this most chaste prince [Kazimierz] could rightly be called a Martyr of Chastity, because he was such a studious observer of chastity that he elected to die an early death).[5] In addition to spending nights prostrate outside on the bare ground meditating on the Passion, he wore a spiked iron chain against his bare skin, and induced death-like ecstasies through intense spiritual devotion to objects and images.[6]

Following the unofficial hiatus in canonisations during the Tridentine era, Jagiellończyk's saintly status was legally finalised post-Trent through a series of piecemeal Vatican documents over the course of the seventeenth century (1602, 1604, 1621, 1636), although the Counter-Reformation reframed him as a

---

2 Sant'Antonio Hilarione di, *Il breve compendio della vita morte, e miracoli del santissimo prencipe Casimiro, figlio del magno Casimiro re di Polonia, riferita da monsignore Zaccaria Ferrerio* (Naples, Aegidio Longo: 1629) 24–25.

3 Important studies on St. Kazimierz's cult and iconography in the Counter-Reformation include Maslauskaitė-Mažylienė S., *Šventojo Kazimiero atvaizdo istorija XVI–XVIII a* (Vilnius: 2010), and eadem, *Dzieje wizerunku św. Kazimierza od XVI do XVIII wieku. Między ikonografią a tekstem, z języka litewskiego przełożyła Katarzyna Korzeniewska* (Vilnius: 2013). See also further citations below on various aspects of his cult.

4 Counter-Reformation perception regarding Jagiellończyk as bloodless martyr was especially shaped by the 1610 hagiography written by Piotr Skarga, S.J., which in turn drew on the first Jagiellonian *vita*, by papal nuncio Zaccaria Ferreri (1520). See Čiurinskas M., "Piotr Skarga's *Żywot Świętego Kazimierza królewica polskiego* (1610) and the Lithuanian hagiographic tradition/Petro Skargos *Šv. Kazimiero, Lenkijos karalaičio, gyvenimas* (1610) ir to meto lietuviškoji hagiografinė tradicija", *Senoji Lietuvos literatūra* 35–36 (2013) 269–301. For the 1520 *vita*, see Ferreri Zaccaria, *Vita Beati Casimiri Confessoris: ex serenissimis Poloni[a]e regibus & magnis [...] Zacharia Ferrerio Vicentino pontifice Gardien[se]: in Polonia[m] & Lituania[m]* (Cracow, Iohannes Haller: 1520). On Counter-Reformation spiritual martyrdom generally, see Noyes R.S., *Peter Paul Rubens and the Counter-Reformation crisis of the Beati moderni* (New York, NY: 2018) 184–185.

5 Ercole Domenico Antonio, *Breue Compendio Della vita di S. Casimiro Confessore, Figliuolo del re di Polonia Cauata da Diuersi Autori* (Rome, Domenico Antonio Ercole: 1687) 8.

6 Sant'Antonio, *Il breve compendio* 23, 81.

venerable (even medieval) pre-Tridentine saint, celebrating his having been awarded sainthood by Leo X (Giovanni di Lorenzo de' Medici) already in 1520.[7] Hagiographies dedicated to the Polish-Lithuanian royal published in Naples and Rome underscore the intercultural role of his cult in connecting ostensibly far-flung historical territories on the Italian peninsula and Baltic littoral.[8] The Grand Duchy of Tuscany under the Medici also maintained a special devotion for the princely saint, whose name rendered in Italian as *Casimiro* was a near homophone for the popular grand ducal name Cosimo, and whose case for canonisation was initiated by a Medici pontiff.[9] Interest from Medicean Tuscany in the saintly would-be king of Poland-Lithuania paralleled grand ducal ambitions to rule the Polish-Lithuanian Commonwealth, a dualistic state consisting of the Grand Duchy of Lithuania and the Kingdom of Poland ruled by a common elected monarch, and one of Europe's largest nations comprising areas of present-day Lithuania, Poland, Latvia, Belarus, and Ukraine.[10] From the late the sixteenth century, the Medici promoted family members for royal elections.[11]

In the following century, Tuscan Grand Duke Cosimo III de' Medici (1642–1723) intended to participate in the 1669 and 1673 Commonwealth royal elections, eventually renounced in favor of his younger brother Francesco Maria de' Medici (1660–1711), whose candidature proved unsuccessful.[12] Renowned among contemporaries for his ardent Catholic religiosity and a zealous collector and devotee of sacred relics, Grand Duke Cosimo III nursed a particular devotion for Casimiro, which manifested as a fervent desire for a relic of the royal saint first expressed in 1673.[13] After a five-year epistolary campaign and protracted diplomatic negotiations, his longing was satisfied, and the largest single known relic of Kazimierz Jagiellończyk was transferred from Vilnius to Florence in 1678 within a majestic reliquary made almost entirely of amber,

---

7   Noyes R.S., "'Purest Bones, Sweet Remains, and Most Sacred Relics.' Re-Fashioning St. Kazimierz Jagiellończyk (1458–84) as a Medieval Saint between Counter-Reformation Italy and Poland-Lithuania", *Religions* 12.1011 (2021) https://doi.org/10.3390/rel12111011.

8   Maslauskaitė-Mažylienė S. (ed.), *Masterpieces of the History of the Veneration of St. Casimir: Lithuania – Italy*, exh. cat., Bažnytinio paveldo muziejus (Vilnius: 2018).

9   Ibidem 56–66.

10   For an overview of Lithuania in the premodern era see Davies N., *Litva: The Rise and Fall of the Grand Duchy of Lithuania: A Selection from Vanished Kingdoms* (New York: 2013).

11   On the Italian candidature for the crown of Poland-Lithuania, see Panella A., "Candidati italiani al trono polacco. I Medici", *Rassegna Nazionale* (16 April 1917) 269–279.

12   Quirini-Popławska D., "La corte di Toscana e la terza elezione in Polonia", *Zeszyty Naukowe Uniwersytetu Jagiellońskiego. Prace Historyczne* 71 (1982) 49–66.

13   On the Medici relic collections see Gennaioli R. – Sframeli M. (eds.), *Sacri Splendori: Il tesoro della 'Cappella delle Reliquie' in Palazzo Pitti* (Livorno: 2014).

MIXED EMOTIONS BETWEEN THE GRAND DUCHIES

with ivory inlay [Figs. 14.1–14.2]. It is worth noting that this gift was not given in isolation; rather, the transfer of Jagiellończyk's remains was part of a larger exchange between Cosimo and members of the Pacowie clan that occurred over nearly a decade, as studied in an important essay by art historian Giovanni Matteo Guidetti.[14] The lavish transfer of gifts culminated in the mutual relocation of relics, with the grand duke dispatching to Vilnius in 1682 a reliquary produced in the Medici workshops, containing a tooth and few hairs of the noble Florentine Carmelite saint and spiritual martyr Maria Maddalena de' Pazzi (1566–1607, canonised 1669), whom the Pacowie especially venerated, claiming a common parentage with the Florentine Pazzi.[15]

This essay takes up this Italo-Baltic relic translation as a case study in the cross-cultural portrayal of entangled emotions during the Counter-Reformation. I consider the transcultural reception and recontextualisation within the Florentine sphere – above all by Grand Duke Cosimo III – of Jagiellończyk's cult, corporeal remains, and the reliquary made to transport, safeguard, and encapsulate the saint's remains between the Lithuanian and Tuscan spheres [Figs. 14.1–14.2]. Drawing on distinct genres of source materials – hagiographies and other period publications, letters and other archival texts, and works of art – this chapter frames the significance of St. Kazimierz as a spiritual martyr, and the symbolic materiality of the reliquary specially made to export his relic from Vilnius to Florence, within the context of the late seventeenth-century Medicean grand ducal ambit. How might Cosimo III's cultural, spiritual, visual, and material milieu equip and condition him to perceive and receive the Polish-Lithuanian saint's relic and its precious container, particularly with regard to the cultivation of shifting emotions in the context of devotion. How might he understand the ways in which the reliquary's constituent materials (ivory and amber) not only represented but also bodied forth the transitions

---

14   Guidetti G.M., "Kultūriniai ir meniniai Lietuvos ir Tuscanos ryšiai XVII a. antroje pusėje: Pacų šeima ir didysis kunigaikštis Kosimas III Medičis", in Mitrulevičiūte D. (ed.), *Lietuva – Italija. Šimtmečių Ryšiai* (Vilnius: 2016) 439–462. See also Noyes R.S., "'The Polar Winds have driven me to the conquest of the Treasure in the form of the much-desired relic.' (Re)moving Relics and Performing Gift Exchange between Early Modern Tuscany and Lithuania", in Strenga G. – Kjar L. (eds.), *Gifts and Materiality: Gifts as Objects in Medieval and Early Modern Europe* (London: 2022) 103–131.

15   For Pazzi, see Copeland C., *Maria Maddalena de'Pazzi: The Making of a Counter-Reformation Saint* (Oxford: 2016). On the saint's Lithuanian cult, see Baniulytė A., "Šv. Marijos Magdalenos de'Pazzi kultas Lietuvos baroko kultūroje: atvaizdai ir istorinė tikrovė", *Darbai ir dienos* 53 (2010) 225–258. On the Pazzi reliquary, see ibidem, and Guidetti G.M., "Il reliquario di santa Maria Maddalena de'Pazzi a Vilnius e l'attività di Giovanni Comparini e Giuseppe Vanni per la corte di Toscana: nuovi documenti", *Bollettino della Accademia degli Euteleti della Città di San Miniato* 79 (2012) 197–215.

FIGURE 14.1 Danzig (Gdańsk) workshop, Reliquary of St. Kazimierz Jagiellończyk, c.1677–1678. Wooden core, amber, silver, ivory, metal. 35 × 56 × 20 cm. Front view. Florence, Palazzo Pitti, Tesoro dei Granduchi
IMAGE © GALLERIE DEGLI UFFIZI

FIGURE 14.2 Danzig (Gdańsk) workshop, Reliquary of St. Kazimierz Jagiellończyk, c.1677–1678. Wooden core, amber, silver, ivory, metal. 35 × 56 × 20 cm. Back view. Florence, Palazzo Pitti, Tesoro dei Granduchi
IMAGE © GALLERIE DEGLI UFFIZ

and/or elisions from emotion to emotion characteristic of St. Kazimierz's penitential devotions, tears, and ecstasies. How might the notion of 'kinaesthetic analogy' be marshaled to explain the reliquary's reliance upon multi-sensory means to convey the mystery of the saint inside to its grand ducal recipient: Cosimo's bodily interaction with and handling of the container gave rise to analogies between the precious materials and the saint's miraculously incorrupt body, and between the artisanal properties of these same materials and the mixed emotional states upon which Jagiellończyk's status as spiritual martyr was largely predicated.[16] Lastly, I explore how the reliquary might also thereby model, monitor, mirror, and ultimately transfer the holy prince's emotional malleability to the pious votary who manipulated the relic – first and foremost Grand Duke Cosimo.

The Tuscan grand duke was the model of an ideal aspirational recipient for a relic container that promised a means to not only imitate but also instantiate the complex emotions experienced by the saint inside, and thus emulate and in a certain lesser sense re-approximate the saint's own martyrdom. Cosimo's Catholic fervor was considered exceptional by contemporaries, who noted his singular piety, pilgrimages to holy sites, attendance at Mass multiple times per day, and frequent reading of martyrologies.[17] As noted above, the grand duke's zealous religiosity, and his particular avidity for relics and reliquaries, was nurtured largely by his mother Vittoria della Rovere, whose own 'infocato devotione' (ardent devotion) to the Church, its saints and their relics has been the subject of an important study by Adelina Modesti.[18] Under Vittoria's aegis, the tutelage of young Cosimo was overseen by Sienese theologian Volunnio Bandinelli, and c.1647 she commissioned a portrait by Justus Sustermans depicting her young son as the Christ child.[19]

That as a young man the future grand duke was known to spend half the day in prayer, that he demonstrated little interest in courtly pursuits, instead visiting sacred Tuscan sites such as Verna, Camaldoli and Vallombrosa, and that he was said to have demonstrated 'segni di una singolare pietà' (signs of a singular piety) – all would suggest that Cosimo was destined for a career in the Church (which was instead the lot of his younger brother Francesco Maria de' Medici), or indeed a life of holiness.[20] After separating irreparably from his wife

---

16 Bhalla N., "Containing the Uncontainable: Kinaesthetic Analogies and an Early Christian Box", *The Art Bulletin* 104.3 (2022) 6–28.

17 Acton H., *The Last Medici* (London: 1988) 45–46.

18 Modesti, *Women's Patronage* 205–262.

19 Modesti, *Women's Patronage* 12.

20 Acton, *The Last Medici* 113.

Marguerite Louise d'Orléans in 1675, he assumed a rigorously devout lifestyle, almost as if aspiring to the status of living sainthood; he also had himself portrayed in the guise of St. Joseph.[21] During the Holy Year 1700, he undertook a pilgrimage to Rome in order to touch the sacred relics of St. Peter's, particularly the Volto Santo, and to this end successfully petitioned Pope Innocent XII to appoint him a Canon of San Giovanni in Laterano, an occasion recorded in a portrait by Carlo Maratta.[22] Later in life, it was reported that Cosimo visited the convent of San Marco daily to perform spiritual exercises.[23]

Cosimo III's own zeal for Kazimierz was perhaps sparked by the homonymy between the saint's name rendered in Italian, *Casimiro*, and his own given name Cosimo, a connection reinforced by the Polish-Lithuanian prince's canonization having been initiated by a Medici pope. His ardor for a piece of the saint was sustained by his profound Counter-Reformation fervor for the rarest holy relics, fostered by his grandmother Maria Maddalena of Austria (1589–1631) and mother Vittoria della Rovere (1622–1694), whose remarkable relic diplomacy impressed even the seasoned ecclesiasts they enlisted to negotiate for numinous treasures.[24] By the time Cosimo asked for a piece of *Casimiro*, his family had already amassed within a jewel-like reliquary chapel consecrated in 1616 within the Medici Palazzo Pitti an impressive array of sacred trophies. This private setting afforded Medici devotees especially close access to the divine through bodily proximity to their sacred relic collection, occasionally enhanced through actual corporal contact.

Complementing the relics themselves was a no less breathtaking collection of priceless reliquaries, some imported to Florence as gifts, other manufactured in the grand ducal *Galleria dei Lavori* (Gallery of Works), Medicean workshops housed within the same palace.[25] Although the conventional claim that Cosimo's many expensive commissions of sacred artworks contributed to Tuscany's financial decline is exaggerated,[26] under his patronage Florentine

---

21   For his religious fervor see Guzmán M.T., *A Medici Pilgrimage: The Devotional Journey of Cosimo III to Santiago De Compostela (1669)* (Turnout: 2018).

22   Ibidem, 222–224. See also Gennaioli – Sframeli (eds.), *Sacri Splendori* 244–245.

23   Acton, *The Last Medici* 240. See also Guarini E.F., "COSIMO III de' Medici, granduca di Toscana", *Dizionario Biografico degli Italiani* 30 (1984), https://www.treccani.it/enciclope dia/cosimo-iii-de-medici-granduca-di-toscana_(Dizionario-Biografico).

24   Sanger A., *Art, Gender and Religious Devotion in Grand Ducal Tuscany* (Burlington, VT: 2014) 71–92, and Modesti A., *Women's Patronage and Gendered Cultural Networks in Early Modern Europe: Vittoria della Rovere, Grand Duchess of Tuscany* (New York, NY: 2020) 205–242.

25   Gennaioli and Sframeli, *Sacri Splendori* 243–338.

26   Acton, *The Last Medici*.

MIXED EMOTIONS BETWEEN THE GRAND DUCHIES 545

sacred arts flourished, including the production of devotional images and multimedia sculpted reliquaries of the utmost refinement.[27] In all these respects, and taken together with the homonymic coincidence between his own given name and that of the saintly Polish-Lithuanian prince *Casimiro*, it would seem that the Tuscan grand duke emulated Kazimierz Jagiellończyk, who at a young age abandoned affairs of state to pursue a life of living sainthood that led to his spiritual martyrdom.

As early as 1670, before beginning his epistolary crusade for a relic of the Polish-Lithuanian saint, Cosimo commissioned from Florentine artist Carlo Dolci (1616–1686) a likeness of Kazimierz as one in a series of saints' portraits. That it was kept in the grand ducal bed chamber suggests his special devotion to the saint, and his particular engagement with this image [Fig. 14.3].[28] The image's iconography sheds light on the Florentine perception of the holy prince, and this provides a context for Cosimo's reception of the relic and its container years later. Dolci's devotional icon descended from an iconographical lineage that derived from a past cult image recorded in Zaccaria Ferreri's 1520 Jagiellonian hagiography composed at the behest of Medici Pope Leo X [Fig. 14.4].[29]

In Ferreri's *vita*, the saintly prince is depicted in a woodcut frontispiece full-length portrait with his face framed by splendorous rays, standing in three-quarter view in long fur-lined mantle set against a landscape marked by desolate rocks and thorny branches. This early likeness endowed him with the crown and white lily symbolizing his status as spiritual martyr, with his right hand tightly clutching a rosary in his left hand symbolically girding his loins in the struggles against temptation. From the bare vegetation spring gracefully curved bows that blossom into florid leaves, echoing the lilies and the botanical pattern woven into his brocade mantle. Starting with Ferreri, hagiography fashioned Jagiellończyk into a composite figure whose advent heralded his native land's conquest over frost, cold, and barrenness.[30] Exemplifying complimentary notions of chill and warmth, chastity and fertility intrinsically linked

---

27   Spinelli R., *Le Committenze Sacre Di Cosimo III De' Medici: Episodi Poco Noti o Sconosciuti (1677–1723)* (Florence: 2019).

28   Gennaioli – Sframeli (eds.), *Sacri Splendori* 272–273, and Maslauskaitė-Mažylienė (ed.), *Masterpieces* 80–83. An undocumented copy by Dolci, today in the Pushkin Museum, may have been made as a gift for the Pacowie: although there is no record of this, we do know that the Medici traded portraits with the Lithuanian nobility, and may have dispatched the copy amongst these exchanges. See Noyes, "Representing the Family of Pacowie".

29   See Ferreri, *Vita Beati Casimiri* [n.p.] and Noyes, "Re-Fashioning St. Kazimierz", fig. 2.

30   Ferreri, *Vita Beati Casimiri* [n.p.].

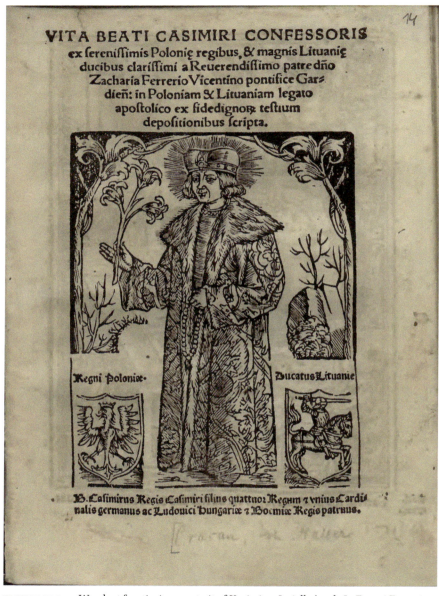

FIGURE 14.3   Woodcut frontispiece portrait of Kazimierz Jagiellończyk. In Ferreri Zaccaria, *Vita Beati Casimiri Confessoris* [n.p]
IMAGE IN THE PUBLIC DOMAIN

FIGURE 14.4 Carlo Dolci, Portrait of St. Kazimierz, 1670–1671. Oil on canvas, 95 × 79 cm
IMAGE © GALLERIE DEGLI UFFIZI

to his homeland, the holy prince embodied a duality attributed to the Baltic region as an 'Indies of the north' during the early modern age of discovery.[31]

Dolci re-envisioned a young spiritual martyr whose angular features are emphasised by his upturned gaze rendered in profile, starkly illuminated by

---

31 Donecker S., "Est vera India septemtrio: re-imagining the Baltic in the age of discovery", in Lehtonen T. – Kaljundi L. (eds.), *Re-forming Texts, Music, and Church Art in the Early Modern North* (Amsterdam: 2016) 393–419.

divine rays that dramatically pierce ominous clouds. The heavenly light reveals an aquiline nose (perhaps hinting at his ancient Roman heritage), protruding jaw, and skeletal countenance with deeply sunken eyes and gaunt cheeks. Marble-white, pearlescent skin is coloured alternately by livid tinges of red at the lips and fingertips, and deep charcoal on the eye sockets, cheeks, and jawline, complemented by black eyebrows, hair, and a satin tunic.

A crimson robe lined with sable fur – another important Baltic luxury export – recalls the cold climate of his homeland, which crucially shaped his suffering through meditative exercises practiced outdoors. Although seated at a red-covered table of sorts, the background setting suggests exposure to the elements. Depicted in an ecstatic pose suggestive of spiritual suffering, gazing heavenward with hand clasped to his bosom, the prince is attended by a spray of white lilies dotted with red carnations signifying his bloodless martyrdom.[32] Having set aside his royal crown and his quill, he is shown as the composer of the devotional hymn to the Virgin, *Omni die dic Mariae*, the so-called *Hymn of St. Kazimierz* in sixty stanzas; the first fourteen lines are inscribed on the parchment scroll he grasps in his left hand:

> Omni die / dic Mariae / Mea laudes anima: / Ejus festa, / ejus gesta / Cole devotissima. / Contemplare / et mirare / Ejus celsitudinem: / Dic felicem / genitricem, / Dic beatam / Virginem. / Ipsam cole, / ut de mole

> Every day, / my soul, / say praises to Mary; / Her feasts / and her feats / honour most devoutly. / Contemplate her / and admire / her exaltation; / Say, 'Happy / Mother'; / say 'Blessed Virgin'. / Honour her, / that she may free you.

The portrait figures a type of martyrdom induced by means of extreme asceticism and spiritual exercises, and characterised by ostensibly antithetical states of suffering and joy, remorse and peace, pain and elation. It is instructive to consider this image's iconography in tandem with the passage cited at the opening of this chapter from the saint's 1629 *Vita*, which gave an account of how the saint cultivated these mixed emotions by means of his pursuit of self-abnegation and devotional practices. Dolci and his grand ducal patron very likely referred to such a hagiographical text as a guide as part of the production of the portrait. In the passage, the bodily perception of alternating winter chill and summer heat functions as correlate to the prince's ostensibly

---

32 Rush A.C., "Spiritual Martyrdom in St. Gregory the Great", *Theological Studies* 23.4 (1962) 569–589, at 585.

opposed emotional fluctuations. During the course of his nightly exercises, Jagiellończyk experienced sweet pleasure during prayerful intonations while accompanied by an angelic host and Christ, then overwhelming tearful pity while meditating on the Passion, which in turn begat recollection of the Passion's sweet fruits that triggered incomparable joy; intoning lauds of the crucified Savior's charity elicited enjoyment and delight.

The cumulative effect of his prolonged and repeated nocturnal exercises was the mystical ecstatic ascent of the saint's spirit to celestial heights, where a feeling of "unspeakable contentment" (*contento indicibile*) pierced his soul. The passage from light (streaming from the upper left) to dark (receding into the right background) across Dolci's composition, and the rosy tinge on the edges of the clouds and the rim of the prince's halo, together suggest that this likeness ventures to capture Kazimierz at the climactic moment when his nighttime exercises and complex emotional state culminated in his rapturous elevation, with the warming luminescence suggestive of impending dawn at the conclusion of his night's travails and ecstasies. The hand raised and pressed to his heart is indicative of the simultaneously stabbing pain and indescribable pleasure he felt within as the celestial light penetrated his soul.[33] Designed to engender similar experiences and sensations in devout beholders, Dolci's portrait encouraged them to emulate spiritual martyrs like Kazimierz – first and foremost, the artist's patron, Cosimo III de' Medici, who beheld the painting regularly in the relatively intimate space of his bed chamber in Palazzo Pitti.

> Vostra Paternità è un grande ascendente per le fortune delle mie honori, poiche tutte sortiscono il più avventuroso adempimento, dove le scorge l'affetto, et favor sia l'uno, e l'altro posso dire, che furono i Venti Polari per condurmi alla conquista del sacro Tesoro nella sospirata reliquia del santo Rè Casimiro, di cui gia mi vedo arricchito, quando remeno il pericolo di mille sisti, e golfi difficili, prima di giugnere à possederlo: nè mi da il cuore d'esplicare alla P.V. tutto il giubilo che inondò l'animo mio all'aprire il dispaccio di Wilna, accompagnato dalla sua carta obbligatiss.ma. Nei tratti cordiali, e gentili co' quali s'esprime quell degno Prelato, mi par di scorgere con auidenza quell Genio, che si inspirò alla mente, e si dettò

---

33   Kazimierz's rapturous nocturnal episodes, during which his spiritual exercises engendered a flow of rapidly shifting, overlapping, and compounded emotions, were not unique to the holy prince amongst his other Counter-Reformation saints: period hagiography for Oratorian founder, white martyr, and mystic St. Filippo Neri (1515–1595, canonized 1622), for example, described nighttime exercises which begat similar mixed emotions, ecstatic visions, and soul-piercing raptures. Noyes, *Peter-Paul Rubens* 184–187.

alla penna di lui; però si contenti V. Ptà, ch'io non abbia minore gratitudine al motore della mano, che alla mano stessa, da cui mi viene un dono sì prezioso, e stimabile, ò sia per l'esser suo spiritual ò per le insigni reali circonstanze, che tanto lo qualificano. Resto adesso in una giusta impazienza, ch'animi qui felicissimamente.

Your Holy Fathership is a great portent for the fortune of my own honours, since they have realised the most adventurous fulfillment, whence emerge both feeling and favour. It was the Polar Winds that led me to the conquest of the sacred Treasure that is the longed-for relic of the saintly King [sic] Casimiro, with which I already see myself rewarded, when I will row my vessel through the danger of a thousand difficult obstacles and abysses before arriving at its possession. My heart cannot find words to express the joy that flooded my soul upon opening the dispatch from Vilnius, accompanied by your most obliging message. In those cordial and kind expressions of that dignified Prelate [the Bishop of Vilnius], it seems to me that I am in the presence of that Genius that inspired his mind and moved his pen. However, Your Fathership should be satisfied that I have no less gratitude for the hand's movement, and for the hand itself from whence comes to me such a precious and inestimable gift, both for the spiritual essence and for the actual honourable circumstances which accompany it. I now remain in a state of righteous impatience, which animates me most joyously.[34]

Tuscan Grand Duke Cosimo III de' Medici composed this exultation early in the new year of 1677, in reply to a letter from Vilnius. Directed to Superior General of the Society of Jesus Giovanni Paolo Oliva, Cosimo's jubilant message responded to a missive ferried via Jesuit networks, from the bishop nominate of Vilnius Mikołaj Stefan Pac (1626–1684). Bishop Pac was a leading member of the powerful Pac (pl. Pacowie) family, whose rise to pre-eminence in Lithuania paralleled that of the Medici in Tuscany, and who dominated Lithuanian politics by the latter half of the seventeenth century.[35] Weaving together rheto-

---

34　ARSI, Epistolae Externorum, vol. 36, fols. 1r–v, 32r–v. For relevant archival sources pertaining to the exchanges taken up in the ensuing sections of this article, see also records preserved in Florence, Archivio di Stato Firenze (hereafter ASF), filza Mediceo del Principato: 1529–1753 (hereafter MP), 4489–4494, especially 4492, fols. 298r–v, 442r–v, 561r, 604r, 697r; 4493, 602r–v, 603r–604v, 608r–v, 609r–v.

35　On the Pacowie, see Baniulytė A., "The Pazzi Family in Lithuania: Myth and Politics in the European Court Society of the Early Modern Age", *Medium aevum quotidianum* 58 (2009) 41–57.

MIXED EMOTIONS BETWEEN THE GRAND DUCHIES 551

ric drawing on entangled period notions of Counter-Reformation religiosity, Catholic crusade, classical maritime epic, and cultural geography of the Baltic region, Cosimo's epistle expressed his compound emotive state intermingling travail and triumph, satisfaction and anticipation. This emotional ambivalence was triggered by news from Bishop Pac that his yearning for a relic of the holy body of St. Kazimierz Jagiellończyk, first expressed as early as 1673, would finally be fulfilled.[36]

Cosimo III de' Medici's avid desire to be granted a piece of *Casimiro* was apparently first expressed in connection with his own ambitions apropos the 1673 Commonwealth royal election, Mikołaj Stefan Pac's 1673 nomination to the episcopate, and the 1673 Polish-Lithuanian military victory against the Ottoman Turks at Chocim (Khotyn), where the bishop's cousin Lithuanian Grand Hetman (i.e., commander of the armed forces) Michał Kazimierz Pac (1624–1682) played a key role.[37] Despite his 1673 nomination to the Vilnius episcopate, Mikołaj Stefan Pac faced opposition from both his own wife (who only reluctantly agreed to annulment) and the Vilnius cathedral chapter charged with custodianship of Jagiellończyk's eponymous reliquary chapel, and was only granted papal ordination in 1682, after multiple trips to Italy in the 1670s. These circumstances and the exceptional nature of Cosimo's request delayed its fulfilment, transforming the holy remains into an transcultural object of desire which could be leveraged from multiple perspectives to serve a wide range of religio-political and ideological ends, implicating multiple middle-men in negotiations over the Italo-Baltic relic translation, including members of the Society of Jesus and court intermediaries.[38] Cosimo's ask was in fact exceptional: the Polish-Lithuanian King's own appeal for a relic of the holy prince was denied in 1672.[39]

A subsequent letter from Vilnius to Florence relayed how, in the presence of witnesses, on 27 October 1677 a femur (or tibia) bone was removed from

---

36   For an initial intercessory letter from Giovanni Paolo Oliva to Bishop Pac see Rome, ARSI, Epistolae Nostrorum, vol. 7, 383.

37   For Grand Hetman Pac see Noyes R.S., "'To see at Least in an Image the Semblance of a Friend ...' Representing the Family of Pacowie Between Baroque Tuscany and Lithuania", *Kaunas History Annals* 20 (2022) 161–176.

38   On the Jesuits in this place and period, see Fordoński K. – Urbański P., "Jesuit Culture in Poland and Lithuania, 1564–1773", *Journal of Jesuit Studies* 5.3 (2018) 341–351. On Lorenzo Domenico Pazzi as court intermediary, see Baniulytė A., "Gli italiani alla corte dei 'Pazzi' in Lituania: mito e politica nel Seicento barocco", *Archivio storico italiano* 168 (2010) 325–348.

39   On King Michał Korybut Wiśniowiecki's unsuccessful relic request, see Maslauskaitė-Mažylienė (ed.), *Masterpieces* 64.

the silver coffin safeguarding the prince's remains and furnished with a certificate of authenticity, illuminated on parchment, which described the relic's enclosure within a silk-lined cypress casket, tied with a golden and silver band marked with the bishop's seal in fourteen places, and upholstered with an opulent red fabric embroidered with gold and silver thread.[40] One year later, Antonio Maria Principati and Aleksander (Alessandro) Buchuiz, envoys of Bishop Pac, delivered the relic to Florence by Christmas 1678. In his missive accompanying the gift, Mikołaj Stefan Pac underscored the prestige of such a large integral first-class corporal relic from a saintly prince, one of 'non meno sublime grandezza e magnificenza, che celebre veneratione et esaltatione, tanto qui che anco e' stato canonizzato dalla Sta Mem.a di Papa Leone x.o della Ser.ma Casa di V.A.' (no less sublime greatness and magnificence, and famous veneration and exultation, for the fact that [Kazimierz] was canonized by His Holiness Pope Leo x of Your Highness's most noble House).[41]

Hagiography around Kazimierz, whose cult enjoyed a seventeenth-century resurgence, interwove his nonviolent martyrdom in heroic resistance against heresy, insurrection and temptation in the far northern Baltic with his spiritual purity.[42] The latter especially materialised in his purported postmortem bodily incorruption, a miraculous manifestation recognised by the Church as an *indicium sanctitatis*, proof that the subject was divinely exempt from the physical process of decomposition and undoubtedly worthy of sainthood; during the Counter-Reformation, this phenomenon, increasingly verified by autopsy, came to be appreciated as a sine qua non of sanctity.[43] On the occasion of Prince Kazimierz's provisional canonisation in Poland-Lithuania in 1604, the ceremonial *translatio* of the saint from the cathedral crypt to the altar entailed the opening of his coffin and inspection of his remains, revealing a body miraculously preserved and sweet-smelling after 120 years.[44]

Thus his bodily dismemberment for the benefit of the Medici represented a noteworthy cultic concession, since a relic separated from an incorrupt corpse held special significance. Key to the saint's hagiography is the claims that he devoutly intoned the Marian melody inscribed in Dolci's portrait of Jagiellończyk during his martyrial episodes, and that the text of the hymn was

---

40   Florence, Archivio della Basilica di San Lorenzo, 73. See Gennaioli – Sframeli (eds.), *Sacri Splendori* 270–271, and Maslauskaitė-Mažylienė (ed.), *Masterpieces* 57–58.

41   ASF, MP, 4493, fol. 608r–v.

42   See further discussion in Noyes, "Re-fashioning St. Kazimierz".

43   Bouley B.A., *Pious Postmortems: Anatomy, Sanctity, and the Catholic Church in Early Modern Europe* (Philadelphia: 2017) 70–90.

44   For these circumstances and the dispersal of Casimir's relics see Maslauskaitė S., "Šv. Kazimiero relikvijos ir relikvijoriai", *Acta academiae artium Vilnensis* 41 (2006) 35–57.

MIXED EMOTIONS BETWEEN THE GRAND DUCHIES   553

found together with his miraculously intact body on the occasion of the aforementioned 1604 translation of his remains.[45] Dolci's inclusion of the Marian
laud thus bears witness before the fact, as it were, to the saint's precious relics, their exceptional state of preservation, and their ceremonial relocation.
Perhaps contemplation of the portrait, and the circumstances surrounding the
hymn it depicts, helped to spark in Grand Duke Cosimo a fervent desire to
obtain part of the prince himself.

The grand duke celebrated the arrival of the Lithuanian prince's body part
in a suite of letters, one addressed to Giovanni Paolo Oliva:

> Io non posso tacere à V. Ptà l'immensa mia contentezza per il felice
> adempimento, che ieri sortirono le mie brame all'arrivo del sacro Tesoro,
> alla cui conquista tanto pellegrinò la penna, e il pensiero di V.Ptà per le
> parti del settentrione, colla volontà d'arricchirmene, dico l'inestimabile
> reliquia del Glorioso Principe S. Casimiro; che accompagnata dal ricco
> ornamento: d'una preziosa suppellettile per l'altare che dovrà custodirla,
> me fù consegnata in questa villa dal Sig.e abate Principati et da un'altro
> Gentilhuomo de Mons.e Vescovo di Vilna, à suo nome, e di quell Capitolo.
> Non è possibile ch'io mi sodisfaccia adesso colla P.V. nel rendere à quell
> Prelato la giustizia che merita lo splendore della sua generosità, per che
> ho le specie troppo confuse, sorpreso dalla nobiltà di si magnifico dono:
> Però solo intendo di appagare il mio spirito nel mostrami tra tanto grato
> à V. Pta che me fù intercessore; e questa piccola espressione sia una
> linea [...] del cuore mio, ove abbonda la riconoscenza, e la consolazione.

> I cannot keep my immense pleasure from Your Fathership, due to the
> joyful satisfaction of my cravings, upon yesterday's arrival of the sacred
> Treasure, whose conquest was sought through the pilgrimage of both
> the pen and the mind desirous of rewarding myself. I speak of the ines-
> timable relic of Glorious Prince St. *Casimiro*, which was accompanied
> by rich ornament: namely, a precious altar furnishing to safeguard the
> relic. These were handed over to me in this city [of Florence] by the Lord
> Abbot and by a gentleman [Antonio Maria Principati and Aleksander
> (Alessandro) Buchuiz] of My Lord the Bishop of Vilnius, on behalf of him
> and the Vilnius Cathedral chapter. It is impossible for me sufficiently to
> thank [Mikołaj Stefan Pac] as much as the splendour of his generosity
> warrants, because my senses are too confused, surprised by the nobility

---

45   Skarga Piotr, *Żywoty Świętych Pańskich na wszystkie dnie roku* (Warsaw: Mikołów, 1910)
     218–219.

of such a magnificent gift. However, I intend only to assuage my spirit in showing myself very grateful to Your Fathership, my intercessor. May this small expression be a first attempt [...] from my heart, whence abounds thanks and consolation.[46]

With a rhetorical flourish coupling crusade and piety, Cosimo implies that he obtained the Baltic treasure through arduous virtual pilgrimage undertaken with 'the pen and the mind'. The grand dukes writes as if, in the manner of a sanctified crusader, he overcame spiritual adversities to win the body of the northern prince as sacred spolia. His mystical struggle and inner journey toward spiritual conquest in the North, which finally results in conferral of the reliquary trophy, resonate with the ambitions of the Medici house to rule over Poland-Lithuania and establish an Italo-Baltic transregional empire. In professing his confused emotional state, intermingling surprise, gratitude, and victorious satisfaction, he registers the significance and tremendous impact of the gift. That the relic and its vessel gained an especially privileged place in the grand duke's daily religious praxis becomes apparent from a subsequent letter to Bishop Pac written in Spring 1679 on the occasion of the saint's feast day (4 March), which solicits counsel regarding the special (Lithuanian) liturgical or devotional offices owed to such a holy prince of the Church:

> Celebrandosi appunto in questo giorno dalla chiesa universale la festività del Glorioso S. Casimiro io pure ebbi divozione di rendere più qualche straordinario culto alla insigne reliquia dello stesso santo, che mi accompagna da per tutto, fin che non sia disposto il luogo ove abbia da stare più degnamente collocarsi: e con [...] opportunità mi è venuto in animo d'intendere se codesto clero, e diocese si reciti in cuor del suo gran Protettore un uficcio particolare, a diversa da quello, che sta registrato nel Brevario Romano.

> As we are today celebrating in accordance with the Universal Church the holy day of the Glorious St. *Casimiro*, I yet devoutly wish additionally to bestow some special cult on the saint's relic which accompanies me everywhere, until a more fitting place for its safekeeping has been made ready. Thus, on this occasion it occurred to me to ask if this cleric [the Bishop of Vilnius] and his diocese recite in their hearts some special office for their great Protector, which may differ from that found in the Roman Breviary.[47]

---

46 ARSI, Epistolae Externorum, vol. 36, fols. 32r–v.
47 ASF, MP, 4493, fol. 615r–v.

MIXED EMOTIONS BETWEEN THE GRAND DUCHIES

Despite the lack of surviving records attesting to Cosimo's potential interactions through habitual devotions with the relic (nor with Dolci's 1670 portrait of Jagiellończyk), it is not difficult to imagine him engaging prayerfully with the prince's relic and its container (itself a tertiary relic by virtue of contact with the saint), on which more below. The grand duke perhaps held, moved, and meditated on Kazimierz's body within its receptacle while gazing at the saint's portrait in his bedchamber, while also contemplating on and emulating the complex emotions that the image puts on show.

No written reply from Bishop Pac is known to survive in response to Cosimo's query regarding a particular mass to be said for the Polish-Lithuanian saint, although the bishop made visits in person to the Medici court, and may have relayed his answer in person. In any case, Pac's most likely reply would have been to refer his pious Tuscan friend back to a special liturgy for the holy prince included in Ferreri's 1520 hagiography, the text of which was then partly reprinted in Vilnius in 1604 on the occasion of Jagiellończyk's provisional canonization in the territories of the Commonwealth, the *translatio* of his body in Vilnius cathedral, and the discovery of his wondrously preserved *corpus*.[48] Thus this liturgy gestured both to the saint's origins with the Medici papacy and interrelations between Italy and the Baltic in the previous century, and to the more recent continuation and confirmation of the saint's cult, as well as the special status of his relics.

The 1520 *Missa de Sancti Casimiro* analogises the passage from one emotion to another by means of figuring of the transition from day to night, light to darkness, and their inverse, in addition to referencing transitional periods of twilight.[49] Alluding to Kazimierz's mixed and shifting emotions as related in his hagiography and adumbrated visually in Dolci's likeness, Ferreri's liturgy is conceived to assist the votary in cultivating these emotions. Central passages of Nocturns turn around the holy prince's compound and shifting emotional state during his nighttime spiritual exercises, when he is alternately consumed with penitential compunction attended by copious tears, and filled with gratitude to praise the Divine. This intermingling of guilt, sadness, despair, grief, happiness, and thankfulness hinges on the coupling of a reference to penitential Psalm 6:7, 'Laboravi in gemitu meo ; lavabo per singulas noctes lectum meum : lacrimis meis stratum meum rigabo' (I am worn out from my groaning; all night

---

48 Święcicki Grzegorz, *Theatrum S. Casimiri: In quo ipsius prosapia, vita, miracula, et illustris pompa in solemni eiusdem apotheoseos instauratione, Vilnae Lithuaniae metropoli, v. Id. Maij, anno D[omi]ni M.DC.IV. instituta graphice proponuntur* ... ([Vilnae]: Typographicis Academiae Societatis Iesu, [1604]) 29–33.

49 E.g. 'Nox redit terries abeunte phoebo' ('Night returns to the earth as the sun departs') 'Surgit aurore nitor' ('The brilliance of dawn rises'). Ferreri, *Vita Beati Casimiri* [n.p.] and Grzegorz, *Theatrum S. Casimiri* 31–32.

I flood my bed with weeping; I drench my couch with tears), with that to the eulogistic Psalm 119:62, 'Media nocte surgebam ad confitendum tibi, super judicia justificationis tuæ' (At midnight I rise to give you thanks for your righteous laws).[50] Bookending the central pairing the liturgy's opening and closing appeal for praises of joy and delight from the votary, are coupled with gestures to the warming fire of Kazimierz's virtue and the brightening arrival of day.

The arrival of Kazimierz's relic and its luminous amber container prompted Grand Duke Cosimo to profess his inexpressible joy and gratitude in another letter thanking Bishop nominate Mikołaj Stefan Pac for the gift of the saint, 'il glorioso Principe e Protettore di codesti Regni' (glorious Prince and Protector of both our Realms). This letter notably couples his fluctuating emotions with the cognitive processes that possession of the relic and reliquary ornamented with the saint's likeness engendered:

> in vedermi al possesso d'un si grande e si qualificato Tesoro che non son'atto per fare all'Eminenza Vostra la corrispondente espressione della gioa e riconoscimento venire dell'animo mio [...] Et poi che l'inestimabile valore del sacro dono non è da pareggiarsi con i sentimenti di qualunque più alta estimazione [...] In ciò poi che riguarda i ricchissimi ornamenti, e la Imagine del santo Principe, con l'Eminenza Vostra volle accompagnare la sopredetta reliquia io non posso se non esaltare grandemente l'istituto della di lei raggiosa Magnificenza, che ben s'adatta al infinito pregio della cosa stessa.

> seeing myself in possession of so great and exceptional a Treasure, I was incapable of expressing to Your Eminence the joy and gratitude issuing from my soul. [...] As for the richest ornaments, and the image of the holy Prince, with which Your Eminence thought fit to accompany the relic, I can only exalt your radiant Magnificence, which adapted to the infinite worth of the [relic] itself.[51]

The additional year that passed between the 1677 retrieval of the Kazimierz relic in Vilnius and its ultimate journey south to Florence in late 1678 was necessitated by the manufacture of the receptacle mentioned repeatedly in Cosimo's effusive epistles, today separated from its original contents and in the collections of the Palazzo Pitti [Figs. 14.1–14.2].[52] In addition to the aforementioned

---

50 Ferreri, *Vita Beati Casimiri* [n.p.].

51 January 1679. ASF, MP, 4493, fols. 609r–v.

52 On the Kazimierz reliquary see Gennaioli – Sframeli (eds.), *Sacri Splendori* 266–267, and Maslauskaitė-Mażylienė (ed.), *Masterpieces* 74–76.

MIXED EMOTIONS BETWEEN THE GRAND DUCHIES

cypress coffer, Jagiellończyk's bone was transported to Tuscany nestled inside a silver coffin (since lost), within an ivory and amber casket commissioned through Jesuit agents at Bishop Pac's behest from the renowned Danzig (Gdańsk) workshops.[53]

It was this second vessel, manufactured from indigenous Baltic materials and measuring an impressive 35.5 cm wide, 58 cm long, and 20 cm high, that required the grand duke to wait another year for his sacred prize. Cosimo's remark that the reliquary 'mi accompagna da per tutto' (accompanies me everywhere) underscores how closely the grand duke guarded the remains and their receptacle, keeping them in proximity to his person: was it carried from room to room, conveyed from one Medici palazzo to another? What remains of this essay takes up the question of his experience of corporeal proximity to the ivory and amber vessel, particularly as regards bodily interaction and how it may have activated the casket's allusive material properties to inspire a pious reenactment or, better, re-approximation of the saint's compound emotions and white martyrdom.

The Kazimierz reliquary consists of a wood frame overlaid with complex inlay composed of thin intricately carved panels of various shades of amber, the object's primary decorative material, and small amounts of ivory, all pieced together into a three-dimensional mosaic, and surmounted by an equestrian portrait of the saint contained within. An entry in the 1698 Medicean inventory of sacred objects in the Palazzo Pitti chapel described the casket thusly:

> Una cassetta impiallacciata d'ambra a spartimenti che alcuni bassi rilievi d'avorio bianco con fondi di tabi nero a onde con colonette, e figurine d'ambra gialla, e bianco con rosette simili, e s'apre d'avanti con due sportelli, con coperchio sopra fermo a sepolcro con quattro gigli, e un cavallino in mezzo d'avorio bianco con figurina sopra d'ambra gialla che rappresenta San Casimiro, foderata dentro di velluto rosso cremisi con palline sotto d'ambra gialla

> A small box encrusted with amber plaquettes and bas-reliefs in white ivory against a black background with spiral columns, and figurines and rosettes of yellow and white amber. It opens from the front with two small doors, and the top is covered in the manner of a sepulcher [or,

---

53   Florence, ASF, MP 4493, fol. 492r. On Danzig amber manufacturing as a mediating force between the Baltic and Italy in this period, see King R., "The Shining Example of 'Prussian Gold': Amber and Cross-Cultural Connections between Italy and the Baltic in the Early Modern Period", in Lipińska A. (ed.), *Materiał rzeźby: Między techniką a semantyką* (Wroclaw: 2009) 456–470.

'with a coffin-type cover'] with four lilies [or iris], and in the centre a horse of white ivory surmounted by a yellow amber figurine representing St. Kazimierz. The inside is lined with red velvet, with ball feet of yellow amber underneath.[54]

By the time the long-awaited relic arrived in Florence, the Medici had amassed in their private reliquary chapel over thirty amber items, many of which also featured ivory accents.[55] The Jagiellończyk casket stands out amongst the encyclopedic gathering of amber objects both due to its large size, and its distinctly archaising style, with figures overwhelmingly conceived either frontally or in profile, schematised and abstracted block-like forms, and geometric monumental silhouette.[56] The reliquary presents as if it were pieced from individual parts that imitate incongruous spolia – including florid carved appliqués, faux gems, and cabochons, and figural plaquettes – all seemingly repurposed from other objects. The casket's construction as a *pseudo*-spoliate object creates a strong visual impression of movement, both in its variegated colours and shapes and animated surfaces, and its gesture to the motility entailed in processes of dismantling and reassembling of other objects (in this case imagined or invented). The container's design imitating a precious thing ostensibly manufactured from other, older reused or altered things, was fitting for the relic's special status as a sacred trophy detached from yet spiritually linked to the saint's venerable and miraculously intact body.

The architectonic design of the casket alludes to the holy prince's inviolate body and its place of burial in Lithuania as *locus sanctus*. Suggestive of medieval architectural sculpture, the stiffly frontal addossed figures of early bishops Augustine and Ambrose guarding the coffin's front opening subtly evoke movement, echoed in the spiral solomonic columns at the four corners, which miniaturized a feature of sacral architecture associated with holy sites and burials.[57] The reliquary was thus a miniaturisation of the saint's eponymous

---

54   ASF, Guardaroba Medicea 1090, fol. 3v. In Gennaioli – Sframeli (eds.), *Sacri Splendori* 266.

55   Hinrichs K., *Bernstein, das 'Preußische Gold' in Kunst- und Naturalienkammern und Museen des 16.–20. Jahrhunderts* (Ph.D. dissertation, Humboldt-Universität: 2007) 266–269.

56   Compare, e.g., Gennaioli – Sframeli (eds.), *Sacri Splendori* 184–193, 224–225. The casket's design is vaguely reminiscent of medieval Byzantine ivory caskets often repurposed as reliquaries: see, e.g., Cutler A., "On Byzantine Boxes", *The Journal of the Walters Art Gallery* 42/43 (1984–1985) 44–46. It is very similar to a smaller and less complex reliquary casket donated in 1691 to the monastery of S. Chiara in Naples: see Gennaioli – Sframeli (eds.), *Sacri Splendori* 266.

57   Ward Perkins, J.B., "The Shrine of St. Peter and its Twelve Spiral Columns", *Journal of Roman Studies* 42 (1952) 21–33.

MIXED EMOTIONS BETWEEN THE GRAND DUCHIES

reliquary chapel in Vilnius cathedral.[58] Described in the Medicean inventory as a cover 'in the manner of a sepulcher' (or 'coffin-type cover'), the top is punctuated by four fleur-de-lis finials on the corners, which adumbrate both the Pacowie *gozdawa* (lily) and Florentine *giglio* (iris).[59] They were likewise symbolic of the saint's special status as spiritual martyr, called *un bianco giglio* (a white iris) in period hagiography.[60]

Although not pictured here, the top features ivory plaques with scenes of the Annunciation and Visitation, and winged cherubim. Crowning the diminutive tomb, the equestrian figurine of Kazimierz recalls the centuries-old Vytis emblem of the Lithuanian Grand Duchy,[61] while also invoking his role a spiritual crusader and his sobriquet of *nobil Cavaliere* (noble Knight) in hagiographic literature.[62] Atop a striding horse, Jagiellończyk is very much on the move, as his steed and steady gaze body forth the peripatetic transregional journeying of the bone inside the box, reifying the emotional motility inherent to his white martyrdom.

Movement is further evoked by the ivory figural cartouches portraying holy persons arranged in interactive quartets on each of the four sides. Although a lack of attributes sometimes hampers identification, storied saints depicted include Lawrence, Barbara, Ursula, Catherine of Alexandria and Margaret of Antioch, Francis and Dominic, Agnes or Constance, and likely St. Stanislaus (Jagiellończyk's remains were long guarded in the chapel of St. Stanislaus, and the relic was solemnly removed on the feast day of Stanislaus).[63] These long-established objects of Catholic devotion are intermingled with more modern holy persons, notably five apparent figurations of holy Jesuits, foregrounding the critical intercessory role of the Society in negotiating the relic's transfer. Three such figures share the middle register on the coffin's front doors with St. Stanislaus (far left, holding crozier and crucifix): from left to right, they recite the Mass, ostend a Crucifix, and consecrate the host.[64]

---

58   Noyes, "(Re)moving relics and performing gift exchange".

59   Czyż A., "The Symbolic and Propaganda Message of the Heraldic Programmes in Two 17th-Century Marriage Prints (Epithalamia) of the Pacas Family", *Knygotyra* 73 (2020) 79–93.

60   Sant'Antonio, *Il breve compendio* 60.

61   Galkus J., *Lietuvos Vytis: albumas* (Vilnius: 2009).

62   Sant'Antonio, *Il breve compendio* 83.

63   Guidetti, "*Kultūriniai ir meniniai Lietuvos ir Tuscanos ryšiai*" 464–465. See also Gennaioli – Sframeli (eds.), *Sacri Splendori* 266–267, and Maslauskaitė-Mažylienė (ed.), *Masterpieces* 76.

64   These three Jesuit types, despite their rather schematic rendering, could depict, respectively, Jesuit founding fathers Ignatius of Loyola and Francis Xavier, and Polish-born novice Stanisław Kostka (1550–1568), beatified in 1605.

While all the plaquettes adhere to a more static than narrative mode of representation, the iconic figures' subtly turned bodies and opposing gazes enliven the compositional surface, putting into play imaginary exchanges between the historically disparate holy personages. For example, on the front side, figures in the central register turn in reverence toward each other (or rather, toward the Medici escutcheon), while those in the bottom and top registers turn to the right, directing the votary's gaze around the box's corner. On the reverse side this directionality is inverted, as the upper and lower figures face toward the left, establishing an antithetical rhythm. Most importantly, they encourage the devotee to interact with the object by turning it, or moving their own body to view the reliquary from all sides.

Ivory was avidly collected by the Medici, and often combined with amber in Baltic-made objets d'art.[65] A substance that had a long historical association with devotion, here the material potentially evoked the body of Jagiellończyk in several ways. Ivory's snowy hue recalls the rendering of the saint's skin in Dolci's portrait, eliciting notions of purity and chastity and the saint's origins in the snowy north and white martyrdom.[66] Ivory's resemblance to bone and flesh, and its origins in living matter, reflexively summoned up thoughts of the mystery of the Incarnation, of saintly incorruption and of the promise of bodily resurrection, making ivory ideally suited to rendering corporeal flesh, but also an appropriate synecdoche for the saint's bone inside, as well as Kazimierz's inviolate corpse preserved in Vilnius.[67] Art historian Sarah Guérin has explored ivory's haptic qualities in relation to embodied devotional practices.[68] In the case of the Kazimierz reliquary, the fine linear carving and highly textured surface of the white plaquettes would have invited interaction by touch, which

---

65   While the type and origin of the ivory used here remain unknown, it could have been sourced from Nordic-Baltic or Sibero-Russian walrus for this work. On the Nordic-Baltic region and Siberia as sources of ivory in this period, see Rijkelijkhuizen M., "Whales, Walruses, and Elephants: Artisans in Ivory, Baleen, and Other Skeletal Materials in Seventeenth- and Eighteenth-Century Amsterdam", *International Journal of Historical Archaeology* 13.409 (2009) 409–429. On Medici ivory collections, see Schmidt E., *Das Elfenbein der Medici: Bildhauerarbeiten für den florentiner Hof* (Munich: 2012). For period mixed amber-ivory objects, see, e.g., Gennaioli – Sframeli (eds.), *Sacri Splendori* 224.

66   Donecker S., "The Lion, the Witch and the Walrus: Images of the Sorcerous North in the 16th and 17th Centuries", TRANS *Internet-Zeitschrift für Kulturwissenschaften* 17 (2010) http://www.inst.at/trans/17Nr/4-5/4-5_donecker.htm (accessed on 4.10.2022).

67   Guérin S.M., "Meaningful Spectacles: Gothic Ivories Staging the Divine", *Art Bulletin* 95 (2013) 53–77.

68   Guérin S., *French Gothic Ivories. Material Theologies and the Sculptor's Craft* (Cambridge: 2022).

MIXED EMOTIONS BETWEEN THE GRAND DUCHIES   561

in turn would transfer heat to the ivory's substance, which would then retain warmth as if enlivened.[69]

In a manner more dramatic than ivory, amber – the primary material of the Kazmierz casket – possessed material properties which made it exegetically suited to reliquaries, enhancing their kinaesthetic qualities. Giovanni Matteo Guidetti persuasively argues that additional amber altar furnishings consisting of a crucifix and candlesticks accompanied the reliquary coffin.[70] That amber was prominently featured in Bishop Pac's extraordinary gift was in keeping with amber diplomatic gift-giving to promulgate the rare and storied substance as the patrimony of the Baltic elite.[71] Bishop Pac may have known that the Tuscan grand duke appeared to have had a special predilection for the substance; by the late seventeenth century the Medici collections boasted a splendid corpus of amber devotional objects.[72] Historically used in incense recipes for its musky, sweet perfume,[73] its smoke used to exorcise demons,[74] amber held a special association with salvation, devotion and spiritual exercises in Italian culture, thanks in part to its long-standing popularity in early modern Italy as a premier material for making rosaries.[75]

As demonstrated in an important study by Rachel King on amber rosaries in Italy, amber's material properties were understood to function exegetically, in helping pious users to understand and approximate divine mysteries in terms of its perceptible qualities, as well as physically and emotionally, in

---

69 Guérin S., "Saisir le sens. Les ivoires gothiques et le toucher", in Palazzo E. (ed.), *Les Cinq Sens au Moyen Âge* (Paris: 2016) 589–622.

70 ASF, Guardaroba Medicea, 1090s, fol. 4r–v. See discussion in Guidetti, "*Kultūriniai ir meniniai Lietuvos ir Tuscanos ryšiai*".

71 Netzer S., "Bernsteingeschenke in der preussischen Diplomatie des 17. Jahrhunderts", *Jahrbuch Der Berliner Museen* 35 (1993) 227–246; King R., "Whose Amber? Changing Notions of Amber's Geographical Origin", *Ostblick* 2 (2014) 1–22.

72 Hinrichs, *Bernstein* 266–269. See also Gennaioli – Sframeli (eds.), *Sacri Splendori* 184–201. Grusiecki T., "Foreign as Native: Baltic Amber in Florence", *World Art* 7, 1 (2017) 3–36. See also King R., "Finding the Divine Falernian: Amber in Early Modern Italy", V&A Online Journal 5 (Autumn 2013) http://www.vam.ac.uk/content/journals/research-journal/issue -no.-5-2013/finding-the-divine-falernian-amber-inearly-modern-italy/.

73 For its use in historical incense recipes see Burridge C., "Incense in medicine: an early medieval perspective", *Early Medieval Europe* 28 (2020) 219–255.

74 Bonardo Giovanni Maria, *La minera del mondo* (Venice, appresso Fabio, & Agostin Zoppini fratelli: 1585) 19v, 25r.

75 King R., "The Beads with Which We Pray Are Made from It: Devotional Ambers in Early Modern Italy", in Göttler C. – Boer W.D. (eds.), *Religion and the Senses in Early Modern Europe* (Leiden: 2013) 153–175. For an example from the Medici collections see Gennaioli – Sframeli (eds.), *Sacri Splendori* 200–201.

encouraging them to engage via their various bodily senses with these qualities, and through pious meditation thereby give rise to certain emotional states.[76] The salvific and prophylactic properties of amber (long used against plague),[77] as well as its applications in modulating and transforming the emotions, were promulgated by the Medicean court during Cosimo III's day: his daughter, Anna Maria Luisa de' Medici (1667–1743), who collected an extensive medicinal and alchemical recipe collection and gifted *materia medica* to elites across Europe, prepared a panacean 'Essenza d'Ambra' (Essence of Amber) that was purported to 'vivifica i sentimenti' (enliven the emotions).[78]

Tuscan natural historian Ulisse Aldrovandi (1522–1605) penned excursuses unfolding the exegetical potential of amber in his *Musaeum metallicum*, a work on mineralogy, geology and palaeology observations.[79] Aldrovandi was a friend of Tuscan Grand Duke Francesco de' Medici (1574–1587), even a guest of the grand duke in his Studiolo in the Palazzo Vecchio in 1577.[80] *Musaeum metallicum* was published postuhumously in 1648 with a dedication to Grand Duke Ferdinando II de' Medici (1610–1670), father of Cosimo III; it is thus safe to assume that the Tuscan scientist's work would have been well known in Medicean circles during the period when Cosimo received the amber vessel.

Aldrovandi fittingly included an exegesis of amber in a natural historical work explicating how amber figured bodily resurrection, and constituted the premier substance to body forth metamorphoses and transmutative or compound states; his fellow natural historians maintained that amber's origins were aqueous, identifying it as a solidified liquid; some even theorized that amber was the congealed tears of aquatic creatures.[81] Aquatic origins notwithstanding, amber was a 'warm' substance according to humoral theory, being called in Low German *bernsten*, from *bernen* (to burn), referring to its fiery

---

76   King, "The Beads with Which We Pray".

77   Riddle, John M. "Pomum Ambrae: Amber and Ambergris in Plague Remedies." Sudhoffs Archiv Für Geschichte Der Medizin Und Der Naturwissenschaften 48, no. 2 (1964): 111–22.

78   ASF, Miscellanea Medicea 1, fol. 214r. On amber in Medicean pharmacopeia during this period see Buchanan A.L., *The Politics of Medicine at the Late Medici Court: The Recipe Collection of Anna Maria Luisa de' Medici (1667–1743)* (PhD Thesis, University of South Florida, Tampa, FL, 2018) 128–129.

79   Aldrovandi Ulisse, *Musaeum metallicum libros IV* (Bologna, Giovanni Battista Ferroni: 1648).

80   Tosi A., ed., *Ulisse Aldrovandi e la Toscana* (Florence: 1989); Findlen P., *Possessing Nature: Museums, Collecting, and Scientific Culture in Early Modern Italy* (Berkeley: 1994) 243–245, 352–365.

81   King R., "Whale's Sperm, Maiden's Tears and Lynx's Urine: Baltic Amber and the Fascination for It in Early Modern Italy", *Ikonotheka* 22 (2009) 168–179.

visual qualities and chemical potential to burn and evaporate.[82] According to Aldrovandi:

> Praeterea humana caro mollem succinic ortum, deinde eius etiam duritiam, et splendorem aemulabitur: quandoquidem in ortu, nimirum dum in his mundi vanitatibus versatur, mollitie delitiarum non caret, sed tempore resurrectionis, divino durata calore rutilans, instar electri, apparebit. Aut dicendum erit, quod, licet homines a primordio sint molles, et ad quaelibet criminal perpetranda proni, nihilominus frigore divini timoris, vel calore humanarum calamitatum perculsi, Constantia et perseverantia durescunt.

> Human flesh imitates amber's soft beginnings and, thereafter, its hardness and brightness, inasmuch as, in its beginning, that is while it is involved in the vanities of the world, it does not lack the softness of pleasures, but at the time of the resurrection, having been hardened by divine heat, and shining, [the flesh] will appear the image of amber. Or it may be said, that although men are soft by their nature and prone to committing certain transgressions, beset by the cold of divine fear or by the heat of human calamities they become hard through constancy and perseverance, nevertheless.[83]

This passage gestures to the fact that contact with human flesh enlivens amber, causing it to retain and transfer warmth, in analogy to the shading of one emotion into another. More specifically, when 'read' metaphorically against Aldrovandi's text, amber's conductivity, and the resulting sensible passage from cool to warm in the handler's hands, invites an analogy to the resurrected flesh of the righteous – radiant, firm, converted by divine heat – and to the transformation effected by the devout who persevere, passing through divine fear (cold) and suffering (heat). Amber possesses another conductive property, whereby it conserves a static charge (amber in Latin and Greek is, respectively, *electrum* and *electron*) when subjected to friction, attracting lighter objects to itself. Aldrovandi analogised this triboelectric effect, whereby amber could produce a sensible electric charge transfer, to Christ's own burning love: 'pariter

---

82   Hammarlund A., "The Amber Road. Center and Periphery", *Baltic Worlds* 3, 1 (2010) 4–10, at 6.

83   Aldrovandi, *Musaeum metallicum*, 414. Cited in King, "The Beads with Which We Pray", 165.

Christus Dominus charitatis aestu ardescens vanos peccantes ad se allicit' (burning with the heat of his love, Christ draws vain sinners to himself).[84]

The substance's inherent duality, imbricating cold liquid and hot fire, is captured in Ovid's *Metamorphoses*, where amber first appears as the tears of the Heliades, daughters of Helios and sisters of the ill-fated Phaeton, after they are transformed into trees, their teardrops solidified by the sun and disseminated by flowing water.[85] In addition to the intrinsic association of amber with tears, the *Metamorphoses* also evinces amber's self-reflexive gesture to its own mixed emotional origins, as the substance derives from the sisters crying in a mixed emotional state of grief, surprise, horror, and painful suffering. The Ovidian account would have been familiar to the Medici court in Cosimo III's day, thanks to the painting *The Creation of Amber*, executed around 1572 by Santi di Tito for the Studiolo of Francesco I where Aldrovandi was also a guest; the work depicted amber's advent and the Heliades' transformation as told in the *Metamorphoses*, and has been discussed in an important study by Tomasz Grusiecki on the reception of Baltic amber in the Tuscan milieu of the Medici court.[86]

As a purportedly solidified marine liquid associated with heat and fire that married ostensibly opposed sates of coldness and warmth according to natural historical knowledge, and as substance inherently linked to tears shed as a result of complex emotions thanks to classical tradition, amber was especially appropriate, in the case of Kazimierz, as both an allegory and proxy for the spiritual martyr inside, whose shifting emotions and pious tears, compound state of chastity and fertility, and dual characterization as at once cold (due to his geographic origins) and warm (due to the ardency of his virtue), were recorded in period hagiography. A hymn in the liturgy recorded in the saint's first 1520 hagiography encapsulates this duality:

> Terra, quae brumam patitur reigentem, / Et caret phoebe radio calente / Sentit accensum boream superni / Sydere amoris. / Nempe, cui clarem genus, et propago / Regia, exurgens Casimirus ignem. / Quo calet frigens aquilo ministrat / Aethere ab alto. / Ignis est virtus animosa: per quam / Mens in authorem calefacta summum / Nil nisi mundam cupit, et beatam / Degere vitam.

---

84 Aldrovandi, *Musaeum metallicum*, 414. In King, "The Beads with Which We Pray", 168.

85 Ovid, *The Metamorphoses*. Translated by Allen Mandelbaum (New York: 1993) 53–54.

86 See further discussion in Grusiecki T., "Foreign as Native", 1–4.

MIXED EMOTIONS BETWEEN THE GRAND DUCHIES

> The land [of the cold north], enduring winter's harsh rule, and lacking the sun's warming rays, feels the north wind ignited with the star of heavenly love. Indeed, of clear lineage and royal offspring, arises Kazmierz, a fire warming the cold north wind, from the high ether. This fire is courageous virtue: through which the mind, warmed toward the Supreme Creator, desires nothing but a pure and blessed life.[87]

It bears consideration that Grand Duke Cosimo maintained close bodily proximity to the amber reliquary once it arrived in his possession; this is suggestive of his deep desire for corporal contact and interaction with the container. Considered in tandem with Dolci's portrait of Kazimierz made for Cosimo, with its evocation of the arrival of a rapturous dawn at the climax of the holy prince's nocturnal spiritual exercises and emotional transformations, the reliquary's material enlivenment in the hands of the Tuscan grand duke would have gained further significance within the context of the liturgy for Jagiellończyk written at the behest of the Tuscan grand duke's ancestor, and which may have contributed to conditioning Cosimo's emotional experience of the reliquary.

His tactile experience of the reliquary casket – touching, turning it, opening the doors to glimpse the wrapped relic inside – would have activated the amber's otherwise latent haptic and olfactory potential. As portions of the radiant ember-like substance heated in his hands, the material's capacity to retain this heat would, upon repeated contact, make it feel as if the casket itself was transfigured from cold to warm, exuding palpable warmth like a living entity and personating both the emotional passage from cold melancholy to warm joy and gratitude and the saint's inherent duality (both 'cold' and 'warm') as framed in hagiography. Likewise, touch would trigger the box's release of a musky fragrance redolent of the sweet smell ascribed to saints' incorrupt bodies, and the commonplace used to describe holy persons like St. Kazimierz who died 'in odour of sanctity'. The perfume might also have elicited the saint's shifting emotions from pain and pity to joy and delight in pleasuring in the 'sweet company of the Angels and his dear Saviour,' meditating on the 'sweet fruits' of the Passion, and singing of 'sweet lauds' to Christ and the Virgin. The scent would have transferred via contact to linger on Cosimo's own prayerful hands, a powerful reminder of the mechanism of contact inherent in relics leaving perceptible traces of the saint's ardent virtue. Caressing the coffin, perceiving the amber's static charge, at once suggestive of the saint's

---

87   Ferreri, *Vita Beati Casimiri* [n.p.].

aura and evocative of the 'unspeakable contentment' of the saint's rapturous transverberation, would perhaps have brought to mind how the saint burns to draw devotees to himself in imitation of Christ.

By way of conclusion, it is worth returning to Cosimo's celebratory passage of 1677, which inflected his own ambivalent emotional state – resonating with triumph and impatience, desire and trepidation, joy and hope – triggered by knowledge of the imminent promise of a relic of St. Kazimierz. This points to both the reliquary's intended emotional utility for and effects on its devout recipient, and its ability physically to register and sensuously reify these effects through manipulation and bodily interaction with the devotee. Like Dolci's portrait, the precious amber casket was designed to encourage emulation of Jagiellończyk, and thereby to engender similar experiences and sensations in pious interactants.

In the case of the painting, this operated by means of the beholder's visual contemplation of the image's formal and iconographical aspects. In addition to pondering the reliquary's form and iconography with the eyes, in holding, manipulating, opening and closing, and carrying the box, the exercitant of spiritual exercises focusing on the relic would have attempted to imitate the exemplary devotions of Kazimierz, sharing as much as possible in the emotional vicissitudes of the holy prince's spiritual martyrdom. The coffin's palpable material transmutations, calling to mind and reifying the saint's emotional ductility, might thereby function simultaneously through touch and smell as a sensible indicator of the devotees' own internal emotional transformations, as they imitated Jagiellończyk's spiritual exercises and attempted to recreate the saint's shifting emotions.

Bibliography

Early Modern Sources

Ulisse Aldrovandi, *Musaeum metallicum libros IV* (Bologna, Giovanni Battista Ferroni: 1648).

Bonardo Giovanni Maria, *La minera del mondo* (Venice, appresso Fabio, & Agostin Zoppini fratelli: 1585).

Ercole Domenico Antonio, *Breue Compendio Della vita di S. Casimiro Confessore, Figliuolo del re di Polonia Cauata da Diuersi Autori* (Rome, Domenico Antonio Ercole: 1687).

Ferreri Zaccaria, *Vita Beati Casimiri Confessoris: ex serenissimis Poloni[a]e regibus & magnis [...] Zacharia Ferrerio Vicentino pontifice Gardien[se]: in Polonia[m] & Lituania[m].* (Cracow, Iohannes Haller: 1520).

Sant'Antonio Hilarione di, *Il breve compendio della vita morte, e miracoli del santissimo prencipe Casimiro, figlio del magno Casimiro re di Polonia, riferita da monsignore Zaccaria Ferrerio* (Naples, Aegidio Longo: 1629).

Skarga Piotr, *Żywoty Świętych Pańskich na wszystkie dnie roku* (Warsaw: Mikołów, 1910).

Święcicki Grzegorz, *Theatrum S. Casimiri: In quo ipsius prosapia, vita, miracula, et illustris pompa in solemni eiusdem apotheoseos instauratione, Vilnae Lithuaniae metropoli, v. Id. Maij, anno D[omi]ni M.DC.IV. instituta graphice proponuntur ...* ([Vilnae]: Typographicis Academiae Societatis Iesu, [1604]).

Secondary Sources

Acton H., *The Last Medici* (London: 1988).

Baniulytė A., "The Pazzi Family in Lithuania: Myth and Politics in the European Court Society of the Early Modern Age", *Medium aevum quotidianum* 58 (2009) 41–57.

Baniulytė A., "Gli italiani alla corte dei 'Pazzi' in Lituania: mito e politica nel Seicento barocco", *Archivio storico italiano* 168 (2010) 325–348.

Baniulytė A., "Šv. Marijos Magdalenos de'Pazzi kultas Lietuvos baroko kultūroje: atvaizdai ir istorinė tikrovė", *Darbai ir dienos* 53 (2010) 225–258.

Bhalla N., "Containing the Uncontainable: Kinaesthetic Analogies and an Early Christian Box", *The Art Bulletin* 104, 3 (2022) 6–28.

Bouley B.A., *Pious Postmortems: Anatomy, Sanctity, and the Catholic Church in Early Modern Europe* (Philadelphia, PA: 2017).

Buchanan A.L., *The Politics of Medicine at the Late Medici Court: The Recipe Collection of Anna Maria Luisa de' Medici (1667–1743)* (PhD Thesis, University of South Florida, Tampa, FL, 2018).

Burridge C., "Incense in medicine: an early medieval perspective", *Early Medieval Europe* 28 (2020) 219–255.

Čiurinskas M., "Piotr Skarga's *Zywot Swiętego Kazimierza królewica polskiego* (1610) and the Lithuanian hagiographic tradition/Petro Skargos *Šv. Kazimiero, Lenkijos karalaičio, gyvenimas* (1610) ir to meto lietuviškoji hagiografinė tradicija", *Senoji Lietuvos literatūra* 35–36 (2013) 269–301.

Copeland C., *Maria Maddalena de' Pazzi: The Making of a Counter-Reformation Saint* (Oxford: 2016).

Cutler A., "On Byzantine Boxes", *The Journal of the Walters Art Gallery* 42/43 (1984–1985) 44–46.

Czyż A., "The Symbolic and Propaganda Message of the Heraldic Programmes in Two 17th-Century Marriage Prints (Epithalamia) of the Pacas Family", *Knygotyra* 73 (2020) 79–93.

Davies N., *Litva: The Rise and Fall of the Grand Duchy of Lithuania: A Selection from Vanished Kingdoms* (New York, NY: 2013).

Donecker S., "The Lion, the Witch and the Walrus: Images of the Sorcerous North in the 16th and 17th Centuries", *TRANS Internet-Zeitschrift für Kulturwissenschaften* 17 (2010) http://www.inst.at/trans/17Nr/4-5/4-5_donecker.htm (accessed on 4.10.2022).

Donecker S., "Est vera India septemtrio: re-imagining the Baltic in the age of discovery", in Lehtonen T. – Kaljundi L. (eds.), *Re-forming Texts, Music, and Church Art in the Early Modern North* (Amsterdam: 2016) 393–419.

Grusiecki T., "Foreign as Native: Baltic Amber in Florence", *World Art* 7, 1 (2017) 3–36.

Findlen P., *Possessing Nature: Museums, Collecting, and Scientific Culture in Early Modern Italy* (Berkeley: 1994).

Fordoński K. – Urbański P., "Jesuit Culture in Poland and Lithuania, 1564–1773", *Journal of Jesuit Studies* 5.3 (2018) 341–351.

Gennaioli R. – Sframeli M. (eds.), *Sacri Splendori: Il Tesoro Della 'Cappella Delle Reliquie' in Palazzo Pitti* (Livorno: 2014).

Guérin S.M., "Meaningful Spectacles: Gothic Ivories Staging the Divine", *Art Bulletin* 95 (2013) 53–77.

Guérin S., "Saisir le sens. Les ivoires gothiques et le toucher", in Palazzo E. (ed.), *Les Cinq Sens au Moyen Âge* (Paris: 2016) 589–622.

Guérin S., *French Gothic Ivories. Material Theologies and the Sculptor's Craft* (Cambridge: 2022).

Guarini E.F., "COSIMO III de' Medici, granduca di Toscana", *Dizionario Biografico degli Italiani* 30 (1984), https://www.treccani.it/enciclopedia/cosimo-iii-de-medici -granduca-di-toscana_(Dizionario-Biografico) (accessed on 10.8.2023).

Guidetti G.M., "Il reliquario di santa Maria Maddalena de'Pazzi a Vilnius e l'attività di Giovanni Comparini e Giuseppe Vanni per la corte di Toscana: nuovi documenti", *Bollettino della Accademia degli Euteleti della Città di San Miniato* 79 (2012) 197–215.

Guidetti G.M., "Kultūriniai ir meniniai Lietuvos ir Tuscanos ryšiai XVII a. antroje pusėje: Pacų šeima ir didysis kunigaikštis Kosimas III Medičis", in Mitrulevičiūte D. (ed.), *Lietuva – Italija. Šimtmečių Ryšiai* (Vilnius: 2016) 439–462.

Guzmán M.T., *A Medici Pilgrimage: The Devotional Journey of Cosimo III to Santiago De Compostela (1669)* (Turnout: 2018).

Hammarlund A., "The Amber Road. Center and Periphery", *Baltic Worlds* 3, 1 (2010) 4–10.

Hinrichs K., *Bernstein, Das 'Preußische Gold' in Kunst- und Naturalienkammern und Museen des 16.–20. Jahrhunderts* (Ph.D. dissertation, Humboldt-Universität: 2007).

King R., "The Shining Example of 'Prussian Gold': Amber and Cross-Cultural Connections between Italy and the Baltic in the Early Modern Period", in Lipińska A. (ed.), *Materiał rzeźby: Między techniką a semantyką* (Wroclaw: 2009) 456–470.

King R., "Whale's Sperm, Maiden's Tears and Lynx's Urine: Baltic Amber and the Fascination for It in Early Modern Italy", *Ikonotheka* 22 (2009) 168–179.

King R., "The Beads with Which We Pray Are Made from It: Devotional Ambers in Early Modern Italy", in Göttler C. – Boer W.D. (eds.), *Religion and the Senses in Early Modern Europe* (Leiden: 2013) 153–175.

King R., "Finding the Divine Falernian: Amber in Early Modern Italy", V&A Online Journal 5 (Autumn 2013)", http://www.vam.ac.uk/content/journals/research-journal/issue-no.-5-2013/finding-the-divine-falernian-amber-inearly-modern-italy/.

King R., "Whose Amber? Changing Notions of Amber's Geographical Origin", *Ostblick* 2 (2014) 1–22.

Maslauskaitė S., "Šv. Kazimiero relikvijos ir relikvijoriai", *Acta academiae artium Vilnensis* 41 (2006) 35–57.

Maslauskaitė-Mažylienė S., *Šventojo Kazimiero atvaizdo istorija XVI–XVIII a* (Vilnius: 2010).

Maslauskaitė-Mažylienė S., *Dzieje wizerunku św. Kazimierza od XVI do XVIII wieku. Między ikonografią a tekstem, z języka litewskiego przełożyła Katarzyna Korzeniewska* (Vilnius: 2013).

Maslauskaitė-Mažylienė S. (ed.), *Masterpieces of the history of the veneration of St. Casimir: Lithuania – Italy*, exh. ciat., Bažnytinio paveldo muziejus (Vilnius: 2018).

Modesti A., *Women's Patronage and Gendered Cultural Networks in Early Modern Europe: Vittoria della Rovere, Grand Duchess of Tuscany* (New York: 2020).

Netzer S., "Bernsteingeschenke in der preussischen Diplomatie des 17. Jahrhunderts", *Jahrbuch Der Berliner Museen* 35 (1993) 227–246.

Noyes R.S., *Peter Paul Rubens and the Counter-Reformation crisis of the Beati moderni* (New York: 2018).

Noyes R.S., "'Purest Bones, Sweet Remains, and Most Sacred Relics.' Re-Fashioning St. Kazimierz Jagiellończyk (1458–84) as a Medieval Saint between Counter-Reformation Italy and Poland-Lithuania", *Religions* 12, 1011 (2021) https://doi.org/10.3390/rel12111011.

Noyes R.S., "'The Polar Winds have driven me to the conquest of the Treasure in the form of the much-desired relic.' (Re)moving relics and performing gift exchange between early modern Tuscany and Lithuania", in Strenga G. – Kjar L. (eds.), *Gifts and Materiality: Gifts as Objects in Medieval and Early Modern Europe* (London: 2022) 103–131.

Noyes R.S., "'To see at Least in an Image the Semblance of a Friend …' Representing the Family of Pacowie Between Baroque Tuscany and Lithuania", *Kaunas History Annals* 20 (2022) 161–176.

Ovid, *The Metamorphoses*. Translated by Allen Mandelbaum (New York: 1993).

Panella A., "Candidati italiani al trono polacco. I Medici", *Rassegna Nazionale* 16 April (1917) 269–279.

Quirini-Popławska D., "La corte di Toscana e la terza elezione in Polonia", *Zeszyty Naukowe Uniwersytetu Jagiellońskiego. Prace Historyczne* 71 (1982) 49–66.

Rijkelijkhuizen M., "Whales, Walruses, and Elephants: Artisans in Ivory, Baleen, and Other Skeletal Materials in Seventeenth- and Eighteenth-Century Amsterdam", *International Journal of Historical Archaeology* 13, 409 (2009) 409–429.

Rush A.C., "Spiritual Martyrdom in St. Gregory the Great" *Theological Studies* 23, 4 (1962) 569–589.

Sanger A., *Art, Gender and Religious Devotion in Grand Ducal Tuscany* (Burlington, VT: 2014).

Schmidt E., *Das Elfenbein der Medici: Bildhauerarbeiten für den florentiner Hof* (Munich: 2012).

Spinelli R., *Le Committenze Sacre di Cosimo III de' Medici: Episodi Poco Noti o Sconosciuti (1677–1723)* (Florence: 2019).

Tosi A. (ed.), *Ulisse Aldrovandi e la Toscana* (Florence: 1989).

SECTION B

Heuristic and Sanative Images of Mixed Emotions

∴

CHAPTER 15

Francisci chorda traxit ad se plurima corda: 'Drawing' the Heart's Emotions in Jan Provoost's Diptych of *Christ Carrying the Cross*

Elliott D. Wise

Abstract

Jan Provoost's diptych of *Christ Carrying the Cross* depicts strikingly distinct emotional states. On the left, a beleaguered Jesus is surrounded by both violence and cruelty, as well as compassion and grief. On the right, a Franciscan friar engages in meditative prayer. Although his countenance is inscrutable, a rebus inscribed on the diptych's frame points to the mixed emotions of his heart. The rebus construes the cord of his Franciscan profession as a tether linking his heart to Christ's and, by extension, to the complex emotions of the Passion. The meditative praxis of St. Bonaventure and the Observant Franciscans, along with the diptych's trope of stone, illuminates the loving, mingled emotions that transit imperceptibly beneath the friar's 'petrified' expression.

Keywords

Jan Provoost – St. Bonaventure – Hendrik Herp – Franciscans (Order of Friars Minor) – rebus – heart – rope – Bruges

Painted in 1522 for an unnamed Franciscan patron, Jan Provoost's diptych of *Christ Carrying the Cross* registers a wide range of emotions [Fig. 15.1]. In the left panel, Jesus shoulders the cross in proximity to leering tormentors, whose deformed features reveal the violent passions of their souls. The creased brows and tear-streaked faces of the Virgin and St. John manifest deep compassion, although the different angles of their heads and varying directions of their gazes imply unique iterations of sorrow. In stark contrast, the Franciscan donor in the adjoining panel is emotionally inscrutable. In the tradition of the Franciscan *Meditations on the Life of Christ* (*Meditationes vitae Christi*), his stare suggests that he is prayerfully inhabiting the mystery of the Lord's Passion before him. With his back erect, neck tense and bent forward, and hands

© ELLIOTT D. WISE, 2025 | DOI:10.1163/9789004694613_016

hovering just apart from each other – the fingers uncomfortably unsupported in midair – he is a model of St. Luke's description of 'those servants, whom the lord when he cometh shall find watching'.[1] 'Watch and pray, that ye enter not into temptation', Christ admonished his sleepy disciples during their vigil with him in Gethsemane. 'The spirit indeed is willing, but the flesh is weak'.[2] Where the apostles failed, this Franciscan succeeds, but while his zealous attention is everywhere manifested in body, the sentiments of his soul are hardly traceable. His blank gaze conforms to the position of the Virgin's eyes, but his tearless face, set jaw, and pressed lips hide further echoes of Marian *Compassio*. Indeed, compared to the tumultuous emotions of the left panel, speckled with blood, tears, and spittle, the donor looks stony by comparison, and in fact, the frame and exterior of the diptych have been rendered in fictive marble and magmatic porphyry, as if troping the opacity that conceals the movements of the friar's heart [Fig. 15.2].

The movement of hearts, however, is at the core of the diptych's argument, as the inscription on the upper edge of the frames makes plain. In ornamental Gothic lettering, the text reads, *Francisci chorda traxit ad se plurima corda* ('Francis's cord draws the most hearts to itself').[3] 'Cord' and 'hearts' are represented as pictograms, the former by the sinuous length of rope used by the Friars Minor to belt their habits and bearing the knots that recall their vows of poverty, chastity, and obedience. The latter pictogram takes the form of two hearts, which, like the Franciscan cord, are emphasised by the shadows they cast and the relatively large amount of space they occupy. 'Cord' and 'hearts', moreover, are homophones in Latin – *chorda* and *corda* – further linking the two words and establishing them as the controlling devotional prompt of the painting. This analogy between cord (singular) and hearts (plural) has, as one of its primary objectives, the delineating and disciplining of the donor's hidden emotions, binding them to Christ, like the cord wrapped around the Lord's hands in Provoost's diptych (one cord, linking two hearts). The affections of the heart are crucial in the Franciscan spiritual tradition, and the writings of the great Franciscan mystic and theologian, St. Bonaventure (1221–1274), identify the suffering Jesus as the ultimate expression of the votary's affective fervor. Analogising the patron's heart to a Franciscan cord, the three knots and tight

---

1   Luke 12:37.

2   Matthew 26:41.

3   Dlabačová A., "The Art of Observance. Jan Provoost's *Diptych of a Franciscan Friar* as an Exponent of the Spirituality and Position of the Franciscan Order in the Low Countries, c. 1520", in Falque I. – Guideroni A. (eds.), *Rethinking the Dialogue between the Verbal and the Visual: Methodological Approaches to the Relationship Between Religious Art and Literature (1400–1700)* (Leiden: 2023) 216–217.

FIGURE 15.1   Jan Provoost, Interior of *Christ Carrying the Cross and Portrait of a Fifty-Four-Year-Old Franciscan*, (1522). Oil on panel, 40 cm × 49.5 cm. Sint-Janshospitaal, Bruges (inv. no. 0000.SJ0191.I). Artwork in the public domain

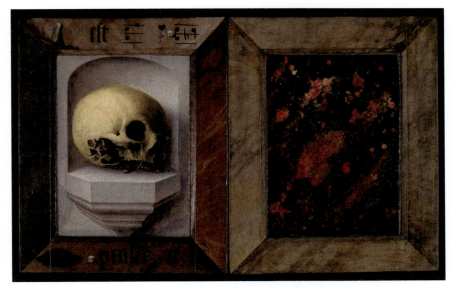

FIGURE 15.2   Jan Provoost, Exterior of *Christ Carrying the Cross and Portrait of a Fifty-Four-Year-Old Franciscan*, (1522). Oil on panel, 40 cm × 49.5 cm. Sint-Janshospitaal, Bruges (inv. no. 0000.SJ0191.I). Artwork in the public domain

cincture give form to the friar's hidden emotions, twisting, tying, and girding his soul as he shuns evil affections and tethers himself to the heart of Christ.

Provoost's diptych, then, elaborates on the theme of 'mixed emotions' in several ways. It reflects on visible emotions, unseen and secret emotions, constancy in navigating perverse and fickle emotions, dying to emotions derived from the corporeal senses, and conformity to the interior emotions of Christ's Passion. Jesus's face – his moist eyes reflecting the light, his cheeks marked with tear-like lines of blood, his slightly creased brow, and barely open lips – registers compassion, grief, and longsuffering love. But these traceable feelings are only part of the depth of his Passion. His intent gaze toward the friar, and specifically toward the friar's heart, invites the Franciscan patron to also perceive the 'inner Passion' that tortured the heart of Jesus with unseen emotions, both his own and those of all humanity for whom he suffered. Indeed, Provoost clusters the anguished faces of Mary and John, as well as the remorseless and belligerent countenances of the tormentors, both along and within the framework of the cross. In this way, Jesus 'bears them', as much as he bears the heavy wooden beams. Their emotions – a mixture of painful empathy and merciless derision – form part of the unseen suffering racking the Lord's soul. He guides the Franciscan votary to this insight through a purposeful composition of scene. The way he pauses in the forward onslaught of his march to Calvary and turns to look penetratingly across the frame dividing the diptych evinces a calculated, instructive revelation.

The intentionality of Christ's gaze also 'tethers' the friar to the Passion, so that he follows each of its movements through building layers of emotion. Although the patron's bodily posture is as immovable and rigid as a rock, the diptych implies that his heart is supple in echoing each emotional inflection in the heart of Jesus. In fact, the friar's unresponsive appearance should be understood as evidence of his constancy and steadfast diligence in these devotions. The tethering stare operates by virtue of the mendicant vocation established by St. Francis of Assisi (ca. 1181–1226). 'Francis's cord draws the most hearts', and in the diptych, the example of the *poverello* (Little Poor Man) of Assisi models a form of *imitatio Christi*, in which the votary unites *internally* with the suffering Jesus. The heart, rather than the body, is martyred, as St. Bonaventure describes in his account of Francis's stigmatisation, when the saint was 'totally transformed into the likeness of Christ crucified, not by the martyrdom of his flesh, but by the fire of his love consuming his soul'.[4] Significantly, Francis

---

4   13.3, *Legenda Sancti Francisci*, in St. Bonaventure, *Doctoris seraphici S. Bonaventurae, S.R.E. episcopus cardinalis. Opera omnia*, ed. Studio et Cura PP. Collegii a S. Bonaventura (Florence: 1882–1902) 8:543: 'ut amicus Christi praenosceret, se non per martyrium carnis, sed per

greeted his stigmatisation with mixed emotions: he was 'overwhelmed and his heart was flooded with a mixture of joy and sorrow'.[5] Uniquely in the case of the *poverello*, the unseen 'fire of his love consuming his soul' was authenticated by the appearance of external wounds in his hands, feet, and side. These marks – Bonaventure describes them in notarial terminology as a 'seal' (*sigillum*) – first 'left in [Francis's] heart a marvelous ardor' and shortly thereafter 'imprinted on his body markings that were not less marvelous'.[6]

Bonaventure reports that St. Francis tried to hide 'the royal secret' (*secreti regalis*) of his stigmata, just as he regularly masked the ecstasies and empathies of his soul throughout his life.[7] The enigma and secrecy of Francis's passion implies special privilege, a point borne out by the *poverello's* refusal to tell his brother friars what the seraphic figure in his stigmatising vision had said to him. Bonaventure posits that 'those things he had been told [...] were so secret that men are not permitted to speak of them'.[8] In the diptych, the insistent delineation between the highly emotional in the left panel and the seemingly emotionless in the right infers a similar privilege of unseen secrecy. For all his stony immunity to the visual, aural, haptic, and olfactory emotions of the left panel, Provoost's friar nonetheless engages in Christ's emotions with martyrizing intensity, albeit on a rarified, internal plane.

1   Volatile Senses and Inscrutable Stone

Relatively little has been written on the life and works of Jan Provoost (ca. 1465–1529). He was unknown to scholars until 1864, when his name was

---

     incendium mentis totum in Christi crucifixi similitudinem transformandum'. English translation in St. Bonaventure, *Bonaventure: The Soul's Journey into God, The Tree of Life, The Life of St. Francis*, trans. E. Cousins, The Classics of Western Spirituality (Mahway, NJ: 1978) 306.

5   13.3, *Legenda Sancti Francisci*, in St. Bonaventure, *Opera omnia* 8:543: 'vehementer obstupuit, mixtumque moerore gaudium cor eius incurrit'. English translation in St. Bonaventure, *Bonaventure* 305.

6   13.3, *Legenda Sancti Francisci*, in St. Bonaventure, *Opera omnia* 8:543: 'in corde ipsius reliquit ardorem, sed et in carne non minus mirabilem signorum impressit effigiem'. English translation in St. Bonaventure, *Bonaventure* 306.

7   13.5, *Legenda Sancti Francisci*, in St. Bonaventure, *Opera omnia* 8:543. English translation in St. Bonaventure, *Bonaventure* 308.

8   13.4, *Legenda Sancti Francisci*, in St. Bonaventure, *Opera omnia* 8:543: 'Credendum sane, tam arcana illa fuisse sacri illius Seraph in cruce mirabiliter apparentis eloquia, quod forte non liceret hominibus ea loqui'. English translation in St. Bonaventure, *Bonaventure* 307.

transcribed from an inventory of the Antwerp guild of St. Luke.[9] A decade later, Henry James Weale (1832–1917) was the first to publish on him and piece together his oeuvre, only one painting of which has been authenticated with documentary evidence.[10] Provoost was born in the city of Mons, capital of the province of Hainaut. He was likely apprenticed to Simon Marmion (1424/25–1489), the celebrated miniaturist of Valenciennes, and he married Marmion's widow approximately two years after the master's death. Provoost was married a total of four times. He acquired substantial wealth through his wives and had a prosperous career in Bruges and likely in Valenciennes as well. He acquired citizenship in Bruges in 1494, and although the Antwerp Guild of St. Luke lists a 'Jan Provoost' in its 1493 registry, Ron Spronk has recently thrown this identification with the Bruges Provoost into question.[11] Documents from the Bruges guild deferentially refer to a 'Mr. Jan Provoest, painter and knight'

---

9   Rombouts P.F. –Lerius T.F.X. van (eds.), *De Liggeren: en andere historische archieven der Antwerpsche Sint Lucasgilde, onder zinspreuk: "Wt ionsten versaemt"* (Antwerp: [1864–1876]) 1:46, 64.

10   Weale H.J., "Jean Prévost, Peintre", *Le Beffroi* 4 (1875) 205–215. Only the Bruges *Last Judgment*, completed in 1525, can be connected to Provoost from archival evidence. For pioneering scholarship on Jan Provoost in general (excluding studies of specific works), see Weale H.J., *Exposition des primitifs flamands et d'art ancient*, exh. cat., (Bruges: 1902) cat. nos. 167–169; Hulin de Loo G., "Geschiedenis der kunst in de Nederlanden (België en Holland), Eenige Brugsche schilders van de eerste helft der XVIe eeuw", *Kunst en Leven* 1.5 (1902) 1–43; Wurzbach A. von, *Niederländisches Künstler-Lexikon auf Grund Archivalischer Forschungen Bearbeitet L–Z* (Vienna: 1910) 2:363–364; Michel É., "À propos de Jean Provost et du Maître de Saint-Gilles", *Gazette des beaux-arts* 17 (1928) 228–237; Parmentier R.A., "Bronnen voor de geschiedenis van het Brugse schildersmilieu in de 16e eeuw. 19 Jan Provost", *Revue Belge d'Archéologie et d'Histoire de l'Art* 11 (1941) 97–118; Becherini B. – Ragghianti C.L. – Collobi-Ragghianti L. – De Witt A., *Mostra d'arte fiamminga e olandese dei secoli XV e XVI catalogo*, exh. cat., Strozzi Palace (Florence, 1947) 131–138; Ragghianti C.L., "Sull'opera di Jan Provost", *Critica d'arte* 8 (1949/1950) 334–340; Bologna F., "Nuove attribuzioni a Jan Provost", *Bulletin des Musées Royaux des Beaux-Arts de Belgique* 5, 1 (1956) 13–31; Speth-Holterhoff S., "Trois panneaux de Jean Provost", *Bulletin Musées Royaux des Beaux-Arts de Belgique* 14 (1965) 15–26; Friedländer M.J., *Early Netherlandish Painting*, vol. 9b, *Joos van Cleve, Jan Provost, Joachim Patenier*, trans. H. Norden (New York: 1973) 85–94; Spronk R., "Jan Provoost: Art Historical and Technical Examinations", 2 vols. (Ph.D. dissertation., Rijksuniversiteit: 1993); idem, "Jan Provoost", in Martens M.P.J. (ed.), *Bruges and the Renaissance: Memling to Pourbus* (Ludion: 1998) 94–106; Schouteet A., *De vlaamse Primitieven te Brugge. Bronnen voor de schilderkunst te Brugge tot de dood van Gerard David*, vol. 2: L–Z, Fontes Historiae Artis Neerlandicae: Bronnen voor de kunstgeschiedenis van de Nederlanden 2 (Brussels: 2004) 127–132; Spronk R., "Jan Provoost before c. 1500: The Documentary Evidence", in Koopstra A. – Seidel C. – Waterman J.P. (eds.), *Tributes to Maryan W. Ainsworth: Collaborative Spirit: Essays on Northern European Art, 1350–1650* (London: 2022) 86–93.

11   Spronk argues convincingly that the Antwerp record refers to a different painter of the same name. Spronk, "Jan Provoost before c. 1500" 86–93.

(*Mr Jan Provoest, scilder ende ruddere*), since he had been inducted into the Knights of the Holy Sepulcher during a pilgrimage to Jerusalem at the end of the fifteenth or beginning of the sixteenth century.[12] He belonged to the Bruges confraternity of Jerusalem Pilgrims and in 1527 served as its master. He owned several homes and wielded considerable influence, such that when Albrecht Dürer (1471–1528) visited Bruges in 1520, it was Provoost who entertained him. The two artists had met the previous year in Antwerp, and Dürer created a portrait of him in charcoal and another in silverpoint.[13] At his death in 1529, Provoost was entombed in the church of St. Gilles.[14]

The diptych of *Christ Carrying the Cross* is a visually complex, mature work, completed twenty-eight years after Provoost obtained Bruges citizenship and just seven years before his death.[15] The panels are precisely dated to 1522 by the inscription on the lower edge of the frame, which also records the friar's age as fifty-four. The reverse of the donor panel includes a rebus that has never been definitively transliterated. Inscribed across the upper and lower frames, it contains a puzzling arrangement of French words, musical notation, and pictorial images (a bluestone boulder, a field pansy, dice, and a bonnet), with a large skull resting on a stone console in the panel's center. Various readings of the rebus have been suggested, all of which recommend the subject of death for the viewer's meditation. In 1902, Georges Hulin de Loo proposed the following reading:

> *Bonne est la pensée de la mort.*
> *Bonnet de penser à la mort.*[16]

---

12   Haute C.V., *La Corporation des peintres de Bruges* (Bruges: n.d. [1913]) 200; Geirnaert N., *Het archief van de familie Adornes en de Jeruzalemstichting te Brugge*, Brugse Geschiedbronnen 19–20 (Bruges: 1987–1989) 1:152; Spronk, "Jan Provoost" 1:94–96; idem, "The Reconstruction of a Triptych of Jan Provoost for the Jerusalem Chapel in Bruges", *Burlington Magazine* 147, 1223 (February 2005) 109–111; Koldeweij J., *Geloof & geluk: Sieraad en devotie in middeleeuws Vlaanderen* (Arnhem: 2006) 189–193; Spronk, "Jan Provoost before c. 1500" 92.

13   The silverpoint is no longer extant, but a charcoal and brown chalk drawing at the British Museum has been suggested as one of the Dürer portraits. British Museum, London, inv. no. SL,5218.52. See Crowe J.A. – Cavalcaselle G.B., *Les anciens peintres flamands, leur vie et leur oeuvres, annoté et augmenté de documents inédits par Alex. Pinchart et Ch. Ruelens* (Brussels: 1862–1863) 2:293–294; Spronk, "Jan Provoost before c. 1500" 88.

14   On Provoost's biography and the historiography of scholarship, see Spronk, "Jan Provoost: Art Historical and Technical Examinations" 1: esp. 9–42.

15   The diptych was attributed to Jan Provoost by Hulin de Loo in 1902. Hulin de Loo G., *Exposition de tableaux flamands des XIVe, XVe et XVIe siècles. Catalogue critique précédé d'une introduction sur l'identité de certaines maîtres anonymes* (Ghent: 1902) 51, cat. no. 189.

16   Hulin de Loo, "Geschiedenis der kunst" 27–28, cat. no. 12.

580   WISE

Good is the thought of death.
Good, it is, to think on death.

Seventy-four years later, the Bruges Sint-Janshospitaal Museum published a
different interpretation:

Dur est la pensée de la mort.
Bonnet (Bon est) de penser à mi (moi).[17]

Hard is the thought of death.
Good, it is, to think of me.

In this reading, 'me' is death personified, as if the skull were speaking. In 1995,
Leo Wuyts suggested another reading, this time interpreting the bluestone pictogram as a navigation device for sailors:

Amer est la pensée de la mort.
Bon est de penser à la mort.[18]

Bitter is the thought of death.
Good, it is, to think on death.

Wuyts's interpretation is compelling, particularly in its allusion to Ecclesiasticus:

O death, how bitter is the remembrance of thee to a man that liveth at
rest in his possessions, unto the man that hath nothing to vex him, and
that hath prosperity in all things: yea, unto him that is yet able to receive
meat! O death, acceptable is thy sentence unto the needy, and unto him
whose strength faileth, that is now in the last age, and is vexed with all
things, and to him that despaireth, and hath lost patience![19]

The condemnation of the 'man that liveth at rest in his possessions' and 'hath
prosperity in all things' is especially consonant with the Franciscan vocation

---

17   Lobelle H., *Sint Janshospitaal Brugge, 1188–1976: Tentoonstelling, Brugge, 5 juni–
     31 augustus 1976*, exh. cat., (Bruges: 1976) 2:579, cat. no. S 74. See also Lobelle-Caluwe H. –
     M. Cumberlege, *Memlingmuseum Bruges*, Musea Nostra (Bruges: 1987) 92.
18   Wuyts L., "Een kanttekening bij de diptiek met de 'Kruisdraging' en het 'Portret van
     een Minderbroeder' van Jan Provoost", *Gentse Bijdragen tot de Kunstgeschiedenis en
     Oudheidkunde* 30 (1995) 220.
19   Ecclesiasticus 41:1–2; Wuyts, "Een kanttekening" 220.

EMOTIONS IN PROVOOST'S DIPTYCH OF CHRIST *CARRYING THE CROSS* 581

of radical poverty. Wuyts also quotes St. Jerome as an important source text for the rebus's second line, when the Church father, citing Plato, asserts that 'a wise man's whole life should be a preparation for death'.[20]

In 2003, Annette Scherer argued that if the bluestone is understood to be a 'touchstone' (*toucheau*), the rebus could be deciphered as follows, still with the final line in the voice of Death personified:

> *Tout chaud est ma pensée dé la.*
> *Bon est de penser à moi.*[21]

> Entirely passionate is my thought there.[22]
> Good, it is, to think on me.

Most recently, Anna Dlabačová has returned the rebus closer to Hulin de Loo's first suggestion, although she acknowledges that the verse may be purposefully ambiguous in meaning. The bluestone boulder is likely a 'border stone' (*borne*, *bosne*, or *bonne*), which would render the first line as *Bonne est la pensée de la mort*.[23] Combined with the Latin pictogram inscription on the diptych's interior, the complexity of the French rebus speaks to the erudition of the Franciscan donor and may suggest connections to the rhetorical chambers of Bruges on the part of both the friar and the artist.[24]

---

20   40.14, *Ad Heliodorum epitaphium Nepoltiani*, in St. Jerome, *Sancti Eusebii Hieronymi epistulae* (*Select Letters of St. Jerome*) Loeb Classical Library 262:1, ed. J. Henderson, trans. F.A. Wright (Cambridge, MA: 1933), 294/295: 'omnem sapienti vitam meditationem esse mortis'.

21   Scherer A., "Fromme Rätsel: Beobachtungen zum Diptychon eines Franziskaners von Jan Provost", Kammel F.M. (ed.), *Im Zeichen des Christkinds. Privates Bild und Frömmigkeit im Spätmittelalter: Ergebnisse der Ausstellung Spiegel der Seligkeit*, exh. cat., Germanisches Nationalmuseum Nürnberg (Nuremberg: 2003) 82–83.

22   This is Dlabačová's translation. Dlabačová, "The Art of Observance" 218.

23   Ibidem, 245.

24   See Hulin de Loo, "Geschiedenis der Kunst" 42–43; Spronk, "Jan Provoost" 94; Scherer A., "Diptychon eines Minoritenbruders", in Kammel F.M. – Curtius A., *Spiegel der Seligkeit. Privates Bild und Frömmigkeit im Spätmittelalter. Ausstellungskatalog Germanisches Nationalmuseum, Nürnberg, 31. Mai bis 8. Oktober 2000*, exh. cat., Germanisches Nationalmuseum (Nuremberg: 2000) 399; idem, "Fromme Rätsel" 78, 83–84; Warnar G., "*Elckerlijc* in beeld: Jan Provoosts 'Rijkaard en de dood'", *Spieghel der Letteren* 57 (2015) 273–289; idem, "Eye to Eye, Text to Image? Jan Provoost's *Sacred Allegory*, Jan van Ruusbroec's *Spieghel der eeuwigher salicheit*, and Mystical Contemplation in the Late Medieval Low Countries", in Melion W.S. – Wandel L.P. (eds.), *Image and Incarnation: The Early Modern Doctrine of the Pictorial Image*, Intersections 39 (Leiden: 2015) 224–226; Dlabačová, "The Art of Observance" 241, 244–245.

The representations of dice, pansies, neumes, a bonnet, and an outcropping of bluestone do not just function as homophonic clues for decoding the rebus. They also serve as secondary *memento mori* devices – the chance of tumbling dice, the ephemeral nature of music, the field pansy that evokes Isaiah 40: 'All flesh is grass and all the goodliness thereof is as the flower of the field [...] The grass withereth, the flower fadeth: but the word of our God shall stand forever'.[25] Even the bluestone outcropping anticipates the grave, as polished bluestone from Provoost's native Hainaut was the favored material for Netherlandish tomb effigies.[26] The skull's gaping eye sockets, nose cavity, and broken jaw underscore the passing of the senses at death: the fragrance of the flower, the sound of music, and the warmth of the hat. The rebus's warning against fleeting senses and the evanescence of life may apply equally to the vagrancies of emotion and shifting passions that move upon the soul. Appearing on the back of the donor portrait, the rebus images advise the friar against fickle mood swings, as illustrated in the facing panel of *Christ Carrying the Cross*, when, in response to Pilate's offer to release Christ from his bonds, 'the chief priests *moved* the people, that he should rather release Barabbas unto them'.[27] The ferocious faces of Jesus's tormentors – pressed so close to the empathetic countenances of his mourners – illustrate how quickly the crowds that hailed Jesus, crying, 'Hosanna to the Son of David: Blessed is he that cometh in the name of the Lord; Hosanna in the highest', at his Triumphal Entry could degenerate to such an extent that, later that week, 'Pilate saw that he could prevail nothing, but rather a tumult was made'.[28]

The swell of worshipful emotion on Palm Sunday had also been tumultuous. St. Matthew writes that 'all the city was moved, saying, Who is this?', echoing the high-pitched exuberance following the raising of Lazarus when the Pharisees had lamented, 'Perceive ye how ye prevail nothing? behold, the world is gone after him'.[29] Jesus himself voiced criticism of fickle exuberance that could rapidly shift to doubt and betrayal when it lacked a deeper foundation of faith. His parable of the sower describes seeds that 'fell upon stony places, where they had not much earth: and forthwith they sprung up, because

---

25   Isaiah 40:6, 8. On the multivalence of the image in sacred rebuses, see Brantley J., "'In Things': The Rebus in Premodern Devotion", *Journal of Medieval and Early Modern Studies* 45, 2 (May 2015) esp. 299–316.

26   On the use of bluestone from the Hainaut province in funerary sculpture and its exportation throughout the Low Countries and France, see Nys L., *La pierre de Tournai. Son exploitation et son usage aux XIIIème, XIV^{éme} et XV^{éme} siècles* (Tournai, Belgium: 1993).

27   Mark 15:11.

28   Matthew 21:9, 27:24.

29   Matthew 21:10; John 12:19.

EMOTIONS IN PROVOOST'S DIPTYCH OF CHRIST *CARRYING THE CROSS*   583

they had no deepness of earth: And when the sun was up, they were scorched; and because they had no root, they withered away'.[30] The Lord explains that these seeds represent 'he that heareth the word, and anon with joy receiveth it; yet hath he not root in himself, but dureth for a while: for when tribulation or persecution ariseth because of the word, by and by he is offended'.[31]

An exemplum of joy morphing 'by and by' to offense unfolds in St. John's gospel when Jesus miraculously multiplied fish and bread to feed 5000 men. Inspired – more by greed for food and supernatural spectacle than by faith – these over-zealous men sought to 'take [Jesus] by force, to make him a king'.[32] The following day, Jesus attempted to satiate their appetite with spiritual food as he discoursed on the 'bread of life', teaching that 'my flesh is meat indeed, and my blood is drink indeed', and 'except ye eat the flesh of the Son of man, and drink his blood, ye have no life in you'.[33] 'Scorched', as it were, by this 'hard saying', their zeal withered like the seedlings in rocky ground, and 'many of his disciples went back, and walked no more with him'.[34] As much as Jesus used stony soil to characterise fair-weather faith, he also uses stone to signify the pinnacle of emotional stability. Upon asking his twelve apostles, 'Will ye also go away?', St. Peter voiced steadfast devotion: 'Lord, to whom shall we go? Thou hast the words of eternal life. And we believe and are sure that thou art that Christ, the Son of the living God'.[35] St. Peter modeled unyielding faith again when, in response to Jesus's query, 'Whom say ye that I am?', he replied, 'Thou art the Christ, the Son of the living God'.[36] Christ's response to this declaration inflects the 'stony' face of Provoost's Franciscan donor with new meaning:

> Blessed art thou, Simon Bar-jona: for flesh and blood hath not revealed it unto thee, but my Father which is in heaven. And I say also unto thee, that thou art Peter, and upon this rock [*petram*] I will build my church; and the gates of hell shall not prevail against it. [...] Then charged he his disciples that they should tell no man that he was Jesus the Christ.[37]

St. Peter's convictions did not derive from the erratic emotions that pertain to 'flesh and blood' but from something surer and steadier: revelation from the

---

30 Matthew 13:5–6.
31 Matthew 13:21.
32 John 6:15.
33 John 6:53, 55.
34 John 6:60, 66.
35 John 6:67–69.
36 Matthew 16:15–16.
37 Matthew 16:17–18, 20.

'Father which is in heaven'. Jesus compares this constancy of faith – St. Peter's anchored emotions – to a rock. I have already alluded to the 'Petrine' watchfulness of Provoost's friar at the beginning of this essay. St. Peter's adamantine nature – unbending on the outside and immovably committed to emotional faith within – is an important model for the patron, especially given the imagery of stone in the diptych. In fact, the scriptural play on the name Peter, which means 'stone' (*Tu es* Peter *et super hanc* petram *aedificabo ecclesiam meam*), employs rhetoric similar to that of Provoost's rebus, in which a rock pictogram gives voice to the word *dur* (hard) and yet simultaneously signals the fleeting sense of touch and the chill of a tombstone. In charging his apostles to keep his identity secret, Christ only further associates their devotion with the muteness of rock and the secrecy of a rebus.

The diptych's stone pictogram thus evokes the 'prince of the apostles' as the model for the friar's 'petrified' expression, which is neither 'tossed to and fro, and carried about with every wind of doctrine', nor swayed by the leering and volatile demonstrations of emotive 'flesh and blood' in the facing panel.[38] At the same time, though, the friar's likeness inspires him to persevere where St. Peter failed. The chief apostle weathered the emotional maelstrom of the Passion more like a swinging pendulum than an immovable boulder. In impetuous fervor, he vowed to 'lay down [his] life for [Jesus's] sake': 'Though I should die with thee, yet will I not deny thee'.[39] A few hours later, his zeal manifested itself in violent indignation as he cut off the ear of the high priest's servant, prompting Jesus to quell the angry assault with the admonition, 'Put up again thy sword into his place: for all they that take the sword shall perish with the sword'.[40] St. Peter's emotions continued to shift dramatically with night progressing to early morning as he thrice denied knowing Jesus, the final time accompanied by fury: 'Then began he to curse and to swear, saying, I know not the man'.[41] Just moments later, upon hearing the cock crow, St. Peter's passions volleyed once again, this time from anger to profound grief: 'And he went out, and wept bitterly'.[42]

The calcified features of Provoost's friar model steadfast affection for Christ in the secret, hidden recesses of the heart. His stony face does not indicate an absence of emotion, nor should we assume a simplistic emotional state, untouched by the kinds of multi-layered emotions Peter experienced during

---

38   Ephesians 4:14.

39   John 13:37; Matthew 26:35.

40   Matthew 26:52.

41   Matthew 26:74.

42   Matthew 26:75.

EMOTIONS IN PROVOOST'S DIPTYCH OF CHRIST *CARRYING THE CROSS*   585

the Passion. As much as mingled emotions – in Peter's case, anger, indignation, and despair – can characterize fickleness, so also can they form the groundwork of rock-like constancy in love. After all, Jesus himself was torn by varying emotions: 'oppressed' and 'afflicted', 'despised and rejected', 'a man of sorrows, and acquainted with grief'.[43] Many of the emotions that racked his soul were not even his own, but experienced vicariously as he 'bor[e] our griefs, and carried our sorrows', 'wounded for our transgressions, [...] bruised for our iniquities: the chastisement of our peace [...] upon him'.[44] His steadfastness – especially in the emotional bombardment of the Passion – makes him the 'chief corner stone', the 'stone which the builders rejected', and the rock that Moses struck in the wilderness, 'and the waters gushed out'.[45] St. Peter's epistle in the New Testament exhorts the followers of Christ to be 'lively stones', and on Palm Sunday, Christ asserts that even solid rock can cry out in emotion for God.[46] When the Pharisees exhorted him to calm the affections of the teeming crowd, Jesus replied, 'I tell you that, if these should hold their peace, the stones would immediately cry out'.[47] It is quite possible, therefore, that spiritual love – of the most immovable, rocky kind – can be construed as a mixed emotion.

2   Iconography of Passion

A half-length close-up of Christ Carrying the Cross was an unusual subject for the sixteenth-century Low Countries. Sixten Ringbom identified Provoost's diptych as the very first of that type north of the Alps, although it is certainly related to larger, more narrative versions of the subject, such as the famous *Christ Carrying the Cross*, attributed to Hieronymus Bosch [Fig. 15.3].[48] The iconography of the half-length Jesus on the *Via dolorosa* (Sorrowful Way) developed in Milan and Venice in the late fifteenth century with devotional

---

43   Isaiah 53:3, 7.

44   Isaiah 53:4–5.

45   Ephesians 2:20; Luke 20:17; Psalm 105:41.

46   1 Peter 2:5.

47   Luke 19:40.

48   Ringbom S., *Icon to Narrative, the Rise of the Dramatic Close-Up in Fifteenth-Century Devotional Painting*, 2nd ed. (Doornspijk, The Netherlands: 1984) 149n27. For similarities to Bosch, see Friedländer, *Joos van Cleve, Jan Provost* 92–93; Spronk R., "Diptiek van een minderbroeder", in Martens M.P.J. (ed.), *Brugge en de Renaissance. Van Memling tot Pourbus. Notities*, exh. cat., St. John's Hopsital and Groeningemuseum (Bruges: 1998) 36; Scherer, "Diptychon eines Minoritenbruders 398; Hand, J.O. – Metzger C.A. –Spronk R., *Prayers and Portraits: Unfolding the Netherlandish Diptych*, exh. cat., National Gallery of Art (Washington: 2006) 210; Dlabačová, "The Art of Observance" 216.

FIGURE 15.3 Hieronymus Bosch or Follower of Hieronymus Bosch, *Christ Carrying the Cross*, (ca. 1510–ca. 1516). Oil on panel, 76.7 × 83.5 cm, Museum voor Schone Kunsten, Ghent (inv. 1902 – H). Artwork in the public domain

paintings by Giovanni Bellini and his followers. Provoost's exposure to Italian examples likely came via his pilgrimage to Jerusalem, on which he would have journeyed through Venice. In Provoost's treatment of the subject, Christ interacts with his Franciscan votary across the frames and hinges linking the two panels. He turns his head and neck and even pivots his left shoulder to face the friar. Significantly, his gaze is not directed to the donor's eyes but rather to his heart, as if assessing its unseen affections and 'binding' them to his own heart by the power of his stare. Christ demonstrates the bondage he enacts with his gaze by displaying his wrists wrapped in rope, fingers intertwined. It is in loving imitation of the bound Christ that the Franciscan donor dons his own rope – the cord of his vocation – as the 'bond of peace' and 'charity, which

EMOTIONS IN PROVOOST'S DIPTYCH OF CHRIST *CARRYING THE CROSS*   587

is the bond of perfectness'.[49] In the words of St. Gregory of Nyssa, the votary is 'led to God by desire, drawn to him as if pulled by a rope'.[50] In the writing of the patristics, holy desire anchors the soul and protects it from fickle and evanescent emotions that can metamorphose with dangerous unpredictability.[51] Desire for God, as a sacred emotion, guides the votary to distinguish between the vagrancies of *eros* and the constancy of love. By so doing, 'the soul clings to [the good] and mingles with it, fashioning itself to that which is being continually grasped and discovered anew'.[52] In Scripture, the act of binding the emotions to God in love is also imitative, for St. John explains that 'we love [God], because he first loved us'.[53] That loving 'bond of peace' ties Christ to the friar and the friar to Christ, and it weathers physical and emotional violence as durably as the granite rendered on the diptych's reverse.

Provoost may well have adapted his conceit of bonds and binding from northern Italian devotional 'close-ups'. He likely would have seen Titian/ Giorgione's *Christ Carrying the Cross* from San Rocco, which, according to Giorgio Vasari (1511–1574), had quickly acquired a reputation as a cult image in Venice [Fig. 15.4].[54] As in Provoost's diptych, the Titian/Giorgione Christ looks beyond the confines of the frame, this time to fix the viewer with a mournful glance, and his gray-violet robe may have been the inspiration for Provoost's garment of nearly the same color. The rope also occupies a central place in the San Rocco composition. Knotted around Christ's neck and held firmly in his captor's left hand, it reinforces the heavy diagonal of the cross resting on the Lord's shoulder. The twisted loops crisscrossing the captor's right arm repeat the cruciform shape and viscerally bolster his vice-like grip on Jesus's garment and his harsh, unyielding stare into Christ's face. Bernardino Luini's half-length diptych of *Christ Carrying the Cross and the Virgin* also features a heavy noose

---

49   Ephesians 4:3, Colossians 3:14.
50   St. Gregory of Nyssa, *On the Soul and the Resurrection*, quoted in Wilken R.L., "Blessed Passion of Love: The Affections, the Church Fathers, and the Christian Life", in Coulter D.M. – Yong A. (eds.), *The Spirit, the Affections, and the Christian Tradition* (Notre Dame, IN: 2016) 35. In this same treatise, St. Gregory compares the shedding of a soul's vices to a rope, caked in mud, being pulled toward God, the 'violent tugging' of which dislodges the mud. St. Gregory of Nyssa, *Ascetical Works*, trans. V.W. Callahan, The Fathers of the Church: A New Translation 58 (Washington, D.C.: 1967) 241–242.
51   Wilken, "Blessed Passion" 29–39, esp. 36.
52   St. Gregory of Nyssa, *On the Soul and the Resurrection*, quoted in Wilken, "Blessed Passion" 36.
53   1 John 4:19.
54   Vasari Giorgio, *Le vite de' più eccellenti pittori, scultori ed architettori scritte da Giorgio Vasari pittore Aretino*, ed. G. Milanesi (Florence: 1906) 7:437; Belting H., *The Image and Its Public in the Middle Ages* (New Rochelle: 1990) 472.

FIGURE 15.4   Titian/Giorgione, *Christ Carrying the Cross*, (1505). Oil on canvas, 68.2 cm × 88.3 cm, Scuola Grande di San Rocco, Venice
IMAGE © CAMERAPHOTO ARTE, VENICE/ART RESOURCE, NY

around the Lord's neck [Fig. 15.5]. Mother and son look at one another, and Mary's crossed arms mirror the placement of the rope on Jesus's shoulders, indicating her desire to share his bonds and the yoke of his cross.[55]

In a similar impulse, Provoost's friar lifts his hands as if waiting for them to be bound. Infrared reflectography reveals that in earlier stages of the composition there was a loop of rope extending from the Franciscan's wrists and brushing suggestively near his heart. The finished painting removes this loop of rope and relegates the evocation of a bound heart to the pictogram in the frame and the unseen cord that the friar would have always worn around his waist.[56] As mentioned earlier, Christ 'tethers' the friar with his gaze, angled downward toward his heart. 'For the Lord seeth not as a man seeth; for man

---

55   For these and other half-length Christ Carrying the Cross images related to the Provoost diptych, see Ringbom, *Icon to Narrative* 148–155.
56   For the infrared reflectogram and its analysis, see Hand – Metzger – Spronk, *Prayers and Portraits* 210.

FIGURE 15.5 Bernardino Luini, *Christ Carrying the Cross and the Virgin*, (1520/1530). Oil on wood, 50.6 cm × 49.7 cm, Museo Poldi Pezzoli, Milan, (inv. no. 1624)
© MUSEO POLDI PEZZOLI, MILAN

looketh on the outward appearance, but the Lord looketh on the heart'.[57] The 'rope' of Christ's sightline gives form to the homophonic relationship between 'hearts' and 'cord' and imbues the 'heart-to-heart' exchange between Jesus and the friar with emotive meaning. Staring into space, rather than making eye contact with Christ, the Franciscan, likewise 'seeth not as a man seeth' and instead, like St. Peter, perceives Christ not by 'flesh and blood' but on a higher emotional plane: by the non-corporeal movements of the spirit.

That wordless, internal communion accords with the account of the Lord's interaction with his mother as he carried the cross along the *Via dolorosa* to Calvary. The *Meditations on the Life of Christ* describe the encounter between mother and son as one of silent, voiceless pathos:

> Because his grief-stricken mother could not get close to see him on account of the crowd of people, she went quickly with John and her companions by another shorter route, to try to meet him by getting there before the others. She intercepted him at a crossroad outside the city gate, picking him out, weighed down by the huge wooden cross which

---

57   1 Samuel 16:7.

she had not seen before. She was stricken half-dead in her anguish, and was incapable of speaking a word to him, nor the Lord to her, hurried along as he was by those who were leading him to be crucified.[58]

In holding his head and gazing at the same angle as the grieving Mary in the facing panel, Provoost's friar suggests that his heart-to-heart communion with the Savior is like hers. Indeed, were Jesus's head turned to the left instead of the right, it would align perfectly with his mother's face, as if he had been gazing at the *Virgo doloris* (sorrowful Virgin) just moments before twisting his eyes to the right and staring with similar intensity – albeit across the centuries – into the eyes of the friar's heart (*oculi cordis*).[59]

3 Franciscan Affects

The Friars Minor are well known for highly emotional spirituality. In Franciscan writings these affects of the soul are treated with nuance and include exterior demonstrations of piety such as weeping, as well as internal and unseen movements of the soul, which sometimes manifest themselves in discernable traces. Prudence was advised in concealing the effects of emotion, and the dangers of errant emotions were warned against. In an attempt to excavate the concealed emotions of Provoost's friar as his heart is 'drawn' by the triple-knotted cord of his vocation, I will now turn to the writings of one of the most ubiquitous authors in Franciscan affective devotion: St. Bonaventure (1221–1274). I will pull primarily from four of his texts: *The Life of St. Francis* (*Legenda Sancti Francisci*), *The Tree of Life* (*Lignum vitae*), *The Mystical Vine* (*Vitis mystica*), and *The Soul's Journey into God* (*Itinerarium mentis in Deum*). The latter three are

---

58 Chapter 77, in Caulibus John of, *Meditations on the Life of Christ*, trans. and ed. F.X. Taney – A. Miller – C.M. Stallings-Taney (Asheville, NC: 2000) 250; Caulibus Iohannis de, *Meditaciones vite Christi olim S. Bonauenturo attributae*, ed. M. Stallings-Taney, Corpus Christianorum Continuatio Mediaeualis 153 (Turnhout: 1997) 269: 'Quia uero mesta mater propter multitudinem gencium ei appropinquare non poterat nec uidere, iuit per aliam uiam breuiorum celeriter cum Iohanne et sociabus suis ut alios precedens eidem approximare ualeret. Cum autem extra portam ciuitatis in concursu uiarum eum habuit obuium, cernens eum oneratum ligno tam grandi quod primo non uiderat, semimortua facta est pre angustia nec uerbum ei dicere potuit nec Dominus ei, acceleratus ab eis qui eum ducebant ad crucifigendum'.

59 On the meditative and timeless nature of gazes and interactions "outside the frames" of Northern diptychs, see Wise E.D., "Cycles of Memory and Circular Compassion in a Germanic Passion Diptych", *Journal of Historians of Netherlandish Art* 10, 1 (Winter 2018) DOI: 10.5092/jhna.2018.10.1.1.

robust works of mysticism, tracking the soul's ascent to unity with the Trinity. St. Bonaventure and the Franciscans are by no means the sole voice extolling the virtues of interior, affective conformity to Christ. Jean Leclercq has written extensively about similar ideas in a variety of monastic and mendicant traditions.[60] In other words, much of the theological and mystical discussion that follows is not unique. It is, however, the language and imagery that would have been most familiar to Provoost's friar, and it stands apart from other monastic writings in recommending, as much implicitly as explicitly, the person of St. Francis as the archetype of loving *imitatio Christi*. The example of the order's founder and the emotional guidance of 'Francis's cord' hover over the devotional conceit of the diptych in much the way that they hover over the treatises of St. Bonaventure and his followers.

An educated Franciscan, like the one who commissioned Provoost's diptych, would certainly have known Bonaventure's work, and that Provoost himself was interested in mysticism, and of a particularly complex sort, is evinced by his *Sacred Allegory* painting from circa 1500 [Fig. 15.6]. This enigmatic and strikingly unusual composition has been explained by Geert Warnar with recourse to Middle Dutch mysticism, particularly the writings of Jan van Ruusbroec (1293–1381).[61] Dlabačová has argued convincingly that Provoost's anonymous friar may be Jean Glapion (ca. 1460/1465–1522), the zealous reformer of the Bruges Franciscans, who brought the Braamberg friary into conformity with the Observance in 1515 and probably instigated the ascetic modifications for its confraternity chapel to Our Lady of the Dry Tree.[62] Glapion served as confessor to Emperor Charles v (1500–1558) who, along with a number of other benefactors, could have provided the funds for a diptych by one of Bruges's most eminent artists, since Glapion himself was vowed to strict poverty.[63] Glapion's exact date of birth is unknown, but he would have been within easy range of the sitter's age of fifty-four in the year 1522.[64] Seeing as Glapion died the same year the diptych was finished, the diptych may have

---

60   See, for instance, Leclercq J., *Contemplative Life* (Kalamazoo, MI: 1978); *Aspects of Monasticism* (Kalamazoo, MI: 1978); *La spiritualité du moyen âge* (Paris: 1961); *The Love of Learning and the Desire for God: A Study of Monastic Culture* (New York: 1961).

61   Warnar "Eye to Eye, Text to Image?" 203–230. See also Reynaud N., "Une allégorie sacrée de Jan Provost", *Revue de Louvre et des musées de France* 25 (1975) 7–16.

62   Dlabačová, "The Art of Observance" esp. 241–248.

63   Ibidem, 242, 247–248. On Glapion in his historical context, see Godin A., "La société au xve siècle, vue par J. Glapion (1460?–1522), frère mineur, confesseur de Charles-Quint", *Revue du Nord* 46 (1964) 341–370.

64   Dlabačová, "The Art of Observance" 243.

FIGURE 15.6   Jan Provoost, *Sacred Allegory*, (ca. 1500). Oil on wood, 50 cm × 40 cm, Musée du Louvre, Paris (inv. no. RF 1973 44)
© 2017 RMN-GRAND PALAIS (LOUVRE)/TONY QUERREC

EMOTIONS IN PROVOOST'S DIPTYCH OF CHRIST *CARRYING THE CROSS*   593

evolved prematurely into an epitaph for him.[65] Like most Observant preachers, Glapion was ardently devoted to the Passion, the Virgin, and affective conformity with Christ, and he would have also known the work of important Netherlandish Franciscans, such as Hendrik Herp (c.1410–1477).[66] The Observance encouraged the Stations of the Cross (*Via crucis*), and narratives of Christ's agony – often parsed into stand-alone distillations for meditation – characterize much of Observant literature.[67] Glapion himself composed such a text. His *Pastimes of the Pilgrim of Human Life* (*Passe-temps du Pèlerin de Vie Humaine*) envision life as a week-long pilgrimage, in which votaries apprehend salvation by diligently imitating Christ.[68] This treatise was written between October of 1521 and February 1522, precisely when Provoost was painting his diptych of *Christ Carrying the Cross*.[69] Indeed, Glapion – if he is the friar represented in the right panel – seems to be engaging in precisely the meditation he advises in his *Pastimes*, or else he appears to 'reflect' on the Lord at a station along the *Via dolorosa*, with Christ halting and turning to look, mirror-like, on Glapion's heart: 'Is it nothing to you, all ye that pass by? behold, and see [as if through a mirror] if there be any sorrow like unto my sorrow'.[70]

---

65   For the memorial function of late fifteenth- and early sixteenth-century diptychs featuring religious, see Engen H. van, "Memor esto mei: Devotional Diptychs and Religious Orders in the Late Medieval Low Countries", in Weijert R. de – Bueren T. van (eds.), *Living Memoria: Studies in Medieval and Early Modern Memorial Culture in Honour of Truus van Bueren* (Hilversum, Netherlands: 2011) 284–287.

66   On the relevance of Herp's *Mirror of Perfection* (*Spieghel der volcomenheit*) to Provoost's diptych, see Dlabačová, "The Art of Observance" esp. 227–240.

67   On Observant devotional themes, including the Stations of the Cross, see Roest B., "Franciscans between Observance and Reformation: The Low Countries (ca. 1400–1600)", *Franciscan Studies* 63 (2005) 428–433. On Herp, more generally, see Short W.J., "Hendrik Herp: The Mirror of Perfection or Directory of Contemplatives", *Franciscan Studies* 64 (2006) 407–433; Dlabačová A., "Tauler, Herp and the Changing Layers of Mobility and Reception in the Low Countries (c. 1460–1560)", *Ons Geestelijk Erf* 84 (2013) 120–152; idem, *Literatuur en observantie. De Spieghel der volcomenheit van Hendrik Herp en de dynamiek van laatmiddeleeuwse tekstverspreiding* (Hilversum: 2014). For Passion themes in early sixteenth-century Netherlandish devotional diptychs, see Engen, "Memor esto mei" 279, 283.

68   Godin A., "Jean Glapion: Le passe-temps de pèlerin de vie humaine", *Bulletin tri-mestriel de la Société académique des antiquaires de La Morinie* 20 (1962–1967) 367–380, 427–430, 481–498; Roest, "Franciscans between Observance and Reformation" 432–433; Dlabačová, "The Art of Observance" 223, 226–227, 236–237, 248.

69   Dlabačová, "The Art of Observance" 226. On the quality of reflection in the diptych and its resonance with Franciscan writings on mirrors, see ibidem, 230, 235–236, 238. See also Spronk, "Diptiek van een minderbroeder" 38.

70   Lamentations 1:12.

594   WISE

For St. Bonaventure, meditation, prayer, and contemplation – as practiced by Provoost's friar – catalysed the affections and enabled the soul to ascend the mystical ladder. In his writing, emotions slip from one to another, forming a chain that commences with compunction and remorseful examination of conscience and then builds, affect upon affect (*transeundum autem est ab uno ad aliud*), until tranquility, serenity (*tranquillitas et serenitas*), and spiritual joy (*spiritualis iucunditas*) are obtained.[71] Importantly, Bonaventure's emotive *catena* does not compartmentalise emotions into isolated categories, fundamentally distinct from one another. It is, rather, a chain of slippage and compound registers. Much of the later spiritual tradition promulgated by the Observants derives from this layering of emotions.[72] In a sermon for the feast of St. Mary Magdalene, whose abundant emotions gave rise to the adjective 'maudlin', Bonaventure taught that 'devotion is the affection of sweet love from the memories of Christ's goodness'.[73] In his *Tree of Life* he cites the Lord's 'tender affection' (*tenero [...] affectu*) mingled with 'vehement anxiety' (*vehemens anxietas*) and 'his most sensitive response to bodily pain' (*passionis corporeae vivacissimum sensum*).[74] Similar emotional compounds ripple across the life of Christ, running together in rapid succession, as in Bonaventure's account of the Crucifixion:

> But with the eye of your mind you saw that divine soul filled with the gall of every form of bitterness, now groaning in spirit, now quaking with fear, now wearied, now in agony, now in anxiety, now in confusion, now oppressed by sadness and sorrow.[75]

A similar building of emotions – one on top of the next – transpires in the hearts of votaries who fix their minds on the Crucified:

---

71   Longpré P.E., *La théologie mystique de Saint Bonaventure* (*À l'occasion du VIIᵉ centenaire: 1221–1291*) (Florence: 1921) 22–24; Dreyer, "'Affectus'" 17; 1.9, in St. Bonaventure, *De triplici via*, quoted in Longpré, *La théologie mystique* 24.

72   Roest, "Franciscans between Observance and Reformation", 432–433.

73   *Sermo* 3.1, *De Sancta Maria Magdalena*, in St. Bonaventure, *Opera omnia* 9:561: 'Nam devotio est affectio amoris suavis proveniens ex memoria beneficiorum Christi'. English translation and quotation in Dreyer, "'Affectus'" 18.

74   *Fructus* 5.18, 7.28, *Lignum vitae*, in St. Bonaventure, *Opera omnia* 8:75,79. English translation in St. Bonaventure, *Bonaventure* 141, 142, 152.

75   *Fructus* 7.28, *Lignum vitae*, in St. Bonaventure, *Opera omnia* 8:79: 'Sed et divinissimam illam animam oculis conspexisti mentalibus omnis amaritudinis felle repletam, nunc spiritu frementem, nunc paventem, nunc taedentem, nunc agonizantem, nunc anxiatam, nunc turbatam, nunc omni tristitia et dolore moestissimam partim'. English translation in St. Bonaventure, *Bonaventure* 152.

O human heart, you are harder than any hardness of rocks, if at the recollection of such great expiation you are not struck with terror, nor moved with compassion nor shattered with compunction nor softened with devoted love.[76]

On occasion, such mixing of emotions is outwardly visible, as in the groans and 'tear-filled prayer' (*magis lacrymosa prece*) of St. Francis and when 'he grieved with such tender pity that he seemed like a mother who was daily in labor pains', but more often these affections transit imperceptibly within the heart.[77] *The Soul's Journey into God* is a treatise on interiority, with the votary gazing inward to contemplate God's image impressed in the soul. The prologue 'invite[s] the reader to the groans of prayer through Christ crucified', enshrining the ardent emotions of the suffering Christ as the prompt for mystical experience: 'There is no other path but through the burning love of the Crucified, a love which so transformed Paul into Christ when he was carried up to the third heaven that he could say: With Christ I am nailed to the cross. I live, now not I, but Christ lives in me'.[78] Such contemplation, although fervent and emotional, is often framed in quiet introspection. The prologue to *The Soul's Journey into God* advises readers to look past rhetoric, beauty, and worldly intellect in order to savour meaning, truth, and affection. 'You should not run rapidly over these considerations', Bonaventure admonishes, 'but should mull them over slowly with the greatest care' so that tranquil and measured meditation – 'the peaceful ecstasy of contemplation', as he calls it in *The Legend of St. Francis* – will mask the intensity of emotion within.[79] Offering the *poverello* of Assisi as an exam-

---

76 *Fructus* 8.29, *Lignum vitae*, in St. Bonaventure, *Opera omnia* 8:79: 'O cor humanum omni lapidum duritia durius, si ad tanti rememorationem piaculi nec terrore concuteris nec compassione afficeris nec compunctione scinderis nec pietate molliris'! English translation in St. Bonaventure, *Bonaventure* 154.

77 8.1, *Legenda Sancti Francisci*, in St. Bonaventure, *Opera omnia* 8:526: 'tanta miserationis teneritudine deplorabat, ut eas tanquam mater in Christo quotidie parturiret'. English translation in St. Bonaventure, *Bonaventure* 251.

78 1.4, *Itinerarium mentis in Deum*, in St. Bonaventure, *Opera omnia* 5:296: 'ad gemitum orationis per Christum crucifixum'; 1.3, *Itinerarium mentis in Deum*, in St. Bonaventure, *Opera omnia* 5:295; 'Via autem non est nisi per ardentissimum amorem Crucifixi, qui adeo Paulum ad tertium caelum raptum transformavit in Chrstum, ut diceret: Christo confixus sum cruci, vivo autem, iam non ego; vivit vero in me Christus'. English translations in St. Bonaventure, *Bonaventure* 54, 55.

79 *Prologus* 5, *Itinerarium mentis in Deum*, in St. Bonaventure, *Opera omnia* 5:296: 'non est harum speculationum progressus perfunctorie transcurrendus, sed morosissime ruminandus'. English translation in St. Bonaventure, *Bonaventure* 57. For *The Legend of St. Francis*, 13.1, *Legenda Sancti Francisci*, in St. Bonaventure, *Opera omnia* 8:542: 'contemplationis tranquillis excessibus'. English translation in St. Bonaventure, *Bonaventure* 303.

ple of hidden affects, Bonaventure explains that 'many times he was lifted up in ecstatic contemplation so that, rapt out of himself and experiencing what is beyond human understanding, he was unaware of what went on about him'.[80] Outwardly, 'he seemed insensible [...] and noticed nothing at all of what was going on around him, as if he were a lifeless corpse'.[81] Bonaventure thus signals that the 'stony' exterior of Franciscan meditative praxis can indicate the presence of complex, mixed emotions within. This counter-intuitive conclusion can also be drawn from the impassive countenance of Provoost's friar.

Bonaventure uses multi-sensory descriptions to signal these unseen emotions, heat and fire being the most prevalent: 'fire that totally inflames and carries us into God by ecstatic unctions and burning affections', 'ablaze with the fire of divine love' and 'warmth and sweetness' 'like a glowing coal [...] totally absorbed in the flame of divine love'.[82] It is significant that Provoost's donor panel once featured an interior with windows, blazing hearth, and pot warming over the fire, analogous to the cell of Abbot Christiaan de Hondt in his diptych from 1499 [Fig. 15.7]. Although Provoost's friar maintains a stony façade as unreadable as that of a 'lifeless corpse', the cozy hearth would have evinced spiritual warmth within the 'house of his heart', much like St. Francis who, in the 'bite of the winter's frost', 'served the Lord in cold and nakedness', all the while warmed within by a 'burning spirit'.[83]

Emotions are volatile in Bonaventure's writing, and the 'flame of desire for our heavenly home' (*supernae patriae flamma per desiderium*) can rapidly give way to the 'flames of sensual pleasure' (*voluptatis incendio*) and other vices

---

80   10.2, *Legenda Sancti Francisci*, in St. Bonaventure, *Opera omnia* 8:533: 'Suspendebatur multoties tanto contemplationis excessu, ut supra semetipsum raptus et ultra humanum sensum aliquid sentiens, quid ageretur circa se exterius, ignoraret'. English translation in St. Bonaventure, *Bonaventure* 273.

81   10.2, *Legenda Sancti Francisci*, in St. Bonaventure, *Opera omnia* 8:533: 'insensibilis videbatur ad omnia et velut exanime corpus de his quae fiebant circa ipsum, nihil penitus advertebat'. English translation in St. Bonaventure, *Bonaventure* 274.

82   7.6, *Itinerarium mentis in Deum*, in St. Bonaventure, *Opera omnia* 5: 'ignem totaliter inflammantem et in Deum excessivis unctionibus et ardentissimis affectionibus transferentem'. English translation in St. Bonaventure, *Bonaventure* 115. *Fructus* 8.32, *Lignum vitae*, in St. Bonaventure, *Opera omnia* 8:80: 'divinae dilectionis igne succensa'. English translation in St. Bonaventure, *Bonaventure* 157. 10.5, *Legenda Sancti Francisci*, in St. Bonaventure, *Opera omnia* 8:534: 'calorem et dulcedinem'. English translation in St. Bonaventure, *Bonaventure*, 277. 9.1, *Legenda Sancti Francisci*, in St. Bonaventure, *Opera omnia* 8:530: 'Totus namque quasi quidam carbo ignitus divini amoris flamma videbatur absorptus'. English translation in St. Bonaventure, *Bonaventure* 262.

83   5.1, 2, *Legenda Sancti Francisci*, in St. Bonaventure, *Opera omnia* 8:516: 'in nuditate Domino serviebat et frigore'; 'hiemalis algoris asperitate tueri, in spiritus fervore respondit'. English translation in St. Bonaventure, *Bonaventure* 219.

FIGURE 15.7   Master of 1499, Interior right panel of *Diptych of Abbot Christiaan de Hondt*, (1499). Oil on panel, 31 cm × 29 cm, Koninklijk Museum voor Schone Kunsten, Antwerp (inv. no. 255-256-530-531). Artwork in the public domain

competing for the believer's heart.[84] The five senses – although certainly distinct from emotions – are, nonetheless, potent manipulators of emotion, and in *The Soul's Journey into God*, they are tempered by faith, hope, and charity until they are refined and transfigured:

> The soul, therefore, now believes and hopes in Jesus Christ and loves Him, who is the incarnate, uncreated, and inspired Word – the Way, the Truth, and the Life. When the soul by faith believes in Christ as in the uncreated Word, who is the Word and the brightness of the Father, she recovers her spiritual hearing and sight to view the splendors of that Light. When the soul longs with hope to receive the inspired Word, she recovers, because of her desire and affections, the spiritual sense of smell. When she embraces with love the Incarnate Word, inasmuch as she receives delight from Him and passes over to Him in ecstatic love, she recovers her sense of taste and touch.[85]

For St. Bonaventure, these 'spiritual senses' are the primary method of discerning God as the soul climbs ever higher on the mystical ladder toward unification with the divine.[86] With transformed senses, the votary conforms to St. Francis, whose joy in evangelisation 'filled [him] with the sweetest fragrance and anointed [him] with precious ointment'; whose gratitude for divine love took the form of music, 'as if an inner chord of his heart had been plucked by the plectrum'; and who, upon hearing or speaking the name of Jesus 'was filled with joy interiorly and seemed to be altered exteriorly as if some honey-sweet flavor had transformed his taste or some harmonious sound had transformed his hearing'.[87]

---

84   1.2, 5.3, *Legenda Sancti Francisci*, in St. Bonaventure, *Opera omnia* 8:516, 517. English translation in St. Bonaventure, *Bonaventure* 219, 220.

85   4.3, *Itinerarium mentis in Deum*, quoted and translated in Dreyer E., "'Affectus' in St. Bonaventure's Theology", *Franciscan Studies* 42 (1982) 16–17: 'Anima igitur credens, sperans et amans Iesum Christum, qui est Verbum incarnatum, increatum et inspiratum, scilicet via, veritas et vita, dum per fidem credit in Christum tanquam in Verbum increatum quod est Verbum et splendor Patris, recuperat spiritualim auditum et visum: auditum ad suscipiendum Christi sermones, visum ad considerandum illius lucis splendores. Dum autem spe suspirat ad suscipiendum Verbum inspiratum, per desiderium et affectum recuperat spiritualem olfactum. Dum caritate complectitur Verbum incarnatum, ut suscipiens ab ipso delectationem et ut transiens in illud per ecstaticum amorem, recuperat gustum et tactum'.

86   Dreyer, "'Affectus'" 18–19.

87   8.3, *Legenda Sancti Francisci*, in St. Bonaventure, *Opera omnia* 8:526: 'suavissimis se dicebat repleri odoribus et quasi unguento pretioso liniri'. English translation in St. Bonaventure,

EMOTIONS IN PROVOOST'S DIPTYCH OF CHRIST *CARRYING THE CROSS*   599

Hendrik Herp, a key contributor to the Netherlandish literature of the Franciscan Observance, was a dedicated student of St. Bonaventure and describes the mystical metamorphosis of the senses similarly. In his *Soliloquy of Divine Love* (*Soliloquium divini Amoris*), he cites the Canticles for their description of the lover chasing after the fragrance of the beloved: 'Draw me (*trahe me*), we will run after thee' 'because of the savour of thy good ointments thy name is as ointment poured forth'.[88] Like the rope that tethers Provoost's friar to Christ, Herp explains that God's love operates on the will of the votary to draw the entire person (*totum hominem trahit*) – including affective and intellective faculties (*tam intellectivas, quam affectivas*) – into unity with the divine will via 'indwelling charity' (*inhabitantem charitatem*).[89] The verb, *traho* (to draw), which is a key component of Herp's exegesis of the Canticles passage, also plays a crucial role in Provoost's diptych: *Francisci chorda traxit ad se plurima corda* ('Francis's cord *draws* the most hearts to itself'). The sitter's vows – emblematised by the cord of his Observant profession – are synonymous with the *drawing* of his will (*tractu voluntatis*), which enables mystical union with Christ.[90] After all, the vows of a religious are, above all else, a free-*will* binding to God in obedience. Herp's notion of mystical ascent includes refashioning the soul into an image of Christ (*reformat animam ad divinum similitudinem*) and 'reflecting' on him and his abundant sweetness (*susceptionum divinarum suavitatum*), as through a mirror.[91] In her analysis of Provoost's diptych, Dlabačová notes that Christ's beneficent demeanor and gentle smile, even in the midst of diabolic tormentors, exemplifies Herp's teaching on unconditional charity to others.[92] Jesus's rope-like gaze leads his Franciscan votary by exemplum through the surrounding storm of emotions, demonstrating

---

Bonaventure, 252. 9.1, *Legenda Sancti Francisci*, in St. Bonaventure, *Opera omnia* 8:530: 'quasi plectro vocis extrinsecae chorda cordis interior tangeretur'. English translation in St. Bonaventure, *Bonaventure* 262. 10.6, *Legenda Sancti Francisci*, in St. Bonaventure, *Opera omnia* 8:535: 'Nomen autem Iesu cum exprimeret vel audiret, iubilo quodam repletes interius, totus videbatur exterius alterari, ac si melifluus sapor gustum, vel harmonicus sonus ipsius imutasset auditum'. English translation in St. Bonaventure, *Bonaventure* 278.

88   Song of Solomon 1:3–4.

89   Chapter 38, in Herp Henricus de, *Soliloquium divini Amoris*, in *Theologiae mysticae libri tres: Addita introductione ad doctrinam secondi libri admodum necessaria, per R.P.F. Petrum Paulum Philippium Ord. Praedic. S. Theologiae Doctorem* (Cologne: 1611) 224.

90   For Herp's use of being "drawn" and the related concept of the "knot", see Van Nieuwenhove R., "Ruusbroec, Jordaens, and Herp on the Common Life: The Transformation of a Spiritual Ideal", in Arblaster J. – Faesen R. (eds.), *A Companion to John of Ruusbroec* (Leiden: 2014) 232–233.

91   Chapter 21, in Herp, *Soliloquium divini Amoris* 2:170; chapter 38, in ibidem, 2:227.

92   Dlabačová, "The Art of Observance" 229.

how to withstand their competitive allurements. Provoost's composition echoes an analogy in Herp's *Soliloquium*, in which the loving bride is drawn (*trahi*) to her suffering bridegroom, just as a hunting dog chases a wounded animal (*sicut canis venaticus feram insequitur recto tramite*), drawn by its scent (*quam odorifera[m] Christus reddidit in sua passione*).[93] In Provoost's diptych it is also a wounded creature whose blood and wounds draw the pious attention of a votary 'hunting dog'. Reading Provoost's pictorial representation of the Passion in tandem with Herp introduces a level of exegetical irony, since Jesus's tormentors are also associated with dogs, albeit vicious and ravening ones: 'for dogs have compassed me', 'they make a noise like a dog [...] Behold, they belch out with their mouth: swords are in their lips'.[94]

The sweetness of Christ and the 'savour of his good ointments' effect such a change on willing hearts that their fallen, carnal senses transform into purified, spiritual ones. Herp writes that the serpent of Eden poisoned mankind's sensory perception with 'noxious taste' (*sapor noxius*) and a predilection to sensuality:

> And now, therefore, the interior, spiritual vision dims, hearing deafens, smell fades, taste becomes bitter, and touch coarsens, as the Psalmist rightly cries, saying, 'Eyes have they, but they see not: they have ears, but they hear not: noses have they, but they smell not'.[95]

Jesus, however, 'who is the savory wisdom of the Father, as in whom is the taste of all sweetness as well as deliciousness, effectively imparts this taste to us'.[96] Herp distinguishes the 'spiritual sense' (*sensus spiritualis*) – or 'inner use of grace' (*usus interior gratiae*), as St. Bonaventure terms it – from the corporeal sense using words drawn from St. Augustine's *Confessions*:

> But what do I love, when I love Thee? Not the prettiness of a body, not the gracefulness of temporal rhythm, not the brightness of light (that friend of these eyes), not the sweet melodies of songs in every style, not the fragrance of flowers and ointments and spices, not manna and honey,

---

93 Chapter 37, in Herp, *Soliloquium divini Amoris* 2:221.

94 Psalm 22:16; 59:6–7.

95 Chapter 37, in Herp, *Soliloquium divini Amoris* 2:222: '& ideo nu[n]c visus spiritualis interior tenebrescit, auditus surdescit, olfactus tabescit, gustus amarescit, et tactus crassescit, ut merito clamet Psalmista, dicens, *Oculos habent, & non videbunt; aures habent, & non audient; nares habent, & non odorabu[n]t*.

96 Ibidem, 2:221–223: 'Iesus Christus, qui est sapida sapientia Patris, utpote in qua est sapor omnis suavitatis, && delectamenti, nobis efficaciter ingerit hunc gustum'.

EMOTIONS IN PROVOOST'S DIPTYCH OF CHRIST *CARRYING THE CROSS*

not limbs which can be grasped in fleshy embraces – these I do not love, when I love my God. Yet I do love something like a light, a voice, an odor, food, and embrace, when I love my God – the light, voice, odor, food, embrace of my inner man, wherein for my soul a light shines, and place does not encompass it, where there is a sound which time does not sweep away, where there is a fragrance which the breeze does not disperse, where there is a flavor which eating does not diminish, and where there is a clinging which satiety does not disentwine. This is what I love, when I love my God.[97]

The disparity between the emotions prompted by refined, spiritual senses and those inspired by base, carnal senses could not be more glaring than in the left panel of Provoost's diptych. Bulging eyes and nostrils, fetid breath, wet spittle, and the tactility of the grinning figure stroking his red beard proffer the 'poison of deceit' (*fraudis veneno*) and 'flame of greed' (*cupiditatis flamma*) for the friar's evaluation, even as the empathy of the Virgin and St. John appeals to the nobler side of his emotions.[98] These two mourners have been isolated to the upper left corner and blockaded by the intersecting planks of the cross, as if to assist the friar in sifting between different emotional responses to Christ's Passion. In *The Tree of Life*, Bonaventure describes another Passion mystery, similarly dilated to implicate the reader in its contrasting responses to the gentle but reproachful gaze of Jesus:

> O whoever you are, who [...] have shamelessly denied Christ, who suffered for you, remember the passion of your beloved Master and go out

---

97   Chapter 38, in ibidem, 2:225; 10.6.8, in St. Augustine, *Confessiones*, ed. F. Ramorino (Rome: 1909) 261: 'Quid autem amo, cum te amo? Non speciem corporis nec decus temporis, non candorem lucis ecce istis amicum oculis, non dulces melodias cantilenarum omnimodarum, non florum et unguentorum et aromatum suaviolentiam, non manna et mella, non membra acceptabilia carnis amplexibus: non haec amo, cum amo Deum meum. Et tamen amo quandam lucem et quandam vocem et quendam odorem et quendam cibum et quendam amplexum, cum amo Deum meum, lucem, vocem, odorem, cibum, amplexum interioris hominis mei, ubi fulget animae meae, quod non capit locus, et ubi sonat, quod non rapit tempus, et ubi olet, quod non spargit flatus, et ubi sapit, quod non minuit edacitas, et ubi haeret, quod non divellit satietas. Hoc est quod amo, cum Deum meum amo'. English translation comes from St. Augustine, *Saint Augustine: Confessions*, trans. V.J. Bourke, The Fathers of the Church: A New Translation 21 (Washington, D.C.: 2008) 269–270. For Herp's excerpt from the St. Augustine quotation, see chapter 38, in Herp, *Soliloquium divini Amoris* 2:225.

98   *Fructus* 5.17, *Lignum vitae*, in St. Bonaventure, *Opera omnia* 8:75. English translation in St. Bonaventure, *Bonaventure* 140.

with Peter to weep most bitterly over yourself. When the one who looked upon the weeping Peter looks upon you, you will be inebriated with the wormwood of a twofold bitterness: remorse for yourself and compassion for Christ, so that having atoned with Peter [...] you will be filled with the spirit of holiness.[99]

Note, in particular, Bonaventure's injunction to experience mixed emotions in the form of 'twofold' bitterness.

It is the gaze of Christ in Provoost's diptych that invites the friar to conform his heart to the heart of the Lord, concordant with St. Bonaventure's words in *The Mystical Vine*: 'I have found the heart of my Lord, my King [...] the heart of my most gracious Jesu! [...] I will boldly say, "His heart is also mine". [...] Jesus and I share one heart'.[100] The two hearts on the diptych's frame, spaced apart from each other, emblematise the souls of Jesus and the friar, drawn together by the cord of Franciscan vocation. In its pictographic form, that cord twists just above Christ's head like a visual echo of his crown of thorns. Significantly, the fourth chapter in *The Mystical Vine* – entitled, "On the Binding of the Vine" (*De ligatura vitis*) – discourses at length on seven bonds, including the 'thorny bonds' of the mocking crown and the rope bond used to take Jesus captive.[101] The bonds of his Incarnation and Passion are the corporeal evidence for the preexisting 'bonds of charity that drew [*tractus fuit*] him from heaven to earth', for long before his advent in the flesh 'his heart had already been bound by bonds of love'.[102] Bonaventure exhorts the faithful to be reciprocally 'bound with the passion-bonds of our good and loving Jesus', their 'hearts [...] bound

---

99   *Fructus* 6.21, *Lignum vitae*, in St. Bonaventure, *Opera omnia* 8:76: 'O quisquis es, qui [...] Christum pro te passum negasti procaciter vel voluntate vel actu; rememorans passionem dilectissimi Magistri, foras cum Petro egredere, ut te ipsum amarissime defleas'. English translation in St. Bonaventure, *Bonaventure* 144.

100 3.4, *Vitis mystica*, in St. Bonaventure, *Opera omnia* 8:163–164: 'Et ego inveni cor regis Domini [...] benignissimi Iesu [...] Orabo utique. Cor enim illius etiam meum est [...] ego cum Iesu cor unum habeo'. English translation in St. Bonaventure, *The Mystical Vine: A Treatise on the Passion of Our Lord*, trans. A friar of S.S.F., Fleur de Lys Series of Spiritual Classics 5 (London: 1955) 19–20.

101 4.3, *Vitis mystica*, in St. Bonaventure, *Opera omnia* 8:167: 'vinculis etiam spineis'. English translation in St. Bonaventure, *The Mystical vine* 25. For the bonds of rope, see 4.1, in St. Bonaventure, *Vitis mystica* 8:166.

102 4.5, *Vitis mystica*, in St. Bonaventure, *Opera omnia* 8:168: 'Vinculis enim caritatis ipse devinctus, ad suscipienda vincula passionis de caelo tractus fuit in terram'. English translation in St. Bonaventure, *The Mystical Vine* 27; 4.1, *Vitis mystica*, in St. Bonaventure, *Opera omnia* 8:166: 'te prius in corde caritatis nexibus fuisse constrictum'. English translation in St. Bonaventure, *The Mystical Vine* 23.

by the chain of his love', so that 'when through the bonds of his passion we have gained the bonds of his charity, we shall have become one with him'.[103]

The noose on the left end of Provoost's pictogram bond resembles the loop around the Lord's hands in the painting below, which, by homophonic implication, is also knotted around Christ's heart, beating just to the right. As in *The Mystical Vine*, the heart of Jesus becomes the guide and anchor for Provoost's friar as he navigates an emotional field in which love, zeal, betrayal, denials, and contrition can twist the soul in quick succession. In that stormy sea, Christ is the 'sure foundation' to which the heart lashes itself – 'a stone, a tried stone, a precious corner stone'.[104] The fictive porphyry on the back of *Christ Carrying the Cross* takes on special meaning here as the corner stone (*lapis angularis*), its crimson mottling like splattered blood from the rivulets dripping down Christ's brow and neck on the reverse. Because of its deep purple/red hue, porphyry has long been connected to blood, and the pink and white granules that fleck the surface of Provoost's slab mingle those associations with flesh, in particular the wounded flesh of Christ.[105]

---

103   4.5, *Vitis mystica*, in St. Bonaventure, *Opera omnia* 8:168: 'Vinciamur ergo vinculis passionis boni et amantissimi Iesu'. English translation in St. Bonaventure, *The Mystical Vine* 27; 3.6, *Vitis mystica*, in St. Bonaventure, *Opera omnia* 8:165: 'cor nostrum [...] amoris sui vinculo constringere'. English translation in St. Bonaventure, *The Mystical Vine* 22; 4.5, *Vitis mystica*, in St. Bonaventure, *Opera omnia* 8:168: 'prius passionis vinculis nostro capiti colligemur, ut per hoc ad caritatis vincula pervenientes, unum cum ipso efficiamur'. English translation in St. Bonaventure, *The Mystical Vine* 28.

104   Isaiah 28:16.

105   On these kinds of "fleshy intrusions" in porphyry, see Barry F., *Painting in Stone: Architecture and the Poetics of Marble from Antiquity to the Enlightenment* (New Haven: 2022) 213–214. Slabs of veined marble signify the flesh of Mother Earth, as if crisscrossed with arteries and capillaries. When a network of colored mineral deposits were vaguely anthropomorphic or zoomorphic, it was viewed as a natural wonder, not dissimilar from an *acheiropoietic* image, *non manufactum* (made without hands). On these points, see Barry, *Painting in Stone* esp. 61–64, 178–184, 212–218. Bonaventure's account of St. Francis's stigmatisation – in which Christ's wounds are impressed *non manufacta* into the *poverello*'s flesh – contains overtones of lapidary wonders, particularly given the event's geological context on the rocky slopes of Mount La Verna. Surely it is not coincidental that Jan van Eyck's *St. Francis Receiving the Stigmata* in Turin (1430–1432) embellishes the mystical wounding on Mount La Verna with fictive stone on the panel's reverse, the mottling of which resembles drops of blood. The obverse also connects stigmatisation to images in stone but this time by way of analogy with the many fossils scattered among the rocks of Mount La Verna, each of which has been impressed with a pictorial trace. See Bé K., "Geological Aspects of Jan van Eyck's 'Saint Francis Receiving the Stigmata'", in Asperen de Boer J.R.J. van (ed.), *Jan van Eyck: Two Paintings of Saint Francis Receiving the Stigmata* (Philadelphia: 1997) 88–95.

Bloody stones were among the most precious relics of the Passion, their natural veining often conflated with rusty stains from Christ's exsanguination.[106] Concerning the Column of the Flagellation, St. Bonaventure notes that the scourging caused Christ's 'blood to be shed so copiously that the column is said still to preserve the red marks (*vestigia*)'.[107] As a prominent confrère in the Brotherhood of Jerusalem Pilgrims, Provoost would have been specially attuned to the relic-like connotations of the faux stone on his diptych.[108] Porphyry plaques, moreover, were often employed as altar stones to allude to the sacramental presence of Christ's blood in the Eucharist.[109] The rectangle of magmatic porphyry on the reverse of Provoost's *Christ Carrying the Cross* is distinctly reminiscent of such an altar stone. Its splattering of bloody marks functions, to use one of Bonaventure's most beloved terms, as *vestigia* – 'vestiges' or 'footprints' – that recall and record the presence of God. In this case, the *vestigia* register the traces of divine emotions: 'the intensity of the anxiety in the Redeemer's spirit [...] testified to by the drops of bloody sweat that ran down to the ground from his entire body'.[110] As the exterior, or 'cover', for Provoost's diptych, the porphyry's expressionistic chromatism sets an affective mood for the votary before the ensemble is even opened. In the words of 1 Peter 2, it has become a 'living stone', speckled with warm blood, that makes 'lively stones' of those tethered to it and 'take[s] the stony heart out of their flesh, and [...] give[s] them an heart of flesh'.[111]

Antonio Leonelli da Crevalcore's *St. Francis as the Man of Sorrows* from ca. 1490 depicts the *poverello* revealing his stigmata on one side and, on the back, a composition of faux porphyry and serpentine [Fig. 15.8 and 15.9]. Fabio Barry has argued that the large, purplish-red circle of stone in the center, set in an expanse of brown rock, is meant to represent one of the stigmata surrounded by the coarse, brown cloth of the Franciscan habit.[112] Like a devotional close-up

---

106   Barry, *Painting in Stone* 3, 212–218.

107   4.2, *Vitis mystica*, in St. Bonaventure, *Opera omnia* 8:166: 'si sanguis tuus in flagellatione fuit copiose effusus, ut columna guttis illius aspersa, sicut asseritur, adhuc rubra servet vestigia'. English translation in St. Bonaventure, *The Mystical Vine* 24.

108   This interpretation is modeled on Barry's analysis of Anselme Adorno, the probable patron of Van Eyck's *St. Francis Receiving the Stigmata* and an inveterate Jerusalem enthusiast. Barry, *Painting in Stone* 218.

109   Ibidem, 157. Barry suggests that a number of faux marble paintings may allude to altar stones. See ibidem, 214–218.

110   *Fructus* 5.18, *Lignum vitae*, in St. Bonaventure, *Opera omnia* 8:75: 'Quanta vero fuerit in spiritu Redemptoris pro diversis cansis anxietas, testes sunt guttae sudoris sanguinei ex toto corpore decurrentis in terram'. English translation in St. Bonaventure, *Bonaventure* 142.

111   1 Peter 2:5, Ezekiel 11:19.

112   Barry, *Painting in Stone* 218.

FIGURE 15.8   Antonio Leonelli da Crevalcore, *St. Francis as the Man of Sorrows*, (ca. 1490). Tempera on wood panel, 74.5 cm × 56 cm, Princeton University Art Museum, Princeton, Museum purchase, Carl Otto von Kienbusch Jr., Memorial Collection (inv. no. y1956-3). Artwork in the public domain

FIGURE 15.9   Antonio Leonelli da Crevalcore, Reverse of *St. Francis as the Man of Sorrows*, (ca. 1490). Tempera on wood panel, 74.5 cm × 56 cm, Princeton University Art Museum, Princeton,Museum purchase, Carl Otto von Kienbusch Jr., Memorial Collection (inv. no. y1956-3). Artwork in the public domain

of St. Francis's side wound with his robe torn away to make a circular viewing window, Leonelli's panel illuminates the lapidary conceit in Provoost's diptych. Since the latter composition depends heavily on hearts – the heart of Jesus, the willing heart of the friar, and their emotions that transit, largely imperceptibly, 'heart to heart', I would argue that the rectangle of magmatic porphyry on the reverse of the Christ panel can likewise allude to a heart. The marks of cream and red that mottle its surface not only have an expressionistic quality, but the splotches also function as rhythmic propulsions of color, like the pumping of a heart. A veritable riot of emotion and feeling lies latent in the chromatic intrusions of this granite heart, fulfilling the Lord's words on Palm Sunday that 'the stones would immediately cry out'.

St. Bonaventure discourses on the hearts of Jesus and his worshipers when *The Mystic Vine* pointedly compares the Savior's heart to a precious treasure – like a fine stone – mined from the earth:

> So they dug and dug, not only through his hands, but his feet also. And then with the lance of their fury they pierced not only his side but the very depths of his most sacred heart [...] Thy heart is a goodly treasure; it is a heart that is precious. It was when the field of thy body had been dug that we found it. Who would cast away such a pearl? Nay, rather I will give all the pearls in my possession for it.[113]

Like a pearl hidden in an oyster, the heart of Jesus is described as a natural wonder – discovered, 'not made'. It is a divine rarity, come down from heaven and sheathed in the stony flesh of Mother Earth. The fictive rock framing Provoost's slab of faux porphyry is, as in Leonelli's panel, coordinated to the color of a Franciscan habit. Here it is the gray of the Observants that surrounds the porphyry, and the brown of the Conventuals that borders the skull. The inscription on the diptych completes its evocation of mendicant dress by citing that most distinctive component of the Franciscan costume: 'the cord of Francis', which 'draws the most hearts to itself'. Both Christ and his votary are dressed in gray and bound with rope to signify the discipline and rigor of the Franciscan profession that, in the diptych, masks the emotions of the soul, as if in a steely

---

113   3.2–3, *Vitis mystica*, in St. Bonaventure, *Opera omnia* 8:162–163: 'Foderunt ergo et perfoderunt non solum manus, sed et pedes, latus quoque et sanctissimi cordis intima furoris lancea perforarunt [...]. Bonus thesaurus, pretiosa margarita cor tuum, optime Iesu, quam fosso agro corporis tui, invenimus. Quis hanc margaritam abiiciat? Quin potius dabo omnes margaritas; cogitationes et affectiones meas commutabo et comparabo illam mihi'. English translation in St. Bonaventure, *The Mystical Vine* 18–19.

'garment' of humility, mortification, and, above all, poverty. 'Blessed are the poor in spirit', Jesus taught, and his own 'meekness and lowliness of heart' is demonstrated by his gentle, unpresuming manner in Provoost's panel, his grisaille robe pulled down at his breast, like a cleft in gray rock, to draw attention to the unseen passion of his heart – that 'excess of love' (*caritate nimia*), which, according to Bonaventure, caused his death.[114] Jesus benignly encounters a mob of abuse and rejection – as 'the stone which the builders rejected' – and, mute as rock, is 'brought as a lamb to the slaughter, and as a sheep before her shearers is dumb, so he opened not his mouth'.[115] In like manner, the friar in the right panel cloaks his emotions in the poverty and simplicity of the Observance, the Franciscan cord binding his heart as securely as the slabs of gray stone that corral the explosive color in the magmatic porphyry plaque.

For Bonaventure, the 'peaceful ecstasy' hidden in the heart finds its truest manifestation in union with Christ, specifically in the wrenching emotions of his Passion. Following the example of St. Francis, whose ecstasy stigmatised his very flesh, Bonaventure calls on votaries to make the crucified Christ the mirror of their souls' zeal: 'His unquenchable fire of love for the good Jesus had been fanned into such a blaze of flames that many waters could not quench so powerful a love [...] and by his sweet compassion he was [...] transformed into him who chose to be crucified'.[116] 'True piety [...] had so filled Francis's heart and penetrated its depths that it seemed to have appropriated the man of God completely into its dominion. This is what drew him up to God [...] [and] transformed him into Christ'.[117] 'In this passing over, [...] all intellectual activities must be left behind and the height of our affection must be totally transferred and transformed into God'.[118]

---

114 Matthew 5:3, 11:29; 13.3, *Legenda Sancti Francisci*, in St. Bonaventure, *Opera omnia* 8:542. English translation in St. Bonaventure, *Bonaventure* 305.

115 Matthew 21:42; Isaiah 53:7.

116 13.2–3, *Legenda Sancti Francisci*, in St. Bonaventure, *Opera omnia* 8:542: 'Excreverat siquidem in eo insuperabile amoris incendium boni Iesu in lampades ignis atque flammarum, ut aquae multae caritatem eius tam validam exstinguere non valerent [...] sursum ageretur in Deum et compassiva dulcedine in eum transformaretur, qui [...] voluit crucifigi'. English translation in St. Bonaventure, *Bonaventure* 305.

117 8.1, *Legenda Sancti Francisci*, in St. Bonaventure, *Opera omnia* 8:526: 'Pietas vera [...] adeo cor Francisci repleverat ac penetraverat viscera, ut totum videretur virum Dei in suum dominum vindicasse. Haec est, quae ipsum per devotionem sursum agebat in Deum, per compassionem transformabat in Christum'. English translation in St. Bonaventure, *Bonaventure* 250.

118 7.4, *Itinerarium mentis in Deum*, in St. Bonaventure, *Opera omnia* 5:312: 'In hoc autem transitu [...] oportet quod relinquantur omnes intellectuales operationes, et apex affectus totus transferatur et transformetur in Deum'. English translation in St. Bonaventure, *Bonaventure* 113.

EMOTIONS IN PROVOOST'S DIPTYCH OF CHRIST *CARRYING THE CROSS*   609

The 'passing over' into God with affections, and the bodily senses that manipulate them, translated into the crucified Christ is Bonaventure's notion of mystical death. In *The Soul's Journey into God*, he writes:

> This fire is God, and his furnace is in Jerusalem; and Christ enkindles it in the heat of his burning passion, which only he truly perceives who says: My soul chooses hanging and my bones death. Whoever loves this death can see God [...] Let us, then, die and enter into the darkness; let us impose silence upon our cares, our desires and our imaginings. With Christ crucified let us pass out of this world to the Father.[119]

The 'stony' silence of mystical death returns us to the diptych's tense balance between caricatured passions and impassive faith, stone and blood, tears and violence. 'He that loseth his life for my sake shall find it', says Christ, and in Provoost's painting the cord of Franciscan vocation trains the heart – through loops, knots, and cincture – to die to worldly senses and degenerate emotions, like the skull on the reverse of the donor panel with its decayed sensory organs – empty cavities where eyes, nose, ears, and mouth once were.[120] The cord's similarity to a hangman's noose becomes eerily pertinent to the painting's argument. In this instance, however, 'the thought of death is good' (*bonne est la pensée de la mort*) because mystical death reforms the emotions into *vestigia* – vestiges – of Christ. To this point, Bonaventure cites the 'divine fire' (*ignis ille divinus*) in Francis's heart, which 'steamed' the stigmata into his flesh (*evaporaret in carne*) or the 'invisible wound of love' (*vulnus amoris invisibile*) to Christ's heart that manifested itself as an exterior, 'visible wound' (*vulnus visibile*) made by the centurion's lance.[121] In his sermon on the days of Creation (*Collationes in Hexaemeron*), Bonaventure describes the swirl of bodily senses sleeping, while the heart 'keeps vigil':

---

119   7.6, *Itinerarium mentis in Deum*, in St. Bonaventure, *Opera omnia* 5:313: 'Qui quidem ignis Deus est, et huius caminus est in Ierusalem, et Christus hunc accendit in fervore suae ardentissimae passionis, quem solus ille vere percipit, qui dicit: Suspendium elegit anima mea, et mortem ossa mea. Quam mortem qui diligit videre potest Deum [...] Moriamur igitur et ingrediamur in caliginem, imponamus silentium sollicitudinibus, concupiscentiis et phantasmatibus; transeamus cum Christo crucifixo ex hoc mundo ad Patrem'. English translations in St. Bonaventure, *Bonaventure* 115–116.

120   Matthew 10:39.

121   *Fructus* 5.18, *Lignum vitae*, in St. Bonaventure, *Opera omnia* 8:75: 'Quanta vero fuerit in spiritu Redemptoris pro diversis cansis anxietas, testes sunt guttae sudoris sanguinei ex toto corpore decurrentis in terram'. English translation in St. Bonaventure, *Bonaventure* 119; 3.5, *Vitis mystica*, in St. Bonaventure, *Opera omnia* 8:164. English translation in in St. Bonaventure, *The Mystical Vine* 20.

I was sleeping, but my heart kept vigil. Only the affective power keeps vigil and imposes silence upon all the other powers; then the man becomes foreign to his senses: he is in ecstasy and hears secret words that man may not repeat, because they are only in the heart.[122]

Sts. Peter, James, and John slumbered in Gethsemane, but Provoost's friar 'watch[es] and pray[s]', his countenance stony but his inner emotions riveted, 'heart to heart', on Christ. Unlike St. Francis, this friar's palms are unmarked, but the awkward way in which he holds them separated from each other draws attention to them and configures the discomfort of his hand gesture as a *vestigium* for internal wounds. In her analysis of St. Bonaventure's notion of mystical death, Elizabeth Dreyer memorably states that 'love silences all discursive activities' so that 'the heart alone remains'.[123] It is tempting to read Provoost's two pictogram hearts in just that way: as the stripped-down essence – the 'vestiges' – of unity between God and the votary. The 'binding' of the patron's heart to Jesus – so that he meditatively replicates each movement in the emotional itinerary of the Passion – is the lofty aspiration of Franciscan spirituality. The 'petrified', passionless appearance of Provoost's patron in no way distances him from Christ's emotions but rather signifies his 'Petrine' constancy and resolution in the unseen movements of the soul. Indeed, when Provoost's diptych is closed, the bodies and hearts of Christ and the friar closely align so that, in the words of Bonaventure's paraphrase of the *Song of Songs*, 'A bundle of myrrh is my beloved to me; he will linger between my breasts'.[124]

Acknowledgements

I express my deep gratitude to Rachel A. Wise and Luke Lyman for their invaluable assistance in the research and preparation of this essay.

---

122 2.30, *Collationes in Hexaemeron*, printed and translated at http://john114.org/Docs/SB_HEX.htm#Hexo2no1: 'Ego dormio, et cor meum vigilat. Sola affectiva vigilat et silentium omnibus aliis potentiis imponit; et tunc homo alienatus est a sensibus et in ecstasi positus et audit *arcana verba, quae non licet homini loqui*, quia tantum sunt in affectu'; *Fructus* 5.18, *Lignum vitae*, in St. Bonaventure, *Opera omnia* 8:75: 'Quanta vero fuerit in spiritu Redemptoris pro diversis causis anxietas, testes sunt guttae sudoris sanguinei ex toto corpore decurrentis in terram'. English translation in St. Bonaventure, *Bonaventure* 142.

123 Dreyer, '"Affectus"' 20.

124 *Prologus* 1, *Lignum vitae*, in St. Bonaventure, *Opera omnia* 8:68: 'Fasciculus myrrhae dilectus meus mihi, inter ubera mea commorabitur'. English translation in St. Bonaventure, *Bonaventure* 119.

Bibliography

Barry F., *Painting in Stone: Architecture and the Poetics of Marble from Antiquity to the Enlightenment* (New Haven: 2022).

Bé K., "Geological Aspects of Jan van Eyck's 'Saint Francis Receiving the Stigmata'", in Asperen de Boer J.R.J. van (ed.), *Jan van Eyck: Two Paintings of Saint Francis Receiving the Stigmata* (Philadelphia: 1997) 88–95.

Becherini B. – Ragghianti C.L. – Collobi-Ragghianti L. – De Witt A., *Mostra d'arte fiamminga e olandese dei secoli XV e XVI catalogo*, exh. cat., Strozzi Palace (Florence, 1947).

Belting H., *The Image and Its Public in the Middle Ages* (New Rochelle: 1990).

Bologna F., "Nuove attribuzioni a Jan Provost", *Bulletin des Musées Royaux des Beaux-Arts de Belgique* 5, 1 (1956) 13–31.

Brantley J., "'In Things': The Rebus in Premodern Devotion", *Journal of Medieval and Early Modern Studies* 45, 2 (May 2015) 287–321.

Caulibus John of, *Meditations on the Life of Christ*, trans. and ed. F.X. Taney – A. Miller – C.M. Stallings-Taney (Asheville, NC: 2000).

Caulibus Iohannis de, *Meditaciones vite Christi olim S. Bonauenturo attributae*, ed. M. Stallings-Taney, Corpus Christianorum Continuatio Mediaeualis 153 (Turnhout: 1997).

Collationes in Hexaemeron, printed and translated at http://john114.org/Docs/SB_HEX.htm#Hexo2no1.

Crowe J.A. – Cavalcaselle G.B., *Les anciens peintres flamands, leur vie et leur oeuvres, annoté et augmenté de documents inédits par Alex. Pinchart et Ch. Ruelens* (Brussels: 1862–1863).

Dlabačová A., *Literatuur en observantie. De Spieghel der volcomenheit van Hendrik Herp en de dynamiek van laatmiddeleeuwse tekstverspreiding* (Hilversum: 2014).

Dlabačová A., "Tauler, Herp and the Changing Layers of Mobility and Reception in the Low Countries (c. 1460–1560)", *Ons Geestelijk Erf* 84 (2013) 120–152.

Dlabačová A., "The Art of Observance. Jan Provoost's *Diptych of a Franciscan Friar* as an Exponent of the Spirituality and Position of the Franciscan Order in the Low Countries, c. 1520", in Falque I. – Guideroni A. (eds.), *Rethinking the Dialogue between the Verbal and the Visual: Methodological Approaches to the Relationship Between Religious Art and Literature (1400–1700)* (Leiden: 2023) 212–254.

Dreyer E., "'Affectus' in St. Bonaventure's Theology", *Franciscan Studies* 42 (1982) 5–20.

Engen H. van, "Memor esto mei: Devotional Diptychs and Religious Orders in the Late Medieval Low Countries", in Weijert R. de – Bueren T. van (eds.), *Living Memoria: Studies in Medieval and Early Modern Memorial Culture in Honour of Truus van Bueren* (Hilversum, Netherlands: 2011) 269–320.

Friedländer M.J., *Early Netherlandish Painting*, vol. 9b, *Joos van Cleve, Jan Provost, Joachim Patenier*, trans. H. Norden (New York: 1973).

Geirnaert N., *Het archief van de familie Adornes en de Jeruzalemstichting te Brugge*, Brugse Geschiedbronnen 19–20 (Bruges: 1987–1989).

Godin A., "Jean Glapion: Le passe-temps de pèlerin de vie humaine", *Bulletin tri-mestriel de la Société academique des antiquaires de La Morinie* 20 (1962–1967) 367–380, 427–430, 481–498.

Godin A., "La société au XVe siècle, vue par J. Glapion (1460?–1522), frère mineur, confesseur de Charles-Quint", *Revue du Nord* 46 (1964) 341–370.

Hand J.O. – Metzger C.A. – Spronk R., *Prayers and Portraits: Unfolding the Netherlandish Diptych*, exh. cat., National Gallery of Art (Washington: 2006).

Haute C.V., *La Corporation des peintres de Bruges* (Bruges: n.d. [1913]).

Herp Henricus de, *Soliloquium divini Amoris,* in *Theologiae mysticae libri tres: Addita introductione ad doctrinam secondi libri admodum necessaria, per R.P.F. Petrum Paulum Philippium Ord. Praedic. S. Theologiae Doctorem* (Cologne: 1611) 224.

Hulin de Loo G., *Exposition de tableaux flamands des XIVe, XVe et XVIe siècles. Catalogue critique précédé d'une introduction sur l'identité de certaines maîtres anonymes* (Ghent: 1902).

Hulin de Loo G., "Geschiedenis der kunst in de Nederlanden (België en Holland), Eenige Brugsche schilders van de eerste helft der XVIe eeuw", *Kunst en Leven* 1.5 (1902) 1–43.

Koldeweij J., *Geloof & geluk: Sieraad en devotie in middeleeuws Vlaanderen* (Arnhem: 2006).

Leclercq J., *Contemplative Life* (Kalamazoo, MI: 1978).

Leclercq J., *Aspects of Monasticism* (Kalamazoo, MI: 1978).

Leclercq J., *La spiritualité du moyen âge* (Paris: 1961).

Leclercq J., *The Love of Learning and the Desire for God: A Study of Monastic Culture* (New York: 1961).

Lobelle H., *Sint Janshospitaal Brugge, 1188–1976: Tentoonstelling, Brugge, 5 juni–31 augustus 1976*, exh. cat., Sint-Janshospitaal, 2 vols. (Bruges: 1976).

Lobelle-Caluwe H. – M. Cumberlege, *Memlingmuseum Bruges*, Musea Nostra (Bruges: 1987).

Longpré P.E., *La théologie mystique de Saint Bonaventure (À l'occasion du VIIe centenaire: 1221–1291)* (Florence: 1921).

Michel É., "À propos de Jean Provost et du Maître de Saint-Gilles", *Gazette des beaux-arts* 17 (1928) 228–237.

Nys L., *La pierre de Tournai. Son exploitation et son usage aux XIIIème, XIV^{éme} et XV^{éme} siècles* (Tournai, Belgium: 1993).

Parmentier R.A., "Bronnen voor de geschiedenis van het Brugse schildersmilieu in de 16e eeuw. 19 Jan Provost", *Revue Belge d'Archéologie et d'Histoire de l'Art* 11 (1941) 97–118.

Ragghianti C.L., "Sull'opera di Jan Provost", *Critica d'arte* 8 (1949/1950) 334–340.

Reynaud N., "Une allégorie sacrée de Jan Provost", *Revue de Louvre et des musées de France* 25 (1975) 7–16.

Ringbom S., *Icon to Narrative, the Rise of the Dramatic Close-Up in Fifteenth-Century Devotional Painting*, 2nd ed. (Doornspijk, The Netherlands: 1984).

Roest B., "Franciscans between Observance and Reformation: The Low Countries (ca. 1400–1600)", *Franciscan Studies* 63 (2005) 409–442.

Rombouts P.F. –Lerius T.F.X. van (eds.), *De Liggeren: en andere historische archieven der Antwerpsche Sint Lucasgilde, onder zinspreuk: "Wt ionsten versaemt"* (Antwerp: [1864–1876]).

St. Augustine, *Confessiones*, ed. F. Ramorino (Rome: 1909).

St. Augustine, *Saint Augustine: Confessions*, trans. V.J. Bourke, The Fathers of the Church: A New Translation 21 (Washington, D.C.: 2008).

St. Bonaventure, *Bonaventure: The Soul's Journey into God, The Tree of Life, The Life of St. Francis*, trans. E. Cousins, The Classics of Western Spirituality (Mahway, NJ: 1978).

St. Bonaventure, *Doctoris seraphici S. Bonaventurae, S.R.E. episcopus cardinalis. Opera omnia*, ed. Studio et Cura PP. Collegii a S. Bonaventura (Florence: 1882–1902).

St. Bonaventure, *The Mystical Vine: A Treatise on the Passion of Our Lord*, trans. A friar of S.S.F., Fleur de Lys Series of Spiritual Classics 5 (London: 1955).

St. Gregory of Nyssa, *Ascetical Works*, trans. V.W. Callahan, The Fathers of the Church: A New Translation 58 (Washington, D.C.: 1967).

St. Jerome, *Sancti Eusebii Hieronymi epistulae* (*Select Letters of St. Jerome*) Loeb Classical Library 262:1, ed. J. Henderson, trans. F.A. Wright (Cambridge, MA: 1933).

Scherer A., "Diptychon eines Minoritenbruders", in Kammel F.M. – Curtius A., *Spiegel der Seligkeit. Privates Bild und Frömmigkeit im Spätmittelalter. Ausstellungskatalog Germanisches Nationalmuseum, Nürnberg, 31. Mai bis 8. Oktober 2000*, exh. cat., Germanisches Nationalmuseum Nürnberg (Nuremberg: 2000).

Scherer A., "Fromme Rätsel: Beobachtungen zum Diptychon eines Franziskaners von Jan Provost", Kammel F.M. (ed.), *Im Zeichen des Christkinds. Privates Bild und Frömmigkeit im Spätmittelalter: Ergebnisse der Ausstellung Spiegel der Seligkeit*, exh. cat., Germanisches Nationalmuseum Nürnberg (Nuremberg: 2003) 78–86.

Schouteel A., *De vlaamse Primitieven te Brugge. Bronnen voor de schilderkunst te Brugge tot de dood van Gerard David*, vol. 2: L–Z, Fontes Historiae Artis Neerlandicae: Bronnen voor de kunstgeschiedenis van de Nederlanden 2 (Brussels: 2004).

Short W.J., "Hendrik Herp: The Mirror of Perfection or Directory of Contemplatives", *Franciscan Studies* 64 (2006) 407–433.

Speth-Holterhoff S., "Trois panneaux de Jean Provost", *Bulletin Musées Royaux des Beaux-Arts de Belgique* 14 (1965) 15–26.

Spronk R., "Diptiek van een minderbroeder", in Martens M.P.J. (ed.), *Brugge en de Renaissance. Van Memling tot Pourbus. Notities*, exh. cat., St. John's Hopsital and Groeningemuseum (Bruges: 1998) no. 22, 36–38.

Spronk R., "Jan Provoost", in Martens M.P.J. (ed.), *Bruges and the Renaissance: Memling to Pourbus* (Ludion: 1998) 94–106.

Spronk R., "Jan Provoost: Art Historical and Technical Examinations", 2 vols. (Ph.D. dissertation., Rijksuniversiteit: 1993).

Spronk R., "Jan Provoost before c. 1500: The Documentary Evidence", in Koopstra A. – Seidel C. – Waterman J.P. (eds.), *Tributes to Maryan W. Ainsworth: Collaborative Spirit: Essays on Northern European Art, 1350–1650* (London: 2022) 86–93.

Spronk R., "The Reconstruction of a Triptych of Jan Provoost for the Jerusalem Chapel in Bruges", *Burlington Magazine* 147, 1223 (February 2005) 109–111.

Van Nieuwenhove R., "Ruusbroec, Jordaens, and Herp on the Common Life: The Transformation of a Spiritual Ideal", in Arblaster J. – Faesen R. (eds.), *A Companion to John of Ruusbroec* (Leiden: 2014) 204–236.

Vasari Giorgio, *Le vite de' più eccellenti pittori, scultori ed architettori scritte da Giorgio Vasari pittore Aretino*, ed. G. Milanesi (Florence: 1906).

Warnar G., "*Elckerlijc* in beeld: Jan Provoosts 'Rijkaard en de dood'", *Spieghel der Letteren* 57 (2015) 273–289.

Warnar G., "Eye to Eye, Text to Image? Jan Provoost's *Sacred Allegory*, Jan van Ruusbroec's *Spieghel der eeuwigher salicheit*, and Mystical Contemplation in the Late Medieval Low Countries", in Melion W.S. – Wandel L.P. (eds.), *Image and Incarnation: The Early Modern Doctrine of the Pictorial Image*, Intersections 39 (Leiden: 2015) 203–230.

Weale H.J., *Exposition des primitifs flamands et d'art ancient*, exh. cat., (Bruges: 1902).

Weale H.J., "Jean Prévost, Peintre", *Le Beffroi* 4 (1875) 205–215.

Wilken R.L., "Blessed Passion of Love: The Affections, the Church Fathers, and the Christian Life", in Coulter D.M. – Yong A. (eds.), *The Spirit, the Affections, and the Christian Tradition* (Notre Dame, IN: 2016).

Wise E.D., "Cycles of Memory and Circular Compassion in a Germanic Passion Diptych", *Journal of Historians of Netherlandish Art* 10, 1 (Winter 2018) DOI: 10.5092/jhna.2018.10.1.1.

Wurzbach A von., *Niederländisches Künstler-Lexikon auf Grund Archivalischer Forschungen Bearbeitet L–Z* (Vienna: 1910).

Wuyts L., "Een kanttekening bij de diptiek met de 'Kruisdraging' en het 'Portret van een Minderbroeder' van Jan Provoost", *Gentse Bijdragen tot de Kunstgeschiedenis en Oudheidkunde* 30 (1995) 219–221.

CHAPTER 16

'Symbolic Anatomies': Hendrick Goltzius and the Ambiguities of Early Modern Disability

Barbara A. Kaminska

Abstract

This essay analyses strategies developed by Hendrick Goltzius and Karel van Mander to orchestrate viewers' responses to Goltzius's deformed right hand. While Goltzius's works that thematise his 'cromme handt' distil fundamental ideas of the Western psychology of artistic creation and of disability, they are also tied to his experiences of the compound condition of melancholy, whose 'overcoming' drove Goltzius's potential for virtuosity, invention, and craftsmanship. By demonstrating that Goltzius and Van Mander encouraged viewers to transcend emotions commonly associated with reactions to disability and disease, such as charity and revulsion, the essay clarifies and expands the affective history of early modern disfigurement and impairment.

Keywords

Hendrick Goltzius – disability – melancholy – disfigurement – Karel van Mander – supercrip

In *Portraits of Violence: War and the Aesthetics of Disfigurement*, Suzannah Biernoff asserts that 'the military body [...] is more than flesh and blood: it is a symbolic site invested with political as well as personal meaning. Valor, heroism, patriotism, courage: these concepts assume visible form, and do their cultural work, when they are personified and embodied'.[1] Biernoff's framework of 'symbolic anatomies', which understands the body – in particular a deformed body – as 'a primary system or microcosm of meaning, whether social, political, or cosmological' accommodates just as easily the artist's body as a site of art theoretical, aesthetic, and cultural tropes. Crucially, 'symbolic anatomies'

---

1 Biernoff S., *Portraits of Violence. War and the Aesthetics of Disfigurement* (Ann Arbor: 2017) 4.

© BARBARA A. KAMINSKA, 2025 | DOI:10.1163/9789004694613_017

do not erase deformity and disability by transforming them into a metaphor; for a 'symbolic anatomy' to operate, the disability must remain embodied. Biernoff's concept provides a unique lens for the analysis of the visual and textual construction of the artistic identity of Hendrick Goltzius (1558–1617), carefully fashioned using his own drawings, prints, and *penwercken*, as well as his biography in Karel van Mander's *Het Schilder-Boeck* (1604). According to Van Mander, as a one-year-old child, Goltzius burned his face in boiling oil and his hands in red-hot coals. The complex impact of this accident on the crafting of Goltzius's artistic persona vis-à-vis physical damage to his body and fluid emotional responses to his 'cromme handt' form the main subject of this essay. Examining the veracity of Van Mander's account, I will argue that Goltzius's disfigured hand distils fundamental ideas of the Western psychology of artistic creation and of disability while encouraging viewers to transcend emotions commonly associated with disability and disfigurement.[2]

Although Van Mander's text and Goltzius's works seem to obliterate the lived experience of disability – which is sublimated into the late-Renaissance trope of *difficoltà* – they in fact illuminate the agency of a person with disability over the agency of non-disabled observers. In the virtuoso displays of his deformity, Goltzius shaped his contemporaries' responses to his 'defect', merging the real and the symbolic aspects of his unusual anatomy. Describing reactions to disability, period sources routinely suggest compound emotions of disgust and fear, and charity and pity. But Goltzius's hand, the instrument of his inimitable skill, resisted these commonplace responses. Analysing Goltzius's works that thematise his 'cromme handt', I will argue that viewers' reactions to his performance of disability and disfigurement are orchestrated not only through the learned appreciation of his transition from martial to artisanal virtue and the employment of the *difficoltà* topos, but also through each of these works' stylistic characteristics.[3] The rewriting of emotional responses to Goltzius's hand proposed by Van Mander is yet another strategy of identifying him as the most

---

2   Disability is often seen as a loss of normative functions of the body while deformity is defined as an aesthetic category, 'a deviation from normal appearance'. Turner D.M. "Introduction. Approaching Anomalous Bodies", in Turner D.M. – Stagg K. (eds.) *Social Histories of Disability and Deformity. Bodies, Images and Experiences* (London – New York: 2006) 2. As Goltzius's 'cromme handt' entailed both the loss of normative function and appearance, I will be using these terms interchangeably.

3   On the theme of martial and artisanal virtue, see: Melion W.S., "Love and Artisanship in Hendrick Goltzius's *Venus, Bacchus and Ceres* of 1606", *Art History* 16.1 (1993) 60–94, and Melion W.S., "Self-Imaging and the Engraver's Virtù: Hendrick Goltzius's *Pietà* of 1598", *Nederlands Kunsthistorisch Jaarboek/Netherlands Yearbook for History of Art* 46 (1995) 104–143.

exceptional among Netherlandish artists; in this regard, its significance lies in the construction of the local canon. But Van Mander's narrative ultimately transcends this immediate goal and challenges our often-reductive understanding of emotions that early modern societies were capable of experiencing when confronted with disability and proves that repulsion and compassion are not innate reactions to bodily difference.[4] Works by Goltzius that thematise his 'cromme handt' are also tied to his experiences of 'swaermoedicheyt' (melancholy), a compound psychosomatic set of emotions which Van Mander presented as the second force whose 'overcoming' drove Goltzius's potential for virtuosity, invention, and craftsmanship. In *Het Schilder-Boeck*, both the impaired hand and the persisting melancholy are introduced as adverse conditions that required an ongoing reshaping of Goltzius's persona and could only be transcended by embracing an equally complex devotion to all manners of artistic creation.

1   Goltzius's Accident and Disfigurement in *Het Schilder-Boeck*[5]

Karel van Mander describes Goltzius as 'a plump, wild and lively child', 'spirited and lively', and thus particularly prone to accidents:

> [Hendrick] is hem vallende niet alleen een stocxken door zijnen neus gevallen, en hem veelmael uyt t'water laten trecken: maer was oock so tot den vuyre gheneghen, dat hy een Iaer oft meer oudt wesende, alleen gaende, op t'vier viel, met t'aensicht boven pan met ghebranden Oly, verbernende in de gloeyende colen beyde zijn handen, welcke hem zijn Moeder vlijtigh pooghde wel te ghenesen, met spalcken, smeeren, en anders, in groote smerten nacht en dagh, tot dat een neus wijse buyr-vrouw quam de spalcken ontbinden, segghende: sy soudet beter

---

4   Here we need to remind ourselves that the early modern period had no overarching term equivalent to what we call 'disability', and instead used words that described specific ways in which bodies and senses did not conform to their normative physiognomies or functions. Early modernity's resistance to grouping these 'anomalies' together is perhaps a more accurate approach towards disability than the one we follow. On disability as an artificial category see, for instance: Garland-Thomson R., *Extraordinary Bodies: Figuring Physical Disability in American Culture and Literature* (New York: 2017) 13.

5   In the writing of this section, I have greatly benefited from the expertise of Pengfei Zhang and other medical professionals, who very kindly offered their interpretation of Van Mander's account of Goltzius's accident and provided an anatomical explanation of Goltzius's 1588 drawing.

beschicken, windende slechs de rechter handt in eenen doeck, waer door de senuwen der selver aen den anderen groeyden, in voegen dat hy zijn leven de handt noyt recht open doen con. Neffens dit ongheluck, jongh kindt wesende, gheschiedet dat zijn Vader door ongeluck oft onbewist hem hiet steken in de mondt Orpriment, oft Aurapigmentum, het welck den Vader ten besten hy mocht weder uyt crabde.[6]

[Hendrick] not only pierced his nose with a stick in falling and often had to be fished out of the water, but he was also so attracted to fire that when he was a year or so old and could walk by himself, he fell into the fire with his face over a pan of boiling oil and burned both his hands in the red-hot coals, which his mother carefully tried to heal with splints, ointments and other things, and he was in much pain day and night, until a well-known female neighbour removed the splints saying that she could do better; she then bound only the right hand in a cloth on account of which the tendons of that hand grew together with the consequence that throughout his life he could never completely open that hand. Besides this accident, it happened that when he was a young child, his father mistakenly or unwittingly let him put orpiment, or auripigmentum, in his mouth, which the father scraped out again the best he could.[7]

If we try to imagine little Hendrick's accident, we can picture a child falling face-first into a pan, then almost immediately lifting himself up by his hands to escape the hot oil. This would likely have caused more damage to the palm than the dorsum of his hands.[8] With few exceptions, the truthfulness of Van Mander's account has gone unquestioned, especially the life-long consequences of the burn and of the incompetent treatment of his right hand.[9] In the historiography of art, Goltzius's right hand has come to symbolise

---

6 Mander Karel van, *Het Schilder-Boeck* (Haarlem, Paschier van Wesbuch: 1604), fols. 281v–282r.

7 Mander Karel van, *The Lives of the Illustrious Netherlandish and German Painters*, ed. – trans. H. Miedema, vol. 1 (Doornspijk: 1994) 385.

8 The plastic surgeon F. Groenvelt has offered a similar conclusion: Hendrick 'probably fell into the fire with the side of the hand striking the coals, after which the hand was twisted outwards so that the back of the fingers was also burned'. Leeflang H. – Luijten G. (eds.), *Hendrick Goltzius (1558–1617): Drawings, Prints and Paintings*, exh. cat., Rijksmuseum Amsterdam – Metropolitan Museum of Art (Waanders: 2003) 244.

9 In his commentary to *The Lives*, however, Hessel Miedema suggested that the resemblance of Goltzius's drawings of his hand to the study of a hand by Bronzino 'conclusively refutes' Van Mander's story about Goltzius's accident and his deformed hand; see Mander, *The Lives*, vol. 5, 180. On Bronzino's drawing, see Goldner G.R., "A New Bronzino Drawing", *Master Drawings* 28.3 (1990) 262–264.

the triumph of *ingenium* and *geest* (spirit) over corporal limitations through *oefeninge* (practice, exercise): the artist successfully trained both hands so that he could use them with the same sureness and precision, drawing with his left hand and engraving with his right. These accomplishments were driven by the more elusive 'great love for art' mentioned by Van Mander and thematised in the 1606 *Sine Cerere et Libero Friget Venus*.[10]

Van Mander tells us that Hendrick 'fell into the fire with his face over a pan of boiling oil'; oil burns, especially to the more sensitive skin of the face – not to mention the skin of a one-year-old child – would typically be more severe than burns on the hands caused by hot coals. And yet, Van Mander never mentions any disfigurement of Goltzius's face, nor do we see any scarring in his self-portraits or portraits of him by other artists. In the construction of Goltzius's identity as an artist, his hands, in particular his right hand, are of far greater importance. Van Mander asserts later in Goltzius's biography that it was indeed his right hand that functioned as his best portrait, an identifying *pars pro toto*. Such a synecdochical representation of a disabled body, in which the deformed or the impaired part stands in for a person, is not unusual: as Allison Hobgood and Elizabeth Bearden have noted, when the bones of Richard III of England were unearthed, it was his war wounds and the curvature of his spine that not only allowed for the identification of his remains but took 'centre stage' in the crafting of his identity across the news in a manner akin to his depiction in William Shakespeare's play.[11] But unlike Richard III, Van Mander's Goltzius claims property over his persona to become more than his disfigured body, as evidenced by another anecdote in *Het Schilder-Boeck*. Goltzius travelled incognito to and across Italy, which led to a quarrel between his friend Jan Mathijssen and the young antiquarian Philips van Winghen, who joined them on the journey from Rome to Naples. Van Winghen, who had learned from Abraham Ortelius that Goltzius was in Italy, wished to see the 'clever engraver from Holland' but refused to believe that it was the man 'whom he saw daily'. Having eventually concluded that 'van Winghen een goet Compagnon met eeren was, en dat hy nu wel behoorde bescheyt te weten, stack zijn rechter cromme handt uyt, toonende met eenen zijnen Neusdoeck, ghemerckt met het teycken dat op zijn Printen staet, te weten, H. en G. in een' ('Van Winghen was a good companion and an honourable man and that he deserved a proper answer, [Goltzius] held out his crippled right hand and also showed him his handkerchief marked with the monogram which is on his prints, that is,

---

10   Melion "Love and Artisanship". See also this essay for the discussion of this topic.

11   Bearden E., "Monstrous Births and Crip Authority: Cervantes, the *Persiles*, and the Representation of Disability", *eHumanista/Cervantes* 5 (2016) 69.

H and G intertwined').[12] Van Winghen was aware of Goltzius's 'rechter cromme handt' as Ortelius had described in his letters 'some distinguishing features of his [Goltzius's] shape and appearance including his deformed right hand'. This raises the question: why did he fail to recognise Goltzius sooner – surely he must have noticed his deformed right hand! In Van Mander's account, this delayed recognition serves to underscore that Goltzius remains fully in control of his identity at all times: he manages to deceive fellow painters and collectors in Germany and Italy by travelling in disguise, for instance, and it is he who decides when and how to show Van Winghen his 'cromme handt', only in conjunction with his monogrammed handkerchief that unmistakably links him to his engravings. The disfigured hand gains its true meaning as an instrument of artistic creation. As the primary locus of Goltzius's 'symbolic anatomy', the hand supersedes his face, which is of far less interest to his contemporaries or to Van Mander.

Goltzius's performance of his disfigurement in the meeting with Van Winghen needs to be considered in the broader context of displays of disability and disease in the early modern Netherlands, which were commonly associated with paupers occupying public spaces. These 'unsightly beggars' had been described as *abiectus* since the late Middle Ages.[13] By 1526 their presence was considered disturbing enough for Juan Luis Vives to comment in *On Assistance to the Poor* on the benefits of regulating charitable giving and removing beggars from the streets: 'It will be safer, healthier, and pleasanter to attend churches and to dwell in the city. The hideousness of ulcers and diseases will no longer be imposed on the general viewing, eliminating a spectacle revolting to nature and even to the most humane and compassionate mind'.[14] Those disabled people who were forced to rely on alms for their livelihood had to navigate contradictory expectations of their potential benefactors. The display of a disabled body was necessary to remove any doubt that the person was genuinely unable to work and deserving of compassion, but, as Vives makes clear, it also provoked disgust. It must be noted here that within the ethical system of early modern Christianity, regardless of denomination, compassion

---

12   Mander, *Het Schilder-Boeck*, fol. 283v. Translated in: Mander, *The Lives*, vol. 1, 393.

13   I use the term 'unsightly beggars' as a nod to Susan Schweik, who introduced it to analyze the so-called 'ugly laws' that barred disabled people from begging in American cities between 1867 and 1974.

14   Vives Juan Luis, *On Assistance to the Poor*, trans. A. Tobriner (Bruges, Hubertus de Croock: 1525; rpt. ed., Toronto: 1999) 55. On disabled paupers as abject, see: Metzler I., "Indiscriminate Healing Miracles in Decline: How Social Realities Affect Religious Perception", in Mesley M.M. – Wilson E. (eds.), *Contextualizing Miracles in the Christian West, 1100–1500* (Oxford: 2014) 169–170.

'SYMBOLIC ANATOMIES': GOLTZIUS AND THE EARLY MODERN DISABILITY

was a precondition of the actionable virtue of charity and had profoundly positive overtones. It should not be understood as equivalent to condescending pity rightfully rejected by contemporary disability scholars and activists.[15] Compassion, activated through the sight of a disabled body, was meant to lead to the religious response of works of mercy listed in Matthew 25:35–45. But the empathy engendered by disabled bodies was often mixed with the fear of unpredictable fate and the possibility that one might become disabled, impoverished, and in need of assistance by no fault of their own. The recognition that this existential uncertainty rather than pure merciful kindness would stand behind actionable charity lurks in the inscription accompanying *Caritas* from the 1559 series of the *Seven Virtues* designed by Pieter Bruegel the Elder and engraved by Philips Galle: 'Speres tibi accidere quod alteri accidit, ita demum excitaberis ad opem ferendam / si sumpseris eius animum qui opem tunc in malis constitutes implorat' ('Expect what happens to others to happen to you; you will then and not till then be aroused to offer help only if you make your own the feelings of the man who appeals for help in the midst of adversity') [Fig. 16.1][16] Although the verses call for compassion, the opening plea can be read both as a paraphrase of Luke 6:31 ('And as you would that men should do to you, do you also to them in like manner') and a reminder of the vicissitudes of life, which was a common trope of the humanistic culture of the early modern Netherlands, thematised, for instance, in a series of prints designed by Maarten van Heemskerck (1564), based on the 1561 Antwerp devotional procession celebrating the Feast of Circumcision.

To feel revulsion toward disabled and deformed bodies was to deny the possibility of falling into the same circumstances. Disgusted rejection of disabled paupers ultimately had its source in the premodern aetiology of impairment, which continued to associate congenital defects with sin (of the parents) and explain disabilities acquired in adulthood as a direct consequence of moral transgressions, for instance, when a sentenced criminal's limb had to

---

15   Scholars such as Bill Hughes have argued that the 'moral and religious duty of decent Christian people to participate in acts of mercy and the provision of alms' transformed disabled people into 'the objects of the pathos of charitable gaze' by offering the benefactors 'the ultimate bonanza of salvation'. Hughes B., "Invalidating Emotions in the Non-Disabled Imaginary. Fear, Pity and Disgust", in Watson N. – Vehmas S. (eds.), *Routledge Handbook of Disability Studies* (Abingdon-on-Thames – New York: 2020) 93. While I acknowledge this argument's intellectual importance for understanding the genesis of contemporary ableism, it presents a form of anachronical ethical reductionism that does not capture the redemptive and the social dynamics of early modern communities.

16   For the English translation see: Orenstein N.M. (ed.), *Pieter Bruegel the Elder: Drawings and Prints* (New York: 2001) 181.

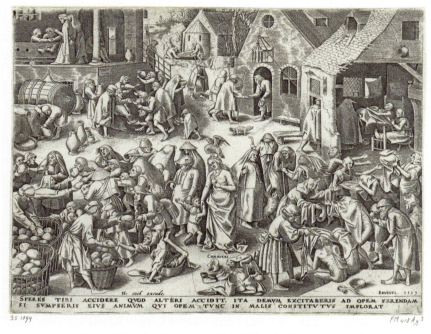

FIGURE 16.1   Philips Galle after Pieter Bruegel the Elder, *Caritas*, 1559–1560. Engraving, 22.3 × 29.1 cm. Amsterdam, Rijksmuseum
IMAGE © PUBLIC DOMAIN

be amputated due to damage caused in prison by chains. This hyperbolical association between impairment and moral and religious shortcomings is well captured in the engraving published around 1570 by Hieronymus Cock in Antwerp, known as *Cripples* or *The Crippled Bishop* [Fig. 16.2]. While physicians and pathologists have identified several diseases that cause the types of impairments and deformities captured by the unknown artist, the print and its accompanying inscription ('All who would gladly live by the blue beggar's sack / Go mostly as cripples') were meant to serve as a warning against beggars feigning their impairments and a deterrent against helping those who did not deserve it.[17] Of course, early modern viewers would encounter disability and deformity beyond the public display of impairment by 'unsightly beggars', within familial and professional networks, religious confraternities and parish

---

17   Dequeker J., Fabry G., Vanopdenbosch L. "Hieronymus Bosch (1450–1516): Paleopathology of the Medieval Disabled and Its Relation to the Bone and Joint Decade 2000–2010", *Israel Medical Association Journal* 3 (2001) 64–71.

'SYMBOLIC ANATOMIES': GOLTZIUS AND THE EARLY MODERN DISABILITY 623

FIGURE 16.2   Anonymous, *Cripples (The Crippled Bishop)*, ca. 1570. Engraving, 30.3 × 21.9 cm

congregations. In those settings, especially among parents of children with disability, impairment evoked sorrow, inspired a quest for treatment, and caused concern not only for the child's comfort and material status, but also salvific prospects. Deafness and blindness in particular continued to be seen as potentially perilous to one's salvation, and often encouraged close family members to become 'facilitators' of religious experiences, whether by acting as interpreters for deaf and mute relatives or funding devotional works of art on their behalf.[18] But while important, these elusive, intimate experiences of disability lack the performative aspect that Vives's 'spectacle[s] revolting to nature' and Goltzius's works have in common.[19]

Goltzius's works that I discuss here sublimate his 'rechter cromme handt' into an epitome of Aristotelian aesthetics, according to which artistic and technical proficiency can make 'things that are ugly in life beautiful in art'.[20] This sublimated perception of Goltzius's body precluded Philips van Winghen from expressing revulsion at the sight of his hand; disgust is in fact completely erased from Karel van Mander's life of Goltzius, as is empathy towards the 'lame' engraver. Van Mander substitutes both emotions with wonder and admiration, augmenting Goltzius's artistic genius by separating it from commonplace responses to disability and deformity. In doing so, Van Mander bolsters Goltzius's self-attained compensatory (ambi)dexterity, to which I turn later in this essay.

The 1588 drawing registers the actual damage to the hand, consistent with what is known about the accident: a line of indentation runs across the dorsum

---

18 On religious donation as a salvific intervention see: Pearson A., "Sensory Piety as Social Intervention in a Mechelen Besloten Hofje", *Journal of Historians of Netherlandish Art* 9.2 (Summer 2017) n.p.

19 Elizabeth Bearden has analyzed another type of performative demonstration of disability in the early modern period, i.e., the 'gainful self-display' of conjoined twins, the most famous among whom were Lazarus and Joannes Baptista Colloredo (1617–after 1646). Period sources describe viewers fascinated by their 'noveltie', 'a Great marvel', and 'so newe a spectacle', alongside the fear of monstrous maternal impressions and revulsion. Bearden E., *Monstrous Kinds: Body, Space, and Narrative in Renaissance Representations of Disability* (Ann Arbor: 2019) 179–227. But relatively few viewers would have been familiar with those displays, and there is a considerable difference between conjoined twins, whose bodies would be often considered monstrous and were connected to the discourse of prodigious births and the much more common displays of disease and disability as described by Vives. For a productive distinction between perceptions of disability and monstrosity in the Middle Ages and entangled emotions generated by severe physical impairments see: Kuuliala J., "Miracle and the Monstrous: Disability and Deviant Bodies in the Late Middle Ages", in Canalis R.F. – Ciavolella M. (eds.), *Disease and Disability in Medieval and Early Modern Art and Literature* (Turnhout: 2021) 107–130.

20 Waugh P. (ed.), *Literary Theory and Criticism: An Oxford Guide* (Oxford: 2006) 45.

of the whole hand, the nail bed of the middle finger is caved in, the phalanges of the index finger are irrevocably bent and distorted, and the damaged muscles around the wrist are unnaturally bulbous [Fig. 16.3]. Although the scarring is hardly noticeable in this monochromatic drawing, it is possible to identify 'excessive traction of scar tissue at the base of this [middle] finger'.[21] The palm of the hand – never depicted by Goltzius – must have been affected the most by the accident, but there is also evidence of contractures between the thumb and the index finger, below the ring finger, and toward the little finger. Though less detailed, the 1589 self-portrait in the British Museum, executed in silverpoint with the addition of graphite and grey and blue-grey wash, gives us a better idea of the effects of the accident on Goltzius's skin: there appears to be vertical scarring on the dorsum of the hand, between the ring and the little fingers, running to Goltzius's wrist [Fig. 16.4]. We see similar scarring and discolouration in the *Four Studies of [Goltzius's] Hand* from ca. 1588–1589 in the Frankfurt Städel Museum, especially in the two hands at the bottom, whose structure most closely resembles the anatomy of the hand in the Teylers Museum drawing [Fig. 16.5]. The scarring and discolouration are most prominent on the right side of the hand; the location of these scars suggests that Goltzius's right hand, which he eventually trained to engrave, must have been his dominant hand, as he instinctively leaned on it during the accident.

If the hand was badly burned and impaired in the accident itself, according to Van Mander, the permanent damage to the tendons and nerves was caused by the incompetent treatment administered by 'a know-all female neighbour'. The splints and ointments used by Goltzius's mother on both hands did not seem to have had any adverse effects, although understandably, the child suffered considerable pain. By the time the neighbour offered her assistance, the less badly burned left hand must already have healed enough not to require any further treatment. However, the removal of splints, which, if properly used, can indeed help to prevent contractures and tissue destruction in burn victims, and their replacement with tightly wrapped cloth, significantly contributed to the life-long impairment and deformity. While it is possible that the burn alone was severe enough to cause the loss of function in Hendrick's right hand, Van Mander is adamant about casting blame on the local 'wise woman'. *Het Schilder-Boeck* was published at a time when medicine was becoming a regulated profession; one could not practice without a guild membership, and university-trained physicians and barber-surgeons warned naïve patients against quacks. Whereas the initial treatment administered by the mother can

---

21   Leeflang, *Hendrick Goltzius*, 244–245.

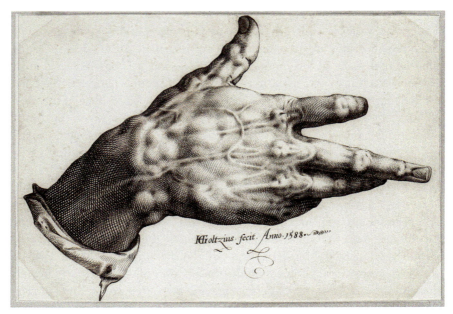

FIGURE 16.3   Hendrick Goltzius, [*Goltzius'*] *Right Hand*, 1588. Pen and brown ink on paper, 22.9 × 32.8 cm. Haarlem, Teylers Museum
IMAGE © PUBLIC DOMAIN

be understood as an instinctive, loving reaction to her young child's pain, the neighbour's meddling signifies gendered medical ignorance. Within this paradigmatic narrative, female ignorance causes Goltzius's impairment, and it takes male *ingenium* and perseverance to overcome it.

Without any doubt, the distorted anatomy of Goltzius's right hand seen in his drawings can be explained as an accurate depiction of the impact of the accident and the failed treatment. Still, his drawings blur the distinction between real and symbolic anatomy. The area around the wrist in the Teylers drawing also epitomises Goltzius's signature style as it imitates the crosshatching used for the depiction of bulging muscles in prints such as the *Roman Heroes* and, most famously, *The Great Hercules* of 1589. More generally, the drawing recreates the exaggerated anatomical features typical of Goltzius's engravings created around the same time. The manner in which the hand is drawn is simultaneously a stylistic choice and an accurate depiction of structural abnormalities – neither only one nor the other. As such, the drawing is also a clever embodiment of *difficoltà*. As David Summers argued in his seminal study, the theoretical category of *difficoltà* began to be associated first and foremost with the representation of the human body in the 1500s: since

FIGURE 16.4 Hendrick Goltzius, *Self-Portrait*, 1589. Silverpoint with graphite, with grey and blue-grey wash, on yellow-prepared vellum, 14.6 × 10.4 cm. London, British Museum
IMAGE © THE TRUSTEES OF THE BRITISH MUSEUM

FIGURE 16.5 Hendrick Goltzius, *Four Studies of [Goltzius'] Right Hand*, 1588–1589. Black and red chalk, on slightly tinted ribbed laid paper, 30.9 × 20.7 cm. Frankfurt am Main, Städel Museum
IMAGE © PUBLIC DOMAIN

'the human figure' was 'the crown and sum of creation', the representation of the human body was seen as the consummate challenge to any visual artist.[22] Conceiving and then creating compositions that allowed for the display of this artistic virtue was, according to Giorgio Vasari, the domain of Michelangelo. In Van Mander's *Lives*, it is of course Goltzius who embodies Buonarroti's relentless insistence on setting 'difficulties before himself'. Goltzius's image of his right hand draws attention to the corporeal limitations of his art making and documents a material trace of their overcoming. The drawing's ingenuity lies in the tension between what's revealed and what's artfully concealed, which recalls the late-Renaissance tension between *facilità* and *difficoltà*.

The tension between the simultaneous display and concealment of the hand's disability through its presentation as an embodiment of mastery over *difficoltà* in the 1588 drawing transforms into the impairment's literal disappearance in *Four Studies of [Goltzius's] Right Hand*. The *Four Studies* was intended as a reference sheet for Goltzius and his assistants, providing them with various correct depictions of a hand. Here, the artist tried different gestures; in leafing through a book, the malformation of the hand can be completely concealed, and Goltzius thus showed us his hand as if it were a normal hand, 'perfected' it. If the drawing testifies to a moment of self-doubt, questioning whether malformed hands deserve to be portrayed, that moment was brief, for as I argue here, Goltzius deliberately shaped his identity vis-à-vis his disability, merging its real and symbolic aspects.

Van Mander clearly signalled the symbolic value of the hand's deformation in his description of the childhood accident. The accident is presented as anything but random: it happened because Goltzius was 'attracted to the fire'. The phrase unmistakably announces his future interest in alchemy, bolstered by the next misfortune that befell him in childhood: the ingestion of the highly toxic orpiment (auripigmentum), a type of yellow pigment which, alongside realgar, was made alchemically.[23] Although orpiment produced a spectacular effect of golden lustre without using actual gold, Van Mander himself warned about orpiment alongside verdigris (Spanish green) in the twelfth chapter of *Den Grondt der edel, vry schilderconst* (*Foundation of the Noble, Free Art of Painting*), calling them pigments 'poisonous by nature, to be avoided'.[24]

---

22   Summers D., *Michelangelo and the Language of Art* (Princeton: 1981) 184.

23   Göttler C., "Yellow, Vermilion, and Gold: Colour in Karel van Mander's *Schilder-Boeck*", in Burghartz S. – Burkart C. – Göttler C. – Rublack U. (eds.), *Materialized Identities in Early Modern Culture, 1450–1750: Objects, Affects, Effects* (Amsterdam: 2021) 257.

24   Mander Karel van, *Den Grondt der Edel vry Schilder-const* in Mander, *Het Schilder-Boeck*, fol. 50r.

Van Mander did not elaborate on this warning, but Goltzius's accident calls to mind a passage from the *Libro dell'Arte* (ca. 1400), in which Cennino Cennini reminds readers willing to risk painting with orpiment: 'watch that you do not spatter your mouth with it lest you do harm'.[25] Still, if used in small doses, both orpiment and realgar could also be administered as remedies.[26] Van Mander tells us that after Goltzius put orpiment in his mouth, his father scraped it out as best he could; Hendrick presumably ingested only a small amount which, literally and symbolically, might even have had a beneficial, medicinal effect on the child. Thus, another mishap that could have been fatal to young Hendrick instead becomes an anecdote about the future artist's attraction to alchemical transmutation: indeed, it serves as the last in a series of accidents involving the elements of air, water, and fire. Among these elements, fire was the most important: Goltzius is transformed in and through fire, as the damage to his right hand becomes the prerequisite of uncommon manual (ambi)dexterity and, as such, exemplifies classical tropes of disability and compensation.

2 Goltzius the Supercrip

The damage to Goltzius's hand likely helped him to become a better engraver for a very simple reason: the strength necessary for engraving must come from the wrist and the forearm, which Goltzius had no choice but to engage. Van Mander might have been aware of this straightforward explanation, as he comments about the beginning of Goltzius's professional career that, after learning to etch in copper, he 'versocht oock met zijn lamme handt in't coper te leeren snijden, t'welck hem soo in't beginsel gheluckte, dat Cornhardt doe ter tijt vier mijlen van daer woonende, hem begheerde aen te nemen te leeren Plaet-snijden' ('also tried with his bad hand to learn to engrave on copper which he from the start managed so well that Cornhardt, who at that time lived four miles from there, wanted to take him on to learn engraving').[27] But ultimately, Van Mander attributes Goltzius's accomplishments to his love of art, commitment to daily practice, and capacity for both imitation and invention.

Over and beyond Goltzius, there are only three other artists with disabilities mentioned in *Het Schilder-Boeck*: the stained-glass painter Pierre Crabais (Pieter Dircksz. Crabeth, active ca. 1507–1542), called 'Krepel Pieter' ('Crippled Pieter'), the deaf student of Frans Floris, Thomas van Coelen from Nijmeghen,

---

25 Göttler, "Yellow, Vermilion, and Gold", 260.
26 Ibidem.
27 Mander, *Het Schilder-Boeck*, fol. 282r. Translated in: Mander, *The Lives*, vol. 1, 385.

'SYMBOLIC ANATOMIES': GOLTZIUS AND THE EARLY MODERN DISABILITY   631

and Rijckaert Aertsz., known as 'Rijk with the peg leg' (1482–1577). Van Mander tells us nothing about Crabais and Van Coelen besides mentioning their names and disabilities, but the short biography of Aertsz. deserves our attention as it adds to the affective history of disability.[28] In his youth, Rijckaert burned his leg which had to be amputated after unsuccessful treatment. A son of a fisherman from Wijk aan Zee, Rijckaert was no longer fit to take up his father's profession and 'often sat by fire', which in Van Mander connotes quietness, lack of activity, and melancholy.[29] Rijckaert's behaviour after his accident is a commonly expected reaction to a new disability, which he nevertheless transcended through art. It was during Rijckaert's contemplative hours by the fireplace that nature 'awaken[ed] him' and 'invit[ed] him to the art of drawing', which he began practicing by drawing with coal on the hearth and the chimney.[30] In the life of Rijckaert, fire once again functions as the catalyst of artistic ingenuity: in Goltzius's biography, it caused an accident that physically preconditioned him to become an excellent engraver, and in Rijckaert's, it created a new intellectual, mental, and emotional desire seemingly *ex nihilo*, in a region of the Netherlands where, according to Van Mander, there was no 'tempting example' that could have inspired young men to art.

Although Van Mander stops short of calling Rijckaert's initial reaction to the amputation 'swaermoedicheyt' (melancholy), his behaviour certainly suggests this 'diagnosis', and deserves a comparison with Goltzius. Early modernity has been famously called 'the Golden Age of melancholy', but there is only a handful of instances when the condition is mentioned in *Het Schilder-Boeck*. Van Mander describes as 'swaermoedich' Carel van Yper, whom inconsiderate banter by fellow painters and excessive drinking pushed to suicide, and in the case of Hendrick Goltzius, he characterises melancholy as a psychosomatic condition, the symptoms of which manifest as tuberculosis.[31] The first onset of Goltzius's melancholy resulted from his forced neglect of art, brought about by family obligations, and was cured by his journey to Italy. When the disease returned, Goltzius alleviated its effects by drinking goat's milk and 'suckl[ing at] women's breasts'. Two years later, he began to paint. This chronology of events suggests that the treatment spurred Goltzius's rebirth as a person and an artist: indeed, as Eric Jan Sluijter has noted, Van Mander treats the mature

---

28   Mander, *Het Schilder-Boeck*, fols. 227v, 242v, and 247r–247v.
29   Mander, *The Lives*, vol. 5, 180.
30   This is similar to Goltzius's drawing 'on walls and elsewhere' when he first showed talent for visual arts.
31   On Carel van Yper, see: Mander, *The Lives*, vol. 1, fol. 253r–253v. The phrase 'golden age of melancholy' was coined by Jean Starobinski in 'Histoire du traitement de la mélancolie, des origines à 1900', *Acta Psychosomatica* 3 (Basel: 1960).

Goltzius as a 'child prodigy', due to his newfound mastery of painting.[32] Van Mander's narration of Goltzius's disease, treatment, relapse, and a second, more successful recovery follows the pattern of religious pilgrimage and healing. In those stories, the afflicted supplicants would gradually regain their health when approaching a wonder-working shrine – in Goltzius's case, works by Italian artists he had longed to see – but would experience only a temporary relief if they failed to fulfil their vow.[33] Likewise, to see, copy, and discuss works of Italian artists was not sufficient to cure Goltzius's illness; he had to master a new medium and reinvent himself as a painter to be fully and permanently cured. In stark contrast to the Dürerian aetiology of melancholy, Goltzius recovers completely from his 'swaermoedicheyt' only through his re-dedication to his work.

Van Mander discusses 'swaermoedicheyt' in predominantly negative terms, focusing on the grave, life-threatening symptoms of the disease. His approach corresponds with the definition of the disease in the 1573 *Schat der Neder-duytscher spraken*, which described 'swaermoedicheyt' as an emotionally mixed condition encompassing 'lassitudo animi' (weariness of the soul) and 'tristitia' (sadness, sorrow), but also 'languor' (inertia, apathy) and 'fastidium' (loathing, disdain).[34] Plantin's thesaurus suggests an increasingly complex understanding of melancholy as a compound of affects, defined only twenty years earlier in *Het Tresoor der Duytschen Talen* simply as 'droefheyt' (sadness).[35] The peril of 'swaermoedicheyt' thus came to be seen in its combination of sorrowful exhaustion with an apathetic inability to overcome it. Still, while early modernity blamed melancholy for somatic suffering and mental imbalance, it was also at times associated with enhanced intellectual and creative prowess, and even seen as a 'necessary adjunct to creativity'.[36] The description of Goltzius as prone to 'swaermoedicheyt' thus implies that he was singularly gifted, and this was augmented by the fact that he ultimately capable of overcoming the disease in its debilitating form. As I argue later, this form

---

32   Sluijter, E.J., "Goltzius, Painting and Flesh; or, Why Goltzius Began to Paint in 1600", in Van den Doel M. – Van Eck N. (eds.), *The Learned Eye: Regarding Art, Theory, and the Artist's Reputation* (Amsterdam: 2005) 160.

33   For instance, in one medieval story, a girl cured from blindness lost her sight again when her mother did not embark on a pilgrimage she pledged. Wheatley E., *Stumbling Blocks before the Blind: Medieval Constructions of Disability* (Ann Arbor: 2010) 166.

34   *Thesaurus Theutonicae linguae; Schat der Neder-duytscher spraken* (Antwerp, Christophe Plantin: 1573) n.p.

35   Werve Jan van den, *Het Tresoor der Duytschen Talen* (Antwerp, Hans de Laet: 1553) 105.

36   Dixon L., *The Dark Side of Genius. The Melancholy Persona in Art, ca. 1500–1700* (University Park: 2013) 13.

of perseverance, located in Goltzius's *ingenium*, is essential to the construction of his artistic persona vis-à-vis his hand's severe deformity.

Both chronic and acute (as in the case of Goltzius) manifestations of melancholy called for similar curatives, ranging from dietary changes to counter the excess of black bile to exercise, conversations with friends, travel, and enjoyment of art and music.[37] Goltzius's diet of milk and journey to Italy, with pranks that he played on fellow artists, thus align with a standard period response to melancholy. The "Life of Rijckaert Aertsz" further solidifies Van Mander's belief in the healing potential of *schilderconst* present in Goltzius's biography, for Rijckaert's embrace of painting counters the negative effects of his disabling amputation. According to *Het Schilder-Boeck*, Rijckaert grew into 'a quiet, moderate, peace-loving, virtuous and pious man who greatly loved Holy Scripture and inner peace', achieving stoic contentment which Van Mander sees as a desirable quality in an artist that predisposes him to creating good works whatever his circumstances. Moreover, Rijckaert 'was very much loved and cheerful, often saying: I am rich and prosperous'; this pleasant demeanour and universal likeability earned him a portrayal as Saint Luke in Frans Floris's famous painting of ca. 1560. Only at a later age when he began to lose his sight and his impaired vision led him to apply paint too thickly, did he become moody and discontented, conscious of his inability to paint well. His biography confirms that emotional reactions to disability can shift over the course of life, depending on the specific type and scope of disability.[38]

Het Schilder-Boeck was published in 1604 and thus too early to include the prominent deaf artists Hendrick Avercamp, Johannes Thopas, and Jan Jansz. de Stomme, but its praise of Goltzius created a striking intersection of disability and artistic virtuosity.[39] For Van Mander, Goltzius was the consummate artist, whose multifaceted oeuvre embodied the pinnacle of the Netherlandish tradition in the same way 'the divine' Michelangelo's art had become

---

37   Early modern authors agreed that melancholy was, in the words of Lodovico Guicciardini, a 'hatelijcke ende onghesonde' (spiteful and unhealthy) condition that had to be treated. While Guicciardini's preferred curative against melancholy was wine, early modern recipe books frequently suggested complex tinctures against the condition. Guicciardini Lodovico, *Beschrijvinghe van alle de Neder-landen* (Antwerp, Willem Jansz: 1612) 29.

38   David Turner calls attention to this 'range of variables' in attitudes towards disablement in a historical context in: Turner D., "Disability history and the history of emotions: reflections on eighteenth-century Britain", *Asclepio* 68.2 (2016) n.p.

39   Curious is the absence from *Het Schilder-Boeck* of Hans Verhagen de Stomme (ca. 1540/ 45–1600), an Antwerp draughtsman and watercolour painter of animals, including the elephant which was paraded in Antwerp in 1566, and whose compositions became an important source for Hans Bol and Joris Hoefnagel.

synonymous with unsurpassable perfection in Giorgio Vasari's *Lives*. Goltzius's disability is effectively framed as a prerequisite of his artistic genius, implicitly bolstered by his 'swaermoedicheyt', and Goltzius himself confirms such a view of his art in his works. In a famous passage of Goltzius's biography, Van Mander praises him as 'a rare Proteus or Vertumnus in art, because he [could] transform himself to all forms of working methods' and, in *Den Grondt*, as 'the only phoenix with golden feathers'.[40] The alchemical associations with the resurrected phoenix which, as Christine Göttler has pointed out, 'was frequently used as a symbol for the philosopher's stone', alongside Goltzius's ingestion of orpiment and his childhood transformation in a hearth fire, makes another mythological comparison suitable: Goltzius can be cast in the role of Vulcan. According to Van Mander, Vulcan discovered 'all the things that are built or created through fire'; in other words, he was the inventor of those artisanal skills associated with fire.[41] Those skills should be seen as attributes compensating for Vulcan's lameness, due to which he could not dwell among the physically perfect Olympians; in the words of Marie Delcourt, his disability was 'the price paid by the magician to acquire his art'.[42] The myth of Vulcan introduced into Western thought two fundamental, intertwined ideas about disability and artistic creation: first, that special gifts that set the disabled person apart can compensate for physical and sensory disabilities; and second, that art as *technē*, the material and technical aspects of the creative process, can serve to overcome disability. Vulcan, in addition to his metallurgic and alchemical skills, possessed 'a powerful torso, muscular arms and ambidextrous fingers'.[43] Goltzius shared the latter trait with him, although, in contrast to Vulcan, he became ambidextrous through his stubborn *oefeninge*, in a sense exerting more control over his destiny than had the disabled god. Both Vulcan and Goltzius were also extraordinarily inventive and imaginative in their metalwork, of which engraving is of course a type.

By mobilizing the compensation trope that interprets Goltzius's impaired hand as the instrument of singular virtuosity, Van Mander and Goltzius further

---

40 Melion W.S., "Karel van Mander's 'Life of Hendrick Goltzius': Defining the Paradigm of Protean Virtuosity in Haarlem around 1600", *Studies in the History of Art* 27 (1989) 113–133; and Göttler C., "Tales of Transformation. Hendrick Goltzius's *Allegory of the Alchemical Arts* in the Kunstmuseum Basel", *Inquiries into Art, History, and the Visual* 2 (2020) 444.

41 Mander Karel van, *Wtlegginge, en sin-ghevende verclaringe op den Metamorphosis Publij Ovidij Nasonis* in Mander, *Het Schilder-Boeck* (Haarlem, Paschier van Wesbuch: 1604), fol. 14v. See also Göttler, "Tales of Transformation" 433.

42 Cited in Stiker H.-J., *A History of Disability* (Ann Arbor: 2000) 59.

43 Ebenstein W., "Toward an Archetypal Psychology of Disability Based on the Hephaestus Myth", *Disability Studies Quarterly* 26.4 (2006) n.p.

erase 'fear, pity and disgust', the three emotions that Bill Hughes has recognised as the 'building blocks of the emotional infrastructure of ableism', and whose origins he and other scholars sought in the long history of Western Christianity.[44] Instead, for his contemporaries, Goltzius, a crippled engraver, must have seemed a curious aberration, what in recent years has been termed a 'supercrip'. A supercrip is an inspiring disabled individual who overcomes their disability and accomplishes things that the non-disabled population considers to be impossible for them to achieve. As Eli Clare asserts, 'the nondisabled world is saturated with' supercrip stories, such as 'a blind man hikes the Appalachian Trail from end to end. An adolescent girl with Down syndrome learns to drive and has a boyfriend. A guy with one leg runs across Canada'.[45] To Clare and many disability scholars and activists such stories 'reinforce the superiority of the nondisabled body and mind', largely because they ignore the oppressive socioeconomic and political conditions that make it difficult for people with disabilities to lead ordinary lives. Essential to the construction of the 'supercrip' persona is the shift in the emotional response from pity and charity to awe and admiration, bolstered by the emphasis on 'individualized attributes such as willpower and determination' that allow the disabled person to 'overcome' their impairment.[46] The importance of these individual characteristics brings together Goltzius's physical impairment and his experiences of melancholy. Goltzius transcended the first onset of his 'swaermoedicheyt' by embarking on a perilous journey to Italy. His dedication to art and desire to see works by Italian masters that inspired his travel negated the grim medical diagnosis of his physicians, none of whom 'had any hope of being able to help him'. While travel was considered a curative for melancholy, the condition's complex relationship to artistic creativity and exceptional ability implies that Goltzius's ability to 'overcome' mental and bodily difference was an innate aspect of his personality. The individual mental attributes play an even bigger role in supercrip narratives if the 'supercrip' accomplishes things that are unusually difficult even for a non-disabled person. Like Clare's 'blind man hiking the Appalachian Trail' and 'a guy with one leg running across Canada' whose feats are extraordinary even from the perspective of 'normative' bodies, Goltzius accomplished things beyond the grasp of most non-disabled artists. But in contrast to many stereotyped supercrip heroes, Goltzius appears to have embraced his supercrip identity and used it to his advantage. Through

---

44   Hughes, "Invalidating Emotions" 91.

45   Clare E., *Exile and Pride: Disability, Queerness, and Liberation* (Durham: 2015) 2.

46   Schalk S., "Reevaluating the Supercrip", *Journal of Literary & Cultural Disability Studies* 10.1 (2016) 77.

his self-assured virtuosity, Goltzius encouraged the conflation of the physical and the symbolic anatomies of his 'rechter cromme handt', all the while keeping firm control over the process of identity-formation, as the anecdote about Van Winghen's incredulity reveals. Van Winghen's reaction confirms that Goltzius, aided by Van Mander, also possessed affective agency in this process: he aimed to evoke wonderment, awe, and admiration.

The process of 'becoming a supercrip' is thematised in one of Goltzius's key works, the 1586 engraving of Gaius Mucius Scaevola, the third print in the series of the *Roman Heroes* [Fig. 16.6]. Scaevola, a Roman youth, plotted to assassinate the Etruscan king Lars Porsenna who had laid siege to Rome, but after mistakenly killing the king's scribe, he was captured. In the face of imminent death, Scaevola put his right hand into a flame to show his fearlessness. This self-sacrificial demonstration of courage saved his life and the city of Rome: after witnessing Scaevola's self-inflicted suffering, the king, who presumed that all Romans were as impervious to suffering, retreated from Rome. In the background of Goltzius's engraving, Scaevola stands by the body of the assassinated scribe, his hand still holding the sword firmly in the fire, his gesture compensating for – though not nullifying – his crime. Rather than saving Rome by assassinating Porsenna, Scaevola transformed the fate of his city and underwent a personal transformation by fire, as the voluntary self-sacrifice became a turning point in the siege. As Walter Melion has convincingly argued, in the series Goltzius chose 'to portray heroes whom he could convert into figures of himself through the mediation of Livy'.[47] This personal connection is then completed by Van Mander, for whom the *Roman Heroes* embodied 'heldighe cracht der Teycken-const, en t'vermoghen des Graef-ijsers' (the 'heroic power of his [Goltzius's] draughtsmanship and the might of his burin').[48] The conflation of Goltzius's 'artisanal virtuosity' with 'martial virtue' is consistent with Valerius Maximus's *Dictorum factorumque memorabilium libri IX* (Antwerp 1574); the story of Scaevola, at the heart of which a 'defect' is transformed, literally and metaphorically into a strength, must have held great appeal to young Goltzius.[49] That Mucius Scaevola functioned for Goltzius as an allegorical image symbolic of his own life, art, and virtue/virtuosity, is clear from Van Mander's inclusion of the *Roman Heroes* among the few early works by Goltzius he discusses. He also mentions that besides the 1586 engraving,

---

47   Melion W.S., "Memorabilia aliquot Romanae strenuitatis exempla: The Thematics of Artisanal Virtue in Hendrick Goltzius's *Roman Heroes*", *Modern Language Notes* 110.5 (1995) 1110.

48   Mander, *The Lives*, vol. 1, 397. Melion, "Love and Artisanship" 67.

49   Ibidem 70.

FIGURE 16.6   Hendrick Goltzius, *Mucius Scaevola*, 1586. Engraving, 36.7 × 23.5 cm. Amsterdam, Rijksmuseum
IMAGE © PUBLIC DOMAIN

Goltzius painted 'a large, oblong canvas in grisaille in oils [...] with the history of the Roman who burns his hand, astonishingly well designed and executed, and it was made for a place in a room in a large, distinguished house in Haarlem, at that time the property of burgomaster Gerit Willemsen but now belonging to Goltzius'.[50]

3 How to Look at Goltzius's Hand

If the engraving of Mucius Scaevola, created when Goltzius was twenty-eight, thematises artisanal virtuosity as masculine, martial virtue, *Sine Cerere et Libero Friget Venus*, created twenty years later, reframes Goltzius's burin-holding burned hand as an offering at the altar of Venus [Fig. 16.7]. In the background, next to the playful adolescent Cupid tending the fire on the altar of Venus, Goltzius tempers burins, sanctifying 'his tools by heating them in love's flame'.[51] As we recall, Goltzius taught himself to etch and engrave in copper thanks to his 'great love for art'; here, he pays homage to the goddess of love. But *Sine Cerere* is also a confident commentary on the symbolic metamorphosis of the childhood accident into the virtuosity of the mature artist. Goltzius's right hand is disturbingly close to the fire and would have been easily obscured by the flames if it weren't for Goltzius's exquisite technique. As a hapless toddler, Goltzius fell into a fire; now, he is in perfect control of his movements, as evidenced by the steadiness of his hands depicted in the *penwerck* and the technique that required steadiness from the hands which created it. The unsettling proximity of Goltzius's hands to the fire serves to engage the viewer in the kind of shifting emotional response to his hand's deformation orchestrated by him and Van Mander for their contemporaries. Our visceral fear of fire is not irrational: the flames on the altar of Venus that envelop Goltzius's right hand create subtle lines across the dorsum where the hand was badly burned. The delicate transparency of those lines creates an illusory effect that blurs the distinction between flames and the scarring of Goltzius's skin. Astonishingly, though obscured, the intermediate and the distal phalanges of his index finger, absent in the drawings from the 1580s, are visible and contracted only as much as required to hold the burins – a gesture perhaps suggesting that the damage to the tendons did indeed make Goltzius uniquely suited for his work as an engraver. The origins of his talent and skills would then be a combination of natural and artificial causes: his attraction to fire, a harbinger of his

---

50   Mander, *The Lives*, vol. 1, 397.
51   Melion, "Love and Artisanship" 69.

'SYMBOLIC ANATOMIES': GOLTZIUS AND THE EARLY MODERN DISABILITY 639

FIGURE 16.7 Hendrick Goltzius, *Sine Cerere et Libero Friget Venus*, 1606. Pencil, pen, and brown wash on grounded canvas, 220 × 170 cm. St. Petersburg, The Hermitage
IMAGE © PUBLIC DOMAIN

alchemical interest, leads to a deformation of his hand that instrumentalises it into the best of all burin-hands. The conversion is then completed through diligent *oefeninge*, and we, the viewers, transcend our fear of fire to embrace admiration for Goltzius's skill.

This transition from the negative instinctive response of fear to learned appreciation is enveloped in the aura of erotic joy and contentment in the service of love, expressed not only through the theme of the *penwerck* but also its style. *Sine Cerere* is a sophisticated spectacle of delicate lines subtly defining the soft curvatures of Venus's, Ceres's, and Bacchus's bodies. The work's precise, robust yet delicate, inimitable technique, along with the draughtsman's self-portrait, makes Goltzius emphatically present. The image can be associated with delight as defined by Van Mander, who attributed it in particular to colour and well-designed figures with decorous poses, gestures, and physical characteristics. Although *Sine Cerere* uses exclusively brown and red ink, its semi-transparency nevertheless gives the *penwerck* 'the lustre of oil-based painting'.[52] The design of the Venus's and Ceres's bodies aligns with Van Mander's recommendations for the *decorum* of representing of mythological female figures in Chapter Four of the *Foundation*: 'Lustich behendich sullen oock verschijnen Van de gracelijcheyt waer te nemen. / Alle roeringhen van leden oft letten / Der Nimphen, Goddinnen en Concubijnen' ('Every motion of the limbs or members / Of Nymphs, Goddesses, and Concubines / Must also appear pleasing and deft').[53] The interaction between Venus and Bacchus adds to the delight achieved through this *decorum* of poses by evoking the feelings of love as outlined in Chapter Six: 'T'affect der Liefden uytbeeldinghe bouwen, Met een vriendelijck toelachend' aenschouwen, Met omhelsinghen, en aermen omvanghen, En de hoofden toeneyghende doen hanghen nae malcander' ('the affect of Love / Between men and women, / With a friendly, smiling visage / With embraces and clasping of arms / And tilting of heads mutually inclined').[54] The complementary curvatures of Venus's and Bacchus's bodies amplify this 'affect of love' and transform it into an erotic image. The two gods are revealed to us by mischievous putti drawing back the curtain that concealed them, thus unsettling our gaze as we are transformed into voyeurs participating in the titillating aura of this scene. Its overtone is, however, overwhelmingly positive. In Book v of *Wtlegginge, en sin-ghevende verclaringe op den Metamorphosis Publij Ovidij Nasonis*, a commentary on Ovid's *Metamorphoses* that forms a part of *Het Schilder-Boeck*, Van Mander

---

52   Melion, "Love and Artisanship", 60.
53   Mander, *Den Grondt*, 14v. For the English translation see: Mander, *Karel van Mander*, 237.
54   Mander, *Den Grondt*, 23r. For the English translation see: Mander, *Karel van Mander*, 261.

describes the multifaceted nature of Venus, whom poets have associated with complex and even contradictory emotions such as joy and sadness, hope and despair, laughter and regret. Beyond distinguishing between the celestial and the earthly Venus – the latter of whom is depicted in Goltzius's 1590 *Venus and Cupid* – Van Mander describes the goddess's potential for arousing unbridled carnal lust, inspiring deception, and bringing on a change of heart.[55] But these negative attributes or incarnations of Venus are countered by fecundity, loveliness, friendliness, and beauty. The joyful nature of Venus is embodied in Philomeides Aphrodite, the laughing Venus. It is she that we see in the 1606 *penwerck*, and her pleasant smile is repeated in the face of Cupid standing next to Goltzius. Executed in the medium that Goltzius invented after his return to Haarlem and perfected after he became a painter, the *penwerck*, through its choice of Philomeides Aphrodite, thematizes not only his burned burin-hand but also the definite overcoming of his melancholy. While in Van Mander's account Goltzius's recovery from his illness was effected by his artistic transformation following his Italian journey – which alone was an insufficient therapeutic – *Sine Cerere* conceptualizes the curative in more specific terms. In his youth, Goltzius identified with the martial virtue of Scaevola, whose fearlessness and intrepidity were unambiguous, straightforward emotions. While embracing the 'supercrip' identity of the Roman hero, Goltzius continued to struggle with the complex psychosomatic condition of melancholy; to transcend it, he had to shift to another complex emotion – love – in the process of becoming a votary in service of Venus.

Whereas Goltzius's disfigured hand was already a central theme of *Mucius Scaevola* and the 1588 drawing in the Teylers Museum, the different pictorial and narrative frameworks that these works employed confirm that disability and deformity are not fixed affective categories, but rather, are co-shaped by a multitude of factors. Together with the 1606 *Sine Cerere*, these works rely on distinct and varied stylistic and compositional characteristics to elicit a specific, if complex and unequivocal, emotional response from their viewers. The self-assured stance of Scaevola, from whose foreground image the mutilated hand has been removed, is an embodiment of Van Mander's advice regarding the depiction of martial figures in *The Foundation of the Noble, Free Art of Painting*: 'Sonderlinghe stercke ghestelde Mannen / Sullen doen gheweldigh' acten en standen' ('Men of specially strong constitution / Will perform powerful

---

55   On the 1590 Venus and Cupid see: Melion W.S., "The Trope of Anthropomorphosis in Hendrick Goltzius's *Venus and Cupid* (1590), *Venus, Bacchus, and Ceres* (1593), and *Portrait of Frederick de Vries* (1597)", in Melion W. – Zell M. – Woodall J. (eds), *Ut Pictura Amor: The Reflexive Imagery of Love in Artistic Theory and Practice, 1500–1700* (Boston: 2017) 159–228.

acts and take forcible positions') and should be 'in stellingh en acty woester ontbonden' ('fiercely unbridled in pose and gesture').[56] The confrontation between Mucius and King Porsenna is depicted in the lower one-third of the composition's background, leaving the rest of the background blank except for a few clouds. Nothing distracts us from the physical prowess of Mucius and his decorously exaggerated muscles and veins, as the austerity of the composition augments the dignity of his martial deeds and projects the emotion of *gravitas* onto his military body. Compositional and stylistic straightforwardness of the print communicates the univocal artistic persona that Goltzius embraced at the time of its creation. But, as we have seen, that persona, grounded in martial boldness, was insufficient to accommodate the complexity of Goltzius's affective relationship to art that at the time took on the form of the extreme condition of melancholy. Juxtaposed with the 1606 *Sine Cerere, Mucius Scaevola* reveals the shortcomings of uncomplicated, unambiguous conceptualization of emotions involved in the act of creation and reception of images.

Goltzius soon abandoned such resolute straightforwardness. In the 1588 drawing of his right hand, the inclusion of the artist's elaborate signature confirms its status as a work of art, but the hand's disembodied state and the physiognomic precision of its representation nevertheless place it within the visual discourse of early modern anatomy. The drawing's ontological status is confounding, as it's suspended between an artist's self-portrait and a medical specimen without conforming to either genre. It invites inquisitive looking that relies on curiosity as a precondition of knowledge, but the depicted hand's anomalies can quickly transform this laudable quest for visual knowledge into 'a visual vice'.[57] In the end, we are not sure what we are supposed to feel when looking at the drawing, or even how long we are supposed to look at it. Goltzius leaves us with several questions. Does the image require prolonged ocular scrutiny in the name of appreciation of the artist's craft, or should we avert our gaze before it instrumentalises Goltzius's hand into a display of a minor freakery? And if we look away, does this mean that we are disgusted by Goltzius's unorthodox anatomy? While evoking the tradition of medical curiosa, the drawing ultimately transgresses the early modern conventions of anatomical illustrations. Alongside detailed images of individual parts of the body, sixteenth-century anatomical treatises routinely used stylised figures engaged

---

56   Mander, *Den Grondt*, fol. 14v. For the English translation see: Mander Karel van, *Karel van Mander and His Foundation of the Noble, Free Art of Painting*, ed. – trans. W.S. Melion (Boston – Leiden: 2023) 238.

57   I borrow this term from Rosemarie Garland-Thomson. Garland-Thomson R., *Staring. How We Look* (Oxford: 2009) 65.

'SYMBOLIC ANATOMIES': GOLTZIUS AND THE EARLY MODERN DISABILITY

in dramatic action or hyperbolic display of emotions to mediate anatomical content, but that content exemplified what the 'normal' human body looked like. The visual rhetoric of 'implicit drama' in these illustrations was meant to convey the *storia*, in Alberti's sense, of the human body.[58] Goltzius's drawing of his hand operates as a synecdoche of the thematic and affective *storia* of his unusual biography that accommodates contradictory and ultimately unresolved modes of looking.

4   Goltzius's Hand and Disability Gain

By way of conclusion, I would like to briefly return to *Mucius Scaevola* and consider it as a work that provides an achronological, summative understanding of Goltzius's 'cromme handt'. The inscription at the bottom of the print's first state reads:

> Errorem caedis pensat dum Mutius igne, Vendicat Iliacos obsidione lares. Civibus absumpta dedit hoc si Scaevola dextra, Quae Iove non laesam restituente daret?

> Because Mucius makes amends in the fire for his murder of the wrong man, he relieves the houses of Troy's descendants from the siege. If Scaevola achieved all this for his fellow citizens by sacrificing his right hand, what would he then achieve if Jupiter were to restore him without an injured hand?[59]

This anonymous inscription was added after Goltzius finished the engraving, and in the second edition of the series, dedicated to Rudolf II, was replaced with an epigram composed by the Gorinchem humanist Franco Estius.[60] Its poetic quality aside, the anonymous inscription implicates us in considering Goltzius's impairment in a way that gradually forces us to acknowledge it as a condition of his virtuosity while activating our memory and understanding of his art. The epigram interprets Scaevola's voluntary self-sacrifice as a

---

58   Kemp M., "Style and Non-style in Anatomical Illustration: From Renaissance Humanism to Henry Gray", *Journal of Anatomy* 216 (2010) 196.

59   Translated in Leeflang – Luijten, *Hendrick Goltzius* 90.

60   On Estius's verses in the *Roman Heroes* prints, see Ost K., "Epigramme als Widmungsträger: Die intermediale Neukonzeptualisierung von Hendrick Goltzius' Römischen Helden", Hammari M. – Pawlak A. – Rüth S. (Re-)*Inventio: The New Edition as a Creative Practice in the North Alpine Printmaking of the Early Modern Period* (Berlin – Boston: 2022) 57–106.

necessary act of penitence that proves his military valour and as a heroic deed that saved the Roman Republic. Praising his martial virtue, the author asks the reader/viewer: what even greater deeds would Scaevola accomplish if his hand were to be miraculously healed? Through the identification of Scaevola with Goltzius, we are invited to participate in this exercise of imaginary artistic invention. Is there anything else that Goltzius could have achieved if his hand's deformity were removed? In the light of all his achievements listed by Van Mander, a true *kunstliefhebber* cannot answer in the affirmative. How does our perplexed inability to imagine any greater inventions affect our perception of disability in general? We have to acknowledge that Goltzius, a crippled engraver and painter, reached his true potential not despite of but thanks to his entangled deformity; thus, we need to look at his deformity as an embodiment not of loss but of gain.[61] Besides removing our own negative responses to impairment, the case of Goltzius's 'lamme handt' destigmatizes the early modern emotions evoked by disability, often seen as unredeemable in their presumed penchant for disgust and charity. Rejecting univocal emotions as a reaction to bodily difference, Goltzius and Van Mander show us that sixteenth- and seventeenth-century non-disabled viewers were capable of seeing disability as more than a pitiful condition that called for assistance or a revolting 'spectacle' that should be hidden from the public eye. But if they engage us in fluid responses to Goltzius's disfigurement, they are also emphatic about the necessarily complex role of melancholy in the shifting of his artistic persona, thus providing an important and extensive correction to the affective history of early modern disfigurement and disease.

Bibliography

Bearden E., "Monstrous Births and Crip Authority: Cervantes, the *Persiles*, and the Representation of Disability", *eHumanista/Cervantes* 5 (2016) 69–84.

Bearden E., *Monstrous Kinds: Body, Space, and Narrative in Renaissance Representations of Disability* (Ann Arbor: 2019).

Biernoff S., *Portraits of Violence. War and the Aesthetics of Disfigurement* (Ann Arbor: 2017).

Clare E., *Exile and Pride: Disability, Queerness, and Liberation* (Durham: 2015).

Dixon L., *The Dark Side of Genius. The Melancholy Persona in Art, ca. 1500–1700* (University Park: 2013).

---

61   On staring as the instrument of shaping perceptions of disability and beauty, see Garland-Thomson, *Staring*.

Ebenstein W., "Toward an Archetypal Psychology of Disability Based on the Hephaestus Myth", *Disability Studies Quarterly* 26.4 (2006) n.p.

Garland R., *The Eye of the Beholder: Deformity and Disability in the Graeco-Roman World* (Ithaca: 1995).

Garland-Thomson R., *Extraordinary Bodies: Figuring Physical Disability in American Culture and Literature* (New York: 2017).

Garland-Thomson R., *Staring. How We Look* (Oxford: 2009).

Goldner G.R., "A New Bronzino Drawing", *Master Drawings* 28.3 (1990) 262–264.

Göttler C., "Tales of Transformation. Hendrick Goltzius's *Allegory of the Alchemical Arts* in the Kunstmuseum Basel", *Inquiries into Art, History, and the Visual* 2 (2020) 403–446.

Göttler C., "Yellow, Vermilion, and Gold: Colour in Karel van Mander's *Schilder-Boeck*", in Burghartz S. – Burkart C. – Göttler C. – Rublack U. (eds.), *Materialized Identities in Early Modern Culture, 1450–1750: Objects, Affects, Effects* (Amsterdam: 2021) 223–280.

Guicciardini Lodovico, *Beschrijvinghe van alle de Neder-landen* (Antwerp, Willem Jansz: 1612).

Hughes B., "Invalidating Emotions in the Non-Disabled Imaginary. Fear, Pity and Disgust", in Watson N. – Vehmas S. (eds.), *Routledge Handbook of Disability Studies* (Abingdon-on-Thames – New York: 2020) 89–101.

Kemp M., "Style and Non-style in Anatomical Illustration: From Renaissance Humanism to Henry Gray", *Journal of Anatomy* 216 (2010) 192–208.

Kuuliala J., "Miracle and the Monstrous: Disability and Deviant Bodies in the Late Middle Ages", in Canalis R.F. – Ciavolella M. (eds.), *Disease and Disability in Medieval and Early Modern Art and Literature* (Turnhout: 2021) 107–130.

Leeflang H. – Luijten G. (eds.), *Hendrick Goltzius (1558–1617): Drawings, Prints and Paintings*, exh. cat., Rijksmuseum Amsterdam – Metropolitan Museum of Art (Waanders: 2003).

Mander Karel van, *Het Schilder-Boeck* (Haarlem, Paschier van Wesbuch: 1604).

Mander Karel van, *The Lives of the Illustrious Netherlandish and German Painters*, ed. and trans. H. Miedema (Doornspijk: 1994).

Mander Karel van, *Karel van Mander and His Foundation of the Noble, Free Art of Painting*, ed. and trans. W.S. Melion (Boston – Leiden: 2023).

Melion W.S., "Karel van Mander's 'Life of Hendrick Goltzius': Defining the Paradigm of Protean Virtuosity in Haarlem around 1600", *Studies in the History of Art* 27 (1989) 113–133.

Melion W.S., "Love and Artisanship in Hendrick Goltzius's *Venus, Bacchus and Ceres* of 1606", *Art History* 16.1 (1993) 60–94.

Melion W.S., "Memorabilia aliquot Romanae strenuitatis exempla: The Thematics of Artisanal Virtue in Hendrick Goltzius's *Roman Heroes*", *Modern Language Notes* 110.5 (1995) 1090–1134.

Melion W.S., "Self-Imaging and the Engraver's Virtù: Hendrick Goltzius's *Pietà* of 1598", *Nederlands Kunsthistorisch Jaarboek/Netherlands Yearbook for History of Art* 46 (1995) 104–143.

Melion W.S., "The Trope of Anthropomorphosis in Hendrick Goltzius's Venus and Cupid (1590), Venus, Bacchus, and Ceres (1593), and Portrait of Frederick de Vries (1597)", in Melion W. – Zell M. – Woodall J. (eds), *Ut Pictura Amor: The Reflexive Imagery of Love in Artistic Theory and Practice, 1500–1700* (Boston: 2017) 159–228.

Metzler I., "Indiscriminate Healing Miracles in Decline: How Social Realities Affect Religious Perception", in Mesley M.M. – Wilson E. (eds.), *Contextualizing Miracles in the Christian West, 1100–1500* (Oxford: 2014) 154–176.

Orenstein N.M. (ed.), *Pieter Bruegel the Elder: Drawings and Prints* (New York: 2001).

Ost K., "Epigramme als Widmungsträger: Die intermediale Neukonzeptualisierung von Hendrick Goltzius' Römischen Helden", in Hammari M. – Pawlak A. – Rüth S. (eds.), *(Re-)Inventio: The New Edition as a Creative Practice in the North Alpine Printmaking of the Early Modern Period* (Berlin – Boston: 2022) 57–106.

Pearson A., "Sensory Piety as Social Intervention in a Mechelen Besloten Hofje", *Journal of Historians of Netherlandish Art* 9.2 (Summer 2017) n.p.

Schalk S., "Reevaluating the Supercrip", *Journal of Literary & Cultural Disability Studies* 10.1 (2016) 71–86.

Schweik S.M., *Ugly Laws: Disability in Public* (New York: 2009).

Sluijter E.J., "Goltzius, Painting and Flesh; or, Why Goltzius Began to Paint in 1600", in Van den Doel M. – Van Eck N. (eds.), *The Learned Eye: Regarding Art, Theory, and the Artist's Reputation* (Amsterdam: 2005) 158–178.

Starobinski J. "Histoire du traitement de la mélancolie, des origines à 1900", *Acta Psychosomatica* 3 (Basel: 1960).

Stiker H.-J., *A History of Disability* (Ann Arbor: 2000).

Summers D., *Michelangelo and the Language of Art* (Princeton: 1981).

Thesaurus Theutonicae linguae; Schat der Neder-duytscher spraken (Antwerp, Christophe Plantin: 1573).

Turner D.M. "Introduction. Approaching Anomalous Bodies", in Turner D.M. – Stagg K. (eds.) *Social Histories of Disability and Deformity. Bodies, Images and Experiences* (London – New York: 2006) 1–16.

Turner D., "Disability History and the History of Emotions: Reflections on Eighteenth-Century Britain", *Asclepio* 68.2 (2016) n.p.

Vives Juan Luis, *On Assistance to the Poor*, trans. A. Tobriner (Bruges, Hubertus de Croock: 1525; rpt. ed., Toronto: 1999).

Waugh P. (ed.), *Literary Theory and Criticism: An Oxford Guide* (Oxford: 2006).

Werve Jan van den, *Het Tresoor der Duytschen Talen* (Antwerp, Hans de Laet: 1553).

Wheatley E., *Stumbling Blocks before the Blind: Medieval Constructions of Disability* (Ann Arbor: 2010).

CHAPTER 17

Exploring Complex Emotions through the Portrayal of Dialogic Exchange: Pieter Lastman's *Paul and Barnabas in Lystra* of 1617

Graham R. Lea

Abstract

This essay addresses the biblical history painting of Pieter Lastman (1583–1633), in particular his preference for showing moments of conflict and moral dilemma expressed in/through dialogue. Lastman's *Paul and Barnabas in Lystra* visualises the complex emotional state of the apostles, brought about by a sudden reversal of fortune. Organised around a conversation between Paul and the pagan priest, Lastman's picture differs markedly from other Netherlandish examples: he dramatises the biblical scene by staging it in the manner codified by the local *rederijkerskamers* (chambers of rhetoric). Through narratological analysis, I demonstrate that Lastman shared with the rhetoricians an interest in representing shifting emotional responses to dramatic turning points in circumstances involving conflict and moral dilemma. Like the rhetoricians, Lastman focuses on Paul's delivery of exasperated speech, which issues from and registers a shifting mixture of love, fear, and anger.

Keywords

painting – rhetoric – Bible – drama – emotion – Pieter Lastman – apostles – narrative

Pieter Lastman (1583–1633) was one of the most celebrated history painters in Amsterdam in the early decades of the seventeenth century. The narrative moments which he chose to depict in his paintings often include circumstances in which the protagonists encounter moments of conflict and moral dilemma. Lastman inventively describes his figures reacting to these circumstances while engaged in conversation; in responding to what is said and heard, as well as to the activities that have given rise to their dialogic exchanges, they externalise complex emotional states. This pictorial strategy is only intensified by his choice to portray essential and crucial moments through which

© GRAHAM R. LEA, 2025 | DOI:10.1163/9789004694613_018

the entire story becomes clear. Consequently, a narratological analysis of his paintings can best serve to elucidate Lastman's approach to history painting. Narratology, the study of the form and function of narrative, naturally concerns itself with the characteristics and structural components of story and how these components function in relation to one another. The narratological component most relevant here is action, that is, the sequence of acts and events which constitutes the plot of a story.[1] It is evident from his history paintings that Lastman prefers to portray a specific moment of suspended action in which he attempts to distil the complete narrative.

These moments typically operate as turning points in the story where the protagonists frequently experience a dramatic reversal from fortune to misfortune or vice versa. These turns of events often precipitate a process whereby a character perceives – and then further recognises – the magnitude and consequences of that change.[2] Lastman, in his depictions of such turning points, almost always focuses attention on the complex emotional reactions writ large upon a protagonist's body, face, and gestures, as a result of the abrupt and tragic change in circumstances. An essential component of Lastman's persuasive portrayal of these turning points is thus his representation of consequent emotions in all their complexity; the abrupt reversal of fortune is presented as the antecedent cause of the mixed and/or shifting emotions that Lastman so tellingly describes. Implicit in his account of the protagonists' reversal of fortune is the transition from one emotion to another. In the moment where the protagonist's fortune reverses, happiness, joy, triumph, and elation can suddenly give way to fear, anxiety, anger, and grief, or to compounds of these various emotions.

To obtain a clearer sense of how Lastman represents the complex emotions brought about by a sudden reversal of fortune, one can do no better than to examine his painting, *Paul and Barnabas in Lystra* of 1617 [Fig. 17.1]. The story Lastman illustrates comes from the Book of Acts, which recounts how the Holy Spirit commissioned Paul and Barnabas to leave the church in Antioch, Syria, and preach the Gospel of Christ throughout Cyrus and Asia Minor.[3] During their ministry-journey, they preached the Christian message in Jewish synagogues, traveling to Seleucia, to the towns of Salamis and Paphos on the island

---

1 For an introduction to narratology, see Prince G., *Narratology: The Form and Functioning of Narrative* (Berlin: 1982), Fludernik M., *An Introduction to Narratology* (New York: 2006), and Liveley G., *Narratology* (Oxford: 2019).
2 Golahny A., "Pieter Lastman: moments of recognition", *Nederlands Kunsthistorisch Jaarboek* 60 (2010) 179–201.
3 Acts 13:2–3.

FIGURE 17.1   Pieter Lastman, *Paul and Barnabas in Lystra* (1617). Oil on panel. 76 × 115 cm. Amsterdam Museum, Amsterdam. Public Domain.

of Cyprus, to the towns of Attalia and Perga in Pamphylia, to Antioch and Iconium in Galatia, and then to Lystra, also located in Galatia.

While in Cyprus, they converted the proconsul, Sergius Paulus, despite opposition from the magician and Jewish false-prophet, Bar-Jesus, also known as Elymas. According to Acts, the Holy Spirit equipped Paul to condemn and rebuke the magician; the blinding of Elymas by the power of Paul's words led to the conversion of the proconsul to Christianity.[4] In the synagogue at Antioch, Galatia, as well as throughout the city, Paul preached the Gospel of Christ, identifying Jesus as the fulfilment of the Hebrew scriptures.[5] As in Cyprus, however, the apostles met opposition when Jewish clerics, who, alarmed at the popularity of the Gospel and the rising number of conversions among both Jews and Gentiles, sought to debate Paul and Barnabas and undermine their arguments. The clerics, having failed to discredit the apostles, incited the religious elite of Antioch to persecute Paul and Barnabas and run them out of town.[6] Paul and Barnabas encountered similar opposition in Iconium. There, they converted

4 Acts 13:9–12.
5 Acts 13:16–41.
6 Acts 13:50–52.

a number of Jews and Gentiles, but ultimately fled from persecution, making their way to Lystra.[7]

The episode Lastman describes in his painting of 1617 is a moment within this extended evangelical journey during which Paul and Barnabas spread the Word in spite of continual opposition and rejection. Undoubtedly, Lastman studied their travels to distinguish the unique circumstances of the event in Lystra. It is notably a situation of complex interactions, in which Paul and Barnabas are not rejected but, rather, are embraced and celebrated. They are accepted, however, for the wrong reasons, as will become evident. Not only does the situation require the apostles to shift their argument abruptly, but it also causes them to undergo a sudden shift of emotions. The apostles are forced urgently to pivot from persuading their audience of the Christian Gospel to dissuading them from false belief and idolatrous activity. A consequence of this sudden change in circumstances and what it requires is the emotional response of the apostles, shifting from a confident and joyful state to one of exasperation and distress. Not only does the complexity of this unique situation demand inventive pictorial solutions in a visual description of the event, but it also provides Lastman with the opportunity to explore how one conveys the shifting emotions the apostles experience.

Upon arriving in Lystra, Paul and Barnabas came upon a man lame since birth, whose faith in the Word inspired Paul to heal him. Seeing this miraculous event, the people of Lystra rejoiced, but instead of recognising it as the work of the Holy Spirit, they ascribed the miracle to their pagan gods; identifying Paul as Hermes (Mercury) and Barnabas as Zeus (Jupiter), they exclaimed, 'The gods have come down in the likeness of men'![8] The error of mistaken identity escalated when a priest, bringing oxen and garlands to the Temple of Zeus, called upon the crowd to offer a sacrifice to the god. Shocked at the people's idolatry and fearing lest they blaspheme against God, Paul and Barnabas tore their garments and rushed into the crowd to stop the sacrifice, all the while lamenting this disastrous turn of events.[9] Avowing their humanity, placing themselves on an equal footing with the people of Lystra, and giving credit for the miracle to God, they attempted to clarify by whose power the lame man was actually healed.[10]

---

7   Acts 14:1–7.
8   Acts 14:8–11.
9   Acts 14:14.
10   Acts 14:15–17.

The narrative reports that the apostles' arguments were persuasive enough to give pause to the people of Lystra and halt the sacrifice to Zeus. However, their success was only partial and temporary. Disgruntled Jews from Iconium and Antioch in Galatia arrived in Lystra and persuaded the people to rise up against the apostles. They stoned Paul and left him for dead on the outskirts of the city, but in spite of their best efforts, he survived. The next day, he continued with Barnabas on their journey and finally arrived in Derbe, the last stop before their return to Antioch in Syria.[11]

Lastman's painting of 1617 focuses on the culmination of the apostles' change in fortune, when the apostles, most notably, Paul, confront the priest of Jupiter (Zeus). Lastman has put stress on Paul: he adorns him with a garment of green and purple, colours which he uses nowhere else in the image, and he places Paul between two figures dressed in white, an acolyte at right who carries a tall candlestick and the temple priest who wears a wreath of laurel and holds a sacrificial vessel. To the left of the priest and acting as the central axis around which the painting is organised, one finds a sacrificial altar, already prepared for an offering.[12] Balancing the image, at left, a procession of enthusiastic Lystrans escorts a white bull adorned with garlands to the altar where with great fanfare the temple priest will read the auspices. The priest, instead of continuing with his preparations for sacrifice or welcoming the arrival of the bull, is shown turning away from the altar, his attention having been seized by the commotion behind him, in particular Paul's protestations against the pagan ceremony.

Paul stands higher than the priest and, emphatically crossing his hands, directs his gaze steeply down towards the priest and his activities [Fig. 17.2]. Not only does Lastman portray Paul affirming by his gesture the cross of Christ and opposing it to idolatry, he also employs this gesture to supplement what is presumably Paul's condemnatory speech of protest. This characterisation of

---

11   Acts 14:19–23.
12   The story offered Lastman the opportunity to represent ancient sacrificial rites accurately by including practices and historical instruments associated with the ancient city of Lystra. See Waiboer A.E., "Lastmans Opferdarstellungen und ihre weit reichende Wirkung", in Sitt M. (ed.), *Pieter Lastman: In Rembrandts Schatten?* exh. cat., Hamburger Kunsthalle (Munich: 2006) 44–45. For a discussion of Lastman's attention to representing ancient sacrificial customs, see Golahny A., "Paired Poems on Pendant Paintings: Vondel and Oudaan Interpret Lastman", in Golahny (ed.), *The Eye of the Poet: Studies in the Reciprocity of the Visual and Literary Arts from the Renaissance to the Present* (Lewisburg: 1996) 154–178, and eadem, "Lastman's 'Dido's Sacrifice to Juno' Identified", *Kroniek van Het Rembrandthuis* 1–2 (1998) 39–48.

FIGURE 17.2   Pieter Lastman, *Paul and Barnabas in Lystra* (1617). Oil on panel. 76 × 115 cm. Detail of apostles. Amsterdam Museum, Amsterdam. Public Domain.

the confrontation between Paul and the priest is the driving focus of Lastman's painting, and it is what distinguishes Lastman's iteration of the story from previous examples. As will become evident, the subtle manner in which Lastman describes the confrontation between Paul and the temple priest suggests the emotional shift the apostles experience: as a result of the apostles' dramatic reversal of fortune, the calm contentment felt during the healing of the lame man suddenly changes to the exasperation and distress experienced as they attempt to clarify their identity and stop an idolatrous sacrifice; the differences in how Lastman visualises the story demands from viewers that they consider the dialogic exchange unfolding between Paul and the priest and what specific pictorial elements Lastman has employed to visualise the emotional tenor and tone of the conflict.

1 The Pictorial Tradition

Lastman's portrayal of the story, organised around a conversation, which mediates the apostles' shifting emotional response to the narrative moment, is distinct from many precedents in the Netherlandish pictorial tradition. A preparatory drawing for a tapestry by Pieter Coecke van Aelst can serve as an initial point of difference. Coecke was a Flemish painter and tapestry designer who was certainly aware of Raphael's tapestry cartoon of *Paul and Barnabas at Lystra* when he designed his own version for a tapestry in ca. 1529–1530.[13] Raphael's *Acts of the Apostles* were woven in Brussels where copies of the cartoons likely remained and were later used for subsequent weavings. Guy Delmarcel has noted that Coecke was inspired by many of Raphael's inventions; there are numerous correspondences between Raphael's and Coecke's compositions, and many similarities in the positioning and posing of figures.[14] In Coecke's preparatory drawing for *The Sacrifice at Lystra*, on the other hand, one finds him inventing his own unique composition [Fig. 17.3]. The Temple of Jupiter dominates the middle-ground, where it mediates between the stoning of Paul in the left background, the healing of the lame man in the right middle ground, and the main event of the sacrifice in the foreground.

The most distinctive feature of Coecke's invention is the manner in which the apostles and the Lystrans interact and respond to each other. Coecke describes the apostles in the throes of strong emotion without the mediation of dialogue, which is a very different approach from that seen in Lastman's painting. To visualise the degree of the apostles' outrage and distress, Coecke poses the figures in dramatic serpentine attitudes, showing how sudden and swift is their 'turn' towards agitated disquiet. To the right of the altar, at the foot of which a lamb has already been slain, the apostles erupt with horror. The faces of Paul and Barnabas express shock and panic; they hasten in opposite directions with such velocity that their garments whip in the air. As they run, Barnabas tears his clothes, and Paul flails his arms helplessly in overwhelming grief. Many of the Lystrans direct their attention to the apostles, gazing and gesturing either in their direction or towards the preparations for the sacrifice. One Lystran points at the apostles, not to condemn or critique but rather to marshal the crowd's attention [Fig. 17.4]. Not only does

---

13   Cleland E.A.H. – Ainsworth M.W. – Alsteens S. – Orenstein N. – Buchanan I. – Delmarcel G. – Grazzini N.F. (eds.), *Grand Design: Pieter Coecke van Aelst and Renaissance Tapestry*, exh. cat., Metropolitan Museum of Art (New York: 2014) 148–149.

14   Delmarcel G., "The Life of Saint Paul", in Cleland – Ainsworth et al., *Grand Design: Pieter Coecke van Aelst* 125.

FIGURE 17.3   Pieter Coecke van Aelst, *The Sacrifice at Lystra* (ca. 1529–1530). Pen and brown ink. 29.5 × 45.7 cm. J. Paul Getty Museum, Los Angeles. Public Domain.

this figure point out the apostles' reactions, he also directs the viewer's eye to another Lystran.

That figure is a bearded Lystran, placed immediately behind the man who points so noticeably. This figure's hand gestures and face provide a more specific indication of the crowd's temper. Although the figure sports a furrowed brow, the angle of his eyebrows suggests more that he is concerned and thoughtful than angry or distressed. This demeanour is made all the more apparent by the way he lightly shrugs his shoulders while gesturing toward the religious rite. With respect to the apostles' outburst of emotion, this figure's attitude, like that of much of the crowd, registers as thoughtful concern about any offense given to the visitors. The Lystrans believed that Paul and Barnabas were Mercury and Jupiter, so the potential for offense was great. Distinct from what will be evident in Lastman's painting, neither the apostles nor anyone acting on their behalf attempts physically to intervene, nor is there a dialogic exchange between the parties. Coecke's design is primarily a straightforward portrayal of emotive responses to a blasphemous and idolatrous act.

Marten de Vos's painting of the subject of 1568 provides an interesting comparison, as it portrays the apostles presenting an earnest and measured argument without the degree of emotional expression one finds in Coecke's example [Fig. 17.5]. Formal and compositional similarities indicate that Lastman knew De Vos's picture. De Vos set the scene in a densely populated

FIGURE 17.4 Pieter Coecke van Aelst, *The Sacrifice at Lystra* (ca. 1529–1530). Pen and brown ink. 29.5 × 45.7 cm. Detail of sacrifice. J. Paul Getty Museum, Los Angeles. Public Domain.

ancient city that recedes towards various grandiose monuments. The group of figures at the right dominates the foreground, while a procession of Lystrans approaches from the left background. The heterogeneous architecture of towers, columns, obelisks, temples, and other ancient structures occupying the background landscape in this painting as well as the companion pieces, *Paul in Ephesus* (1568) and *Paul on Malta* (1568), is evocative of the ancient ruins De Vos studied during his time in Rome; he typically used such buildings to evoke the biblical past.[15] Paul and Barnabas stand at right, surrounded by a

---

15 Zweite A., *Marten de Vos Als Maler* (Berlin: 1980) 76; Freedberg D., "Art after Iconoclasm. Painting in the Netherlands between 1566 and 1585", in Jonckheere K. – Suykerbuyk R. (eds.), *Art after Iconoclasm: Painting in the Netherlands between 1566 and 1585* (Turnhout, 2012) 37–38. It is likely that De Vos's three paintings, *Paul and Barnabas in Lystra, Paul in*

FIGURE 17.5   Marten de Vos, *Paul and Barnabas in Lystra* (ca. 1568). Oil on panel.
140 × 185 cm. Château d'Olivier, Gironde; as illustrated in Jonckheere K. – Suykerbuyk R. (eds.), *Art after Iconoclasm: Painting in the Netherlands between 1566 and 1585* (Turnhout, 2012) 39.

group of laurel-crowned Lystrans, two of whom extend crowns over the apostles' heads to honour them. The sacrificial bull has not yet arrived nor has the temple priest prepared the altar. These departures from other pictures of the subject are crucial details that downplay the urgent need for intervention to prevent an imminent sacrifice. De Vos focuses instead on the crowd and their interaction with Paul and Barnabas who expostulate with them.

Paul, dressed in dark colours, argues with two Lystrans. With one hand, he rips open his tunic in response to the pagans' mistake of identity and misplaced gratitude; with the other, finger raised, he directs the Lystrans' attention to God, the true source of the miracle [Fig. 17.6]. That the figure is a variation of Raphael's Plato from the *School of Athens* (1509–1511), indicates how concerned De Vos was to portray Paul as a classical rhetor. Barnabas, a step behind

Ephesus, and *Paul on Malta*, formed part of a series painted for Gilles Hooftman, a wealthy Protestant merchant in Antwerp.

FIGURE 17.6
Marten de Vos, *Paul and Barnabas in Lystra* (ca. 1568). Oil on panel. 140 × 185 cm. Details of apostles. Château d'Olivier, Gironde; as illustrated in Jonckheere – Suykerbuyk (eds.), *Art after Iconoclasm*, 39.

Paul and facing in the opposite direction, likewise rends his garments, looking deep into the eyes of the Lystran attempting to honour him. Notably, De Vos describes both Paul and Barnabas tearing their tunics, a clear and conventional expression of grief, but neither apostle is so overcome with the emotion that he departs from engaging in reasoned and measured argument to dissuade the Lystrans. Without the exigent circumstances of an imminent sacrifice, Paul is free to deliver his argument calmly and carefully, remonstrating with the priest who addresses him.

In Jan Saenredam's engraving after Karel van Mander's design of *Paul and Barnabas at Lystra*, one finds the urgent nature of an imminent idolatrous sacrifice that might compel the apostles to respond emotionally with distress and disgust, but as in De Vos's example, one discovers a relatively calm scene wherein Paul delivers an earnest and measured argument. Distinctively, however, Van Mander's design describes a captivated pagan crowd attentively and patiently listening to Paul's words. In this print, the composition directs the viewer's eye down the middle of the image to the background where a crowd stones Paul by the city gates [Fig. 17.7]. Interrupting this view into the image are the gold and silver vessels associated with the sacrifice unfolding in the foreground. Here, Jupiter's priest sets down his thurible and kneels over a basin as he welcomes the arrival of two bulls, the closest of which looks at the priest warily, the other, out at the viewer. Across from the bulls and the procession of pagan celebrants stand Paul, Barnabas, a group of disciples, and the formerly lame man [Fig. 17.8].

FIGURE 17.7   Jan Saenredam after Karel van Mander, *Paul and Barnabas in Lystra* (1589–1607). Engraving. 26.7 × 41 cm. Rijksmuseum, Amsterdam. Public Domain.

Prominently featured among this group is Barnabas who directs his attention heavenward and rives his tunic in atonement for the Lystrans' sin of idolatry. Indeed, Paul and the entire company around Barnabas express their distress at what is happening, as their furrowed brows reveal. Bent at the waist, his lips parted, his right arm and hand, palm open, Paul protests vehemently against the preparations of the impending sacrifice. His words have caught the attention of the many figures kneeling at his feet, as the positions of their heads imply. His delivery strikes home – in this respect, Van Mander's image differs from those of Coecke and De Vos – as is evident from the fact that the Lystrans, even though they still kneel, as if before a god, have stopped their preparations and give their undivided attention to the apostle. Whereas they listen closely, the children's attention wanders, for they are too young to understand.

There is little emotional activity in Van Mander's characterisation of the apostles, and to the degree that emotion is described – for instance, Barnabas tearing his tunic and directing his gaze to heaven – it is visualised in a manner that neither undermines nor distracts from the methodical delivery of Paul's words. Notably, the static and rigid figures of Paul and Barnabas are highly disparate from Coecke's flamboyant figures. To a receptive crowd, Paul delivers his

FIGURE 17.8 Jan Saenredam after Karel van Mander, *Paul and Barnabas in Lystra* (1589–1607). Engraving. 26.7 × 41 cm. Detail of apostles. Rijksmuseum, Amsterdam. Public Domain.

argument boldly and sternly, indicative of his confidence and absent of panic or desperation.

Notably, Van Mander's composition follows the precepts of *historie* he sets out in *Den grondt der edel vry Schilder-const*, and it is this organisational strategy that highly informs Lastman's painting. There, Van Mander conceives his ordering (*ordinanty*) of the pictorial constituents making up a history painting.[16] Following these precepts, Van Mander organises his composition by setting the scene outside and placing the main activity in the foreground.

---

16 Mander Karel van, "Over de Ordening en de Inventie van de Figuurstukken. Het Vijfde Hoofdstuk", in Miedema H. (ed. and trans.), *Den Grondt Der Edel Vry Schilder-Const*. vol. 1 (Utrecht: 1973) 126–157 and Melion W.S., *Shaping the Netherlandish Canon: Karel van Mander's Schilder-Boeck* (Chicago: 1991) 1–12.

He then integrates into his design several objects and leading lines to direct the beholder's eyes through the image towards the horizon. He also populates his composition with diverse figures, each distinct in their physiognomy and temperament. Van Mander's *ordinanty* is only amplified further by the primary figures who participate in the principal event, the secondary figures who direct their gaze at the primary figures, and those who cast their gaze outside the picture plane towards the beholder. It is this multiplication of gazes, according to Van Mander, that not only directs the beholder's looking but also adds to the variety (*verscheydenheyt*) of the composition and the appeal to the beholder's eyes.[17]

What one sees in Lastman's painting is how inventively he integrates the various strands of the pictorial tradition into Van Mander's conception of *ordinanty*. Lastman combines the emotional expression and movement found in Coecke's design with the delivery of argument found in the designs by De Vos and Van Mander. Notably, however, Lastman does not merely visualise Paul's delivery of argument, but rather describes a dialogic exchange between Paul and the temple priest through which the apostle's emotions are made apparent. As will become evident, this dialogic exchange, in which Paul's emotional response is embedded, is heightened by the presence of the idolatrous sacrifice and the crowd, who continuously remain unresponsive to Paul's words. Lastman characterises Paul as having undergone a dramatic emotional shift since his conversion and healing of the lame man. Distinctively, Lastman depicts Paul's emotional shift by focusing on his confrontation with the temple priest; Lastman describes the apostle engaged in a heightened state of exasperated speech as he attempts to persuade the pagan crowd of their error – both in their failure to recognise the true nature of the apostles and in their insistence on performing an idolatrous sacrifice.

In examining Lastman's painting of 1617, we are reminded of some of the compositional similarities it shares with the examples I have enumerated, but several divergences are immediately striking: mentioned earlier, one is the height from which Paul addresses the temple priest; another is the defensive posture and gesture the temple priest adopts in response; and finally, there is the very specific hand gesture that Paul performs, which is not the common trope of the extended or raised hand indicative of speech – that is, it is not just speech that Lastman visualises, but a particular kind of speech that is inflected by the shifting emotions with which Paul responds to his reversal of fortune.

Distinct from the pictorial tradition, Lastman's representation of the episode targets a specific type of verbal exchange, and because he organises

---

17   Melion, *Shaping the Netherlandish Canon* 7–11.

his scene around speech, it would be helpful to gain insight into Lastman's painting by considering the strategy local rhetoricians employed when representing the same scene.[18] That is, because Lastman uses speech to convey the shifting emotions in response to the dramatic change of circumstances and its consequences – notably the imminent performance of an idolatrous sacrifice – insights into how Lastman conceptualises his picture will reveal themselves as one examines the work of the rhetoricians. How the rhetoricians' theatrical performance of the same narrative episode dramatises speech to convey shifting emotions serves as an analogy to understanding what Lastman visualises in his picture. Like Lastman, the rhetoricians of the chambers of rhetoric in the Netherlands were also interested in representing shifting emotional responses to rhetorical situations involving conflict and dilemma, and it will therefore prove useful to consider how the Haarlem chamber of rhetoric, The Pelican, dramatised the story in their play *Paulus ende Barnabas*.[19]

2   The Rhetoricians' Play, *Paulus ende Barnabas*

Principal among the rhetoricians' representation of the story and crucial to how they portray the apostles' reversal of fortune is their emphasis on Paul's increasing fear, anxiety, and frustration, which leads to his heightened use of exasperated speech. Initially, the playwright indicates the persuasiveness and success of Paul and Barnabas's ministry by employing verse, characterised primarily by harmony and balance. As the events turn against the apostles and as the situation becomes more dire, however, the playwright heightens the apostles' language and tone to describe their emotional response to the misfortune they experience. As will become evident, the playwright's image of Paul suffering in despair, desperately pleading, and speaking exasperatedly is similar to Lastman's image of Paul responding to his attendant circumstances in the painting of 1617. Because the play's escalation of emotions is accomplished through the delivery of increasingly exasperated speech and dramatised through a progression of events increasing in exigency and articulated by

---

18 For recent studies on the rhetoricians in the Netherlands, see Dixhoorn A. van, *Lustige Geesten: Rederijkers in de Noordelijke Nederlanden (1480–1650)* (Amsterdam: 2009) and Dixhoorn A. van – Mareel S. – Ramakers B. (eds.), "The Knowledge Culture of the Netherlandish Rhetoricians", *Renaissance Studies* 32.1 (2018).

19 Hummelen W.M.H., *Repertorium van Het Rederijkersdrama 1500–ca. 1620*, no. 1 OB 4 (Assen: 1968); Hüsken, W.N.M. – Ramakers B. – Schaars F.A.M. (eds.), *"Paulus ende Barnabas"*, in Hüsken, W.N.M. – Ramakers B. – Schaars F.A.M. (eds.), *Trou Moet Blijcken: Bronnenuitgave van de Boeken Der Haarlemse Rederijkerskamer "de Pellicanisten". 2: Boek B* (Assen: 1992) 210–66.

several exchanges of dialogue, I will proceed by analysing how this progression of events unfolds in the play. Such analysis anticipates a discussion of what Lastman accomplishes in his painting of the story.

The playwright's primary tool for developing the main characters of Paul and Barnabas is speech, and to convey their emotional response to the crisis they face, the playwright employs distressed and frustrated speech. At the start of the play, however, the apostles' speech is very different. Paul and Barnabas are featured on stage, delivering orations. Each delivery presents a complicated rhyme scheme, ababb / cbcc / dcdd / edee, and so forth, sometimes also including inner-rhymes. These speeches begin with Paul appealing to God to reveal Himself to the pagans of Lycaonia and thereby impel them to renounce their false religion.[20] Barnabas joins Paul in his prayer and petitions God for the Holy Spirit to aid them in preaching the Gospel. These opening speeches incorporate a prayer, followed by an exhortation, and conclude with a long refrain. Through the playwright's characterisation of the apostles as calm and self-assured, the tone is set for the unfolding of the plot. The story is given a methodical, clear, rhythmic, and lyrical beginning that creates a harmonious and balanced tone, and it suggests the strength, confidence, and emotional composure with which Paul and Barnabas enter their ministry work in Lystra.

Following the initial speeches of Paul and Barnabas, the *sinnekens* arrive – Feigned Virtue (*Deuchdelijck schijn*) and Covert Falsehood (*Bedeckte valscheijt*) – who, in accordance with this character type, plot to thwart the protagonists' mission.[21] As foils to Paul and Barnabas, they desire that the people of Lystra resist the apostles' preaching and continue their practice of the pagan religion. The way in which the playwright has the *sinnekens* present this desire, however, reinforces his emphasis on Paul and Barnabas's opening speeches, underscored by their emotional composure. Multiple times, the *sinnekens* offer arguments against the apostles by repeating Paul and Barnabas's critique of the Lystrans' heresy. In other words, the *sinnekens* restate the arguments featured in the apostles' opening speeches but in an unrestrained, impolite, reactionary, and combative tone, thereby embellishing and amplifying the apostles' critique of false religion. By repeating the apostles' remonstrance and juxtaposing their balanced and harmonious delivery with the combative delivery

---

20   Note that there are various cues in the play's text that suggest the author is persuaded by the Reform movement, as he likely addresses the religious strife in the sixteenth-century Netherlands.

21   *Sinnekens* are characters who figure prominently in the work of the rhetoricians, and they personify the propensity of human beings to sin. They figure evil desires, motivations, and intentions, and, through their mischievous acts, they persuade the narrative's protagonist(s) to make choices that inevitably lead to their doom or despair.

of the *sinnekens*, the playwright highlights the sanguine and self-assured emotional state of the apostles. Pursuing this strategy of repetition, even from the mouths of the antagonists, the playwright emphasises his concern for the spiritual power, rhetorical efficacy, and emotional composure of the apostles' speech.

This tone and composure continue in the Paul's delivery of the gospel message to the inhabitants of Lystra, culminating in the conversion of the lame man and Paul's healing of his physical infirmities. Immediately following the healing of the lame man, however, the reversal of the apostles' fortune occurs. In the space of 11 lines, the audience witnesses the silence and stillness of the lame man standing in awe of his healing, the proclamation that such a miracle was effectuated by the persuasive delivery of Paul's gospel message and the lame man's faith in Christ, the pagan crowd's misrecognition of the apostles as Jupiter and Mercury, and the arrival of the temple priest and a sacrificial bull. Essentially, the audience views the abrupt shift from the apostles voicing their sense of elation and triumph through harmonious and balanced verse in the first half of the play to expressions of fear and anger in their response to the sudden misfortune. This shift of emotions culminates in Paul's three attempts to implore the Lystrans to curtail their sacrifice. Each attempt becomes more desperate and more urgent, which externalises Paul's increasing sense of frustration and distress.

Paul's first of three attempts at intervention begins with a rebuke to cease the impending sacrifice. In an attempt to clarify who he is and with what power he acts, Paul continues his argument by contrasting the impotence of the pagan gods, who are incapable of healing the lame man, with the Christian God, who not only has the power to heal but also the capability to remedy their suffering. He condemns their idolatrous practices and moral failures:

> *na u eijgen oppijnie met boossheijt bedocht*
> *want het brengt niet voort dan alle wellusticheijt*
> *Met haet en nijt is het doorvlocht*
> *Ende beseten met groote giericheijt*

> after your own opinion conceived with perversity
> because it brings forth nothing but carnal pleasure
> With hate and envy it is entangled
> And beset with great avarice[22]

---

22 Hüsken – Ramakers – Schaars (eds.), *"Paulus ende Barnabas"* lines 495–498.

Concluding his first intervention, Paul argues that because the people of Lystra have suffering in their hearts, they feel compelled to sacrifice to Jupiter and Mercury. He begs the crowd to give up their idolatry and trust in the gospel promise that Christ will liberate them from sin and suffering, granting peace of heart:

> *Aldus uwe harten daer van doch Leijt*
> *sonder verbeijt // en hangt hem aen*
> *die u door sijn Conincklijcke majesteijt*
> *van alle u sonden bevrijen can*
> *en verlaet alle het affgodissche gespan*
> *soo salt u welgaen verstaet mijn rede*
> *ende u brengen uuijt desen verdoemelijcken ban*
> *in een plaetse daer rust is ende vrede*

> Thus indeed lead your hearts from there
> without delay // and hang them on him
> who, through his kingly majesty,
> can liberate you from all sin
> and who can forsake all the idolatrous bonds
> so you shall favourably understand my reasoned speech
> and cast out these damn spells
> in their place there is rest and peace[23]

At this point in the play, one can characterise Paul's confrontation with the Lystrans as stern but reasoned and measured in argument, evocative of the images by De Vos and Van Mander discussed above. The climax of the scene, however, corresponds more closely with Lastman's visualisation of the episode.

After a brief interlude in which Barnabas explicitly refutes the identification of himself and Paul with Jupiter and Mercury, Paul launches into a second speech of abjuration. Much like the first, this oration begins with a rebuke, followed by an exhortation, and ends with the proclamation of the Gospel. Again, he implores the pagan crowd to cease the preparations for the sacrifice, insisting that such a rite will bring honour neither to him nor Barnabas but only pain, suffering, and idolatry's other ill effects. Paul exhorts the crowd to remember how the one, true God has blessed them with rains and fruitful seasons of harvests that have filled their hearts with food and cheerfulness. It is

---

23 Hüsken – Ramakers – Schaars (eds.), *"Paulus ende Barnabas"* lines 499–506.

DIALOGIC EXCHANGE IN LASTMAN'S *PAUL AND BARNABAS IN LYSTRA*   665

to this God, Paul concludes, that the people of Lystra now have an intercessor (*onsen middelaer*) who shows mercy and heals suffering.

Continuing to stand on stage, the pagans still fail to realise their initial mistake of misidentifying the apostles and summoning the priest of Jupiter. Having heard Paul and Barnabas speak for seventy-six lines, the pagans reply but fail to respond to the points propounded by the apostles. In reaction to Paul's rebukes, exhortations, and gospel claims, the two pagan characters on stage deliver an alternating speech, affirming Paul and Barnabas as Mercury and Jupiter and insisting that the preparations for the sacrifice be expedited.

> *Spoet u toch [...] want het sijn de goden*
> *Brengt die die stieren [...] met die cransen*

> Hurry up [...] because they are gods
> Bring the bulls [...] with the wreaths[24]

It is almost as if the apostles had said nothing, for the preparations of the sacrifice continue uninterrupted. Not only do the pagans fail to heed Paul's warnings, but they are even emboldened. Paul's preaching to the crowd, healing of the lame man, and now his two long counter-orations have failed to stop the preparations for the sacrifice and convince the pagans of the apostles' true identities. As the Lystrans continue to ignore the apostles, the situation becomes more dire. The sense of urgency the apostles feel is only further exacerbated by the increasing disregard shown by the pagans, and the apostles thus become more distraught. In Lastman's painting as in this play, the people's unresponsiveness to Paul and Barnabas's exhortations serves as a catalyst for the two men's response to the increasingly urgent situation, in particular Paul's shifting emotional response to the exigency of the impending idolatry. Lastman's painting associates Paul's delivery of his emotionally-charged speech with the unheeding crowd and the insistent temple priest.

The playwright is very conscious of the setting and staging of the scene. He begins with the lame man rising to use his legs, followed immediately by his stillness and silence. This moment is instantly succeeded by the chaos of the pagans' failure to discern the identities or message of the apostles, and they continue enthusiastic preparations for the idolatrous sacrifice. What once looked like a glorious victory of the Gospel has now reversed course towards blasphemy. It is a course that continuously escalates as the pagans insistently

---

24   Hüsken – Ramakers – Schaars (eds.), "*Paulus ende Barnabas*" lines 557–558.

666   LEA

ignore Paul's admonitions and fail to discern the apostles' true nature; the events reach their breaking point when the priest of Jupiter speaks:

> *Met alle naersticheijt wil ick mijn daer toe pijnen*
> *om dat te volbrengen nae mijn vermeugen*
> *siet ick gae mijn spoen recht als den fijnen*
> *ick seght u Certeijn al sonder Leugen*

> With all perseverance, I will strive
> to accomplish this to the best of my ability.
> Behold, I will hurry as best as I can
> I tell you, for sure, without a lie[25]

Accompanying the text of the dialogue, a stage direction reveals that the priest has begun to perform the sacrifice.[26]

Having elevated the crisis of the reversal of fortune to its climax, the playwright has Paul deliver his third and final expostulatory speech. The apostle's language has changed; his speech is exasperated and desperate; he begins with the exclamation, '*O mannen broeders* [O men, brothers]'.[27] Once more, he advises them that the sacrifice is offered to their detriment, elevating his speech to a stern alarum: '*ick waerschou u* [I warn you]'.[28] And he begins to speak both positively and negatively about the serious consequences that will potentially result from what they decide to do next. Beginning with positive affirmations, he speaks of God's desire permanently to imprint himself on their hearts: '[...] *met goods woort het sal u wel gerijven / en wilt dat wel vast in u harte schrijven* [...] [... with God's word, you shall triumph over it well / and he graciously wants to write that permanently in your heart]'.[29] The people's rejection of their idolatrous sacrifice, argues Paul, should be based on their consciousness of divine love. In his last-ditch effort to persuade the people of Lystra of the grave consequences of their actions, he declares that the penalty for continuing with the sacrifice is extreme. Paul's anger escalates in his final appeal with his most harsh and irate words.

> *dus bid ick u wiltse toch Laeten // vaeren*
> *en aenbidt dien godt hoort dese sentencije*

---

25   Hüsken – Ramakers – Schaars (eds.), "*Paulus ende Barnabas*" lines 588–591.
26   '*Hier bereijtmen om te offeren* [Prepare to sacrifice here]'.
27   Hüsken – Ramakers – Schaars (eds.), "*Paulus ende Barnabas*" line 593.
28   Hüsken – Ramakers – Schaars (eds.), "*Paulus ende Barnabas*" line 595.
29   Hüsken – Ramakers – Schaars (eds.), "*Paulus ende Barnabas*" lines 596–597.

DIALOGIC EXCHANGE IN LASTMAN'S *PAUL AND BARNABAS IN LYSTRA* 667

die machtich is met sijn sijentije
u te behouden oft te verdoemen deur sijn stercke hant
maer voor al compt hij u waerschouwen door mijn Eloquencije
Op dat ghij niet en raeckt in dese schant
Daerom verwerpt doch met groote verstant

so I pray that you do get rid of them
and worship this God [only], hear this verdict,
who has the power through his wisdom
to preserve or damn you by his strong hand.
But he comes especially to warn you through my eloquence
Lest you fall into disgrace.
Therefore, reject this [idolatry] wisely[30]

Before concluding his speech, he characterises their idolatry as covert false-hood (*bedeckte valscheijt*) and feigned virtue (*schijnt deucht*), which are in turn embodied by the *sinnekens* who, according to a stage direction, have coincidently just joined the scene.[31] One can only imagine that Paul points to them as he speaks with condemnation. Building to the scene's final crescendo, Paul ends his speech by offering one last exhortation:

daerom bidt ick u doet doch nae mijn raet
en verlaet desen grouwel groot
voor des heeren ogen en hout het geen maet
noch oock geenen staet maer tis seer snoot
staet wij vercondigen u de rechte waerheijt bloot
sonder werderstoot meught ghijse nu ontfangen
en doet ghij het oock niet / met die alderwreetste doot
sult ghiij gepijnicht worden met groot verstrangen

therefore I pray that you follow my advice yet
and abandon this great horror
before the eyes of the Lord it is immoderate
and respectless, but it is very nefarious
Get up, we proclaim to you, the naked truth.

---

30   Hüsken – Ramakers – Schaars (eds.), "*Paulus ende Barnabas*" lines 603–609.
31   '*Hier comen die neefgens. uuijt. met twed. Joden. ende overvallense ende stenigen paulus*
      ende als sij hen gestenicht hebben slepen sij hem op het ander ent. vant taneel. end laeten
      hem voor doot leggende [Here, the *sinnekens* come out with two Jews, and they overwhelm
      them and stone Paul. And after they have stoned him, they drag him to the other side of
      the stage and leave him for dead]'.

Without protest you must now accept it,
but if you do not, you will pay for it / with the most cruel death,
you shall be punished for it with great sorrow[32]

His words intensify: calling their actions a great horror, he claims to offer them
the naked truth. If they proceed with their blasphemy and idolatry, they will be
punished and, suffering great sorrow, will die a most cruel death.

The verbal confrontation ends abruptly. For a third time, the people of
Lystra fail to respond to Paul's arguments. They do not question, nor do they
revise their initial mistaken identity of the apostles. Not only do they fail to
re-evaluate their actions in preparing the sacrifice to Jupiter, they also never
slow down nor pause to reflect.

3   Lastman's *Paul and Barnabas in Lystra* of 1617

Like the playwright of *Paulus ende Barnabas*, who describes the shifting emotions of the apostles as they experience the dramatic change of their fortune,
so too does Lastman in his painting of 1617. The focus on Paul's delivery of exasperated speech, indicative of the fear, anger, and distress he experiences, is an
approach to describing the narrative moment that both Lastman and the playwright share. To see what Lastman does to visualise intense emotion mediated
by speech, I must return to a description of how he constructs the scene and
positions the figures. He places Paul and Barnabas just below the apex of the
surrounding crowd gathered on the temple steps to view the sacrifice. In order
to discern the identities of Paul and Barnabas, one must look intently at all the
figures, examining their attire, facial expressions, gestures, accoutrements, as
well as each character's position within the overall arrangement.

Adhering to Van Mander's precepts for organising a history painting in
chapter 5 of *Den grondt der edel vry Schilder-const*, Lastman has placed the two
apostles on steps, in the manner that a merchant displays his wares on shelves;
he elevates them so as to indicate their importance but does not situate them
at the peak of his arrangement of figures [Fig. 17.1].[33] He combines his commit-

---

32   Hüsken – Ramakers – Schaars (eds.), "*Paulus ende Barnabas*" lines 615–622.
33   See Broos B.P.J., "Rembrandt and Lastman's Coriolanus: The History Piece in 17th-Century
Theory and Practice", *Simiolus: Netherlands Quarterly for the History of Art* 8 (1976–1975)
202 and Golahny, "Paired Poems on Pendant Paintings" 156; See Mander, "Over de Ordening
en de Inventie van de Figuurstukken" 126–157 and Melion, *Shaping the Netherlandish
Canon* 1–12.

ment to narrative fidelity with his pursuit of narrative invention. As Scripture records that Paul and Barnabas addressed the crowd, Lastman positions the apostles where they can best be seen to address the collected group of Lystrans at the right, but he also indicates that they are surrounded, perhaps even overwhelmed by the people crowding near them. By outnumbering and encircling the apostles, Lastman captures the high tension of the moment, showing how Paul and Barnabas make a desperate appeal against the impending rites offensive to God. It is not only out of fear or imminent threat, however, that Paul and Barnabas act with this degree of desperation. Like the playwright of *Paulus ende Barnabas*, Lastman describes a more profound impetus for the apostles' actions: the Lystrans fail to hear the apostles' arguments or to identify their miracles as assertions of Christ and the truth of the Gospel, and nor do they cease preparing for the pagan sacrifice.

Lastman places the apostles at the right side of the frame, standing on the same side of the altar as the temple priest. This arrangement of figures emphasises the conversation between Paul and the priest of Jupiter, and it also shows the exchange as a face-to-face confrontation, heightening the tension and drama of their disagreement. Unlike the arrangement of figures in the examples by De Vos and Van Mander, Lastman employs an aggressively steep angle from which Paul looks and speaks to the priest, indicative of the emotional fervour with which he delivers his words. The anxious exasperation and distress presumably expressed in Paul's words is further reinforced by the crossing of his hands. Lastman's characterisation of Barnabas exhibits a different response to the circumstances. One finds that the event unfolding before Barnabas has caused him to tear his clothes and contort his face. He lacks the rhetorical skill of his colleague, and instead of arguing the case against the Lystrans, he expresses despair and grief. Lastman elects to visualise Barnabas's mixed emotions by employing the oft-used rhetorical figure of *apostrophe*: he cries out to the heavens and addresses his suffering to God.

Relevant to how Lastman portrays Paul and Barnabas is his characterisation of the temple priest. In the painting, the priest stands in an open, frontal posture, facing the beholder and slightly turned to engage Paul's protest. He wears a priestly tunic and a wreath, and he holds a vessel intended for use in the sacrifice: his position between Paul and the altar, along with his need to turn away from his sacrificial preparations in order to address Paul, suggest that the performance of the sacrifice is imminent. This imminence is further emphasised by the presence of the bull that is processed in from the left, decked in a ceremonial headdress, garlands, and sacrificial vestment. The bull is not relegated to the processional train in the middle ground or the background of the image; it has arrived and awaits to be sacrificed at the command from Jupiter's priest.

Lastman's posing, positioning, and characterisation of the figures, amplify the stakes governing the verbal exchange upon which the image focuses; he heightens the sense of urgency that drives Paul and Barnabas to intervene. The imminence of the sacrifice requires urgent action on their part, which results in a chaotic situation wherein the lame man is at the mercy of the crowd's frenetic energy. He is neither featured as an embodiment of the power of the Gospel nor as the miraculous proof of what the apostles and the priest are arguing; rather, the story's abrupt turn of events and the urgency it brings have rendered him almost indistinguishable amongst the surrounding crowd. Similar to the playwright in *Paulus ende Barnabas*, Lastman emphasises that it is the approaching sacrifice that provokes the growing emotional distress of the apostles and Paul's desperate attempt at intervention.

The Book of Acts reports that Paul and Barnabas rushed into the crowd to prevent the Lystrans from carrying out the sacrifice. Lastman was a close reader of the Bible, and it is no surprise that his painting of 1617 shows the apostles rushing into the crowd.[34] They do so, however, in a manner that demands close attention from the viewer. Lastman's inventive inclusion of the apostles engaging with the crowd is more than an instance of narrative fidelity, of course. It also serves to convey how urgent is their emotional state as they face the pending moment of idolatry. As already noted, Lastman positions Paul and Barnabas not at the apex of the crowd on the temple steps but rather, embedded among the throng. The man wearing a turban standing just behind Paul displays a curious pose. He reaches out with his left hand so as to contest Paul's speech while simultaneously trying to block Paul's approach towards the priest. His right hand not only impedes Paul but can also be read as an endorsement of the sacrifice. Another figure, framed by the two acolytes' candlesticks, stands behind Barnabas and is positioned in a manner that corresponds with the action of the man wearing the turban. He raises his hands across his chest, a gesture which similarly suggests rejection of the apostles' pleas but simultaneously acts as a defensive response. By describing the figures that flank the apostles in this way – one attempting to intervene, the other exhibiting a defensive reaction – Lastman suggests that Paul and Barnabas, having suddenly startled these two figures, have just, in this moment, rushed

---

34   See Seifert C.T., *Pieter Lastman: Studien Zu Leben Und Werk: Mit Einem Kritischen Verzeichnis Der Werke Mit Themen Aus Der Antiken Mythologie Und Historie* (Petersberg: 2011) 104–106. Seifert persuasively shows Lastman's propensity to include details in his paintings which are taken directly from the source text, and it is not surprising to see that Lastman includes the detail of the apostles rushing into the crowd when his predecessors avoided depicting such a pivotal moment.

into the crowd to express their frustration and desperation as they intervene to stop the sacrifice.

This reading of the scene is further supported by the poses of various surrounding figures. Consider the position of the temple priest. Immediately prior to the arrival of the apostles, the priest was presumably facing the altar, anticipating the arrival of the sacrificial bull. It is only due to Paul's sudden interruption and distressed speech, delivered as he rushes into the crowd, that the priest suspends his activities, turning his body in response. The dynamic entry of the apostles becomes even more apparent from the figures located in the bottom right foreground. Various attendants stop in mid-action, and the figure farthest to the right pauses as he lifts a bundle of sticks. Rather than having him complete the motion and stand upright, Lastman directs the figure's attention towards the confrontation at the altar, leaving him still bent over, his lower back taking the weight of his load, his neck contorted in a pose of great discomfort. By depicting this figure almost but not quite standing, as if in a state of suspended animation, Lastman has made the suddenness of the apostles' arrival, along with the urgency of their emotions, all the more explicit. He has visualised a protracted narrative moment that turns on Paul voicing his exasperation, and his emotions are further corroborated by most of the other figures in the painting who acknowledge the urgency with which the apostles behave.

Most other figures in the crowd either direct their attention to the sudden confrontation between Paul and the temple priest or address the beholder. These figures challenge the beholder to identify the apostles, parse the pressing and complex situation unfolding in the scene, and discern the apostles' emotional response to it. The apostles' dramatic expression of emotions, conveyed by their rushing into the crowd and Paul's delivery of urgent and exasperated speech, fails to persuade the Lystrans, but, through Lastman's pictorial invention, it has the persuasive power to convince the beholder to cease idolatrous activity and heed the truth of the Gospel.

4 Conclusion

Lastman and the playwright pursue the same rhetorical strategy in telling the story of Paul and Barnabas's ministry in Lystra. They both focus on the climax of the dramatic turn of events that leads from the healing and conversion of the lame man to the pagans' mistaken identities of the apostles and the imminence of an idolatrous sacrifice. They both do this by visualising Paul's exasperated speech and the mixed emotions that ensue as he confronts the temple priest and the people of Lystra.

In pursuing this shared rhetorical approach to portray the biblical story, however, Lastman and the playwright also employ different means. The playwright uses a series of speeches wherein the apostles speak in a harmonious and balanced tone that characterises the calm and confident manner in which Paul converts and heals the lame man. Paul's emotional composure is abruptly interrupted by the sudden reversal of fortune; the urgent and desperate tone that ensues, exemplified by Paul's three attempts at intervention, causes his exasperation to escalate as he attempts to rectify the turn of events. Lastman visualises Paul's delivery of exasperated speech by emphasising the imminence of the sacrifice and protracting the moment of Paul's rush into the crowd to implore the priest to desist. Lastman does not describe the apostles engaged in the measured delivery of argument as seen in De Vos's painting or Van Mander's print. Instead, he incorporates pictorial elements that indicate the exigency and urgency of the situation; rather than measured and reasoned disputation, there is desperate, anxious, and urgent pleading similar to what the playwright stages in his play. The portrayal of exasperated speech is uniquely suited to indicate that the apostles' circumstances and their awareness of the situation has radically changed, as it externalises the desperation and anxiety felt during their misfortune.

Furthermore, Lastman describes certain characters, including the temple priest and the celebrants in the lower right foreground of his painting, as caught in an interrupted and incomplete action – that is, he implies that had it not been for the abrupt interruption of Paul, the priest and the celebrants would have continued to complete their sinful activity. His description of the Lystrans differs from that by Coecke, De Vos, and Van Mander, in whose works the inhabitants of Lystra are shown holding back from their activity as they consider the emotional display and arguments of the apostles. Lastman instead dilates the narrative moment in which Paul voices his distress and condemns the idolatrous sacrifice. Most of the other figures in the painting corroborate what Paul expresses. They either direct their attention to the sudden confrontation between Paul and the temple priest or directly address the beholder, making a show of the contretemps.

In his painting of 1617, Lastman does not describe the apostles engaging in the measured delivery of an argument to a captive audience. On the contrary, he incorporates pictorial elements indicative of the dire situation in which Paul finds himself: his desperate and anxious plea issues from his complex emotional state, which can best be described as a shifting mixture of love, fear, and anger. Love, instilled by his faith and confidence in the Gospel, motivates Paul to confront and persuade the Lystrans; it is this element that primarily informs the iterations of the scene by De Vos and Van Mander. Paul's love is quite complex as it stems from his desire for the Lystrans to join him in a community in

DIALOGIC EXCHANGE IN LASTMAN'S *PAUL AND BARNABAS IN LYSTRA* 673

Christ, sharing with him one mind and faith in the Gospel. Paul's love is also analogous to a nursing mother who cares for her child with gentleness and affection and without pretence, as he later informs the church at Thessalonica. It is a love that allows Paul to give himself to the Lystrans – offering his talents and gifts in service, which may require his exhaustion or even his death.[35]

It is not just the apostles' love that Lastman incorporates into his painting, however, he also focuses on the imminence of the sacrifice and the exigent circumstances it creates, thereby activating a high degree of fear experienced by the apostles. Not only does his composition and arrangement of figures indicate the anxiety and anguish the apostles experience at the impending act of idolatry, but they also suggest the urgent need for the apostles' immediate intervention. The necessary intervention is both physical and verbal, as Lastman shows the apostles having just rushed into the crowd and Paul remonstrating the temple priest. Through his staging of the scene, Lastman suggests that the Lystrans would continue in their failure to hear and heed the apostles' words were it not for the apostles' action of rushing into the crowd and forcing the pagans' attention. The continued disregard shown by the Lystrans and the ensuing need for such a dramatic intervention justifies the anger that, along with love, also motivates the apostles' action and Paul's speech. A consideration of the apostles' shifting mixture of emotions, as evoked by Lastman, and a comparison of how he and the playwright of *Paulus ende Barnabas* dramatised the same moment reveal that Paul's speech is simultaneously a petition, condemnation, and exhortation. These types of address respectively correspond with Paul's multi-layered mix of emotions: his fear motivates his petition to cease the sacrifice to Jupiter, his anger motivates a condemnation of the idolatry, and his love motivates an exhortation to turn away from such idolatry and embrace Christ. Inventively, Lastman's portrayal of exasperated speech externalises the complex mix of emotions that Paul and Barnabas felt as they attempted to combat idolatry.

Bibliography

Broos B.P.J., "Rembrandt and Lastman's Coriolanus: The History Piece in 17th-Century Theory and Practice", *Simiolus: Netherlands Quarterly for the History of Art* 8 (1976–1975) 199–228.

---

35   See Philippians 1–2:2 and 1 Thessalonians 2:1–8.

Cleland E.A.H. – Ainsworth M.W. – Alsteens S. – Orenstein N. – Buchanan I. – Delmarcel G. – Grazzini N.F. (eds.), *Grand Design: Pieter Coecke van Aelst and Renaissance Tapestry* (New York: 2014).

Delmarcel G., "The Life of Saint Paul", in Cleland E.A.H. – Ainsworth M.W. – Alsteens S. – Orenstein N. – Buchanan I. – Delmarcel G. – Grazzini N.F. (eds.), *Grand Design: Pieter Coecke van Aelst and Renaissance Tapestry* (New York: 2014) 124–35.

Dixhoorn A. van, *Lustige Geesten: Rederijkers in de Noordelijke Nederlanden (1480–1650)* (Amsterdam: 2009).

Dixhoorn A. van – Mareel S. – Ramakers B. (eds.), "The Knowledge Culture of the Netherlandish Rhetoricians", *Renaissance Studies* 32.1 (2018).

Fludernik M., *An Introduction to Narratology* (New York: 2006).

Freedberg D., "Art after Iconoclasm. Painting in the Netherlands between 1566 and 1585", in Jonckheere K. – Suykerbuyk R. (eds.), *Art after Iconoclasm: Painting in the Netherlands between 1566 and 1585* (Turnhout, 2012) 21–49.

Golahny A., "Paired Poems on Pendant Paintings: Vondel and Oudaan Interpret Lastman", in Golahny A. (ed.), *The Eye of the Poet: Studies in the Reciprocity of the Visual and Literary Arts from the Renaissance to the Present* (Lewisburg: 1996) 154–78.

Golahny A., "Lastman's 'Dido's Sacrifice to Juno' Identified", *Kroniek van Het Rembrandthuis* 1–2 (1998) 39–48.

Golahny A., "Pieter Lastman: moments of recognition", *Nederlands Kunsthistorisch Jaarboek* 60 (2010) 179–201.

Hummelen W.M.H., *Repertorium van Het Rederijkersdrama 1500–ca. 1620* (Assen: 1968).

Hüsken W.N.M. – Ramakers B. – Schaars F.A.M. (eds.), "*Paulus ende Barnabas*", in Hüsken W.N.M. – Ramakers B. – Schaars F.A.M. (eds.), *Trou Moet Blijcken: Bronnenuitgave van de Boeken Der Haarlemse Rederijkerskamer "de Pellicanisten". 2: Boek B* (Assen: 1992) 210–66.

Liveley G., *Narratology* (Oxford: 2019).

Mander Karel van, "Over de Ordening en de Inventie van de Figuurstukken. Het Vijfde Hoofdstuk", in Miedema H. (ed. and trans.), *Den Grondt Der Edel Vry Schilder-Const.* vol. 1 (Utrecht: 1973) 126–157.

Melion W.S., *Shaping the Netherlandish Canon: Karel van Mander's Schilder-Boeck* (Chicago: 1991).

Prince G., *Narratology: The Form and Functioning of Narrative* (Berlin: 1982).

Seifert C.T., *Pieter Lastman: Studien Zu Leben Und Werk: Mit Einem Kritischen Verzeichnis Der Werke Mit Themen Aus Der Antiken Mythologie Und Historie* (Petersberg: 2011).

Waiboer A.E., "Lastmans Opferdarstellungen und ihre weit reichende Wirkung", in Sitt M. (ed.), *Pieter Lastman: In Rembrandts Schatten?* exh. cat., Der Hamburger Kunsthalle (Munich: 2006) 40–49.

Zweite A., *Marten de Vos Als Maler* (Berlin: 1980).

CHAPTER 18

Between Despair and Hope: Raising Emotions with Dutch Seventeenth-Century Marine Paintings and Prints

Stijn Bussels and Bram Van Oostveldt

Abstract

Many Dutch seventeenth-century paintings and prints depict tempests with shipwrecks. Till today these images are often interpreted by reference to metaphorical readings. This essay explores the ways in which a metaphorical reading work in tandem with the arousal of mixed emotions. We go from sea to shore, so to speak, looking beyond the precarious situation of the sailors adrift in the turbulent water. Art historians have largely ignored the marine painters' frequent inclusion of spectators perched on the rocky coast and of sailors whose tenacity and resilience have brought them safely to shore. These figures can be seen to function as epitomes of mixed emotion, conveyors not only of despair but also of hope, the emotional poles between which the viewer is placed. Moreover, by studying the diverse ways in which spectators are represented *in* these images, we can learn more about the intended responses of the beholders *of* the images. Through the shoreside figures, the artists explore a range of possible responses to viewing natural disaster, inviting analogies between the viewers both in the image and before it.

Keywords

marine painting and print – seventeenth century – Dutch Republic – tempests – despair and hope

In a painting of 1655, now in the National Maritime Museum at Greenwich, the Leiden painter Hendrick Staets (active in the period 1626–1659) manages to aptly depict how sailors are facing death and destruction due to a fierce tempest [Fig. 18.1]. Nature is shown at its most threatening by the violent waves that push a ship off the rocks close to an intimidating rock arch. The anthropomorphic, monstrous features of these rocks increase their aggressive appearance. The painter has put everything at stake to portray the reactions

© STIJN BUSSELS AND BRAM VAN OOSTVELDT, 2025 | DOI:10.1163/9789004694613_019

FIGURE 18.1 Hendrick Staets, *Ships Wrecked on a Rocky Shore*, 1655. Oil on panel, 50,8 × 68,6 cm. National Maritime Museum, Greenwich, London

of those affected by the threat. The sailors still on board of the sinking ship are trying to save what is left to save, but it looks like their efforts will soon prove to be fruitless and most of them will meet a certain death. Others have already jumped off the ship or are swung away by the raging wind or water. In their urge to survive, they have clung to the ship's debris; a few are grasping a torn-off mast that floats on the wild water [Fig. 18.2]. Another ship has become the plaything of the waves too, but it looks like this ship can still be saved. Its sails are lowered, but the pressure on the cable of the anchor accentuates the life-threatening challenges the crew must deal with. Staets, however, presents optimism in all this predicament. Whereas above the sinking ship an ominous lightning strikes, the anchored ship is accompanied by the brightness of the sun appearing through the dark clouds. If the courageous sailors manage to hold out for a while longer, the storm might subside, and salvation could be at hand. Thus, the painter plays despair and hope against each other.

Staets does not only try to evoke the contrasting emotions of despair and hope by depicting the different conditions of the two ships and the changing

FIGURE 18.2   Detail from Hendrick Staets, *Ships Wrecked on a Rocky Shore*

weather. He also shows different reactions in the two small figures ashore depicted in the left corner below. With their bodily gestures the painter emphasises how these witnesses of the disaster are confronted with strong, but divergent emotions. One of the two has slipped to his knees in pure dismay, his back turned on the tempest. His placement at the utmost front of the painting makes him stand out. His red attire reinforces this focal point and corresponds to the red dress of a man in the water clinging to the mast. Repulsed by the fierceness with which nature shows itself, the figure ashore fails to face the calamities. The other spectator is also overwhelmed by what is brought right before his eyes, but in contrast with the first one, he holds tight to a rock, mesmerized by what is happening, his eyes fixed on the misfortunes of the drowning men clinging to the floating mast. As they are closest in his field of vision, the effect the tempest has on him seems to be defined by the uncertain state these men are in. This spectator can only hope for the sailors' rescue but must also face the fact that this will be a particularly difficult task because of the violent waves that threaten to smash the men against the rocks.

Staets's oeuvre reveals his preference for these depictions of sea storms,[1] and he was not the first, nor the last to express this preference. Many Dutch

---

1   "Hendrick Staets," RKD artists, https://rkd.nl/explore/artists/74550 (accessed 23 June 2022).

seventeenth-century paintings have tempests with shipwrecks watched by spectators on a rocky coast as their subject.[2] Early precursors can be found in the sixteenth century in the oeuvre or milieu of Herri met de Bles (c.1510–after 1556) and the Bruegel dynasty.[3] These works already emphasise the changing weather conditions in contrasting colours and put spectators in the foreground to demonstrate despair and hope about the fate of the sailors. From the 1630s onwards, thanks to Dutch painters as Jan Porcellis (1584–1632), Simon de Vlieger (1600/1601–1653), and Adam Willaerts (1577–1664) the tempest scenes developed to their full potential and increased in popularity. The subject peaks in the mid-seventeenth century but remains important until the end of the century and even afterwards, as the work of Ludolf Bakhuizen (1630–1708) illustrates.

One of the many other examples was painted in the 1660s by the Rotterdam painter Jacob Bellevois (1621–1676) and is in the collection of the National Maritime Museum as well [Fig. 18.3]. It is three times as large as Staets's painting and uses a richer range of colours, but it relies on the same conventions; Once again, we see a ship on the verge of being entirely wrecked perishing with all hands on deck. Next to the sinking ship, there is a fishing boat at risk too, but not definitely lost yet. As in Staets's painting, clearing skies and dark clouds alternate. Further, we can see again the eyewitnesses in the foreground expressing to be mesmerised or repulsed. However, if we concentrate on the figure that has turned his back on the sea in Bellevois's painting, a variation in this convention turns up [Fig. 18.4]. This figure does not seem to be merely a

---

2   Beer, G. de – Veen, J. van der – Ossing, F. – Dumas, C. (eds.), *The Golden Age of Dutch Marine Painting. The Inder Rieden Collection* (Leiden: 2019), Bol L.J., *Die holländische Marinemalerei des 17. Jahrhundrets* (Braunschweig: 1973) and Giltaij J. – Kelch J., *Praise of Ships and the Sea: The Dutch Marine Painters of the 17th Century* (Seattle: 1996).

3   See Vézilier-Dussart S. – Laffon C., *La Flandre et la mer: De Pieter Bruegel l'Ancien à Jan Breughel de Velours* (Kassel: 2015). E.g. Bol mentions an anonymous Flemish painting in the collection of the Alte Pinakothek, Munich (http://www.sammlung.pinakothek.de/en/artwork/8eGVn voGWQ, accessed 23 June 2022) and Lawrence Goedde discusses a work by a follower of Herri met de Bles in the Museo di Capodimonte, Naples in his *Tempest and Shipwreck in Dutch and Flemish Art: Convention, Rhetoric, and Interpretation* (University Park, PA – London: 1989) 51 (https://www.bridgemanimages.com/en-US/noartistknown/landscape-with-stormy-sea -by-herri-met-de-bles-ca-1510-died-after-1550-oil-on-panel-29-5x43-cm-16th/nomedium /asset/1086823, accessed 23 June 2022). Both works are situated in the mid 16th century, but there is also an impressive sea storm painting that Jan Breughel the Elder (1568–1625) made about 1595–6, now on loan in the National Gallery London from a private collection (https://www.nationalgallery.org.uk/paintings/jan-brueghel-the-elder-a-sea-storm, accessed 23 June 2022).

FIGURE 18.3   Jacob Bellevois, *A Fishing Boat off a Rocky Coast in a Storm with a Wreck*, c.1665. Oil on canvas, 82,5 × 121,9 cm. National Maritime Museum, Greenwich, London

person who happens to be ashore, but a sailor who has just managed to bring himself into safety. The painter follows a popular tradition by contrasting his rescue with the hopeless situation for the crew of the ship that will run into ominous cliffs soon. The steepness of these cliffs contrasts with the low rocks in the foreground of the painting. The high cliffs cannot offer any relief for those seeking salvage. These cliffs are crowned with a tower and few houses that do not seem to be endangered by the storm. Thus, the safety of the land is contrasted with the risks at sea.

Till today the Dutch images of sea storms are often interpreted via metaphorical readings. For instance, at its webpage devoted to Staets's painting the National Maritime Museum proposes the following interpretation:

> In Dutch marine painting, prominently featured rocks in a stormy sea could be understood to stand as symbols of constancy in virtue and political principles. Although they could imply man's steadfast endurance, where rocks were shown in association with cliffs they implied a deadly

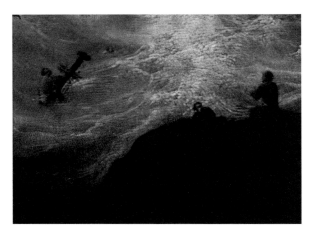

FIGURE 18.4   Detail from Jacob Bellevois, *A Fishing Boat off a Rocky Coast in a Storm with a Wreck*

danger to man. Rocks could be interpreted as an allegory, either warning of the power of the storm to undermine and destroy the seemingly immovable, or be emblematic of God's supreme power. There is ambivalence in the depiction of the rocks here since although they constitute a danger-made clear by the ship which has already gone aground on the treacherous coast, the presence of land could also represent salvation for the men on board, and thus stand as a symbol of hope.[4]

In this quote, despair and hope are not merely seen as emotions, but are part of a deeper reading. As in many other modern analyses of Dutch marine paintings, the different elements are believed to present meaning on two levels, the literal level of the sea storm and a deeper level that provides generalizations about human existence. Already in 1989, however, the American art historian Lawrence Goedde pointed in his seminal book *Tempest and Shipwreck in Dutch and Flemish Art* at the limitations of considering the different elements in depictions of sea storms as metaphors and has brought empathy to the fore as intended response. In other words, Goedde does not merely focus on the reader interpreting an image as a set of metaphors, but that of a person who gets concerned for the misfortunes of the sailors depicted.[5]

---

4   "Ships Wrecked on a Rocky Shore," Royal Museums Greenwich, https://www.rmg.co.uk/collections/objects/rmgc-object-12273 (accessed 23 June 2022).
5   Goedde, *Tempest and Shipwreck*.

We want to add to this discussion and explore the extent to which a metaphorical reading and the arousal of mixed emotions could reinforce each other. Therefore, we will go beyond the focus on the precarious situation in which the sailors in the turbulent water find themselves. Although popular in Dutch depictions of sea storms, art historians have largely ignored the representation of the spectators on the rocky coast, as well as the sailors who have just overcome nature's challenges reaching the safe shores. By looking at these figures, we do not only consider the expression of despair in the storm scenes, but also hope. Moreover, by studying the diverse ways in which spectators were represented *in* these images, we can learn more about the intended responses of the viewers *of* the images. With the figures on the shore, the Dutch artists could express their ideas about possible responses to viewing natural disaster and their audience had to face these possibilities. The artist invites his audience to reflect whether they assume a similar position as one of the spectators in the image.

Before focusing on Dutch visual culture of the seventeenth century, we can briefly take a look at Dutch literature where we find the shipwreck with spectator repeatedly. The German philosopher Hans Blumenberg made it clear that eyewitnessing life-threatening sea storms from a safe position ashore had been used since antiquity as a metaphor to discuss the possibilities of finding peace in life.[6] Among others, Lucretius (*c*.99–*c*.55 BC) used the metaphor in his *De rerum natura* to name the joy that we feel when we escape from the hustle and bustle of everyday life by following Epicurus's teachings. The Dutch Latinist Piet Schrijvers has shown how in the Dutch Republic the ancient metaphor was picked up by Joost van den Vondel (1587–1679) and Constantijn Huygens (1596–1687), among several other authors, but placed in a religious framework.[7] For them, it is primarily God who provides man with order in chaos. This religious interpretation of Lucretius's philosophical ideas is connected with the seventeenth-century Dutch and, more broadly, European reception of biblical passages on ships in danger or shipwrecked, such as Paul's shipwreck or the storm on the Lake of Galilee in the New Testament, and in the Old Testament especially in Corinthians and Ezekiel.[8]

6　Blumenberg H., *Shipwreck with Spectator: Paradigm of a Metaphor for Existence*, trans. S. Rendall (Cambridge, MA: 1997).

7　Schrijvers P., "Schildknaap en tolk van Epicurus. Lucretius in Nederland," in Lucretius, *De natuur van de dingen*, trans. and ed. Schrijvers P. (Groningen: 2008).

8　Goedde, *Tempest and Shipwreck*, chapter 2.

Thus, the early modern literary use of the shipwreck with spectator is closely linked to divine providence.

Text and Image

We can begin our exploration of Dutch visual culture by looking at some of the many prints which depict spectators of shipwrecks in the foreground. In contrast with painting, the prints are often accompanied by texts. Therefore, they also give an insight into contemporary interpretations of the images, or at least they offer us an insight into the views of printmakers and publishers. In his popular emblem book *Sinnepoppen* of 1614, the Amsterdam merchant Roemer Visscher (1547–1620) uses an image of a sea storm to point out that we should beware of making the same mistakes twice [Fig. 18.5].[9] Next to the engraving it reads:

> He is foolish who knocks him to the stone over which he once fell, that is: That each one should be careful not to sail badly twice, as they say: *Frustra Neptunum accusat, qui Iterum naufragium facit.* Meaning: *In vain he laments Neptune or the adventure of the Sea, who makes the second lost voyage.*[10]

Roemer Visscher plays on the Dutch expression 'er kwalijk bij varen' (literally 'sailing badly') by showing who sailors are shipwrecked, but also by using it in its figural sense of 'turning out badly'. Further on, he uses a widespread proverb, originally from Publius Syrus's *Sententiae*, to relate the shipwreck even more to the idea of making a mistake. Thus, he discourages embarking on a sea voyage when the risks are too high. In the light of the general tenor of *Sinnepoppen* where divine providence is presented as central objective for mankind, we can argue that Roemer Visscher condemns an overly strong penchant for exploring the world because it would disregard God's will; By getting absorbed in

---

9   https://www.dbnl.org/tekst/viss004sinn01_01/viss004sinn01_01_0111.php (accessed 23 June 2022).

10   'Hy is dwaes die hem aen de steen stoot daer hy eens over ghevallen heeft, dat is: Dat elck moet wachten voor de tweede mael te doen, daer hy eens qualijck by ghevaren heeft, gelijckmen seyt: *Frustra* Neptunum *accusat, qui Iterum naufragium facit.* Dat is te segghen: *Te vergheefs beklaeght hy* Neptunum *of het avontuur van de Zee, die de tweede verloren reijs doet'.* Visscher Roemer, *Sinnepoppen* (Amsterdam, Willem Jansz. Blaeu, 1614), vol. 2, emblem 47.

FIGURE 18.5   Claes Jansz. Visscher (printmaker), *Frustra qui iterum*, emblem XLVII, in Visscher Roemer, *Sinnepoppen* (Amsterdam, Willem Jansz. Blaeu, 1614), Rijksmuseum

adventures, we show hubris.[11] God warns us against it, but he does not do that endlessly. In the engraving for this emblem, however, we can again see that despair is juxtaposed with hope. The Amsterdam engraver of the image accompanying Roemer Visscher's text, Claes Jansz. Visscher (c.1587–1652, not related to Roemer), renders light in a similar way as we saw in the paintings by Staets and Bellevois. The sun falls on the drowning men trying to pull themselves to safety. They seem to gain control over the life-threatening situation, thus Claes Jansz. Visscher visualises they are rescued.

This engraving again shows that Dutch artists often foreground figures outside the life-threatening danger of sea storms and, with their choice of light, draw extra attention to these figures. In turn, the text makes it clear that Roemer Visscher finds sailors careless, even reckless. Here, then, we encounter the complexity of emblems. The relationship between the image and the

11   Porteman K., "Het embleem als 'genus iocosum'. Theorie en praktijk bij Cats en Roemer Visscher", *De Zeventiende Eeuw* 11 (1995) 184–196.

text makes an unambiguous interpretation not evident. Although we cannot speak of an explicit contradiction, the text emphasises the stupidity of seeking adventure at sea and the engraving the rescue from such adventure. The two sides of the coin that the emblem presents exposes a tension in Dutch society around seafaring. More concretely, it poses an identity question for the young Republic: In a nation that relies largely on the sea for its economic prosperity, such an emblem deals with the problem of putting limits to exploring the world.

But in how far can we extrapolate our analysis of this emblem to other prints and paintings? This move has been a hot topic for Netherlandish art historians for decades already.[12] Ever since Eddy de Jongh's plea for the use of emblem books in iconographic analyses of paintings, including in his *Zinne-en minnebeelden in de schilderkunst van de zeventiende eeuw* of 1967, the question has lingered whether we can fruitfully transfer the layered meanings that emblems indicate to painting to which concrete texts can rarely be attached.[13] We do not want to further explore this discussion on its general level, but will preserve our focus on the figures shown out of danger of death at the front of storm scenes. In doing so, we aim to make it clear that in seventeenth-century visual culture, these figures were a popular means of prompting the Dutch to reflect on what was becoming increasingly essential to their identity formation. Just as we saw that the emblem from *Sinnepoppen* showed a tension between despair and hope regarding the adventures/dangers of the sea, we want to clarify that in other images similar tensions are put to the fore. Just as the emblem, these images encourage the viewer to think about their own position, but the images rarely nail down a particular position themselves.

Thanks to an engraving by Pieter Nolpe (1613–1652), we can take an intermediate step between emblem and painting. In fact, the Amsterdam artist excelled in creating engravings inspired by paintings, adding text. Thus, in one of his series, he connects the months, seasons and elements and comments on human doings. For example, the month of January links Nolpe to the element of air, and in the caption he encourages his audience to put on their skates to have fun on the frozen water in the fresh air. His engraving therefore plays on all the snow and ice fun celebrated in print and painting since Pieter Bruegel the Elder (1525–1530–1569). But in another print in this series, the engraver also

---

12   Harbison C., "Iconography and Iconology", in Veen Henk van – Ridderbos Bernard (eds.), *Early Netherlandish Paintings: Rediscovery, Reception and Research* (Amsterdam: 2004), 378–406.

13   Jongh Eddy de, *Zinne- en minnebeelden in de schilderkunst van de zeventiende eeuw* (Amsterdam: 1967).

FIGURE 18.6   Pieter Nolpe, *Shipwreck: The Month March and the Element water*, 1640s or early 1650s. Engraving, 405 × 519 mm. Rijksmuseum, Amsterdam

plays on the popularity of tempest scenes in the Low Countries. Nolpe attributes the month of March to sea storms and shipwrecks and evidently links it to the element of water [Fig. 18.6].

The Dutch historian Charles Dozy as well as the German print specialist Friedrich Hollstein present Nolpe's *Shipwreck* as being made after a painting of Jan Beerstraten (1622–1666), now in the Alte Pinakothek in Munich.[14] However, the least we can say is that Nolpe handled his model freely.[15] Actually, if he took that painting as his model, the engraver only took over its composition and

---

14   Dozy C.M., "Pieter Nolpe", *Oud Holland* 15 (1897), 151, cat.nr. 173: https://brill.com/view/journals/oh/15/1/article-p94_7.xml?language=en (accessed 23 June 2022) and Hollstein F.W.H., *Hollstein's Dutch and Felmish etchings, engravings and woodcuts*, vol. 14 (Amsterdam: 1956) 151, cat. nr. 173.
15   https://www.sammlung.pinakothek.de/en/artwork/QrLWePD4NO/jan-abrahamsz-beerstraaten/seesturm (accessed 23 June 2022).

FIGURE 18.7   Detail from Pieter Nolpe, *Shipwreck: The Month March and the Element water*

some of its common places. For example, the safe and steadfast castle on high cliffs takes a prominent role in the engraving, just as in the painting. Besides this topos, Nolpe follows convention in, among others, the changing weather conditions, the spectators watching the disaster mesmerised from the safe shores, and the sailors coming ashore [Fig. 18.7]. There is, however, variation as well, since we see an exceptional large number of sailors who manage to reach the mainland in one piece. Moreover, while the two ships are in danger, these will not necessarily be wrecked, as in the paintings by Staets, Bellevois and Beerstraten. So, in the image hope prevails over despair.

To come to a better understanding of these variations, we need to take into consideration that Nolpe's engraving responds to a tradition showing the order of the world. In early modern Europe, the months, seasons, and elements are often presented as prominent examples of God creating structure out of chaos.[16] From this, the viewer of the image could have interpreted Nolpe's

---

16   For a discussion of this expression in Netherlandish painting, see Bakker B., "Order or Variety? Pieter Bruegel and the Aesthetics of Landscape", in Enenkel K.A.E. – Melion W. (eds.), *Landscape and the Visual Hermeneutics of Place, 1500–1700*, Intersections 75 (Leiden: 2021) 158–94 with the latest bibliography.

emphasis on the large number of sailors finding solid grounds, the lack of a real shipwreck, and the emphasis on the safe castle as an expression of the belief in God's good intentions. However, the texts under the engraving do not predominantly connect the image to such a religious metaphorical reading. The French caption ignores divine benevolence and encourages its readers to go on a sea voyage by saying that it is the best way to show one's ability and boldness precisely because the tempest is at first sight the summum of disorder:

> It is easy to boast with art and courage,
> By a fire, with a drink in hand, far from perils and water.
> Art and bravery are seen atop a ship,
> In the midst of chaos, near a shipwreck.[17]

So, in this quote, the importance of God's providence is not the underlying thought as it is in the Dutch appropriation of ancient texts or in emblem books as the *Sinnepoppen*, but a belief in human heroism taking up a fight against the natural forces is put to the fore. There is also a Dutch caption which similarly points at the fact that on a safe place it is hard to show bravery. However, it diverts from the French caption by focusing on the life-threatening dangers of the sea that cause emotions to run high. In contrast with the French text, the Dutch text does not encourage to go on a sea voyage to express oneself as a hero:

> Out of harm's way, it is easy to be a warrior
> And a steersman while chattering away,
> But [it is hard to be that] in hate, sorrow and pain.
> As everything perishes in the water.[18]

The combination of the central image with its spectators and many saved sailors ashore, the title, and the French and Dutch texts shows a complexity that must have urged seventeenth-century viewers to reflect on their own position. The variations from the conventional tempest depictions point them at the safety of the mainland and diminished the dangers of the sea. Mentioning the month March and the element water could have been taken to interpret this

---

17   "A l'aise on peut venter son art & son courage, / Dos au feu, verre en main, loin des coups & de l'eau, / L'Art & le coeur se voit sur le haut du vaisseau, / Au fort de la meslée, & deux doits du naufrage".

18   'Tis buyten Schoots, goed kryghsman sijn. / En stierman met de snater / Maer, inde Haet, Verdriet en Pijn. / Daar 't al vergaet int Water'.

accentuation of safety religiously, but the captions focus on the human capabilities and limitations. Thus, Nolpe's engraving skippers between several textual and visual traditions and conventions encouraging the viewers eventually to make up their minds. The figure in the front centre of the engraving has firmly clung to a rock to view the sea storm. His efforts to find a solid foundation to cope with the forces of nature may have been exemplary for the onlookers to get a grip on the unpredictability of life themselves from the image, face the facts as confronting as these might be, and choose positions between devotion, heroism and restraint.

Providence in Painting

The texts accompanying Nolpe's engraving make it possible to map the complexities in coming to an understanding of how the depiction of the figures on the rocky shores watching a sea storm in despair and hope can be connected with the viewers of the image. But even without explicit text and image relations, we can study these complexities by taking the artists' interactions with traditions and conventions further into consideration. Therefore, we can analyse a painting attributed to Hans Savery the Elder (1564–1622) that is dated circa 1630, once again preserved in the National Maritime Museum [Fig. 18.8]. It has an impressive size, being seven times larger than Staets's painting, but once again shows the same common places. We see a three-master about to capsize dramatically. The white waves besiege the prow like a multitude of monstrous claws. On the stern there is the coat of arms of the city of Amsterdam. Whereas those aboard this ship can still hope for salvation, for the sailors on the neighbouring ship, all hope is futile. The stern of the latter ship shows that it would be under the protection of the Virgin Mary, but the certainty of a shipwreck renders this supernatural protection meaningless. Indeed, the ship is about to disappear completely under the raging water.

The catalogue of the exhibition *Turmoil and Tranquility* of the National Maritime Museum takes a metaphorical reading into consideration by stating that the painting 'may be read as a parable of the precariousness of human life', but it mainly focusses on the contrast between the two ships to interpret the work as a metaphorical rendition of a historical situation.[19] The painting might allude to the Eighty Years' War, so that the ship with the Virgin Mary being wrecked stands for the Spanish and therefore Catholic defeat. The first

---

19   Gaske (ed.), *Turmoil and Tranquility* 70, cat. nr. 2.

FIGURE 18.8   Hans Savery the Elder (attr.), *The Wreck of the* Amsterdam, ca. 1630. Oil on canvas, 125,7 × 177,8 cm. National Maritime Museum, London

ship could represent the policy of Amsterdam, as it was one of the last cities in the Netherlands to align itself with the Dutch Protestant revolt against Spain. This ship is in great danger, but the sailors can still save it. So, in the painting the tension might resonate of a city that doubted for a painfully long time to choose the right side. Nevertheless, the catalogue has to conclude: 'Lack of documentary information relating to the picture has meant that the intended subject, as well as the identity of the artist, remain elusive'.

Besides this politico-metaphorical reading, we can pay attention to the people on the rocky shores to come to a religious interpretation [Fig. 18.9]. Catholic faith already seems to be renounced by the sinking of a ship prominently carrying an image of the Virgin Mary, but the figures on the high cliffs further clarify that a gradation can be made in how to believe in God, as they react differently to the threads of the tempest. Through his rendering of sunlight, the painter has put a spotlight on them. The lowest figure is climbing the rocks trying to escape the violent waves, and two other figures seem to have just preceded him. They follow a fourth figure that has started climbing even

FIGURE 18.9   Detail from Hans Savery the Elder (attr.), *The Wreck of the* Amsterdam

higher rocks. Desperately, they seem to want to move as far away from the sea as possible and escape from all the risks it contains. An alternative is expressed in the two figures who are situated on the same platform as the foursome. They have knelt down and folded their hands together in prayer. Are they addressing a prayer of thanks to God for their own rescue from the raging waters or are they expressing the hope that others still can be saved through prayer? A last figure is praying as well. We find him behind the high rock, he is a hermit kneeling and holding his head up to heaven. Because he is furthest away from the sea storm, he does not need to ask God to be saved and can concentrate fully on the heavenly realms.

Thus, different reactions to the perils of the sea are presented side by side to the viewer. These reactions are far from the call in the French caption of Nolde's engraving for fearless behaviour. The figures express a relation to God that range from pure panic of being abandoned by him over fervent hope praying for his coming to rescue to an expression of solid faith in him and an acceptance of the unfathomability of his plans. So, instead of heroism, the artist shows despair and hope in the face of divine providence. Whereas in the engraving we had to infer divine intervention from the title, here we get a clearer presentation of the different ways people can react to terrible disasters. The viewers see following options: They can try to avoid the fate God has in store for them, they can beg for his mercy, or they can put their fate in his hands. The artist helps the viewers in making up their mind as due to the placement of the figures closer or further from the tempest a hierarchy is shown between those who flee, those who pray for instant relief, and finally those who correctly anticipate his will.

Conclusion

By laying the works of Staets, Bellevois, Nolpe and Savery side by side, a difference in style becomes apparent. The first three artists seem to pursue naturalism, even if their use of colour, as well as brushwork, differ markedly. The latter painter, by contrast, emphasises the drama of the event, transcending a naturalistic effect. This led to the painting being labelled as Dutch because of the subject matter, but at the same time also appearing Flemish because of the flamboyant colours and the extreme positioning of the central ship in the water. In addition, the figure of the hermit is taken into consideration, which seems to have been plucked from a sixteenth-century Flemish landscape painting. Savery who came from Kortrijk, but made a career in Amsterdam, so incorporating both the Dutch and the Flemish tradition, seems a designated candidate, but a watertight attribution is impossible to give. However, the strangeness in style prompts us to think further and see to what extent style played a role in the reading of the depictions of shipwrecks with spectators on rocky shores. As divergent as the style, as well as the measures and media of the images might be, the artists encouraged their audience to reflect on the existential challenges everyone faces. Whatever style, size or medium is eventually taken, the thought process is paramount where the viewer is challenged by the artist. The viewer is given elements to reflect on how natural disasters relate to divine providence and human self-control and to choose between despair and hope.

The figures ashore watching the sea storms that are depicted in many Dutch seascapes may have encouraged the viewers of these images to read the images metaphorically. This metaphorical reading, however, did not exclude a straightforward engagement with the emotions and actions depicted. Viewers of the Dutch marines might have felt the urge to identify with the characters, or at least interrelate with their reactions. The deadly risks faced by the sailors in the water would have received much attention. Many viewers will have been absorbed in the thrill of the spectacle in which man is reduced to a plaything of nature. However, the figures on the shore in the foreground of the prints and paintings must also have been into consideration. Here, the viewers of the print or painting are linked to eyewitnesses of the disaster. The attention with which the images depict diverse ways in which the latter relate to the natural disaster and the plight of their fellow human beings in distress will have caused reflection among the former. The figures on the foreground invited the viewers of the prints and paintings to ask themselves what they would do if faced with a sea storm, another natural disaster, or any other kind of harsh, life-threatening challenge. The options were presented in divergent ways, but often it came down to the following choice: they could remain paralyzed by the overwhelming choice between feeling despair or hope; they could pray to God to be spared of all the perils and even come to a full acceptance of his unfathomability, or they could accept the possibility of the dangers and go aboard to heroically start a voyage at sea.

Bibliography

Bakker B., "Order or Variety? Pieter Bruegel and the Aesthetics of Landscape", in Enenkel K.A.E. – Melion W. (eds.) *Landscape and the Visual Hermeneutics of Place, 1500–1700*, Intersections 75 (Leiden: 2021), 158–194.

Beer G. de – Veen J. van der – Ossing, F. – Dumas C. (eds.), *The Golden Age of Dutch Marine Painting. The Inder Rieden Collection* (Leiden: 2019).

Blumenberg H., *Shipwreck with Spectator: Paradigm of a Metaphor for Existence*, trans. S. Rendall (Cambridge, MA: 1997).

Bol L.J., *Die holländische Marinemalerei des 17. Jahrhundrets* (Braunschweig: 1973).

Dozy C.M., "Pieter Nolpe", *Oud Holland* 15 (1897) 24–50.

Giltaij J. – Kelch J., *Praise of Ships and the Sea: The Dutch Marine Painters of the 17th Century* (Seattle: 1996).

Goedde L., "Convention, Realism, and the Interpretation of Dutch and Flemish Tempest Painting", *Simiolus: Netherlands Quarterly for the History of Art* 16/2–3 (1986) 139–149.

Goedde L., "Natural Metaphors and Naturalism in Netherlandish Marine Painting", in Gaske J. (ed.), *Turmoil and Tranquility. The Sea Through the Eyes of Dutch and Flemish Masters, 1550–1700* (London: 2008) 23–31.

Goedde L., "Seascape as History and Metaphor", in Giltaij J. – Kelch J., *Praise of Ships and the Sea: The Dutch Marine Painters of the 17th Century* (Seattle: 1996) 59–73.

Goedde L., *Tempest and Shipwreck in Dutch and Flemish Art: Convention, Rhetoric, and Interpretation* (University Park, PA – London: 1989).

Harbison C., "Iconography and Iconology", in Veen Henk van – Ridderbos Bernard (eds.), *Early Netherlandish Paintings: Rediscovery, Reception and Research* (Amsterdam: 2004), 378–406.

Hollstein F.W.H., *Hollstein's Dutch and Felmish etchings, engravings and woodcuts*, vol. 14 (Amsterdam: 1956).

Jongh Eddy de, *Zinne- en minnebeelden in de schilderkunst van de zeventiende eeuw* (Amsterdam: 1967).

Porteman K., "Het embleem als 'genus iocosum'. Theorie en praktijk bij Cats en Roemer Visscher", *De Zeventiende Eeuw* 11 (1995) 184–196.

Schrijvers P., "Schildknaap en tolk van Epicurus. Lucretius in Nederland," in Lucretius, *De natuur van de dingen*, trans. and ed. Schrijvers P. (Groningen: 2008).

Vézilier-Dussart S. – Laffon C., *La Flandre et la mer: De Pieter Bruegel l'Ancien à Jan Breughel de Velours* (Kassel: 2015).

Index Nominum

Abraham Hermit, Saint   458, 484
Acciarini, Tideo   156, 164
Achilles Tatius, of Alexandria   36n80
Acquaviva, Claudio   328, 330
Adonis   191, 234
Adorno, Francesco   355–356
Aelst, Pieter Coecke van   653
Aertssens, Hendrik   412
Aertsz., Rijckaert   631
Agrippa d'Aubigné, Théodore   31,
   32nn68–69, 33–34
Alberti, Leon Battista   251n4
Albin, Johan   509n12
Aldrovandi, Ulisse   562–564
Alsted, Johann Heinrich   331
Altdorfer, Albrecht   224, 404
Ammon Nitriota, Saint   458, 469, 484
Amyot, Jacques   320
Anguilla, Michael   228–229, 245
Anthony Hermit, Saint   465n24, 492
Apelles   239, 242
Aquinas, Thomas, Saint   5, 75, 235, 294, 297,
   332, 394–395
Aristotle   49, 67, 70, 85, 92, 111, 115–116, 119,
   162n49, 176, 311, 389–392, 394–395,
   459n15
Arsenius, Saint   455, 484
Athanasius of Alexandria, Saint   465
Attis   191
Augustine of Hippo, Saint (Aurelius
   Augustinus Hipponensis)   54, 110, 187n9,
   202, 316, 376, 395, 399, 466, 493, 511n16,
   516, 558
Aulnoy, Marie – Catherine d'   285–286
Aulus Gellius   321
Ausonius   230
Azor, Juan   333

Baïf, Jean Antoine de   318
Bakhuizen, Ludolf   678
Balde, Jakob, s.j.   36, 220–223, 227–235,
   238n52, 239, 243n68
Bar-Jesus   649
Barnabas, Saint   648–651, 653–658, 662,
   664–665, 668–670, 673

Bascapè, Carlo, Bishop   337, 355–356
Basilius Magnus, Saint (Basil the Great)   464
Bautista, Pedro, Saint o.f.m.   503, 509,
   516–517, 534
Beerstraten, Jan   685–686
Beham, Sebald   404
Bellarmino, Roberto   340
Bellevois, Jacob   678, 683, 686, 691
Benedict of Nursia, Saint   412
Berg, Adam   504n6
Berinzaga, Isabella   327, 331, 337–340,
   342–343, 345–347, 350, 357–358, 360
Beza, Theodore   194
Binck, Jakob   385
Birken, Sigmund von   221n2
Bles, Herri met de   678
Bloemaert, Abraham   410–412, 453, 455,
   457–459, 461–464, 471, 474, 480,
   484–486, 488, 490–492, 494, 495n96,
   497–498
Boethius, Anicius Manlius Severinus   202
Bol, Hans   633n39, 678n3
Bolswert, Boëtius à   411–412, 480, 485
Bolswert, Schelte Adamsz.   526, 529–531
Bonaventure, Saint   510–512, 573–574,
   576–577, 590–591, 594–596, 598–604,
   607–610
Bonosus, Saint   453, 455, 484, 492–494
Borromeo, Carlo, Saint   327, 334, 336–338,
   355–357, 360
Borromeo, Federico   356
Brant, Sebastian   383, 385
Bruegel the Elder, Pieter   7, 9, 13, 621, 678, 684
Buchanan, George   184–187, 190, 192,
   194–195, 197–211, 213
Burch, Adriaan van der   213–214
Burton, Robert   6, 11

Caesar, Gaius Julius   54, 58, 60, 82, 190, 321,
   482
Cagnacci, Guido   532
Callot, Jacques   512, 517
Camerota, Giovanni, s.j.   519
Candid, Peter   221, 227
Carlino, Giacomo   329

INDEX NOMINUM

Cassian, John   465n24
Castellani, Alberto   380n19
Catherine of Alexandria, Saint   220,
    223–224, 228–233, 241, 242n62, 559
Catullus, Gaius Valerius   200
Caussin, Nicolas, s.j.   28, 29n62, 30, 34
Cennini, Cennino   630
Cervantes, Miguel de   286, 289, 295
Charles d'Orléans   314
Charles of Blois – Châtillon   320
Charles the Bold (Duke of Burgundy)   320
Charles v (Holy Roman Emperor)   591
Chelidonius, Benedict   383
Christ, Jesus   10–11, 14–15, 17, 19, 29–30,
    37, 48, 65, 193, 202, 229–230, 234,
    292, 340–341, 345, 347, 355–356, 359,
    370–371, 373, 375–376, 378–383, 385,
    387, 389, 393, 395–397, 401, 404–406,
    411n1, 453, 455, 457–461, 466, 470, 472,
    478, 484, 487–493, 496, 498, 503–506,
    509–512, 514, 516–517, 522, 525, 532, 538,
    543, 549, 563–566, 573–574, 576–577,
    582–589, 591, 593–595, 598–604,
    607–610, 648–649, 651, 663–664, 669,
    673
Cicero, Marcus Tullius   110–111, 114, 376
Claudian (Claudius Claudianus)   240n56,
    242n64
Coelen, Thomas van   630–631
Coligny, Louise de   132
Constantine vii (Byzantine Emperor)   117
Coornhert, Dirk Volckertszoon   54, 56,
    73–76
Corvinus, Mathias (King of Hungary)   154
Crabeth, Pieter Dircksz.   630
Cranach, Lucas the Elder   404

David (King)   125–129, 140, 143, 188, 200, 202
David, Jan, s.j.   17, 19
Deguileville, Guillaume de   377
Delrio, Martin Antonio, s.j.   29, 465n24
Democritus   12, 56, 312, 317
Descartes, René   12–13
Desportes, Philippe   318
Dolci, Carlo   545, 547–549, 552–553, 555,
    560, 565–566
Dominic, Saint (Dominic de Guzmán)   412,
    559

Donati, Alessandro, s.j.   235
Dousa, Janus   195, 209, 214
Du Bellay, Jean   253
Du Bellay, Joachim   36, 250–258, 261, 264,
    268–272, 274–275, 277–278
Dürer, Albrecht   383, 579
Duym, Jacob   130–131

Elias Aegyptius, Saint   432
Elymas   649
Engebrechtsz, Cornelis   378–379
Ens, Kaspar   130
Ephraem, Saint   464
Epictetus   109–110, 114, 336–337
Erasmus, Desiderius   61–62, 65, 73, 75–76,
    79, 313
Estius, Franco   643
Evagrius Ponticus, Abbot   465n24, 471–472
Evelyn, John   2
Eyck, Jan van   397, 603n104

Ferreri, Zaccaria   539n4, 545, 555, 556n50,
    565n87
Figini, Ambrogio Giovanni   334
Filelfo, Francesco   158
Flaminio, Marcantonio   185, 194–196
Floris, Frans   630, 633
Florus, Lucius Annaeus   117
Florus of Lyon (Florus Lugdunensis)   193
Fontana, Giovanni   360n91
Francis Xavier, Saint, s.j.   2, 503–504,
    522–523, 526, 534, 559n64
Francis, Saint (Giovanni di Pietro di
    Bernardone)   502, 504, 510–512, 534,
    576–577, 591, 595–596, 598, 603n104,
    604, 608, 610
Francken, Frans the Younger   55, 85–86,
    88, 90
Fróis, Luís, s.j.   508–509
Froissart, Jean   321, 323
Frontonius, Saint   458, 484
Fugger, Octavianus Secundus   222
Fulgosus, Baptista   321, 323

Gagliardi, Achille   36, 327, 330n7, 333,
    337–341, 343–352, 354, 356–358,
    359–360
Galen (Galenus of Pergamon)   59, 293n33

INDEX NOMINUM

Ganeius, Johannes   196, 197n52
Garcilaso de la Vega   284n1, 297n49
Gerards, Balthasar   132–140, 142
Giussano, Giovanni Pietro   355–356,
    357n84
Glapion, Jean   591, 593
Goltzius, Hendrick   37, 90, 480, 615–621,
    624–626, 629–636, 638, 640–644
Gorcum, Jan van, s.j.   485
Goto, João, Saint, s.j.   521, 529, 532
Gregory of Nyssa, Saint   397, 587
Gregory the Great (Pope)   399, 401
Greuter, Matthäus   519, 521
Greuter, Matthäus   519, 521
Grotius, Hugo   107, 131
Guzmán, Francisco Tello de   504, 505n7,
    506n10, 509, 512, 514, 525

Hainhofer, Philipp   222
Hazart, Cornelius, s.j.   531n52
Heinrich of Sankt Gallen   373, 387
Heinsius, Daniel   105–108, 115–117, 119,
    125, 129–132, 134–135, 136n92,
    137n94, 138, 140, 142–143, 459n15,
    495n96
Helenus, Saint   458, 484
Heliodorus   36
Henri III (King of France)   310, 318–319,
    321–322, 324–325
Heraclides, Bishop   465n24
Heraclitus   12, 56, 311–312, 317
Herp, Hendrik   593, 599–600, 601n97
Hessus, Eobanus   207
Hideyoshi, Toyotomi   503
Hilarion, Saint   455, 484
Hoefnagel, Joris   633n39
Holbein, Hans the Elder   371, 373, 374n8,
    376, 379
Höltzel, Hieronymus   383
Hondt, Christiaan de (Abbot)   596
Honert, Rochus van den   105, 107–108,
    125–126
Hoogstraeten, Samuel van   7
Horace (Quintus Horatius Flaccus)   159, 162,
    171n71, 175, 191, 211, 221, 228, 273
Houbraken, Arnold   7
Housebook Master (Master of the
    Amsterdam Cabinet)   377
Hout, Jan van   195

Huber, Wolf   404
Huygens, Constantijn   681
Hyella   210–212

Ignatius of Loyola, Saint, s.j. (Íñigo López de
    Oñaz y Loyola)   1–2, 356, 494, 497, 504,
    512, 518, 522–523, 526, 527n48, 534,
    559n64
Isaac of Stella   396
Isaiah   183, 373n5, 393, 582, 585nn43–44,
    603n103, 608n114
Isidore of Seville   187, 189

Jagiellończyk, Kazimierz (Casimir), Saint
    37, 538–545, 549, 551–552, 555–560,
    564–566
Jamyn, Amadis   318
Jerome, Saint (Eusebius Hieronymus)
    187–190, 196n50, 224, 387, 412, 465, 488,
    492–493, 511n16, 581
Johann Wilhelm II (Elector Palatine)
    223n12
John of Lyco, Saint   464
John the Baptist, Saint   453, 458
Junius, Franciscus   7

Kilian, Wolfgang   523–525, 529
King João III (King John of Portugal)   197
Kisai, Diogo, Saint, s.j.   521, 529, 532
Kunigunde of Prague (Abbess)   387

Landino, Cristoforo   162, 238
Lang, Franz, s.j.   227
Langhe, Karel de   109
Lapide, Cornelius a, s.j.   234
Lastman, Pieter   xiii, 37, 647–648, 650–652,
    654, 660–662, 668–673
Leo X (Pope, Giovanni di Lorenzo de' Medici)
    540, 545, 552
León, Luis de   285
Lernutius, Janus   184, 190, 192, 209–213
Lipsius, Justus   54, 82–83, 109–114, 209
Lomazzo, Gian Paolo   9–11, 34, 337
Lope de Vega, Félix   287, 296
Lowth, Robert   189n14
Lucan (Marcus Annaeius Lucanus)   230, 321
Lucretius (Titus Lucretius Carus)   681
Ludolph of Saxony   458, 459nn12–13

INDEX NOMINUM

Macarius Aegyptius, Saint 464
Macarius Alexandrinus, Saint 455, 463, 484
Malchus, Saint 455, 463, 484
Mander, Karel van xi, 6–7, 9, 13, 37, 410,
  453, 454n6, 455–458, 460–462, 486,
  488, 490n87, 497, 615–620, 624–625,
  629–634, 636, 638, 640–641, 644,
  657–660, 664, 668–669, 672
Maria Maddalena of Austria (Grand Duchess
  of Florence) 544
Marmion, Simon 578
Marot, Clément 264, 270
Martial (Marcus Valerius Martialis) 242n64
Marulić, Marco 155–158, 164, 175
Mary, Saint xvii, 19, 193, 201, 223–224, 230,
  245, 292, 373n7, 380–381, 458–459, 576,
  588, 590, 688–689
Mary Magdalene, Saint 460n16, 495n96,
  497, 594
Mathijssen, Jan 619
Maupin, Paul 519, 521
Maxentius (Roman Emperor) 232
Maximus, Valerius 636
Meckenem, Israhel van 14–15, 383
Medici, Cosimo III de' (Grand Duke of
  Florence) 37, 540, 549–551, 553–557,
  559–560, 562–566
Medici, Ferdinando de' 334, 562
Miki, Paul, Saint, s.J. 521–523, 525, 529, 532
Montaigne, Michel de 5, 36, 54, 56,
  58, 60–62, 76, 84, 254, 310–312,
  318–325
Montemayor, Jorge de 36, 283, 287–288,
  290, 298n53, 299–300, 302–303
Morales (Morais), Sebastiano 338
Morel, Frédéric 275
Moretus, Joannes 518n33
Morra, Bernardino 356
Moschus, Johannes 465
Moses 187–188, 189n17, 492, 585
Mostaert, Jan 404–405
Myron 230

Natalis, Franciscus (Božićević, Frano) 157
Nero (Roman Emperor) 79–82, 93
Nieulandt, Willem van II 47, 50, 55, 79, 86,
  93
Nolpe, Pieter 684–686, 691
Núñez de Reinoso, Alonso 288

Oliva, Giovanni Paolo s.J. 550, 551n36, 553
Onuphrius, Saint 411, 458, 467–468, 471,
  484
Opitz, Martin 194
Ortelius, Abraham 619–620
Ovid (Publius Ovidius Naso) 159n36,
  168–169, 176, 200, 204, 234

Pac, Michał Kazimierz, Lithuanian Grand
  Hetman 551
Pac, Mikołaj Stefan, Bishop 550–556, 561
Pace, António 512n18
Pachomius, Saint 467–471, 492
Parrhasius 245–246
Passe, Crispijn van de 458
Passe, Willem de 458
Paul Hermit, Saint 465n24
Paul the Apostle, Saint 236n40, 460n16,
  493, 595, 648–658, 660–673, 681
Paulinus of Nola, Bishop (Pontius Meropius
  Anicius Paulinus) 193, 354
Paulus Simplex, Saint 464
Paulus, Sergius (Proconsul of Cyprus) 649
Pazzi, Lorenzo Domenico de' 551n38
Pazzi, Maria Maddalena de', Saint 541
Pelagius, Cardinal Deacon 465n24, 471, 476,
  481, 483
Peletier du Mans, Jacques 273
Pellegrini, Lelio 327, 331–334, 336–337, 348,
  355–356, 359–360
Pepys, Samuel 2
Perrault, Charles 251
Peter the Apostle, Saint 401, 460n16, 544,
  583–585, 589, 601–602, 610
Petrarch, Francesco (Francesco Petrarca)
  112, 186–187, 189–190, 208, 210–211, 251,
  256, 258, 261, 263, 321, 323
Phileul, Vasquin 251
Pibrac, Guy Du Faur, Seigneur de 318
Piccolomini, Enea Silvio 154
Pindar 188, 191
Pius III (Pope, Todeschini – Piccolomini,
  Francesco Nanni) 157
Plato 581, 656
Plempius, Cornelis 461
Plutarch 320–321, 323
Pontano, Giovanni Gioviano 154
Poschasius (Paschasius), Radbertus, Saint
  465

INDEX NOMINUM

Propertius, Sextus   159n37, 191, 200, 234
Provoost, Jan   573–574, 576–579, 582–588, 590–591, 593–594, 596, 599–604, 607, 609–610
Prudentius, Aurelius Clemens   240n56
Publilius Syrus   321
Pyrrhus of Epirus   320

Rabelais, François   36, 269, 310–313, 315–318, 320, 325
Rabia, Girolamo   338
Raphael (Raffaello Sanzio da Urbino)   653, 656
René II (Duke of Lorraine)   320
Rhodes, Georges de, s.j.   235n38
Ribadeneira, Marcelo de, o.f.m.   503, 504n5, 509n13, 514n24, 518n31, 521, 523n44
Ribadeneyra, Pedro de, s.j.   521
Ricci, Bartolomeo, s.j.   518
Richeome, Louis, s.j.   521
Rigaud, Pierre   520n35
Risius (Ryser), Joannes, s.j.   410–412, 485 488, 490–491, 493, 497
Robortello, Francesco   116
Rode, Hermen   387
Rogers, Daniel   195
Ronsard, Pierre de   250–251, 254, 269n26, 271n28, 274, 318–319
Rosweyde, Heribert, s.j.   410–411, 453, 464–467, 469, 476, 479, 480n66, 481, 483, 485–487, 497
Rovere, Vittoria della (Grand Duchess of Florence)   543–544
Rubens, Peter Paul   4, 19, 23, 83, 86, 118, 221, 229
Rudolf II (Holy Roman Emperor)   222, 263
Rufinus of Aquileia (Tyrannius Rufinus) 465n24
Ruusbroec, Jan van   591

Sadeler, Raphaël (II)   517, 525
Saenredam, Jan   90, 462–463, 657
Saint – Paul, Eustache de   235n38
Salutati, Coluccio   190
Sandrart, Joachim von   232
Sandys, George   146
Sannazaro, Jacopo   290m18, 300
Santos, Francisco de los   27–28, 34

Savery the Elder, Hans   688
Scaliger, Iulius Caesar   54–55, 70, 75, 77–78, 159, 190
Scève, Maurice   251, 256, 257n17
Schönfeld, Johann Heinrich   529
Schongauer, Martin   385
Schrevelius, Theodoor   462–464
Schwarz, Christoph   36, 220–223, 227–228, 231–232, 245
Secundus, Janus   207–209, 212–213
Sel, Toussaint du   130
Seneca, Lucius Annaeus   77, 79–82, 85, 109–114, 121, 124, 133–134
Shakespeare, William   48, 390, 619
Sidney, Philip   190, 195
Silius Italicus   241n60
Simeon Stylita, Saint   464
Sisgoreus, Georgius (Bishop)   36, 151, 158, 163–166, 168–171, 173–179
Sixtus IV (Pope, Della Rovere, Francesco) 164
Skarga, Piotr, s.j.   539n4
Sluter, Claus   388–389
Soarez, Cyprian, s.j.   33, 35
Solomon (King)   189n17, 202–203, 462
Sosa, Francisco de, o.f.m. (Bishop)   514n24
Spenser, Edmund   253
Spinoza, Benedictus de   13
Spinula, Franciscus   194
Staets, Hendrick   675–679, 683, 686, 688, 691
Statius, Publius Papinius   234, 242n66
Stomme, Hans Verhagen de   633n39
Stomme, Jan Jansz. de   633
Suárez, Francisco, s.j.   5, 30
Suetonius (Gaius Suetonius Tranquillus) 77, 117
Sulpicius Severus   465n24
Surius, Laurentius   465n24
Swanenburg, Willem van   459

Terence (Publius Terentius Afer)   106
Teresa of Avila, Saint (Teresa Sánchez de Cepeda y Ahumada)   495, 497
Theocritus   228
Theodoretus of Cyrus   465
Theodoricus (monk)   386
Theonas, Saint   464
Thopas, Johannes   633

INDEX NOMINUM

Tibullus, Albius   168–169, 175, 191, 201, 203, 234
Titian   19, 23, 224, 587
Traut, Wolf   383

Vair, Guillaume du   109–110
Valerius Flaccus   240n58
Valier, Agostino   337
Vasari, Giorgio   587, 629, 634
Velázquez, Diego   23, 26–27, 34
Venus   212, 232, 243, 266, 461, 638, 640–641
Verdussen, Hieronymus   465
Veronese, Paolo   224
Villon, François   252n5, 263–264, 270
Virgil (Publius Virgilius Maro)   294, 298
Visscher, Claes Jansz.   683
Visscher, Roemer   682–683
Vives, Juan Luis   293, 298, 620, 624
Vlieger, Simon de   678
Vondel, Joost van den   4, 76, 80n126, 495n96, 681
Vos, Marten de   654–658, 660, 664, 669, 672

Walker, Henry   1
Weyer, Johann   112, 124
Willaerts, Adam   678
Willemsen, Gerit   638
William I (Prince of Orange)   129–130, 132–133, 139–140, 142–143
William of Auxerre   316
William V (Duke of Bavaria)   222–223
Winghe, Antonius de   412, 453n5, 490–491
Winghen, Philips van   619–620, 624, 636

Xavier, Francis, S.J., Saint. *See* Francis Xavier, Saint, S.J.

Zachaeus (Penitent)   459–461, 495
Zeno   333
Zeuxis   227, 229, 239, 242
Zevecote, Jacob van   105, 107–108, 117–119, 129, 134, 143
Zovenzoni, Raffaele   164
Zutphen, Gerard Zerbolt van   402